Body Image, Eating Disorders, and Obesity

Body Image, Eating Disorders, and Obesity

AN INTEGRATIVE GUIDE
FOR ASSESSMENT AND TREATMENT

Edited by J. Kevin Thompson

AMERICAN PSYCHOLOGICAL ASSOCIATION
WASHINGTON, DC

First printing February 1996
Second printing June 1997
Third printing April 2000

Published by
American Psychological Association
750 First Street, NE
Washington, DC 20002

Copies may be ordered from
APA Order Department
P.O. Box 92984
Washington, DC 20090-2984

In the UK, Europe, Africa and the Middle East, copies may be ordered from
American Psychological Association
3 Henrietta Street
Covent Garden, London
WC2E 8LU England

Typeset in Goudy by PRO-Image Corporation, Techna-Type Division, York, PA

Printer: Data Reproductions Corporation, Auburn Hills, MI
Jacket Designer: Berg Design, Albany, NY
Technical/Production Editor: Edward B. Meidenbauer

Library of Congress Cataloging-in-Publication Data
Body image, eating disorders, and obesity : an integrative guide for assessment and
    treatment / J. Kevin Thompson, editor.
        p.   cm.
    Includes bibliographical references and index.
    ISBN 1-55798-324-0 (cloth: acid-free paper)
    ISBN 1-55798-726-2 (pbk: acid-free paper)
    1. Eating disorders. 2. Body image. 3. Obesity. I. Thompson, J. Kevin.
    [DNLM: 1. Body Image. 2. Eating Disorders—psychology. 3. Eating Disorders—
therapy. 4. Obesity—psychology. 5. Obesity—therapy.
    BF 697.5.B63   B667   1996]
    RC552.E18B63   1996
    616.85′26—dc20
    DNLM/DLC
    for Library of Congress   95-36117
                                                                                CIP

British Cataloguing-in-Publication Data
A CIP record is available from the British Library.

Printed in the United States of America

CONTENTS

v

CONTRIBUTORS

David B. Allison, PhD, Obesity Research Center, St. Luke's Roosevelt Hospital, Columbia University College of Physicians and Surgeons

Madeline N. Altabe, PhD, Department of Psychology, University of South Florida

Drew A. Anderson, MA, Department of Psychology, Louisiana State University

Thomas F. Cash, PhD, Department of Psychology, Old Dominion University

Alicia J. Clarke, BA, Department of Psychology, Towson State University

Scott J. Crow, MD, Department of Psychiatry, University of Minnesota

Margaret DeBon, Universities Prevention Center, Department of Psychology, University of Memphis

Myles S. Faith, PhD, Obesity Research Center, St. Luke's Roosevelt Hospital, Columbia University College of Physicians and Surgeons

Patricia H. Fettes, PhD, Department of Psychiatry and Psychology, Mayo Clinic

David M. Garner, PhD, Central Behavioral Healthcare; Department of Psychology, Bowling Green State University

David H. Gleaves, PhD, Department of Psychology, Texas A&M University

Carlos M. Grilo, PhD, Yale Psychiatric Institute, Yale University School of Medicine

Leslie J. Heinberg, PhD, Department of Psychiatry and Behavioral Sciences, Johns Hopkins University School of Medicine

William G. Johnson, PhD, Department of Psychiatry and Human Behavior, University of Mississippi Medical Center

Robert C. Klesges, PhD, Universities Prevention Center, Department of Psychology, University of Memphis

Katharine Loeb, BA, Department of Psychology, Rutgers University

Andrew W. Meyers, Universities Prevention Center, Department of Psychology, University of Memphis

James E. Mitchell, MD, Department of Psychiatry, University of Minnesota

Lawrence D. Needleman, PhD, Department of Psychology, Ohio State University

Kathleen M. Pike, PhD, Department of Psychiatry, College of Physicians and Surgeons of Columbia University

Claire Pomeroy, MD, Department of Medicine, University of Minnesota Medical Center

Thomas Pruzinsky, PhD, Department of Psychology, Quinnipac College; Department of Plastic Surgery, New York University

James C. Rosen, PhD, Department of Psychology, University of Vermont

Laine J. Torgrud, PhD, Department of Psychology, University of Manitoba

Kelly Vitousek, PhD, Department of Psychology, University of Hawaii at Manoa

Donald E. Williams, PhD, Department of Psychiatry and Psychology, Mayo Clinic

Donald A. Williamson, PhD, Department of Psychology, Louisiana State University

PREFACE

On the second week of the first semester of my first year of graduate school, I saw my first psychotherapy patient. She was 5 ft. 7 in. tall and weighed approximately 85 lb. My cotherapist, a second-year student, and I expressed our concern with her emaciated state. However, she discounted this as a therapeutic issue, maintaining that she did not understand why people focused on her body size. This formative experience stimulated my initial interest in body image and eating disorders.

In the almost 20 years since that time, I have had the opportunity to work with hundreds of individuals with some manifestation of an eating disturbance, including anorexia nervosa, bulimia nervosa, obesity, and binge eating disorder. These interactions led to an awareness of the particular problems encountered by these patients, which often served as the starting point for an empirical investigation. This book brings together the findings from my own collaborations with numerous colleagues, along with those from many noted researchers in the field.

I decided to develop and edit this book because of my growing belief, supported by clinical experience as well as recent research, that body image is of central importance in the effective assessment and management of eating disorders and obesity. Thus, body image became a major unifying theme of the book.

A second reason for undertaking this work was to provide empirically supported state-of-the-art information about the most effective assessment and treatment strategies for body image disturbance, eating disorders, and obesity. With regard to assessment, this has resulted in an emphasis on psychometrically sound assessment instruments, interview methodologies, and medical evaluation of physical status. With regard to treatment, the emphasis is on cognitive–behavioral and pharmacologic interventions, although other approaches are also discussed, because cognitive–behavioral and pharmacological therapies have the most empirical support.

Finally, I wanted a book that would provide assessment and treatment information in a detailed and concrete fashion, so that it could be applied to actual clinical cases. One goal was to provide information at differing levels of clinician sophistication, so that graduate students and beginning clinicians—as well as seasoned practitioners—would find the book useful. I believe the contributors to this book have developed a unique resource for anyone involved in the assessment and treatment of body image disturbance, eating disorders, and obesity.

My thanks go to a number of individuals who made the completion of this book possible. Susan Reynolds and Peggy Schlegel were instrumental in providing feedback regarding structure, initial chapter content, and thematic direction. All of the chapter contributors deserve a tremendous amount of credit for the quality of their writing. However, special mention has to go to James Rosen for his uncredited editorial assistance. Many research findings cited in my chapters are from my own research group; the thousands of hours work that went into the completion of these investigations is largely owed to the graduate students whose names accompany mine on these publications. Finally, none of this would have been possible without the input, feedback, and cooperation of the research subjects and patients who participated in the process.

J. KEVIN THOMPSON, PhD
jthomps1@luna.cas.usf.edu

1

INTRODUCTION: BODY IMAGE, EATING DISORDERS, AND OBESITY—AN EMERGING SYNTHESIS

J. KEVIN THOMPSON

Consider the following cases:

J. M. is a 21-year-old Caucasian woman with a 3-year history of anorexia nervosa. She is 5 ft 5 in. and weighs 80 lb. She began restricting her food intake at 15 when her gymnastics coach told her she would not be competitive if she continued gaining weight. Currently, she exercises 3 hours a day and restricts her food consumption to 900 calories a day. She expresses a strong subjective dissatisfaction with her body size, stating that she "feels fat" most of the time. In addition, on an apparatus that allows her to match the width of light beams to her estimation of the width of body sites, she overestimates the size of her waist, hips, and thighs by 60%.

R. K. is a 24-year-old African American woman who binges and purges (by self-induced vomiting) an average of three times each day. She is average weight (5 ft 4 in., 120 lb), but desperately wants to lose 5 lb. She is particularly unhappy with the size of her thighs, stating that it upsets her that they rub together when she walks. In addition, she is concerned that her cheeks are "fat," relating the onset of this concern to teasing from an uncle when she was an adolescent. Her bulimic behavior is exacerbated on days that she is particularly disturbed by the appearance of her cheeks. On a questionnaire of cognitions related to body image she states that she "often" thinks, "How I look ruins everything for me."

A. T. is a 29-year-old Caucasian man, 6 ft 2 in. and 200 lb., and has an athletic build. He has a port wine birthmark that is located near his right eyebrow. His concern about this aspect of his appearance is of long-standing duration. Currently, he attempts to deflect attention to the site by wearing large-rimmed glasses and a cap that he pulls low over his forehead. He also worries that his chest is not large enough, a concern that has not abated even though he recently began a weight-lifting program. His anxiety about the birthmark and his chest size has produced marked social anxiety, and many days he refuses to leave his house. On an interview designed to index his degree of social avoidance, he states that his appearance "severely" interferes with his life.

B. A. is a 40-year-old Hispanic woman who is 5 ft 8 in., 240 lb. She has been overweight since childhood and remembers with distress summers spent in "fat camps." In recent years, she has tried a number of diets, losing and regaining "hundreds" of pounds. She also has developed a problem with "binge eating" in the past 3 months, which she characterizes as "out of control eating" following several days of caloric restriction and exercise. She is so ashamed of her size that she avoids many social occasions and public outings. Her dissatisfaction with her overall figure is reflected in the significant discrepancy between her choice of "ideal" and "actual" size on a series of schematic figures ranging from underweight to morbidly obese.

A wealth of recent research from diverse regions of psychology—including social, clinical, experimental, and child development—indicates the critical role of body image issues in the onset and maintenance of eating disorders and obesity. As these four cases illustrate, appearance-related concerns occur in different types of eating, shape, and weight-related disorders. An examination of these cases reveals that even though the particular manifestation of the eating dysfunction may vary (starvation, purging, overeating), the locus of body image disparagement is often thematically and descriptively quite similar. The vignettes also reflect the fact that body image concerns and eating disturbances are not limited to Caucasian females. Evidence now strongly suggests that these disorders are present in both genders and in individuals of many different ethnicities. (Probable diagnoses for the above cases are, in order, anorexia nervosa, bulimia nervosa, body dysmorphic disorder, and binge eating disorder.)

Leading researchers now believe that assessing and treating body image issues should be integral aspects of assessment and clinical management of eating disorders and obesity (Brownell & Rodin, 1994; Garner & Wooley, 1991; Rosen, 1990, in press). This book aims to synthesize theory, data, and practice with regard to body image as it relates to specific body image disturbances and also as it relates to the assessment and treatment of eating disorders and obesity. This is done both in chapters specifically devoted to body image and in chapters that describe assessment procedures for eating disorders and obesity and interventions for these disorders, such as those on cognitive–behavioral treatments.

This introductory chapter is designed primarily to offer a broad overview of the history and recent developments that have led to the integration of body image into assessment and treatment programs for eating and weight-related problems. A secondary goal is to examine briefly the particular role of gender and ethnicity in body image and eating-related disorders. I will conclude the chapter with a discussion of the general scope and organization of this book.

A BRIEF HISTORY

Whenever there is intense empirical interest in a specific area of research, it is enlightening to trace the historical roots of such a movement. Often there is evidence of early inquiry and exploration, but little systematic follow-up of these seminal ideas. Such a scenerio of early promise without consequent product would be too harsh a characterization of the past 30 years of research on the connection between body image, obesity, and eating disorders. However, a brief review of this area supports the view that the current groundswell of attention took years to coalesce.

Bruch (1962) provided the first systematic theoretical position on the role of body image problems in the phenomenology of eating disorders, delineating a disturbance in this sphere as one of the three necessary factors for the development of anorexia nervosa. She maintained that it was the single most important pathognomonic feature of the disorder and also noted that improvement in anorexic symptomatology might be temporary "without a corrective change in the body image" (Bruch, 1962, p. 189). During this same time period, Stunkard and colleagues provided their seminal observations on body dissatisfaction in adult obese patients, including a finding that the majority of individuals with juvenile-onset obesity had severe adult levels of dissatisfaction with body image, whereas none of the subjects with adult-onset obesity had severe dissatisfaction (Stunkard & Burt, 1967; Stunkard & Mendelson, 1967).

Unfortunately, these early investigations led to only a smattering of studies in the late 1960s and early 1970s (e.g., Fisher, 1986; Thompson, 1990). However, an investigation of size perception in individuals with anorexia nervosa by Slade and Russell (1973) generated a tremendous amount of interest. Using an apparatus designed to document the perceptual accuracy of estimation of body size (see chapter 3, this volume), they found that patients with anorexia nervosa, despite their emaciated state, overestimated the size of their physical dimensions when compared with non-eating-disordered control subjects. The wealth of subsequent research can be credited with leading to the inclusion of a body image criterion for the diagnosis of anorexia nervosa in the *Diagnostic and Statistical Manual of Mental Disorders-III* (*DSM-III*) (American Psychiatric Association, 1980).

On the heels of Slade and Russell's (1973) findings, most of the research in the 1970s and early 1980s was devoted to generating assessment methodologies for measuring the accuracy of the size perception aspect of body image (Cash & Brown, 1987; Garner & Garfinkel, 1981; Slade, 1985; Thompson, 1992; 1995). Some of these studies included samples of obese individuals, along with samples of people with anorexia nervosa and bulimia nervosa (Thompson, Berland, Linton, & Weinsier, 1986). During this time period, bulimia nervosa rapidly emerged as a clinical entity (for an excellent historical review, see Vandereycken, 1994); findings of an associated body image disturbance led researchers to include a body image criterion for its diagnosis in the *DSM-III-R* (American Psychiatric Association, 1987). It is interesting to note that in the *DSM-IV* (American Psychiatric Association, 1994), the body image criterion for anorexia nervosa contains three different components, whereas only one of these manifestations is required for bulimia nervosa (see Exhibit 1). Perhaps this can

EXHIBIT 1
Diagnostic Criteria for Anorexia Nervosa and Bulimia Nervosa

Anorexia Nervosa
1. Refusal to maintain body weight at or above a minimally normal weight for age and height (e.g., weight loss leading to maintenance of body weight less than 85% of that expected; or failure to make expected weight gain during period of growth, leading to body weight less than 85% of that expected).
2. Intense fear of gaining weight or becoming fat, even though underweight.
3. Disturbance in the way in which one's body weight or shape is experienced, undue influence of body weight or shape on self-evaluation, or denial of the seriousness of the current low body weight.
4. In postmenarcheal females, amenorrhea (i.e., the absence of at least three consecutive menstrual cycles). A woman is considered to have amenorrhea if her periods occur only following hormone (e.g., estrogen) administration.

Bulimia Nervosa
1. Recurrent episodes of binge eating. An episode of binge eating is characterized by both of the following:
    a) eating, in a discrete period of time (e.g., within any 2-hour period) an amount of food that is definitely larger than most people would eat during a similar period of time and under similar circumstances,
    b) a sense of lack of control over eating during the episodes (e.g., a feeling that one cannot stop eating or control what or how much one is eating).
2. Recurrent inappropriate compensatory behavior in order to prevent weight gain, such as self-induced vomiting; misuse of laxatives, diuretics, enemas, or other medications; fasting; or excessive exercise.
3. The binge eating and inappropriate compensatory behaviors both occur, on average, at least twice a week for 3 months.
4. Self-evaluation is unduly influenced by body shape and weight.
5. The disturbance does not occur exclusively during episodes of anorexia nervosa.

---

be attributed to the early findings of size misperception in anorexia nervosa and the prominence of the denial of a low body weight among those who have anorexia nervosa. Interestingly, in a recent meta-analysis by Cash and Deagle (1995), anorexic and bulimic samples were not found to differ in size estimation levels. However, bulimics had higher levels of subjective disturbance than anorexics.

As noted earlier, the work in the 1970s and early 1980s focused almost exclusively on size perception. The potentially important role of subjective dissatisfaction with appearance was virtually ignored. The prevailing mind-set appeared to be that the perceptual overestimation of size was most important for eating disorders. Any subjective dissatisfaction present in obesity was perceived to be an expected correlate of the enlarged size for these individuals and of no great clinical interest: If subjects lost weight, their body satisfaction would improve. It is quite intriguing that the real onset of interest in subjective dissatisfaction of body appearance can be traced to researchers' location of widespread body size dsyphoria in normal weight, non-eating-disordered females (Altabe & Thompson, 1994; Cash, Winstead, & Janda, 1986; Rodin, Silberstein, & Striegel-Moore, 1985). Rodin et al. (1985) felt the dysphoria was so commonplace as to represent a "normative discontent" (p. 267); Cash et al. (1986) found that only 7% of women expressed little concern over their physical appearance.

This emergence of substantial interest in the appearance dissatisfaction of "normal" individuals, without an accompanying eating disorder or obesity, paradoxically fueled the return to research on the subjective body image concerns of individuals with anorexia nervosa, bulimia nervosa, and obesity. Researchers also began to question the distinctiveness of the body image disturbances present in normal versus clinical populations. For instance, methodological issues are now offered as one explanation for the specificity of perceptual overestimation in anorexic samples (Penner, Thompson, & Coovert, 1991; see also chapter 3, this volume). In addition, levels of subjective body image distress in nonclinical samples have been shown to be predictive of eating dysfunction and global psychological distress (e.g., depression) in adults and adolescents (McCarthy, 1990; Nolen-Hoeksema & Girgus, 1994; Thompson, Coovert, Richards, Johnson, & Cattarin, 1995). Longitudinal analyses indicate the importance of body dissatisfaction in the development of eating disturbance and of obesity in the development of subjective body size dysphoria (Attie & Brooks-Gunn, 1989; Cattarin & Thompson, 1994).

A new active area of investigation involves an examination of body image concerns in binge eating when it occurs as a syndrome independent from bulimia nervosa. Binge eating disorder is contained in the appendix of the *DSM-IV* as a category needing further study (American Psychiatric Association, 1994). The criteria for binge eating disorder are similar to that of bulimia nervosa. However, there is an exclusionary criterion requiring the absence of "inappropriate compensatory behaviors" such as purging, fasting, or excessive exercise. It is interesting to note that there is no body image criterion for binge eating disorder, despite evidence that it may be an important component of the clinical symptomatology (Grilo, Wilfley, Jones, Brownell, & Rodin, 1994; Smith, Marcus, & Eldridge, 1994; see also chapter, 13, this volume).

Finally, many years after Stunkard's early observations (Stunkard & Burt, 1967; Stunkard & Mendelson, 1967), leading obesity researchers are calling for the inclusion of body image treatment strategies as a component of weight control programs (Brownell & Rodin, 1994; Brownell & Wadden, 1991; Garner & Wooley, 1991). This refocus can be traced to a number of findings, including evidence that (a) body dissatisfaction accompanies weight regain (Wadden, Stunkard, & Liebschutz, 1988), (b) biological factors make it virtually impossible to achieve the current cultural ideal (Brownell, 1991), and (c) the one consistent psychological difference between obese and normal-weight individuals may be in the area of body image (Stunkard & Wadden, 1992).

AN INTEGRATION

Evidence supporting the integration of body image, eating disorders, and obesity is present in a wide variety of emerging research designs and empirical findings. Developmental studies with adolescents provide strong empirical support for the integral role of body image in the formation of eating disorders (Heinberg, Wood, & Thompson, 1995; see also chapter 2, this volume). It also has been found that weight loss may not be associated with changes in body image, but improvements in body image satisfaction may occur in the absence of weight loss (Rosen, Orosan, & Reiter, 1995; see chapters 4 and 16, this volume). In this section, I will review recent work suggesting an integrative conceptualization of body image, eating disturbance, and obesity.

Over the past 15 years, a large number of correlational investigations have found an association between body image problems and eating disturbance (e.g., Rosen, 1990; Thompson, 1990). These findings recently have been supported by longitudinal analyses. For instance, in a 2-year longitudinal study of adolescent girls, Attie and Brooks-Gunn (1989) found that initial levels of body dissatisfaction—not family relationships, maturational status (early physical development), or psychopathology—predicted an increase in eating disturbance at the end of the 2-year period. Cattarin and Thompson (1994), in a 3-year longitudinal study of adolescent girls, found that body image dissatisfaction, not maturational status, was predictive of eating disturbance.

These findings have been replicated with adult samples. In a 2-year longitudinal study, Garner, Garfinkel, Rockert, and Olmsted (1987) found that only body dissatisfaction and restrictive eating tendencies predicted the development of eating-disordered symptoms in ballet students. Striegel-Moore, Silberstein, Frensch, and Rodin (1989), in a sample of women tested before and after their first year of college, determined that disordered eating was associated with weight dissatisfaction and decreased ratings of attractiveness. Covariance structure modeling studies also support the possible causal role of body image problems in the development of eating disturbance (Thompson et al., 1995). The interaction between body image and other risk factors (e.g., sociocultural pressures for thinness, athletic performance anxiety, and negative self-appraisal of athletic achievement) enhances the probability of eating disturbance in female athletes (Williamson et al., 1995).

In perhaps the most extensive longitudinal investigation of causal factors for the development of disordered eating, the findings for an etiological role for body image disturbance are inconclusive. Leon and colleagues currently are examining more than 800 boys and 800 girls who were assessed initially in Grades 7 to 10 (Leon, Fulkerson, Perry, & Cudeck, 1993; Leon, Fulkerson, Perry, & Early-Zald, 1995). For both boys and girls, the researchers found that body dissatisfaction was one of the few variables to predict concurrent risk status (eating disturbance) at three different time periods (Years 1, 2, and 3 of the study). However, body dissatisfaction at Year 1 and Year 2 was not a significant predictor of the development of risk status at Year 3. Leon et al. suggested that the predictive ability may have "dissipated in the prospective analyses because body dissatisfaction is so commmonly found in normal as well as eating disordered adolescent populations" (1995, p. 147). It should be noted that the researchers' sole measure of body image consisted of a nine-item subscale of the Eating Disorder Inventory, which indexes specific dissatisfaction with weight-relevant body sites (waist, hips, thighs, etc.) (see chapter 3, this volume).

The role of obesity in the development of body image problems is supported strongly by findings with adolescents and adults. Cattarin and Thompson (1994) found that an initial overweight status at the first testing predicted size and weight dissatisfaction 3 years later for female adolescents. Being overweight also predicted which girls would receive the most negative social feedback in the form of teasing about weight and size. The role of teasing as a mediator between weight status and the development of body dissatisfaction was found by Thompson et al. (1995). Covariance modeling studies indicated a directional relationship between weight status and teasing, but no causal relation between level of obesity and body image. However, teasing significantly predicted body image disturbance. In a sample of adult obese patients, Grilo, Wilfley, Brownell, and Rodin (1994) found that levels of teasing during adolescence were strongly predictive of concurrent levels of appearance dissatisfaction. Taken together, these findings indicate that overweight status, alone and in conjunction with its social consequences (i.e., teasing), contribute to the development of subjective distress regarding appearance. In their review, Friedman and Brownell (1995) concluded that teasing history was a potential risk factor for the development of body dissatisfaction and general psychological distress in obese individuals.

Alleviating the body image disturbances that may occur with excessive weight is not as simple as producing weight loss. In fact, there is evidence that body image may not change in tandem with weight modification. Cash (chapter 4, this volume) has referred to these residual problems of body disparagement after weight loss as *vestigial body image*. Cash, Counts, and Huffine (1990) tested this proposition by contrasting three groups of subjects: (a) currently overweight; (b) average weight, formerly overweight; and (c) average weight, never overweight. On multiple measures of body image, the two former groups were generally equivalent, with levels of disturbance higher than the group that was never overweight. The formerly overweight subjects appeared as distressed about appearance as the currently obese individuals.

Despite the possibility of an intractable vestigial disturbance consequent to weight loss, there is some evidence that supports the positive body image effects from a successful weight reduction program (Cash, 1994). However, regain of weight also is associated with a return of body dissatisfaction (Wadden et al., 1988). Rosen and colleagues (Rosen, Orosan, & Reiter, 1995; see also chapter 17, this volume) found positive effects from using cognitive–behavioral techniques to treat body image problems in obesity without accompanying procedures designed to produce weight loss (i.e., modify eating or exercise behavior). A specific targeting of body image problems as a component of weight loss programs may be especially important for overweight individuals with associated binge eating (Grilo, Wilfley, Jones, Brownell, & Rodin, 1994; see also chapter 13, this volume), avoidant personality characteristics (Thompson, 1992) or enrollees in rapid, commercial weight loss programs (Cash, 1993).

It is clear that body image problems are integral aspects of the presenting symptomatology of eating disorders and obesity. Therefore, an understanding of the many theoretical and practical issues related to the various types of body image disturbances is crucial for the practitioner involved in treating eating disorders and obesity. In addition, body image concerns, in the absence of an accompanying eating disorder or weight problem, nonetheless may be associated with considerable psychological distress and deserve psychotherapeutic intervention (see chapter 4, this volume).

Up to this point, I have not focused on any particular at-risk population group. However, no discussion of body image, in any context, would be complete without including issues related to gender and ethnicity. Evidence indicates that women, particularly Caucasian women, may be at greater risk for experiencing weight and shape dissatisfaction than men. It is clear that women account for the vast majority of individuals with anorexia nervosa and bulimia nervosa. It is also clear that eating problems and problems of shape and weight satisfaction affect individuals of diverse ethnic backgrounds. Because of its importance for understanding much of the treatment-oriented material to appear in subsequent chapters, I will discuss briefly the role of gender and ethnicity in shape and weight-related disorders.

THE ROLE OF GENDER AND ETHNICITY

For many years, the literature has reported that women with eating disorders, particularly anorexia nervosa, far outnumber men, perhaps by a 9 to 1 ratio (Fairburn & Beglin, 1990; Wolf, 1991). For women, there appears to be a prevalence ratio of .5% to 1.0% for anorexia nervosa and a ratio of 1.0% to 3.0% for bulimia nervosa (American Psychiatric Association, 1994). Rates of body dissatisfaction, indicated by levels of dieting behavior and subjective reports of appearance concern, also reveal gender differences. A national survey of 11,467 high school students and 60,861 adults by the Centers for Disease Control and Prevention provides the most comprehensive information for gender differences (Serdula et al., 1993). Among the adults, 38% of the women and 24% of the men were trying to lose weight. Among high school students, the differences were even more extreme: 44% of the females and 15% of the males were attempting to lose weight. In a recent national survey of females, Cash and Henry (1995) found that more than 40% had a negative body image; the sites of dissatisfaction were primarily in the weight-relevant areas of the body (waist, hips, thighs). Although these numbers do not reveal that weight- and appearance-related disorders are an exclusively female problem, they do suggest that females are at relatively greater risk.

There are a number of gender differences in development, social pressures, and biology that may explain these differences in the incidence of poor body image and eating disorders (Rolls, Fedoroff, & Guthrie, 1991). Striegel-Moore and Marcus (1995) offer an excellent summary of these influences, which include such factors as the central role of beauty in femininity, pubertal changes, and the expectation that women should be more interpersonally oriented. Currently, researchers are attempting to pinpoint the special risk factors in females that may explain their differential susceptibility to eating disorders and body image disturbance. For instance, in a longitudinal study of high school students (Leon et al., 1995), interoceptive awareness (poor interpretation of internal bodily signals, urges, and feelings) was found to be a significant predictor of eating disturbance for females but not for males. McCarthy (1990) and Nolen-Hoeksema and Girgus (1994) have also proposed that cultural pressures regarding appearance and body image disparagement may explain in part the greater incidence of depression in adolescent and adult females.

A consequence of the focus on societal and cultural factors that might explain the gender differences has been a fairly recent intensive focus on the articulation of feminist approaches (Fallon, Katzman, & Wooley, 1994; Gleaves & Eberenz, 1994; Levine, 1994; Schwartz, 1994). In general, these writers focus on the unique sociocultural pressures faced by women that set the stage for the development and maintenance of eating disturbances. For instance, the role of sexual abuse has received a great deal of attention (Kearney-Cooke & Striegel-Moore, 1994). Gilbert and Thompson (in press) recently identified five common themes of feminist explanations for eating disorders: a culture of thinness, weight as power and control, anxieties about female achievement, eating disorders as self-definition, and women as nurturers. Heinberg (chapter 2, this volume) and Garner and Needleman (chapter 10, this volume) introduce some of the important contributions of the feminist approach, both in terms of developmental and treatment implications.

Although the current data are largely supportive of historical gender differences in the occurrence of these disorders, there appears to be an increase in recent years in men with eating disorders. In a direct comparison of male and female eating-disordered patients, Powers and Spratt (1994) found no difference in the occurrence of sexual abuse, and determined that a history of physical and verbal abuse was more common in the male patients. Nemeroff, Stein, Diehl, and Smilack (1994) reviewed recent evidence that suggests males may be receiving increasing media messages regarding dieting, an ideal of muscularity, and plastic surgery options (such as pectoral and calf implants). They concluded that these changes "remain unexplored empirically, because there has been an assumption that body image problems are neither prevalent nor consequential for males" (p. 169). Furthermore, body image concerns may be important predictors of eating dysfunction for males. Wertheim and colleagues found that a desire to be thinner was a more important predictor of weight loss behaviors than psychological or family variables, for both male and female adolescents (Wertheim et al., 1992).

For both sexes, athletic status may be a risk factor for eating disorders and body image concerns. Gymnasts, runners, body builders, rowers, and wrestlers have all been found to have elevated levels of disturbance (Andersen, Bartlett, Morgan, & Brownell, 1995; McDonald & Thompson,

1992; Pasman & Thompson, 1988; Sykora, Grilo, Wilfley, & Brownell, 1993). Another particular at-risk group may be gay men (Gettelman & Thompson, 1993). Brand, Rothblum, and Solomon (1992) found that heterosexual women and gay men had lower ideal weights and were more preoccupied with their weights than heterosexual men and lesbians. However, lesbians and heterosexual women reported higher levels of overall body dissatisfaction and dieting than the two male samples.

As noted earlier, ethnicity also appears to be a moderator of disturbance in eating disorders and weight and shape disturbance. In recent years, a number of articles have addressed the occurrence of body dissatisfaction and symptoms of eating disturbance in individuals of different ethnic backgrounds. Although most of this research has determined that Caucasian females remain at relatively greater risk (Abrams, Allen, & Gray, 1993; Akan & Grilo, 1995; Leon et al., 1995; Powell & Kahn, 1995; Rucker & Cash, 1992), some findings indicate equivalent or even higher levels of disturbance in African American females (Pumariega, Gustavson, Gustavson, Motes, & Ayers, 1994; Striegel-Moore, Schreiber, Pike, Wilfley, & Rodin, 1995). In the report by the Centers for Disease Control and Prevention (Serdula et al., 1993) the number of women trying to lose weight was quite similar across the four ethnicities examined: Caucasian (38.4%), black (38.6%), Hispanic (37.7%), and "other" (38.9%). In addition, a number of studies reported clinical cases of eating disorders with individuals of a variety of different backgrounds (Ahmad, Waller, Verduyn, 1994; Ford, 1992; Schmidt, 1993). Researchers in future years will need to examine the relevance of extant measurement and treatment approaches, which have been validated on primarily Caucasian female samples, for individuals of a different background (see chapter 6, this volume).

In sum, gender appears to be a stronger moderator than ethnicity for the presence of eating disorders and body image disturbance. However, there appears to be little selectivity in the types of individuals who develop binge eating disorder and obesity. Binge eating disorder is somewhat more common than bulimia nervosa (Spitzer et al., 1993), but occurs equally in males and females in community samples (although slightly more women than men who attend weight control programs present with binge eating disorder). It also occurs among Caucasians and African Americans at similar rates (Yanovski, Nelson, Dubbert, & Spitzer, 1993). Obesity has increased dramatically in recent years and occurs roughly more often in men (31%) than women (24%) (National Academy of Sciences National Research Council, 1989). Some surveys put the prevalence among African American and Hispanic women as two or three times that of Caucasian females (Allison, Hoy, Fournier, & Heymsfield, 1993; see also chapter 18, this volume).

It now appears that individuals of both sexes and from diverse ethnic backgrounds are at risk for the development of eating disorders, obesity, and body image disturbance. Although the specific causative factors may vary across these different types of eating- and shape-related clinical problems, there is little doubt that body image disturbances are crucial to the development of the traditional eating disorders of anorexia nervosa and bulimia nervosa. In addition, body image concerns play an important role in the clinical presentation and management of binge eating disorder and obesity (Brownell & Rodin, 1994; Grilo et al., 1994; Smith et al., 1994). The likelihood that body image issues will present as a core feature of *any* patient with an eating problem, regardless of their background or the specific manifestation of the eating disturbance, should guide the clinician to assess carefully for the presence of a body image disturbance and consider its relevance for any treatment plan.

SCOPE AND ORGANIZATION OF THIS BOOK

As described in the preface, one goal of this book is to examine the role of body image disturbance in eating and weight-related disorders. However, a closely aligned second goal is to provide a contemporary review of empirically supported assessment and treatment approaches for these disorders. Therefore, chapters within individual sections on body image, eating disorders, and obesity will focus selectively on reliable and valid measurement methodologies and intervention strategies that have been proven effective in well controlled evaluative studies.

This book will not present, as do many other books, a series of chapters offering different psychotherapeutic approaches for body image disturbance, eating disorders, and obesity. Instead, the focus is on behavioral, cognitive–behavioral, and pharmacological interventions, because these have received the most empirical support in the literature. An obvious limitation of this approach is the potential of shortchanging new or potentially useful methodologies that have not been studied much. For instance, feminist approaches (as discussed earlier) and interpersonal psychotherapies for eating disorders currently are receiving a great deal of attention (Fallon, Katzman, & Wooley, 1994; Kearney-Cooke & Striegel-Moore, 1994; Wilfley et al., 1993), along with cognitive models of information processing that may alter future assessment procedures (Altabe & Thompson, in press; Vitousek & Hollon, 1990). The current status and future potential of these areas, along with other rapidly emerging approaches, although not a primary focus of this book, are nonetheless explored in several chapters (e.g., chapters 2, 10, and 12).

The book is divided into three parts: body image disturbance, eating disorders, and obesity. A brief introduction precedes each part, offering a guide to the organization of that content area, with a specific focus on the location of body image issues. Part I provides a broad overview of body image disturbance, designed to lay the foundation for later discussions on the relevance of body image for eating disorders and obesity. This section, which easily might be expanded to form a single book, covers assessment and treatment issues and also provides background on theories, the role of plastic surgery, the importance of cross-cultural issues in assessment and treatment, and a comprehensive review of the assessment and treatment of body dysmorphic disorder.

Part II focuses on eating disorders, including the newly emergent binge eating disorder diagnostic category. It offers a chapter on assessment methods particular to eating disorders, including structured interview and questionnaire strategies. A chapter also is devoted to the assessment of physical status; it contains a wide variety of medically related symptoms and features, a crucial area of expertise for the mental health professional. This part also thoroughly examines cognitive–behavioral treatments for anorexia nervosa and bulimia nervosa, as befits their strong empirical support. However, chapter 10 will evaluate the role of other therapeutic procedures, including feminist and interpersonal approaches, in a more integrative fashion that focuses on stepped-care and decision-tree models of treatment selection.

Because of its status as a relatively new disorder that is currently under consideration for *DSM* inclusion, chapter 13 explores the unique issues surrounding the etiology, assessment, and treatment of binge eating disorder. Although each treatment chapter contained in this part pays special attention to the modification of body image problems, chapter 12 devotes particular attention to the status of methods designed to change body image disturbance in individuals with eating disorders. Finally, chapter 14 reviews pharmacological treatments and examines the effect of various medications on body image.

Part III provides a review of assessment and treatment for various aspects of the obese condition. An assessment chapter deals with measurement of psychological factors in obesity as well as the ongoing research controversy regarding psychological disturbances in overweight individuals. This part includes an extensive discussion of various treatment approaches, and individual chapters are also offered for the unique situation of morbid obesity and the particular concerns of individuals of various ethnicities. Finally, although virtually ignored until recently, the management of body image issues in the obese is now seen as a major aspect of treatment. Therefore, chapter 17 covers the exciting developments in this area of research.

Each chapter and part is constructed to stand on its own. There is no requirement that the reader digest part I on body image as a prerequisite for understanding the following material. Body image is only one component of the symptomatic picture that is examined in chapters that outline assessment and treatment procedures for eating disorders and obesity. However, an examination of the material in part I may foster an appreciation of the newly emerging role of body image as an integral factor in the management of these disorders.

CONCLUSION

More than 30 years ago, clinicans and researchers noted the important role of body image in the development and treatment of eating and weight-related problems. As we approach the next millenium, a confluence of factors have aligned to produce intense investigative activity in this field. A number of psychometrically sound instruments for assessing body image disturbance have emerged recently. Several well controlled, comparative-outcome studies have clearly indicated the effectiveness of cognitive–behavioral approaches for treating body image problems. These two accomplishments, achieved primarily with non-eating-disordered, normal-weight samples, laid the foundation for the timely application of the methodologies to the body image problems associated with obesity and eating disorders.

In addition, as noted earlier in this chapter, longitudinal analyses have established the important role of body image and obesity as precursors to eating dysfunction and psychological distress in adolescents. Body image concerns, while also present in non-eating-disordered individuals, play a particularly important role in the psychopathology and prognosis of individuals with eating disorders. Finally, although often dismissed as a by-product of overweight status, research now shows that body image concerns remain following weight loss, whereas treatments for body image concerns may lessen disturbance in the absence of weight reductions.

This book underscores the importance of a common feature—body image disturbance—in the etiology, assessment, and treatment of eating and weight-related disorders. As the subsequent sections and chapters will make clear, researchers and clinicians have made great strides in developing sound technologies of assessment and treatment. However, important research avenues remain, especially with regard to extending findings to a variety of population groups differing in age, gender, ethnicity, and socioeconomic status. The integration of body image assessment and modification procedures with extant psychotheraputic approaches will surely continue to occupy researchers and practitioners in future years.

REFERENCES

Abrams, K. K., Allen, L. R., & Gray, J. J. (1993). Disordered eating attitudes and behaviors, psychological adjustment, and ethnic identity: A comparison of black and white female college students. *International Journal of Eating Disorders, 14*, 49–58.

Ahmad, S., Waller, G., & Verduyn, C. (1994). Eating attitudes among Asian schoolgirls: The role of perceived parental control. *International Journal of Eating Disorders, 15*, 91–97.

Akan, G. E., & Grilo, C. M. (1995). Sociocultural influences on eating attitudes and behaviors, body image, and psychological functioning: A comparison of African-American, Asian-American, and Caucasian college women. *International Journal of Eating Disorders, 18*, 181–187.

Allison, D. B., Hoy, M. K., Fournier, A., & Heymsfield, S. B. (1993). Can ethnic differences in men's preferences for women's body shapes contribute to ethnic differences in female adiposity? *Obesity Research, 1*, 425–431.

Altabe, M. N., & Thompson, J. K. (in press). Body image: Is there a cognitive self-schema? *Cognitive Therapy and Research.*

Altabe, M. N., & Thompson, J. K. (1994). Body image. In V. S. Ramachandran (Ed.), *Encyclopedia of human behavior* (Vol. 1, pp. 407–414). San Diego, CA: Academic Press.

American Psychiatric Association. (1980). *Diagnostic and statistical manual of mental disorders* (3rd ed.). Washington, DC: Author.

American Psychiatric Association.(1987). *Diagnostic and statistical manual of mental disorders* (3rd ed., rev.). Washington, DC: Author.

American Psychiatric Association. (1994). *Diagnostic and statistical manual of mental disorders* (4th ed.). Washington, DC: Author

Andersen, R. E., Barlett, S. J., Morgan, G. D., & Brownell, K. D. (1995). Weight loss, psychological and nutritional patterns in competitive male body builders. *International Journal of Eating Disorders, 18*, 49–57.

Attie, I., & Brooks-Gunn, J. (1989). Development of eating problems in adolescent girls: A longitudinal study. *Developmental Psychology, 25*, 70–79.

Brand, P. A., Rothblum, E. D., & Solomon, L. J. (1992). A comparison of lesbians, gay men, and heterosexuals on weight and restrained eating. *International Journal of Eating Disorders, 11*, 253–260.

Brownell, K. D. (1991). Dieting and the search for the perfect body: Where physiology and culture collide. *Behavior Therapy, 22*, 1–12.

Brownell, K. D., & Rodin, J. (1994). The dieting maelstrom: Is it possible and advisable to lose weight? *American Psychologist, 49*, 781–791.

Brownell, K. D., & Wadden, T. A. (1991). The heterogeneity of obesity: Fitting treatments to individuals. *Behavior Therapy, 22*, 153–177.

Bruch, J. (1962). Perceptual and conceptual disturbances in anorexia nervosa. *Canadian Journal of Psychiatry, 26*, 187–194.

Cash, T. F. (1993). Body-image attitudes among obese enrollees in a commercial weight-loss program. *Perceptual and Motor Skills, 77*, 1099–1103.

Cash, T. F. (1994). Body image and weight changes in a multisite comprehensive very-low calorie diet program. *Behavior Therapy, 25*, 239–254.

Cash, T. F., & Brown, T. A. (1987). Body image in anorexia nervosa and bulimia nervosa: A review of the literature. *Behavior Modification, 11,* 487–521.

Cash, T. F., Counts, B., & Huffine, C. E. (1990). Current and vestigial effects of overweight among women: Fear of fat, attitudinal body image, and eating behaviors. *Journal of Psychopathology and Behavioral Assessment, 12,* 157–167.

Cash, T. F., & Deagle, E. A. (1995). The nature and extent of body-image disturbances in anorexia nervosa and bulimia nervosa: A meta-analysis. Unpublished manusrcipt.

Cash, T. F., & Henry, P. E. (1995). Women's body images: The results of a national survey in the U.S.A. *Sex Roles, 33,* 19–28.

Cash, T. F., Winstead, B. A., & Janda, L. J. (1986, April). Body image survey report: The great American shape-up. *Psychology Today, 24,* 30–37.

Cattarin, J. A., & Thompson, J. K. (1994). A three-year longitudinal study of body image, eating disturbance, and general psychological functioning in adolescent females. *Eating Disorders: The Journal of Treatment and Prevention, 2,* 114–125.

Fairburn, C. G., & Beglin, S. J. (1990). Studies of the epidemiology of bulimia nervosa. *American Journal of Psychiatry, 147,* 401–408.

Fallon, P., Katzman, M., & Wooley, S. C. (Eds.). (1994). *Feminist perspectives on eating disorders.* New York: Guilford Press.

Fisher, S. (1986). *Development and structure of the body image.* Hillsdale, NJ: Erlbaum.

Ford, K. A. (1992). Bulimia in an Egyptian student: A case study. *International Journal of Eating Disorders, 11,* 407–411.

Friedman, M. A., & Brownell, K. D. (1995). Psychological correlates of obesity: Moving to the next research generation. *Psychological Bulletin, 117,* 3–20.

Garner, D. M., & Garfinkel, P. E. (1981). Body image in anorexia nervosa: Measurement, theory, and clinical implications. *International Journal of Psychiatry in Medicine, 11,* 263–284.

Garner, D. M., Garfinkel, P. E., Rockert, W., & Olmsted, M. P. (1987). A prospective study of eating disturbances in the ballet. *Psychotherapy and Psychosomatics, 48,* 170–175.

Garner, D. M., & Wooley, S. C. (1991). Confronting the failure of behavioral and dietary treatments for obesity. *Clinical Psychology Review, 11,* 729–780.

Gettelman, T. E., & Thompson, J. K. (1993). Actual differences and stereotypical perceptions in body image and eating disturbance: A comparison of male and female heterosexual and homosexual samples. *Sex Roles, 29,* 545–562.

Gilbert, S., & Thompson, J. K. (in press). Feminist explanations of the development of eating disorders: Common themes, research findings, and methodological issues. *Clinical Psychology: Science and Practice.*

Gleaves, D. H., & Eberenz, K. P. (1994). Sexual abuse histories among treatment-resistant bulimia nervosa patients. *International Journal of Eating Disorders, 15,* 227–232.

Grilo, C. M., Wilfley, D. E., Brownell, K. D., & Rodin, J. (1994). Teasing, body image, and self-esteem in a clinical sample of obese women. *Addictive Behaviors, 19*, 443–450.

Grilo, C. M., Wilfley, D. E., Jones, A., Brownell, K. D., & Rodin, J. (1994). The social self, body dissatisfaction, and binge eating in obese females. *Obesity Research, 2*, 24–27.

Heinberg, L. J., Wood, K. C., & Thompson, J. K. (1995). Body image. In V. I. Rickert (Ed.), *Adolescent nutrition: Assessment and management* (pp. 136–156). New York: Chapman and Hall.

Kearney-Cooke, A., & Striegel-Moore, R. H. (1994). Treatment of childhood sexual abuse in anorexia nervosa and bulimia nervosa: A feminist psychodynamic approach. *International Journal of Eating Disorders, 15*, 305–320.

Leon, G. R., Fulkerson, J. A., Perry, C. L., & Cudeck, R. (1993). Personality and behavioral vulnerabilities associated with risk status for eating disorders in adolescent girls. *Journal of Abnormal Psychology, 102*, 438–444.

Leon, G. R., Fulkerson, J. A., Perry, C. L., & Early-Zald, M. B. (1995). Prospective analysis of personality and behavioral vulnerabilities and gender influences in later development of disordered eating. *Journal of Abnormal Psychology, 104*, 140–149.

Levine, M. P. (1994). Beauty myth and the beast: What men can do and be to prevent eating disorders. *Eating Disorders: The Journal of Treatment and Prevention, 2*, 101–113.

McCarthy, M. (1990). The thin ideal, depression and eating disorders in women. *Behaviour Research and Therapy, 28*, 205–215.

McDonald, K., & Thompson, J. K. (1992). Eating disturbance, body image dissatisfaction, and reasons for exercising: Gender differences and correlational findings. *International Journal of Eating Disorders, 11*, 289–292.

National Academy of Sciences, National Research Council. (1989). *Diet and health: Implications for reducing chronic disease risk.* Washington, DC: National Academy Press.

Nemeroff, C. J., Stein, R. I., Diehl, N. S., & Smilack, K. M. (1994). From the Cleavers to the Clintons: Role choices and body orientation as reflected in magazine article content. *International Journal of Eating Disorders, 16*, 167–176.

Nolen-Hoeksema, S., & Girgus, J. S. (1994). The emergence of gender differences in depression during adolescence. *Journal of Abnormal Psychology, 115*, 424–443.

Pasman, L., & Thompson, J. K. (1988). Body image and eating disturbance in obligatory weightlifters, obligatory runners, and sedentary individuals. *International Journal of Eating Disorders, 7*, 759–768.

Penner, L., Thompson, J. D., & Coovert, D. L. (1991). Size estimation among anorexics: Much ado about very little? *Journal of Abnormal Psychology, 100*, 90–93.

Powell, A. D., & Kahn, A. S. (1995). Racial differences in women's desires to be thin. *International Journal of Eating Disorders, 17*, 191–195.

Powers, P. A., & Spratt, E. G. (1994). Males and females with eating disorders. *Eating Disorders: The Journal of Treatment and Prevention, 2*, 197–214.

Pumariega, A. J., Gustavson, C. R., Gustavson, J. C., Motes, P. S., & Ayers, S. (1994). Eating attitudes in African American women: The *Essence* eating disorders survey. *Eating Disorders: The Journal of Treatment and Prevention, 2*, 5–16.

Rodin, J., Silberstein, L. R., & Striegel-Moore, R. H. (1985). Women and weight: A normative discontent. In T. B. Sonderegger (Ed.), *Psychology and gender. Nebraska Symposium on Motivation, 1984* (pp. 267–307). Lincoln: University of Nebraska Press.

Rolls, B. J., Fedoroff, I. C., & Guthrie, J. F. (1991). Gender differences in eating behavior and body weight regulation. *Health Psychology, 10*, 133–142.

Rosen, J. C. (1990). Body image disturbance in eating disorders. In T. F. Cash & T. Pruzinsky (Eds.), *Body images: Development, deviance, and change* (pp. 190–214). New York: Guilford Press.

Rosen, J. C. (in press). Cognitive behavioral body image therapy for eating disorders. In D. M. Garner and P. E. Garfinkel (Eds.), *Handbook of treatment for eating disorders*. New York: Guilford Press.

Rosen, J. C., Orosan, P., & Reiter, J. (1995). Cognitive behavior therapy for negative body image in obese women. *Behavior Therapy, 26*, 25–42.

Rucker, C. E., & Cash, T. F. (1992). Body images, body-size perceptions, and eating behaviors among African American and White college women. *International Journal of Eating Disorders, 12*, 291–299.

Schmidt, U. (1993). Bulimia nervosa in the Chinese. *International Journal of Eating Disorders, 14*, 505–510.

Schwartz, M. (Ed.). (1994). Special double issue on eating disorders and sexual abuse. *Eating Disorders: The Journal of Treatment and Prevention, 2*, 195–333.

Serdula, M. K., Collins, M. E., Williamson, D. F., Anda, R. F., Pamuk, E. R., & Byers, T. E. (1993). Weight control practices of U.S. adolescents and adults. *Annals of Internal Medicine, 119*, 667–671.

Slade, P. D. (1985). A review of body-image studies in anorexia nervosa and bulimia nervosa. *Journal of Psychiatric Research, 19*, 255–265.

Slade, P. D., & Russell, G. F. M. (1973). Awareness of body dimensions in anorexia nervosa: Cross-sectional and longitudinal studies. *Psychological Medicine, 3*, 188–199.

Smith, D. E., Marcus, M. D., & Eldridge, K. L. (1994). Binge eating syndromes: A review of assessment and treatment with an emphasis on clinical application. *Behavior Therapy, 25*, 635–658.

Spitzer, R. L., Yanovski, S. Z., Wadden, T., Wing, R., Marcus, R., Marcus, M. D., Stunkard, A., Devlin, M., Mitchell, J., Hasin, D., & Horne, R. L. (1993). Binge eating disorder: Its further validation in a multisite study. *International Journal of Eating Disorders, 13*, 137–153.

Striegel-Moore, R. H., & Marcus, M. D. (1995). Eating disorders in women: Current issues and debates. In A. L. Stanton & S. J. Gallant (Eds.), *The psychology of women's health: Progress and challenges in research and application* (pp. 445–487). Washington, DC: American Psychological Association.

Striegel-Moore, R. H., Schreiber, G. B., Pike, K. M., Wilfley, D. E., & Rodin, J. (1995). Drive for thinness in Black and White preadolescent girls. *International Journal of Eating Disorders, 18*, 59–69.

Striegel-Moore, R. H., Silberstein, L. R., Frensch, P., & Rodin, J. (1989). A prospective study of disordered eating among college students. *International Journal of Eating Disorders, 8*, 499–509.

Stunkard, A. J., & Burt, V. (1967). Obesity and the body image: II. Age at onset of disturbances in the body image. *American Journal of Psychiatry, 123*, 1443–1447.

Stunkard, A. J., & Mendelson, M. (1967). Obesity and body image: I. Characteristics of disturbances in the body image of some obese persons. *American Journal of Psychiatry, 123*, 1296–1300.

Stunkard, A. J., & Wadden, T. A. (1992). Psychological aspects of severe obesity. *American Journal of Clinical Nutrition, 55*, 5245–5325.

Sykora, C., Grilo, C. M., Wilfley, D. E., & Brownell, K. D. (1993). Eating, weight, and dieting disturbances in male and female lightweight and heavyweight rowers. *International Journal of Eating Disorders, 14*, 203–211.

Thompson, J. K. (1990). *Body image disturbance: Assessment and treatment.* Elmsford, NY: Pergamon Press.

Thompson, J. K. (1992). Body image: Extent of disturbance, associated features, theoretical models, assessment methodologies, intervention strategies, and a proposal for a new DSM-IV category—body image disorder. In M. Hersen, R. M. Eisler, & P. M. Miller (Eds.), *Progress in behavior modification* (Vol. 28, pp. 3–54). Sycamore, IL: Sycamore Press.

Thompson, J. K. (1995). Assessment of body image. In D. B. Allison (Ed.), *Handbook of assessment methods for eating behaviors and weight-related problems* (pp. 119–148). Thousand Oaks, CA: Sage.

Thompson, J. K., Berland, N. W., Linton, P. H., & Weinsier, R. (1986). Assessment of body distortion via a self-adjusting light beam in seven eating disorder groups. *International Journal of Eating Disorders, 7*, 113–120.

Thompson, J. K., Coovert, M. D., Richards, K. J., Johnson, S., & Cattarin, J. A. (1995). Development of body image, eating disturbance, and general psychological functioning in female adolescents: Covariance structure modeling and longitudinal investigations. *International Journal of Eating Disorders, 18*, 221–236.

Vandereycken, W. (1994). Emergence of bulimia nervosa as a separate diagnostic entity: Review of the literature from 1960 to 1979. *International Journal of Eating Disorders, 16*, 105–116.

Vitousek, K. B., & Hollon, S. D. (1990). The investigation of schematic content and processing in eating disorders. *Cognitive Therapy and Research, 14,* 191–214.

Wadden, T. A., Stunkard, A. J., & Liebschutz, J. (1988). Three year follow-up of the treatment of obesity by very low calorie diet, behavior therapy, and their combination. *Journal of Consulting and Clinical Psychology, 56,* 925–928.

Wertheim, E. H., Paxton S. J., Maude, D., Szmukler, G. I, Gibbons, K., & Hiller, L. (1992). Psychosocial predictors of weight loss behaviors and binge eating in adolescent girls and boys. *International Journal of Eating Disorders, 12,* 151–160.

Wilfley, D. E., Agras, W. S., Telch, C. F., Rossiter, E. M., Schneider, J. A., Cole, A. G., Sifford, L., & Raeburn, S. D. (1993). Group cognitive–behavioral therapy and group interpersonal psychotherapy for the nonpurging bulimic individual: A controlled comparison. *Journal of Consulting and Clinical Psychology, 61,* 296–305.

Williamson, D. A., Netemeyer, R. G., Jackman, L. P., Anderson, D. A., Funsch, C. L., & Rabalais, J. Y. (1995). Structural equation modeling of risk factors for the development of eating disorder symptoms in female athletes. *International Journal of Eating Disorders, 17,* 387–393.

Wolf, N. (1991). *The beauty myth.* New York: William Morrow.

Yanovski, S. Z., Nelson, J. E., Dubbert, B. K., & Spitzer, R. L. (1993). Association of binge eating disorder and psychiatric comorbidity in obese subjects. *American Journal of Psychiatry, 150,* 1472–1479.

I

BODY IMAGE DISTURBANCE

INTRODUCTION

BODY IMAGE DISTURBANCE

This section covers a broad range of topics related to body image disturbance. These range from dissatisfaction with body shape and weight to distress over real and imagined facial disfigurement that may result in requests for cosmetic surgery.

Heinberg begins in chapter 2 by providing an overview of individual and sociocultural factors involved in body shape and weight-related concerns. She looks at perceptual factors believed to be involved, such as those related to cortical deficits, adaptive failure, and perceptual artifacts. She also examines more subjective factors, such as those explained by self-ideal discrepancy and social comparison theory, and a particular trauma that may disturb normal body image development—childhood sexual abuse. Heinberg focuses on contemporary and historical sociocultural ideals of thinness and the influences of gender-role socialization. She discusses briefly the role of the mass media in perpetuating unattainable ideals and describes the feminist perspective on body image and eating disorders. This includes the important influence of culturally reinforced ideals of thinness on women's self-esteem, coping, and sense of control, all of which are believed to be involved with body image, body dissatisfaction, and eating disorders.

In chapter 3, I provide an overview of the variety of assessment methods available for measuring body image disturbance. Methods target perceptual (size estimation), subjective (affective, cognitive), and behavioral aspects of body image. I provide descriptions of measures, along with a table of reliabilities, normative reference groups, and addresses for obtaining further information from the developers of scales. I discuss a number of methodological issues that determine the selection and use of specific measures and offer recommendations for compiling an initial assessment battery. However, I also advocate an individually based procedure, predicated on specific client concerns.

Cash follows in chapter 4 with an in-depth analysis of treatment of body image in non-eating-disordered individuals. This is the first of several intervention-oriented chapters, and his discussion of cognitive–behavioral strategies provides a solid background for the material on modifying body image disturbance covered in the rest of this book. His early presentation of developmental and concurrent activating events that affect body image complements the material provided in chapter 2. The information on assessment also builds on my coverage in chapter 3. However, the major focus of this chapter is Cash's step-by-step guide for using cognitive–behavioral treatment strategies. The components of this empirically validated approach include exposure and desensitization procedures, identifying and challenging faulty appearance assumptions and cognitive errors, modifying self-defeating body image behaviors, developing body image enhancement activities, and programming for relapse prevention and maintenance of changes.

The next three chapters focus on special populations and their distinct body image concerns. In chapter 5, Pruzinsky provides a broad coverage of the rapidly evolving field of cosmetic surgery. Experts predict that the number of individuals considering and choosing plastic surgery as a treatment for body image concerns will continue to increase in future years. This chapter is essential reading for the clinician who encounters such a patient. Pruzinsky first discusses the types of surgery and the multiple issues involved in patient selection, such as patient expectations. He advocates a multimodal assessment, consisting of screening for psychological disorders, eating disorders, body dysmorphic disorder, depression, and personality disorders. He then examines the special concerns of male patients, adolescents, and women with breast implants.

In chapter 6, Altabe provides one of the first reviews of the role of ethnicity in body image disturbance. In recent years, several investigations have compared directly individuals of different ethnicities or people from different countries. These findings, although preliminary, suggest that body image disturbances are found within many ethnic and geographical groups. She reviews the literature comparing body image from diverse ethnic groups in both Western and non-Western countries. One limitation she notes is the reliance on measures developed on primarily Caucasian samples to evaluate individuals from a different background. The chapter offers suggestions for researching body image in culturally diverse groups and provides guidance in assessing body image and in assessing and treating body image disturbances in members of these groups.

In chapter 7, Rosen closes the section with a comprehensive exploration of body dysmorphic disorder, a clinical phenomenon that inhabits the extreme end of the continuum of body image disturbance. His overview of the clinical features includes the various types of dysmorphia and cognitive, affective, and behavioral features. Rosen presents information on the differential diagnosis and development of this disorder and follows with a presentation of the Body Dysmorphic Disorder Examination, which was developed by Rosen and colleagues and rapidly has become the standard for assessment in this area. Treatment guidelines include cognitive restructuring, behavioral exposure to avoided situations, and response prevention.

2

THEORIES OF BODY IMAGE DISTURBANCE: PERCEPTUAL, DEVELOPMENTAL, AND SOCIOCULTURAL FACTORS

LESLIE J. HEINBERG

Theories of body image disturbance can be divided usefully for discussion into three major categories: perceptual, developmental, and sociocultural. The last two focus on a more subjective aspect of body image than does the first theory. The distinction between developmental and sociocultural factors, although useful in organizing a discussion, is to some degree artificial because it is clear that both categories of factors can interact to influence and maintain body image disturbance in a particular individual.

Researchers in the field of body image disturbance generally delineate between a perceptual aspect of body image and a subjective aspect (Cash & Brown, 1987; Thompson, 1990; chapter 3, this volume). In the first section, I will review research supporting the perceptual theories of body image disturbance. These include cortical deficits, adaptive failure, and perceptual artifact theories. Then, under subjective aspects of individual etiology, I will address aspects of developmental theory (i.e., the effects of early maturation and of teasing). I also will describe in brief the influence of sexual abuse on the development of body image disturbance.

The next section, and the majority of the chapter, will focus on sociocultural theory. This analysis will review socioculturally endorsed ideals, feminist theories, the influence of gender roles and the mass media, and laboratory studies. Finally, self-ideal discrepancy, social comparison theory, and other socioculturally based theories will be discussed.

PERCEPTUAL THEORIES

Perceptual theories of body image disturbance address the accuracy of perceptions regarding one's size (e.g., the belief that one is larger than one's actual size). This perceptual aspect is often discussed in reference to eating disorders, and is a recognized diagnostic feature of anorexia nervosa in the *Diagnostic and Statistical Manual of Mental Disorders* (4th edition, American Psychiatric Association, 1994). The following three theories have been offered to explain this perceptually related dimension of body image disturbance.

Cortical Deficits

Researchers have done few studies to examine the cortical components of appearance-related body image. In one study, Thompson and Spana (1991) developed a theory of cortical disturbance to explain perceptual disturbance. They hypothesized that size overestimation relies on visuospatial ability and may be the result of more general visuospatial deficits that can be measured via neuropsychological testing. Their results indicated that size overestimation was related positively to more general visuospatial abilities, as measured by the Benton Visual Retention Test (Thompson & Spana, 1991). In contrast, a study by Dolce, Thompson, Register, and Spana (1987) found that subjects demonstrated greater overestimation for themselves than for a mannequin. Thus, accuracy of size perception may not be simply a consequence of visuospatial ability. Instead, as Dolce et al. (1987) concluded, cognitive and affective influences may interact with perceptual skills to produce size perception estimates.

Other researchers point to neurological disorders of body image or body schema, such as those associated with irritative parietal lobe foci caused by epilepsy or migraine, and posit that the perceptual body image disturbance in anorexia nervosa may be the result of neuropsychological disorders (Braun & Chouinard, 1992; Trimble, 1988). These researchers further hypothesize that people with anorexia nervosa may suffer from automacrosomatognosia, which consists of a hallucination or delusion of one's body being larger than it actually is. Automacrosomatognosia often is associated with brain paroxysms; its focus is within or contiguous with the parietal lobe and requires both subcortical and cortical involvement (Braun & Chouinard, 1992).

Adaptive Failure

Proponents of adaptive failure theory, another explanation for overestimation of body size, maintain that subjects' perceptions of their body size may not change at the same rate as their actual size changes (as they lose or gain weight). Crisp and Kalucy (1974) hypothesized that individuals maintain the perception of their body size at its maximum weight and size. Following weight loss, perception of body size was predicted to remain constant: The greater the size changes, the higher the overestimation of body size. Slade (1977) found partial support for this hypothesis by testing women at 4 and 8 months of pregnancy, finding greater accuracy at 8 months. However, no measurements were taken prior to 4 months of pregnancy, and it is possible that weight and size changes already took place. However, perhaps because of the difficulty of following subjects from their maximum weight through various stages of weight loss, adaptive failure theory has not been empirically tested adequately (Thompson, 1990).

Perceptual Artifact

Researchers favoring perceptual artifact theory propose that a tendency to overestimate one's body size is related to one's actual body size. That is, individuals who are of a smaller size overestimate to a larger extent than individuals of average or larger sizes (Coovert, Thompson, & Kinder, 1988; Penner, Thompson, & Coovert, 1991; chapter 3, this volume). To test this theory, Penner et al. (1991) matched control subjects with anorexic subjects on actual size, selecting a dispositionally thin non-eating-disordered group that was size-matched to the anorexic subjects. Results revealed no differences in the level of overestimation for the anorexic and small-sized control subjects, but both groups overestimated more than randomly selected average-sized control subjects. Coovert et al. (1988) tested perceptual artifact theory in a large sample of normal subjects by correlating actual body size with degree of overestimation. Results indicated that larger levels of overestimation were associated with smaller body sizes. An implication of the Penner et al. (1991) and Coovert et al. (1988) findings is the need to covary out actual size in any study of size estimation of different sized groups (i.e., obese vs. normal, anorexic vs. normal).

SUBJECTIVE THEORIES

A subjective component of body image addresses satisfaction with one's body size or specific body parts. It is often the more subjective aspects of body image that are examined in nonclinical populations. In the past several years, multiple theories have been offered to explain the prevalence of subjective body image disturbance in non-eating-disordered individuals. These theories can be divided into developmental and sociocultural factors.

Developmental Theories

A great deal of research has focused upon the important role of childhood and adolescent development in later body image disturbance. Under the rubric of developmental theories, I will review pubertal and maturational timing, teasing and negative verbal commentary, and early sexual abuse or sexualization.

Puberty and Maturational Timing

Much of the work in the area of body image development focuses on the importance of puberty and maturational timing. Pubertal development is associated with multiple physical and psychological changes for both genders and often is considered to be an important milestone in body image development. For example, Fabian and Thompson (1989) compared subjective and perceptual measures of body image for premenarcheal and postmenarcheal girls and found that postmenarcheal girls were more likely to overestimate the size of their thighs. In addition, for postmenarcheal girls, size overestimation was correlated positively with a history of being teased about body size (Fabian & Thompson, 1989).

Several studies have documented the relationship between maturational timing and body image dissatisfaction. In general, girls who mature later than their peers (i.e., experience menarche after the age of 14) have a more positive body image than those who reach menarche early (before the age of 11) or on time (between the ages of 11 and 14). For example, Brooks-Gunn and Warren (1985) noted that late maturers reported less dissatisfaction, more eating-disordered behavior, and higher overall weight than girls who matured on time or early.

A variety of explanations have been offered to interpret these results. J. K. Thompson (1992) explains that late maturation appears to result in less body fat and weight. What may be even more important is that early maturation and the resulting physical changes may place an adolescent at higher risk for being teased (the following section will explore teasing and negative verbal commentary) (Fabian & Thompson, 1989). As evidence for this latter explanation, Cattarin and Thompson (1994) found, in a 3-year longitudinal study of adolescent body image, that teasing history, but not pubertal timing, predicted later body image dissatisfaction.

Additional research suggests that a synchronous model (one that emphasizes the synchronous stressful events that occur during puberty) is supported over a model emphasizing the timing of puberty (early vs. late) as a possible explanation for the development of body image disturbance (Levine, Smolak, Moodey, Shuman, & Hessen 1994; Smolak, Levine, & Gralen, 1993). Smolak et al. (1993) demonstrated that girls with synchronous onset of menstruation and dating had greater eating disturbance and body image dissatisfaction than those with onset of menstruation alone. Girls for whom puberty was early and coincided with dating had the highest levels of body image dissatisfaction and eating disturbance. Regression analyses of longitudinal data by Levine et al. (1994) suggest a complex equation in which the addition of academic stress to the confluence of advanced pubertal status and dating onset resulted in an even more significant increase in risk for disturbed eating.

Negative Verbal Commentary and Teasing

An additional developmental factor that has gained attention recently is the important role that teasing, or negative verbal commentary, plays in the formation of body image. In an adolescent sample, Fabian and Thompson (1989) found that teasing was related significantly to body satisfaction, eating disturbance, and self-esteem. It appears that teasing during developmentally sensitive periods may have lasting effects. For instance, Brown, Cash, and Lewis (1989) reported that adolescents with eating disturbances had a greater history of being teased by peers than control subjects without bingeing or purging symptoms. As noted earlier, Cattarin and Thompson (1994) found that teasing predicted the development of body dissatisfaction in adolescent females. Cash, Winstead, and Janda (1986) found that adult women who had been teased about their appearances during childhood were more dissatisfied with their appearance than women who had been teased rarely. In addition, in adult samples, several studies indicate that teasing during adolescence is related to adult levels of body dissatisfaction, eating disturbance, and overall psychological functioning (Thompson, Fabian, Moulton, Dunn, & Altabe, 1991). Thompson, Coovert, Richards, Johnson, and Cattarin (1995), using exploratory causal modeling procedures, found that teasing history had a direct influence on body image, eating disturbances, and overall psychological functioning. In an explanation of the negative effects of teasing, Giles (1988), in a case report of a patient with bulimia nervosa, suggested the trauma of a teasing experience may have been an etiological mechanism for the patient's conditioned fear of social disapproval regarding body shape. A relationship between teasing and body image also has been found among obese individuals (Grilo, Wilfley, Brownell, & Rodin, 1994).

More recently, researchers have examined aspects of negative feedback more subtle than teasing (e.g., commentary on food intake). Tantleff-Dunn, Thompson, and Dunn (1995) have developed a measure assessing this type of negative verbal commentary and have demonstrated that even more subtle aspects are associated with body image dissatisfaction and eating disturbance.

Early Sexual Abuse and Sexualization

A few studies have examined the relationship between childhood sexual abuse and the development of body image disturbance. Although there is mixed evidence that eating-disordered patients have a higher incidence of childhood sexual abuse (Hastings & Kern, 1994), Pope and Hudson (1992) reviewed the literature and concluded that early sexual abuse is not a risk factor for eating-disordered behavior. However, interest has remained in the possible relationship between abuse history, body image, and eating disturbance (Hastings & Kern, 1994).

Waller, Hamilton, Rose, Sumra, and Baldwin (1993) found no difference between eating disturbed patients with and without sexual abuse histories on body size overestimation. However, women who reported more recent abuse had significantly greater body size overestimation than both women without an abuse history and those who had been abused prior to the age of 14. Gardner, Gardner, and Morrell (1990) found no differences when comparing degree of overestimation among children who had histories of physical abuse, sexual abuse, or no abuse history. Weiner and Thompson (1995) examined the relationship between overt sexual abuse, covert sexual abuse (such as sexually inappropriate commentary or sexually related teasing), and body image. Women who reported a history of both types of abuse demonstrated greater body image dissatisfaction. Clearly, more research, particularly work examining more subjective indices of body image dissatisfaction, is necessary to examine a possible link between early sexual abuse and body image disturbance.

Sociocultural Theories

Sociocultural theories of body image disturbance examine the influence of common or culture-wide social ideals, expectations, and experiences on the etiology and maintenance of body image disturbance. Most researchers appear to agree that the strongest influences on the development of body image and body image disturbance in Western societies are sociocultural factors (Fallon, 1990; Heinberg, Thompson, & Stormer, 1995). This explanation of body image disturbance is also best supported by available data, although much of this data is correlational in nature. In this section, I examine socioculturally endorsed ideals of thinness and attractiveness, feminist theories, gender-role socialization, and the influence of mass media. I will also examine self-ideal discrepancy, social comparison, and other socioculturally based theories.

Sociocultural Ideals

The current societal standard for thinness in women is pervasive and, unfortunately, often out of reach for the average woman. In a society in which "what is beautiful is good" (Franzoi & Herzog, 1987, p. 19), thinness has become almost synonymous with beauty (Striegel-Moore, McAvay, & Rodin, 1986; Thompson, 1990). Researchers have found that although thinness is valued by society, its opposite—obesity—is seriously denigrated (Rand & Kuldau, 1990; Rodin, Silberstein, & Striegel-Moore, 1985). As a result of this current societal pressure, Vandereycken (1993) asserts that Western cultures have become *lipophobic*. Although current societal ideals promote thinness, additional evidence suggests that women are pressured to achieve appearance goals that are sometimes contradictory to thinness—for example, the possession of large breasts (Thompson & Tantleff, 1992) or a muscular physique (Striegel-Moore, Silberstein, & Rodin, 1986). One's somatotype often conflicts with society's prescribed ideal (Brownell, 1991). And, although thinness is partially under an individual's control, many other socioculturally endorsed aspects of appearance—such as youth and height—are less amenable to alteration. Although some changes may be possible through cosmetics or plastic surgery, sociohistorical changes favoring an aging population and increasing prevalence of obesity (see chapter 18, this volume) will result inevitably in increasingly fewer women who are able to meet the "ideal."

Recent trends. The ideals of feminine beauty have varied and changed in accordance with the aesthetic standards of the particular period of time, and a great percentage of women have attempted to alter themselves to meet these ideals (Mazur, 1986). Previous research has suggested that there has been movement away from a preference for an hourglass figure to a less curvaceous and angular body shape (Garner, Garfinkel, Schwartz, & Thompson, 1980). Additional research (Wiseman, Gray, Mosimann, & Ahren, 1992) has corroborated past findings—for example, demonstrating that Miss America contestants from 1979 to 1988 weighed 13% to 19% below expected weights for women their height. Wiseman et al. (1992) concluded that the majority of "ideal" women in our society, based on their low body weight, meet one of the *DSM-IV* criteria for anorexia nervosa (American Psychiatric Association, 1994).

Similar studies also have examined historical changes in ideal body shapes and document women's interest in conforming to the ideal of their particular point in history. In examinations of popular women's magazines, past research has demonstrated trends toward increasing slenderness of models and increases in articles and advertisements addressing dietary issues (Silverstein, Perdue, Peterson, & Kelly, 1986; Silverstein, Peterson, & Perdue, 1986). Wiseman et al. (1992) updated these studies by tabulating the number of diet-for-weight-loss, exercise, and diet and exercise articles from

1959 to 1989 for leading women's magazines, demonstrating an overall increase in the emphasis on weight loss over the 30-year period. It is interesting to note, as can be seen in Figure 1, the proportion of exercise and diet and exercise references has increased, and from 1983 onward, the prevalence of exercise articles has surpassed that of diet articles (Wiseman et al., 1992).

Wiseman, Gunning, and Gray (1993) tabulated the number of television commercials for diet foods, aids, products, and weight loss programs for the years 1973 to 1991, demonstrating a steady increase in the prevalence of these advertisements. The authors concluded that the sociocultural pressure to lose weight and conform to the thin ideal remains strong; however, alternative methods (such as exercise) are being offered in addition to, or in place of, traditional dieting (Wiseman et al., 1992; Wiseman et al., 1993).

Although the ideal figure has become thinner while the average woman's figure has become larger (Garner et al., 1980), it appears that many women continue to accept the thinner ideal as a goal. In addition, dissatisfaction and distress regarding one's body size has been shown in adolescent girls (Wardle & Marsland, 1990) and in woman of all ages (Pliner, Chaiken, & Flett, 1990).

Feminist Theories and Gender-Role Socialization

Feminist theorists offer new insights into the etiology and maintenance of body image dissatisfaction and disturbance. In general, feminists assert that an important aspect of a woman's social learning is the equating

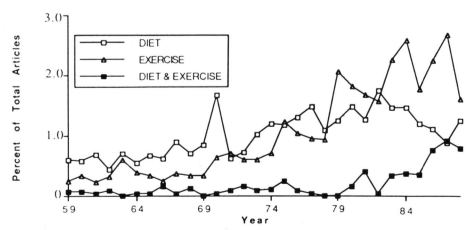

Figure 1. Number of articles as a percent of total articles in six women's magazines. From "Cultural Expectations of Women: An Update" by C. V. Wiseman, J. J. Gray, J. E. Mosimann, & A. H. Ahrens, 1992, International Journal of Eating Disorders, 11, p. 88. Copyright 1992 by John Wiley & Sons, Inc. Reprinted by permission.

of physical attractiveness with self-esteem (Franks, 1986; Nagel & Jones, 1992). These theorists assert that in general women have overidentified with their bodies and that a woman's sense of self-worth often is contingent on conforming to the prevailing norms for thinness and attractiveness (Bergner, Remer, & Whetsell, 1985; Striegel-Moore & Marcus, 1995). In the same way, women are socialized to place higher priority on interpersonal relationships than men (Striegel-Moore & Marcus, 1995). That is, a woman's identity is organized around valuing, seeking out, maintaining, and nurturing social relationships. Women also are taught to believe that they are responsible for the success of their relationships. Socializing experiences (e.g., the media; parental and peer pressures) link success in interpersonal relationships with perceived physical attractiveness (Striegel-Moore & Marcus, 1995).

The feminist perspective is seen a great deal within the literature on eating disorders, perhaps as a result of the preponderance of women who have such disorders (Gilbert & Thompson, in press). Feminists assert that women are vulnerable to the *culture of thinness* that many maintain permeates Western society (Nagel & Jones, 1992; J. K. Thompson, 1992). Feminist authors argue that the denigration of fatness and overvaluation of thinness in our society constitute forms of sexism and misogyny because women typically have 10% to 15% more body fat than men (Brown, 1989; Gilbert & Thompson, in press). Dieting, eating disorders, and dissatisfaction with one's body are seen as natural responses to pathological societal pressures to be thin.

Other authors (Orbach, 1978; Szekely, 1989) have asserted that many women, in their efforts to achieve control in their lives, define themselves by their appearance and body shape. Wooley and Wooley (1982) reported that 63% of the women that they surveyed stated that their weight affected how they generally felt about themselves. Chernin (1981) asserted that women's body images relate to the power differential between men and women, with men attempting to grow larger and therefore more powerful and women attempting to grow smaller, more dependent, and invisible. According to this theory, women define their ideal weight according to their needs for power and control (Gilbert & Thompson, in press). Some feminists argue that eating problems may result from maladaptive coping strategies in response to sexism, racism, abuse, and poverty (B. W. Thompson, 1992).

Gender-role orientation, a widely investigated phenomenon, has been proposed to be of etiological significance in the development of body image dissatisfaction. Timko, Striegel-Moore, Silberstein, and Rodin (1987) demonstrated that femininity as measured by the Personal Attributes Questionnaire (Spence & Helmreich, 1978), significantly correlated with perceived importance of appearance, whereas masculinity did not. Further, gender-typed women have been found to have lower body satisfaction than their more masculine or androgynous peers (Jackson, Sullivan, & Rostker, 1988; van Strien, 1989). Glidden and Tracey (1989) demonstrated that tailoring treatment programs for body image and weight concerns to different gender role attitudes may be beneficial. Women with nontraditional gender role attitudes preferred interventions focusing on internal personal causes. Women with more traditional gender-role attitudes preferred an intervention attributing weight issues to more external, sociocultural etiologies (Glidden & Tracey, 1989).

Finally, recent research has demonstrated the importance of sexual orientation in body image dissatisfaction (Siever, 1994). In a sample of lesbians, gay men, heterosexual women, and heterosexual men, lesbians were the least concerned about physical appearance and gay men and heterosexual women showed significantly higher concern for physical attractiveness (Siever, 1994).

The Role of Mass Media in Body Image Disturbance

Mass media plays a powerful role in communicating the thin standard to the average woman (Mazur, 1986). Freedman (1986) explained that although beauty ideals have been modeled throughout history, the "impact of today's visual media is different from the effect of Botticelli's *Venus*" (p. 14). She noted that historically figures of art were romanticized as unattainable, but today's media blurs the boundaries between glorified fiction and reality. Lakoff and Scherr (1984) asserted that television and magazines have an especially negative influence because models in these media are seen as realistic representations of actual people rather than carefully manipulated, artificially developed images. Furthermore, women may fail to consider that models on television or in print spend many hours with professional hair and makeup artists for a single photograph and employ a rigidly controlled diet and exercise program, seeing these models as realistic and as appropriate comparisons (Jasper, 1993; Lakoff & Scherr, 1984).

Striegel-Moore, Silberstein, and Rodin (1986), in a review of risk factors for bulimia nervosa, hypothesized that the media not only teaches women about the ideal figure but teaches them how to attain it, "including how to diet, purge and engage in other disregulating behaviors" (p. 256). For example, a popular diet book in the 1980s advised women to eat large quantities of fruit after a binge in order to induce diarrhea. In addition, the fitness movement of the past decade has generated a redefinition of the ideal female body which is characterized not only by thinness but firmness as well (Streigel-Moore, Silberstein, & Rodin, 1986). Silverstein, Perdue, Peterson, and Kelly (1986) countered the argument that the media only gives people what they want. They asserted that "even if it were true that the presentations of a thin standard of bodily attractiveness for women appear only when media decision makers believe many women desire such presentations, these decisions would still feed back to affect other women" (Silverstein et al., 1986, p. 531). Although the thin ideal is not promoted only by the media, and may not even originate within the media, the popularity of television, movies, and magazines leads the media to be among the most influential and efficacious communicators of the thin ideal (Raphael & Lacey, 1992; Silverstein et al., 1986).

Numerous authors have recognized the powerful influence of cultural standards of beauty and, specifically, the role the mass media plays in communicating these societal expectations (Jasper, 1993; Lakoff & Scherr, 1984; Thompson, 1990). Historically, many women have been willing to alter their bodies to conform to the societal ideal (Mazur, 1986). The ideal has moved away from a more curvaceous standard to a more angular figure, as discussed earlier (Garner et al., 1980; Morris, Cooper, & Cooper, 1989). As Rodin et al. (1985) discuss, concern over weight and dissatisfaction with one's body has become so prevalent that it can be considered a *normative discontent*. Although all women in American society are presented the thin ideal through a variety of media, individuals fall on the continuum of normative discontent (Rodin et al., 1985), with some women reporting very little body image dissatisfaction and others developing eating disorders.

One measure that purports to examine these individual differences was developed recently by Heinberg et al., (1995). The Sociocultural Attitudes Towards Appearance Scale (SATAQ) was developed to assess women's awareness and acceptance of standards of thinness and attractiveness. This measure has two distinct subscales measuring recognition and internalization of societal standards of appearance. Both subscales converged with other measures of body image and eating disturbance. However, regression analyses indicated that the internalization subscale significantly predicted body image disturbance and eating-disordered behavior (Heinberg et al., 1995).

Laboratory Studies of Sociocultural Theory

The vast majority of research providing support for the sociocultural theoretical model is correlational in nature. However, a handful of controlled laboratory investigations have been conducted. These empirically rigorous studies provide more convincing support for sociocultural theories.

An investigation by Waller, Hamilton, and Shaw (1992) found that subjects with eating disorders showed an increase in body size overestimation (a perceptual body image disturbance) following exposure to photographs of models from popular fashion magazines. In a similar study, Irving (1990) exposed subjects of varying levels of self-reported bulimic symptomatology to photographs of thin, average, and oversize models. Regardless of severity of bulimic symptomatology, the participants shown photographs of thinner models reported lower levels of self-esteem and weight satisfaction than subjects shown photographs of larger models (Irving, 1990).

Heinberg and Thompson (1995) had college-aged women view 10-minute videotapes of commercials that either contained stimuli emphasizing societal ideals of thinness and attractiveness or contained neutral stimuli not related to appearance. Results indicated that subjects who viewed the videotape stressing the importance of thinness and attractiveness reported greater depression, anger, and appearance dissatisfaction than subjects given the neutral manipulation (Heinberg & Thompson, 1995). Subjects who possessed high dispositional levels of body image disturbance showed increases in appearance dissatisfaction following exposure to the experimental tape, whereas subjects with low body image disturbance showed decreases in appearance dissatisfaction following the experimental stimuli. All subjects exposed to the neutral, control video demonstrated a decrease in appearance-related dissatisfaction.

Other Socioculturally Based Theories

The next two theories, self-ideal discrepancy and social comparison theory, are direct outgrowths of sociocultural theory. They propose that individual differences account for differing levels of dissatisfaction within cultures that endorse thinness and attractiveness.

Self-Ideal Discrepancy. Many researchers have used assessment measures that consist of comparing one's actual perceived size on a schematic drawing with a selected ideal size (Fallon & Rozin, 1985; Thompson, 1990). Based in part on these studies and on the importance of socioculturally endorsed ideal weights and appearances, Thompson (1990) proposed a self-ideal discrepancy hypothesis to explain the development and maintenance of body image disturbance. This theory focuses on individuals' tendency to compare their perceived appearance with an imagined ideal or with an ideal other (J. K. Thompson, 1992). The result of such a comparison process may be a discrepancy between the perceived self and the ideal self and thus may lead to dissatisfaction. It is assumed by this theoretical model that the greater the discrepancy between one's perceived self and the perceived ideal, the greater the dissatisfaction. Research supports the hypothesis that a self-ideal discrepancy exists and that a greater discrepancy may be related to higher levels of eating disturbance and body image dissatisfaction (Altabe & Thompson, 1992; Fallon & Rozin, 1985; Thompson & Psaltis, 1988). Silberstein, Striegel-Moore, and Rodin (1987) discussed the importance of this conceptualization and indicated that this discrepancy may lead to a body image dissatisfaction in nonclinical populations that is so frequent that it is thought to be the normative experience for most women.

Social Comparison. A theoretical model using social comparison processes helps explain how exposure to the sociocultural ideal leads to increased body dissatisfaction. Festinger (1954) theorized that humans have an innate tendency to derive information regarding themselves through the process of social comparison. More recent research posits that comparisons with others who are superior to oneself on the attribute of interest (e.g., an upward comparison) often are associated with increases in emotional distress and decreases in self-esteem (Major, Testa, & Bylsma, 1991).

Additional research maintains that a tendency to compare one's physical appearance to others seems to be related strongly to body dissatisfaction (Striegel-Moore, McAvay, & Rodin, 1986). High scores on a measure assessing the tendency to compare physical appearance to others have been shown to be related strongly to high scores of eating disturbance, self-esteem, and body image dissatisfaction (Heinberg & Thompson, 1992a; Thompson, Heinberg, & Tantleff, 1991). In a study by Heinberg and Thompson (1992b), subjects who compared themselves to more similar others (e.g., friends or classmates) reported greater body image anxiety and distress than subjects who compared themselves to generic others (e.g., the average person in the United States), regardless of whether it was an upward or downward comparsion (Heinberg & Thompson, 1992b). A more recent investigation indicates that the majority of variance in body image and eating disturbance can be accounted for by the tendency to make social comparisons and the tendency to be aware of and internalize sociocultural norms regarding thinness and attractiveness (Stormer & Thompson, 1995).

CONCLUSION

Several theoretical models have been proposed to explain the normative discontent of body image (Rodin et al., 1985). It is likely that each of the theoretical approaches discussed in this chapter has some merit, at least for particular individuals (J. K. Thompson, 1992). However, the sociocultural approach most likely accounts for much of the body image disturbance in Western society. As discussed earlier, the mass media, gender socialization, and verbal commentary communicate at an almost constant rate sociocultural messages regarding one's ideal weight and appearance. Nevertheless, individuals exposed to the same ideals of thinness fall on a continuum of dissatisfaction, with some individuals reporting very little disturbance and others developing eating-disordered behavior.

Although sociocultural factors may play the greatest role in body image, for the majority of the population, individual factors also appear to influence the development and maintenance of body image disturbance, particularly for at-risk individuals. Cortical deficits, adaptive failure, and perceptual artifact theory may be unable to explain the prevalence of subjective body image disturbance. However, they provide important information regarding perceptual disturbance, particularly for those individuals with anorexia nervosa. In addition, developmental factors such as early maturation along with synchronous stressful events, negative verbal commentary, and early sexualization may be powerful moderating variables that act to amplify the sociocultural pressure for thinness and attractiveness. It is possible to conceptualize the present sociocultural climate as a *setting condition* for the development of subjective body image disturbance (J. K. Thompson, 1992). That is, although exposure to a culture where appearance and thinness are accorded high regard may not result in body image disturbance, this setting in combination with other factors (e.g., perceptual deficits, sexual abuse, etc.) may result in body image disturbance or eating disorders. Integrative hypotheses should be developed and tested empirically to examine how these multiple factors interplay in the development of body image disturbance.

Although several models have been proposed to explain the development and maintenance of body image dissatisfaction, little work has attempted to evaluate competing theories. Two recent studies have attempted to elucidate further the varying contribution of competing theoretical models. Thompson and Heinberg (1993) evaluated social comparison theory and teasing history to predict variance associated with eating disturbance and body image dissatisfaction. Results indicated that specific teasing about weight and body size, but not general appearance, was a significant predictor of body image dissatisfaction and eating disturbance. In addition, the rated importance of others as comparison targets, but not general frequency of comparison, predicted unique variance (Thompson & Heinberg, 1993).

Stormer and Thompson (in press) had subjects complete measures designed to assess four theoretical models, including maturational timing, teasing, social comparison, and awareness and internalization of sociocultural standards toward thinness and attractiveness. Social comparison and acceptance of socioculturally endorsed standards were found to be significant predictors of body image and eating disturbance. Teasing also accounted for a small portion of the variance, whereas maturational timing did not. Although these studies provide important preliminary data, many more examinations are necessary to determine successfully which etiological factors are important for which individuals.

As discussed earlier, the vast majority of research providing support for the sociocultural theoretical model is anecdotal, descriptive, and correlational in nature. Although recent research has begun to investigate this model in a more empirically rigorous manner, systematic investigation still is needed to endorse sociocultural theories as the predominant explanation of body image disturbance. In addition, the majority of sociocultural studies have examined the standards for thinness, with fewer examining other dimensions of attractiveness. More research is necessary to examine sociocultural standards for specific body sites, age, coloring, and ethnicity (see chapter 6, this volume).

A variety of populations have been neglected by body image research, particularly research examining various theoretical models. A lifespan perspective, examining body image and the influence of society at all ages, is necessary. The majority of works I reviewed in this chapter used adolescent and college-aged participants. However, as individuals age they are likely to move increasingly farther away from an ideal body size (Kumanyika, 1994), and research needs to determine the effect this has on aging persons. Research has also neglected examining body image in deformed, injured or disfigured individuals (Cash & Pruzinsky, 1990), and studies need to focus on the societal standards that are virtually impossible for such individuals to meet. Recent research (Fauerbach, Heinberg, Spence, & Hackerman, 1995; Heinberg, Fauerbach, Spence & Hackerman, 1995) suggests that indices of body image may play an important role in psychological adjustment to burn injury and decisions to undergo reconstructive surgery. However, these populations, as well as more broadly defined medical populations, have been largely ignored.

In this chapter I have reviewed a variety of theoretical models and the research supporting or refuting their potency. Although the sociocultural model is the best supported by available data, much more work is necessary to examine which individuals are at highest risk, how individuals without body image disturbance manage to refute societal messages of thinness and appearance, and how the sociocultural influence varies in a variety of populations. Additional factors, such as the effect of teasing and social comparison, may serve to make individuals more sensitive to sociocultural influences or lead individuals to be less efficacious in refuting unrealistic societal demands for thinness and attractiveness.

REFERENCES

Altabe, M., & Thompson, J. K. (1992). Size estimation versus figural ratings of body image disturbance: Relation to body dissatisfaction and eating dysfunction. *International Journal of Eating Disorders, 11,* 397–402.

American Psychiatric Association. (1994). *Diagnostic and statistical manual of mental disorders* (4th ed.). Washington, DC: Author.

Bergner, M., Remer, P., & Whetsell, C. (1985). Transforming women's body image: A feminist counseling approach. *Women & Therapy, 4,* 25–38.

Braun, C. M. J., & Chouinard, M. (1992). Is anorexia nervosa a neuropsychological disease? *Neuropsychology Review, 3,* 171–212.

Brooks-Gunn, J., & Warren, M. P. (1985). Effects of delayed menarche in different contexts: Dance and nondance students. *Journal of Youth and Adolescence, 14,* 285–300.

Brown, L. S. (1989). Fat oppressive attitudes and the feminist therapist: Directions for change—Fat oppression and psychotherapy: A feminist perspective [Special issue]. *Women and Therapy, 8,* 19–30.

Brown, T. A., Cash, T. F., & Lewis, R. J. (1989). Body-image disturbances in adolescent female binge-purgers: A brief report of the results of a national survey in the U.S.A. *Journal of Clinical Psychology and Psychiatry, 30,* 605–613.

Brownell, K. D. (1991). Dieting and the search for the perfect body: Where physiology and culture collide. *Behavior Therapy, 22,* 1–12.

Cash, T. F., & Brown, T. A. (1987). Body image in anorexia nervosa and bulimia nervosa: A review of the literature. *Behavior Modification, 11,* 487-521.

Cash, T. F., & Pruzinsky, T. (Eds.). (1990). *Body images: Development, deviance, and change.* New York: Guilford Press.

Cash, T. F., Winstead, B. A., & Janda, L. H. (1986, April). Body image survey report: The great American shape-up. *Psychology Today, 20,* 30-44.

Cattarin, J., & Thompson, J. K. (1994). A three-year longitudinal study of body image and eating disturbance in adolescent females. *Eating Disorders: Journal of Treatment and Prevention, 2,* 114–125.

Chernin, K. (1981). *The obsession: Reflections on the tyranny of slenderness.* New York: Harper & Row.

Coovert, D. L., Thompson, J. K., & Kinder, B. N. (1988). Interrelationships among multiple aspects of body image and eating disturbance. *International Journal of Eating Disorders, 7,* 495–502.

Crisp, A. H., & Kalucy, R. S. (1974). Aspects of the perceptual disorder in anorexia nervosa. *British Journal of Medical Psychology, 47,* 349-361.

Dolce, J. J., Thompson, J. K., Register, A., & Spana, R. E. (1987). Generalization of body size distortion. *International Journal of Eating Disorders, 6,* 401–408.

Fabian, L. J., & Thompson, J. K. (1989). Body image and eating disturbance in young females. *International Journal of Eating Disorders, 8,* 63-74.

Fallon, A. E. (1990). Culture in the mirror: Sociocultural determinants of body image. In T. F. Cash and T. Pruzinsky (Eds.), *Body images: Development, deviance, and change.* New York: Guilford Press.

Fallon, A. E., & Rosen, P. (1985). Sex differences in perceptions of desirable body shape. *Journal of Abnormal Psychology, 94,* 102–105.

Fauerbach, J. A., Heinberg, L. J., Spence, R. J., & Hackerman, F. (1995, March). *Deformity location, age and adjustment of patients seeking burn reconstructive surgery.* Paper presented at the Annual meeting of the Society of Behavioral Medicine, San Diego, CA.

Festinger, L. (1954). A theory of social comparison processes. *Human Relations, 7,* 117–140.

Franks, V. (1986). Sex stereotyping and diagnosis of psychopathology. *Women and Therapy, 5*, 219–232.

Franzoi, S. L., & Herzog, M. E. (1987). Judging physical attractiveness: What body aspects do we use? *Personality and Social Psychology Bulletin, 13*, 19–33.

Freedman, R. (1986). *Beauty Bound*. Lexington, MA: D.C. Heath.

Gardner, R. M., Gardner, E. A., & Morrell, J. A. (1990). Body image of sexually and physically abused children. *Journal of Psychiatric Research, 24*, 313–324.

Garner, D. M., Garfinkel, P. E., Schwartz, D., & Thompson, M. (1980). Cultural expectations of thinness in women. *Psychological Reports, 47*, 483-491.

Gilbert, S., & Thompson, J. K. (in press). Feminist explanations of the development of eating disorders and obesity: Common themes, research findings, and methodological issues. *Clinical Psychology: Science and Practice*.

Giles, T. R. (1988). Distortion of body image as an effect of conditioned fear. *Journal of Behavior Therapy and Experimental Psychiatry, 19*, 143–146.

Glidden, C. E., & Tracey, T. J. (1989). Women's perceptions of personal versus sociocultural counseling interventions. *Journal of Counseling Psychology, 36*, 54–62.

Grillo, C. M., Wilfley, D. E., Brownell, K. D., & Rodin, J. (1994). Teasing, body image, and self-esteem in a clinical sample of obese women. *Addictive Behavior, 19*, 443–450.

Hastings, T., & Kern, J. M. (1994). Relationships between bulimia, childhood sexual abuse, and family environment. *International Journal of Eating Disorders, 15*, 103–111.

Heinberg, L. J., Fauerbach, J. A., Spence, R. J., & Hackerman, F. (1995, April). *Psychological factors predict the decision to undergo reconstructive surgery following burn injury*. Paper presented at the Annual Convention of the Society of Behavioral Medicine, San Diego, CA.

Heinberg, L. J., & Thompson, J. K. (1992a). Social comparison: Gender, target importance ratings, and relation to body image disturbance. *Journal of Social Behavior and Personality, 7*, 335–344.

Heinberg, L. J., & Thompson, J. K. (1992b). The effects of figure size feedback (positive vs. negative) and target comparison group (particularistic vs. universalistic) on body image disturbance. *International Journal of Eating Disorders, 12*, 441–448.

Heinberg, L. J., & Thompson, J. K. (1995). Body image and televised images of thinness and attractiveness: A controlled laboratory investigation. *Journal of Social and Clinical Psychology, 14*, 325–338.

Heinberg, L. J., Thompson, J. K., & Stormer, S. (1995). Development and validation of the Sociocultural Attitudes Towards Appearance Questionnaire (SATAQ). *International Journal of Eating Disorders, 17*, 81–89.

Irving, L. M. (1990). Mirror images: Effects of the standard of beauty on the self- and body-esteem of women exhibiting varying levels of bulimic symptoms. *Journal of Social and Clinical Psychology, 9*, 230–242.

Jackson, L. A., Sullivan, L. A., & Rostker, R. (1988). Gender, gender role, and body image. *Sex Roles, 19,* 429–443.

Jasper, K. (1993). Monitoring and responding to media messages. *Eating Disorders: The Journal of Treatment and Prevention, 1,* 109–114.

Kumanyika, S. K. (1994). The cultural aspects of weight control. *The Weight Control Digest, 4,* 347–360.

Lakoff, R. T., & Scherr, R. L. (1984). *Face value: The politics of beauty.* Boston: Routledge & Kegan Paul.

Levine, M. P., Smolak, L., Moodey, A. F., Shuman, M. D., & Hessen, L. D. (1994). Normative developmental challenges and dieting and eating disturbances in middle-school girls. *International Journal of Eating Disorders, 15,* 11–20.

Major, B., Testa, M., & Bylsma, W. H. (1991). Responses to upward and downward social comparisons: The impact of esteem-relevance and perceived control. In J. Suls & T. A. Wills (Eds.), *Social comparison: Contemporary theory and research* (pp. 237–260). Hillsdale, NJ: Erlbaum.

Mazur, A. (1986). U.S. trends in feminine beauty and overadaptation. *The Journal of Sex Research, 22,* 281–303.

Morris, A., Cooper, T., & Cooper, P. J. (1989). The changing shape of female fashion models. *International Journal of Eating Disorders, 8,* 593–596.

Nagel, K. L., & Jones, K. H. (1992). Sociological factors in the development of eating disorders, *Adolescence, 27,* 107–113.

Orbach, S. (1978). *Fat is a feminist issue.* New York: Paddington Press.

Penner, L. A., Thompson, J. K., & Coovert, D. L. (1991). Size estimation among anorexics: Much ado about very little? *Journal of Abnormal Psychology, 100,* 90–93.

Pliner, P., Chaiken, S., & Flett, G. L. (1990). Gender differences in concern with body weight and physical appearance over the lifespan. *Personality and Social Psychology Bulletin, 16,* 263–273.

Pope, H. G., & Hudson, J. I. (1992). Is childhood sexual abuse a risk factor for bulimia nervosa? *American Journal of Psychiatry, 149,* 455–463.

Rand, C. S. W., & Kuldau, J. M. (1990). The epidemiology of obesity and self-defined weight problem in the general population: Gender, race, age, and social class. *International Journal of Eating Disorders, 9,* 329–343.

Raphael, F. J., & Lacey, J. H. (1992). Cultural aspects of eating disorders. *Annals of Medicine, 24,* 293–296.

Rodin, J., Silberstein, L. R., & Striegel-Moore, R. H. (1985). Women and weight: A normative discontent. In T. B. Sonderegger (Ed.), *Psychology and gender: Nebraska Symposium on Motivation, 1984* (pp. 267–307). Lincoln: University of Nebraska Press.

Siever, M. D. (1994). Sexual orientation and gender as factors in socioculturally acquired vulnerability to body dissatisfaction and eating disorders. *Journal of Consulting and Clinical Psychology, 62,* 252–260.

Silberstein, L. R., Striegel-Moore, R. H., & Rodin, J. (1987). Feeling fat: A woman's shame. In H. B. Lewis (Ed.), *The role of shame in symptom formation.* Hillsdale, NJ: Erlbaum.

Silverstein, B., Perdue, L., Peterson, B., & Kelly, E. (1986). The role of the mass media in promoting a thin standard of bodily attractiveness for women. *Sex Roles, 14,* 519–532.

Silverstein, B., Peterson, B., & Perdue, L. (1986). Some correlates of the thin standard of bodily attractiveness for women. *International Journal of Eating Disorders, 5,* 895–905.

Slade, P. D. (1977). Awareness of body dimensions during pregnancy: An analogue study. *Psychological Medicine, 7,* 245–252.

Smolak, L., Levine, M. P., & Gralen, S. (1993). The impact of puberty and dating on eating problems among middle-school girls. *Journal of Youth and Adolescence, 22,* 355–368.

Spence, J. T., & Heimreich, R. L. (1978). Gender, sex roles, and the psychological dimension of masculinity and femininity. In J. T. Spence & R. L. Heimreich (Eds.), *Masculinity and femininity* (pp. 3–18). Austin, TX: University of Texas Press.

Stormer, S., & Thompson, J. K. (in press). A further test of theoretical models of body image disturbance. *International Journal of Eating Disorders.*

Striegel-Moore, R., & Marcus, M. (1995). Eating disorders in women: Current issues and debates. In A. Stanton & S. Gallant (Eds.), *Psychology of women's health: Progress and challenges in research and application* (pp. 445–487). Washington, DC: American Psychological Association.

Striegel-Moore, R., McAvay, G., & Rodin, J. (1986). Psychological and behavioral correlates of feeling fat in women. *International Journal of Eating Disorders, 5,* 935-947.

Striegel-Moore, R., Silberstein, L. R., & Rodin, J. (1986). Toward an understanding of risk factors for bulimia. *American Psychologist, 41,* 246–263.

Szekely, E. A. (1989). From eating disorders to women's situations: Extending the boundaries of psychological inquiry—Counseling women and ethnic minorities [Special issue]. *Counseling and Psychology Quarterly, 2,* 167–184.

Tantleff-Dunn, S., Thompson, J. K., & Dunn, M. F. (1995). Development and validation of the Feedback on Physical Appearance Scale (FOPAS). *Eating Disorders: The Journal of Treatment and Prevention, 3,* 341–350.

Thompson, B. W. (1992). A way outa no way: Eating problems among African-American, Latina, and White women. *Gender and Society, 6,* 546–561.

Thompson, J. K. (1987). Body size distortion in anorexia nervosa: Reanalysis and reconceptualization. *International Journal of Eating Disorders, 6,* 379–384.

Thompson, J. K. (1990). *Body image disturbance: Assessment and Treatment.* Elmsford, NY: Pergamon Press.

Thompson, J. K. (1992). Body image: Extent of disturbance, associated features, theoretical models, assessment methodologies, intervention strategies, and a proposal for a new DSM-IV diagnostic criteria-body image disorder. In M. Hersen, R. M. Eisler, and P. M. Miller (Eds.), *Progress in behavior modification* (pp. 3–54). Sycamore, IL: Sycamore.

Thompson, J. K., Coovert, M. D., Richards, K. J., Johnson, S., & Cattarin, J. (1995). Development of body image, eating disturbance, and general psychological functioning in female adolescents: Covariance structure modeling and longitudinal investigations. *International Journal of Eating Disorders, 18,* 221–236.

Thompson, J. K., Fabian, L. J., Moulton, D. O. , Dunn, M. F., & Altabe, M. N. (1991). Development and validation of the physical appearance related teasing scale. *Journal of Personality Assessment, 56,* 513–521.

Thompson, J. K., & Heinberg, L. J. (1993). A preliminary test of two hypotheses of body image disturbance. *International Journal of Eating Disorders, 14,* 59–64.

Thompson, J. K., Heinberg, L. J., & Tantleff, S. (1991). The physical appearance comparison scale (PACS). *The Behavior Therapist, 14,* 174.

Thompson, J. K., & Psaltis, K. (1988). Multiple aspects and correlates of body figure ratings: A replication and extension of Fallon and Rozin (1985). *International Journal of Eating Disorders, 7,* 813-818.

Thompson, J. K., & Spana, R. E. (1991). Visuospatial ability and size estimation accuracy. *Perceptual and Motor Skills, 73,* 335–338.

Thompson, J. K., & Tantleff, S. (1992). Female and male ratings of upper torso: Actual, ideal, and stereotypical conceptions. *Journal of Social Behavior and Personality, 7,* 345–354.

Timko, C., Striegel-Moore, R. H., Silberstein L. R., & Rodin, J. (1987). Femininity/masculinity and disordered eating in women: How are they related? *International Journal of Eating Disorders, 6,* 701–712.

Trimble, M. R. (1988). Body image and the temporal lobes. *British Journal of Psychiatry, 153,* 12–14.

Vandereycken, W. (1993). The sociocultural roots of the fight against fatness: Implications for eating disorders and obesity. *Eating Disorders: The Journal of Treatment and Prevention, 1,* 7–16.

van Strien, T. (1989). Dieting, dissatisfaction with figure, and sex role orientation in women. *International Journal of Eating Disorders, 8,* 455–462.

Waller, G., Hamilton, K., Rose, N., Sumra, J., & Baldwin, A. (1993). Sexual abuse and body-image distortion in the eating disorders. *British Journal of Clinical Psychology, 32,* 350–352.

Waller, G., Hamilton, K., & Shaw, J. (1992). Media influences on body size estimation in eating disordered and comparison subjects. *British Review of Bulimia and Anorexia Nervosa, 6,* 81–87.

Wardle, J., & Marsland, L. (1990). Adolescent concerns about weight and eating: A social-developmental perspective. *Journal of Psychosomatic Research, 34,* 377–391.

Weiner, K., & Thompson, J. K. (1995). *Body image and sexual abuse.* Unpublished manuscript.

Wiseman, C. V., Gray, J. J., Mosimann, J. E., & Ahren, A. H. (1992). Cultural expectations of thinness in women: An update. *International Journal of Eating Disorders, 11*, 85–89.

Wiseman, C. V., Gunning, F. M., & Gray, J. J. (1993). Increasing pressure to be thin: 19 years of diet products in television commercials. *Eating Disorders: The Journal of Treatment and Prevention, 1*, 52–61.

Wooley, S., & Wooley, O. (1982). The Beverly Hills eating disorder: The mass marketing of anorexia nervosa. *International Journal of Eating Disorders, 2*, 57–69.

3

ASSESSING BODY IMAGE DISTURBANCE: MEASURES, METHODOLOGY, AND IMPLEMENTATION

J. KEVIN THOMPSON

The development of theoretical conceptualizations and treatment strategies for body image disturbance has been paralleled by the construction of a wealth of methodologies designed to assess some aspect of the complex construct of body image (Altabe & Thompson, 1995). In this chapter I will provide a broad overview of these measurement indices and their use, in particular for individuals with eating disorders, obesity, body dysmorphic disorder, and clinically significant levels of body image disturbance (see chapter 7, this volume, for a description of an interview method for body dysmorphic disorder). A number of other comprehensive reviews have offered a detailed analysis of measurement procedures and methodological issues pertaining to assessment (e.g., Cash & Brown, 1987; Slade, 1985, 1994; Thompson, 1990, 1992, 1995; Thompson, Penner, & Altabe, 1990); these articles provide useful ancillary reading to some of the areas covered in this chapter.

At the outset, I will address the definitions of different aspects of the overall construct of body image. I will also review the most widely used and psychometrically sound assessment measures, and I will mention briefly new, potentially fruitful, procedures. In the second section, I will examine methodological issues regarding the appropriate use of the measures I reviewed in the first section. Finally, I will offer specific recommendations for creating a clinical assessment battery.

MEASURES OF BODY IMAGE DISTURBANCE

In past reviews, researchers generally have dichotomized the vast number of assessment strategies into two categories: (a) perceptual measures, which focus on the size perception accuracy component of body image; and (b) subjective indices, which tap into an attitudinal, affective, or cognitive aspect of disturbance (Cash & Brown, 1987; Thompson, 1990). In recent years, a third component, consisting of behavioral avoidance of body dysphoric-producing situations (for example, looking in a mirror, social situations involving physical scrutiny, etc.) has also received attention (Rosen, Srebnik, Saltzberg, & Wendt, 1991; Thompson, Heinberg, & Marshall, 1993).

However, recent factor–analytic studies question the validity of these distinctions (Thompson, Altabe, Johnson, & Stormer, 1994; Williamson, Barker, Bertman, & Gleaves, 1995), indicating considerable overlap among many questionnaire measures that were thought to measure a distinctive affective, cognitive, or behavioral aspect of disturbance. In addition, the perceptual index does not appear to correlate highly with subjective levels of dissatisfaction (Altabe & Thompson, 1992; Keeton, Cash, & Brown, 1990; Thompson et al., 1990) and is affected by a number of factors, including the affective versus cognitive nature of the instructional protocol (Slade & Brodie, 1994; Thompson, 1991; Thompson & Dolce, 1989). Therefore, several methodological issues currently occupy researchers in this area. Following a review of widely used assessment strategies, I will discuss these concerns further.

Subjective and Attitudinal Measures

A number of measures provide a global or generic estimate of size, weight, or overall appearance dissatisfaction. For instance, the Body Areas Satisfaction Scale of the Multidimensional Body–Self Relations Questionnaire (Brown, Cash, & Mikulka, 1990) assesses satisfaction with eight specific body areas, including weight- and non-weight-related areas. The Body Dissatisfaction subscale of the Eating Disorder Inventory–2 (Garner, 1991) measures satisfaction with nine weight-relevant areas (hips, thighs, buttocks, etc.). Other measures, such as the Appearance Evaluation (AE) scale of the Multidimensional Body–Self Relations Questionnaire (MBSRQ) (Brown et al., 1990), Body Shape Questionnaire (Cooper, Taylor, Cooper, & Fairburn, 1987), and the Physical Appearance subscale of the Extended Satisfaction with Life Scale (Alfonso & Allison, 1993), provide a more global, comprehensive assessment of appearance satisfaction. (Sample item from the MBSRQ-AE: "I like my looks just the way they are.") Specific information for all of the instruments discussed, and many other widely used measures, is contained in Table 1.

TABLE 1

Widely Used Measures for the Assessment of Different Components of Body Image Disturbance

Name of Instrument	Author(s)	Description	Reliability 1, 2	Standardization Sample	Address of Author
		Measures of Size Estimation Accuracy			
Adjustable Light Beam Apparatus	1) Thompson & Spana (1988) 2) Thompson (1990)	Adjust width of four light beams projected on wall to match perceived size of cheeks, waist, hips, and thighs	1) IC: (.83) TR: Immediate (.83–.92); 1 week (.56–.86) 2) IC: (.75)	1) 159 female undergraduates 2) 63 female adolescents (10–15 years old)	J. Kevin Thompson, PhD Department of Psychology University of South Florida Tampa, FL 33620-8200
Body Image Detection Device	1) Ruff & Barrios (1986) 2) Barrios, Ruff, & York (1989)	Adjust width of light beam projected on wall to watch perceived size of specific body site	1) IC: (.91, .93) TR: 3 weeks (bulimics; .82–.87, controls; .72–.85) 2) IC: (.21–.82) TR: 3 weeks (.34) 4 weeks (.94) 7 weeks (.37)	1) 20 normal and 20 bulimic undergraduates 2) female undergraduates	Billy A. Barrios, PhD College of Liberal Arts Department of Psychology University of Mississippi Oxford, MS 38677
Movable Caliper Technique: Visual Size Estimation	1) Slade & Russell (1973) 2) Slade (1985) 3) Ben-Tovim & Crisp (1984); Ben-Tovim, Walker, Murray, & Chin (1990)	Adjust distances between two lights to match perceived size	1) IC: (anorexics; .72–.93) (controls; .37–.79) 2) IC: (anorexics; .72) (controls; .63) 3) TR: 2 weeks (.79–.95)	1) 14 female anorexics and 20 female postgraduates and secretaries 2) anorexics 3) normal females	1) Peter Slade, PhD Department of Psychiatry and Department of Movement Science Liverpool University Medical School Ashton Street, P.O. Box 147 Liverpool L69 3BX, England

TABLE 1 (Continued)

Name of Instrument	Author(s)	Description	Reliability 1, 2	Standardization Sample	Address of Author
					2) David I. Ben-Tovim, PhD Department of Psychiatry Repatriation General Hospital Daws Road, Daw Park South Australia, 5041 Finn Askevold, PhD Psychosomatic Department Oslo University Hospital Oslo (Norway)
Image Marking Procedure	1) Askevold (1975) 2) Barrios et al. (1989) 3) Gleghorn, Penner, Powers, & Schulman (1987) 4) Bowden, Touyz, Rodriguez, Hensley, & Beumont (1989)	Subjects indicate their perceived size by marking two endpoints on a lifesize piece of paper	2) IC: (.25–.62) TR: 3 weeks (.17) 4 weeks (.33) 7 weeks (.14) 3) TR: Immediately (.72–.92) 4) TR: 1 day (.38–.85)	2) college females 3) bulimics, normal females 4) 12 anorexics, 12 bulimics, 24 controls	
TV–Video Method	1) Gardner, Martinez, & Sandoval (1987) 2) Gardner & Moncrieff (1988)	Subjects adjust the horizontal dimensions of a television image of themselves to match perceived size	1) IC: not applicable TR: none given	1) 38 normal and eating-disordered adults 2) normal and anorexic females	Rick M. Gardner, PhD Department of Psychology University of Southern Colorado Pueblo, Colorado 81001
Distorting Videocamera	1) Freeman, Thomas, Solyom, & Hunter (1984) 2) Brodie, Slade, & Rose (1989)	Subjects adjust a video image varied from 60% larger to 25% thinner	1) IC: front profile (.62) TR: 7–22 days (frontal; bulimics and anorexics—.91; Controls—.83) 2) IC: (.56–.84) TR: 4 day (.17–.70)	1) 20 eating-disordered females (bulimics and anorexics) and 20 normal females 2) female controls	Richard J. Freeman, PhD Department of Psychology Simon Fraser University Burnaby, BC Canada V5A 1S6

Measure	Studies	Description	Reliability	Population	Contact
Distorting Photograph Technique	1) Glucksman & Hirsch (1969) 2) Garfinkel, Moldofsky, Garner, Stancer, & Coscina (1978) 3) Garfinkel, Moldofsky, & Garner (1979)	Subjects indicate size by adjusting a photograph that is distorted from 20% under to 20% over actual size	1) IC: not applicable 2) TR: 1 week (anorexics—.75; controls—.45) 3) 1 year (anorexics—.70; controls—.14)	1) obese patients 2) anorexics and controls 3) anorexics and controls	David M. Garner, PhD c/o Psychological Assessment Resources, Inc. P.O. Box 998 Odessa, FL 33556
Distorting Video Technique	1) Touyz, Beaumont, Collins, & Cowie (1985)	Subjects indicate size by adjusting photograph that is distorted by 50% under to 50% over actual size	1) IC: not applicable TR: Immediately (.82); 1 day (.63); 8 weeks (.61)	1) anorexics and bulimics	S. W. Touyz, PhD Department of Clinical Psychology Westmead Hospital Westmead 2145 New South Wales, Australia
Distorting Television Method	1) Bowden et al. (1989)	Photograph distorted by videocamera to 50% over and under actual size	1) IC: not applicable TR: 1 day (.92)	1) anorexics, bulimics, controls	J. K. Collins, PhD School of Behavioral Science Macquarie University North Ryde, NSW Australia 2113
Distorting Mirror	1) Brodie et al. (1989)	Distorting mirror (thinner–fatter images)	1) IC: (.61–.92) TR: 4 days (.34–.84)	1) 29 female university students	D. A. Brodie, PhD School of Movement Science University of Liverpool P.O. Box 147 Liverpool L69 3BX England

Subjective / Attitudinal Measures
1) Figural Schema / Silhouettes

Measure	Studies	Description	Reliability	Population	Contact
Figure Rating Scale	1) Stunkard et al. (1983) 2) Thompson & Altabe (1991)	Subjects select from nine figures that vary in size from underweight to overweight	1) IC: not applicable 2) TR: 2 weeks: ideal (males—.82; females—.71); self-think (males—.92; females—.89); self-feel (males—.81; females—.83)	1) 125 males and 204 females (undergraduates)	Albert J. Stunkard, MD University of Pennsylvania Department of Psychiatry 133 S. 36th Street Philadelphia, PA 19104

TABLE 1 (Continued)

Name of Instrument	Author(s)	Description	Reliability 1, 2	Standardization Sample	Address of Author
Contour Drawing Rating Scale	1) Thompson & Gray (1995)	9 male and 9 female schematic figures, ranging from underweight to overweight	1) IC: not applicable TR: 1 week: self (.79)	1) Undergraduates, 40 males and females	James J. Gray, PhD American University Department of Psychology Asbury Building Washington, DC 20016-8062
Breast/Chest Rating Scale	1) Thompson & Tantleff (1992)	5 male and 5 female schematic figures, ranging from small to large upper torso	1) IC: not applicable TR: current (.85) ideal breast (.81) ideal chest (.69)	1) 57 males and 73 females	J. Kevin Thompson, PhD Department of Psychology University of South Florida Tampa, FL 33620-8200
None given	1) Collins (1991) 2) Wood et al. (in press)	7 boy and 7 girl figures that vary in size	1) IC: not applicable TR: 3 days (self = .71; ideal self = .59, ideal other child = .38; ideal adult = .55; ideal other adult = .49) 2) TR: 2 weeks (self = .70; ideal self = .63)	1) 1,118 preadolescent children 2) 109 males and 95 females (age 8–10)	M. E. Collins, HSD, MPH Centers for Disease Control & Prevention 4770 Buford Highway, NE Mailstop K26 Atlanta, GA 30341-3724
Body Image Assessment	1) Williamson, Davis, Bennett, Goreczny, & Gleaves (1989)	Subjects select from 9 figures of various sizes	1) IC: not applicable TR: Immediately–8 weeks (.60–.93) bulimics (ideal—.74; current—.83); obese (ideal—not significant; current—.88; binge-eaters (ideal—.65; current—.81)	1) 659 females including bulimics, binge-eaters, anorexics, normals, obese subjects, and atypical eating-disordered subjects	Donald A. Williamson, PhD Department of Psychology Louisiana State University Baton Rouge, LA 70803-5501

2) Questionnaire Measures

Instrument	Reference	Description	Sample	Reliability	Contact
Eating Disorders Inventory-Body Dissatisfaction Scale	1) Garner, Olmsted, & Polivy (1983) 2) Shore & Porter (1990) 3) Wood et al. (in press)	Subjects indicate their degree of agreement with nine statements about body parts being too large (seven items)	1) 113 female anorexics and 577 female controls 2) 196 boys and 414 girls 3) 109 males and 95 females	1) IC: (anorexics: .90) (controls; .91) 2) IC: adolescents (11–18) (females: .91) (males: .86) 3) IC: children (8–10) (females: .84) (males: .72)	David M. Garner, PhD c/o Psychological Assessments Resources, Inc. P.O. Box 998 Odessa, FL 33556
Color-A-Person Body Dissatisfaction Test	1) Wooley & Roll (1991)	Subjects use five colors to indicate level of satisfaction with body sites by masking on a schematic figure	1) 102 male and female college students; 103 bulimics	1) IC: .74–.85 TR: 2 weeks (.72–.84) 4 weeks (.75–.89)	Orland W. Wooley, PhD Department of Psychiatry University of Cincinnati College of Medicine Cincinnati, OH 45267
Extended Satisfaction With Life Scale-Physical Appearance Scale	1) Alfonso & Allison (1993)	Subjects rate general satisfaction with appearance on a 7-point scale (five items)	1) male and female undergraduates (N = 170)	1: IC: .91 TR: 2 weeks (.83)	David B. Allison, PhD Obesity Research Center St. Luke's/Roosevelt Hospital Columbia University College of Physicians and Surgeons New York, NY 10025
Body Mapping Questionnaire and Colour-the-Body-Task	1) Huon & Brown (1989)	Subjects rate feelings (strongly dislike–strongly like) about 21 body regions. Subjects also color red body sites "liked" and black body sites "disliked."	1) 67 female bulimics 67 female controls	1) IC: not applicable TR: none given	G. F. Huon, PhD Department of Psychology University of Wollongong P.O. Box 1144 Wollongong, NSW 2500 Australia

TABLE 1 (Continued)

Name of Instrument	Author(s)	Description	Reliability 1, 2	Standardization Sample	Address of Author
Body Satisfaction Scale	1) Slade, Dewey, Newton, Brodie, & Kiemle (1990)	Subjects indicate degree of satisfaction with 16 parts (3 subscales: general, head, body)	1) IC: range (.79–.89) TR: none given	1) Females: undergraduates, nursing students, volunteers, overweight subjects, anorexics, bulimics	P. D. Slade, PhD Department of Psychiatry and Department of Movement Science Liverpool University Medical School P.O. Box 147 Liverpool, L69 3BX England
Body Esteem Scale	1) Mendelson & White (1985) 2) D. R. White (personal written communication 9/5/90)	Subjects report their degree of agreement with various statements about their bodies	1) IC: split-half reliability (.85) 2) TR: 2 years (.66)	1) 97 boys and girls (ages: 8.5–17.4) 48 overweight, 49 normal weight 2) 105 boys and girls (ages 8–13)	Donna Romano White, PhD Department of Psychology Concordia University 1455 de Maisonneuve West Montreal, Quebec Canada H3G-1M8
Body Shape Questionnaire	1) Cooper et al. (1987)	34 items that determine concern with body shape	1) IC: none given TR: none given	1) Bulimics, several control samples	Peter Cooper, PhD University of Cambridge Department of Psychiatry Addenbrooke's Hospital, Hills Road Cambridge, CB22QQ England
Self-Image Questionnaire for Young Adolescents Body Image Subscale	1) Peterson, Schulenberg, Abramowitz, Offer, & Jarcho (1984)	Designed for 10–15 year olds; 11-item body image subscale assesses positive feelings toward the body	1) IC: (boys: .81) (girls: .77) TR: 1 year (.60) 2 years (.44)	1) 335 6th-grade students who were followed through the 8th grade	Anne C. Peterson, PhD College of Health and Human Development 101 Henderson Building Pennsylvania State University University Park, PA 16802

Instrument	Reference	Description	Reliability	Sample	Contact
Overweight Preoccupation Scale	1) Cash, Wood, Phelps, & Boyd (1991)	Four items selected from Cash's MBSRQ (Brown et al. 1990)	1) IC: .73 TR: 2 weeks (.89)	1) 79 female undergraduates	Thomas F. Cash, PhD Department of Psychology Old Dominion University Norfolk, VA 23529-0267
Goldfarb Fear of Fat Scale	1) Goldfarb, Dykens, & Gerrard (1985)	10 statements (very untrue to very true) that reflect overconcern with fatness and body size	1) IC: .85 TR: 1 week (.88)	1) 98 high school females	Meg Gerrard Department of Psychology Iowa State University Ames, IA 50011
Bulimia Cognitive Distortions Scale–Physical Appearance Subscale	1) Schulman et al. (1986)	Subjects indicate degree of agreement with 25 statements that measure physical appearance-related cognitions	1) IC: (.97) (for entire scale)	55 female outpatient bulimics aged 17–45 and 55 normal females aged 18–40	Bill N. Kinder, PhD Department of Psychology University of South Florida 4202 Fowler Avenue Tampa, FL 33620-8200
Body Image Automatic Thoughts Questionnaire	1) Cash et al. (1987) 2) T. F. Cash (personal written communication, 4/11/90)	Subjects indicate frequency with which they experience 37 negative and 15 positive body image cognitions	1) IC: (.90) for bulimic and normal subjects for both positive and negative subscales 2) TR: 2 weeks (positive scales: males—.73; females—.71) (negative scale: males—.84; females—.90)	33 female bulimic inpatients and 79 female undergraduates	Thomas F. Cash, PhD Department of Psychology Old Dominion University Norfolk, VA 23529-0267
Mirror Focus Procedure	1) Butters & Cash (1987); Keeton et al. (1990)	Subjects look at themselves in a three-way mirror and then rate their level of discomfort	1) IC: not applicable 2) TR: none given	Undergraduates with elevated body dissatisfaction	Thomas F. Cash, PhD Department of Psychology Old Dominion University Norfolk, VA 23529-0267

TABLE 1 *(Continued)*

Name of Instrument	Author(s)	Description	Reliability 1, 2	Standardization Sample	Address of Author
Physical Appearance State and Trait Anxiety Scale	1) Reed et al. (1991)	Subjects rate the anxiety associated with 16 body sites (8 weight-relevant; 8 non-weight-relevant; trait and state versions available	1) IC: (trait: .88–82) (state: .82–.92) TR: 2 weeks (.87)	Undergraduate females	J. Kevin Thompson, PhD Department of Psychology 4202 Fowler Avenue University of South Florida Tampa, FL 33620-8200
Feelings of Fatness Questionnaire	1) Roth & Armstrong (1993)	Subjects rate extent to which they feel "Thin–Fat" for 61 situations; two scales: troubles (38 items); satisfactions (23 items)	1) IC: troubles: .96 satisfaction: .98 TR: none given	132 undergraduate females	David Roth, PhD Sheppard Pratt Hospital 6501 N. Charter Street P.O. Box 6815 Baltimore, MD 21285-6815
Situational Inventory of Body Image Dysphoria	1) Cash (1994b)	Subjects rate "how often" they experience negative feelings (never–always or almost always) for a total of 48 situations	1) IC: males (.96) females (.96) TR: 1 month males (.87) females (.86)	1) college student normal controls: 110 men; 177 women	Thomas F. Cash, PhD Department of Psychology Old Dominion University Norfolk, VA 23529-0267
Body Image Ideals Questionnaire	1) Cash & Szymanski (1995)	For 10 physical attributes, subjects rate how well they match a "personal ideal." They also rate the importance they place on each ideal. A *discrepancy* score reflects self-ideal discrepancies. There is also an *importance* and *weighted discrepancy* score.	1) IC: discrepancy (.75) importance (.82) weighted discrepancy (.77) TR: none given	1) college student normal controls: 284 women	Thomas F. Cash, PhD Department of Psychology Old Dominion University Norfolk, VA 23529-0267

Measure	Reference	Description	Reliability	Sample	Contact
Appearance Schemas Inventory	1) Cash & LaBarge (in press)	14 items assess "core beliefs or assumptions" about appearance; three subscales: vulnerability, self-investment, and appearance stereotyping	1) IC: .84 2) TR: .71	1) college student normal controls: 274 women	Thomas F. Cash, PhD, Department of Psychology, Old Dominion University, Norfolk, VA 23529-0267

Behavioral Measures

Measure	Reference	Description	Reliability	Sample	Contact
Body Image Avoidance Questionnaire	1) Rosen et al. (1991)	Subjects indicate the frequency with which they engage in body image-related avoidance behaviors	1) IC: (.89) TR: 2 weeks (.87)	1) 145 female undergraduates	James C. Rosen, PhD, Department of Psychology, University of Vermont, Burlington, VT 05405
Physical Appearance Behavioral Avoidance Test	1) Thompson, Heinberg, & Marshall (1993)	Subjects approach own image in a mirror, from a distance of 20 feet; SUDS ratings and approach distance are dependent measures	1) IC: not applicable TR: none given	1) female undergraduates	J. Kevin Thompson, PhD, Department of Pathology, University of South Florida, 4202 Fowler Avenue, Tampa, FL 33620-8200

Miscellaneous Measures

Measure	Reference	Description	Reliability	Sample	Contact
Physical Appearance Related Teasing Scale	1) Thompson, Fabian, et al. (1991)	18-item scale that assesses history of weight and size and general appearance-related teasing	1) IC: weight/size scale: .91; appearance scale: .71 2) TR: 2 week (weight/size: .86; appearance scale: .87)	1) female undergraduates	J. Kevin Thompson, PhD, Department of Pathology, University of South Florida, 4202 Fowler Avenue, Tampa, FL 33620-8200
Perception of Teasing Scale	1) Thompson, Cattarin, et al. (1995)	12 items index general weight, teasing, and competency teasing	1) IC: general weight (.94) competency (.78)	1) 277 female undergraduates	J. Kevin Thompson, PhD, Department of Pathology, University of South Florida, 4202 Fowler Avenue, Tampa, FL 33620-8200

TABLE 1 (Continued)

Name of Instrument	Author(s)	Description	Reliability 1, 2	Standardization Sample	Address of Author
Physical Appearance Comparison Scale	1) Thompson, Heinberg, et al. (1991)	5-item scale that assesses degree subject compares own appearance to that of other individuals	1) IC: .78 TR: 2 weeks (.72)	1) female undergraduates	J. Kevin Thompson, PhD Department of Pathology University of South Florida 4202 Fowler Avenue Tampa, FL 33620-8200
Hand Appearance Scale	1) Vamos (1990)	16-item scale to measure hand appearance concerns: four factors (evaluation, negative emotions, concealment, display)	1) IC: none given 2) TR: none given	1) 84 patients with rheumatoid arthritis	Marina Vamos Department of Psychiatry and Behavioral Sciences School of Medicine University of Auckland Auckland, New Zealand
Sociocultural Attitudes Towards Appearance Scale	1) Heinberg et al. (1995)	14 items assess subjects' recognition and acceptance of societal standards of appearance; two subscales: awareness, internalization	1) IC: awareness (.71) internalization (.88)	1) college students normal controls: 344 women	J. Kevin Thompson, PhD Department of Pathology University of South Florida 4202 Fowler Avenue Tampa, FL 33620-8200

| Feedback on Physical Appearance Scale | 1) Tantleff, Thompson, & Dunn (in press) | 8 items assess appearance-related commentary (verbal, nonverbal) | 1) IC: .84
2) TR: 2 weeks (.82) | 1) college students: 237 women; 161 men | J. Kevin Thompson, PhD
Department of Pathology
University of South Florida
4202 Fowler Avenue
Tampa, FL 33620-8200 |
| Body Exposure in Sexual Activities Questionnaire | 1) Faith, Schare, & Cash (1993) | 28 items measure physical self-consciousness and avoidance of body exposure in sexual situations; two subscales: worry and self-consciousness, comfort with body exposure | 1) IC: .98 (total scale)
.97 (WSC scale)
.92 (CBE scale) | 1) college student normal controls: 401 women; 129 men | Thomas F. Cash, PhD
Department of Psychology
Old Dominion University
Norfolk, VA 23529-0207 |

Note. IC = internal consistency; TR = test–retest reliability. Internal consistency estimates are not applicable for measures that yield a single index or conceptually distinct indices (e.g., some whole-body adjustment methods and figural rating scales). This is a revision of the table presented in Thompson (1990, 1992, 1995).

A number of schematic stimuli, consisting of human figures ranging in size from underweight to overweight, have been created to assess overall size satisfaction (Stunkard, Sorenson, & Schulsinger, 1983; Thompson & Gray, 1995). The difference between an individual's current self-size rating and ideal size rating is a widely accepted index of dissatisfaction level (Thompson, 1995; Williamson, Gleaves, Watkins, & Schlundt, 1993). However, as I will discuss, the type of instructional protocol used for current size may affect ratings. Appendix A contains an example of a figural stimulus material. Schematic figures also have been developed for overall body size ratings for children and adolescents (Collins, 1991; Heinberg, Wood, & Thompson, 1995) and the upper torso region (breast, chest) for adult males and females (Thompson & Tantleff, 1992).

Assessing overall or site-specific body satisfaction may be augmented by including a measure consisting of a ratio between the sizes of relevant body sites. For instance, it is possible that the source of discomfort may lie in the proportionate relationship of the size of one part of the body to a second body site. One such measure is the waist-to-hips ratio. A waist-to-hips ratio of 1.0 would indicate equal circumferences for both sites. Typically, these ratios are somewhat less than 1.0 for women, indicating that the hips are usually larger than the waist. Radke-Sharpe, Whitney-Saltiel, and Rodin (1990) determined that a low waist-to-hips ratio (larger hips than waist) was associated with higher levels of overall body dissatisfaction. However, research with this index is minimal, and some findings indicate that high waist-to-hip ratios (larger waist than hips) are also problematic (Joiner, Schmidt, & Singh, 1994). It is also possible that level of obesity may be an important variable. The ratio may not be an important index of dissatisfaction in cases in which both weight-relevant sites are large. However, in individuals of average weight who, for example, may have proportionately larger hips than waist, the ratio may capture more of the dissatisfaction than reliance on single-site ratings of dissatisfaction (which are yielded by an item analysis of the Eating Disorder Inventory–2 or the Multidimensional Body–Self Relations Questionnaire–Body Areas Satisfaction Scale).

Several researchers have attempted to broaden the range of assessment beyond a singular focus on specific or global estimates of *satisfaction*. For instance, the Appearance Orientation subscale of the Multidimensional Body–Self Relation Questionnaire (Brown et al., 1990) provides a measure of the "cognitive behavioral investment in one's appearance" (Cash & LaBarge, in press). (Sample item: "I am careful to buy clothes that will make me look my best.") Reed, Thompson, Brannick, and Sacco (1991) developed a measure that specifically addressed the anxiety regarding weight- and non-weight-relevant body sites (for example, waist, hips, and thighs vs. lips, hands, and ears). A copy of this scale is contained in Appendix B. Butters and Cash (1987) developed an in vivo measure of body image anxiety that consists of requiring subjects to rate discomfort level (on a scale of 0 to 100) following 30 seconds of self-evaluation in front of a mirror. Fisher and Thompson (1994) modified the measure slightly by allowing subjects merely to imagine themselves in front of the mirror. However, the relation between imaginal and in vivo ratings has not been established.

An even broader assessment of subjective body image disturbance is provided by the Eating Disorder Examination, which consists of symptom ratings made by an interviewer (Fairburn & Cooper, 1993). Two of the four subscales of this measure are related to body image: weight concern and shape concern. This measure is currently in its 12th revision and is used widely and considered a reliable assessment tool. Because it is primarily an index of eating disturbance, more information is presented by Williamson, Gleaves, and Anderson in chapter 9.

Behavioral Assessment

Behavioral assessment has lagged behind other strategies for measuring body image disturbance. Rosen et al. (1991) developed the Body Image Avoidance Questionnaire, a self-report measure of behavioral avoidance, which contains four scales: (a) clothing, (b) social activities, (c) eating restraint, and (d) grooming and weighing. They found that ratings by roommates correlated with a subject's self-reported levels of avoidance (Rosen et al., 1991). However, because Rosen et al.'s (1991) measure is not based on actual behavioral observations, but rather self-reports of behavior, it is not technically a behavioral rating. Weiner, Seime, and Goetsch (1989) provided such a measure via the use of an escape button subjects used to terminate the presence of a video of their image increasing in size. Thompson et al. (1994) attempted to develop a Physical Appearance Behavioral Avoidance Test by progressively requiring subjects (at intervals of 2 ft from a 20-ft distance) to confront their image in a full-length mirror. Subjects' anxiety ratings during this behavioral exposure correlated highly with subjective measures of dissatisfaction. However, even subjects with high levels of body image dissatisfaction generally failed to terminate the exposure (i.e., avoid approaching the mirror). In more recent work in this area, Winfield and Thompson (1995) found that subjects who thought their attractiveness was being rated by experimenters behind a one-way mirror did engage in behavioral avoidance. Thus, although there are a number of excellent subjective and attitudinal measures available, researchers continue to search for a widely applicable behavioral measure.

Measurement of Size Perception

This aspect of body image captured the attention of researchers long before they began to focus on the subjective, attitudinal, and behavioral components just discussed (Thompson, 1990, 1992). Beginning with the seminal work of Slade and Russell (1973), researchers have invented numerous methodologies to test the accuracy of size estimation (historically referred to as *body size distortion*). These methods have ranged from whole-image adjustment procedures (e.g., producing a smaller or larger size via the modification of a photographic or video image) to single-site assessment methods (involving the estimation of a specific body site dimension) (Cash & Brown, 1987; Slade & Brodie, 1994; Thompson, 1990, 1992, 1995).

Although the whole-image adjustment procedures often intrigue clinicians, patients may experience distress at the sight of their image increasing in size (Thompson, 1992). These measures also may be expensive, whereas many single-site measures are financially feasible. The Body Image Detection Device (Ruff & Barrios, 1986) allows subjects to adjust a single beam of light to match their estimation of the size of a certain body region. Thompson and Thompson (1986) modified this apparatus to allow the simultaneous presentation of four beams of light, representing an outline of the human body (cheeks, waist, hips, thighs) and, unaware of the Body Image Detection Device nomenclature, referred to the measure as the Adjustable Light Beam Apparatus. In general, the two measures are comparable (Mizes, 1991). However, Cash and Brown (1987), in support of the Adjustable Light Beam Apparatus, noted that the "simultaneous representation of body-part estimates, would seem more valid than the techniques involving piecemeal estimates without the formation of a gestalt" (p. 506). Thompson and Spana (1988) presented normative data and instructions for constructing the Adjustable Light Beam Apparatus. (See Figure 1 for a demonstration of the use of this procedure.)

Recent Innovations in Assessment

Several new developments indicate that the next few years will produce a variety of creative instruments and assessment methodologies (Altabe & Thompson, 1995). One important area involves the development of measures to test certain theories of body image disturbance (Heinberg et al., 1995; Thompson, 1992; see also chapter 2, this volume). For example, Cash (1994a) has hypothesized that situational (contextual) events may activate schematic processing of appearance-related information, leading him to develop measures to test this theory. The Appearance Schemas Inventory measures core beliefs and assumptions about the importance, meaning, and effects of appearance (Cash & LaBarge, in press); the Situational Inventory of Body-Image Dysphoria (Cash, 1994b) measures negative feelings about appearance in 48 different contexts; and the Body-Image Ideals Questionnaire (Cash & Szymanski, 1995) assesses degree of investment in personal body ideals (see also chapter 4, this volume).

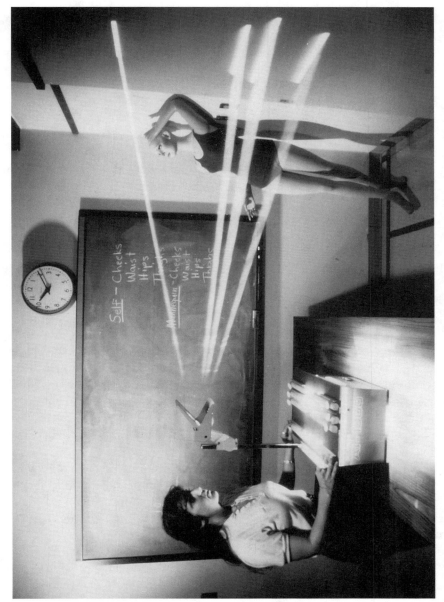

Figure 1. Dr. Lisa J. Fabian uses the Adjustable Light Beam Apparatus to adjust the width of light beams to match her own estimate of the width of her cheeks, waist, hips, and thighs (see Table 1).

The negative verbal commentary (teasing) theory of body image also has received a good deal of support (Akan & Grilo, 1995; Cattarin & Thompson, 1994; Fabian & Thompson, 1989; Grilo, Wilfley, Brownell, & Rodin, 1994; Thompson & Psaltis, 1988), leading my colleagues and me to develop measures of appearance-related teasing (Thompson, Cattarin, Fowler, & Fisher, 1995; Thompson, Fabian, Moulton, Dunn, & Altabe, 1991). Cash (1995) has expanded on these teasing assessment questionnaires by offering an idiographic strategy for measuring teasing frequency and effect. In addition, Rosen (1991) offered the Critical Events Interview, which captures a wide variety of experiences that initially may have fostered body image concerns.

As Heinberg noted in chapter 2, sociocultural and social comparison factors also play a significant role in developing and maintaining body image disturbance, and measures of these variables are also available (Heinberg & Thompson, 1992a, 1992b; Heinberg, Thompson, & Stormer, 1995; Thompson, Heinberg, & Tantleff, 1991). For example, the Sociocultural Attitudes Towards Appearance Questionnaire has two subscales: the awareness scale indexes subjects' cognizance of the pressures on women in Western society to appear attractive, and the internalization scale documents their acceptance and rejection of these sociocultural messages. (A sample item on the internalization scale: "Photographs of thin women make me wish that I were thin" (Heinberg et al., 1995)).

Researchers have begun to emphasize a state versus trait body image distinction (Altabe & Thompson, 1995). With few exceptions, the development of assessment methods has been predicated on the belief that body image is quite static and consistent over time (Cash & Brown, 1987; Thompson, 1992). However, research now supports the notion that body image is malleable and responsive to a variety of contextual and emotional variables, such as information regarding size in relation to peers (Heinberg & Thompson, 1992b) and food consumption (McKenzie, Williamson, & Cubic, 1993; Thompson, Coovert, Pasman, & Robb, 1993).

Therefore, from a clinical perspective, it is advisable to take repeated measures of body image over time to provide a clearer indication of specific problems or to track the effects of treatment. Some measures lend themselves to such repeated use; these include the Physical Appearance State and Trait Anxiety Scale (Reed et al., 1991; see also Appendix B) and the Mirror Distress Rating (Butters & Cash, 1987). The Situational Inventory of Body Image Disturbance (Cash, 1994b) also could be used to make repeated assessments of a patient's distress level in specific situations.

In addition, Heinberg and Thompson (1995) found that a visual analogue rating could be used as a quick and reliable measure of weight and size and overall appearance dissatisfaction. A visual analogue scale is a straight line, 100 millimeters in length, that is anchored at each end by the extremes of disturbance (i.e., "none" vs. "extreme"). Subjects make a slash at the point on the continuum that they feel best captures their state level of discomfort. Their score is measured from left to right; higher scores indicate greater disturbance. Appendix C contains the two visual analogue scales used by Heinberg and Thompson (1995).

Improvements in methodology and instrumentation offer exciting prospects for future research and investigation, and are also expanding the range of assessment targets to many non-weight-related aspects of appearance. In particular, Gardner and colleagues have pioneered the use of a signal detection methodology and instrumentation designed to monitor eye movements associated with visual scanning of the body (Gardner & Morrell, 1991; Gardner, Urrutia, Morrell, Watson, Sandoval, 1990). Researchers have also begun to develop measures to assess aspects of appearance that have received little scrutiny, including baldness (Cash, Price, & Savin, 1993), hand appearance (Vamos, 1990), and skin complexion (Cash & Szymanski, 1994).

METHODOLOGICAL ISSUES

A number of methodological issues should be considered when using many body image assessment measures, particularly the size perception approaches (Touyz & Beaumont, 1987; Thompson, 1992). Several factors affect size estimates, including visuospatial abilities (Thompson & Spana, 1991), repeated testings (practice) (Fisher & Thompson, 1994), type of clothing worn, available illumination, and food consumption (Thompson, Coovert, Pasman, & Robb, 1993). In addition, the specific instructional protocol and the individual's actual size are two factors that have received a great deal of research attention because they affect perceptual *and* subjective measures of body image.

Subjects asked to make an affective rating ("How large do you feel?") tend to produce larger estimates than when asked to make a cognitive rating ("How large do you think you look?"). These findings hold true for eating-disordered and non-eating-disordered subjects (Slade & Brodie, 1994; Thompson & Dolce, 1989). Therefore, it is important to choose a specific instruction and use it consistently over time, in cases in which repeated measures are necessary—otherwise, changes may not be a reflection of treatment but of a specific method variation. Affective versus cognitive instructional differences also have been found with figural ratings. Therefore, it is important to be consistent across time in the instructions given to subjects for completion of these measures (Thompson, 1991; Thompson & Psaltis, 1988).

The actual size of the individual has been shown to affect figural ratings and perceptual size estimation components of body image (Coovert, Thompson, & Kinder, 1988; Penner, Thompson, & Coovert, 1991;

Thompson, 1987; Williamson, Cubic, & Gleaves, 1993). Anorexic patients were found to overestimate body size and select smaller schematic figures than control subjects when the actual size of subjects was not considered as a variable in analyses (Penner et al., 1991; Williamson et al., 1993). However, Penner et al. included a dispositionally thin control group and found overestimation of body size equivalent to that of anorexic patients: both groups overestimated more than a normal-sized control group. Williamson et al. covaried body mass index; the change produced equal current-figure size ratings for patients with anorexia nervosa and bulimia nervosa. These authors offered a number of theories to explain their findings, but from a practical assessment viewpoint, the results argue strongly for attention to this issue.

Actual body size may also be an important confound for some questionnaire measures that assess size and weight satisfaction. Garner, Garner, and Van Egeren (1992) proposed a statistical correction for the Body Dissatisfaction subscale of the Eating Disorder Inventory–2. Their proposed adjustment, which involves adding points to the overall score based on the degree to which an individual's weight falls below the matched population mean weight (Garner et al., 1992) allows for a valid comparison of clinical groups differing in weight (i.e., people with anorexia nervosa, bulimia nervosa, obesity).

Many of the extant questionnaire measures are limited because of their development and validation on a narrow range of subject samples. The great majority of the measures I discuss in this chapter were constructed on female, Caucasian samples, and their generalizability to males or individuals of various ethnicities and ages is questionable. For example, because initial item pools for questionnaire validation often are created by interviewing subjects or asking them to list body image concerns, it is possible that the resultant questionnaires may reflect only the specific concerns of the gender, age, and ethnicity of the subjects sampled. A related concern with some figural stimuli is the obvious Caucasian ethnicity of the figures, a problem that might be handled by using figural silhouettes or blocking out faces (Thompson, 1995; Wood, Becker, & Thompson, in press). Altabe (chapter 6, this volume) provides a detailed discussion of the limitations of available methodology for the investigation of body image in diverse populations, along with an idiographically tailored assessment approach as a possible solution to this problem. Table 1, which notes subject characteristics of the samples used for standardization of the measures discussed in this chapter, can be used as a guide for the selection of a psychometrically sound and appropriate scale for particular cases or samples.

A final pertinent methodological issue involves the reliability and validity of the measures discussed throughout this chapter and contained in Table 1. The great majority of these measures, indeed all of the strategies discussed throughout this chapter, meet Nunnally's (1970) criterion of .70 as a minimally acceptable reliability coefficient for a psychometrically sound measurement instrument. In general, it is inadvisable to use a measure that has a reliability index below this cutoff level. The issues of validity are more complicated and include issues of convergence with other extant measures and clinicians' ratings of distress. In the following section, I will make recommendations based on instruments' proven reliability and validity, with a special focus on those measures that have received the greatest research attention, proven clinically useful, and that possess normative data for comparative purposes.

CONCLUSION

A large number of measures have been created to measure various facets of body image disturbance. Although the great majority of extant indices focus on assessing a weight or size component, several questionnaires also document a more global appearance construct. Furthermore, researchers are in the process of developing instruments to measure specific aspects of body image, such as breast or chest preference, hair or balding concern, and hand appearance.

It is difficult to specify a particular optimal assessment battery because of the multifaceted nature of body image problems likely to present in any unique case. I advocate an initial interview tailored to gather a general idea of a specific patient's body image concerns, followed by a judicious selection of appropriate assessment measures as a hypothesis-testing strategy. However, this approach may not be possible in all circumstances, and the clinician may wish to have some type of standardized assessment, which is then followed by a more idiographic selection of follow-up tests.

I advocate using an initial battery measure that provides a broad and comprehensive assessment. The Eating Disorder Examination 12.00 (Fairburn & Cooper, 1993) can be conducted during the initial interview to yield information regarding shape and weight concerns. This measure often is used in treatment outcome studies for eating disorders and appears to be responsive to psychotherapeutic interventions (see chapter 12, this volume). Perhaps the most widely used questionnaire measure, which also has excellent psychometric properties and normative data for males and females, is the Multidimensional Body–Self Relations Questionnaire (Brown et al., 1990). Three of its scales provide a broad assessment of body image, including: (a) site weight and size satisfaction (Body Areas Satisfaction Scale), (b) global appearance concerns (Appearance Evaluation), and (c) cognitions and behaviors that reflect the importance of appearance to the individual (Appearance Orientation).

A second widely used comprehensive measure of subjective distress is the Body Shape Questionnaire (Cooper, Taylor, Cooper, & Fairburn, 1987). This 34-item measure of body shape disparagement also has 16- and 8-item alternate forms with excellent reliabilities (Evans & Dolan, 1993). I also recommend that the self-report behavioral measure developed by Rosen et al. (1991)—the Body Image Avoidance Questionnaire—be considered for inclusion in a preliminary battery. This measure provides data regarding behaviors in four domains: (a) clothing, (b) social activities, (c) eating restraint, and (d) grooming and weighing.

An initial evaluation also should include some measure of the perceptual accuracy component of body image. There are numerous methodological concerns associated with this aspect of body image (as discussed earlier), and findings indicate that subjective body image distress is tied more closely to eating disturbance (Altabe & Thompson, 1992). In addition, the general movement in the field is toward greater use of subjective and attitudinal measures. However, there is still evidence that size overestimation is associated with relapse (i.e., weight loss) in anorexic patients after an initially positive treatment response (Rosen, 1990). In addition, some treatment strategies focus on improving size estimation accuracy (see chapter 12, this volume). The selection of a specific procedure from those listed in Table 1 is somewhat arbitrary because many have adequate psychometrics. Thompson (1990), noting the variability in size overestimation across sites, advocated the use of a single-site procedure because of its ability to pinpoint discrete sites of inaccuracy. In addition, the single-site procedures are more financially feasible.

In cases in which time is limited and size or weight satisfaction appears to be the dominant theme, the use of schematic figures (see Appendix A) or brief measures of size or weight satisfaction are indicated (Garner, 1991). There also may be instances in which affective (anxiety) or cognitive components appear to be connected to complaints of appearance distress. Therefore, measures such as the Physical Appearance State and Trait Anxiety Scale (Reed et al., 1991; Appendix B) or the Body Image Automatic Thoughts Questionnaire (Cash, Lewis, & Keeton, 1987) might be indicated.

It is also important to include measures that reflect state distress and the situational context of disturbance (Altabe & Thompson, in press). State measures facilitate the determination of treatment efficacy because they can be repeated at regular intervals, and scales focusing on the context of disturbance yield concrete areas for intervention planning. The Mirror Distress Rating (Butters & Cash, 1987), the Physical Appearance State and Trait Anxiety Scale (Reed et al., 1991), and Visual Analogue scales (Heinberg & Thompson, in press; Appendix C) are ideal for state assessments. The Situational Inventory of Body Image Disturbance (Cash, 1994b), which allows a clinician to assess disturbance in 48 different situations, should vastly improve the understanding of the contexts that are most distressing for individual cases. State measures are ideal for pinpointing particular within-subject dispositional factors that may affect body image, such as mood or menstrual cycle effects (Altabe & Thompson, 1990; Carr-Nangle, Johnson, Bergeron, & Nangle, 1994; Thompson, Coovert, et al., 1993).

The foregoing suggestions should not be taken as a blanket endorsement of these measures and a rejection of other assessment approaches. It is important to consider carefully the specific case before conducting an assessment. Table 1 should be examined to ensure that measures are used appropriately given a patient's age, gender, and ethnicity. Caution should be used when a measure is considered for an individual who varies drastically from the sample on which the measure has received empirical testing. When in doubt, the reader is encouraged to contact the authors of particular instruments (addresses are provided in Table 1) for information regarding the appropriate use of measures under consideration. In addition, Altabe (chapter 6, this volume) should be consulted for an idiographically tailored approach that is appropriate for assessing body image concerns, regardless of ethnicity.

REFERENCES

Akan, G. E., & Grilo, C. M. (1995). Sociocultural influences on eating attitudes and behaviors, body image, and psychological functioning: A comparison of African-American, Asian-American, and Caucasian college women. *International Journal of Eating Disorders, 18*, 181–187.

Alfonso, V. C., & Allison, D. B. (1993, August). *Further Development of the Extended Satisfaction With Life Scale.* Paper presented at the annual meeting of the American Psychological Association, Toronto, Canada.

Altabe, M., & Thompson, J. K. (1990). Menstrual cycle, body image, and eating disturbance. *International Journal of Eating Disorders, 9*, 395–402.

Altabe, M. N., & Thompson, J. K. (1992). Size estimation vs. figural ratings of body image disturbance: Relation to body dissatisfaction and eating dysfunction. *International Journal of Eating Disorders, 11*, 397–402.

Altabe, M. N., & Thompson, J. K. (1994). In V. S. Ramachandran (Ed.), *Encyclopedia of human behavior, 1*, 407–414. San Diego, CA: Academic Press.

Altabe, M. N., & Thompson, J. K. (1995). Advances in the assessment of body image disturbance: Implications for treatment strategies. In L. Vandecreek (Ed.), *Innovations in clinical practice* (pp. 89–110). Sarasota, FL: Professional Resource Press.

Askevold, R. (1975). Measuring body image: Preliminary report on a new method. *Psychotherapy and Psychosomatics, 26*, 71–77.

Barrios, B. A., Ruff, G. A., & York, C. I. (1989). Bulimia and body image: Assessment and explication of a promising construct. In W. G. Johnson (Ed.), *Advances in eating disorders* (Vol. 2, pp. 67–89). New York: JAI Press.

Ben-Tovim, D. I., & Crisp, A. H. (1984). The reliability of estimates of body width and their relationship to current measured body size among anorexic and normal subjects. *Psychological Medicine, 14,* 843–846.

Ben-Tovim, D. I., Walker, M. K., Murray, H., & Chin, G. (1990). Body size estimates: Body image or body attitude measures? *International Journal of Eating Disorders, 9,* 57–68.

Bowden, P. K., Touyz, S. W., Rodriguez, P. J., Hensley, R., & Beumont, P. J. V. (1989). Distorting patient or distorting instrument? Body shape disturbance in patients with anorexia nervosa and bulimia. *British Journal of Psychiatry, 155,* 196–201.

Brodie, D. A., Slade, P. D., & Rose, H. (1989). Reliability measures in disturbing body image. *Perceptual and Motor Skills, 69,* 723–732.

Brown, T. A., Cash, T. F., & Mikulka, P. J. (1990). Attitudinal body-image assessment: Factor analysis of the Body Self Relations Questionnaire. *Journal of Personality Assessment, 55,* 135–144.

Butters, J. W., & Cash, T. F. (1987). Cognitive behavioral treatment of women's body-image dissatisfaction. *Journal of Consulting and Clinical Psychology, 55,* 889–897.

Carr-Nangle, R. E., Johnson, W. G., Bergeron, K. C., & Nangle, D. W. (1994). Body image changes over the menstrual cycle in normal women. *International Journal of Eating Disorders, 16,* 267–273.

Cash, T. F. (1994a). Body-image attitudes: Evaluation, investment, and affect. *Perceptual and Motor Skills, 78,* 1168–1170.

Cash, T. F. (1994b). The Situational Inventory of Body-Image Dysphoria: Contextual assessment of a negative body image. *The Behavior Therapist, 17,* 133–134.

Cash, T. F. (1995). Developmental teasing about physical appearance: Retrospective descriptions and relationships with body image. *Social Behavior and Personality, 23,* 123–130.

Cash, T. F., & Brown, T. A. (1987). Body image in anorexia nervosa and bulimia nervosa: A review of the literature. *Behavior Modification, 11,* 487–521.

Cash, T. F., & Labarge, A. S. (in press). Development of the Appearance Schemas Inventory: A new cognitive body-image assessment. *Cognitive Therapy and Research.*

Cash, T. F., Lewis, R. J., & Keeton, W. P. (1987, March). *The Body Image Automatic Thoughts Questionnaire: A measure of body-related cognitions.* Paper presented at the annual meeting of the Southeastern Psychological Association, Atlanta, GA.

Cash, T. F., Price, V. H., & Savin, R. C. (1993). Psychological effects of androgenetic alopecia on women: Comparisons with balding men and with female control subjects. *Journal of the American Academy of Dermatology, 29,* 568–575.

Cash, T. F., & Szymanski, M. L. (1995). The development and validation of the Body-Image Ideals Questionnaire. *Journal of Personality Assessment, 64*, 466–477.

Cash, T. F., Wood, K. C., Phelps, K. D., & Boyd, K. (1991). New assessments of weight-related body image derived from extant instruments. *Perceptual and Motor Skills, 73*, 235–241.

Cattarin, J. A., & Thompson, J. K. (1994). A three-year longitudinal study of body image, eating disturbance, and general psychological functioning in adolescent females. *Eating Disorders: The Journal of Treatment and Prevention, 2*, 114–125.

Collins, M. E. (1991). Body figure perceptions and preferences among preadolescent children. *International Journal of Eating Disorders, 10*, 199–208.

Cooper, P. J., Taylor, M. J., Cooper, Z., & Fairburn, C. G. (1987). The development and validation of the Body Shape Questionnaire. *International Journal of Eating Disorders, 6*, 485–494.

Coovert, D. L., Thompson, J. K., & Kinder, B. N. (1988). Interrelationships among multiple aspects of body image and eating disturbance. *International Journal of Eating Disorders, 7*, 495–502.

Evans, C., & Dolan, B. (1993). Body Shape Questionnaire: Derivation of shortened "alternate forms." *International Journal of Eating Disorders, 13*, 315–321.

Fabian, L. J., & Thompson, J. K. (1989). Body image and eating disturbance in young females. *International Journal of Eating Disorders, 8*, 63–74.

Fairburn, C. G., & Cooper, Z. (1993). The Eating Disorder Examination (12th ed.). In C. G. Fairburn and G. T. Wilson (Eds.), *Binge eating: Nature, assessment, and treatment* (pp. 3–14). New York: Guilford Press.

Faith, M. S., Schare, M. L., & Cash, T. F. (1993, November). *The Body Exposure in Sexual Activities Questionnaire: Psychometrics and sexual correlates.* Paper presented at the annual meeting of the Association for the Advancement of Behavior Therapy, Atlanta, GA.

Fisher, E., & Thompson, J. K. (1994). A comparative evaluation of cognitive–behavior therapy (CBT) versus exercise therapy (ET) for treatment of body image disturbance: Preliminary findings. *Behavior Modification, 18*, 171–185.

Freeman, R. F., Thomas, C. D., Solyom, L., & Hunter, M. A. (1984). A modified video camera for measuring body image distortion: Technical description and reliability. *Psychological Medicine, 14*, 411–416.

Gardner, R. M., Martinez, R., & Sandoval, Y. (1987). Obesity and body image: An evaluation of sensory and non-sensory components. *Psychological Medicine, 17*, 927–932.

Gardner, R. M., & Moncrieff, C. (1988). Body image distortion in anorexics as a non-sensory phenomena: A signal detection approach. *Journal of Clinical Psychology, 44*, 101–107.

Gardner, R. M., & Morrell, J. A. (1991). Body-size judgments and eye movements associated with looking at body regions in obese and normal-weight subjects. *Perceptual and Motor Skills, 73,* 675–682.

Gardner, R. M., Urrutia, R., Morrell, J., Watson, D., & Sandoval, S. (1990). Children's judgments of body size and distortion. *Cognitive Development, 5,* 385–394.

Garfinkel, P. E., Moldofsky, H., & Garner, D. M. (1979). The stability of perceptual disturbances in anorexia nervosa. *Psychological Medicine, 9,* 703–708.

Garfinkel, P. E., Moldofsky, H., Garner, D. M., Stancer, H. C., & Coscina, D. U. (1978). Body awareness in anorexia nervosa: Disturbances in "body image" and "satiety." *Psychosomatic Medicine, 40,* 487–498.

Garner, D. M. (1991). *Eating Disorder Inventory—2: Professional manual.* Odessa, FL: Psychological Assessment Resources.

Garner, D. M., Garner, M. V., & Van Egeren, L. F. (1992). Body dissatisfaction adjusted for weight: The Body Illusion Index. *International Journal of Eating Disorders, 12,* 263–271.

Garner, D. M., Olmsted, M. P., & Polivy, J. (1983). Development and validation of a multi-dimensional eating disorder inventory for anorexia nervosa and bulimia. *International Journal of Eating Disorders, 2,* 15–34.

Gleghorn, A. A., Penner, L. A., Powers, P. S., & Schulman, R. (1987). The psychometric properties of several measures of body image. *Journal of Psychopathology and Behavioral Assessment, 9,* 203–218.

Glucksman, M., & Hirsch, J. (1969). The response of obese patients to weight reduction: III. The perception of body size. *Psychosomatic Medicine, 31,* 1–17.

Goldfarb, L. A., Dykens, E. M., & Gerrard, M. (1985). The Goldfarb Fear of Fat scale. *Journal of Personality Assessment, 49,* 329–332.

Grilo, C. M., Wilfley, D. E., Brownell, K. D., & Rodin, J. (1994). Teasing, body image, and self-esteem in a clinical sample of obese women. *Addictive Behaviors, 19,* 443–450.

Heinberg, L. J., & Thompson, J. K. (1992a). Social comparison: Gender, target importance ratings, and relation to body image disturbance. *Journal of Social Behavior and Personality, 7,* 335–344.

Heinberg, L. J., & Thompson, J. K. (1992b). The effects of figure size feedback (positive vs. negative) and target comparison group (particularistic vs. universalistic) on body image disturbance. *International Journal of Eating Disorders, 12,* 441–448.

Heinberg, L. J., & Thompson, J. K. (1995). Body image and televised images of thinness and attractiveness. *Journal of Social and Clinical Psychology, 14,* 325–338.

Heinberg, L. J., Thompson, J. K., Stormer, S. (1995). Development and validation of the Sociocultural Attitudes Towards Appearance Questionnaire. *International Journal of Eating Disorders, 17,* 81–89.

Heinberg, L. J., Wood, K. C., & Thompson, J. K. (1995). Body image. In V. I. Rickert (Ed.), *Adolescent nutrition: Assessment and management* (pp. 136–156). New York: Chapman and Hall.

Huon, G. F., & Brown, L. B. (1986). Body images in anorexia nervosa and bulimia nervosa. *International Journal of Eating Disorders, 5,* 421–439.

Huon, G. F., & Brown, L. B. (1989). Assessing bulimics' dissatisfactions with their body. *British Journal of Clinical Psychology, 28,* 283–284.

Joiner, T. E., Schmidt, N. B., & Singh, D. (1994). Waist-to-hip ratio and body dissatisfaction among college women and men: Moderating role of depressed symptoms and gender. *International Journal of Eating Disorders, 16,* 199–203.

Keeton, W. P., Cash, T. F., & Brown, T. A. (1990). Body image of body images? Comparative multidimensional assessment among college students. *Journal of Personality Assessment, 54,* 213–230.

McKenzie, S. J., Williamson, D. A., Cubic, B. A. (1993). Stable and reactive body image disturbances in bulimia nervosa. *Behavior Therapy, 24,* 195–207.

Mendelson, B. K., & White, D. R. (1985). Development of self-body-esteem in overweight youngsters. *Developmental Psychology, 21,* 90–96.

Mizes, J. S. (1991). Validity of the Body Image Detection Device. *Addiction Behaviors, 16,* 411–417.

Nunnally, J. (1970). *Psychometric theory.* New York: McGraw-Hill.

Penner, L. A., Thompson, J. K., & Coovert, D. L. (1991). Size estimation among anorexics: Much ado about very little? *Journal of Abnormal Psychology, 100,* 90–93.

Petersen, A. C., Schulenberg, J. E., Abramowitz, R. H., Offer, D., & Jarcho, H. D. (1984). A self-image questionnaire for young adolescents (SIQYA): Reliability and validity studies. *Journal of Youth and Adolescence, 13,* 93–11.

Radke-Sharpe, Whitney-Saltiel, D., & Rodin, J. (1990). Fat distribution as a risk factor for weight and eating concerns. *International Journal of Eating Disorders, 9,* 27–36.

Reed, D., Thompson, J. K., Brannick, M. T., & Sacco, W. P. (1991). Development and validation of the Physical Appearance State and Trait Anxiety Scale (PASTAS). *Journal of Anxiety Disorders, 5,* 323–332.

Rosen, J. C. (1990). Body-image disturbance in eating disorders. In T. F. Cash and T. Pruzinsky (Eds.), *Body images: Development, deviance, and change* (pps. 190–214). New York: Guilford Press.

Rosen, J. C. (1991, November). *Body image disorder and social anxiety.* Paper presented at the annual meeting of the Association for Advancement of Behavior Therapy, New York.

Rosen, J. C., Srebnik, D., Saltzberg, E., & Wendt, S. (1991). Development of a Body Image Avoidance Questionnaire. *Psychological Assessment: A Journal of Consulting and Clinical Psychology, 3,* 32–37.

Roth, D., & Armstrong, J. (1993). Feelings of Fatness Questionnaire: A measure of the cross-situational variability of body experience. *International Journal of Eating Disorders, 14,* 349–358.

Ruff, G. A., & Barrios, B. A. (1986). Realistic assessment of body image. *Behavioral Assessment, 8,* 237–252.

Schulman, R. G., Kinder, B. N., Powers, P. S., Prange, M., & Gleghorn, A. A. (1986). The development of a scale to measure cognitive distortions in bulimia. *Journal of Personality Assessment, 50,* 630–639.

Shore, R. A., & Porter, J. E. (1990). Normative and reliability data for 11 to 18 year olds on the Eating Disorder Inventory. *International Journal of Eating Disorders, 9,* 201–208.

Slade, P. D. (1985). A review of body-image studies in anorexia nervosa and bulimia nervosa. *Journal of Psychiatric Research, 19,* 255–265.

Slade, P. D. (1994). What is body image? *Behaviour Research and Therapy, 32,* 497–502.

Slade, P., & Brodie, D. (1994). Body-image distortion and eating disorder: A reconceptualization based on the recent literature. *Eating Disorders Review, 2,* 32–46.

Slade, P. D., Dewey, M. E., Newton, T., Brodie, D., & Kiemle, G. (1990). Development and preliminary validation of the Body Satisfaction Scale (BSS). *Psychology and Health, 4,* 213–220.

Slade, P. D., & Russell, G. F. M. (1973). Awareness of body dimensions in anorexia nervosa: Cross-sectional and longitudinal studies. *Psychological Medicine, 3,* 188–199.

Stunkard, A., Sorenson, T., & Schulsinger, F. (1983). Use of the Danish Adoption Register for the study of obesity and thinness. In S. Kety, L. P. Rowland, R. L. Sidman, & S. W. Matthysse (Eds.), *The genetics of neurological and psychiatric disorders* (pp. 115–120). New York: Raven Press.

Tantleff-Dunn, S., Thompson, J. K., & Dunn, M. (1995). Development and validation of the Feedback on Physical Appearance Scale (FOPAS). *Eating Disorders: The Journal of Treatment and Prevention, 3,* 341–350.

Thompson, J. K. (1987). Body size distortion in anorexia nervosa: Reanalysis and reconceptualization. *International Journal of Eating Disorders, 6,* 379–384.

Thompson, J. K. (1990). *Body image disturbance: Assessment and treatment.* Elmsford, NJ: Pergamon Press.

Thompson, J. K. (1991). Body shape preferences: Effects of instructional protocol and level of eating disturbance. *International Journal of Eating Disorders, 10,* 193–198.

Thompson, J. K. (1992). Body image: Extent of disturbance, associated features, theoretical models, assessment methodologies, intervention strategies, and a proposal for a new *DSM-IV* diagnostic category—Body Image Disorder. In M. Hersen, R. M. Eisler, and P. M. Miller (Eds.), *Progress in Behavior Modification* (Vol. 28, pp. 3–54). Sycamore, IL: Sycamore Press.

Thompson, J. K. (1995). Assessment of body image. In D. B. Allison (Ed.), *Handbook of assessment methods for eating behaviors and weight-related problems* (pp. 119–148). Newbury Park, CA: Sage.

Thompson, J. K., & Altabe, M. N. (1991). Psychometric qualities of the Figure Rating Scale. *International Journal of Eating Disorders, 10*, 615–619.

Thompson, J. K., Altabe, M. N., Johnson, S., & Stormer, S. (1994). A factor analysis of multiple measures of body image disturbance: Are we all measuring the same construct? *International Journal of Eating Disorders, 16*, 311–315.

Thompson, J. K., Cattarin, J., Fowler, B., & Fisher, E. (1995). The Perception of Teasing Scale (POTS): A revision and extension of the Physical Appearance Related Teasing Scale (PARTS). *Journal of Personality Assessment, 65*, 146–157.

Thompson, J. K., Coovert, D. L., Pasman, L., & Robb, J. (1993). Body image and food consumption: Three laboratory studies of perceived caloric content. *International Journal of Eating Disorders, 14*, 445–457.

Thompson, J. K., & Dolce, J. J. (1989). The discrepancy between emotional vs. rational estimates of body size, actual size, and ideal body ratings: Theoretical and clinical implications. *Journal of Clinical Psychology, 45*, 473–478.

Thompson, J. K., Fabian, L. J., Moulton, D. O., Dunn, M. F., & Altabe, M. N. (1991). Development and validation of the physical appearance related testing scale. *Journal of Personality Assessment, 56*, 513–521.

Thompson, M. A., & Gray, J. J. (1995). Development and validation of a new body image assessment scale. *Journal of Personality Assessment, 64*, 258–269.

Thompson, J. K., Heinberg, L., & Marshall, K. (1994). The Physical Appearance Behavior Avoidance Test (PABAT): Preliminary findings. *The Behavior Therapist, 17*, 9–10.

Thompson, J. K., Heinberg, L., & Tantleff, S. (1991). The Physical Appearance Comparison Scale (PACS). *The Behavior Therapist, 14*, 174.

Thompson, J. K., Penner, L., & Altabe, M. N. (1990). Procedures, problems, and progress in the assessment of body images. In T. F. Cash & T. Pruzinsky (Eds.), *Body images: Development, deviance, and change* (pp. 21–48). New York: Guilford Press.

Thompson, J. K., & Psaltis, K. (1988). Multiple aspects and correlates of body figure ratings: A replication and extension of Fallon and Rozin (1985). *International Journal of Eating Disorders, 7*, 813–818.

Thompson, J. K., & Spana, R. E. (1988). The adjustable light beam method for the assessment of size estimation accuracy description, psychometrics, and normative data. *International Journal of Eating Disorders, 7*, 521–526.

Thompson, J. K., & Spana, R. E. (1991). Visuospatial ability, accuracy of size estimation, and bulimic disturbance in a noneating-disordered college sample: A neuropsychological analysis. *Perceptual and Motor Skills, 73*, 335–338.

Thompson, J. K., & Tantleff, S. (1992). Female and male ratings of upper torso: Actual, ideal, and stereotypical conceptions. *Journal of Social Behavior and Personality, 7*, 345–354.

Thompson, J. K., & Thompson, C. M. (1986). Body size distortion and self-esteem in asymptomatic normal weight males and females. *International Journal of Eating Disorders, 5,* 1061–1068.

Touyz, S. W., & Beumont, P. J. V. (1987). Body image and its disturbance. In P. J. V. Beumont, G. D. Burrows, & R. C. Casper (Eds.), *Handbook of eating disorders* (pp. 171–187). New York: Elsevier Science Publishers.

Touyz, S. W., Beaumont, P. J. V., Collins, J. K., & Cowie, L. (1985). Body shape perception in bulimia and anorexia nervosa. *International Journal of Eating Disorders, 4,* 261–265.

Vamos, M. (1990). Body image in rheumatoid arthritis: The relevance of hand appearance to desire for surgery. *British Journal of Medical Psychology, 63,* 267–277.

Wiener, A., Seime, R., & Goetsch, V. (1989, March). *A multimethod assessment of fear of weight gain in bulimic and low risk females.* Paper presented at the annual meeting of the Southeastern Psychological Association, Washington, DC.

Williamson, D. A., Barker, S. E., Bertman, L. J., & Gleaves, D. H. (1995). Body image, body dysphoria, and dietary restraint: Factor structure in nonclinical subjects. *Behaviour Research and Therapy, 33,* 85–93.

Williamson, D. A., Cubic, B. A., & Gleaves, D. H. (1993). Equivalence of body image disturbances in anorexia and bulimia nervosa. *Journal of Abnormal Psychology, 102,* 177–180.

Williamson, D. A., Davis, C. J., Bennett, S. M., Goreczny, A. J., & Gleaves, D. H. (1989). Development of a simple procedure for assessing body image disturbances. *Behavioral Assessment, 11,* 433–446.

Williamson, D. A., Gleaves, D. H., Watkins, P. C., & Schlundt, D. G. (1993). Validation of the self-ideal body size discrepancy as a measure of body dissatisfaction. *Journal of Psychopathology and Behavioral Assessment, 15,* 57–68.

Winfield, C., & Thompson, J. K. (1995). *Recent developments in the search for a behavioral measure of body image disturbance.* Unpublished manuscript.

Wood, K. C., Becker, J. A., & Thompson, J. K. (in press). Body image dissatisfaction in preadolescent children. *Journal of Applied Developmental Psychology.*

Wooley, O. W., & Roll, S. (1991). The Color-a-Person Body Dissatisfaction test: Stability, internal consistency, validity, and factor structure. *Journal of Personality Assessment, 56,* 395–413.

APPENDIX A
CONTOUR DRAWING RATING SCALE

Instructions: Subjects are asked to rate their "ideal" figure and their "current" size. As noted in the text, it may be useful to consider other instructional protocols, such as a "think" and "feel" rating. The discrepancy between "ideal" and "current" size is an index of body size dissatisfaction (Thompson & Gray, 1995; see Table 1).

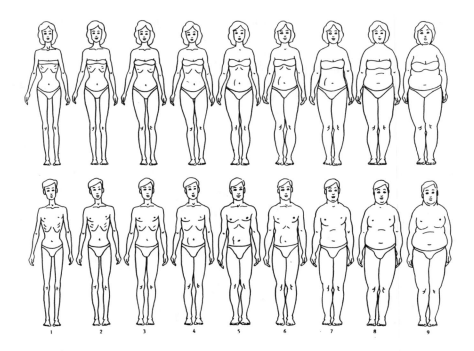

APPENDIX B
PHYSICAL APPEARANCE STATE AND
TRAIT ANXIETY SCALE
TRAIT VERSION

The statements listed below are used to describe how anxious, tense, or nervous you feel *in general* about your body or specific parts of your body. Use the following scale:

0	1	2	3	4
Never	Rarely	Sometimes	Often	Almost Always

In general, I feel anxious, tense, or nervous about:

1. The extent to which I look overweight	0	1	2	3	4
2. My thighs	0	1	2	3	4
3. My buttocks	0	1	2	3	4
4. My hips	0	1	2	3	4
5. My stomach (abdomen)	0	1	2	3	4
6. My legs	0	1	2	3	4
7. My waist	0	1	2	3	4
8. My muscle tone	0	1	2	3	4
9. My ears	0	1	2	3	4
10. My lips	0	1	2	3	4
11. My wrists	0	1	2	3	4
12. My hands	0	1	2	3	4
13. My forehead	0	1	2	3	4
14. My neck	0	1	2	3	4
15. My chin	0	1	2	3	4
16. My feet	0	1	2	3	4

The State version has the same items. However, the instructions *right now* replace *in general*. In addition, the following are the response choices:

0	1	2	3	4
Not at all	Slightly	Moderately So	Very Much So	Exceptionally

Items 1 to 8 make up the weight subscale, and items 9 to 16 make up the non-weight subscale (Reed et al., 1991). (For further information, see Table 1.)

APPENDIX C
VISUAL ANALOGUE SCALES

Instructions: Subjects mark their level of disturbance on the 100 millimeter line. The distance from 0, measured from the left in millimeters, indicates the level of distress (For further information, see Heinberg & Thompson, 1995).

| |_____|

NO
Weight/Size
Dissatisfaction

EXTREME
Weight/Size
Dissatisfaction

| |_____|

NO
Overall Appearance
Dissatisfaction

EXTREME
Overall Appearance
Dissatisfaction

4

THE TREATMENT OF BODY IMAGE DISTURBANCES

THOMAS F. CASH

Our society's unrelenting emphasis on physical appearance drives many people's pursuits of physical perfection. They are consumers of the newest fashions in clothing, the latest promises of lasting weight loss, the exercise products and programs for attaining the "right shape," and ultimately the sculpting services of cosmetic surgeons. One would think that with all these tools for transforming appearance, people would like their looks. But this could not be further from the truth. Body image disturbances range from relatively benign discontent with some physical feature to an obsessive, perhaps delusional, conviction that one's appearance is grotesque. A negative body image is a prevalent problem today, and its possible psychological solutions are just beginning to emerge.

The principal purpose of this chapter is to foster a practical understanding of body image, its dysfunctions, and its treatment. I will first establish conceptual and empirical foundations for clinicians working with a range of clients with body image problems. Then I will delineate my program of cognitive–behavioral body image therapy (Cash, 1991b, 1995b; Cash & Grant, 1995).

THE PREVALENCE AND PREDICAMENTS OF BODY DISSATISFACTION

A 1985 national body image survey (Cash, Winstead, & Janda, 1986) revealed that about two out of of every five women and about one out of three men were dissatisfied with their overall looks. Discontent with weight-related body areas were salient for both sexes, and most respondents were unhappy with at least one aspect of their appearance. Only 28% of men and 15% of women were satisfied with *all* body areas listed in the survey. Comparisons with a survey conducted more than a decade earlier (Berscheid, Walster, & Bohrnstedt, 1973) and with one done more recently (Cash & Henry, 1995) suggest that Americans' body images are not improving.

The clinical implications of body image disturbances are considerable (Rosen, 1992; Thompson, 1992). Moderate associations exist for both sexes between body dissatisfaction and poor psychological adjustment in general (Cash & Pruzinsky, 1990; Thompson, 1990). Pruzinsky (1990), Cash and Grant (1995), and contributors to this volume offer discussions of body image and specific psychopathologies. In the Diagnostic and Statistical Manual of Mental Disorders, 4th edition (*DSM-IV*) (American Psychiatric Association, 1994), body image disturbances are a primary defining feature in anorexia nervosa, bulimia nervosa, body dysmorphic disorder, and transsexualism, as well as certain forms of somatic delusional disorder and the culture-bound Koro syndrome. Furthermore, body dissatisfaction entails vulnerabilities to poor self-esteem, depression, social anxiety and inhibition, and sexual dysfunctions (Cash & Grant, 1995). The link between body image and well-being is especially strong among persons who are more psychologically invested in their appearance (e.g., Cash & Szymanski, 1995; Pliner, Chaiken, & Flett, 1990; Rosen & Ross, 1968).

THE DEVELOPMENT OF A NEGATIVE BODY IMAGE

The causes of dysfunctional body experiences may be divided into two categories. First are the historical, developmental influences that shape the acquisition of particular body image attitudes. Second are the current or proximal influences that govern the flow of body experiences in everyday life. Formulated from a cognitive–social learning framework, these past and present forces are depicted in Figure 1.

Historical, Developmental Determinants

One's sense of self is rooted in the basic experience of embodiment (Cash & Pruzinsky, 1990). The body is the boundary that separates a per-

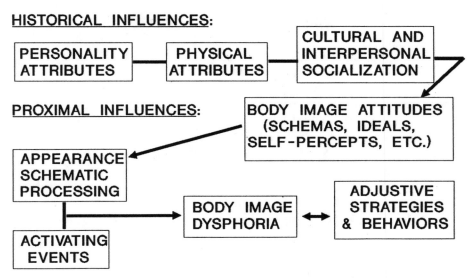

HISTORICAL INFLUENCES:

PERSONALITY ATTRIBUTES — PHYSICAL ATTRIBUTES — CULTURAL AND INTERPERSONAL SOCIALIZATION

PROXIMAL INFLUENCES: BODY IMAGE ATTITUDES (SCHEMAS, IDEALS, SELF-PERCEPTS, ETC.)

APPEARANCE SCHEMATIC PROCESSING

ACTIVATING EVENTS

BODY IMAGE DYSPHORIA ↔ ADJUSTIVE STRATEGIES & BEHAVIORS

Figure 1. Causal processes in the development of body image disturbances.

son from all that is not the person—from the outside world. By 2 years of age, most children recognize their bodily self in a mirror (e.g., Schulman & Kaplowitz, 1977). This physical reality increasingly becomes a self-representation.

Body image develops in a cultural context (Fallon, 1990), taking shape as children internalize the messages and physical standards of society. From childhood on, people evaluate their appearance in terms of how well it matches the "shoulds" (Lerner & Jovanovic, 1990). Likewise, they may judge self-worth based on these standards. Ideals often reflect distorted beliefs about what the other gender truly finds attractive (Fallon & Rozin, 1985). Others' expectations are seldom as extreme or as stringently held as most people assume.

Socialization also involves interpersonal modeling and the vicarious acquisition of values and attitudes about appearance (see Cash & Grant, 1995; Rieves & Cash, 1995). The parent who expends great effort to make the kids look perfect conveys the necessity of good looks for social acceptance. Family members who constantly fret about their looks convey that looks are something to worry about. Having a sibling doted on for being attractive may foster one's implicit social comparisons that diminish body satisfaction.

Recurrent teasing about one's appearance during childhood may have an enduring effect on body image (e.g., Cash, 1995a; Cash et al., 1986; Fabian & Thompson, 1989; Grilo, Wilfley, Brownell, & Rodin, 1994; Rieves & Cash, 1995; Thompson & Psaltis, 1988; see also chapter 2, this volume). Many adults with a strong dislike of their appearance recall distressing childhood episodes of teasing or criticism of their appearance (Cash, 1995a; Rieves & Cash, 1995; Thompson, 1991). Indeed, the most common content of social teasing in childhood concerns physical appearance (Shapiro, Baumeister, & Kessler, 1991).

Puberty brings dramatic changes in appearance. It also can bring an intense preoccupation with these changes and how others will perceive them (Pruzinsky & Cash, 1990). The timing of physical maturation can affect the emotional meaning that teenagers attach to their changing bodies (Downs, 1990; Lerner & Jovanovic, 1990). Early maturing girls and late maturing boys are prone to have less favorable body experiences. Common facial acne also contributes to teenagers' body image concerns (Krowchuk, Stancin, Keskinen, & Walker, 1991).

The human body and its appearance are ever-changing. Whereas people frequently initiate aesthetic changes to improve or gain a sense of control over their looks, other less controllable changes are a natural part of aging or are the result of heredity or life's misfortunes. Unwanted changes can precipitate acute or persistent body image disturbances. For example, "normal" hereditary hair loss can have a deleterious effect on men's and women's body images (Cash, Price, & Savin, 1993; Cash & Pruzinsky, 1995). People with stigmatizing conditions such as obesity are also at risk for developing a negative body image (Friedman & Brownell, 1995; Cash, 1990, 1993; Cash & Hicks, 1990; see also chapter 17, this volume). A history of being overweight may have residual body image effects well after weight loss (Cash, Counts, & Huffine, 1990), with body image fragility in the face of small weight gains (Cash, 1994a). Body image can also be impaired by traumatic disfigurements, such as mastectomy or severe facial injuries (Bernstein, 1990; Cash, 1992b; Pruzinsky, 1992).

A final source of influence on body image development pertains to certain moderating personality traits (Cash, 1990). Most prominent is the extent to which persons are appearance schematic, defining much of their selfhood in terms of their physical attributes (Altabe & Thompson, in press; Cash & Labarge, in press). Self-esteem and social confidence are pivotal. Children, adolescents, or adults who have acquired a positive sense of self are less vulnerable to societal "shoulds" or assaults on their physical acceptability. Public self-consciousness can lay the foundation for a negative body image. This predisposition to view oneself as an audience would potentiates self-scrutiny and preoccupation with one's appearance.

Proximal Determinants

Cultural, social, developmental, and personality factors serve as predisposing causes of body image attitudes. How these attitudes affect day-to-day body experiences depend on precipitating, cognitive mediational, and maintaining factors (see Figure 1).

From my perspective (Cash, 1994b, 1994c, 1995b; Cash & Grant, 1995; Labarge, Cash, & Brown, in press), contextual events serve to activate schema-driven processing of information about and self-appraisals of one's appearance. Activating events may involve body exposure, social scrutiny, social comparisons, wearing certain clothing, looking in the mirror, eating, exercising, weighing, or some unwanted change in one's appearance. Self-evaluations draw on extant body image attitudes and discrepancies between self-perceived and idealized physical characteristics. Implicit or explicit *internal dialogues* (i.e., automatic thoughts, interpretations, and conclusions) reflect habitual and faulty patterns of reasoning—namely, the commission of cognitive errors. These cognitions potentiate various body image emotions (and vice versa), which motivate adjustive, emotion-regulating actions. Such actions include avoidant and concealment behaviors, appearance-correcting rituals, social reassurance seeking, and compensatory actions. They function as maintaining causes via negative reinforcement because they enable the person to escape, reduce, or regulate dysphoric experiences.

BODY IMAGE TREATMENT STUDIES

Prior to the mid-1980s, the few studies evaluating body image therapies had methodological shortcomings (Butters & Cash, 1987). Fortunately, the past decade has brought better research. Cash and Grant (1995) have provided a detailed discussion of body image treatment research, which is summarized in the next section.

Body Image Outcomes in Eating Disorder Treatments

Although the nature of the body image disturbances in anorexia nervosa and bulimia nervosa has been controversial (Cash & Brown, 1987; Hsu & Sobkiewicz, 1991), a recent meta-analysis (Cash & Deagle, 1995) revealed that attitudinal body image dissatisfaction is much stronger than perceptual size distortion among these patients. Investigators (Fairburn, 1987; Garfinkel, 1992; Wilson & Smith, 1989) also have proposed that a central distinctive feature of eating-disordered women is their investment in weight and body shape for defining self-worth. Despite the importance of body image disturbances in eating disorders, few controlled treatment studies with these patients have incorporated body image interventions and measurements (see Cash & Grant, 1995; Rosen, 1990; see also chapter 11, this volume). To my knowledge, no study has compared the *same* treatment with and without a systematic body image therapy component. Nevertheless, Cash and Grant (1995) made several noteworthy observations:

- Psychoeducational approaches in treating eating disorders have produced varied results in altering body image.
- Successful targeted changes in eating behavior or weight are not necessarily indicative of body image changes.
- Eating-disordered patients with the greatest residual, posttreatment body image disturbances are prone to relapse.
- Cognitive and cognitive–behavioral therapies that explicitly address body image issues produce modestly favorable body image changes of uncertain clinical significance. Usually, only one or two sessions and little extra-therapeutic homework are devoted to body image.

Psychotherapy Outcome Studies for Body Dysmorphic Disorder

In her review of case studies of body dysmorphic disorder, Phillips (1991) concluded that behavioral, psychodynamic, and supportive interventions have yielded mixed results. Subsequently, Neziroglu and Yaryura-Tobias's (1993) treatment of five such patients with exposure, response prevention, and cognitive restructuring produced improvements in four patients, including their overvalued ideation of ugliness. The patients maintained the changes a year later.

Unique in the literature is Rosen, Reiter, and Osoran's (1995) controlled-outcome study of cognitive–behavioral body image therapy. As Rosen details in chapter 7, treatment led to a significant decrement of body dysmorphic symptoms and improvement in evaluative body image. Changes generalized to psychological well-being and were sustained at 4 months. Cognitive–behavioral body image therapy appears to hold promise as an effective treatment for body dysmorphic disorder.

Body Image Therapy With Obese Persons

Most clinicians probably regard dieting and weight loss as the proper route to a better body image among obese people. Most weight management programs focus on eating behavior, nutrition, and exercise but virtually ignore body image. The notion of body acceptance without weight reduction is seldom a consideration, though some professionals (Brownell & Wadden, 1991; Cash, 1992a; Garner & Wooley, 1991) now argue for such alternative treatments in view of the biogenetic determinants of obesity and the rather poor long-term maintenance of weight loss.

Rosen, Orosan, and Reiter (1995) found that cognitive–behavioral body image therapy appears helpful for obese persons (see chapter 17, this volume). After treatment and at a 4.5-month follow-up, clients treated with cognitive–behavioral therapy, relative to control subjects, reported significantly improved weight and shape satisfaction, reduced size overestimation, fewer body dysmorphic symptoms, enhanced global adjustment and self-esteem, and less dysfunctional eating patterns. These changes occurred without significant weight modification.

Body Image Therapy With Average-Weight, Body-Dissatisfied Women

Given the prevalence of body image discontent among women, most body image therapy outcome studies have been conducted with "nonclinical," body-dissatisfied women who were neither obese nor met diagnostic criteria for eating disorders (Freedman, 1990). I will summarize the results of studies comparing cognitive–behavioral body image therapy with a control or alternative treatment condition.

In 1987, Dworkin and Kerr compared the efficacy of cognitive, cognitive–behavioral, and reflective therapies relative to a wait-list control group in increasing college women's body satisfaction and self-concept. Gains in body satisfaction and self-concept for those participating in treatment were significantly greater than occurred for the wait-list group. Cognitive therapy was the most effective in producing positive body image changes, and the other two treatments were comparably effective. Cognitive–behavioral and cognitive therapy were equally effective in enhancing self-concept, and both were superior to reflective therapy.

Concurrent with Dworkin and Kerr (1987), Butters and Cash (1987) independently examined the effectiveness of a more extensive cognitive–behavioral body image therapy program. They compared a 6-week individual treatment with a wait-list control group, which subsequently was treated with a 3-week cognitive version of the program. The results confirmed significant body image improvements for the 6-week cognitive–behavioral therapy group, relative to the control subjects, and changes were maintained at a 7-week follow-up. Outcomes entailed more favorable and satisfying body image evaluations, less appearance investment, reductions in dysfunctional body image cognitions, and less mirror exposure distress. Self-evaluations of fitness, sexuality, social self-esteem, and global functioning also were differentially enhanced by treatment. The 3-week program produced comparable outcomes.

In 1989, Rosen, Saltzberg, and Srebnik examined the efficacy of cognitive–behavioral body image therapy compared to a minimal treatment that controlled for demand characteristics and nonspecific treatment elements. The minimal therapy condition was similar in format to cognitive–behavioral therapy except that it excluded structured exercises to correct maladaptive body image cognitions, behaviors, and perceptions. For both treatments, 2-hour group sessions lasted 6 weeks.

Relative to minimally treated clients, those obtaining body image cognitive–behavioral therapy showed significant reductions in their perceptual size overestimation over time. Although clients in both conditions reported significant decrements in body image discontent, only those who had received cognitive–behavioral therapy changed from a clinical to normal range. At a 2-month follow-up, the same between-group difference was evident. Only the cognitive–behavioral therapy group made significant changes on reported body image avoidance. Rosen et al. (1989) concluded that group treatment with cognitive–behavioral therapy effectively produced positive changes in perceptual, evaluative, and behavioral aspects of body image. Unlike Dworkin and Kerr (1987), they found cognitive–behavioral therapy to be more effective than minimal, nondirective therapy.

In a subsequent dismantling study, Rosen, Cado, Silberg, Srebnik, and Wendt (1990) compared two versions of cognitive–behavioral therapy to determine the necessity to include exercises to correct perceptual body image distortion. Both conditions produced equally significant improvements in all measured aspects of body image, psychological adjustment, and dysfunctional eating patterns (except for average caloric intake). All outcomes were maintained after 3 months, with the exception of meal frequencies and binge episodes. The authors concluded that perceptual size-estimation training is a nonessential ingredient of effective body image cognitive–behavioral therapy.

Fisher and Thompson (1994) treated body-dissatisfied women with either cognitive–behavioral therapy or a physical exercise program that included body image education, aerobics, and weight-lifting. Both 6-week treatments produced significant decreases in body image anxiety and dissatisfaction, whereas an untreated control group was unchanged. For treatment *and* control groups, however, significant and equivalent decreases occurred in body image avoidance behaviors and size overestimation. The authors expressed concern, however, about the clinical meaningfulness of the improvements. An attrition rate in excess of 50% at the 3-month follow-up unfortunately prevented conclusions about the stability of outcomes.

Grant and Cash (1995) evaluated therapy in two formats—a group therapy modality versus a largely self-directed format with modest therapist contact. Recent meta-analytic evidence revealed that, for a variety of psychological problems, largely self-administered, structured interventions with minimal therapist contact can produce outcomes that are often as favorable as therapist-administered treatments (Gould & Clum, 1993; Scogin, Bynum, Stephens, & Calhoon, 1990).

Grant and Cash (1995) used Cash's (1991b) published audiocassette program *Body Image Therapy: A Program for Self-Directed Change*, which consists of eight 30-minute cassette sides, a client workbook, and clinician's manual. Clients were assigned randomly to 11-week, modest-contact treatments or to group cognitive–behavioral therapy treatments. Both completed the audiocassette program. The modest-contact group met for 15 to

20 minutes weekly with an assistant who explained and reviewed the assigned tapes and homework procedures, answered questions, reinforced compliance, and facilitated any needed problem-solving with homework compliance. In the group therapy condition, clients met for 90 minutes weekly in therapy groups that, in addition to the conditions described in the previous therapy plan, solicited clients' discussions of their body image experiences, goal setting, behavioral rehearsal, and problem solving. Sessions involved (a) self-assessment of body image developmental influences; (b) self-monitoring of body image experiences—antecedents, cognitions, and consequences; (c) multimodal relaxation training; (d) body image desensitization (imaginal and in vivo); (e) identifying and monitoring of cognitive body image errors; (f) cognitive restructuring to alter dysfunctional internal dialogues; (g) self-assessment of self-defeating body image behaviors; (h) exposure, response prevention, stress inoculation, self-regulation, and mastery-and-pleasure activities to decrease avoidant or compulsive patterns and to increase positive body image behaviors; (i) review and integration of acquired skills and problem solving and assertion with "difficult" situations; and (j) development of relapse-prevention and maintenance strategies.

Grant and Cash (1995) found equivalent therapeutic outcomes for the two cognitive–behavioral therapy formats. All outcomes were sustained at a 2-month follow-up and included significant gains in body image evaluation and satisfaction and reductions in negative body image affect across a range of situations (including mirror and weigh-in exposures). Clients further reported less schematic investment in their appearance, fewer cognitive body image errors and negative body image thoughts, and less body image focus and avoidance during sexual relations. They became less anxiously preoccupied with their weight and reported more congruence between self and ideal body size percepts. Improvements generalized to self-esteem, social–evaluative anxiety, depression, and eating disturbance. Unlike previous studies, Grant and Cash (1995) statistically examined the clinical significance of body image changes and confirmed that the reliable or functional improvements were quite favorable for both treatment modalities.

These outcome studies attest to the efficacy of cognitive–behavioral therapy procedures in the amelioration of a negative body image among women of average weight without clinical eating disorders. The treatment has been found to be successful when implemented by relatively inexperienced therapists in group, individual, and supervised self-directed formats. Because all investigations used what typically would be referred to as nonclinical samples, it is important to note that subjects often manifested subclinical symptoms associated with their extremely negative body images—namely, poor self-esteem, anxiety, depression, and eating disturbances. Cognitive–behavioral therapy appears effective in improving cognitive, evaluative, affective, perceptual, and self-reported behavioral aspects of body image. Furthermore, body image changes consistently generalize to other areas of psychosocial functioning linked with a negative body image. Although most changes are maintained at least 2 or 3 months after therapy, longer follow-ups have not been conducted.

COGNITIVE–BEHAVIORAL BODY IMAGE THERAPY: A PRACTICAL GUIDE

The remainder of this chapter is a practitioner-oriented description of Cash's (1995b) most recent version of the body image therapy program, also presented in detail by Cash and Grant (1995). Body image cognitive–behavioral therapy can be conducted in either individual or group modalities. Practitioners may find it useful to be familiar with Cash's (1995b) self-help book or earlier audiocassette version of the program (1991b). Materials from these sources can be used as a supplement assigned to clients in therapy.

The program assumes that the clinician has conceptual and technical competencies in cognitive–behavioral therapy, the essential therapeutic relationship skills, and acumen in clinical problem solving. The clinician must acquire an accurate understanding of the functional significance of body image disturbances in relation to other aspects of the clients' problems. The program's steps should be implemented in a manner that cumulatively builds skills and integrates techniques.

Step 1: A Comprehensive Body Image Assessment

Soon after the initial interview in which the clinician and client have decided that body image will be a principal focus of therapy, a battery of body image measures should be given. These serve as (a) baseline indices of multiple facets of the client's body experiences, (b) information for feedback to educate the client about strengths and vulnerabilities and as evidence of the causal processes in the client's body experiences, and (c) crucial data for treatment planning. Most are self-report inventories that clients can complete and return the following session. In this volume (chapter 3) and elsewhere, Thompson (1990, 1992; Thompson, Penner, & Altabe, 1990) has provided excellent consumer guides to many of these instruments. A list of reliable and valid body image assessments that I often use follows (see also Cash & Grant, 1995).

One set of measures tap clients' body image evaluations, body image affect, and cognitive–behavioral investment in and reactions to appearance: (a) the Multidimensional Body–Self Relations Questionnaire

(Brown, Cash, & Mikulka, 1990; Cash, 1994d); (b) the Body-Image Automatic Thoughts Questionnaire (Cash, Lewis, & Keeton, 1987); (c) the Appearance Schemas Inventory (Cash & Labarge, in press); (d) the Situational Inventory of Body-Image Dysphoria (Cash, 1994c); (e) the Body Image Avoidance Questionnaire (Rosen, Srebnik, Saltzberg, & Wendt, 1991); (f) the Body Shape Questionnaire (Cooper, Taylor, Cooper, & Fairburn, 1987); (g) the Body-Image Ideals Questionnaire (Cash & Szymanski, 1995; Szymanski & Cash, 1995).

Additional useful measures are these clinician-administered procedures: (a) the Body Dysmorphic Disorder Examination (Rosen & Reiter, 1992); (b) the Body Image Assessment Procedure (Williamson, Davis, Bennett, Goreczny, & Gleaves, 1989); (c) in vivo distress ratings during mirror exposure and during weighing (Butters & Cash, 1987; Cash, Counts, & Huffine, 1990; Grant & Cash, 1995; Keeton, Cash, & Brown, 1990).

The clinician should also select measures of psychosocial functioning known to be associated with a negative body image. Pertinent are assessments of global adjustment, self-esteem, social–evaluative anxiety and self-consciousness, depression, eating disturbance, and sexual functioning.

Step 2: Body Image Education and Self-Discoveries

Early on, clinicians should explain the tenets of cognitive–behavioral therapy in terms of unlearning and relearning patterns of thinking, feeling, and behaving. Clients must come to see themselves as active participants in change and view the therapist as a catalyst and teacher who collaboratively helps them develop specific competencies and create corrective experiences.

The aim of the next few sessions is to enhance clients' understanding of their body image experiences. This is achieved through several psychoeducational activities.

1. The client receives bibliotherapeutic information on the psychology of physical appearance (e.g., chapter 1 of Cash, 1995b; or tape side 1 of Cash, 1991b). This information (a) promotes a rational view of the effects of objective appearance on people's lives and stresses the stronger effects of subjective body image, (b) normalizes the client's body image concerns, and (c) provides a framework (from Figure 1) to understand the components and causes of a negative body image.
2. Through discussions, therapist and client begin to apply this information to personalize the client's knowledge in terms of both predisposing and proximal influences. With respect to

the former, clients keep a body image diary to record critical events and experiences, from early childhood to the present, regarded as formative in their body image development.

3. Drawing on results of the body image assessments (from Step 1), the therapist and client collaborate to discover *activators*—salient precipitating events and situations; *beliefs*—thoughts, perceptions, and inferences in the client's internal dialogues ("private body talk"); and *consequences*—the resultant emotions and adjustive behaviors. The therapist instructs clients in self-monitoring and assigns diary keeping. Body image emotions are self-rated in terms of intensity and duration. The client records these sequences for typical past episodes of body image distress. The client then reviews this information with the therapist, who collaborates in identifying apparent themes. Next, the client makes diary entries for ongoing body image experiences and brings the diary to each session for discussion.

4. From these increasingly precise revelations of patterns and processes, the therapist and client set explicit, written therapeutic goals.

Step 3: Body Image Exposure and Desensitization

The goal of Step 3 is to facilitate clients' exposure to the bodily foci and situational events that provoke discontent and dysphoria. This is conducted as self-control desensitization (Goldfried & Davison, 1976), rather than as passive, reciprocal inhibition. Clients actively use acquired relaxation skills to reduce and manage negative body image emotions. The following procedures are used.

1. Body-and-mind relaxation (Cash, 1991b, 1995b) training includes progressive muscle relaxation, diaphragmatic breathing, imagery exercises, and self-instructional and autogenic techniques (for cued relaxation). After an initial in-session induction, clients receive a 30-minute tape (e.g., tape side 3 from Cash, 1991b) or a transcript for making their own tape (Cash, 1995b). For a week they practice relaxation daily, rate their mental and physical relaxation, and note any problems as well as components that are most helpful.

2. In the next session, the therapist guides the client in cue-controlled relaxation, without a tape, and begins hierarchy development. Two hierarchies are created, with 6 to 12 items each. The first lists body areas or features that are the foci of

varying degrees of discontent. The second hierarchy concerns situations or events that trigger body image distress.

3. In the initial desensitization trials, clients use relaxation skills to manage discomfort as they progressively picture disaffected body areas, from least to most disliked. The goal each time is *not* to be anxiety-free but to control and reduce discomfort. Clients begin in-session and continue as daily homework, noting progress and difficulties. Each item is imagined for 15 seconds, then 30 seconds, and then 1 minute, moving up the hierarchy with reasonable control of discomfort.

4. The next trials involve the client's completing the hierarchy during in vivo, full-length mirror confrontation, while fully dressed. Again, in-session trials can initiate the procedure, which the client completes as homework and records problems and progress for review with the therapist.

5. Next, mirror desensitization is carried out privately at home, while the client is entirely or mostly undressed. For obvious professional reasons, this should *never* be done as an in-session exercise. Even in total privacy, many clients will experience substantial distress and resist this procedure. Clinical judgment is essential for deciding when these trials should be attempted.

6. A final, imaginal desensitization procedure targets the contexts of body image distress. Again, most trials can be conducted in a self-directed homework assignment, with an emphasis on controlling rather than eliminating discomfort. Clients' diary records should be examined and discussed to reinforce successes and resolve difficulties.

Step 4: Identifying and Challenging Appearance Assumptions

Cognitive therapy draws on the techniques of Beck (1976) and Ellis (1977) to identify and alter maladaptive cognitive phenomena at various interdependent levels—from automatic thoughts to cognitive errors to underlying beliefs, assumptions, or schemas. Most persons with a negative body image are highly appearance-schematic, having an elaborate array of emotion-laden, implicit beliefs or assumptions (see Cash, 1995b; Cash & Grant, 1995; Cash & Labarge, in press) that tie their looks to their basic sense of self. For example, they may believe, "The only way I could ever like my looks would be to change my looks." Or, "If people knew how I really look, they'd like me less."

This phase of therapy targets the assumptions that clients endorsed previously on the Appearance Schemas Inventory (Cash & Labarge, in press). The goal is for clients to discover the personal maladaptivity and tenuous veracity of their core assumptions, which serve to guide dysfunctional body image thoughts, feelings, and behaviors. Homework assignments support this process of discovery and questioning, which Cash (1995b) referred to as establishing "reasonable doubt":

1. The therapist reintroduces the framework that regards cognitive processes as pivotal in body image difficulties. The aim of unearthing potential sources of fuel for distress is emphasized.

2. Appearance Schemas Inventory items that the client had endorsed are targeted. The client is asked to expand briefly on his or her personal belief in each. Drawing on specific episodes of body image distress, the therapist helps make connections between the underlying assumptions and their experiential effects.

3. The therapist initially selects assumptions that are espoused less vehemently and engages in a Socratic dialogue that guides the client's exploration of the evidence of the truth and falsity of the belief. In effect, questions concern, "What's wrong with this picture?" "Can you think of instances that contradict this?" "If you didn't believe this, how would you have reacted differently?"

4. The therapist reiterates the importance of the client's questioning these underlying assumptions. A homework assignment asks the client to write, for each endorsed assumption, "When I assume _____, then I think _____, and I feel _____." The client then writes out possible exceptions, contradictions, and flaws with each assumption.

5. In the next session, the therapist reviews the homework, reinforcing and elaborating (a) evidence of the body-image implications of the client's assumptions and (b) instances of effective challenging of these assumptions. Client and therapist collaborate to develop more rational, accurate statements, which the client will write down and rehearse. The therapist listens for and ferrets out other implicit beliefs. The therapist must recognize the kernel of truth in some assumptions and not take incredulous stances. Exploring the need for and consequences of an assumption is more effective than attacking its absurdity.

Step 5: Identifying and Correcting Cognitive Errors

The next level of cognitive therapy focuses on the client's problematic private body talk. This step flows logically from the previous one, and a number of cognitive strategies are employed to help the client capture and correct faulty body image thoughts and inferences.

1. The client learns to identify specific cognitive body image errors (Cash, 1992c) and develops strategies to correct them with more rational internal dialogues. The therapist provides a description and examples of each of 12 errors—from Cash's (1991b) tape side 5 or the pertinent chapter in Cash (1995b). Errors are given mnemonically useful names (e.g., *beauty or beast* error rather than *dichotomous reasoning,* and *blind mind* instead of *minimization*). The client reviews his or her body image diary for A-B-C sequences that reflect each error.

2. The therapist coaches and models to help the client develop corrective thinking strategies for typically faulty private body talk. The client also is encouraged to link his or her cognitive errors to the higher-order appearance assumptions identified earlier. Before working on corrective thinking strategies in vivo, the client first expounds them on homework sheets for representative episodes of body image dysphoria—adding a *D* for *disputing* to the A-B-C sequence. The client writes down the self-statements and interpretations that reflect each error, followed by disputational counterarguments to each.

3. During the next session, the client and therapist elaborate and rehearse these counterarguments. To prepare the client for in vivo self-monitoring and cognitive restructuring, the therapist introduces the "stop, look, and listen" technique. This refers to (a) *stopping* the negative self-talk in mid-stream, (b) *looking* at activating events and maladaptive private body talk to discern the inherent cognitive errors that are producing body image emotional reactions, and (c) *listening* to more rational, accurate self-statements that correct the errors.

4. The client is asked to audiotape corrective thinking dialogues and listen to them daily to facilitate acquisition. The client continues to keep a body image diary to record the use of corrective thinking in the daily management of dysfunctional body image experiences. Now the client adds entries for in vivo disputations and their emotional *effects,* which completes an A-B-C-D-E sequence.

Step 6: Modifying Self-Defeating Body Image Behaviors

This facet of therapy targets clients' maladaptive behaviors associated with a negative body image. Two types of self-defeating actions are avoidant behaviors and obsessive–compulsive patterns. Although these maneuvers may offer temporary emotional relief, they serve to perpetuate body image discontent and dysphoria. They are motivated by desires to escape, reduce, or manage negative body image experiences (e.g., self-consciousness, embarrassment, anxiety). Body image avoidance may involve avoiding certain practices (e.g., weighing, wearing revealing clothing), people (e.g., those who match one's physical ideals), places (e.g., exercise class, the beach or pool), or poses that accentuate one's disliked features. In addition are "grooming to hide" behaviors in which clothing, cosmetics, or hairstyles are used inflexibly to conceal or camouflage perceived flaws. The compulsive, *appearance-preoccupied rituals* are of two types. *Fixing* behaviors are time-consuming efforts to manage, repair, or alter one's appearance, usually by perfectionistic grooming regimens. *Checking* rituals include frequent mirror inspection, weighing, or social reassurance seeking. Step 6 applies cognitive and behavioral strategies to decrease avoidant and compulsive patterns and fortify clients' control over them.

1. Drawing on the conceptual model (Figure 1), the therapist helps the client understand the function and maladaptivity of these behaviors. The therapist and client collaborate to identify maladaptive behaviors of each type. As homework, the client inventories these.
2. The therapist helps the client construct hierarchies of each type of pattern. There are two hierarchies of avoidant behaviors—one for practices, persons, poses, and places avoided, and another for grooming-to-hide behaviors. Items are arranged in order of the client's efficacy expectations that he or she will be able to confront or execute whatever is avoided. In a similar way, a third hierarchy arranges compulsive patterns in order of efficacy expectations that the client can refrain from performing the ritual under cued or probable circumstances.
3. Next, the client is taught a strategy derived from stress inoculation training (Meichenbaum, 1985). This "PACE yourself" strategy (Cash, 1995b) entails four steps— *prepare* (and rehearse an exact plan for confronting the avoidance or resisting the ritual), *act* (on the plan), *cope* (using relaxation, imagery, corrective thinking to manage any discomfort), and *enjoy* (pre-determined self-rewards).
4. One item at a time, the client develops a detailed PACE strategy for confronting each item on the avoidance and grooming-to-hide hierarchies, mentally rehearses the plan, and then carries out the strategy. After each attempt at changing a self-defeating pattern, the client notes the results in his or her diary and makes strategic changes as needed.

The client progresses up the hierarchy, from easiest to most difficult activities.

5. A similar procedure is followed in developing and implementing graduated exposure and response prevention strategies for reducing appearance-preoccupied, compulsive rituals (Steketee & White, 1990). The therapist and client creatively tailor plans that control rituals by means of delay tactics, time restriction, frequency rationing, obstruction, or scheduling of the specific fixing and checking behaviors (see Cash, 1995b). Throughout, the client uses the PACE strategy, incorporates acquired skills in corrective thinking and coping, and records plans and results in the diary.

Step 7: Body Image Enhancement Activities

Therapeutic steps thus far have targeted negative cognitive and behavioral patterns. In Step 7, the client works on increasing positive body experiences. Many people with a negative body image overemphasize their appearance and fail to derive rewarding experiences from aspects of bodily functioning. For example, if they exercise they focus on weight loss or body definition rather than on the mastery and pleasure of the experience itself. The therapist introduces this phase of therapy with a dysfunctional relationship metaphor for framing how the client relates to his or her body (Cash, 1995b). The goal is to improve this relationship by expanding the client's mastery and pleasure in "treating the body right."

1. The client completes a survey (Cash, 1991b, 1995b) of the frequency of various body-related activities over the past year, rating the mastery and the pleasure derived from each. The client classifies activities associated with at least a moderate sense of mastery or pleasure into appearance, health and fitness, and sensate categories.
2. The client selects two or three activities for mastery and for pleasure in each of the three categories, and then schedules and enacts one or two per day. The client records the mastery or pleasure experiences for each.
3. The therapist reviews the results of these activities, reinforcing the client's self-regulatory abilities to expand the sources of his or her positive body-related experiences. If the client has difficulty carrying out an activity, the therapist helps develop appropriate cognitive and behavioral strategies to overcome resistance.
4. Next, a series of experiential exercises (Cash, 1991a, 1995b) are carried out to promote positive body experiences. For ex-

ample, in a "Writing Wrongs" exercise, the client writes his or her body a letter in an effort to improve the relationship. Brief mirror affirmations can bolster a positive body image also. Another exercise, "I Am Becoming," requires that the client discern how he or she would think, feel, and act differently if his or her body image ideals were actually attained. The client then spends a day enacting this body image script.

Step 8: Relapse Prevention and Maintenance of Changes

Finally, the client evaluates progress, sets future goals, and develops strategies for high-risk situations and set-backs (Marlatt & Gordon, 1984; Meichenbaum, 1985).

1. It is expected that the therapist will have continuously monitored the client's cognitive, affective, and behavioral progress during the program, using diary records and other assessments. Nevertheless, at this stage, the therapist should readminister all pretreatment assessments. To promote a sense of accomplishment, the therapist reinforces the areas of greatest improvement in light of the specific goals that the client had set. Together, the client and therapist then identify lingering problem areas and set new goals, such as feeling better about particular body areas or gaining more control over certain distressing thoughts, feelings, or situations.

2. Troublesome interactions, such as those with nagging or critical friends and relatives, can be chronic sources of body image distress. With therapist modeling and with behavioral rehearsal, the client learns interpersonal problem solving and assertiveness skills in managing these difficult people. For example, a client acquires the means to manage a loved one who hurls regular insults that undermine the client's body image.

3. The therapist helps the client use the PACE strategy in anticipating difficulties and developing plans that take into account current vulnerabilities and areas of potential set-backs. The therapist and client prepare together for high-risk situations by drawing on cognitive–behavioral strategies that the client previously found to be helpful. The therapist further normalizes temporary set-backs as "lapses not relapses" and as signals to use skills imparted by the program. An important attitude to instill in the client is, "Don't give yourself a hard time for having a hard time!"

Termination and Follow-Up Issues

At this point, as throughout therapy, the therapist should facilitate the generalization of cognitive and behavioral skills from body image to other areas of the client's life. Moreover, attributing improvements to the client's efforts and skills is important to prevent the client's leaving with a "What will I do without you" view of the therapist. The therapist may wish to keep the door open for booster sessions to attend any problems the client has in attaining the new goals. As a bridge to foster continued change, the therapist may wish to schedule a 3- to 6-month follow-up session.

CONCLUSION

The past decade has brought conceptual and empirical advances in our understanding of body image and its dysfunctions and treatment. Still, further progress is needed. Dismantling studies must determine the most efficacious elements of this multifaceted treatment. The evaluation of body image cognitive–behavioral therapy as an addition to extant treatments for obesity and eating disorders is crucial. Its continued evaluation as a treatment for body dysmorphic disorder is a priority. Its value as an adjunct or alternative to elective cosmetic surgery should be examined. Clinicians and researchers also should consider the helpfulness of cognitive–behavioral body image therapy to persons challenged by physical disfigurements. Finally, in view of the known risk factors in the development of prevalent body image disturbances, there is potential value in a psychoeducational adaptation of body image cognitive–behavioral therapy for the prevention of problems among children and early adolescents.

REFERENCES

Altabe, M., & Thompson, J. K. (in press). Body image: Is there cognitive self-schema? *Cognitive Therapy and Research.*

American Psychiatric Association. (1994). *Diagnostic and statistical manual of mental disorders* (4th ed.). Washington, DC: Author.

Beck, A. T. (1976). *Cognitive therapy and the emotional disorders.* New York: International Universities Press.

Bernstein, N. R. (1990). Objective bodily damage: Disfigurement and dignity. In T. F. Cash & T. Pruzinsky (Eds.), *Body images: Development, deviance, and change* (pp. 131–148). New York: Guilford Press.

Berscheid, E., Walster, E., & Bohrnstedt, G. (1973, November). Body image. The happy American body: A survey report. *Psychology Today, 7*, 119–131.

Brown, T. A., Cash, T. F., & Mikulka, P. J. (1990). Attitudinal body-image assessment: Factor analysis of the Body–Self Relations Questionnaire. *Journal of Personality Assessment, 55*, 135–144.

Brownell, K. D., & Wadden, T. A. (1991). The heterogeneity of obesity: Fitting treatments to individuals. *Behavior Therapy, 22*, 153–177.

Butters, J. W., & Cash, T. F. (1987). Cognitive–behavioral treatment of women's body-image dissatisfaction. *Journal of Consulting and Clinical Psychology, 55*, 889–897.

Cash, T. F. (1990). The psychology of physical appearance: Aesthetics, attributes, and images. In T. F. Cash & T. Pruzinsky (Eds.), *Body images: Development, deviance, and change* (pp. 51–79). New York: Guilford Press.

Cash, T. F. (1991a). Binge-eating and body images among the obese: A further evaluation. *Journal of Social Behavior and Personality, 6*, 367–376.

Cash, T. F. (1991b). *Body-image therapy: A program for self-directed change.* New York: Guilford Press.

Cash, T. F. (1992a). Body images and body weight: What is there to gain or lose? *Weight Control Digest, 2*(4), 169ff.

Cash, T. F. (1992b). Body-image therapy for persons with facial disfigurement: A cognitive–behavioral approach. In R. E. Bochat (Ed.), *Special faces: Understanding facial disfigurement* (pp. 25–33). New York: National Foundation for Facial Reconstruction.

Cash, T. F. (1992c). *The Private Body Talk Questionnaire: An instrument to assess cognitive body-image errors.* Unpublished manuscript, Old Dominion University, Norfolk, VA.

Cash, T. F. (1993). Body-image attitudes among obese enrollees in a commercial weight-loss program. *Perceptual and Motor Skills, 77*, 1099–1103.

Cash, T. F. (1994a). Body image and weight changes in a multisite comprehensive very-low-calorie diet program. *Behavior Therapy, 25*, 239–254.

Cash, T. F. (1994b). Body-image attitudes: Evaluation, investment, and affect. *Perceptual and Motor Skills, 78*, 1168–1170.

Cash, T. F. (1994c). The Situational Inventory of Body-Image Dysphoria: Contextual assessment of a negative body image. *The Behavior Therapist, 17*, 133–134.

Cash, T. F. (1994d). *The users' manual for the Multidimensional Body–Self Relations Questionnaire.* Unpublished manuscript, Old Dominion University, Norfolk, VA.

Cash, T. F. (1995a). Developmental teasing about physical appearance: Retrospective descriptions and relationships with body image. *Social Behavior and Personality, 23*, 123–130.

Cash, T. F. (1995b). *What do you see when you look in the mirror?: Helping yourself to a positive body image.* New York: Bantam Books.

Cash, T. F., & Brown, T. A. (1987). Body image in anorexia nervosa and bulimia nervosa: A review of the literature. *Behavior Modification, 11,* 487–521.

Cash, T. F., Counts, B., & Huffine, C. E. (1990). Current and vestigial effects of overweight among women: Fear of fat, attitudinal body image, and eating behaviors. *Journal of Psychopathology and Behavioral Assessment, 12,* 157–167.

Cash, T. F., & Deagle, E. (1994). *The nature and extent of body-image disturbances in anorexia nervosa and bulimia nervosa: A meta-analysis of extant research.* Manuscript submitted for publication.

Cash, T. F., & Grant, J. R. (1995). The cognitive–behavioral treatment of body-image disturbances. In V. Van Hasselt & M. Hersen (Eds.), *Sourcebook of psychological treatment manuals for adults* (pp. 567–614). New York: Plenum Press.

Cash, T. F., & Henry, P. (1995). Women's body images: The results of a national survey in the U.S.A. *Sex Roles, 33,* 19–28.

Cash, T. F., & Hicks, K. L. (1990). Being fat versus thinking fat: Relationships with body image, eating behaviors, and well-being. *Cognitive Therapy and Research, 14,* 327–341.

Cash, T. F., & Labarge, A. (in press). Development of the Appearance Schemas Inventory: A new cognitive body-image assessment. *Cognitive Therapy and Research.*

Cash, T. F., Lewis, R. J., & Keeton, P. (1987, March). *Development and validation of the Body-Image Automatic Thoughts Questionnaire.* Paper presented at the meeting of the Southeastern Psychological Association, Atlanta, GA.

Cash, T. F., Price, V., & Savin, R. (1993). The psychosocial effects of androgenetic alopecia among women: Comparisons with balding men and female controls. *Journal of the American Academy of Dermatology, 29,* 568–575.

Cash, T. F., & Pruzinsky, T. (Eds.). (1990). *Body images: Development, deviance, and change.* New York: Guilford Press.

Cash, T. F., & Pruzinsky, T. (1995). The psychosocial effects of androgenetic alopecia and their implications for patient care. In D. Stough (Ed.), *Hair replacement: Surgical and medical* (pp. 1–13). St. Louis, MO: Mosby.

Cash, T. F., & Szymanski, M. (1995). Development and validation of the Body-Image Ideals Questionnaire. *Journal of Personality Assessment, 64,* 466–477.

Cash, T. F., Winstead, B. W., & Janda, L. H. (1986, April). The great American shape-up: Body image survey report. *Psychology Today, 20,* 30–37.

Cooper, P. J., Taylor, M. J., Cooper, Z., & Fairburn, C. G. (1987). The development and validation of the Body Shape Questionnaire. *International Journal of Eating Disorders, 6,* 485–494.

Downs, A. C. (1990). The social biological constructs of social competency. In T. P. Gullotta, G. R. Adams, & R. Montemayor (Eds.), *Developing social competency in adolescence* (pp. 43–94). New York: Sage.

Dworkin, S. H., & Kerr, B. A. (1987). Comparison of interventions for women experiencing body image problems. *Journal of Counseling Psychology, 34,* 136–140.

Ellis, A. (1977). *Techniques for disputing irrational beliefs*. New York: Institute for Rational Living.

Fabian, L. J., & Thompson, J. K. (1989). Body image and eating disturbance in young females. *International Journal of Eating Disorders, 8*, 63–74.

Fairburn, C. G. (1987). The definition of bulimia nervosa: Guidelines for clinicians and research workers. *Annals of Behavioral Medicine, 9*, 3–7.

Fallon, A. E. (1990). Culture in the mirror: Sociocultural determinants of body image. In T. F. Cash & T. Pruzinsky (Eds.), *Body images: Development, deviance, and change* (pp. 80–109). New York: Guilford Press.

Fallon, A. E., & Rozin, P. (1985). Sex differences in perceptions of body shape. *Journal of Abnormal Psychology, 94*, 102–105.

Fisher, E., & Thompson, J. K. (1994). A comparative evaluation of cognitive–behavioral therapy (CBT) versus exercise therapy (ET) for the treatment of body-image disturbance: Preliminary findings. *Behavior Modification, 18*, 171–185.

Freedman, R. (1990). Cognitive–behavioral perspectives on body-image change. In T. F. Cash & T. Pruzinsky (Eds.), *Body images: Development, deviance, and change* (pp. 272–295). New York: Guilford Press.

Friedman, M. A., & Brownell, K. D. (1995). Psychological correlates of obesity: Moving to the next research generation. *Psychological Bulletin, 117*, 3–20.

Garfinkel, P. E. (1992). Evidence in support of attitudes to shape and weight as a diagnostic criterion of bulimia nervosa. *International Journal of Eating Disorders, 1*, 321–325.

Garner, D. M., & Wooley, S. C. (1991). Confronting the failure of behavioral and dietary treatments for obesity. *Clinical Psychology Review, 11*, 729–780.

Goldfried, M., & Davison, G. C. (1976). *Clinical behavior therapy*. New York: Holt, Rinehart and Winston.

Gould, R. A., & Clum, G. A. (1993). The meta-analysis of self-help treatment approaches. *Clinical Psychology Review, 13*, 169–186.

Grant, J., & Cash, T. F. (1995). Cognitive–behavioral body-image therapy: Comparative efficacy of group and modest-contact treatments. *Behavior Therapy, 26*, 69–84.

Grilo, C. M., Wilfley, D. E., Brownell, K. D., & Rodin, J. (1994). Teasing, body image, and self-esteem in a clinical sample of obese women. *Addictive Behaviors, 19*, 443–450.

Hsu, L. K., & Sobkiewicz, T. A. (1991). Body image disturbance: Time to abandon the concept for eating disorders? *International Journal of Eating Disorders, 10*, 15–30.

Jacobi, L., & Cash, T. F. (1994). In pursuit of the perfect appearance: Discrepancies among self- and ideal-percepts of multiple physical attributes. *Journal of Applied Social Psychology, 24*, 379–396.

Keeton, W. P., Cash, T. F., & Brown, T. A. (1990). Body image or body images?: Comparative, multidimensional assessment among college students. *Journal of Personality Assessment, 54,* 213–230.

Krowchuk, D. P., Stancin, T., Keskinen, R., & Walker, T. M. (1991). The psychosocial effects of acne on adolescents. *Pediatric Dermatology, 8,* 332–338.

Labarge, A. S., Cash, T. F., & Brown, T. A. (in press). Use of a modified Stroop task to examine appearance-schematic information processing in college women. *Cognitive Therapy and Research.*

Lerner, R. M., & Jovanovic, J. (1990). The role of body image in psychosocial development across the life span: A developmental contextual perspective. In T. F. Cash & T. Pruzinsky (Eds.), *Body images: Development, deviance, and change* (pp. 110–127). New York: Guilford Press.

Marlatt, G. A., & Gordon, J. (1984). *Relapse prevention: A self-control strategy for the maintenance of behavior change.* New York: Guilford Press.

Meichenbaum, D. (1985). *Stress inoculation training.* Elmsford, NY: Pergamon Press.

Neziroglu, F. A., & Yaryura-Tobias, J. A. (1993). Exposure, response prevention, and cognitive therapy in the treatment of body dysmorphic disorder. *Behavior Therapy, 24,* 431–438.

Phillips, K. A. (1991). Body dysmorphic disorder: The distress of imagined ugliness. *American Journal of Psychiatry, 148,* 1138–1149.

Pliner, P., Chaiken, S., & Flett, G. L. (1990). Gender differences in concern with body weight and physical appearance over the life span. *Personality and Social Psychology Bulletin, 16,* 263–273.

Pruzinsky, T. (1990). Psychopathology of body experience: Expanded perspectives. In T. F. Cash & T. Pruzinsky (Eds.), *Body images: Development, deviance, and change* (pp. 170–189). New York: Guilford Press.

Pruzinsky, T. (1992). Social and psychological challenges for individuals with facial disfigurement. In R. E. Bochat (Ed.), *Special faces: Understanding facial disfigurement* (pp. 15–24). New York: National Foundation for Facial Reconstruction.

Pruzinsky, T., & Cash, T. F. (1990). Medical interventions for the enhancement of adolescents' physical appearance: Implications for social competence. In T. P. Gullotta, G. R. Adams, & R. Montemayor (Eds.), *Developing social competency in adolescence* (pp. 220–242). New York: Sage.

Rieves, L., & Cash, T. F. (1995). *Reported social developmental factors associated with women's body-image attitudes.* Manuscript submitted for publication.

Rosen, G. M., & Ross, A. O. (1968). Relationship of body image to self-concept. *Journal of Consulting and Clinical Psychology, 32,* 100.

Rosen, J. C. (1990). Body-image disturbances in eating disorders. In T. F. Cash & T. Pruzinsky (Eds.), *Body images: Development, deviance, and change* (pp. 190–214). New York: Guilford Press.

Rosen, J. C. (1992). Body image disorder: Definition, development, and contribution to eating disorders. In J. H. Crowther, D. L. Tennenbaum, S. E. Hobfoll, & M. A. P. Stephens (Eds.), *The etiology of bulimia: The individual and family context* (pp. 157–177). Washington, DC: Hemisphere.

Rosen, J. C., Cado, S., Silberg, N. T., Srebnik, D., & Wendt, S. (1990). Cognitive behavior therapy with and without size perception training for women with body image disturbance. *Behavior Therapy, 21*, 481–498.

Rosen, J. C., Orosan, P., & Reiter, J. (1995). Cognitive behavioral body image therapy for negative body images in obese women. *Behavior Therapy, 26*, 25–42.

Rosen, J. C., & Reiter, J. (1992). *Body dysmorphic disorder examination*. Unpublished manuscript, University of Vermont, Burlington.

Rosen, J. C., Reiter, J., & Orosan, P. (1995). Cognitive behavioral body-image therapy for Body Dysmorphic Disorder. *Journal of Consulting and Clinical Psychology, 63*, 263–269.

Rosen, J. C., Saltzberg, E., & Srebnik, D. (1989). Cognitive behavior therapy for negative body image. *Behavior Therapy, 20*, 393–404.

Rosen, J. C., Srebnik, D., Saltzberg, E., & Wendt, S. (1991). Development of a body image avoidance questionnaire. *Psychological Assessment, 3*, 32–37.

Schulman, A. H., & Kaplowitz, C. (1977). Mirror-image responses during the first two years of life. *Developmental Psychobiology, 10*, 133–142.

Scogin, F., Bynum, J., Stephens, G., & Calhoon, S. (1990). Efficacy of self-administered treatment programs: Meta-analytic review. *Professional Psychology: Research and Practice, 21*, 42–47.

Shapiro, J. P., Baumeister, R. F., & Kessler, J. W. (1991). A three-component model of children's teasing: Aggression, humor, and ambiguity. *Journal of Social and Clinical Psychology, 10*, 459–472.

Steketee, G., & White, K. (1990). *When once is not enough: Help for obsessive–compulsives*. Oakland, CA: New Harbinger.

Szymanski, M. L., & Cash, T. F. (1995). Body-image disturbances and self-discrepancy theory: Expansion of the Body-Image Ideals Questionnaire. *Journal of Social and Clinical Psychology, 14*, 134–146.

Thompson, J. K. (1990). *Body-image disturbance: Assessment and treatment*. Elmsford, NY: Pergamon Press.

Thompson, J. K. (1991). Body shape preferences: Effects of instructional protocol and level of eating disturbance. *International Journal of Eating Disorders, 10*, 193–198.

Thompson, J. K. (1992). Body image: Extent of disturbance, associated features, theoretical models, assessment methodologies, intervention strategies, and a proposal for a new DSM-IV category—body image disorder. In M. Hersen, R. M. Eisler, & P. M. Miller (Eds.), *Progress in behavior modification* (vol. 28, pp. 3–54). Sycamore, IL: Sycamore Press.

Thompson, J. K., Penner, L. A., & Altabe, M. N. (1990). Procedures, problems, and progress in the assessment of body images. In T. F. Cash & T. Pruzinsky (Eds.), *Body images: development, deviance, and change* (pp. 21–48). New York: Guilford Press.

Thompson, J. K., & Psaltis, K. (1988). Multiple aspects and correlates of body figure ratings: A replication and extension of Fallon and Rozin (1985). *International Journal of Eating Disorders, 7,* 813–818.

Williamson, D. A., Davis, C. J., Bennett, S. M., Goreczny, A. J., & Gleaves, D. H. (1989). Development of a simple procedure for assessing body image disturbances. *Behavioral Assessment, 11,* 433–446.

Wilson, G. T., & Smith, D. (1989). Assessment of bulimia nervosa: An evaluation of the Eating Disorders Examination. *International Journal of Eating Disorders, 8,* 173–179.

5

COSMETIC PLASTIC SURGERY AND BODY IMAGE: CRITICAL FACTORS IN PATIENT ASSESSMENT

THOMAS PRUZINSKY

Cosmetic plastic surgery is body image surgery (Pruzinsky & Edgerton, 1990). A patient's request for cosmetic surgery is motivated by their experience of body image dysphoria. In addition, the goal of any cosmetic surgical procedure is to produce positive changes in body-related cognitions, behaviors, and emotions. This is the magic of cosmetic plastic surgery: By modifying the body, psychological change can result (Goin & Goin, 1981; Pruzinsky & Edgerton, 1990).

Extensive clinical experience and the available empirical literature documents that the majority of individuals who undergo cosmetic plastic surgery do not evidence blatant psychopathology and are satisfied with the surgical outcome (e.g., Burk, Zelen, & Terino, 1985; Cline, 1990; Goin & Goin, 1981; Goin & Rees, 1991; Kilmann, Sattler, & Taylor, 1987; Robin, Copas, Jack, Kaeser, Thomas, 1988; Slator & Harris, 1992; Wengle, 1986a). This may surprise some mental health professionals who assume that if a patient is dissatisfied with their body, then the safest and most efficacious intervention is to change body image (i.e., the patient's perception of their body)—*not* to change the body itself. It is interesting to note, however, that clinicians experienced in evaluating cosmetic surgery patients often see these patients as having psychological strengths and will describe them as *doers* "because of their tendency to react to things that happen to them by taking some positive action" (Goin & Goin, 1987; p. 1129).

Of course, there are many important exceptions to these generalizations, and there are many limitations to our understanding of the psychological changes occurring in cosmetic surgery. Nonetheless, it is clear that the motivation to undergo cosmetic surgery is to change body image and that cosmetic surgery is often associated with improvements in body image.

The primary goal of this chapter is to provide a structure for clinically evaluating cosmetic plastic surgery patients. Mental health professionals are most likely to evaluate these patients when a plastic surgeon is concerned that they are not proper candidates for surgery or when patients have a negative response to a surgical procedure already completed. Both situations are clinically challenging and require an understanding of body image variables (and other psychological and social variables) influencing the patient. The focus of this chapter is on the preoperative patient evaluation of cosmetic surgery patients. However, the information on preoperative evaluation also provides important suggestions for evaluating patients post-operatively.

TYPES OF SURGICAL PROCEDURES

There are many types of cosmetic surgery procedures, including such traditional and routine operations as rhinoplasty (nose surgery), rhytidectomy (face-lifting), mentoplasty (chin augmentation), liposuction (fat removal), hair transplants, blepharoplasty (eyelid surgery), abdominoplasty (tummy tuck), mastopexy (breast lift), breast augmentation, and breast reduction.[1] New cosmetic procedures are being developed constantly. For example, surgical procedures to widen or reduce the width of the head recently have been employed for cosmetic purposes (Edgerton, Langman, & Pruzinsky, 1990; Pertschuk, 1993) and the development of surgical implants for augmenting calf muscles or the pectoral regions are also relatively new (Couzens, 1992). However, the surgical procedures most frequently performed by board-certified plastic surgeons today are liposuction (fat removal from various body locations), rhinoplasty, and face-lifting (American Society for Plastic and Reconstructive Surgery (ASPRS), 1992).

The number of cosmetic surgery procedures conducted in 1992 by board-certified plastic surgeons (ASPRS, 1992) is estimated to be more than 650,000. However, the actual number of individuals undergoing cosmetic surgery is much higher because many surgeons who conduct these

---

[1]In this chapter, I am not discussing reconstructive plastic surgery (i.e., surgery for congenital or acquired forms of objective disfigurement). However, it is important to mention the profound body image issues evident in these patient populations. It is hoped that in the future more attention will be given to these individuals by researchers and clinicians with expertise in body image (Pruzinsky, 1989, 1990, 1992, 1994; Pruzinsky & Doctor, 1994).

procedures are not board certified by the American Society for Plastic and Reconstructive Surgery.

PATIENT SELECTION FOR COSMETIC SURGERY

The most frequent role for mental health professionals in caring for cosmetic surgery patients is conducting psychological screening—usually referred to as *patient selection for surgery*. The vast majority of evaluations of cosmetic surgery patients are conducted by plastic surgeons with no consultation from a mental health professional. The "typical" cosmetic surgery patient (who often experiences mild to moderate anxiety and self-consciousness) does not require (nor do they desire) formal psychological evaluation.

However, there are some instances in which a surgeon detects that patients have a greater degree of psychological dysphoria than the typical cosmetic surgery patient and requires that the patients undergo psychological evaluation to determine their appropriateness for surgery. In general, the primary goals of patient selection are to ensure that the patient does not evidence known contraindications for cosmetic surgery and to evaluate the degree to which they are likely to benefit from the requested operation.

There are many factors to consider in patient selection (e.g., Goin & Goin, 1981; Pruzinsky & Persing, 1991; Wengle, 1986b). Some patient-selection factors are specific to patient populations, including the elderly (Napoleon & Lewis, 1990), adolescents (Goldwyn, 1991), and patients evidencing significant psychopathology (Edgerton, Langman & Pruzinsky, 1990, 1991; Napoleon & Lewis, 1989). Some patient-selection factors are specific to the type of operation requested—for example, breast reduction (Cline, 1990), breast augmentation (Kaslow & Becker, 1992), or rhinoplasty (Copas & Robin, 1989; Goin & Rees, 1992; Slator & Harris, 1992).

Plastic surgeons often will try to obtain from their mental health professional colleagues a brief and highly reliable psychological method (i.e., a formula) for screening out patients who are not likely to benefit from surgery. However, such a method does not exist. Mental health professionals should not attempt to provide such a quick fix for their surgeon colleagues. Rather, the most professional and efficacious way to proceed in evaluating cosmetic surgery patients is to adhere to the basic principles of psychological selection. This involves evaluating four critical domains: (a) assessment of patient expectations, (b) multimodal assessment (Lazarus, 1981) of body image variables, (c) screening for psychological disorders, and (d) evaluation of the patient's ability to weigh the potential risks and benefits of the operation (see Exhibit 1).

EXHIBIT 1
Critical Variables in Psychological Selection of Cosmetic Surgery Patients

I. Assessing patient expectations
    A. Surgical expectations
    B. Social expectations
    C. Psychological expectations
II. Multimodal body image evaluation (Lazarus, 1981)
    A. Behavioral
    B. Affect
    C. Sensation
    D. Imagery
    E. Cognition
    F. Interpersonal
    G. Biological
III. Screening for psychological disorders and dysfunction
    A. Body dysmorphic disorder
    B. Eating disorders
    C. Personality disorders
    D. Depression
IV. Patient evaluation of surgical risk and benefit
    A. Surgical risks and benefits
    B. Social risks and benefits
    C. Psychological risks and benefits

ASSESSING PATIENT EXPECTATIONS

Assessing patient expectations for surgery is the single most important aspect of patient selection. Patient expectations for cosmetic surgery can be grouped into surgical, social, and psychological motivations.

Surgical Expectations

The starting point for evaluating patients is to understand their body perception and requested surgical change. Patients should have a clear image of the desired surgical change and should be able to describe the desired change in considerable detail. Health care providers must be beware of the patient who is uncertain or vague. For example, it is problematic if the patient is willing to defer to the aesthetics of the surgeon (e.g., "Doctor, do what you think would make me look my best").

When evaluating surgical expectations of a patient, the health professional's goal is to perceive, to the degree it is possible, the "deformity" and anticipated surgical change from the patient's perspective. It is often helpful for the patient to use a mirror to point out the exact anatomical areas of concern and to illustrate the desired change. The patients' responses to viewing themselves in the mirror also can provide insight into their automatic thoughts related to body image (Cash, 1991) and a clearer understanding of the emotions associated with their body perceptions.

Some patients bring photographs from magazines depicting the desired surgical change, which is also helpful in understanding the patient's projected future body image. In some instances, it is helpful to use photographs taken of the patient in the surgeon's office to illustrate the desired surgical change (e.g., by having the patient or surgeon draw on the photograph to specify the requested anatomical change).

Another method of assessing patient's surgical expectations is through the use of three dimensional imaging in which a patient's image is captured on videotape, which then can be modified to illustrate varying surgical scenarios (e.g., bigger or smaller nose, lips, etc). This technique has been used with increasing frequency and is well received by cosmetic surgery patients (Thomas, Freeman, Remmler, & Ehlert, 1989). However, it is not clear if these techniques influence the patient's surgical request or body image perception.

A unique approach to assessing surgical expectations is the Napoleon Somatoprojection Test (NST; Napoleon, 1989). This test is based in part on the tradition of using projective drawings to evaluate body image (e.g., Machover, 1949). The NST requires patients to draw their conception of their current body image, their ideal body image, and the body image that they believe can be achieved realistically through surgery. This technique requires only a few minutes to administer and can be used by the surgeon, plastic surgery nurse, or mental health professional.

There are numerous advantages to including this type of assessment. Most important, the NST provides information unavailable when using a standard clinical interview. In his description of the test, Napoleon addressed this issue.

> Why not just ask the patient what they expect [from the operation]? Though this might work with some patients, most people cannot readily verbalize their expectations. Frequently a patient's expectancies are held unconsciously, rather like a magical wish that defies description. Others may not come right out and say that they demand perfection, when that is really what they might expect. (1989, p. 2)

When assessing patient surgical expectations, it is also important to know how long patients have been considering surgery (i.e., if this a persistent or transient body image concern). In addition, if they previously have undergone any cosmetic surgery, it is essential to understand the full nature of their responses to the operations.

In summary, the starting point for patient selection is an evaluation of patient expectations for the outcome of surgery. Any method (e.g., the use of mirrors, photographs, video-imaging, or projective drawings) that constructively facilitates an understanding between the patient and health professionals helps to clarify expectations and should be used.

Social Expectations

A frequently made distinction in the cosmetic surgery literature is between *internal* and *external* motivations (Edgerton & Knorr, 1971). This distinction is based on the common-sense observation that the best motivations for cosmetic surgery (i.e., motives that are healthy and achievable) are internal to the individual ("I want the operation to feel better about myself"). In contrast, external motivations, (i.e., undergoing an operation to please someone else or to change someone else's behavior) are regarded as negative, unrealistic expectations that likely cannot be achieved.

However, it must be understood that plastic surgery can change social perceptions of appearance (Cash & Horton, 1983; Kalick, 1979) and that even patients who will benefit from cosmetic surgery often have expectations for how other people will respond to the surgical change. Therefore, when evaluating cosmetic surgery patients it is critical to understand these social expectations, including understanding the type of social response they expect from family, friends, and coworkers; knowing if they would be pleased if no one noticed the surgical change; and understanding if they hope to elicit some specific social reaction. Knowledge of these expectations provides a clearer understanding of the patients' social motivations regarding the outcome of cosmetic surgery.

Psychological Expectations

The vast majority of cosmetic surgery patients expect that as a result of the operation they will think and feel differently about themselves. Patients often hope, at minimum, to reduce the cognitions, beliefs, and emotions associated with the self-consciousness that is at the heart of their desire for surgery. In addition, many patients expect to experience behavioral changes, often focused on being more socially active or assertive and less sexually inhibited. However, most patients do not clearly articulate how they will be psychologically different after the operation. The degree to which the patient is aware of these hopes and expectations, and the degree to which they can be realistically accomplished by surgery, are critical to consider in the preoperative period. The surgery clearly cannot be deemed a success if the patients do not experience some of the more important changes for which they were hoping.

There are many dimensions to consider when evaluating the critical factor of patient expectations for cosmetic surgery. There is no "quick and easy" and psychometrically sound measure that can assess each of the expectations. However, by using a structured approach to patient evaluation (outlined in the next section), psychologists can integrate the use of some of the currently available body image assessment technologies discussed elsewhere in this book.

MULTIMODAL ASSESSMENT OF BODY IMAGE VARIABLES

A helpful approach to understanding the motivations for and outcomes associated with cosmetic surgery is to conduct a multimodal evaluation (i.e., Lazarus' BASIC ID (1981)) of body image functioning.[2] A multimodal evaluation of the body image experience of cosmetic surgery patients partially overlaps with assessing patient expectations. However, multimodal evaluation emphasizes that body image is a multidimensional experience (Pruzinsky & Cash, 1990) involving behavior, affect, sensation, imagery, and cognition, as well as interpersonal and biological components. Evaluating each of these areas of functioning provides a relatively comprehensive understanding of the patient's body image experience.

Examples of critical issues to evaluate when conducting a multimodal body image evaluation of cosmetic surgery patients are illustrated in Exhibit 2. This exhibit provides an initial structure for evaluating the body image experience of cosmetic surgery patients but is not intended to review comprehensively such an evaluation process. Established questionnaire measures of affective, cognitive, and behavioral components of body image may also prove helpful (Thompson, 1992; see also chapters 3, 4, this volume).

A multimodal evaluation is often instructive to the patient, and when successful can illustrate the multiple ramifications of body image dysphoria, some of which they have not thought about or discussed previously. A preoperative evaluation of these body image dimensions makes it more likely the individual undergoing cosmetic surgery will experience positive postoperative psychological change. Using a multimodal analysis is also helpful for structuring postoperative evaluations.

SCREENING FOR PSYCHOLOGICAL DISORDERS

As mentioned earlier, the vast majority of cosmetic surgery patients do not evidence blatant psychopathology. However, patients requiring formal preoperative psychological evaluation should be screened for body dysmorphic disorder, eating disorders, personality disorders, and depression. Of course, there are other psychological problems that should be considered

---

[2] I would like to thank Thomas F. Cash, PhD, for his suggestion to apply traditional multimodal evaluation strategies to body image issues.

EXHIBIT 2

Multimodal Evaluation of Body Image Variables in Cosmetic Plastic Surgery

Behavior	How does the person's body image affect behavior? Which behaviors are occurring in the pre- and postoperative period that are associated with body image dysphoria or change? For example, does body image experience affect the use of cosmetics, clothing, mannerisms, or posture? Does the patient avoid mirrors or other reflecting surfaces? Does the patient spend an inordinate amount of time looking at his or her reflection? Does the patient avoid viewing photographs or videotapes of himself or herself? The Situational Inventory of Body Image Dysphoria (SIBID) (Cash, 1994) is especially helpful in evaluating these variables.
Affect	What is the primary emotional experience associated with the patient's body image dysphoria and with changes in the postoperative period? To what degree does the individual experience anxiety, depression, guilt, and shame regarding the perceived disfigurement or anticipated surgical change? What is the primary emotion associated with the perceived disfigurement? What is the individual's emotional response to the postoperative changes, and how do these emotions vary over time?
Sensation	What types of body sensations affect the person in the preoperative period? For example, women requesting breast reduction or breast augmentation surgery will refer to the way clothing feels on their body. In addition, in the postoperative period, changes in sensation are quite common (though most often transient) in liposuction (Courtiss & Donelan, 1988) and other procedures (Goin & Goin, 1981) and can be a focus of attention.
Imagery	How does the person "see" his or her appearance and how does he or she perceive himself or herself from the perspective of others or when looking at photographs or videotapes? How does the person picture the anticipated change in appearance? In the postoperative period, how does the person "imagine" the preoperative appearance?
Cognition	What are the patient's automatic thoughts and beliefs about their physical appearance in general (Cash, 1991) and about the specific body area they would like changed? How are these cognitive patterns associated with emotional experience and behavior? How and to what degree do these cognitive patterns change in the postoperative period?
Interpersonal	How do people in the patient's life perceive the patient's "deformity"? Does the patient seek reassurance from others regarding appearance? What is the social response to the request for cosmetic surgery? Are family members supportive of the planned operation? Are family members pushing the patient toward having the operation? How does the patient's perception of appearance influence social interaction—at home, with friends, or in occupational functioning? How does the patient's body experience affect sexual functioning? Is the patient anticipating changes in social interaction as a result of the operation?
Biological	What surgical (biological) changes are anticipated? How much pain, swelling, or discoloration will occur in the postoperative period? What will be the aesthetic, functional, or kinesthetic outcome of the operation? How will the patient look and feel (i.e., physically) differently? Is the patient aware of the surgical risks and limitations, and to what degree is the patient accurately evaluating these factors?

in this patient population—for example, a history of abuse (Morgan & Froning, 1990) and anxiety disorders (especially social phobia). However, the four problems described in the sections that follow are among the most common in this patient population.

Body Dysmorphic Disorder

The diagnosis and conceptualization of body dysmorphic disorder (BDD) is still being refined (American Psychiatric Association, 1994; Hollander & Phillips, 1993; Phillips, 1991; see also chapter 7, this volume). In addition, there is no clear estimate of the incidence of BDD in the cosmetic surgery population. Differential diagnosis of BDD from normative discontent with appearance is especially challenging and relevant to evaluating cosmetic surgery patients.

Some patients seeking cosmetic surgery evidence the key characteristic of BDD—an exaggerated emotional response to minimal (i.e., hardly noticeable) physical deformity or an intense emotional response to a "deformity" that does not exist (American Psychiatric Association, 1994). Some patients manifest more extreme variants of BDD and may be diagnosed with obsessive–compulsive disorder, and some may be delusional (e.g., Edgerton et al., 1991).

Patients meeting *DSM-IV* criteria for BDD (American Psychiatric Association, 1994) should undergo a more thorough evaluation and also be evaluated for possible medication or psychological treatment (Hollander & Phillips, 1993; chapter 7, this volume). However, existence of the disorder is not necessarily an *absolute* contraindication for surgery, though these patients certainly must receive intensive psychological support and evaluation in the context of any surgical treatment (Edgerton et al., 1991).

Eating Disorders

At least one publication suggests a possible relationship between eating disorders and cosmetic surgery (Yates, Shisslak, Allender, & Wolman, 1988), though no data regarding the possible overlap between these patient populations currently exists. On the basis of clinical experience, my colleagues and I are concerned about the possible under-diagnosis of eating disorders in patients (especially young women) undergoing liposuction procedures. Many demographic and psychological similarities exist between women with eating disorders and those requesting this most popular plastic surgery procedure (ASPRS, 1992). Therefore, it seems prudent to screen for eating disorder symptoms in the liposuction patient population, though little is known about the incidence of eating disorders in this or other groups of cosmetic surgery patients.

Depression

Many patients requesting cosmetic surgery often report mild to moderate depression (Goin & Goin, 1981). It is apparent that a small subset of these patients can be diagnosed with a *DSM-IV* mood disorder. However, epidemiological estimates of co-occurring mood disorders in this patient population are not available.

One concern among clinicians experienced in evaluating these patients is that their body image dysphoria is a masked form of depression and they exhibit symptoms of a somatizing process that very likely will not be treated successfully with surgery. In some instances, it is clinically prudent to undertake psychotherapeutic treatment (possibly with medication) prior to considering surgical intervention. If the patient's desire for surgery remains after a positive outcome in treating depression, then their request should be given full consideration.

Personality Disorders

There is a long clinical tradition of examining the motivations for and responses to plastic surgery in terms of patterns of personality malfunctioning (Goin & Goin, 1987). An empirical investigation (Napoleon, 1993) of the *DSM-III-R* (American Psychiatric Association, 1987) defined personality styles of 133 patients seeking plastic surgery found a very high incidence (more than 70% of this sample) of personality disorder (or characteristics of personality disorder) in a representative surgery practice. The most common diagnoses were narcissistic (25%), dependent (12%), histrionic (9.7%), and borderline (9.0%) personality patterns (Napoleon, 1993). Napoleon (1993) described these patients in terms of the most common body areas of concern, the patient's demeanor, and the relationship the patient had with the surgeon. On the basis of the patient's specific personality style, Napoleon also suggested the most helpful approach to interacting with each patient type. These suggestions are very helpful for understanding the range of plastic surgery patients and for suggesting the most efficacious methods of interacting with them.

PATIENT EVALUATION OF SURGICAL RISK AND BENEFIT

It is important to consider the process of informed consent when striving to understand patient decision making regarding cosmetic surgery. A brief review of the informed consent process is helpful because it integrates all of the considerations previously discussed.

Informed consent involves patients weighing the risks and benefits of undergoing surgery. Informed consent is a process of communication and is based on a mutual understanding between the patient and the health care provider; it is not simply the event of a patient signing an informed consent form (Connelly, 1988).

Informed consent requires clear communication between the patient and the surgeon. The surgeon must understand the patient's surgical request and expectations for social and psychological change. The surgeon also must clearly communicate the surgical, social, and psychological limits and risks associated with the proposed surgery. To fully engage in informed consent, the patient must understand these surgical risks, have a clear understanding of benefits, and be capable of weighing these risks and benefits. Such a decision must include an evaluation of the patient's body image experience.

It is very difficult to offer specific recommendations regarding the relative importance of all the variables that can and should be considered when evaluating the prospective cosmetic surgery patient. Any single variable could be a potentially absolute contraindication for surgery. For example, if the surgery will violate or fail to fulfill one of the patient's primary expectations for surgery, this is a definite surgical contraindication. In addition, the patient who is unable to provide a truly informed consent should be refused surgery.

The ultimate decision to grant or refuse the patient's request for surgery depends on the specific characteristics of the patient, the surgeon's personality and experience, as well as the ability of the psychological consultant to be involved regularly in the patient's care. It is reasonable to expect that the psychologist involved in such an evaluation will render an opinion regarding the suitability of the patient for surgery. However, in most cases, the ultimate decision is up to the surgeon.

If the patient is going to be provided surgery, it is important that the psychologist who has conducted the evaluation be apprised of the patient's treatment so that the psychologist can be available if needed. In those situations in which patients are refused surgery, the psychologist consultant should be involved in reinforcing the reasons for the refusal as well as offering the patients alternative methods of addressing their body image dysphoria—ideally in a conjoint meeting between patients, surgeon, and psychologist. When such patients are turned down they are often very upset and angry. It is widely assumed that the vast majority of patients refused surgery will go on to seek out consultations with other plastic surgeons until they find one who will operate on them. The clinical reality is that such patients are usually turned down by plastic surgeons without the input of mental health consultants.

SPECIAL GROUPS OF COSMETIC SURGERY PATIENTS

All cosmetic surgery patients are unique and have special personality, body image, and social characteristics that need to be considered during their evaluations. However, patients with breast implants, male cosmetic surgery patients, and adolescent patients each have unique body image considerations warranting more detailed discussion.

Women With Breast Implants

Patients with silicone gel-filled breast implants represent the group of cosmetic surgery patients with the most pressing psychological and body image concerns. For many years, breast augmentation using silicone gel-filled breast implants was the most frequently requested surgical procedure (ASPRS, 1992). Estimates of the total number of women with breast implants are remarkably imprecise and range from 1 to 2 million (Hilts, 1992, 1993). In 1993, the Food and Drug Administration imposed a moratorium on the use of these devices because significant issues regarding their safety and efficacy were raised (Hilts, 1992, 1993).

Mental health professionals are increasingly likely to have contact with these women, partially as a result of the tremendous impact of mass media coverage of the purported medical risks associated with such implants (Handel, Wellisch, Silverstein, Jensen, & Waisman, 1993; Larson, Anderson, Maksud, & Grunert, 1994). At least three types of breast augmentation patients may come to the attention of mental health professionals: (a) the patient with physical symptoms (e.g, chronic fatigue, joint pain, symptoms of scleroderma) undergoing evaluation for surgical explantation of the breast implants; (b) the patient who currently reports no negative physical symptoms but who is concerned about the potential medical risks of her breast implants; and (c) the patient considering breast augmentation who is weighing the risks and benefits of undergoing the procedure (most likely with saline-filled implants).

Mental health professionals experienced in evaluating these patients describe them as having a range of body image and health related concerns. These concerns are often exaggerated by the existence of preoperative vanity guilt (Goldywn, 1991). That is, prior to undergoing surgery, some women feel guilty because they have let such a "small" concern bother them; nonetheless, they felt self-conscious enough to undertake the costs, risks, and discomforts associated with the operation. Now, with the often reported health threatening risks of silicone gel-filled breast implants, these women have an even greater sense of guilt and fear. The massive amounts of litigation against breast implant manufacturers complicate the clinical and quality-of-life issues surrounding body image and breast implants.

Male Cosmetic Surgery Patients

Men undergo cosmetic surgery much less often than women, making up approximately 15% of all procedures conducted by board-certified plastic surgeons (ASPRS, 1992). However, this represents a significant increase over the past 10 to 15 years (ASPRS, 1992).

Male patients historically were considered to be more psychologically disturbed than females and at greater risk for psychological problems in response to cosmetic plastic surgery (Edgerton & Langman, 1982; Goin & Goin, 1981; Wright, 1987). A leading researcher and clinician in the psychology of cosmetic surgery, Wright, stated

> male patients bring to the surgeon an array of unexplored motivations and expectations along with unresolved emotional conflicts. These feelings of ambivalence, emotional instability, and sometimes even hostility toward the surgeon make the male aesthetic patient more of a psychological risk than the female aesthetic patient. (1987, p. 724)

One possible explanation for this observation is that when compared to females, males experience greater body image vulnerability (Fisher, 1986). Fisher's (1986) extensive review of the body image literature revealed that "despite being consistently more critical of their physical appearance, females are generally more comfortable with their bodily experiences (including body change) than are males" (p. 106). However, there currently are no reliable data to document gender differences in the motivations for or response to cosmetic surgery. The perception that males are more likely to be psychologically disturbed persists, and males often are given greater scrutiny during the preoperative evaluation process.

Adolescent Cosmetic Surgery Patients

An increasing number of adolescents undergo cosmetic surgery (ASPRS, 1992). This has led to some debate regarding the appropriateness of cosmetic surgery for an age group that so often experiences body image dysphoria. The debate focuses on the observations that undergoing surgery always entails some potential health risk and is also expensive. Critics argue that the surgeon should simply wait to see if adolescents grows out of their discontent with their appearances. Advocates argue that adolescents should not have to suffer with body image dysphoria, which may establish negative patterns of interpersonal functioning and self-perception, when the physical change can be reliably and safely made through surgery. They believe that the surgery will spare the youngster the emotional suffering during a developmentally sensitive period, as long as the family can afford the operation.

The youngster's specific personality characteristics and social situation must be taken into account when deciding such issues. The available data and clinical experience indicate that the vast majority of adolescent patients are pleased with the outcome of their operations (e.g., Fodor, 1988; Goldwyn, 1991). However, there are currently no available data to indicate the long-term psychological or body image functioning of these patients, nor are there any available data regarding the existence of co-occurring mental disorders or the degree to which the individuals' concerns will abate over time if no operation is conducted. When evaluating adolescents for cosmetic surgery, all of the considerations outlined earlier in the chapter must be explored, in addition to evaluating the patient's parents and assessing their expectations and perceptions.

POSTOPERATIVE PROBLEMS IN COSMETIC SURGERY

There are a number of potential body image problems that can emerge postoperatively for cosmetic surgery patients (Pruzinsky & Edgerton, 1990). These problems include "patient dissatisfaction with results of a technically successful surgery" (Macgregor, 1981) (i.e., surgery in which there were no surgical complications and that resulted in the patient's appearance being improved). Such patients usually have had one of their unspoken preoperative expectations violated, or they manifest psychopathology that went undetected (Macgregor, 1981).

One of the more vexing clinical challenges in the area of cosmetic surgery is the assessment of *insatiable* patients (Groenman & Sauer, 1983; Knorr, Edgerton, & Hoopes, 1967). These patients undergo multiple operations and are apparently unable to develop an overall positive body image. They repeatedly seek out multiple surgical procedures, sometimes on the same body area or on a wide range of body areas.

There are no clear clinical guidelines for treating these individuals, other than to recommend the standard evaluation described earlier in the chapter. It appears that some of these individuals do in fact become satiated over time (Edgerton, Langman, & Pruzinsky, 1995), though it is not currently possible to predict this outcome.

An even more extreme (and infrequent) example of a negative postoperative outcome is patient loss-of-identity in which patients report that they do not recognize themselves when they look in the mirror (e.g., Knorr, 1972). The loss of identity response is more common in surgical procedures that result in a fundamental change in the person's appearance (e.g., in rhinoplasty) in contrast to surgical procedures that are restorative, returning patients to a previous appearance (e.g., face-lifting) (Goin & Goin, 1981). The symptoms most often reported by such patients are similar to depersonalization and derealization; though there is no evidence of a psychotic decompensation, which can occur in some cosmetic surgery patients. In persistent cases of loss-of-identity, it may be helpful to surgically return the patient to their preoperative appearance (Edgerton et al., 1995).

CONCLUSION

Evaluating and treating cosmetic surgery patients provides a unique opportunity to make important clinical contributions and to learn about body image, particularly body image change. A thorough evaluation of these patients involves assessing their preoperative expectations, conducting a multimodal assessment of body image functioning, screening for psychopathology, and ensuring that full informed consent has taken place. Obtaining these pieces of information provides a solid foundation for assessing these patients both pre- and postoperatively.

REFERENCES

American Psychiatric Association. (1987). *Diagnostic and statistical manual of mental disorders* (3rd ed., rev.). Washington, DC: Author.

American Psychiatric Association. (1994). *Diagnostic and statistical manual of mental disorders* (4th ed.). Washington, DC: Author.

American Society for Plastic and Reconstructive Surgery. (1992). *Report of surgical procedures conducted by Board Certified Plastic and Reconstructive Surgeons.* Arlington Heights, IL: Director of Communications Executive Office.

Burk, J., Zelen, S. L., & Terino, E. O. (1985). More than skin deep: A self-consistency approach to the psychology of cosmetic surgery. *Plastic and Reconstructive Surgery, 76,* 270–275.

Cash, T. F. (1991). *Body-image therapy: A program for self-directed change.* New York: Guilford Press.

Cash, T. F. (1994). The Situational Inventory of Body Image Dysphoria (SIBID). *The Behavior Therapist, 17,* 133–134.

Cash, T. F., & Horton, C. E. (1983). Aesthetic surgery: Effects of rhinoplasty on the social perception of patients by others. *Plastic and Reconstructive Surgery, 72,* 543–548.

Cline, C. J. (1990). Psychological aspects of breast reduction surgery. In R. M. Goldwyn (Ed.), *Reduction Mammaplasty* (pp. 45–56). Boston: Little, Brown.

Connelly, J. E. (1988). Informed consent: An improved perspective. *Archives of Internal Medicine, 148,* 1266–1268.

Copas, J. B., & Robin, A. A. (1989). The Facial Appearance Sorting Test (FAST): An aid to the selection of patients for rhinoplasty. *British Journal of Plastic Surgery, 42,* 65–69.

Courtiss, E. H., & Donelan, M. B. (1988). Skin sensation after suction lipectomy: A prospective study of 50 consecutive patients. *Plastic and Reconstructive Surgery, 81*, 550–553.

Couzens, G. S. (1992). Surgically sculpting athletic physiques: Liposuction and calf and pectoral implants. *The Physician and Sportsmedicine, 20*, 153–166.

Edgerton, M. T., & Knorr, N. J. (1971). Motivational patterns of patients seeking cosmetic (aesthetic) surgery. *Plastic and Reconstructive Surgery, 48*, 551–557.

Edgerton, M. T., & Langman, M. W. (1982). Psychiatric considerations. In E. H. Courtiss (Ed.), *Male aesthetic surgery* (pp. 17–38). St Louis, MO: Mosby.

Edgerton, M. T., Langman, M. W., & Pruzinsky, T. (1990). Patients seeking symmetrical recontouring for "perceived" deformities in the width of the face and skull. *Aesthetic Plastic Surgery, 14*, 59–73.

Edgerton, M. T., Langman, M. W., & Pruzinsky, T. (1991). Plastic surgery and psychotherapy in the treatment of 100 psychologically disturbed patients. *Plastic and Reconstructive Surgery, 88*, 594–608.

Edgerton, M. T., Langman, M. W., & Pruzinsky, T. (1995). *Cosmetic plastic surgery for the emotionally disturbed patient.* Manuscript submitted for publication.

Fisher, S. (1986). *Development and structure of the body image.* Hillsdale, NJ: Erlbaum.

Fodor, P. B. (1988). Aesthetic rhinoplasty in early adolescence. *Aesthetic Plastic Surgery, 12*, 207–216.

Goin, J. M., & Goin, M. K. (1981). *Changing the body: Psychological effects of plastic surgery.* Baltimore: Williams & Wilkens.

Goin, J. M., & Goin, M. K. (1987). Psychological understanding and management of the plastic surgery patient. In N. G. Georgiade, G. S., Georgiade, R. Riefkohl, & W. J. Barwick (Eds.), *Essentials of plastic, maxillofacial, and reconstructive surgery* (pp. 1127–1143). Baltimore: Williams & Wilkens.

Goin, M. K., & Rees, T. D. (1991). A prospective study of patients' psychological reactions to rhinoplasty. *Annals of Plastic Surgery, 27*, 210–215.

Goldwyn, R. M. (1978). Patient selection: The importance of being cautious. In E. H. Courtiss (Ed.), *Aesthetic surgery trouble: How to avoid it and how to treat it* (pp. 14–16). St. Louis, MO: Mosby.

Goldwyn, R. M. (1991). *The patient and the plastic surgeon* (2nd ed.). Boston: Little, Brown.

Groenman, N. H., & Sauer, H. C. (1983). Personality characteristics of the cosmetic surgical insatiable patient. *Psychotherapy and Psychosomatics, 40*, 241-245.

Handel, N., Wellisch, D., Silverstein, M. J., Jensen, J. A., & Waisman, E. (1993). Knowledge, concern, and satisfaction among augmentation mammaplasty patients. *Annals of Plastic Surgery, 30*, 13–20.

Hilts, P. J. (1992, January 8). Vigilance is called essential for women with breast implants. *New York Times*, p. A16.

Hilts, P. J. (1993, January 7). FDA questions safety of saline breast implants. *New York Times*, A16.

Hollander, E., & Phillips, K. A. (1993). Body image and experience disorders. In E. Hollander (Ed.), *Obsessive-compulsive-related disorders* (pp. 17–48). Washington, DC: American Psychiatric Press.

Kalick, S. M. (1979). Aesthetic surgery: How it affects the way patients are perceived by others. *Annals of Plastic Surgery, 2*, 128–133.

Kaslow, F., & Becker, H. (1992). Breast augmentation: Psychological and plastic surgery considerations. *Psychotherapy, 29*, 467–473.

Kilmann, P. R., Sattler, J. I., & Taylor, J. (1987). The impact of augmentation mammoplasty: A follow-up study. *Plastic and Reconstructive Surgery, 80*, 374–378.

Knorr, N. J. (1972). Feminine loss of identity in rhinoplasty. *Archives of Otolaryngology, 96*, 11–15.

Knorr, N. J., Edgerton, M. T., & Hoopes, J. E. (1967). The "insatiable" cosmetic surgery patient. *Plastic and Reconstructive Surgery, 40*, 285–288.

Larson, D. L., Anderson, R. C., Maksud, D., & Grunert, B. K. (in press). What influences public perceptions of silicone breast implants? *Plastic and Reconstructive Surgery*.

Lazarus, A. A. (1981). *The practice of multimodal therapy*. New York: McGraw-Hill.

Macgregor, F. C. (1981). Patient dissatisfaction with results of technically satisfactory surgery. *Aesthetic Plastic Surgery, 5*, 27–32.

Machover, K. (1949). *Personality projection in the drawing of the human figure*. Springfield, Ill. Charles C. Thomas.

Morgan, E., & Froning, M. L. (1990). Child sexual abuse sequelae and body-image surgery. *Plastic and Reconstructive Surgery, 86*, 475–478.

Napoleon, A. (1989). *Napoleon Somatoprojection Test (NST): A measure of expectancy in cosmetic surgery*. Unpublished manuscript.

Napoleon, A. (1993). The presentation of personalities in plastic surgery. *Annals of Plastic Surgery, 31*, 193–208.

Napoleon, A., & Lewis, C. M. (1989). Psychological considerations in lipoplasty: The problematic or "special care" patient. *Annals of Plastic Surgery, 23*, 430–432.

Napoleon, A., & Lewis, C. M. (1990). Psychological considerations in the elderly cosmetic surgery candidate. *Annals of Plastic Surgery, 24*, 165–169.

Pertschuk, M. (1993). Psychosocial considerations in interface surgery. *Clinics in Plastic Surgery, 18*, 11–18.

Phillips, K. A. (1991). Body dysmorphic disorder: The distress of imagined ugliness. *American Journal of Psychiatry, 148*, 1138–1149.

Pruzinsky, T. (1988). Collaboration of plastic surgeon and medical psychotherapist: Elective cosmetic surgery. *Medical Psychotherapy: An International Journal, 1*, 1–13.

Pruzinsky, T. (1989). Collaboration of plastic surgeon and medical psychotherapist: Reconstructive surgery for burn injuries. *Medical Psychotherapy: An International Journal, 2*, 11–22.

Pruzinsky, T. (1990). Collaboration of plastic surgeon and medical psychotherapist: Reconstructive surgery for congenital craniofacial deformities. *Medical Psychotherapy: An International Journal, 3*, 103–116.

Pruzinsky, T. (1992). Social and psychological effects of major craniofacial deformity. *Cleft Palate and Craniofacial Journal, 29*, 578–584.

Pruzinsky, T. (1994). Psychosocial aspects of facial deformity for advanced skin cancer of the head and neck. In R. S. Weber, M. Miller, & H. Goepfert (Eds.), *Basal and squamous cell skin cancers of the head and neck.* Philadelphia: Lea & Febiger.

Pruzinsky, T., & Cash, T. F. (1990). Integrative themes in body image development, deviance, and change. In T. F. Cash & T. Pruzinsky (Eds.), *Body images: Development, deviance, and change* (pp. 337–349). New York: Guilford Press.

Pruzinsky, T., & Doctor, M. (1994). Body images and pediatric burn injury. In K. Tarnowski (Ed.), *Psychological aspects of childhood burn injury.* Elmsford, NY: Pergamon Press.

Pruzinsky, T., & Edgerton, M. T. (1990). Body image change and cosmetic plastic surgery. In T. F. Cash & T. Pruzinsky (Eds.), *Body images: Development, deviance, and change* (pp. 217–236). New York: Guilford Press.

Pruzinsky, T., & Persing, J. A. (1991). Psychological perspectives on aesthetic applications of reconstructive surgery techniques. In D. K. Ousterhout (Ed.), *Aesthetic applications of craniofacial techniques* (pp. 43–56). Boston: Little, Brown.

Robin, A. A., Copas, J. B., Jack, A. B., Kaeser, A. C., Thomas, P. J. (1988). Reshaping the psyche: The concurrent improvement in mental state after rhinoplasty. *British Journal of Psychiatry, 152*, 539.

Slator, R., & Harris, D. L. (1992). Are rhinoplasty patients potentially mad? *British Journal of Plastic Surgery, 45*, 307–310.

Thomas, J. R., Freeman, M. S., Remmler, D. J., & Ehlert, T. K. (1989). Analysis of patient response to preoperative computerized video imaging. *Archives of Otolaryngology: Head and Neck Surgery, 115*, 793–796.

Thompson, J. K. (1992). Body image: Extent of disturbance, associated features, theoretical models, assessment methodologies, intervention strategies, and a proposal for a new DSM-IV diagnostic category-Body image disorder. In M. Hersen, R. M. Eisler, & P. M. Miller (Eds.), *Progress in behavior modification* (pp. 3–54). Sycamore, IL: Sycamore.

Wengle, H. P. (1986a). The psychology of cosmetic surgery: A critical overview of the literature 1960–1982—Part 1. *Annals of Plastic Surgery, 16*, 435–443.

Wengle, H. P. (1986b). The psychology of cosmetic surgery: Old problems in patient selection seen in a new way—Part 2. *Annals of Plastic Surgery, 16,* 487–493.

Wright, M. R. (1987). The male aesthetic patient. *Archives of Otolaryngology and Head and Neck Surgery, 113,* 724-727.

Yates, A., Shisslak, C. M., Allender, J. R., & Wolman, W. (1988). Plastic surgery and the bulimic patient. *International Journal of Eating Disorders, 7,* 557–560.

6

ISSUES IN THE ASSESSMENT AND TREATMENT OF BODY IMAGE DISTURBANCE IN CULTURALLY DIVERSE POPULATIONS

MADELINE N. ALTABE

The past several years have seen an increase in attention to cultural diversity in many areas of psychology. The study of body image is one of the areas in which cultural issues are being explored. It is important to study cultural diversity in body image for many reasons. The face of the client with a body image disturbance or eating disorder is not always Caucasian, as was believed in the past (Hsu, 1987) when very few cases of eating disorders in non-Caucasians were reported. However, more recent estimates of the prevalence of eating disorders in non-Caucasian patients range from 1% to 4%, depending on age, ethnicity, and location (Dolan, 1991). Moreover, some studies of individuals of African descent suggest that their body image disturbance is equal to that of Caucasians (Dolan, 1991; Pumariega, Gustavson, Gustavson, Motes, & Ayers, 1994). Clearly, it is important to understand the factors associated with body image in diverse populations. However, most of the previous research on body image has focused on Caucasian samples. Therefore, models developed to understand body image disturbance may or may not apply to diverse populations.

An important framework for the study of body image is the sociocultural model. As noted by Heinberg (chapter 2, this volume), this model states that the prevalence of eating disorders and body image disturbance in Western countries is partially attributable to cultural ideals of beauty that value thinness. The sociocultural model arose out of early research showing that eating disorders increased in prevalence over the same decades that Miss Americas and *Playboy* centerfolds became thinner (Garner, Garfinkel, Schwartz, & Thompson, 1980). Thus, cultural ideals of thinness may represent a causal factor in the etiology of eating disorders and body image disturbance. The clearest test of the sociocultural model, however, is to evaluate whether diverse populations, with diverse ideals for appearance, differ in the prevalence of body image disturbance or eating disorders. Cross-cultural studies are essential to evaluate the sociocultural model. Such studies may also help to explain why thinness is the ideal in Western countries today.

Thus, there is a need to explore cultural factors in body image for both practical and theoretical considerations. The literature I will review in this chapter will aid in this exploration. I will examine two general types of cross-cultural comparisons: Caucasians compared with non-Caucasians living in Western countries (other English-speaking nations and Europe) and Caucasians compared with native inhabitants of non-Western countries. Finally, I will discuss issues in research, assessment, and treatment of body image disturbance in diverse populations.

ETHNIC GROUPS IN WESTERN COUNTRIES

In this chapter, intercountry groups are described using the ethnic origin and country of residence format: Asian American, African British, Caucasian Australian, and so on. If the ethnic origin matches the country of residence, I use the format "native-country of origin."

Ethnically diverse groups living in Western countries are important to understand because they are most likely to come in contact with psychological researchers and practitioners. These diverse groups are unique because their attitudes may be a reflection of their ethnic culture, the majority culture, or some combination thereof. The following studies yield some information about the body image disturbance of various groups.

Studies in Which Non-Caucasian Ethnic Groups Show Less Body Image Disturbance

Although some studies show that non-Caucasians have as much body image or eating disturbance as Caucasians, this result is not uniformly supported. Some studies have shown that individuals of African and Asian descent have less body image disturbance than their Caucasian counterparts. For example, Rucker and Cash (1992) compared Caucasian and African American college women on several subjective measures of body image disturbance. They found that the African American women had less body dissatisfaction, fewer negative body cognitions, less negative evaluation of appearance, and reported fewer body image avoidance behaviors.

Nevo (1985) compared Asian American, African American, and Caucasian American college women in this country. The Asian women in Nevo's (1985) sample exhibited less eating disturbance and weight concerns than the Caucasian women. African Americans were a small subsample in this study—too small to do a statistical comparison. However, they tended to have less weight-related eating disturbance than Caucasians. Rosen et al. (1991) compared African American and Caucasian college women with regard to body image disturbance. The African American women were significantly less dissatisfied with their body weight as measured by the Eating Disorder Inventory (Garner, Olmsted, & Polivy, 1983). In comparing subjects of both groups who had bulimic tendencies, the Caucasian women showed more body dissatisfaction than the African American women. The ethnic differences between the groups may have been accentuated because the African American women were attending a predominantly African American college. Presumably, such an environment would reinforce ethnic culture rather than the dominant culture, which values thinness. Abrams, Allen, and Gray (1993) found that Caucasians had more eating disturbance, regardless of weight, than African Americans. In the African American group, eating-disordered behaviors were related more closely to overweight status.

Wardle and Marsland (1990) investigated the weight-related body image attitudes of British girls of varying ethnic backgrounds. The Caucasian girls showed more weight concern than girls from Afro Caribbean or Asian descent. Similarly, Ahmad, Waller, and Verduyn (1994) compared Asian and Caucasian schoolgirls living in Britain. The Caucasian girls had significantly more body dissatisfaction than the Asian girls (after family variables were partialed out of the analysis). The Asian girls did have more eating disturbance, but the authors related the differences in eating disturbance to parenting styles, rather than cultural standards for thinness.

In a study of adults, Rand and Kuldau (1990) investigated perceptions of overweight status in a random sample of Caucasian and African American adults living in a rural county. They found that Caucasian women who described themselves as having "no weight problem" tended to be low normal weight, whereas African American women and men of both ethnic groups who described themselves in the same way were overweight.

Using a figure rating task, Furnham and Alibhai (1983) examined the ideal weights of Caucasian British, Kenyan British and Asian British individuals who had emigrated to Britain from Kenya. The Caucasians attributed more positive characteristics to the thin figures, whereas the non-Caucasians had more positive things to say about the heavy figures. The authors made the point that their results may differ from some American studies because African British subjects may have lived in Western countries for fewer generations than African Americans.

In general, these studies suggest that non-Caucasians living in Western countries have a more positive body image than their Caucasian counterparts, particularly in terms of weight-related body image. Their ideals for beauty are heavier. Their general body satisfaction and weight satisfaction are greater.

Studies Showing No Differences Between Caucasians and Other Ethnic Groups

Fewer studies suggest no differences between ethnic groups living in Western countries. However, the number of studies showing no differences may simply reflect the tendency to publish findings reflecting significant differences. But in regard to ethnic comparisons, findings of no difference can be meaningful.

In a study of U.S. college students, Dolce, Thompson, Register, and Spana (1987) found that size overestimation was similar for African American and Caucasian individuals. However, African American women tended to overestimate a mannequin's waist more than their own.

In a study using subjective body image measures, Dolan, Lacey, and Evans (1990) found no difference in concern for weight and body shape among Caucasian, Afro Caribbean, and Asian individuals residing in London. However, Caucasians had significantly more disordered eating, suggesting that they may have acted on their body image concerns more often.

Verkuyten (1990) compared Turkish and Dutch adolescents living in the Netherlands. In this Arab versus Caucasian comparison, there was a significant difference in self-esteem. However, no differences were found for satisfaction with various body parts.

Pumariega et al. (1994) used the popular African American beauty magazine, *Essence*, to survey the eating and body image attitudes of African American women. These authors compared their results with those of the 1984 *Glamour* magazine survey (presumably a predominantly Caucasian sample). Levels of body dissatisfaction were similar for both groups of magazine readers.

These studies suggest that sometimes there are no differences in body image disturbance between ethnic groups. Specifically, studies show that the groups do not differ in perceptual accuracy and general appearance satisfaction. This contrasts with studies cited in the previous section that show that Caucasians have higher levels of weight dissatisfaction. Thus, ethnic groups may differ on some aspects of body image, but not others. The issue warrants further study.

Factors Related to Body Image in Ethnic Groups Living in Western Countries

Some researchers have tried to understand why some members of ethnic groups are more prone to body image disturbance than others. For example, Rao and Overman (1984) looked at the relationship between weight and gender roles in African American women. Their results showed that increased weight was correlated with a traditional female role orientation in these women. Rao and Overman suggested that a desire to be thin may be related to a desire to break out of a traditional female role.

The study by Pumariega et al. (1994) of the body image of *Essence* readers investigated ethnic identification as it relates to body image disturbance. A strong Black identity, defined by a single item rating, was negatively correlated with a "preoccupation with a desire to be thinner" (p. 13). It should be noted that there was no correlation between Black identification and overall eating or body image disturbance. However, the relationship that was established can be taken as a suggestion that ethnic identity may affect body image disturbance. Abrams et al. (1993) found a related result. Specifically, among African Americans, disordered eating was related to assimilation to Caucasian culture, as measured by the Racial Identity Attitude Scale for Blacks (Helms, 1990). Akan and Grilo (1995) also tested the hypothesis that racial identification is related to eating disturbance. The authors found that Asian American and African American subjects had less disturbance than Caucasian Americans. However, this was unrelated to racial identification for either group.

Another factor investigated in relation to ethnic groups is socioeconomic status. Nagel and Jones (1992) reviewed several studies that support the traditional view that a thin ideal is associated with higher socioeconomic status. Wardle and Marsland's (1990) study of British schoolgirls also supported this relationship. Across ethnic groups, girls attending high socioeconomic status schools showed more body image concern. However, not all studies support this association. In particular, Schmolling (1988) investigated the body image of individuals with a lower socioeconomic status than the typical college student samples. Subjects with eating and body image disturbance were evenly distributed across socioeconomic groups. Caucasian women did score significantly higher than the group of non-Caucasian women, which primarily consisted of African American and Hispanic American students.

There are some factors that may affect the relationship between ethnicity and body image disturbance, but the previous studies conflict, suggesting that much more research is required.

BODY IMAGE COMPARISONS ACROSS COUNTRIES

Eating disorders and body weight dissatisfaction are generally associated with Western countries in which thin ideals dominate. The following studies examined how Western countries compare with non-Western countries. In addition, comparisons are made among Western countries. These studies may help to clarify what aspects of the cultures promote thin ideals.

Western Versus Non-Western Countries

Some studies confirm the Western versus non-Western difference in weight ideals. For example, Furnham and Baguma (1994) used a method similar to Furnham and Alibhai (1983) in comparing the traits ascribed to thin and fat figures. Their subjects were Native Ugandan and Native British college students. The Ugandan subjects rated the heavier figures more positively. In fact, they rated the obese figures as healthy despite the prevalence of health information that suggests that obesity is a health risk. Clearly, these two groups differ in their values regarding weight.

Ford, Dolan, and Evans (1990) also used a figure rating task to examine the size ideals of non-Western individuals. Their method was similar to that of Fallon and Rozin (1985) in which individuals choose from among figures of different sizes the ones that represent their current and ideal size. The subjects in the Ford et. al (1990) study were Arab students attending an English-speaking university in Egypt. The authors considered this a slightly Westernized Arab environment. The Arab students were compared to Fallon and Rozin's (1985) American college students. Like Fallon and Rozin's (1985) female subjects, Arab women's ideal size differed significantly from their current size. However, their ideals were heavier than those of the American students, making their overall level of actual–ideal size discrepancy smaller. Arab males, like their American counterparts, showed almost no difference between actual and ideal size.

As with intracountry comparisons, some intercountry comparisons show that diverse groups have similar body image attitudes. For example, Gustavson et al. (1993) examined the perceptual accuracy of body size estimation using a computer imaging methodology. The American, Costa Rican, and Japanese students in this study had similar levels of perceptual accuracy. As with intracountry comparisons, perceptual accuracy in intercountry comparisons is similar across groups.

Another type of study involves the effect of emigration to Western countries on body image. Several early case studies (e.g., Buchanan & Gregory, 1984; Silber, 1986) suggested that the stress of being an outsider in a new place, combined with extreme ideals of thinness, promoted body image disturbance and eating disorders. Nasser (1986) compared Arab women attending school in London and Cairo. Twelve percent of the women living in London developed eating disorders; none of the women living in Egypt did.

In an empirical examination of this hypothesis, Furukawa (1994) examined the reactions of Japanese high school students who lived in other countries as part of foreign exchange student program. The host countries were spread across North America, Europe, South America, and Asia. There were no significant changes in body dissatisfaction, even though the students gained weight. Some students did develop maladaptive eating patterns. However, students with these problems were evenly distributed across Western and non-Western countries. The author suggested that eating disturbances resulted from pressure to be thin, which the students learned in their own Japanese culture, combined with the stress of living in a foreign country.

Few studies have compared different cultures' attitudes toward appearance. Two indicated that the people of non-Western countries prefer heavier figures. A third showed no differences in perceptual accuracy between groups. Thus, these studies support the idea that Western countries have thinner weight ideals. Other studies have investigated the effects of emigration to Western countries with mixed results about how stressful that is for an individual's body image. Intercountry comparisons are important tests of the sociocultural hypothesis. More research is necessary to begin to draw conclusions based on this research methodology.

Comparisons Among Different Western Countries

Several studies have compared the body image of individuals living in different Western countries. For example, Hamilton and Chowdhary (1989) compared American women with rural Scottish women. The two groups were equally dissatisfied with their body weight; however, Scottish women had less variability in the range of ratings for different body parts than the American women. Their lack of variability in ratings may have reflected a lack of detailed focus on physical appearance. A main difference between American women and the Scottish women cited by the authors is lack of media exposure, which may increase attention to appearance.

Tiggemann and Rothblum (1988) compared American and Australian college students. They found that American students dieted more and showed more weight concern and body consciousness than Australians.

The authors caution that sampling differences may account for this difference. However, these studies suggest that among Western nations, Americans have greater body image concerns.

There are many hypotheses about the prevalence of eating disorders and body image disturbance. One hypothesis is that non-Caucasian groups in Western countries suffer less from these problems. This may be true for some non-Caucasians. A second hypothesis is that these problems are less significant in non-Western countries. This is probably true for some countries. Finally, there is the hypothesis that emigration promotes eating disorders and body image disturbance. This notion requires further study. Unfortunately, the research has not progressed to the point of unequivocally supporting any of these hypotheses. Caution on the part of the practitioners, and more work on the part of researchers, is recommended.

IMPLICATIONS FOR RESEARCH, ASSESSMENT, AND TREATMENT

The studies reviewed in the last section begin to give some information about the body images of diverse groups. At the same time, the studies highlight some of the problems in trying to understand a complex construct, body image disturbance, as it manifests in different groups. Researchers and practitioners need to move forward in an informed way in understanding body image in different ethnicities. In this section, I review specific recommendations for how that approach can be achieved.

ISSUES IN RESEARCHING BODY IMAGE IN CULTURALLY DIVERSE GROUPS

The literature review presented earlier demonstrated the need for more study of ethnic diversity in body image. Conflicting results and a lack of attention to non-weight related aspects of body image are the two main problems with previous studies. In this section I review the goals and questions important to the future of this area of research, as well as the methodology available to achieve these goals.

Research Goals

A major goal of multicultural research in body image is to determine the incidence of body image disturbance and eating disorders in different ethnic groups. Levels of body image disturbance equal to those of Caucasians have been observed in other ethnic groups.

Other questions relating to prevalence are also important. One question is whether body image and eating disorders have a different etiology and symptom pattern in different groups. To answer this question researchers may need to assess a variety of body image and eating disturbance variables when making cross-cultural comparisons.

The other major goal of cross-cultural comparisons is to explore the sociocultural hypothesis. As the studies discussed earlier illustrate, many cross-cultural comparisons are conducted within Western countries, where the differences between ethnic groups are blurred. Cross-country comparisons make for clearer conclusions but are more difficult for any single researcher to complete. It may be necessary for cross-cultural researchers to collaborate across countries to make stronger comparisons.

A secondary goal relating to the sociocultural hypothesis is to try to understand the nature of body image ideals in different cultures. Some measures of body image, such as the figure ratings (chapter 3, this volume), do yield some information about group ideals. Only a few studies have used figure ratings in their cross-cultural comparisons. Even so, figure rating scales only assess weight ideals, not other physical appearance traits. Future studies aimed at understanding the sociocultural hypothesis may need to examine the range of beliefs about ideal physical appearance.

Methods of Researching Body Image in Culturally Diverse Groups

The research to date has used participants from a variety of ages, but most have been students. The instruments used have been those developed primarily for Caucasian groups. These design limitations have implications for the types of information collected and the conclusions that can be drawn regarding the body image of ethnically diverse groups.

Participants

College students are the most common sample for cross-cultural comparisons. This choice of subjects helps to ensure that individuals of different ethnic groups are similar in age, educational level, and current living situation. However, college is itself a cultural environment, which can cloud distinctions between groups. Other factors, such as attending a predominantly African American college may also affect findings. Moreover, in some countries, college students may be a more privileged sample of young adults than they are in the United States. It may be important in future studies to clearly describe cultural backgrounds, as well as the current cultural environment of the students. Whenever possible, it would be helpful to find non-student samples.

A second issue is the distinctiveness of ethnic groups within any one country. In intracountry comparisons, all individuals have been influenced by the collective culture as well as by their ethnic subgroup. Individuals may also belong to more than one subgroup. Cross-country comparisons make for better cross-cultural comparisons.

Measures

There are several issues relating to the instruments used to assess body image in diverse populations. One of these issues arises strictly in the context of diverse groups living in Western countries. As discussed earlier, members of a non-Caucasian ethnic group may endorse the values of their ethnic group, the values of the Caucasian culture, or some combination of ethnic values. This confusion limits the generalizability of ethnic comparisons within Western countries. It would be helpful for intracountry comparisons to include measures that assess ethnic identification. Perhaps only those individuals with greater ethnic identification ought to be used in some studies—for example, those studies that are investigating the ideals of ethnic subgroups. For questions of prevalence of beliefs, ethnic identification may be less important. Some of the studies that have assessed ethnic identification have shown that it does affect the results. African American women with a strong Black identity appear to be protected from body image disturbance (Abrams et al., 1993; Pumariega et al., 1994). The measures used to assess ethnic identification include Likert ratings and tests of identification with specific ethnic groups (Abrams et al., 1993; Akan & Grilo, 1995). Measures such as this may continue to be useful in cross-ethnic studies.

Another issue involves the body image instruments that have been used in studies of cultural differences. These measures include diverse indexes of weight satisfaction, eating disorders, figure selection, and other aspects of body image. Many of these measures, and indeed most of the measures of body image that are commonly used, have been developed using a primarily Caucasian sample or a generic college student sample with unspecified proportions of various ethnic groups (chapter 3, this volume). Future development of measures should at least specify the ethnic composition of the norming sample.

Even with a multicultural sample for test development there may still be problems with the test items. Are they equally reliable and valid in each subgroup? For example, Hamilton and Chowdhary (1989) showed that American women had more differentiation in their satisfaction with body parts than Native Scottish women. A body satisfaction measure developed using these Scottish women would probably fail to pinpoint the body image concerns of Caucasian American women. Some other culture that was more focused on a particular body site might need an even more detailed questionnaire than that developed for Americans. A culture that focuses on discrete body parts (e.g., the Chinese ideal of small feet for women) would necessitate the use of such a protocol. Other cultures may be less focused on weight than Western cultures. This is not to say that the questionnaires that currently exist are not valuable, but they may be limited to explaining how non-Caucasians rate on a measure of primarily Caucasian body image concerns.

Proposed Model for Assessment of Body Image in Diverse Samples

Because of the problems inherent in assessing the body image of diverse populations, alternative methods need to be considered. One alternative derives from the cognitive model. The cognitive model has some similarity to the sociocultural hypothesis on a conceptual level. Stated in cognitive terms, the sociocultural hypothesis asserts that individuals develop beliefs (cognitions) about physical appearance through experience with a particular culture. Once learned, these beliefs affect how people feel about, perceive, and attend to the physical appearance of themselves and others. The ability to develop a body image belief system may be common across cultures, but the content of this system will vary across cultures. In addition, the importance of that set of beliefs may vary. The notion that a belief system can have effects on day-to-day perception and reactions is an inherently cognitive one (Altabe & Thompson, in press). In this section, I will present a cognitive model for multicultural assessment.

First, a distinction needs to be made between cognitive assessment measures and cognitive-based assessment techniques. Cognitive assessment instruments measure the typical cognitions associated with a particular disorder or construct (e.g., a test that measures the thoughts associated with panic disorder). A cognitive-based assessment technique attempts to understand specific thoughts of individuals. These assessments are often done to study the effects of individual knowledge, such as the knowledge contained in self-schemas.

An example of a cognitive-based assessment technique is self-discrepancy assessment. In *self-discrepancy theory*, the self is described as containing a representation of the actual self, ideal self, and other selves (Higgins, 1987). These selves can be taken from different standpoints such as one's own view of the *actual* self or the *ideal* self. Discrepancies between aspects of the self are said to cause specific emotions when activated. An *actual–ideal* discrepancy from one's own standpoint is hypothesized to relate to depressive affect. An example of this type of discrepancy is believing that one is stupid but wanting to be highly intelligent. A poor grade may activate this discrepancy and cause depressive affect. This phenomenon has been empirically validated (Strauman & Higgins, 1987).

The format for assessing physical appearance self-discrepancy is depicted in Exhibit 1. This instrument is a modification of the method described in Strauman and Higgins (1987). Individuals are asked to complete three trait lists: one for their own view of their actual appearance, one for their own ideal, and one for their perception of their cultural ideal. For example, a Caucasian American woman might describe herself as medium-sized, her ideal self as thin, and her view of the cultural ideal may include the trait of large breasts (for a complete example, see Table 1). Scoring guidelines adapted from Strauman and Higgins (1987) yield numerical discrepancy levels between these appearance selves (see Exhibit 2). This method can be useful in assessing what physical attributes are important to individuals of different culture groups. The numerical discrepancy scores can be averaged and compared across groups. The larger the discrepancy is between actual and ideal, the greater the body image disturbance.

Previous application of these theories to body image confirmed the existence and mood-inducing effects of priming an individual's body image discrepancies (Altabe & Thompson, in press). There seems to be an overlap in conceptual meaning between a discrepancy between aspects of the self and the way in which people become distressed over failing to meet their own physical appearance ideals.

As part of an ethnic diversity study using this method, recently emigrated Chinese male college students were compared with Caucasian American men (Altabe, 1993). There were no significant differences in the *level* of discrepancy for these two groups. The groups did differ on other body image measures, such as frequency of thinking about physical appearance and the figure size preferred by men. The Chinese American men thought about their appearance less and believed that most men preferred a heavier figure than the Caucasian American men indicated. The groups also differed in the content of their body image selves. One of the most common ideal traits listed by the Chinese American men was "big eyes"; for Caucasian American men, a common ideal trait was "muscular build."

Thus physical appearance discrepancy assessment can answer two questions relating to diversity: *What* different groups are concerned about and *how much* they are concerned about certain appearance traits.

ISSUES IN ASSESSMENT AND TREATMENT OF BODY IMAGE DISTURBANCE IN CULTURALLY DIVERSE GROUPS

The literature I reviewed pinpoints some key issues in the treatment of body image disturbance and eating disorders in ethnically diverse groups. A first issue is accessibility of treatment to various groups. Dolan and colleagues' (1990) study of British women showed that although African and Caucasian women had similar levels of eating and body image disturbance,

EXHIBIT 1
Appearance Discrepancy Assessment Format

Please list the physical appearance attributes of the type of person YOU believe you ACTUALLY are NOW.

1. _____   _____
2. _____   _____
3. _____   _____
4. _____   _____
5. _____   _____
6. _____   _____
7. _____   _____
8. _____   _____
9. _____   _____
10. _____   _____

For each physical appearance attribute above, rate the extent to which YOU believe you ACTUALLY possess the attribute, using the following scale.

1	2	3	4
slightly	moderately	a great deal	extremely

Please list the physical appearance attributes of the type of person YOU believe you would IDEALLY like to be (i.e., wish, desire, or hope to be).

1. _____   _____
2. _____   _____
3. _____   _____
4. _____   _____
5. _____   _____
6. _____   _____
7. _____   _____
8. _____   _____
9. _____   _____
10. _____   _____

For each physical appearance attribute above, rate the extent to which YOU believe you would IDEALLY like to possess the trait, using the following scale.

1	2	3	4
slightly	moderately	a great deal	extremely

Please list the physical appearance attributes of the type of person YOUR SOCIETY/CULTURE would IDEALLY like you to look like.

1. _____   _____
2. _____   _____
3. _____   _____
4. _____   _____
5. _____   _____
6. _____   _____
7. _____   _____
8. _____   _____
9. _____   _____
10. _____   _____

For each physical appearance attribute above, rate the extent to which YOUR SOCIETY/CULTURE would IDEALLY like you to possess the attribute, using the following scale.

1	2	3	4
slightly	moderately	a great deal	extremely

TABLE 1
Physical Appearance Discrepancy Case Example: 18 Year Old Caucasian American Female

Actual		Own Ideal			Cultural Ideal		
Trait	Extent	Trait	Extent	(Score)	Trait	Extent	(Score)
short	2	tall	1	(4)	tall	2	(4)
overweight	3	slim	2	(4)	slender	2	(4)
redhead	4	redhead	4	(−2)	redhead	2	(2)
freckled	4	freckled	4	(−2)	freckled	0	(4)
fair skinned	3	fair skinned	3	(−2)	tan	3	(4)
larger than avg. frame	2	avg. frame	2	(2)	avg. frame	2	(2)
Total Discrepancy				4			20

African British individuals were underrepresented in seeking mental health services for eating disorders. Dolan (1991) related this finding to other reports that ethnic minorities in Britain feel uncomfortable seeking help from the national health service. Sue, Zane, and Young (1994) reviewed studies of utilization of all mental health services by non-Caucasians in the United States. Most of the studies they reviewed indicated that Asian and Hispanic Americans have a lower rate of utilization, whereas African American and Native Americans had higher rates of utilization in proportion to the total population in a given area.

There were also differences in the types of settings from which help was sought. Only African Americans used private psychiatric facilities as much as Caucasians. Other non-Caucasians sought help from public settings such as medical, state, and veterans affairs hospitals. These settings may be less sensitive to eating disorders because eating disorders and body image disturbance have traditionally been problems of the upper-classes, who seek psychological help from private sources. There is no simple answer to this problem other than for clinicians to be sensitive to this issue for those seeking counseling. It is also important to remember that no ethnic group is immune to these problems.

In the assessment phase of treatment with non-Caucasians, several factors need to be evaluated. Most assessments for eating disorders and body image disturbance include an evaluation of body dissatisfaction. With individuals of non-Caucasian descent it may be important to assess satisfaction with a wider range of appearance traits than many measures provide. The assessment model described in the last section may be useful. Another possibility is to use a structured interview. A third possibility is to look for assessments that measure satisfaction with a wide range of body sites, such as a body parts satisfaction scale (chapter 3, this volume). It should be

EXHIBIT 2
Scoring Rules for Physical Appearance Discrepancy Questionnaire

The goal of scoring is to assess the extent to which the subjects' ideal differs from their actual appearance. The focus is on the ideal list as it compares to the actual trait list. Use the following scoring guidelines in the order of priority given. Begin by comparing the actual ideal trait list. At least four traits must be on the ideal list. If there are fewer than four traits, do not score. Note, however, that "compound" ideals such as "long brown hair" would count as 2 different traits (long hair and brown hair).

The Non-Discrepancy Rule
If the ideal trait exactly matches an actual trait (the same word or a synonym and the same extent number), score it as "−2."

Actual list: blue eyes, 3   Ideal list: blue eyes, 3   Score of "−2"

The Value Discrepancy Rule
If the ideal trait is the same as or a synonym of an actual trait but differs in extent number, take the absolute value of the difference in extent numbers.

Actual list: blue eyes, 4   Ideal list: blue eyes, 2   Score of "2"

The Opposing Discrepancy Rule
If the ideal trait is the exact opposite of an actual trait, score it as "4," regardless of extent numbers. Also consider different hair color and different eye color to be opposites.

Actual list: fat, 2   Ideal list: thin, 4   Score of "4"

The Relative Discrepancy Rule
A term usually stated with a suffix of "er" indicating a desire for more of this trait is called a *relative discrepancy*. A desire for less of a trait would fall into this area as well. Examples include, taller, thinner, more muscular, etc. To score these, take the extent number of the ideal trait.

Actual list: tan, 2   Ideal list: more tan, 3   Score of "3"
Actual list: nothing   Ideal list: lighter hair, 2   Score of "2"

The Ambiguous Discrepancy Rule
If the trait listed on the ideal list is not a synonym or antonym of a trait listed on actual list, but clearly describes the same trait, this is scored as "2."

Actual list: medium height, 3   Ideal list: tall, 4   Score of "2"

For each trait on the ideal list, try to apply one of these rules. If none of the rules apply to an ideal trait, score it as "0." Then add up the total for that ideal list. This is the discrepancy score.

---

noted that the body image subscales of the commercially available eating disorders measures, such as the Eating Disorder Inventory, primarily measure weight dissatisfaction. Practitioners should include questionnaires that measure more than weight dissatisfaction.

An additional part of the assessment phase for ethnically diverse groups includes measuring cultural and family variables that may be different from those found in the typical Caucasian client. During both assessment and treatment, clinicians may need to continue to be sensitive to acculturation issues and differences in family structure. There is an important distinction between behavior typical for different ethnic groups and pathogenic for the individual. For example, Asian parents may exert more control over their children. This behavior may be typical for this ethnic group but has also been linked to eating disturbance (Ahmad et al., 1994).

Another set of issues centers around the experience of non-Caucasian individuals in predominantly Caucasian countries. Non-Caucasians in these countries are typically exposed to more than one set of body image ideals, and this requires that therapists be sensitive to individual issues of both the ethnic and the majority culture. Studies do not support the notion that switching cultures necessarily creates body image problems, but some individuals may develop disorders in trying to adapt to the Western ideal of thinness. A related issue is the effect of simultaneously being exposed to Caucasian and non-Caucasian values. Some studies have indicated that identification with African American culture is a protective factor against eating and body image disturbance for that ethnic group. Perhaps for some individuals, treatment could involve increasing non-Caucasian ethnic identification (for example, encouraging the individual to get involved with ethnically oriented activities). Although no studies directly assess the problem, biracial individuals may be particularly stressed by acculturation issues related to body image.

While issues of culture in body image disturbance are central questions, they take on a very individualized form when it comes to assessment and treatment. Ethnic identification and acculturative stress may play a role in an individual case of body image disturbance. However, non-Caucasians may present with none of these cultural issues. Each case must be evaluated individually. The use of a variety of assessments may be helpful.

CONCLUSION

Many ongoing issues remain in understanding ethnic diversity in body image. A central issue is whether there is a distinct difference between Caucasians and non-Caucasians in Western countries in terms of either weight or non-weight related body image. Alternatively, do multiethnic societies result in an entire continuum of cultural influences such that ethnic identification represents a better explanatory variable than ethnicity? More intercountry comparison studies are needed to understand the culture of thinness in Western countries and to test the sociocultural hypothesis. As researchers undertake these questions, it is important to consider whether the current methods and test instruments are valid for use with non-Caucasians. Hopefully, it is a disappearing issue that some professionals still believe that Caucasians are the only ones to suffer from eating disorders or body image disturbance. These issues are central to understanding the nature of body image and its disturbances in all people. They also challenge researchers and clinicians alike to collaborate to gain a greater understanding.

REFERENCES

Abrams, K. K., Allen, L. R., & Gray, J. J. (1993). Disordered eating attitudes and behaviors, psychological adjustment, and ethnic identity: A comparison of Black and White female college students. *International Journal of Eating Disorders, 14*, 49–57.

Ahmad, S., Waller, G., & Verduyn, C. (1994). Eating attitudes among Asian schoolgirls: The role of perceived parental control. *International Journal of Eating Disorders, 15*, 91–97.

Akan, G. E., & Grilo, C. M. (1995). Sociocultural influences on eating attitudes and behaviors, body image, and psychological functioning: A comparison of African-American, Asian-American, and Caucasian college women. *International Journal of Eating Disorders, 18*, 181–187.

Altabe, M. (1993, November). The subjective view of body image: Multicultural application of a cognitive–schema assessment method. In T. Pruzinsky & T. F. Cash (Co-Chairs), *Body image: Diverse populations, theoretical perspectives, and change processes.* Symposium conducted at the annual meeting of the Association for the Advancement of Behavior Therapy, Atlanta, GA.

Altabe, M., & Thompson, J. K. (in press). Body image; A cognitive self-schema construct? *Cognitive Therapy and Research.*

Buchanan, T., & Gregory, L. D. (1984). Anorexia nervosa in a black Zimbabwean. *British Journal of Psychiatry, 145*, 326–330.

Dolan, B. (1991). Cross-cultural aspects of anorexia nervosa and bulimia: A review. *International Journal of Eating Disorders, 10*, 67–78.

Dolan, B., Lacey, J. H., & Evans, C. (1990). Eating behaviour and attitudes to weight and shape in British women from three ethnic groups. *British Journal of Psychiatry, 157*, 523–528.

Dolce, J. J., Thompson, J. K., Register, A., & Spana, R. E. (1987). Generalization of body size distortion. *International Journal of Eating Disorders, 6*, 401–408.

Fallon, A., & Rozin, P. (1985). Sex differences in the perceptions of desirable body shape. *Journal of Abnormal Psychology, 94*, 102–105.

Ford, K. A., Dolan, B. M., & Evans, C. (1990). Cultural factors in the eating disorders: A study of body shape preferences of Arab students. *Journal of Psychosomatic Research, 34*, 501–507.

Furnham, A., & Alibhai, N. (1983). Cross-cultural differences in the perception of female body shapes. *Psychological Medicine, 13*, 829–837.

Furnham, A., & Baguma, P. (1994). Cross-cultural differences in the evaluation of male and female body shapes. *International Journal of Eating Disorders, 15,* 81–89.

Furukawa, T. (1994). Weight changes and eating attitudes of Japanese adolescents under acculturative stresses: A prospective study. *International Journal of Eating Disorders, 15,* 71–79.

Garner, D. M., Garfinkel, P. E., Schwartz, D., & Thompson, M. (1980). Cultural expectations of thinness in women. *Psychological Reports, 47,* 483–491.

Garner, D. M., Olmsted, M. P., & Polivy, J. (1983). Development and validation of a multidimensional eating disorder inventory for anorexia nervosa and bulimia. *International Journal of Eating Disorders, 2,* 15–34.

Gustavson, C. R., Gustavson, J. C., Pumariega, A. J., Herrera-Amighetti, L., Pate, J., Hester, C., & Gabaldon, M. P. (1993). Body image distortion among male and female American and Costa Rican students and female Japanese students. *Perceptual and Motor Skills, 76,* 127–130.

Hamilton, J. A., & Chowdhary, U. (1989). Body cathexis assessments of rural Scottish and American women. *Perceptual and Motor Skills, 69,* 11–16.

Helms, J. E. (1990). *Black and White racial identity: Theory, research, and practice.* New York: Greenwood Press.

Higgins, E. T. (1987). Self-discrepancy: A theory relating self and affect. *Psychological Review, 94,* 319–340.

Hsu, L. K. (1987). Are the eating disorders becoming more common in Blacks? *International Journal of Eating Disorders, 6,* 113–124.

Nagel, K. L., & Jones, K. H. (1992). Sociological factors in the development of eating disorders. *Adolescence, 27,* 107–111.

Nasser, M. (1986). Comparative study of the prevalence of abnormal eating attitudes among Arab female students at both London and Cairo universities. *Psychological Medicine, 16,* 621–625.

Nevo, S. (1985). Bulimic symptoms: Prevalence and ethnic differences in college women. *International Journal of Eating Disorders, 4,* 153–168.

Pumariega, A. J., Gustavson, C. R., Gustavson, J. C., Motes, P. S., and Ayers, S. (1994). Eating attitudes in African-American women: The *Essence* eating disorders survey. *Eating Disorders: The Journal of Treatment and Prevention, 2,* 5–16.

Rand, C. S. W., & Kuldau, J. M. (1990). The epidemiology of obesity and self-defined weight problem in the general population: Gender, race, age, and social class. *International Journal of Eating Disorders, 9,* 329–343.

Rao, V. V. P., & Overman, S. J. (1984). Sex-role perceptions among black female athletes and nonathletes. *Sex Roles, 11,* 601–611.

Rosen, E. F., Anthony, D. L., Booker, K. M., Brown, T. L., Christian, E., Crews, R. C., Hollins, V. J., Privette, J. T., Reed, R. R., & Petty, L. C. (1991). A comparison of eating disorder scores among African-American and White college females. *Bulletin of the Psychonomic Society, 29,* 65–66.

Rucker, C. E., & Cash, T. F. (1992). Body images, body-size perceptions and eating behaviors among African-American and White college women. *International Journal of Eating Disorders, 12,* 291–299.

Schmolling, P. (1988). Eating Attitude Test scores in relation to weight, socioeconomic status, and family stability. *Psychological Reports, 63,* 295–298.

Silber, T. J. (1986). Anorexia nervosa in Blacks and Hispanics. *International Journal of Eating Disorders, 5,* 121–128.

Strauman, T. J., & Higgins, E. T. (1987). Automatic activation of self-discrepancies and emotional syndromes: When cognitive structures influence affect. *Journal of Personality and Social Psychology, 53,* 1004–1014.

Sue, S., Zane, N., & Young, K. (1994). Research on psychotherapy with culturally diverse populations. In A. E. Bergin & S. L. Garfield (Eds.), *Handbook of psychotherapy and behavior change* (pp. 783–817). New York: John Wiley & Sons.

Tiggemann, M., & Rothblum, E. D. (1988). Gender differences in social consequences of perceived overweight in the United States and Australia. *Sex Roles, 18,* 78–86.

Verkuyten, M. (1990). Self-esteem and the evaluation of ethnic identity among Turkish and Dutch adolescents in the Netherlands. *The Journal of Social Psychology, 130,* 285–297.

Wardle, J., & Marsland, L. (1990). Adolescent concerns about weight and eating; A social–developmental perspective. *Journal of Psychosomatic Research, 34,* 377–391.

7

BODY DYSMORPHIC DISORDER: ASSESSMENT AND TREATMENT

JAMES C. ROSEN

Body dissatisfaction is so common today that it has become a normal sign of living in a society that glorifies beauty, youth, and health. Yet some people develop an excessive preoccupation with their physical appearance to the point that it causes them real distress or disability. The diagnostic category that can accommodate such people is body dysmorphic disorder (BDD).

The concept of pathologic concerns about physical appearance has a long history, although BDD is new to the diagnostic nomenclature. The term preceding BDD was dysmorphophobia, which was introduced by Morselli in 1886 (Morselli, 1886). The phobia in Morselli's cases was not described clearly, but the term he coined literally meant *fear of ugliness*. In Janet's description (1903), he referred to an *obsession de la hontu de corps* (obsession with shame of the body) that involved distressing fears of being viewed as ridiculous. The first English language paper on dysmorphophobia was not published until 1970 (Hay, 1970). The essence of the disorder eventually was clarified not as a fear of *becoming* deformed but as an irrational conviction of being abnormal already and fear of other people's reactions. The *phobia* suffix was removed from the *DSM* terminology when body dysmorphic disorder was introduced as a diagnosis in that system (American Psychiatric Association, 1987). Cases of dysmorphophobic complaints were also were described under the term *monosymptomatic hy-*

pochondriacal psychosis (Munro, 1980, 1988), a disorder involving an encapsulated somatic delusion. The other forms of monosymptomatic hypochondriacal psychosis were delusions of infestation (e.g., with insects) and delusions of odor (e.g., body sweat). At this time, this would be diagnosed as delusional disorder, somatic subtype (American Psychiatric Association, 1994).

The purpose of this chapter is to describe the clinical features of BDD and its development and treatment, although empirical information on these topics is very limited at the present time. Detailed recommendations are given for cognitive–behavior therapy. Intervention consists of cognitive restructuring of private body talk and undue importance given to physical appearance, exposure to avoided body image situations, and response prevention of body checking and grooming behaviors.

CLINICAL FEATURES OF BODY DYSMORPHIC DISORDER

The essential feature of BDD is, "Preoccupation with an imagined defect in appearance. If a slight physical anomaly is present, the person's concern is markedly excessive" (American Psychiatric Association, 1994, p. 468). Unlike normal concerns about appearance, the preoccupation with appearance in BDD is excessively time consuming and causes significant distress or impairment in social situations.

Types of Appearance Complaints

Patients with BDD can be distressed about virtually any aspect of their physical appearance (Phillips, 1991), though they are normal appearing. Some patients report vague complaints of being ugly, misshapen, or odd looking and cannot locate or specify the nature of the defect. In contrast, others localize their concern exactly to features or blemishes, such as a big nose, crooked mouth, asymmetrical breasts, fleshy thighs, protruding buttocks, small penis, birthmark, hairline, acne, scars, and so forth. Dislike of body weight or shape is common today (Cash, Winstead, & Janda, 1986), but these complaints can be diagnosed as BDD if the defect is imagined or exaggerated and is accompanied by the required distressing and disabling preoccupation (Crisp, 1988). Although preoccupation with appearance can be similar in BDD and eating disorders (Rosen, 1992), weight and shape concerns that occur exclusively during the course of anorexia nervosa or bulimia nervosa are not diagnosed separately as BDD. However, there are case studies of patients shifting from one diagnosis to the other, indicating that the disorders are related (Pantano & Santonastaso, 1989; Sturmey & Slade, 1986).

The frequency of appearance complaints in two larger case series by Phillips and Rosen and their colleagues (Phillips, McElroy, Keck, Pope, & Hudson, 1993; Rosen, Reiter, & Orosan, 1995) is presented in Table 1. This is a rough comparison because Rosen and colleagues' (1995) subjects were all women and Phillips and colleagues (1993) reported their frequencies for both men and women. Also, Rosen et al. reported only the primary and one secondary appearance complaint, whereas Phillips et al. reported all complaints. The main difference is that more subjects in Rosen's study reported weight concerns compared to Phillip's patients who were more concerned about facial features, skin, and hair. The fact that women are more likely than men to be concerned about weight, as has been explored elsewhere in this book, accounts for some of the difference.

TABLE 1
Type of Appearance Complaints in Patients With Body Dysmorphic Disorder (in percentage of subjects)

Phillips et al., 1993 (17 men, 13 women)	Rosen et al., 1995 (54 women)
hair[a] (63)	thighs (38)
nose (50)	abdomen (35)
skin[b] (50)	breast size or shape (20)
eyes (27)	skin[b] (17)
head/face shape (20)	buttocks (15)
overall body build (20)	facial features (12)
lips (17)	overall weight (9)
chin (17)	scars (8)
stomach (17)	aging (7)
teeth (13)	hair[a] (7)
legs (13)	height (6)
breasts–pectoral muscles (10)	hips (5)
ugly face (10)	teeth (4)
ears (7)	arms (3)
cheeks (7)	
buttocks (7)	
penis (7)	
arms (7)	
neck (3)	
forehead (3)	
facial muscles (3)	
shoulders (3)	
hips (3)	

[a]Head and body hair.
[b]Acne, blemishes, wrinkles.
Note. Total is greater than 100% because subjects reported more than one defect. From "Body Dysmorphic Disorder: 30 Cases of Imagined Ugliness," by K. A. Phillips, S. L. McElroy, P. E. Keck, H. G. Pope, and J. I. Hudson, 1993, *American Journal of Psychiatry, 150*, pp. 302–308 and "Cognitive Behavioral Body Image Therapy for Body Dysmorphic Disorder," by J. C. Rosen, J. Reiter, and P. Orosan, 1995, *Journal of Consulting and Clinical Psychology, 63*, 263–269.

The type of appearance complaint is one of the most concrete and often fascinating features of BDD. A detailed assessment of the meaning the patient gives to the defect could reveal important information about other dysfunctions or self-images and, as a consequence, could be helpful in diagnosis or treatment. For example, Birtchnell, Whitfield, and Lacey (1990) reported that some women who requested breast reductions are uncomfortable with sexuality. Nonetheless, at present there is no study of BDD patients that has examined differences in severity of body image symptoms, psychopathology, or response to treatment when grouped according to body parts or appearance features. As with other somatoform disorders, the problem in BDD may not be where on the body the patient sees a physical defect, but the very fact that the patient is preoccupied with it.

Cognitive and Affective Features

Unlike normal self-consciousness about physical appearance, BDD involves a preoccupation that is time consuming, distressing, and interfering. Although it can occur throughout the day, appearance preoccupation is even more intense in social situations in which the person feels self-conscious and expects to be scrutinized by other people. This attention makes patients feel anxious, embarrassed, and ashamed because they believe the defect reveals some personal inadequacy. Although a striking feature of BDD is the person's conviction in the existence (or severity) of the physical defect, this distorted perception is only the first step in a sequence of BDD beliefs. The typical thought pattern is, "I look defective, other people notice and are interested in my defect, they view me as unattractive (ugly, deformed, deviant, etc.), and evaluate me negatively as a person, and consequently my appearance proves something negative about my character and worth to other people." The exaggeration of a flaw in appearance is only consequential in BDD because it leads to other maladaptive beliefs.

BDD beliefs have been described inconsistently as either obsessions, overvalued ideas, or delusions (de Leon, Bott, & Simpson, 1989). Indeed, there appears to be no single type of thought process that accounts for all BDD patients. Phillips and McElroy (1993) presented case examples of BDD, including a patient who was "absolutely convinced" of a nonexistent abnormality of her nose and a patient who thought she had excessive facial hair but resisted asking people for reassurance in fear that people would think she was "crazy." The authors concluded that the thought process in BDD varies on a continuum of insight from fair to delusional. Delusional thinking in BDD refers to distortions of reality that are held with complete conviction and, if present, the patient can also be diagnosed with delusional disorder, somatic type. Unlike delusions in schizophrenia or other psychotic disorders, the content of BDD delusions is not bizarre (e.g., a preoccupation with "ugly" vascular marks on the skin rather than skin marks of the Devil). The preoccupation with appearance, no matter how unrealistic, is understandable given the patient's culture and personal history (McKenna, 1984; Thomas, 1984, 1985).

Behavioral Features

Most patients with BDD avoid some social situations they believe might call attention to their appearance. A small portion become housebound (Phillips et al., 1993). However, most patients are capable of at least limited social and vocational functioning, using ways to avoid full exposure of their appearance in public by wearing concealing clothes, grooming, or contorting body posture and movements to hide the defect. Various kinds of body checking behaviors are common, such as inspecting the defect in the mirror, grooming rituals, comparing one's appearance to other people, and asking others for reassurance. As with compulsions, these behaviors are difficult to resist, and in some extreme cases body checking can last hours each day. Finally, BDD patients are convinced the only way to improve their self-esteem is to improve they way they look. Thus, most BDD patients undertake beauty remedies such as skin or hair treatments, cosmetic surgery, weight reduction, and other measures to eliminate the defect, which usually are unnecessary and ineffective measures to eliminate the symptoms of BDD.

DIAGNOSTIC CLASSIFICATION OF BODY DYSMORPHIC DISORDER

So similar are the features of BDD in some patients to obsessive–compulsive disorder (OCD) that it has been proposed as a variant of OCD (Hollander, Liebowitz, Winchel, Klumer, & Klein, 1989; Neziroglu & Yaryura-Tobias, 1993a; Phillips et al., 1993), the difference being that BDD patients' obsessions and compulsions are about their appearance rather than contamination, order, or unacceptable impulses. The other arguments for categorizing BDD under OCD is the high comorbidity for the two disorders and the fact that serotonin-reuptake inhibitors and exposure plus response prevention—two treatments of choice for OCD—seem to be effective for BDD as well.

Body dysmorphic disorder also has a high comorbidity with several other disorders. In particular, BDD patients appear to have diagnoses of social phobia even more often than OCD (Phillips et al., 1993). Social phobics and BDD patients share similar pathology. They both experience deep feelings of shame and embarrassment, fear they appear odd or foolish to others, and avoid situations that might call attention to their perceived inadequacies.

Body dysmorphic disorder remains classified as a somatoform disorder (American Psychiatric Association, 1994), the main rationale being that the pathology revolves around preoccupation with physical symptoms. Indeed, BDD has strong parallels to hypochondriasis. Both disorders involve a belief in having a bodily defect that is exaggerated and not accounted for by an organic abnormality. In both disorders, thoughts of the defect provoke anxiety that the patient attempts to alleviate with reassurance seeking and body checking. Patients with BDD typically seek out beauty remedies (e.g., cosmetic surgery, skin treatments, weight reduction) as hypochondriacal patients overutilize medical services in pursuit of a diagnosis or cure.

These analogies to other disorders are useful because the pathology of BDD is not well understood. However, neither OCD, social phobia, nor hypochondriasis is the best or only model for BDD. The disorder has many features and may appear in different forms, but it is important to keep in focus that the unique and core pathology of BDD is a disorder of body image.

DEVELOPMENT OF BODY DYSMORPHIC DISORDER

Little is known about the development of BDD. No prospective, longitudinal study of BDD symptoms has been undertaken, nor has a theoretical model of BDD been articulated clearly. Nonetheless, the published case studies offer some insights into the course of BDD development that, in combination with other knowledge about body image development, lead me to offer the following perspective.

The BDD patient's preoccupation with physical appearance is likely to begin during adolescence (Andreasen & Bardach, 1977; Munro & Stewart, 1991; Phillips, 1991; Thomas, 1984) when concerns regarding physical and social development peak (Pliner, Chaiken, & Flett, 1990). Self-consciousness about appearance is often more intense for adolescents who possess some remarkable physical characteristic—such as being unusually tall or unusually short, maturing early or late, having an exceptionally large nose, having severe acne, having big breasts or small breasts, being overweight, and so forth. Deviations, imperfections, and perfections in appearance can elicit more than the usual amount of interest and feedback from other people. The two factors together—physical appearance and social feedback—influence body image development (Lerner & Jovanovic, 1990). Indeed, BDD patients describe noticeable features that draw attention from others (Hay, 1970).

Many adolescents have conspicuous features, but some become more self-conscious as a result of other basic psychological vulnerabilities such as negative self-esteem or shyness. These are two problems that are noted with some frequency in cases of BDD (Phillips, 1991). The risk for developing BDD is even greater if the appearance feature is coupled with more traumatic incidents. The most common cited in the BDD literature is being teased about appearance (e.g., case examples by Braddock, 1982; Hay, 1970; Munjack, 1978; Philippopoulos, 1979). Some BDD patients are subjected to repeated criticism of their appearance, generally by family members. Others trace the beginning of their preoccupation to a single instance, a passing remark that perhaps was not meant to be critical. Nonetheless, the patient experiences the comment as humiliating or ridiculing. Other critical incidents reported by our patients (Rosen et al., 1995) include physical and sexual abuse or assault, sexual harassment, public failure in athletics or dance, and physical injury or illness. These experiences can condition body image distress in similar situations through generalization. Furthermore, dysfunctional assumptions are triggered in BDD patients about the normality of their physical appearance and the implications of appearance for personality, self-worth, and acceptance.

Once developed, dysfunctional beliefs about appearance are strengthened by focusing selectively on information that is consistent with being defective and negatively evaluated because of it (Vitousek & Hollon, 1990). Patients rehearse negative and distorted self-statements about physical appearance to such an extent that such statements become automatic and believable. Avoidance behavior prevents the patients from habituating to the sight of their appearances, especially in social situations in which there is the possibility of attention from other people. Finally, checking behavior may provide immediate relief, but in the long run it keeps the person's attention focused on aspects of appearance that elicit anxiety (Marks & Mishan, 1988; Pruzinsky & Edgerton, 1990). These are the cognitive and behavioral factors that perpetuate the disorder.

ASSESSMENT OF BODY DYSMORPHIC DISORDER

To adequately assess BDD, one must evaluate the severity of the body image disturbance and determine if the condition meets the diagnostic criteria. Because the *DSM* criteria for BDD are vague, the need for a standardized assessment is even greater. Popular measures of body image, such as those used in assessing eating-disordered patients, are not completely suitable for BDD because they either are biased toward measuring weight dissatisfaction in women or do not tap into many of the BDD symptoms. The development of standardized assessment techniques specific to BDD has been extremely limited.

The Yale–Brown Obsessive Compulsive Scale was modified by Phillips (1993) to measure obsessions and compulsions in BDD. Among other changes, the phrase "thoughts about body defect" was inserted into the standard questions. The 10-item scale is relevant to several important BDD symptoms. It taps into the distress and interference of thoughts about the defect and the efforts made to control them, and it measures time spent engaged in activities related to the defect. BDD patients usually score lower on the measure after therapy (Neziroglu & Yaryura-Tobias, 1993a). These preliminary findings are encouraging, but formal psychometric studies of the modified scale are needed.

Neziroglu and Yaryura-Tobias (1993a) reported a simple rating scale they called the Overvalued Ideation Scale, with which patients rate the strength of their beliefs in the existence of the defects. They state this is a measure of insight into their distorted body image. Patients with BDD report a high level of conviction on this scale. The scale does not tap into other typical BDD beliefs about the importance of appearance to self-worth but could be modified to do so. No psychometric studies of the Overvalued Ideation Scale are available.

Body image distortion in the perceptual sense is central to the concept of BDD, yet only two applications of perceptual tests have been reported. In both cases, figure drawings were used to measure size distortion of body parts: distortion of nose size in rhinoplasty patients (Jerome, 1992) and distortion of penis size in patients with Koro syndrome (Chowdhury, 1989).

Rosen and Reiter (in press) developed the Body Dysmorphic Disorder Examination. It is a 33-item semistructured clinical interview that requires 15 to 30 minutes to administer. Subjects are asked at the beginning to describe any aspect of physical appearance that they have disliked during the past 4 weeks. The interviewer rates the reported physical defect as either "not observable," "observable but minimally defective—not abnormal," or "definitely abnormal." The complaint also is rated by the interviewer as delusional or not delusional. Subjects are asked to check from a list of beauty or corrective remedies (e.g., cosmetic surgery) that they have tried at anytime. The remaining 28 items are questions about BDD symptoms over the past 4 weeks that can be summed for a total score of BDD severity. In addition, there is a set of recommended criteria for the diagnosis of BDD using cutoff scores on individual items. These items were selected by an independent panel as best representing the diagnostic criteria and clinical features of BDD as described in the *DSM-IV* (American Psychiatric Association, 1994). Exhibit 1 lists the content of diagnostic items on the examination.

The Body Dysmorphic Disorder Examination has adequate internal consistency and test–retest and interrater reliability. It correlates with measures of body dissatisfaction, negative self-esteem, and psychological symp-

- Physical defect is not observable or is minimal,
- Upsetting preoccupation with appearance,
- Self-consciousness and embarrassment about appearance in social or public situations,
- Excessive importance given to appearance in self-evaluation,
- Negative self-evaluation attributed to appearance,
- Distress when appearance noticed by others,
- Avoidance of activities because of self-consciousness about appearance

toms and is sensitive to change following treatment. It distinguishes between clinical and nonclinical groups and agrees with other clinicians' diagnosis of BDD. The examination provides unique information in predicting clinical status when controlling for psychological adjustment and other measures of body image. A self-administration version that requires minimal clinician time has been developed. Preliminary studies indicate that is has acceptable reliability and validity.[1]

TREATMENT OUTCOME RESEARCH IN BODY DYSMORPHIC DISORDER

Case reports on treatment of patients with dysmorphophobic symptoms have appeared in psychiatric literature for nearly a century. However, until recently, few studies have examined treatment in cases that were clearly diagnosed as BDD. Several different treatments have been tested, but much more research is needed in order to understand how best to treat BDD patients.

Pharmacotherapy

Reports of pharmacotherapy for BDD have been based on uncontrolled case studies and informal clinical impressions of the investigators. Several attempts at treating BDD with various neuroleptic, antidepressant and antianxiety medications have been unsuccessful (Phillips, 1991). The most promising pharmacotherapy appears to be serotonin-reuptake inhibitors (Clomipramine and Fluoxetine), which were effective in all five of Hollander's cases (Hollander et al., 1989). Phillips et al. (1993) reported

---

[1]The Body Dysmorphic Disorder Examination (interview and self-administration versions) and the cognitive–behavior therapy manual for BDD are available by writing the author at Department of Psychology, University of Vermont, Burlington, VT 05405. (My e-mail address is j_rosen @dewey.uvm.edu).

that 58% of their patients achieved a complete or partial reduction of BDD symptoms with Clomipramine or Fluoxetine. Other investigators reported these medications to be ineffective with their patients (Neziroglu & Yaryura-Tobias, 1993a; Thomas, 1984; Vitiello & de Leon, 1990). On balance, the use of serotonin-reuptake inhibitors with BDD patients is encouraging. However, more rigorous study of pharmacotherapy is needed before any conclusions can be made.

Psychotherapy

In regard to psychotherapy, Bloch and Glue (1988) reported reduced BDD symptoms in one case of psychodynamic therapy, whereas two reports of other nonbehavioral therapies were unsuccessful (Braddock, 1982; Philippopoulos, 1979). Systematic desensitization was effective in one case (Munjack, 1978). Marks and Mishan (1988) reported exposure plus response prevention was successful in four of five cases, although only two of their cases were treated purely with behavior therapy and no medication. In comparison, Neziroglu and Yaryura-Tobias (1993b) and Watts (1990) reported the use of exposure plus response prevention alone, resulting in decreased BDD symptoms in five of six cases.

The only controlled treatment study for BDD was conducted by Rosen et al. (1995) using the cognitive–behavioral treatment that will be described in the next section. Fifty-four female patients with body dysmorphic disorder were assigned randomly to cognitive behavior therapy or no treatment. Patients were treated in small groups for eight 2-hour sessions. Symptoms of BDD were decreased significantly in therapy subjects, and the disorder was eliminated in 82% of cases at posttreatment and 77% at 4-month follow-up, according to the Body Dysmorphic Disorder Examination. Overall psychological symptoms and self-esteem also improved in therapy subjects. In sum, cognitive–behavior therapy appears to be effective for BDD, though not uniformly so.

TREATMENT GUIDELINES FOR BODY DYSMORPHIC DISORDER

The purpose of this section is to provide an overview of cognitive–behavior therapy procedures. Psychologists have administered this therapy in various formats including group and individual therapy, mixed gender groups, groups that also involved patients with non-BDD body image problems (e.g., more substantial appearance defects), therapists of the same or different gender as the patient(s), and as an adjunct to other concurrent psychotherapy. Each of these circumstances presents unique challenges and opportunities and requires some adjustment in the therapy.

Initial Phase of Treatment

Therapy should begin by providing the patient with basic information on the psychology of physical appearance, the concept of body image, and the development of BDD (Cash & Pruzinsky, 1990). At the outset, the therapist will have to deal with typical forms of resistance to treatment to gain the patient's cooperation and investment in therapy. Most notably, BDD patients believe that on entering therapy they cannot feel any different about themselves until they eliminate the defect. This must be countered at the beginning by stressing that the problem in BDD is how patients view themselves from the inside and that therapy is designed to change body image, not appearance. The patients also must understand that although cultural messages about appearance and personal historical events (e.g., being teased as a child) might be important in their BDD development, therapy will have to focus on overcoming the attitudes and behaviors that maintain the disorder. In our group therapy program for BDD (Rosen et al., 1995), we educate our patients and examine their body image history in the first two sessions using mini-lectures, discussion, and homework from an audiotape series on body image therapy (Cash, 1991). However, the basic facts need repetition as the therapist addresses irrational beliefs later.

Cognitive Restructuring

Therapy requires a detailed behavioral assessment in order to pinpoint the dysfunctional attitudes and the situations in which they occur. A self-monitoring diary, such as the kind used in treating depression (Beck, Rush, Shaw, & Emery, 1979) can greatly facilitate cognitive restructuring. The patient should record the body image situations, the thoughts or beliefs, and the effect of these on mood and behavior. For example, a patient might write, "I was talking to people at work and they seemed to be looking closely at me. They were fixating on my lips. I kept wondering if they thought, 'She is really odd looking—she must be terrible at her job.' I felt ashamed and tried to cover my mouth. Later I made up an excuse and left the room."

If patients have trouble identifying these experiences in day-to-day circumstances, the therapist might first sensitize them by administering questionnaires that list common negative body image attitudes and situations. The Body Image Automatic Thoughts Questionnaire (Cash, 1991) is a self-assessment form that suggests typical self-criticisms, and the Situational Inventory of Body-Image Dysphoria (Cash, 1994) is a self-report measure of 48 situations that often provoke negative body image feelings, including being around other people, eating, sight of body, sex, and certain clothes or makeup. A behavioral assessment using questionnaires and self-monitoring will narrow the problem to a set of distressing circumstances.

The patient eventually should be taught to recognize maladaptive thoughts that occur in these situations and to record alternative thoughts in the diary. To begin, as much as possible, patients should be encouraged to interrupt intrusive negative self-statements of body dissatisfaction such as, "The shape of my mouth is really weird; I look clownish." Ask the patient to construct more objective, neutral, sensory self-descriptions that are free of emotionally loaded self-criticisms. For example, the patient might rehearse descriptions of her mouth as being "wide" and "full-lipped" rather than "weird." Positive self-descriptions are unnecessary at first and generally are rejected by the patient. A slip back to self-criticism should be a cue to the patient to follow it with a corrective self-statement. The therapist should avoid arguing with the patient about the reality of the defect and instead try to eliminate the negative body talk that causes distress.

This type of thinking is difficult to extinguish completely because some degree of body dissatisfaction is normal, and in some cases the self-descriptions of BDD patients are accurate. Therefore, instead of remaining focused on the aesthetics of appearance, the therapist should continue on to the more damaging beliefs related to the implications of physical appearance. Here is where the problem of BDD departs from the much more common problem of body dissatisfaction. To begin, using the body image diary, patients should elaborate on their appraisal of situations in which the dissatisfaction occurred. In other words, if the patient thought, "I look disgusting, weird," the therapist would encourage the patient to follow this thought to where it leads. The sequence of thinking typically leads to beliefs that the defect proves something negative about the patient's character and worth to other people. Common examples are thinking that the defect is evidence of being unlovable, foolish, stupid, promiscuous, immoral, disgusting, freakish, alien, weak, unmasculine, unfeminine, and so forth. These are the types of beliefs that account for the deep feelings of shame and embarrassment in BDD patients.

To overcome distress, patients will have to examine all their assumptions in a more objective, dispassionate manner through questioning by the therapist. A patient, for example, should be asked to evaluate the evidence for and against the idea that everyone is keenly interested in the appearance of his hair. The patient should evaluate the evidence that if other people did notice his hair carefully, they would in fact view him as unlikable. The standard cognitive restructuring techniques used in treating depression and anxiety disorders (Barlow, 1988; Beck et al., 1979) are applicable to BDD. This work should be continued by the patient in the self-monitoring diary, which the therapist can use as an ongoing assessment of the patient's progress. Gradual changes in attitudes might be assessed by asking the patients to rate believability on a 0 to 100 scale next to the written disputing thought in the diary. Repeated assessment with the Overvalued Ideation Scale used by Neziroglu and Yaryura-Tobias (1993a) would give an indication of changes in the problematic assumptions. For patients who have difficulty recognizing these irrational beliefs or constructing alternatives, Cash (1991) laid out a model of the process in a self-assessment of typical cognitive errors.

As with other somatoform disorder patients, persons with BDD attribute most of their troubles to their physical defect. Recovery from the disorder will be facilitated if the patient can identify explanations for their distress other than their appearance. For example, the patient who feels his hair makes him look undesirable and repulsive should be asked about other behavioral traits that might push people away. He might indicate that he never initiates conversations or discloses information about himself and that he has nothing interesting to say. He should be asked to consider the possibility that these factors are even more important than appearance in developing communication with other people. Arriving at other explanations can be a juncture at which the patient will abandon the idea that he must change his appearance to be more happy and successful.

Behavioral Procedures

Strong emotions of anxiety and accompanying avoidance behavior, body checking, and grooming rituals make BDD suitable for exposure and response prevention techniques.

Exposure to Avoided Situations

We recommend that before facing anxiety-provoking situations in public, patients should begin with exposure to the sight of their bodies, unsupervised in the privacy of their own homes. A hierarchy of body parts, from satisfying to most distressing, can be created by interviewing the patient or using a simple body satisfaction scale such as the Body Cathexis Scale (Secord & Jourard, 1953) or the Body Areas Satisfaction Scale of the Multidimensional Body–Self Relations Questionnaire (Brown, Cash, & Mikulka, 1990). Patients should practice viewing each step in the hierarchy for as long as a minute or two until they are able to do so without significant distress. The exposure should be carried out clothed and then unclothed in front of a full-length mirror. Cash (1991) recommended that the subject first learn relaxation and progress through the hierarchy using a systematic desensitization. Giles (1988) reported a similar desensitization therapy in a woman with bulimia nervosa who imagined viewing a hierarchy of distressing body areas in a mirror.

Patients should be sure to view the satisfying and mildly dissatisfying areas in order to take in the whole picture of themselves, rather than focus immediately on the offensive locations. Many BDD patients avoid looking at their defects and will find this assignment to be extremely challenging. The exposure may need to be conducted over several weeks. Other BDD patients already scrutinize themselves in the mirror. In those cases, the exposure assignment should be conducted anyway; however, patients should be instructed to practice neutral, objective body talk while viewing themselves.

Avoidance behavior in BDD can take many forms. Some patients avoid public or social outings altogether and are quite disabled. Others function socially, but avoid full participation or full exposure of the defect. Because avoidance techniques can be quite subtle, a thorough assessment is needed. The more avoidance habits that can be identified, the more opportunities the therapist can concoct for the patient to unlearn self-consciousness. The body image self-monitoring diary can give evidence of avoidance; in an earlier example the patient wrote that she covered her mouth and left a conversation. The Body Dysmorphic Disorder Examination asks about general categories of avoidance (e.g., social and public places, clothing, nudity, physical activities, touching the body). Detailed examples of these types of avoidance should be obtained. Contextual cues that influence the difficulty—such as familiarity of people, physical proximity to others, and type of social interaction (e.g., speaking to a group vs. speaking to an individual)–should be taken into account when finally arriving at a hierarchy of distressing situations. An example of a hierarchy was presented by Munjack (1978) in his desensitization of a man concerned about attention to redness in his face.

Some BDD patients have successfully avoided unwanted attention to their appearance for so long, they are unaware of situations that will be difficult to manage. In these circumstances, it might be useful to begin with a series of behavioral avoidance tests to probe for distress. Thompson, Heinberg, and Marshall (1994) gave an example of such an assessment that involved having the subject rate distress at increasing proximity to a mirror and measuring the distance she was able to approach.

Examples of exposure assignments we have used are wearing a form-fitting outfit instead of baggy clothes, undressing in front of a spouse, not hiding facial features with hands or combed-down hair, dressing to reveal scars, exercising in public wearing workout clothes, showering at the health club rather than home, drawing attention to appearance with more trendy clothes, accentuating a distressing feature (e.g., eyebrows) with makeup or not wearing makeup at all, standing closer to people, and trying on clothes or makeup in stores and then asking sales clerks for feedback on their looks.

An example of graded exposure with a patient who was overly self-conscious about his hands was (a) keep hands out of pockets while in the presence of others, (b) allow a stranger to greet him by shaking his hand, (c) wearing a wrist watch and rings to attract more attention to his hands, (d) signing a check in front of the bank teller, (e) trying on rings in a jewelry store in front of the sales clerk, and (f) allowing dirty fingernails to be seen by a supervisor at work.

Marks and Mishan (1988) reported five cases treated with exposure techniques. Their patient with concerns about her red lips and complexion gradually reentered avoided social situations, from riding on buses to sitting close to others to eventually leaving bits of toothpaste on her lips to call more attention to them. Neziroglu and Yaryura-Tobias (1993a, 1993b) described several patients with hair concerns who were required to go in public with their hair messed up, while thoughts of needing to be perfect and approved were challenged by the therapist.

A self-defeating aspect of avoidance in BDD is that efforts to camouflage or hide the defect actually can worsen appearance by locking the patient into a rigid lifestyle of inhibited dressing, grooming, nonverbal behavior, physical activities, and so forth. Many of our patients who fear being viewed as unattractive, uninteresting, ugly, odd, and so on, create their own reality by avoiding the very behaviors that might make them more attractive. In the course of exposure therapy, patients typically discover that not only can they tolerate the anxiety, but they experience a sense of liberation when they incorporate new styles of dress and physical activity into their repertoire.

Response Prevention

Most BDD patients engage in some form of body checking that involves deliberate efforts to inspect, scrutinize, measure, or correct their appearance. Typical behaviors are inspecting oneself in the mirror, weighing, measuring body parts with measuring tapes, trying on certain outfits to test size, and pinching body fat. Excessive grooming behavior coupled with checking is common. Examples are checking oneself in several outfits before finishing dressing in the morning, straightening hair repeatedly, applying makeup many times in one day, trimming nails excessively, and plucking hairs or picking at skin. Like compulsions, in some instances the BDD patient will engage in body checking as a ritual to undo a distressing thought about the defect. For example, a patient might run to the mirror and scrutinize himself on having the thought that he looked hideous to someone with whom he just spoke. In other instances, the behavior lacks compulsive features. Nonetheless, the checking perpetuates a negative preoccupation with appearance. For example, a patient berates herself while she weighs herself three times a day.

The severity of these behaviors varies widely. Several cases have been described in which compulsions occupied so much time the patients were unable to leave home or carry out normal activities (Hollander et al., 1989; Neziroglu & Yaryura-Tobias, 1993a, 1993b). More typically, the frequency of the behavior is much lower and, although self-defeating, the rituals do not grossly impair daily functional activities. Checking behavior in BDD can be assessed briefly with the Body Dysmorphic Disorder Examination or the modified Yale–Brown Obsessive Compulsive Scale, which also assesses the degree of interference caused by the behavior. No case reports of BDD have used extensive behavioral measures of the frequency and time spent engaged in grooming and checking rituals, although such an assessment might be useful during the course of treatment. Behavioral avoidance tests also could be used to measure the patient's ability to resist the behavior. For example, one could measure the time a patient could view himself in the mirror while refraining from adjusting his hair. These behavioral assessments could help the therapist devise a planned reduction in the behaviors and provide an objective measure of treatment gains.

Checking and grooming behaviors generally can be decreased using simple self-management techniques. Examples are reducing the frequency of weighing, covering mirrors, leaving home without a make up kit, setting a fixed time for dressing, allowing oneself only two changes of clothes, refraining from inspecting skin blemishes, and so forth. A situational assessment of these behaviors, recorded in the body image self-monitoring diary, is helpful to identify the cues that trigger checking behavior and to incorporate these into the behavior change plan. For example, a patient might report weighing herself after every meal in addition to morning and evening weighings. Based on degree of urge to engage in the behavior, the patient might start by eliminating weighings at night and morning and later practice eating without weighing. In general, these interventions can be conducted without supervision by the therapist. Afterward, the therapist should debrief the patients by asking them about the actual effect of not checking as compared with the prediction they feared. For instance, a patient might be relieved to discover that his weight remained stable even though he did not monitor it closely. Or a patient might find that people treated her no differently even though she ventured out without makeup. Cash (1991) provided a monitoring form on which patients could identify their behavior, their plan to manage without it, and the effect of not engaging in the behavior. A work sheet such as this doubles as a cue for change in the patient and an assessment of progress for the therapist.

In cases in which the frequency is high or the urge to engage in the behavior is strong, a supervised exposure plus response prevention procedure will be necessary. Marks and Mishan (1988) described a woman who worried that her sweat smelled terribly. They accompanied her at first to help her go on public outings without bathing or applying deodorant. To strengthen resistance to the behavior, it might be useful to first accentuate the desire to correct the defect and then prevent the behavior. For example, Neziroglu and Yaryura-Tobias (1993b) had a woman exaggerate the vascular markings around her nose with a red pen and then refrain from applying make-up while she viewed herself in the mirror. Messing hair and then refraining from grooming in front of the mirror was used in several cases (Neziroglu & Yaryura-Tobias, 1993a).

Another form of checking behavior is seeking reassurance from other people, usually by asking if the defect is noticeable or worse than before. Seeking reassurance can reach high frequencies, to the point a patient might ask his spouse dozens of times if he looked okay before leaving home. This behavior is another example of negative body talk, only verbalized aloud to others. Reassurance seeking is self-defeating because it does not eliminate the preoccupation (the patient does not believe the reassurance), it inadvertently trains other people to take even more of an interest in their appearance, and it can strain relationships with partners and family members. It is usually possible and desirable to eliminate this behavior completely. Patients might need to be convinced to cooperate with the intervention by emphasizing the negative consequences of reassurance seeking on their relationships. Also, it helps to explain how therapy is designed to make them feel more self-confident and that to do so, they must learn not to depend on other people's opinions. In most cases, the patient can simply be instructed to stop asking for feedback. Indirect attempts to elicit reassurance need to be eliminated as well. For example, a patient should refrain from saying aloud, "Honey, my hair looks so uneven today." Exposure plus response prevention might be required as well. For example, the patient might practice walking in front of his spouse, dressed imperfectly, and refrain from asking her opinion. Medical reassurance seeking, such as repeated dermatology consultations, should be eliminated as one might do in the cognitive–behavioral treatment of hypochondriasis (Warwick & Salkovskis, 1989).

Related to reassurance seeking is the problem of BDD patients discounting positive feedback they receive on a spontaneous basis. As a result of distorted cognitive processes, patients typically overlook or refuse any feedback that is discrepant from their negative body images. Because other people can be more objective—and usually more positive—about patients' appearances, it would be desirable for patients to attend to such information and incorporate it into their self-images. To attack this problem on a behavioral level, we train patients using role-played conversations to refrain from discounting statements (e.g., "Oh, you can't mean that. I really look terrible today."). Instead, the patient practices accepting the compliment (e.g., "Thank you very much. It *is* a new hair style."). The patient then rehearses it subvocally to allow it to be absorbed.

A final type of checking behavior is comparing oneself with others. Some BDD patients try to reassure themselves by comparing their defect to the body part in other people. The frequency of comparing can reach high levels, to the point the patient is unable to look at other people without focusing on their appearance. Looking at pictures in fashion and fitness magazines is another common cue for comparing. Comparisons usually are flawed because the patient's distorted body image perception makes the comparison nonobjective. Also, patients selectively focus on people who are more perfect looking than they are rather than comparing themselves to a normal range of people. Finally, comparing is another body image situation that provokes negative body talk. Because it is so self-defeating, an effort should be made to control this form of checking. Behavioral self-control strategies can be devised to suit the patient's habit. Patients might be asked to avoid buying fashion magazines, to stand at the front of the aerobics class where they will not be able to watch the other participants, and not to verbalize aloud comparison statements to other people (e.g., "You look so great, I wish I had your skin color."). A difficulty in reducing comparing is that it is typically manifested more cognitively than behaviorally. Cognitive strategies might include focusing on an aspect of the person's appearance other than the one related to the patient's defect (looking at her smile rather than the size of her nose); interrupting negative comparisons ("I wish I had his build") with self-accepting statements; appreciating the beauty in others ("What a lovely figure she has") instead of dwelling on hostile, jealous thoughts ("I can't stand these skinny women"); and focusing on nonappearance features in other people ("How friendly he seems"). Because comparing is a subjective experience, it may be difficult for the patient to recognize the extent of the problem. To facilitate assessment, the therapist might administer the Physical Appearance Comparison Scale, a simple self-report inventory of comparing (Thompson, Heinberg, & Tantleff, 1991) or ask patients to begin recording comparing thoughts and behaviors in their body image self-monitoring diaries.

CONCLUSION

Body dysmorphic disorder is a distressing condition that can impair functioning to a considerable degree. The disorder is more common than generally recognized, and there probably is an unmet need for treatment because BDD is unknown to most mental health practitioners. Systematic research into BDD only recently has begun, and most basic questions about the prevalence, pathology, etiology, assessment, and treatment of the disorder remain unanswered. Despite different conceptualizations of the disorder, behavior therapy that makes use of cognitive restructuring, exposure, and response prevention appears to be effective in eliminating the symptoms, although long-term improvement has not been established. Another treatment for BDD that warrants study at this point is pharmacotherapy with serotonin-reuptake inhibitors. A controlled trial of medication, using objective measures, is needed. Further knowledge about BDD and its treatment will benefit the people who suffer from this disorder and also people in other clinical populations in which concerns about body image are common.

REFERENCES

American Psychiatric Association. (1987). *Diagnostic and statistical manual of mental disorders* (3rd ed., rev.). Washington, DC: Author.

American Psychiatric Association. (1994). *Diagnostic and statistical manual of mental disorders* (4th ed.). Washington, DC: Author.

Andreasen, N. C., & Bardach, J. (1977). Dysmorphophobia: Symptom or disease? *American Journal of Psychiatry, 134,* 673–676.

Barlow, D. H. (1988). *Anxiety and its disorders: The nature and treatment of anxiety and panic.* New York: Guilford Press.

Beck, A. T., Rush, A. J., Shaw, B. F., & Emery, G. (1979). *Cognitive therapy of depression.* New York: Guilford Press.

Birtchnell, S., Whitfield, P., & Lacey, J. (1990). Motivational factors in women requesting augmentation and reduction mammaplasty. *Journal of Psychosomatic Research, 34,* 509–514.

Bloch, S., & Glue, P. (1988). Psychotherapy and dysmorphophobia: A case report. *British Journal of Psychiatry, 152,* 271–274.

Braddock, L. E. (1982). Dysmorphophobia in adolescence: A case report. *British Journal of Psychiatry, 140,* 199–201.

Brown, T. A., Cash, T. F., & Mikulka, P. J. (1990). Attitudinal body-image assessment: Factor analysis of the Body Self-Relations Questionnaire. *Journal of Personality Assessment, 35,* 134–144.

Cash, T. F. (1991). *Body image therapy: A program for self-directed change.* New York: Guilford Press.

Cash, T. F. (1994). The Situational Inventory of Body Image Dysphoria: Contextual assessment of a negative body image. *The Behavior Therapist, 17,* 133–134.

Cash, T. F., & Pruzinsky, T. (Eds.). (1990). *Body images: Development, deviance and change.* New York: Guilford Press.

Cash, T. F., Winstead, B. A., & Janda, L. H. (1986, April). Body image survey: The great American shape-up. *Psychology Today, 20,* 30–44.

Chowdhury, A. N. (1989). Dysmorphic penis image perception: The root of Koro vulnerability. *Acta Psychiatrica Scandinavica, 80,* 518–520.

Crisp, A. H. (1988). Some possible approaches to prevention of eating and body weight/shape disorders, with particular reference to anorexia nervosa. *International Journal of Eating Disorders, 7,* 1–17.

de Leon, J., Bott, A., & Simpson, G. M. (1989). Dysmorphophobia: Body dysmorphic disorder of delusional disorder, somatic subtype? *Comprehensive Psychiatry, 30,* 457–472.

Giles, T. R. (1988). Distortion of body image as an effect of conditioned fear. *Journal of Behaviour Therapy and Experimental Psychiatry, 19*, 143–146.

Hay, G. G. (1970). Dysmorphophobia. *British Journal of Psychiatry, 116*, 399–406.

Hollander, E., Liebowitz, M. R., Winchel, R., Klumer, A., & Klein, D. F. (1989). Treatment of body-dysmorphic disorder with serotonin reuptake blockers. *American Journal of Psychiatry, 146*, 768–770.

Janet, P. (1903). *Les obsessions et la psychasthenine.* Paris: Felix Alcan.

Jerome, L. (1992). Body dysmorphic disorder: A controlled study of patients requesting cosmetic rhinoplasty [Letter to the editor]. *American Journal of Psychiatry, 149*, 577.

Lerner, R. M., & Jovanovic, J. (1990). The role of body image in psychosocial development across the life span: A developmental contextual perspective. In T. F. Cash & T. Pruzinsky (Eds.), *Body images: Development, deviance and change* (pp. 110–130). New York: Guilford Press.

Marks, I., & Mishan, J. (1988). Dysmorphophobic avoidance with disturbed bodily perception: A pilot study of exposure therapy. *British Journal of Psychiatry, 152*, 674–678.

McKenna, P. J. (1984). Disorders with overvalued ideas. *British Journal of Psychiatry, 145*, 579–585.

Morselli, E. (1886). Sulla dismorfofobia e sulla tafefobia. *Nolletinno della Accademia di Genova, 6*, 110–119.

Munjack, D. J. (1978). The behavioral treatment of dysmorphophobia. *Journal of Behavior Therapy and Experimental Psychiatry, 9*, 53–56.

Munro, A. (1980). Monosymptomatic hypochondriacal psychosis. *British Journal of Hospital Medicine, 24*, 34–38.

Munro, A. (1988). Monosymptomatic hypochondriacal psychosis. *British Journal of Psychiatry, 153* (Suppl. 2), 37–40.

Munro, A., & Stewart, M. (1991). Body dysmorphic disorder and the DSM IV: The demise of dysmorphophobia. *Canadian Journal of Psychiatry, 36*, 91–96.

Neziroglu, F. A., & Yaryura-Tobias, J. A. (1993a). Body dysmorphic disorder: Phenomenology and case descriptions. *Behavioural Psychotherapy, 21*, 27–36.

Neziroglu, F. A., & Yaryura-Tobias, J. A. (1993b). Exposure, response prevention, and cognitive therapy in the treatment of body dysmorphic disorder. *Behavior Therapy, 24*, 431–438.

Pantano, M., & Santonastaso, P. (1989). A case of dysmorphophobia following recovery from anorexia nervosa. *International Journal of Eating Disorders, 8*, 701–704.

Philippopoulos, G. S. (1979). The analysis of a case of dysmorfophobia. *Canadian Journal of Psychiatry, 24*, 397–401.

Phillips, K. A. (1991). Body dysmorphic disorder: The distress of imagined ugliness. *American Journal of Psychiatry, 148*, 1138–1149.

Phillips, K. A. (1993). *Body dysmorphic disorder modification of the Y-BOCS, McLean version.* Belmont, MA: McLean Hospital.

Phillips, K. A., & McElroy, S. L. (1993). Insight, overvalued ideation, and delusional thinking in body dysmorphic disorder: Theoretical and treatment implications. *Journal of Nervous and Mental Disease, 181,* 699–702.

Phillips, K. A., McElroy, S. L., Keck, P. E., Pope, H. G., & Hudson, J. I. (1993). Body dysmorphic disorder: 30 cases of imagined ugliness. *American Journal of Psychiatry, 150,* 302–308.

Pliner, P., Chaiken, S., & Flett, G. L. (1990). Gender differences in concern with body weight and physical appearance over the life span. *Personality and Social Psychology Bulletin, 16,* 263–273.

Pruzinsky, T., & Edgerton, M. T. (1990). Body-image change in cosmetic plastic surgery. In T. F. Cash & T. Pruzinsky (Eds.), *Body images: Development, deviance and change* (pp. 217–237). New York: Guilford Press.

Rosen, J. C. (1992). Body image disorder: Definition, development, and contribution to eating disorders. In J. H. Crowther, D. L. Tennenbaum, S. E. Hobfoll, & M. A. P. Stephens (Eds.), *The etiology of bulimia: The individual and familial context* (pp. 157–177). Washington, DC: Hemisphere.

Rosen, J. C., & Reiter, J. (in press). Development of the Body Dysmorphic Disorder Examination. *Behaviour Research and Therapy.*

Rosen, J. C., Reiter, J., & Orosan, P. (1995). Cognitive behavioral body image therapy for body dysmorphic disorder. *Journal of Consulting and Clinical Psychology, 63,* 263–269.

Secord, P. F., & Jourard, S. M. (1953). The appraisal of body-cathexis: Body-cathexis and the self. *Journal of Consulting Psychology, 17,* 343–347.

Sturmey, P., & Slade, P. D. (1986). Anorexia nervosa and dysmorphophobia. *British Journal of Psychiatry, 149,* 780–782.

Thomas, C. S. (1984). Dysmorphophobia: A question of definition. *British Journal of Psychiatry, 144,* 513–516.

Thomas, C. S. (1985). Dysmorphophobia and monosymptomatic hypochondriasis [Letter to the editor]. *American Journal of Psychiatry, 142,* 1121.

Thompson, J. K, Heinberg, L. J., & Marshall, K. (1994). The Physical Appearance Behavioral Avoidance Test (PABAT): Preliminary findings. *Behavior Therapist,* 9–10.

Thompson, J. K., Heinberg, L., & Tantleff, S. (1991). The Physical Appearance Comparison Scale (PACS). *The Behavior Therapist, 14,* 174.

Vitiello, B., & de Leon, J. (1990). Dysmorphophobia misdiagnosed as obsessive–compulsive disorder. *Psychosomatics, 31,* 220–221.

Vitousek, K. B., & Hollon, S. D. (1990). The investigation of schematic content and processing in eating disorders. *Cognitive Therapy and Research, 14,* 191–214.

Warwick, H. M. C., & Salkovskis, P. M. (1989). Hypochondriasis. In J. Scott, J. M. G. Williams, & A. T. Beck (Eds.), *Cognitive therapy: A clinical casebook* (pp. 78–102). London: Routledge.

Watts, F. N. (1990). Aversion to personal body hair: A case study in the integration of behavioural and interpretative methods. *British Journal of Medical Psychology, 63,* 335–340.

II

EATING DISORDERS

INTRODUCTION

EATING DISORDERS

This section focuses on the comprehensive assessment and treatment of anorexia nervosa, bulimia nervosa, and binge eating disorder. Although considering body image problems is essential in managing eating disorders, empirically grounded assessment and treatment programs involve a broader focus and also target a number of the severe symptoms of eating disorders, such as starvation and purging. Therefore, most chapters in this part do not focus exclusively on body image issues. In addition to general psychological approaches to assessment and treatment, chapters also consider physical and medical assessment and pharmacological interventions.

This part will take a somewhat hierarchical approach to the presentation of material, which is based on a logical model for the evaluation of an individual case. For instance, in chapter 8, Pomeroy offers an analysis from the medical perspective, cataloging and describing the important physical symptoms and signs likely to be associated with an eating disorder. She also examines the role of the physician, initial medical evaluation, medical complications, associated behaviors and their physiological correlates (laxatives, diuretics, diet pills), and medical management.

Williamson, Gleaves, and Anderson in chapter 9 follow with a corollary examination of important psychological measurement issues. A number of psychometric issues are important in selecting a diagnostic measure. This discussion on reliability and validity sets the stage for an examination of interview methods, self-monitoring procedures, and psychological tests. A large number of assessments are available that document the many features of eating disorders, including an interview measure that assesses weight and shape concerns (providing an elaboration of my discussion of this instrument in chapter 3). This chapter emphasizes that reliable and valid diagnoses of eating disorders are predicated on the accurate selection and use of assessment measures. It is interesting to note that the authors found that there has been little systematic use of these measures in treatment-outcome research.

Garner and Needleman in chapter 10 encourage a decision-tree and stepped-care logic to the initial selection of treatment options. The stepped-care approach consists of ordering empirically or logically derived interventions based on factors such as probability of success and cost. The decision-tree provides choice points that result in a number of paths for treatment that are dependent on factors such as the specific clinical features of the patient and response to treatment. Their flowchart is a much needed addition to the literature on patient–treatment matching. They also discuss the use and merits of the various options available to the clinician for the treatment of eating disorders, including inpatient therapy, day treatment regimens, educational interventions, self-help manuals, family therapy, and the various individual therapy approaches (cognitive–behavioral, behavioral, interpersonal, supportive-expressive, psychodynamic, feminist, and pharmacotherapy). Although they detail the timely use of each of these therapeutic approaches, the authors also clearly cite the greater empirical documentation of cognitive–behavioral procedures.

The presentation of cognitive–behavioral interventions for anorexia nervosa and bulimia nervosa is contained in chapter 11. Pike, Loeb, and Vitousek lay out a comprehensive examination of the multiple components of their cognitive–behavioral approach. This model has a number of elements that address body image concerns. They begin, however, with background material on the theory and practice of behavioral and cognitive therapy. A cognitive–behavioral model of eating disorders and a review of the outcome research sets the stage for the lengthy and involved description of the fundamental features of cognitive–behavioral therapy. There are three phases to their approach. In phase one, they focus on issues such as orienting the patient to therapy, prescribing normalized eating, and addressing binge eating and purging and delay strategies and alternatives. Several other phase one strategies include a large body image component. They directly address and challenge faulty assumptions about weight and shape, along with attempts to modify excessive weight monitoring behaviors (such as excessive weighing). In phases two and three, along with strategies designed to eliminate forbidden foods, train problem-solving skills, and reduce relapse, the authors specifically address body image issues via cognitive restructuring procedures. Their clinical material in this section includes case examples and excerpts. Finally, they offer a relatively new approach, based on cognitive processing models of psychopathology, for identifying and challenging self-schema that perpetuate an eating disorder.

In chapter 12, Heinberg, Clark, and I build on the presentation of body image interventions in chapter 11 by offering a chapter devoted solely to the treatment of body image disturbance in anorexia nervosa and bulimia nervosa. Although there are a large number of outcome studies, few of these investigations either targeted body image issues or measured changes in body image. However, there is preliminary evidence that cognitive–behavioral approaches are effective in modifying maladaptive attitudes toward weight and shape. Other procedures include image confrontation methods, training in accurate size perception, challenging societal expectations, and experiential approaches. A recent focus on prevention of body image problems involves early education programs with children and adolescents. The role of parents and romantic partners in the formation and maintenance of body image has also received recent attention. My evaluation of the research on treatment of body image disturbance in anorexia nervosa and bulimia nervosa concludes with a strong call for including the programs developed by Cash and Rosen (see Chapters 4, 7, and 16).

Johnson and Torgrud offer one of the first examinations of the relatively new binge eating disorder in chapter 13. They begin with an overview of its clinical characteristics, including binge eating (frequency, amount, duration, loss of control issues, and antecedents and consequences), distinctiveness from bulimia nervosa, and concomitant psychopathology. Although research is just emerging, there is evidence that body image problems are an important area of assessment and intervention. The authors review assessment methods that focus on the features of this disorder and examine treatment strategies that primarily include cognitive–behavioral components. There likely will be a dramatic increase in research on this disorder in the years to come. Johnson and Torgrud provide a framework for conducting these investigations and offer clinical guidelines for contemporary treatment strategies.

Crow and Mitchell in chapter 14 close this section with a review of pharmacological treatments for anorexia nervosa and bulimia nervosa. In addition to the pharmacotherapy comparative studies, they examine the investigations that evaluate combined psychotherapy and pharmacological interventions. Their summation of treatment efficacy includes a detailing of effects on body image measures. There is little evidence that the reviewed studies were powerful in modifying body image concerns. The authors end by discussing the practical issues involved in prescribing medication, such as compliance and comorbidity.

8

ANOREXIA NERVOSA, BULIMIA NERVOSA, AND BINGE EATING DISORDER: ASSESSMENT OF PHYSICAL STATUS

CLAIRE POMEROY

It is critical to assess carefully the physical status of patients with eating disorders throughout therapy (Comerci, 1990; de Zwaan & Mitchell, 1992; Pomeroy & Mitchell, 1989; Sharp & Freeman, 1993). Too often therapists focus exclusively on psychological aspects of care and overlook medical complications, with potentially devastating consequences (Colling & King, 1994; Crisp, Callender, Halek, & Hsu, 1992; Ratnasuriya, Eisler, Szmukler, & Russell, 1991). The goal should be a multidisciplinary treatment program that incorporates medical management as an integral part of the overall care of eating-disordered patients.

This chapter reviews the physical symptoms and signs of anorexia nervosa, bulimia nervosa, and binge eating disorder, and highlights the critical role of the medical physician. Potential medical complications of each organ system are discussed, including the adverse consequences of associated laxative, diuretic, and ipecac abuse. Specific recommendations for medical management are presented, emphasizing nutritional counseling, indications for hospitalization, interactions with coexistent illnesses, and ongoing monitoring of physical status.

PHYSICAL SYMPTOMS AND SIGNS OF EATING DISORDERS

Recognizing and accurately diagnosing eating disorders can be challenging. Many patients with eating disorders will not present with symptoms obviously attributable to the eating disorder. Indeed, patients with anorexia nervosa may actively deny food restriction, and bulimics may be quite secretive about binging and purging behaviors. When eating-disordered patients do present with physical complaints, they may adamantly resist the physician's attempt to relate the medical problems to disordered eating. Compounding these problems, physicians and other health care professionals may fail to recognize symptoms and signs that are clues to an underlying eating disorder. Alert physicians will find that eating disorders can be detected accurately if they maintain vigilance and compassion.

Anorexia Nervosa

In anorexia nervosa, physical symptoms and signs usually reflect the effects of caloric restriction and subsequent weight loss (see Tables 1 and 2). However, given Western society's current emphasis on thinness, many patients—and even their families and friends—may not appreciate the serious implications of the weight loss. The cornerstone of diagnosis lies in delineating that the patient has a body image disturbance (see chapters 3 and 4, this volume). Nevertheless, patients with anorexia nervosa may

TABLE 1
Common Symptoms of Eating Disorders

Anorexia Nervosa	Bulimia Nervosa	Binge Eating Disorder
■ Patients often deny complaints, including concern about low body weight	■ Patients may be secretive about disordered eating, binging, and purging	■ Request for diet advice or concern about overweight
■ Fatigue, decreased energy	■ Fatigue, decreased energy	■ Depression
■ Anxious energy	■ Depression	■ Abdominal pain, bloating
■ Sleep disturbances	■ Headaches	
■ Irritability, depression, personality changes	■ Abdominal pain, bloating	
■ Headaches	■ Recurrent vomiting	
■ Abdominal pain, constipation	■ Heartburn	
■ Cold intolerance	■ Constipation	
■ Amenorrhea	■ Irregular menses	
	■ Swelling of hands, feet	

TABLE 2
Common Physical Examination Signs of Eating Disorders

Anorexia Nervosa	Bulimia Nervosa	Binge Eating Disorder
▪ Inanition ▪ Bradycardia ▪ Low blood pressure ▪ Low body temperature ▪ Dry skin ▪ Brittle hair, hair loss on scalp ▪ Lanugo hair ▪ Brittle nails ▪ Yellow skin, especially palms ▪ Signs of estrogen deficiency on gynecologic examination	▪ Often appear healthy ▪ Russell's sign ▪ Parotid gland swelling ▪ Erosion of dental enamel ▪ Periodontal disease, dental caries ▪ Absent gag reflex ▪ Peripheral edema	▪ Often overweight ▪ Otherwise usually appear healthy

present with physical complaints—for example, headaches and fatigue are common. Other patients may report feeling anxious or agitated, and a history of excess exercise is common. Abdominal pains or evidence of gastrointestinal bleeding may concern the patient. Many patients with anorexia nervosa note intolerance to cold. Although most female patients with established anorexia nervosa have amenorrhea, few will present with this complaint. Indeed, return of menses is often a feared consequence of weight gain. When establishing medical history, it is important to discuss sexual practices and birth control.

On physical examination, signs of anorexia nervosa are often quite obvious (see Table 2). The marked inanition of these patients is usually painfully clear to the physician, despite attempts by some patients to disguise their weight loss by wearing loose fitting or oversized clothing. Vital signs are characteristically abnormal; blood pressure is often low because of the dehydrated state; and in the extreme, orthostatic changes may be detected. Bradycardia is common, with pulse rates of 30 to 50 beats per minute frequently observed. A careful integumentary examination in patients with anorexia nervosa may reveal brittle hair and nails and loss of scalp hair. Fine, downy hair, called *lanugo hair*, may be present on the face (Gupta, Gupta, & Haberman, 1987). Yellow discoloration of the skin, especially on the palms, may occur. Nonspecific discomfort during palpation of the abdomen is common. Finally, in female patients signs of estrogen deficiency can usually be detected on gynecologic examination.

Bulimia Nervosa

Patients with bulimia nervosa often appear healthy and may have few obvious symptoms or signs of illness (see Tables 1 and 2). Patients with bulimia nervosa occasionally present to the health care system requesting help for recurrent binge–purge cycles. More often, patients are quite secretive about these behaviors. Patients may complain of depression, fatigue, or headaches. Some may suffer from abdominal pain, bloating, or heartburn; these symptoms are usually directly attributable to binge–purge cycles. Irregular menses in females may also be of concern to the bulimic patient. Most often, physical symptoms in these patients can be attributed to the effects of associated diuretic, laxative, diet pill, or ipecac use (Mitchell, Pomeroy, & Huber, 1988). If diuretic or laxative abuse results in significant electrolyte abnormalities, patients may notice fatigue, weakness, or cardiac palpitations. Chronic laxative abuse can result in constipation. Discontinuing diuretics and laxatives can result in reflex edema formation that may be quite troubling for the patient. Finally, ipecac use can cause myopathy and lead to complaints of muscle fatigue, weakness, or decreased exercise tolerance (Dresser, Massey, Johnson, & Bossen, 1993).

Physical signs of bulimia nervosa may be difficult to detect, and many bulimic patients have entirely normal physical examinations (see Table 2). The classical sign of bulimia nervosa is Russell's sign—the presence of bruises or calluses on the thumb or hand, secondary to trauma from self-induced vomiting (Mitchell, Seim, Colon, & Pomeroy, 1987). Swelling of the parotid and salivary gland has been linked to recurrent vomiting (Buchanan & Fortune, 1994). Erosion of dental enamel on the posterior surfaces of the teeth, as a result of damage by acidic gastric contents during recurrent vomiting, is characteristic in bulimia nervosa.

Binge Eating Disorder

Binge eating disorder is the most recently described eating disorder and the least studied (de Zwaan & Mitchell, 1992). Most of these patients are overweight but usually appear healthy otherwise (see Table 1). Many of these patients never seek medical help for disordered eating. However, they often visit physicians seeking diet advice. Such requests should prompt a careful evaluation by the medical physician to discern eating patterns, including binging. These patients may present with depression or fatigue, probably related to stress about body image or other life events. Obesity is the sole physical examination sign of binge eating in most patients (see Table 2).

ROLE OF THE MEDICAL PHYSICIAN

The exact role of the medical physician depends on the particular needs of the patient as well as the organization of the eating disorders team (Thompson, 1984). Mental health professionals may elect to select an internist, pediatrician, or family practitioner to whom they refer eating-disordered patients for medical care. When care is provided by an eating disorders team, as is common in many larger clinics or hospitals, it is advisable to include an internist, pediatrician, or family practitioner as a member of the team. In either case, identification of a designated medical physician facilitates communication between the health care professionals providing the psychiatric and other medical care. It also helps to ensure that the medical physician has the adequate experience and training to provide good medical care for this challenging group of patients.

INITIAL MEDICAL EVALUATION

All patients beginning treatment for an eating disorder should receive an initial complete medical examination. This allows the physician to confirm the diagnosis of an eating disorder and exclude other underlying medical illnesses that may mimic eating disorders. In addition, early detection of medical complications and coexisting medical conditions facilitates arrangements for appropriate medical follow-up. This includes informing other health care professionals of medical conditions that might alter the treatment approach, such as avoiding tricyclic antidepressants in patients with serious cardiac conduction disturbances or recognizing anticipated changes in insulin requirements in diabetics after normalizing eating patterns. Finally, the initial medical assessment provides an opportunity to develop a strong physician–patient relationship, serving as a basis for optimal management of medical complications that may arise during treatment.

Assessment of Physical Status

At the initial medical evaluation, the physician should perform a complete history and physical examination (see Table 3). The routine medical history should be expanded to include special emphasis on aspects potentially related to eating disorders. A weight history and diet history will provide clues to the severity and chronicity of the eating disorder. It is important to review actual body weights from childhood to the present. A menstrual and obstetrical history in female patients is essential to help interpret the extent of hypothalamic–pituitary axis dysfunction. Given the

TABLE 3
Initial Medical Assessment

History	Laboratory
■ General medical history, emphasizing 　Weight 　Diet 　Menstrual patterns 　Sexual activity 　Psychiatric illnesses 　Chemical dependence 　Use of diuretics, laxatives, diet 　pills, ipecac	■ Complete blood count with differential ■ Electrolytes, glucose ■ Calcium, magnesium, phosphorus ■ Liver tests—hepatic transaminases, bilirubin, alkaline phosphatase ■ Albumin, transferrin ■ Blood, urea, nitrogen, creatinine ■ Thyroid function tests—total triiodothyronine (T3), total thyroxine (T4), thyroid stimulating hormone, index ■ Urinalysis ■ Stool guaiac
Physical Examination ■ Complete physical examination, emphasizing 　Weight (degree of inanition, overweight) 　State of hydration 　Skin and hair examination 　Cardiac, pulmonary, and abdominal examinations 　Neurologic examination 　Gynecologic examination	■ Electrocardiogram ■ Chest X ray ■ Other laboratory tests as indicated by history or physical: 　Abdominal X ray 　Follicle-stimulating hormone, leutinizing hormone, estrogen, prolactin 　Amylase 　Muscle enzymes (creatinine phosphokinase, aldolase) 　Bone densitometry 　Urine drug screen (illicit drugs, diuretics)

high frequency of comorbid psychiatric conditions, especially depression and chemical dependency, a psychiatric, alcohol, and illicit drug use history is critical. The physician also should place particular emphasis on compiling an accurate history of use and abuse of other legal medications—especially diuretics, laxatives, diet pills, and ipecac.

A thorough physical examination should be performed for all patients. The physician should assess degree of inanition or overweight by careful height and weight measurements and document vital signs (blood pressure, including orthostatic changes, pulse, respirations, and temperature). State of hydration can be estimated by examining mucous membranes and skin turgor. Abnormalities of skin and hair can provide clues to eating disorders. A thorough cardiac, pulmonary, abdominal, musculoskeletal, and neurologic examination are important. For women, a gynecologic examination is important. Occasionally, it may be necessary to defer this examination until a trusting patient–physician relationship has been established, but the importance of the examination should not be overlooked.

Screening laboratory examinations are appropriate for nearly all eating-disordered patients at the time of the initial medical assessment (see Table 3). A complete blood count is important to detect anemia or leukopenia. If the patient is found to be anemic, the physician should order a peripheral smear and consider checking serum, iron, folate, and vitamin B12 levels. Serum electrolytes—including sodium, potassium, chloride, and bicarbonate—should be measured, as well as glucose, calcium, magnesium, and phosphorus. Tests of liver and renal function also are indicated. Albumin, transferrin, and total protein are useful indicators of nutritional status. Thyroid function tests are recommended, especially because many of the symptoms of hypo- or hyperthyroidism can be mimicked by eating disorders. Urinalysis and stool guaiac examination are also important. An electrocardiogram and a chest roentgenogram should be checked at baseline in most patients (Beumont, Russell, & Touyz, 1993).

Other laboratory tests should be performed as guided by historical and physical examination findings. For example, in patients with amenorrhea, it may be appropriate to evaluate the status of the hypothalamic–pituitary–gonadotropin axis by measuring serum follicle-stimulating hormone, leutinizing hormone, or estrogen levels. Abdominal symptoms may prompt abdominal X rays or, in severe cases, evaluation with endoscopy. Patients with anorexia nervosa with low weight of more than 1-year duration may develop osteoporosis, and some authorities recommend assessing them with bone densitometry to evaluate fracture risk. Urine drug screening can be used to detect surreptitious diuretic or laxative abuse in patients who deny use of these drugs but have symptoms or electrolyte abnormalities suggesting abuse of these medications.

Differential Diagnosis

Because a variety of other medical illnesses can mimic eating disorders, a major goal of the initial medical assessment is to rule out other causes of disordered eating or abnormal weight. Misdiagnosis can be devastating, and valuable time can be lost treating an apparent eating disorder while the real illness remains undetected (Marshall & Russell, 1993). A variety of medical illnesses, including malignancies, endocrine disorders, chronic infections, gastrointestinal disorders, and hypothalamic lesions can simulate anorexia nervosa and bulimia nervosa (see Table 4). Some rare syndromes may also mimic binge eating. For the most part, these diseases can be detected during a comprehensive history and physical examination performed by an experienced clinician, augmented by judicious use of screening laboratories. It is important to remember that there are specific criteria for diagnosing eating disorders and that exhaustive workups to rule out rare or unusual diseases in the differential generally are not appropriate. Nevertheless, the astute clinician plays a critical role in avoiding potentially tragic misdiagnosis.

TABLE 4
Differential Diagnosis of Eating Disorders

Anorexia Nervosa	Bulimia Nervosa	Binge Eating Disorder
▪ Malignancies, especially lymphoma, stomach cancer ▪ Endocrine diseases— thyrotoxicosis, Addison's disease, diabetes mellitus, Simmond's disease (hypophyseal cachexia) ▪ Chronic infections, especially tuberculosis, AIDS ▪ Gastrointestinal diseases— malabsorption syndromes, inflammatory bowel disease (Crohns, ulcerative colitis), parasitic infections ▪ Hypothalamic lesions or tumors ▪ Undiagnosed cystic fibrosis, superior mesenteric artery syndrome, zinc deficiency	▪ Gastrointestinal diseases— inflammatory bowel disease, peptic ulcer disease, pancreatitis, parasitic infections ▪ Connective tissue diseases with GI involvement leading to abnormal gut motility, especially scleroderma and achalasia ▪ Hypothalamic lesions or tumors	▪ Klein–Levin syndrome ▪ Prader–Willi syndrome ▪ Temporal lobe or limbic seizures ▪ Lesions of the hypothalamus, frontal lobes, or temporal lobe (e.g., bilateral temporal lobe ablation of Kluver–Bucy)

MEDICAL COMPLICATIONS

Eating disorders are associated with serious and even fatal medical complications. Mortality in anorexia nervosa is quite high, ranging from 6% to 20% (Crisp et al., 1992; Ratnasuriya et al., 1991). Recent studies have shown that even with treatment, only one half of patients with anorexia nervosa recover and that up to 25% of patients are disabled severely by chronic sequalae of their disease (Beumont et al., 1993). Death is most often a result of inanition, fluid and electrolyte abnormalities, or suicide. A distressing number of patients with bulimia nervosa also die, usually of cardiac arrhythmias related to electrolyte disturbances. Although death secondary to binge eating is uncommon, fatalities do occur (for example, as a result of gastric rupture after a large binge), and significant morbidity may occur from obesity and its associated medical complications. The high mortality and morbidity secondary to eating dis-

TABLE 5
Medications Abused by Eating Disordered Patients: Over-the-Counter Preparations

Drug	Brand Names	Active Ingredient	Major Complications
Laxatives (stimulant)	Agoral, Correctol, Dialose Plus, Doxidan, Exlax, Feen-A-Mint, Philip's Gelcaps	Phenolphthalein	Diarrhea Constipation Excess stool losses leading to electrolyte abnormalities, metabolic acidosis, dehydration, cathartic colon, melanosis coli, protein-losing gastroenteropathy
	Dulcolax	Bisacodyl	
Diuretics[a]	Bayer Select Menstrual, Midol, Pamprin, Premsyn-PMS, Odrinal, Diurex-2, Diurex-MPR	Pamabron	Dehydration, electrolyte abnormalities, metabolic (contraction) alkalosis
Diet pills	Acutrim, Appedrine, Control, Dexatrim, Hungrex, Permathene, Thinz	Phenylpropanolamine	Agitation, anxiety, cardiac arrhythmias
Ipecac	Ipecac	Emetine base	Skeletal muscle myopathy, cardiomyopathy

[a]Usually marketed as components of medications for premenstrual symptoms.

orders emphasizes the need for close ongoing monitoring of the patient to facilitate early diagnosis of medical complications in individuals with eating disorders.

Cardiovascular

Cardiac complications are the most common cause of death in patients with eating disorders, especially in patients with anorexia nervosa with very low weight and in patients with bulimia nervosa with electrolyte abnormalities as a result of purging and diuretic or laxative abuse (Kreipe & Harris, 1992; Schocken, Holloway, & Powers, 1989). Dehydration secondary to decreased oral intake, purging, or diuretic and laxative abuse is common and is manifested by low blood pressure and orthostatic changes.

A variety of electrocardiogram abnormalities have been reported in eating-disordered patients, but the true frequency and significance remain controversial. Nonspecific ST-T wave changes and waves are frequent but of uncertain clinical importance. More serious electrocardiogram abnormalities usually reflect electrolyte abnormalities, especially low serum levels of potassium (hypokalemia), and less frequently, sodium (hyponatremia), calcium (hypocalcemia), phosphate (hypophosphatemia), or magnesium (hypomagnesemia). Of most concern are conduction disturbances, such as heart blocks (especially second degree) or junctional escape rhythms. Prolongation of the QT interval (after correction for cardiac rate) is an ominous sign predicting a significant risk for serious cardiac arrhythmias and sudden cardiac death. Since cardiac arrhythmias are a frequent cause of death in eating-disordered patients, careful monitoring of the electrocardiogram in high-risk individuals is recommended, especially in patients with protracted low weight, active purging, diuretic and laxative abuse, or electrolyte abnormalities.

Mitral valve prolapse has been reported to be common in patients with anorexia nervosa. Prolapse apparently results from the decreased left ventricular size, which accompanies dramatic weight loss, resulting in disproportion between the ventricle and mitral valve (Meyers, Starke, Pearson, & Wilken, 1986). This abnormality appears to be reversible with weight gain. The true importance of the apparently increased incidence of mitral valve prolapse is difficult to discern since echocardiographic evaluation for evidence of mitral valve prolapse may be pursued more aggressively in eating-disordered patients.

Refeeding cardiomyopathy complicated by heart failure is a dreaded complication of overaggressive refeeding regimens in low-weight anorexia nervosa patients, and deaths have been reported. Treatment plans for very low weight anorexia nervosa patients should include cardiac evaluation by an experienced clinician during early refeeding and should emphasize awareness of the importance of gradual increases in caloric replacement. Another cause of cardiomyopathy in eating-disordered patients is ipecac-induced myocardial failure (Palmer & Guay, 1985). Because the active ingredient, emetine, accumulates in the body and has a prolonged half-life, recovery of cardiac function can take weeks to months, and permanent impairment has been reported.

Gastrointestinal

Bowel dysfunction is a major cause of morbidity and occasionally mortality in the eating-disordered patient (Ceuller & VanThiel, 1986; Crowell, Cheskin, & Mosial, 1994; McClain, Humphries, Hill, & Nickl, 1993). Many patients with anorexia nervosa and bulimia nervosa complain of abdominal pains and bloating, probably related to the impaired gastrointestinal motility and delayed gastric emptying times documented in many of these individuals (Ceuller, Kaye, Hsu, & VanThiel, 1988; Geliebter et al., 1992; Kamal et al., 1991). Recurrent vomiting can lead to esophageal irritation with heartburn symptoms and evidence of erosive esophagitis.

When severe, vomiting can lead to esophageal perforation (Boerhooves syndrome) with spillage of acidic contents, sepsis, and death. Gastric dilatation and rupture has also been described in patients after episodes of binge eating (Roseborough & Felix, 1994). Mallory-Weiss tears with gastrointestinal bleeding, ranging from mild to life-threatening, are additional serious complications of forceful vomiting. Chronic sequalae of recurrent vomiting include esophageal strictures or Barrett's esophagus. Colonic complications, especially constipation and abdominal pain, may be attributable to decreased oral intake, dehydration or gut dysmotility.

Laxative abuse is another major cause of gastrointestinal pathology in eating-disordered patients (Mitchell & Boutacoff, 1986). Long-term use of stimulant laxatives may result in loss of normal peristaltic function and laxative dependence. Melanosis coli (black discoloration of the colon) may be seen on endoscopy. Cathartic colon with severe constipation eventually may require resection of the colon.

Elevated serum amylase levels are common in eating-disordered patients (Kinzl, Biebl, & Herold, 1993). It is important that the clinician recognize that hyperamylesemia can result either from parotid or salivary glands (Mandel & Kaynar, 1992) or from the pancreas. Determining amylase isoenzymes can be helpful in differentiating the source of the amylase. Since pancreatitis can complicate eating disorders, especially during refeeding, the clinician should carefully evaluate patients with abdominal pain and elevated serum amylase levels for pancreatitis. Conversely, extensive workups for pancreatic pathology are inappropriate in most eating-disordered patients in whom hyperamylesemia is attributable to recurrent vomiting and parotid gland hypertrophy.

Renal, Fluid, and Electrolytes

Disordered eating can result in a variety of dangerous fluid and electrolyte abnormalities. Restricted intake, recurrent vomiting, and abuse of diuretics and laxatives can all result in serious fluid imbalance. Contracted blood volume leads to a reduced glomerular filtration rate in the kidneys (Boag, Weerakoon, Ginsburg, Havard, & Dandona, 1985), with elevated blood urea nitrogen and creatinine levels. Renal dysfunction can be a result of kaliopenic nephropathy in which prolonged low serum potassium levels lead to polyuria, polydipsia, and even chronic renal failure.

Electrolyte abnormalities are a major problem in many eating-disordered patients (Mitchell, Pyle, Eckert, Hatsukami, & Lentz, 1983). Clinicians caring for the eating-disordered patient must make a significant effort to restore potassium balances. Life-threatening potassium losses can occur as a result of recurrent vomiting or abuse of laxatives and diuretics. The most common electrolyte abnormality is hypokalemia accompanied by a metabolic (contraction) hypochloremic alkalosis. Effectiveness of potassium replacement therapy is markedly attenuated by contraction of extra-cellular fluid volume. Thus, the clinician and patient must understand that cessation of purging and correction of fluid status is an essential prerequisite to restoring serum potassium levels to normal.

Hyponatremia, hypocalcemia, and hypomagnesemia can also compli-cate eating disorders and should be monitored carefully by the physician. Excess vomiting may result in elevated serum phosphate levels (hyper-phosphatemia). Conversely, potentially life-threatening hypophosphatemia may occur during refeeding, resulting in cardiac arrhythmias or neurological complications. Although metabolic contraction alkalosis is the most com-mon acid–base imbalance in purging or diuretic- and laxative-abusing pa-tients, individuals who abuse large amounts of laxatives may develop a metabolic acidosis (Mitchell, Hatsukami, Pyle, Eckert, & Boutacoff, 1987).

Endocrine and Metabolic

Alterations of endocrine function are characteristic of eating disorders (Fichter & Pirke, 1990; Thomas & Rebar, 1990), especially in anorexia nervosa and to a lesser extent in bulimia nervosa. In anorexia nervosa, sustained hypercortisolism is the norm, reflecting persistant activation of the hypothalamic–pituitary–adrenal axis (Boyar et al., 1977; Gold et al., 1986; Gwirtsman et al., 1989). As a result, nonsuppression is expected on the dexamethasone suppression test in these patients. The etiology of hy-pothalmic–pituitary–adrenal axis stimulation is incompletely defined—a primary central nervous system defect, effects secondary to starvation, or stress manifestations all have been hypothesized.

Less consistently, abnormal dexamethasone suppression test results have been reported in bulimics (Mitchell, Pyle, Hatsukami, & Boutacoff, 1984). It is unclear if this is attributable to hypercortisolism (Hudson et al, 1983; Mortola, Rasmussen, & Yen, 1989) or merely represents a failure to absorb dexamethasone from the gastrointestinal tract in patients with bulimia nervosa (Mitchell et al., 1984). Finally, obesity itself (as observed in many binge eaters) has been associated with abnormal dexamethasone suppression test results, possibly because of a requirement for higher doses of dexamethasone in obese patients with a large volume of distribution. For this reason, in such patients a repeat test should be performed with a double dose of dexamethasone before the test is interpreted definitively as abnormal.

Abnormalities of the hypothalmic–pituitary–gonadotropin axis also are observed in patients with anorexia and in some with bulimia nervosa (Devlin et al., 1989). Amenorrhea is a diagnostic criterion for anorexia nervosa in women. Because the onset of amenorrhea occasionally precedes significant weight loss, some authorities have implicated primary central nervous system dysfunction; however, amenorrhea is also quite common in other forms of starvation and may be attributable to caloric restriction per se. In any case, cessation of menses should be considered an adaptive physiologic response to starvation. In patients with anorexia nervosa, hypoestrogenemia with low leutinizing hormone and follicle-stimulating hormone levels is frequent. An immature pattern of the responsivity of these hormones to gonadotropin-releasing hormones is characteristic. Abnormal menstrual cycles also occur in a subset of patients with bulimia nervosa and also have been associated with abnormal gonadotropin hormone production (Pirke, Fichter, Chlond, & Doerr, 1987).

The results of thyroid function tests are abnormal in many individuals with anorexia and in some with bulimia nervosa (Curran-Celentano, Erdman, Nelson, & Grater, 1985; Spalter, Gwirtsman, Demitrack, & Gold, 1993). The most common pattern is a *euthyroid sick* pattern with low total triiodothyronine (T3) but relatively normal total thyroxine (T4) and thyroid-stimulating hormone. This pattern represents a physiologic down-regulation as a result of starvation and should not be treated with thyroid hormone replacement. However, a few eating-disordered patients will have true thyroid dysfunction. Since the signs and symptoms of hypo- and hyperthyroidism can mimic findings in eating disorders, all patients should have screening tests for thyroid function.

Accelerated osteoporosis is a serious medical problem that is often underdiagnosed in anorexic patients (Biller et al., 1989; Putukian, 1994; Rigotti, Nussbaum, Herzog, & Neer, 1984). Hypoestrogenemia, hypercortisolism, and decreased calcium intake all may contribute to osteoporosis in these patients. The risk of fractures, especially Colle's fracture of the wrist, is increased significantly.

Other endocrine and metabolic abnormalities are also reported. Anorexia nervosa is associated with impaired or erratic release of vasopressin. Polyuria and polydipsia may reflect the development of nephrogenic diabetes insipidus. An elevated cholesterol level (hypercholesterolemia) is a frequent finding in anorexic patients, in contrast to other forms of starvation in which low serum cholesterol values are expected. In atypical cases, cholesterol testing may assist in the differential diagnosis of weight loss in a young woman. Elevated serum carotene levels are frequent in anorexia nervosa and may result in frank carotenodermia (orangish discoloration of the skin). Other metabolic abnormalities, such as zinc deficiency or low vitamin K levels, have been reported in eating-disordered patients, but these are unusual.

Pulmonary

Recurrent vomiting places the eating-disordered patient at risk for aspiration of gastric contents and the development of chemical or bacterial pneumonitis. In addition, high thoracic pressures created by forceful vomiting can cause rupture of the pleura and formation of pneumomediastinum (air in the mediastinum), pneumopericardium (air surrounding the heart), and subcutaneous emphysema (air in the soft tissues of the head, neck, or chest) as a result of the escape of air into surrounding tissues. Ventilatory failure, presumably as a result of decreased energy reserves as well as electrolyte abnormalities, has been reported in severe anorexia nervosa (Ryan, Whittaker, & Road, 1992).

Dermatologic

Dermatologic signs may provide important clues to the diagnosis of eating disorders but are not usually life threatening (Gupta et al., 1987). Especially in patients with anorexia nervosa, the skin and nails often become dry and brittle. Hair loss on the scalp may be quite distressing to the patient, as may the formation of lanugo hair on the face. Other dermatologic signs may suggest bulimia nervosa. As discussed earlier, bruises and calluses on the thumb, fingers, or hand may be inflicted by the teeth during self-induced vomiting (Russell's sign). Facial petechiae (tiny skin hemorrhages) or ecchymoses (bruises) and conjunctival hemorrhages may also result from forceful vomiting.

Dental

Consulting with a dental expert experienced in evaluating patients with eating disorders should be routine in patients who purge (Roberts & Li, 1987; Simmons, Grayden, & Mitchell, 1986; Touyz et al., 1993). Recurrent exposure to gastric acid from vomiting will cause permanent damage and erosion of tooth enamel. This decalcification is referred to as perimylolysis. Acid-resistant amalgams will appear increasingly prominent as damage to the teeth progresses. Many eating-disordered patients also have an increased incidence of gingivitis and periodontal disease, at least in part because of malnutrition. Some authorities have noted an increase in dental caries in patients with anorexia nervosa, but others have disputed this finding.

Hematologic and Immunologic

Anemia in anorexia nervosa is common and usually multifactorial (Howard, Leggat, & Chaudhry, 1992). Starvation-induced bone marrow suppression is perhaps most frequent, but blood loss from the gastrointestinal tract, iron deficiency, and nutritional abnormalities such as vitamin B12 or folate deficiency are all possible etiologies. Transfusions should be used only for the unusual patient with serious medical consequences of anemia, such as high-output congestive heart failure or severe anemia with hemoglobin less than 7–8 g/dL. Leukopenia with a relative lymphocytosis is a well described finding in anorexia nervosa. Finally, thrombocytopenia occurs, albeit less frequently, and can manifest as minor bleeding from the gums or skin, but only very rarely as major hemorrhage.

Immune function in eating-disordered patients remains poorly defined (Pomeroy, Mitchell, & Eckert, 1992). Some studies report an increased incidence of bacterial infections such as pneumonia, tuberculosis, and staphylococcal infections, especially in neutropenic (low white blood cell counts) patients (Devuyst, Lambert, Rodhain, Lefebvre, & Coche, 1993). However, other studies suggest that the incidence of infection is not increased, and, in fact, patients with anorexia nervosa may be protected against viral infections when their weight is very low, and then develop viral illness during weight gain (Bowers & Eckert, 1978). Laboratory studies suggest evidence of impaired cell-mediated immunity with skin test anergy documented in many patients under about 60% of ideal body weight. Low complement values and abnormal helper and suppressor lymphocyte counts (CD4$^+$: CD8$^+$ ratio) counts also have been reported (Pomeroy et al., 1992). Most recently, defective production of cytokines such as γ-interferon and interleukin-2 has been reported (Bessler, Karp, Notti, Apter, Tyano, Djaldetti, et al., 1993; Polack, Nahmod, Emeric-Sauval, Bello, Costas, Finkielman, et al., 1993). However, other cytokines such as interleukin-6 and transforming growth factor-β appear to be elevated in anorexic patients who are starving (Pomeroy et al., 1994). Since cytokines mediate interactions between the brain, endocrine, and immune systems, it is not surprising that their production is aberrant in eating disorders, but much remains to be learned in this emerging area.

Neurologic

Sleep disorders have been reported in patients with eating disorders, but the true frequency and the extent to which they are a result of the eating disorder itself versus coexisting psychopathology remain controversial. Some studies have reported abnormal electroencephalographic patterns, but others have refuted this finding. Computerized tomography scans have revealed more consistent abnormalities, especially enlarged ventricles and external cerebrospinal fluid spaces in many patients with anorexia nervosa and some with bulimia nervosa (Krieg, Irke, Lauer, & Backmund, 1988; Krieg et al., 1989). This *pseudoatrophy* usually resolves with weight gain. Pituitary glands of patients with anorexia nervosa and bulimia nervosa appear to be smaller than those of control subjects on magnetic resonance imaging (Doraiswamy et al., 1991). The advent of position emission tomography scanning has allowed exciting glimpses into the actual function of brain tissue and characteristic abnormalities have been identified in eating-disordered patients (Andreason et al., 1992; Herholz et al., 1987; Nozoe et al., 1993). The most reliable studies show hypermetabolism of glucose in the caudate region of the brain of patients with anorexia nervosa during the starvation phase of their illness.

Miscellaneous

Many patients with anorexia nervosa complain of impaired tolerance to extremes of temperature. Cold intolerance may be manifested by numbness and discoloration of the fingers and toes (Raynaud's phenomenon) and has been attributed to a combination of decreased body fat plus possible impaired central nervous system thermoregulation.

ASSOCIATED BEHAVIORS: ABUSE OF LAXATIVES, DIURETICS, DIET PILLS, AND IPECAC

The clinician must be aware of the remarkable frequency with which eating-disordered patients abuse a variety of medications in attempts to augment weight loss (see Table 5 on page 185). Eating-disordered patients may consume large numbers of stimulant laxatives. Symptoms of alternating diarrhea and constipation can be quite uncomfortable for the patient. Chronic use of stimulant laxatives has a number of long-term adverse consequences. Most important, cathartic colon results, requiring ever increasing amounts of laxatives to maintain even normal bowel function, and eventually colonic resection may be required. Steatorrhea (fatty stools) and protein-losing gastroenteropathy also can result. Enemas are also used by some patients in attempts to promote weight loss. A variety of over-the-counter enemas or tap water enemas may be used as frequently as every day.

Eating-disordered patients often abuse diuretics as well. Most commonly, these patients have access to diuretics in the form of over-the-counter preparations marketed for treatment of premenstrual symptoms. Other patients, often health care workers, may abuse prescription diuretics such as hydrochlorathiazide, loop diuretics, or potassium-sparing diuretics (Pomeroy, Mitchell, Seim, & Seppala, 1988). The overuse of these diuretics frequently results in severe and life-threatening electrolyte abnormalities. Hyponatremia and hypokalemia with a metabolic (contraction) alkalosis are observed most often. These electrolyte imbalances place the patient at risk of cardiac arrhythmias, as well as renal and gastrointestinal dysfunction.

Neither laxative nor diuretic use causes effective long-term weight loss. The initial transient loss of fluid is rapidly offset by the body's normal homeostatic mechanisms. Fluid loss and the associated volume contraction stimulate the renin–angiotension–aldosterone system, resulting in elevated aldosterone levels (secondary hyperaldosteronism) (Mitchell, Pomeroy,

Seppala, & Huber, 1988). This compensatory mechanism encourages fluid and electrolyte retention by the kidney (Mitchell et al., 1984). Once the body achieves this new set-point, a larger fraction of fluid is retained as the body attempts to restore fluid balance. Therefore, when diuretics or laxatives are discontinued, persistent hyperaldosteronism promotes reflex peripheral edema accumulation. The associated weight gain and bloating often trigger an unfortunate resumption of abusive behaviors in a dangerous self-perpetuating cycle.

Over-the-counter diet pills may be taken in dangerously high numbers by patients with eating disorders. Large quantities of the active ingredient, phenylpropanolamine, can result in agitation, anxiety, and personality changes. In some patients, abuse of diet pills may precipitate potentially lethal cardiac rhythm disturbances or neurologic abnormalities. Patients may also surreptitiously ingest large amounts of illicit amphetamines or synthetic thyroid hormone in misguided attempts to cause weight loss.

Ipecac is a potentially dangerous drug when used frequently and in large quantities to induce vomiting. Long-term use can cause serious cardiac and skeletal muscle myopathy (Mitchell et al., 1988; Palmer & Guay, 1985). The drug is available in an over-the-counter formulation, and eating-disordered patients may consume hundreds or even thousands of doses. The active ingredient, emetine base, accumulates in muscles over time with chronic use and causes a progressive myopathy. Fatalities as a result of ipecac-induced cardiomyopathy are well documented.

MEDICAL MANAGEMENT

The medical physician plays a critical role in the therapeutic management of the eating-disordered patient, in conjunction with the other members of the eating disorders team. After the initial medical assessment, the medical physician should continue to be an active participant in the ongoing care of the patient (see Table 6).

Nutritional Counseling

The medical physician should be involved in planning the nutritional portion of the treatment plan. Gradual caloric increases for patients with anorexia, healthy meal planning for patients with bulimia nervosa, and appropriate weight-reduction diets for binge eaters must be individualized to the patient's medical condition. In anorexia nervosa, normal feeding is clearly preferable to nasogastric nutrition or parenteral hyperalimentation, except for rare emergencies (Mehler & Weiner, 1993). Gradual caloric increases are needed because rapid caloric replacement can be complicated by life-threatening refeeding cardiomyopathy or pancreatitis. All therapeu-

TABLE 6
Medical Management of Patients With Eating Disorders[a]

Laboratory Test	Usual Frequency	Comments
■ History and physical examination, nutritional counseling, follow-up of medical complications	1–3 months	More often (up to daily) if patient medically unstable
■ Complete blood count	6 months–1 year	More often if abnormal or evidence of bleeding or possible infection
■ Electrolytes, blood urea nitrogen, creatinine, glucose	3–6 months	More often if diuretic, laxative abuse; up to daily–weekly if abnormal
■ Thyroid function tests	1 year	More often if receiving replacement therapy
■ Liver function tests	1 year	More often if abnormal
■ Albumin, transferrin	6 months–1 year	More often if inadequate nutrition suspected
■ Urinalysis	1 year	More often if abnormal; immediately if symptoms of infection
■ Electrocardiogram	1 year	More often if abnormal
■ Other laboratory tests that were abnormal at initial assessment	Variable	Individualized monitoring

[a]These are guidelines only. Laboratory monitoring must be individualized for each patient by the physician. Follow-up evaluation should be done more frequently if the patient is unstable.

tic plans should be individualized with weight gain strategies tailored to the patient's medical stability and extent of weight loss; traditionally a weight gain of 1 to 2 pounds per week was considered reasonable in anorexia nervosa but more rapid weight gain in the hospitalized patient may be appropriate. The physician should play an active role in counseling the patient about the medical need for healthy eating behaviors and maintaining good nutrition.

Need for Hospitalization

The medical physician is responsible for determining when the patient's physical status necessitates hospitalization. Indications for hospitalization of the eating-disordered patient include medical emergencies such as cardiac arrhythmias, serious electrolyte disturbances, or major gastrointestinal bleeding. Patients should remain on a medical unit until their physical condition is stable. The goal is to transfer the patient to an inpatient eating disorders ward as soon as it is medically safe because treatment appears to be more effective in these specialized units (Beumont et al., 1993).

The medical physician also consults in the decision to hospitalize the eating-disordered patient for other indications. Hospitalization is appropriate when the prognosis is considered poor secondary to medical, psychiatric, and social factors. It is typical to consider hospitalization for anorexic patients who weigh less than 70% to 75% of their ideal body weight or who have a rapidly decreasing weight. Patients with high suicide risk or other severe comorbid psychiatric conditions such as serious depression or major chemical dependency issues also may require inpatient treatment. A poor social or family situation may indicate a need for hospitalization if treatment is to be successful. Finally, failure of outpatient therapy signals the need for inpatient treatment. Generally, anorexic patients are most likely to require hospitalization; inpatient monitoring is also necessary in bulimic patients whose medical condition is unstable because of recurrent purging or abuse of laxatives or diuretics.

On-Going Medical Care

During treatment, especially during major changes in eating, the medical physician should monitor the patient's physical condition frequently. The exact frequency of physician visits will be detected by the fragility of the patient's physical status. Low weight anorexic patients with electrolyte abnormalities may need to be seen daily as inpatients, whereas relatively stable binge eaters may require only occasional outpatient visits.

For many patients, monitoring and treatment of electrolyte abnormalities will be the major focus of the medical physician's attention. Mild decreases in serum potassium may be corrected with dietary manipulation—such as eating bananas and other foods high in potassium. However, many bulimic patients require oral potassium supplements. Therapy must be individualized but should be considered when serum potassium levels fall below about 3.3 mEq/L (normal range 3.5 to 4.5 mEq/L). When levels fall below about 2.8 to 3.0 mEq/L, hospitalization and intravenous potassium supplements may be necessary. However, it is critical to emphasize that no level of hypokalemia can be considered safe; therapy must be individualized; and all patients must be followed closely.

Monitoring the patient's cardiac status is also critical. During major weight changes, patients remain at-risk for life-threatening cardiac arrhythmias. Patient complaints of palpitations or chest pain should prompt immediate evaluation with a focused history, physician examination, and possibly electrocardiogram. If significant arrhythmias or cardiac failure are suspected, it is appropriate to consult with a cardiologist. Although continuous cardiac monitoring on a medical unit is usually not necessary, it can be lifesaving in the particularly high-risk patient.

The medical physician should also evaluate abdominal complaints. Gastrointestinal bleeding is not uncommon in anorexic and bulimic patients. If suspected, a physician visit with history and physical examination, stool guaiacs, and monitoring of serial hemoglobins is necessary. Endoscopy performed by a trained gastroenterologist is appropriate to detect sites of bleeding in the unstable patient. Suspected gastric or esophageal perforation is a medical emergency requiring immediate surgical consultation.

In general, the endocrine complications of eating disorders are treated most successfully by correction of the aberrant eating patterns. However, osteoporosis is a major concern in the patient with anorexia nervosa, and, left untreated, may predispose the patient to a lifelong legacy of increased fracture risk. The best treatment of osteoporosis in anorexic patients is unknown, but clearly, normalization of eating behaviors and weight gain is the desired goal. Extrapolating from standards of treatment for postmenopausal osteoporosis, supplementing calcium and replacing estrogen have been advocated for anorexic patients, but definitive studies are not yet available.

Patients must be counseled to discontinue laxative, diuretic, diet pill, or ipecac use. Many eating-disordered patients are extremely reluctant to give up these behaviors. When laxative or diuretic use is ceased, reflex peripheral edema may result. As discussed previously, the resultant discomfort and fear of associated weight gain may precipitate a self-perpetuating cycle of escalated use of laxatives or diuretics. The physician should emphasize that the fluid retention is a transient problem that will resolve as the body reestablishes homeostatic fluid balance. Temporary use of a mild sodium restriction may be useful in attenuating the severity of edema formation. In some laxative abusers, temporary use of bulk-type laxatives such as Metamucil after stopping stimulant laxative preparations may help normalize bowel function.

A dentist experienced in treating patients with eating disorders should evaluate all eating-disordered patients and provide close follow-up of patients who purge. The dentist can evaluate extent of enamel erosion, treat periodontal disease, and repair dental caries. Counseling the patient about the dental consequences of recurrent vomiting is critical. The benefit of brushing the teeth immediately after vomiting has been questioned because it may actually lead to increased damage. Bicarbonate rinses can decrease acidic damage to teeth, but should not be used as a substitute for behavioral changes.

Other Coexistent Medical Illnesses

Other coexistent medical illnesses can exacerbate or be exacerbated by an eating disorder. Illnesses that require the patient to carefully manage their diet or weight can be quite challenging to treat in the eating-disordered patient. The physician must work closely with the dietitian and other members of the treatment team to counsel the patient about the importance of consistent, well balanced nutritional intake and the need to avoid recurrent binging or vomiting.

Managing eating-disordered patients with coexisting diabetes mellitus can be particularly challenging (Rodin & Daneman, 1992). The usual struggles with body image and control issues in adolescent diabetics are magnified by a simultaneous eating disorder. Eating-disordered patients may withhold insulin deliberately to induce loss of glucose in the urine (glycosuria) and weight loss, placing themselves at risk for diabetic ketoacidosis. In addition, erratic caloric intake, either as a result of restriction in anorexic patients or binging in bulimic patients and binge eaters, can make determination of insulin dosages difficult. The medical physician must work with the eating disorder team to provide stable, nonjudgmental medical care in these extremely high-risk patients.

Reproductive function is frequently disrupted in the eating-disordered patient (Stewart, 1992). Infertility can result from anorexia nervosa, bulimia nervosa, or obesity associated with binge eating. Physicians are advised to search for historical or physical examination clues to an eating disorder in the infertile patient. If the diagnosis of an eating disorder is established, complex, painful, and costly workups for other etiologies of infertility may be avoided.

If the eating-disordered patient does become pregnant, medical care should be provided by the obstetrician in close collaboration with the eating disorders team (Stewart, Raskin, Garfinkel, MacDonald, & Robinson, 1987). The preoccupation with body image characteristic of the eating-disordered patient is often exacerbated by the physiologic changes of pregnancy. In turn, this may accelerate abnormal eating behaviors that can adversely affect both mother and baby. Hyperemesis gravidarium (excess vomiting in pregnancy), inadequate maternal weight gain, and pregnancy-induced hypertension all appear to be more frequent in patients with eating disorders, especially anorexia nervosa. Labor and delivery is often more difficult for this patient population. Prolonged labor and increased requirement for cesarean section have been anecdotally reported in anorexic patients. Women with an active eating disorder at the time of conception are at increased risk of delivering distressed babies. Eating-disordered women also appear to have more difficulty with breast feeding and may have difficulty providing appropriate diets for their babies later in life.

Advice regarding pregnancy must be individualized. However, for many patients, it may be best to advise postponing pregnancy until the eating disorder has been appropriately treated. When women with an active eating disorder do become pregnant, careful and compassionate medical care should be provided in a coordinated fashion between the obstetrician and the eating disorders team to ensure the best outcome for the patient and her baby.

CONCLUSION

Assessing physical status is an integral component of the care of the patient with anorexia nervosa, bulimia nervosa, or binge eating disorders. Specific symptoms and physical examination signs characterize each of the eating disorders and should be evaluated carefully by all members of the eating disorder team. In addition, a variety of medical conditions can complicate eating disorders. Cardiac arrhythmias, electrolyte disturbances, gastrointestinal dysfunction, endocrine abnormalities, and abuse of laxatives, diuretics, diet pills, and ipecac are major potential sources of morbidity and even mortality in the eating-disordered patient. Ideally, a medical physician will be included as a member of the eating disorder team and will be responsible for identifying, treating, and preventing of these medical complications. Working together, coordinated care can be provided for patients with eating disorders in order to optimize the prognosis in these potentially devastating illnesses.

REFERENCES

Andreason, P. J., Altemus, M., Zametkin, A. J., King, A. C., Lucino, J., & Cohen, R. M. (1992). Regional cerebral glucose metabolism in bulimia nervosa. *American Journal of Psychology, 149*, 1506–1513.

Bessler, H., Karp, L., Notti, I., Apter, A., Tyano, S., Djaldetti, M., & Weizman, R. (1993). Cytokine production in anorexia nervosa. *Clinical Neuropharmacology, 16*, 237–243.

Beumont, P. J., Russell, J. D., & Touyz, S. W. (1993). Treatment of anorexia nervosa. *Lancet, 341*, 1635–1640.

Biller, B. M. K., Saxe, V., Herzog, D. B., Rosenthal, D. I., Holzman, S., & Klibanski, A. (1989). Mechanisms of osteoporosis in adult and adolescent women with anorexia nervosa. *Journal of Clinical Endocrinology and Metabolism, 68*, 548–554.

Boag, F., Weerakoon, J., Ginsburg, J., Havard, C. W. H., & Dandona, P. (1985). Diminished creatinine clearance in anorexia nervosa. Reversal with weight gain. *Journal of Clinical Pathology, 38*, 60–63.

Bowers, T. K., & Eckert, E. (1978). Leukopenia in anorexia nervosa: Lack of increased risk of infection. *Archives of Internal Medicine, 138*, 1520–1523.

Boyar, R. M., Hellman, L. D., Roffwarg, H., Katz, J., Zumoff, B., O'Connor, J., Bradlow, H. L., & Fukushima, D. K. (1977). Cortisol secretion and metabolism in anorexia nervosa. *New England Journal of Medicine, 296,* 190–193.

Buchanan, J. A., & Fortune, F. (1994). Bilateral parotid enlargement as a presenting feature of bulimia nervosa in a post-adolescent male. *Postgraduate Medical Journal, 70,* 27–30.

Ceuller, R., Kaye, W. H., Hsu, L. K., & VanThiel, D. H. (1988). Upper gastrointestinal tract dysfunction in bulimia. *Digestive Diseases Science, 33,* 1549–1553.

Ceuller, R. E., & VanThiel, D. H. (1986). Gastrointestinal consequences of the eating disorders. Anorexia nervosa and bulimia. *American Journal of Gastroenterology, 81,* 1113–1124.

Colling, S., & King, M. (1994). Ten-year follow-up of 50 patients with bulimia nervosa. *British Journal of Psychology, 164,* 80–87.

Comerci, G. (1990). Medical complications of anorexia nervosa and bulimia. *Medical Clinics of North America, 74,* 1293–1310.

Crisp, A. H., Callender, J. S., Halek, C., & Hsu, L. K. G. (1992). Long-term mortality in anorexia nervosa. *British Journal of Psychiatry, 161,* 104–107.

Crowell, M. D., Cheskin, L. J., & Mosial, F. (1994). Prevalence of gastrointestinal symptoms in obese and normal weight binge eaters. *American Journal of Gastroenterology, 89,* 387–391.

Curran-Celentano, J., Erdman, J. W., Nelson, R. A., & Grater, S. J. E. (1985). Alteration in Vitamin A and thyroid hormone status in anorexia nervosa and associated disorders. *American Journal of Clinical Nutrition, 42,* 1183–1191.

de Zwaan, M., & Mitchell, J. E. (1992). Binge eating in the obese. *Annals of Medicine, 24,* 303–308.

Devlin, M. J., Walsh, B. T., Katz, J. L., Roose, S. P., Linkie, D. M., Wright, L., Wiele, R. V., & Glassman, A. H. (1989). Hypothalamic–pituitary–gonadal function in anorexia nervosa and bulimia. *Psychiatry Research, 28,* 11–24.

Devuyst, O., Lambert, M., Rodhain, J., Lefebvre, C., & Coche, E. (1993). Haematological changes and infectious complications in anorexia nervosa: A case-control study. *Quarterly Journal of Medicine, 86,* 791–799.

Doraiswamy, P. M., Krishnan, K. R., Boyko, O. B., Husain, M. M., Figiel, G. S., Palese, V. J., Escalona, P. R., Shah, S. A., McDonald, W. M., Rockwell, W. J. K., & Ellinwood Jr., E. H. (1991). Pituitary abnormalities in eating disorders: Further evidence from MRI studies. *Progress in Neuro-Psychopharmacology and Biologic Psychiatry, 15,* 351–356.

Dresser, L. P., Massey, E. W., Johnson, E. E., & Bossen, E. (1993). Ipecac myopathy and cardiomyopathy. *Journal of Neurology Neurosurgery and Psychiatry, 56,* 560–562.

Fichter, M. M., & Pirke, K. M. (1990). Endocrine dysfunction in bulimia nervosa. In M. M. Fichter, *Bulimia nervosa: Basic research, diagnosis, and therapy* (pp. 235–257). Chichester, England: John Wiley & Sons, Ltd.

Geliebter, A., Melton, P. M., McCray, R. S., Gallagher, D. R., Gage, D., & Hashim, S. A. (1992). Gastric capacity, gastric emptying, and test-meal intake in normal and bulimic women. *American Journal of Clinical Nutrition, 56*, 656–661.

Gold, P. W., Gwirtsman, H., Avgerinos, P. C., Nieman, L. K., Gallucci, W. T., Kaye, W., Jimerson, D., Ebert, M., Rittmaster, R., Loriaux, D. L., & Chrousos, G. P. (1986). Abnormal hypothalamic–pituitary–adrenal function in anorexia nervosa. *New England Journal of Medicine, 314*, 1334–1342.

Gupta, M. A., Gupta, A. K., & Haberman, H. F. (1987). Dermatologic signs in anorexia nervosa and bulimia nervosa. *Archives of Dermatology, 123*, 1386–1390.

Gwirtsman, H. E., Kaye, W. H., George, D. T., Jimerson, D. C., Ebert, M. H., & Gold, P. W. (1989). Central and peripheral ACTH and cortisol levels in anorexia nervosa and bulimia. *Archives of General Psychiatry, 46*, 61–69.

Herholz, K., Krieg, J. C., Emrich, H. M., Pawlik, G., Beil, C., Pirke, K. M., Pahl, J. J., Wagner, R., Wienhard, K., Ploog, D., & Heiss, W. D. (1987). Regional cerebral glucose metabolism in anorexia nervosa measured by positron emission tomography. *Biological Psychiatry, 22*, 43–51.

Howard, M. R., Leggat, H. M., & Chaudhry, S. (1992). Haematological and immunological abnormalities in eating disorders. *British Journal of Hospital Medicine, 48*, 234–239.

Hudson, J., Pope, H. G., Jr., Jonas, J. M., Laffer, P. S., Hudson, M. S., & Melby, J. C. (1983). Hypothalamic–pituitary–adrenal axis hyperactivity in bulimia. *Psychiatry Research, 8*, 111–117.

Isner, J. M., Roberts, W. C., Heymsfield, S. B., & Yager, J. (1985). Anorexia nervosa and sudden death. *Annals of Internal Medicine, 102*, 49–52.

Kamal, N., Chami, T., Andersen, A., Rosell, F. A., Schuster, M. M., & Whitehead, W. E. (1991). Delayed gastrointestinal transit times in anorexia nervosa and bulimia nervosa. *Gastroenterology, 101*, 1320–1324.

Kinzl, J., Biebl, W., & Herold, M. (1993). Significance of vomiting for hyperamylasemia and sialadenosis in patients with eating disorders. *International Journal of Eating Disorders, 13*, 117–124.

Kreipe, R. E., & Harris, J. P. (1992). Myocardial impairment resulting from eating disorders. *Pediatric Annals, 21*, 760–768.

Krieg, J. C., Irke, K. M., Lauer, C., & Backmund, H. (1988). Endocrine, metabolic, and cranial computed tomography findings in anorexia nervosa. *Biological Psychiatry, 23*, 377–387.

Krieg, J. C., Lauer, C., Leinsinger, G., Pahl, J., Schreiber, W., Pirke, K. M., & Moser, E. A. (1989). Brain morphology and regional cerebral blood flow in anorexia nervosa. *Biological Psychiatry, 25*, 1041–1048.

Mandel, L., & Kaynar, A. (1992). Bulimia and parotid swelling: A review and case report. *Journal of Oral and Maxillofacial Surgery, 50*, 1122–1125.

Marshall, J. B., & Russell, J. L. (1993). Achalasia mistakenly diagnosed as eating disorder and prompting prolonged psychiatric hospitalization. *Southern Medical Journal, 86*, 1405–1407.

McClain, C. J., Humphries, L. L., Hill, K. K., & Nickl, N. J. (1993). Gastrointestinal and nutritional aspects of eating disorders. *Journal of the American College of Nutrition, 12,* 466–474.

Mehler, P. S., & Weiner, K. L. (1993). Anorexia nervosa and total parenteral nutrition. *International Journal of Eating Disorders, 14,* 297–304.

Meyers, D. G., Starke, H., Pearson, P. H., & Wilken, M. K. (1986). Mitral valve prolapse in patients with anorexia nervosa. *Annals of Internal Medicine, 105,* 384–386.

Mitchell, J. E., & Boutacoff, L. I. (1986). Laxative abuse complicating bulimia: Medical and treatment implications. *International Journal of Eating Disorders, 5,* 325–334.

Mitchell, J. E., Hatsukami, D., Pyle, R. L., Eckert, E. D., & Boutacoff, L. I. (1987). Metabolic acidosis as a marker for laxative abuse in patients with bulimia. *International Journal of Eating Disorders, 6,* 557–560.

Mitchell, J. E., Pomeroy, C., & Huber, M. (1988). A clinician's guide to the eating disorders medicine cabinet. *International Journal of Eating Disorders, 7,* 211–223.

Mitchell, J. E., Pomeroy, C., Seppala, M., & Huber, M. (1988). Pseudo-Bartter's syndrome, diuretic abuse, idiopathic edema and eating disorders. *International Journal of Eating Disorders, 7,* 225–237.

Mitchell, J. E., Pyle, R. L., Eckert, E. D., Hatsukami, D., & Lentz, R. (1983). Electrolyte and other physiological abnormalities in patients with bulimia. *Psychiatry of Medicine, 13,* 273–278.

Mitchell, J. E., Pyle, R. L., Hatsukami, K., & Boutacoff, L. I. (1984). The dexamethasone suppression test in patients with bulimia. *Journal of Clinical Psychiatry, 45,* 508–511.

Mitchell, J. E., Seim, H. C., Colon, E., & Pomeroy, C. (1987). Medical complications and medical management of bulimia. *Annals of Internal Medicine, 107,* 71–77.

Mortola, J. F., Rasmussen, D. D., & Yen, S. S. C. (1989). Alterations of the adrenocorticotropin–cortisol axis in normal weight bulimic women: Evidence for a central mechanism. *Journal of Clinical Endocrinology and Metabolism, 68,* 517–522.

Nozoe, S., Narvo, T., Nakabeppu, Y., Soejima, Y., Nakajo, M., & Tanaka, H. (1993). Changes in regional cerebral blood flow in patients with anorexia nervosa detected through single photon emission tomography imaging. *Biological Psychiatry, 34,* 578–580.

Palmer, E. P., & Guay, A. T. (1985). Reversible myopathy secondary to abuse of ipecac in patients with major eating disorders. *New England Journal of Medicine, 313,* 1457–1459.

Pirke, K. M., Fichter, M. M., Chlond, C., & Doerr, P. (1987). Disturbances of the menstrual cycle in bulimia nervosa. *Clinical Endocrinology, 27,* 245–251.

Polack, E., Nahmod, V. E., Emeric-Sauval, E., Bello, M., Costas, M., Finkielman, S., & Arzt, E. (1993). Low lymphocyte interferon-gamma production and variable proliferative response in anorexia nervosa patients. *Journal of Clinical Immunology*, *13*, 445–451.

Pomeroy, C., Eckert, E., Hu, S., Eiken, B., Mentink, M., Crosby, R., & Chao, C. C. (1994). Role of interleukin-6 and transforming growth factor-β in anorexia nervosa. *Biological Psychiatry*, *36*, 836–839.

Pomeroy, C., & Mitchell, J. E. (1989). Medical complications and management of eating disorders. *Psychiatric Annals*, *19*, 488–493.

Pomeroy, C., Mitchell, J. E., & Eckert, E. D. (1992). Risk of infection and immune function in anorexia nervosa. *International Journal of Eating Disorders*, *12*, 47–55.

Pomeroy, C., Mitchell, J. E., Seim, H., & Seppala, M. (1988). Prescription diuretic abuse in patients with bulimia nervosa. *Journal of Family Practice*, *27*, 493–496.

Putukian, M. (1994). The female triad. Eating disorders, amenorrhea, and osteoporosis. *Medical Clinics of North America*, *78*, 345–356.

Ratnasuriya, R. H., Eisler, I., Szmukler, G. I., & Russell, G. F. M. (1991). Anorexia nervosa: outcome and prognostic factors after 20 years. *British Journal of Psychiatry*, *158*, 495–502.

Rigotti, N. A., Nussbaum, S. R., Herzog, D. B., & Neer, R. M. (1984). Osteoporosis in women with anorexia nervosa. *New England Journal of Medicine*, *311*, 1601–1606.

Roberts, M. W., & Li, S. H. (1987). Oral findings in anorexia nervosa and bulimia nervosa: A study of 47 cases. *Journal of the American Dental Association*, *115*, 407–410.

Rodin, G. M., & Daneman, D. (1992). Eating disorders and IDDM. A problematic association. *Diabetes Care*, *15*, 1402–1412.

Roseborough, G. S., & Felix, W. A. (1994). Disseminated intravascular coagulation complicating gastric perforation in a bulimic woman. *Canadian Journal of Surgery*, *37*, 55–58.

Ryan, C. F., Whittaker, J. S., & Road, J. D. (1992). Ventilatory dysfunction in severe anorexia nervosa. *Chest*, *102*, 1286–1288.

Schocken, D. D., Holloway, J. D., & Powers, P. S. (1989). Weight loss and the heart. *Archives of Internal Medicine*, *149*, 877–881.

Sharp, C. W., & Freeman, C. P. L. (1993). The medical complications of anorexia nervosa. *British Journal of Psychiatry*, *162*, 452–462.

Simmons, M. S., Grayden, S. K., & Mitchell, J. E. (1986). The need for psychiatric–dental liaison in the treatment of bulimia. *American Journal of Psychiatry*, *143*, 783–784.

Spalter, A. R., Gwirtsman, H. E., Demitrack, M. A., & Gold, P. W. (1993). Thyroid function in bulimia nervosa. *Biological Psychiatry*, *33*, 408–414.

Stewart, D. E. (1992). Reproductive functions in eating disorders. *Annals in Medicine*, *24*, 287–291.

Stewart, D. E., Raskin, J., Garfinkel, P. E., MacDonald, O. L., & Robinson, G. E. (1987). Anorexia nervosa, bulimia, and pregnancy. *American Journal of Obstetrics and Gynecology, 157,* 1194–1198.

Thomas, M. A., & Rebar, R. W. (1990). The endocrinology of anorexia nervosa and bulimia nervosa. *Current Opinion in Obstetrics and Gynecology, 2,* 831–836.

Thompson, J. K. (1984). The psychologist as a member of a clinical nutrition outpatient services team. *Journal of Practical Application in Clinical Nutrition, 4,* 20–24.

Touyz, S. W., Liew, V. P., Tserg, P., Friskin, K., Williams, H., & Beumont, P. J. (1993). Oral and dental complications in dieting disorders. *International Journal of Eating Disorders, 14,* 341–347.

9

ANOREXIA NERVOSA AND BULIMIA NERVOSA: STRUCTURED INTERVIEW METHODOLOGIES AND PSYCHOLOGICAL ASSESSMENT

DONALD A. WILLIAMSON, DREW A. ANDERSON, and DAVID H. GLEAVES

This chapter summarizes methods for assessing the psychological and behavioral characteristics of anorexia nervosa and bulimia nervosa. Over the past 15 years, research on the assessment of eating disorders has expanded greatly (Williamson, 1990). This chapter describes the structured interview methods, self-monitoring procedures, and self-report inventories that have been tested most extensively. The first section reviews the basic psychometric concepts by which these methods are evaluated. The next three sections describe the instruments that have been developed. We review psychometric research pertaining to each method. The final section reviews the methodology that has been used for evaluating therapeutic procedures for anorexia and bulimia nervosa. We summarize recommendations for future research and clinical applications in the final section.

PSYCHOMETRIC RESEARCH ISSUES

According to the *Standards for Educational and Psychological Testing* (American Psychological Association, 1985), the *reliability* of an instrument is the degree to which derived scores are free from errors of measurement. Such measurement errors lead to inconsistencies in derived data and reduce the reliability of an instrument. Estimates of reliability can be based on several different types of evidence, all of which relate to the consistency of derived scores. The consistency that is examined may be across repeated administration of the same test over time (test–retest reliability), across administration of alternate forms of the test, or within individual administrations of a test (split-half reliability or internal consistency). These different types of evidence for consistency have somewhat different meanings. Reliability coefficients for the first three types of data are reported as correlations between the two sets of scores. Internal consistency can be reported by alpha coefficients or, when the items are dichotomous, Kuder–Richardson–20 coefficients. For structured interviews, another relevant concept is *interrater reliability*, which is the degree of agreement among two or more interviewers or raters. When data obtained from an interview are nominal in nature, the appropriate statistic for calculating interrater reliability is the kappa coefficient, which is a measure of chance-corrected agreement (Landis & Koch, 1977). When quantitative variables are used, the *intraclass correlation* is most appropriate to measure interrater reliability (Shrout & Fleiss, 1979). If interviews yield ranked data, Kendall's rank correlation coefficient can be used to determine interrater agreement.

Validity may be the most important concept in developing and evaluating tests. The term generally refers to the appropriateness, meaningfulness, and usefulness of the inferences that can be made from the instrument (American Psychological Association, 1985). As this definition implies, a test may be valid for one purpose and invalid for another. Evidence for validity is frequently grouped into three categories: content-related, criterion-related, and construct-related evidence of validity.

Content validity refers to the degree to which an instrument samples a relevant domain of content. Evidence for criterion-related validity demonstrates that test scores are significantly related to one or more relevant variables. Evidence supporting construct related validity is that which suggests that the instrument actually measures the construct that it purports to measure.

Reliability and validity have an important relationship. Reliability is necessary but not sufficient for validity. That is, an instrument must be reliable to be valid, but can be reliable and still be invalid. The reliability of an instrument can be conceptualized as setting the upper bound for its validity.

The process of *psychometric development* involves a series of steps. These include identifying the intended use of test scores, identifying behaviors to represent the construct in question, sampling the domain, preparing test specifications, constructing items, and reviewing items (Crocker & Algina, 1986). These steps are generally followed by field tests with large numbers of examinees representative of the target population. Based on these field tests, item analyses can be performed, resulting in item refinement or elimination. Once a final form of the instrument is developed, the developer must thoroughly examine the reliability and validity of the instrument. Ideally, test validation involves several types of evidence, spanning all three categories of validity. In the following sections, we discuss psychometric research pertaining to structured interviews and psychological tests for eating disorders.

STRUCTURED INTERVIEWS

Four structured interviews for evaluating symptoms of eating disorders have been reported in the research literature: (a) Eating Disorder Examination, (b) Interview for Diagnosis of Eating Disorder, (c) Clinical Eating Disorder Rating Instrument, and (d) Structured Interview for Anorexia and Bulimia Nervosa. Table 1 describes the subscales and summarizes psychometric research for the Eating Disorder Examination and the Interview for Diagnosis of Eating Disorder. Research on the Clinical Eating Disorder Rating Instrument (Palmer, Christie, Cordle, Davies, & Kenrick, 1987) and the Structured Interview for Anorexia and Bulimic Nervosa (Fichter et al., 1989) is limited, and we will not review it.

Eating Disorder Examination

The Eating Disorder Examination (Fairburn & Cooper, 1993) is a well developed interview format for assessing the symptoms of anorexia nervosa and bulimia nervosa. It has been revised twelve times and its psychometric properties have been tested in many empirical studies (Fairburn & Cooper, 1993). It was first described by Cooper and Fairburn (1987).

The four subscales are described as (a) restraint, (b) eating concern, (c) shape concern, and (d) weight concern. Internal consistency of the subscales was found to be relatively high in a series of investigations (Fairburn & Cooper, 1993). The items derived from the interview are 23 symptom ratings made by the interviewer. Interrater reliability of the individual symptom ratings has been reported to be quite high (Cooper & Fairburn, 1987). As shown in Table 1, interrater reliability for subscale scores also has been found to be high (Fairburn & Cooper, 1993). Evidence for discriminant and concurrent validity has also been reported (Fairburn & Cooper, 1993).

The Eating Disorder Examination was originally developed to assess the outcome of therapy and to evaluate the psychopathology of anorexia and bulimia nervosa. It has been recently expanded to enable the clinician to diagnose anorexia nervosa and bulimia nervosa using the diagnostic criteria of the *Diagnostic and Statistical Manual of Mental Disorders* (American Psychiatric Association, 1994). The procedure for its use as a diagnostic instrument was described by Fairburn and Cooper (1993). There

TABLE 1
Summary of Psychometric Research for Structured Interviews

Name of Instrument	Author(s)	Description	Reliability	Validity
Eating Disorders Examination, 12th ed.	Cooper & Fairburn (1987); Fairburn & Cooper (1993)	4 scales assess eating disorder symptoms: restraint, eating concern, shape concern, & weight concern	IC: >.65 for all 4 scales TR: unknown IR: >.80 for all 4 scales	Content: Y Criterion: Y Construct: Y
Interview for Diagnosis of Eating Disorders, 4th ed.	Williamson (1990); Williamson, Davis, Norris, & Van Buren (1990)	Assesses for a diagnosis of AN, BN, BED using DSM-IV criteria	IC: unknown TR: >.85 for all ratings and total score IR: >.85 for all ratings and total score	Content: Y Criterion: Y Construct: Y

Note. IC = internal consistency, TR = test–retest reliability, IR = interrater reliability, Y = yes, N = no, AN = anorexia nervosa, BN = bulimia nervosa, BED = binge eating disorder.

have been no formal tests of its validity as a tool for diagnosing eating disorders, however.

Interview for Diagnosis of Eating Disorders

The Interview for Diagnosis of Eating Disorders (IDED) (Williamson, 1990) was developed specifically for diagnosing eating disorders. This interview format has undergone four revisions and is currently being tested for the diagnoses of anorexia nervosa, bulimia nervosa, and binge eating disorder using *DSM-IV* criteria. In the original version the IDED, described in Williamson (1990), the term *compulsive overeating* was used to describe binge eating disorder. In the fourth revision of the IDED, the diagnoses of subtypes for anorexia nervosa and bulimia nervosa are operationalized, and the *DSM-IV* criteria for binge eating disorder were used for structuring the questions and symptom ratings of the interview.

In this fourth revision, diagnoses are based on the interviewer ratings for 21 symptoms. Diagnoses are based on high symptom ratings that match the criteria for a diagnosis of anorexia nervosa, bulimia nervosa, or binge eating disorder (American Psychiatric Association, 1994). Total scores for anorexia nervosa, bulimia nervosa, and binge eating disorder subscales are derived by summing the ratings for each symptom within each diagnostic category.

Table 1 summarizes the psychometric data for the original Interview for Diagnosis of Eating Disorders (Williamson, Davis, Norris, & Van Buren, 1990). Interrater reliability and test–retest (1 week) reliability have been reported to be high. Total scores for diagnostic subscales have differentiated clinical eating disorder groups from normal and obese subjects. Also, evidence for concurrent validity with other measures of eating disorder symptoms has been reported.

SELF-MONITORING PROCEDURES

Self-monitoring of eating behavior and nutrient intake has been used frequently in psychological studies of eating disorders (Williamson, 1990). Schlundt (1989) reviewed this research literature and concluded that self-monitoring data could be used to conduct a functional analysis of eating behavior. In a functional analysis, the environmental, cognitive, and emotional antecedents of binge eating, purging, and restrictive eating can be identified. This type of analysis is individualized and leads directly to treatment planning. In two earlier studies, Schlundt and colleagues (Schlundt, Johnson, & Jarrell, 1985, 1986) provided support for the predictive validity of this assessment approach.

Williamson (1990) and Schlundt (1989) provided the details of two self-monitoring procedures that have been developed and tested psychometrically. In Exhibit 1, the self-monitoring forms developed by Williamson (1990) are illustrated. Using this procedure, the subject is instructed to monitor each eating episode on a separate form. The environmental and emotional antecedents and consequences of eating and purging are documented in this procedure. Also, the amount and type of food consumed in each eating episode are recorded. From this nutrient intake data, caloric and nutrient analysis can be conducted. Recent research studies (Williamson, Davis, et al., 1990; Williamson, Gleaves, Lawson, 1991) have provided support for the predictive and concurrent validity of this self-monitoring procedure.

Most psychological studies that have employed self-monitoring procedures have not used validated methods. Thus, the psychometric properties of these methods are generally unknown. This problem is especially noteworthy when attempting to evaluate self-monitoring procedures that have been used to judge the effectiveness of treatment methods.

PSYCHOLOGICAL TESTS

For purposes of review, we selected eight self-report inventories that have been developed to measure symptoms related to anorexia nervosa and bulimia nervosa. Psychometric research pertaining to each instrument is summarized in Table 2.

Eating Disorder Inventory–2

The Eating Disorder Inventory–2 (Garner, 1991) is a 91-item multidimensional self-report inventory designed to assess the symptoms of anorexia nervosa and bulimia nervosa. The original version (Garner, Olmsted, & Polivy, 1983) contained 64 questions divided into 8 scales: (a) drive for thinness, (b) bulimia, (c) body dissatisfaction, (d) ineffectiveness, (e) perfectionism, (f) interpersonal distrust, (g) interoceptive awareness, and (h) maturity fears. The revision retained these original 8 scales and added 27 items to form 3 additional scales: (a) asceticism, (b) impulse regulation, and (c) social insecurity. Eating Disorder Inventory–2 items are answered using a 6-point rating scale ranging from "always" to "never."

Garner (1991) found Cronbach's alphas for the eight original subscales to be generally high; however, Eberenz and Gleaves (in press) found internal consistency for the three additional scales of the revised inventory to be much lower. Test–retest reliability has been found to be satisfactory at 1 week (Welch, 1988), 3 weeks (Wear & Pratz, 1987), but lower at 1 year (Crowther, Lilly, Crawford, Shepherd, & Olivier, 1990). Most validity

EXHIBIT 1

Illustration of Self-Monitoring Procedure for Eating Behavior and Nutrient Intake

FOOD MONITORING INSTRUCTIONS

RECORD EACH DRINK, MEAL, OR SNACK ON A SEPARATE PAGE AT THE TIME OF EATING. BE SURE TO INCLUDE ALL LIQUIDS (EVEN WATER). BE ACCURATE IN YOUR DESCRIPTION OF FOOD OR DRINK. FOR EXAMPLE, INCLUDE "RYE" BREAD, "FRIED BREADED" CHICKEN "BREAST, "DUNCAN HINES" CHOCOLATE CHIP COOKIES, ETC. DON'T FORGET TO INCLUDE THE AMOUNT.

ABBREVIATION KEY

DESCRIBE EACH EATING EPISODE BY CIRCLING ONE CHOICE FOR EACH DESCRIPTOR BELOW.

MEAL (BREAKFAST, LUNCH, DINNER, SNACK).
ACTIVITY PRIOR (SOCIAL, WORK, RELAXATION, TV, EXERCISE, CLASS, OTHER). IF OTHER, WRITE IN THE ACTIVITY.
WITH WHOM (FRIEND, FAMILY, DATE/SPOUSE, ALONE, OTHER). IF OTHER WRITE IN WHO.
WHERE (BEDROOM, WORK, RESTAURANT, KITCHEN, DINING ROOM, LIVING ROOM, DEN, OTHER). IF OTHER WRITE IN WHERE.
MOOD (VERY NEGATIVE, NEGATIVE, NEUTRAL, POSITIVE, VERY POSITIVE).
DESCRIBE YOUR MOOD (SAD, DEPRESSED, HAPPY, GUILTY, ETC.).
HUNGER (VERY HUNGRY, MODERATELY HUNGRY, NEUTRAL, NOT HUNGRY, FULL).
AMOUNT EATEN - BASED ON YOUR EVALUATION OF WHETHER YOU ATE MORE OR LESS THAN A NORMAL AMOUNT FOR THAT MEAL OR SNACK.

INITIALS _____

NUMBER _____

Day _____ Date _____ Time _____ PM, AM Meal (B, L, D, S)

ACT. PRIOR (SOC., SK., REL., TV, EX., CL., OTHER) _____

WHO WITH (FRIEND., FAM., DATE/SP., ALONE, OTHER) _____

WHERE (BDRM., WK., REST., KIT., DR., LR., DEN., OTHER) _____

MOOD PRIOR (- -, -, N, +, + +) DESCRIBE _____

HUNGER PRIOR (VH, MH, N, NH, F) _____

AMT EATEN--UNDEREAT, NORMAL, SLIGHT OVEREAT, MOD OVEREAT, BINGE

MOOD AFTER EATING (- -, -, N, +, + +) DESCRIBE _____

HUNGER AFTER EATING (VH, MH, N, NH, F) _____

PURGE (NO, YES (CIRCLE ONE) VOMIT, LAXATIVES, OR DIURETICS?)
IF LAX. OR DIURETICS - HOW MANY? _____

TIME OF PURGE _____ PM, AM

MOOD AFTER PURGING (- -, -, N, +, + +) DESCRIBE _____

HUNGER AFTER PURGING (VH, MH, N, NH, F) _____

ACCURATE DESCRIPTION OF FOOD OR DRINK ITEM   AMOUNT

_____

_____

_____

_____

_____

_____

_____

COMMENTS: _____

_____

TABLE 2
Summary of Psychometric Research for Psychological Tests

Name of Instrument	Author(s)	Description	Reliability	Validity
Eating Disorder Inventory–2	Eberenz & Gleaves (in press); Garner (1991)	91 items (11 subscales) concerning symptoms of both AN and BN	IC: .65–.93 TR: 1 week (.67–.95) 3 week (.65–.92) 1 year (.41–.75) (from EDI)	Content: Y Criterion: Y Construct: Y
Eating Attitudes Test	Carter & Moss (1984); Garner & Garfinkel (1979)	40 items concerning attitudes and behaviors associated with AN and BN	IC: .79 TR: 2–3 wk. (.84)	Content: Y Criterion: Y Construct: Y
Bulimia Test–Revised	Smith & Thelen (1984); Thelen et al. (1991)	36 items (8 unscored) concerning symptoms of BN	IC: .97 TR: 2 months (.95)	Content: Y Criterion: Y Construct: Y
Setting Conditions for Anorexia Nervosa Scale	Slade & Dewey (1986)	40 items (5 subscales) designed to identify individuals at risk for developing AN or BN	IC: >.66 for all 5 scales TR: unknown	Content: Y Criterion: Y Construct: Y
Bulimia Cognitive Distortions Scale	Schulman et al. (1986)	25 items that measure cognitive distortions associated with BN	IC: .97 TR: unknown	Content: Y Criterion: Y Construct: unknown
Eating Questionnaire–Revised	Williamson et al. (1989)	15 items concerning the symptoms of BN	IC: .87 TR 2 week (.90)	Content: Y Criterion: Y Construct: unknown
Bulimic Investigatory Test, Edinburgh	Henderson & Freeman (1987); Waller (1992)	33 items (2 subscales) designed to measure symptoms of BN	IC: symptom (.96) severity (.62) TR: 1 week (.86) 15 week (.68)	Content: Y Criterion: Y Construct: unknown
Mizes Anorectic Cognitions Scale	Mizes (1991); Mizes & Klesges (1989)	33 items (3 subscales) designed to measure cognitions associated with AN and BN	IC: subscales (.75–.89) total (.91) TR: 2 months (.78)	Content: Y Criterion: Y Construct: Y

Note. IC = internal consistency, TR = test–retest reliability, Y = yes, N = no, AN = anorexia nervosa, BN = bulimia nervosa studies of the Eating Disorder Inventory have tested the original eight-factor version; these studies have supported the validity of the scales. The scales most directly concerned with eating behavior and attitudes (drive for thinness, bulimia, and body dissatisfaction) were found to be more highly correlated with other measures of eating disorder symptoms. Other Eating Disorder Inventory scales, which measure general psychopathology, were found to be more highly correlated with criterion measures of general psychopathology. The inventory has been found to distinguish anorexia nervosa from nonclinical subjects as well as distinguishing purging from nonpurging anorexic patients (Garner et al., 1983).

Eating Attitudes Test

The Eating Attitudes Test (Garner & Garfinkel, 1979) is a 40-item self-report inventory designed to assess thoughts and behaviors related to anorexia nervosa. Items are scored on a 6-point Likert-type format ranging from "always" to "never." A 26-item version was developed following factor analysis to eliminate unnecessary items; Eating Attitudes Test and Eating Attitudes Test–26 scores have been found to be highly correlated (Garner, Olmstead, Bohr, & Garfinkel, 1982).

As shown in Table 2, internal consistency of the Eating Attitudes Test has been found to be high (Garner & Garfinkel, 1979). Test–retest reliability has also been shown to be satisfactory (Carter & Moss, 1984). The test has been found to be correlated positively with other self-report measures of eating disorder symptoms (e.g., Gross, Rosen, Leitenberg, & Willmuth, 1986; Henderson & Freeman, 1987; Mizes, 1988). It has also been found to distinguish clinical eating-disordered patients from normal subjects and binge eating patients from anorexic and bulimic patients, but did not differentiate anorexic subjects from bulimic subjects (Williamson, Prather, McKenzie, & Blouin, 1990).

Bulimia Test–Revised

The Bulimia Test–Revised (Thelen, Farmer, Wonderlich, & Smith, 1991) is a 28-item self-report inventory designed to assess the symptoms of bulimia nervosa. Responses are scored on a 5-point rating scale. The revised test (Smith & Thelen, 1984) reflects *DSM-III-R* diagnostic criteria for bulimia nervosa (American Psychiatric Association, 1987). The Bulimia Test and the Bulimia Test–Revised are highly correlated (Thelen et al., 1991).

Most research studies have been conducted with the original version. Thelen et al. (1991) found the revised version to have good internal consistency and good test–retest reliability over a 2-month period. The revised version has been found to be highly correlated with a diagnosis of bulimia nervosa (Thelen et al., 1991). Validity studies have found the original Bulimia Test to correlate highly with other self-report measures of bulimic symptoms, including body image disturbance (Williamson, Anderson, Jackman, & Jackson, 1995).

Setting Conditions for Anorexia Nervosa Scale

The Setting Conditions for Anorexia Nervosa Scale (Slade & Dewey, 1986) is a 40-item self-report inventory designed to measure five constructs that Slade (1982) identified as setting conditions for the development of anorexia nervosa. The following five constructs form the five scales: (a) dissatisfaction and loss of control, (b) social and personal anxiety, (c) perfectionism, (d) adolescent problems, and (e) need for weight control. Items are rated on a 5-point scale. The authors suggested that scores above 42 on the dissatisfaction and loss of control scale or 22 on the perfectionism scale indicated an "at-risk" status for the development of an eating disorder. A computerized version is also available (Butler, Newton, & Slade, 1988).

Internal consistency for the subscales of the Setting Conditions for Anorexia Nervosa Scales has been shown to be satisfactory for both clinical and nonclinical subjects. No test–retest studies have been reported. The scale does not differentiate bulimic from anorexic subjects (Slade & Dewey, 1986).

Bulimia Cognitive Distortions Scale

The Bulimia Cognitive Distortions Scale (Schulman, Kinder, Powers, Prange, & Gleghorn, 1986) is a 25-item self-report inventory developed to assess irrational beliefs and cognitive distortions associated with bulimia nervosa. The items were developed after interviewing bulimic subjects about binge eating, purging, dieting, and concerns about appearance. The items are rated using a 5-point Likert-type scale.

Coefficient alpha has been found to be high. No studies of test–retest reliability have been reported. It has been correlated with other self-report measures of irrational thoughts as well as depression. Schulman et al. (1986) found the scale to both discriminate bulimic individuals from normal individuals and to be correlated with bulimic symptoms.

Eating Questionnaire–Revised

The Eating Questionnaire–Revised (Williamson, Davis, Goreczny, McKenzie, & Watkins, 1989) is a 15-item self-report instrument that was designed as a symptom checklist for bulimia as defined in the *DSM-III* (American Psychiatric Association, 1980). The test assesses both individual symptoms of bulimia (e.g., binge eating, purging, loss of control) and overall severity of a bulimic symptom profile.

Williamson et al. (1989) reported adequate internal consistency and test–retest reliability of the total score and individual items. In a test of predictive validity, Williamson et al. (1989) found that the Eating Questionnaire–Revised total score discriminated subjects with clinical binge eating problems (bulimia nervosa and obese binge eaters) and those without significant binge eating (obese and nonclinical controls). In a test of concurrent validity, total scores were found to be highly correlated with the Bulimia Test and the Eating Attitudes Test.

Bulimic Investigatory Test, Edinburgh

The Bulimic Investigatory Test, Edinburgh (Henderson & Freeman, 1987) is a 33-item self-report instrument developed for the detection and description of binge eating. The instrument yields both symptom and severity subscales. To define bulimia, the authors suggested a cutoff score of 20 for the symptom scale and a cutoff score of 5 on the severity score.

Using a combined clinical and nonclinical sample, Henderson and Freeman (1987) reported high internal consistency coefficients for the symptom subscale but significantly lower internal consistency coefficients for the severity subscale. Test–retest correlations (15-week intervals) were reported to be higher for nonclinical subjects than for bulimic subjects. The Bulimic Investigatory Test has been found to discriminate bulimic patients and normal controls accurately and to correlate significantly with other indices of binge eating (Henderson & Freeman, 1987; Waller, 1992).

Mizes Anorectic Cognitions Questionnaire

The Mizes Anorectic Cognitions Questionnaire (Mizes & Klesges, 1989) is a 33-item questionnaire designed to measure cognitions associated with anorexia and bulimia nervosa. The instrument yields a total score and three empirically derived factors: (a) rigid weight regulation, (b) self-worth and self-control, and (c) weight and approval. The factor structure has been found to be consistent in clinical and nonclinical samples, and internal consistency was found to be adequate in both samples (Mizes & Klesges, 1989; Mizes et al., 1993). In tests of validity, the questionnaire has been found to be strongly correlated with other measures of eating disorder symptoms, irrational thinking, and cognitions associated with binge eating (Mizes, 1991). The scores of patients diagnosed with anorexia nervosa and bulimia nervosa were not found to differ (Mizes, 1991).

MEASURES OF TREATMENT OUTCOME

Many treatment outcome studies have been reported for bulimia nervosa. A survey of these published studies shows considerable diversity in the measures selected to evaluate treatment outcome. For the purpose of reviewing the literature pertaining to this issue, we identified 28 controlled treatment-outcome studies of bulimia nervosa. Table 3 summarizes the outcome measures used in these 28 studies. Measures are listed by name if they were used in at least five studies; otherwise, the measure was categorized as "other." From these data, frequency total and percentages were calculated for the use of each assessment instrument.

In these studies, the frequency of binge eating and purging was measured by a variety of methods, including self-report, self-monitoring of food intake, and unvalidated questionnaires. These measures of treatment outcome were used most frequently (75% and 64%, respectively). From a psychometric perspective, most of these self-report measures have not been shown to have adequate reliability or validity. Body weight was reported as an outcome measure in only 25% of the studies. Ten psychometrically developed questionnaire measures of eating disorder symptoms were found to have been used in these 28 studies. Of these, the Eating Attitudes Test was used in 14 studies and the Eating Disorder Inventory was used in 11 studies. Other measures were selected for use in 2 or fewer studies. One of the dangers of using unvalidated measures of binge eating is the subjectivity used by subjects in defining *binge*. For example, the term *binge* can have several meanings—for example, eating an objectively large amount of food or eating only a subjectively large amount of food (Williamson et al., 1991). Cooper and Fairburn (1987) developed the Eating Disorder Examination to develop more objective measures of binge eating. (As noted earlier, this examination was developed for the purpose of evaluating treatment outcome.) It defines binge eating using four descriptions of overeating; no other measure of binge eating allows for this level of specificity. As noted earlier, the Eating Disorder Examination has undergone extensive psychometric development. Yet, we found only 5 of 28 studies selected it as a measure of treatment outcome.

In most of these studies, other psychopathological symptoms were also measured. The Beck Depression Inventory (Beck & Beamesderfer, 1974) and Hamilton Rating Scale–Depression (Hamilton, 1960) were the most frequently selected indices of depression (57% and 25%, respectively). In five other studies, depression was assessed using other measures. The Rosenberg Self-Esteem Scale (Rosenberg, 1979) was used in 28% of the studies and the Symptom Checklist-90 or SCL-90-R (Derogatis, 1977) was used in 23% of the studies. In 20 of the 28 studies, general psychopathology was evaluated using a diverse set of measures. From this review, it is clear that the measurement of treatment outcome for bulimia nervosa has used

TABLE 3

Summary of Treatment Outcome Measures for Bulimia Nervosa

Author(s)	Measures of Eating Disorder Symptoms							Measures of Other Symptoms					
	Frequency of binging	Frequency of purging	EDE	EAT	EDI	wt	Other eating	HSD	BDI	Other dep	RSS	SCL-90	Other
Lacy (1983)	X	X				X				X			X
Pope et al. (1983)	X	X					X	X					X
Walsh et al. (1984)	X	X		X			X	X	X				X
Yates & Sambrillo (1984)	X	X		X								X	X
Kirkley et al. (1985)	X	X		X	X		X		X	X			X
Hughes et al. (1986)	X	X			X								X
Fairburn et al. (1986)	X	X		X		X	X			X			X
Lee & Rush (1986)	X	X						X	X			X	X
Wilson et al. (1986)	X	X				X	X					X	X
Wolchik et al. (1986)	X	X					X		X		X		
Agras et al. (1987)	X	X		X									
Freeman et al. (1988)	X	X		X	X		X	X		X	X	X	
Horne et al. (1988)		X				X							
Leitenberg et al. (1988)	X	X		X	X		X		X				X
Walsh et al. (1988)				X	X			X	X			X	
Agras et al. (1989)	X	X		X	X			X	X				X
Mitchell et al. (1990)	X	X			X			X	X				X
Pyle et al. (1990)	X												
Fairburn et al. (1991)			X				X		X				X
Laessle et al. (1991)	X	X		X			X						X
Wilson et al. (1991)			X				X	X	X		X	X	X
Agras et al. (1992)	X			X	X	X	X		X	X			X
Kettlewell et al. (1992)	X	X		X	X		X		X			X	X
Wolf & Crowther, (1992)	X		X				X		X		X	X	X
Fairburn, Jones, et al. (1993)			X				X		X		X	X	X
Fairburn, Peveler, et al. (1993)			X				X		X		X	X	X
Garner et al. (1993)				X	X							X	
Thackwray et al. (1993)	X			X	X				X				
Total (percent)	21 (75)	18 (64)	5 (18)	14 (50)	11 (39)	5 (18)	16 (57)	8 (29)	16 (57)	5 (18)	6 (21)	11 (39)	20 (71)

Note. EDE = Eating Disorder Examination; EAT = Eating Attitudes Test (original or 26 question revision); EDI = Eating Disorders Inventory; Other eating = other self-report eating measures; HSD = Hamilton Rating Scale-Depression (Hamilton, 1960); BDI = Beck Depression Inventory; Other dep = other depression measures; RSS = Rosenberg Self-Esteem Scale (Rosenberg, 1979); SCL-90 = original Symptom Checklist-90 (Derogatis, 1977) or revision; Other = other measures of secondary psychopathology, global rating scales. When a measure was reported in a study, its use is designated by an X.

a wide variety of measures across investigations. As a result, it is difficult to compare outcomes across studies—for example, through the use of meta-analysis.

CONCLUSION

Of the structured interviews that have been developed to assess anorexia nervosa and bulimia nervosa, the Eating Disorder Examination is most highly developed. There is a strong need for an interview method that yields reliable diagnoses based on *DSM-IV* diagnostic criteria (American Psychiatric Association, 1994). The addition of restricting and binge–purge subtypes to the diagnostic nomenclature for anorexia nervosa and purging and nonpurging subtypes for bulimia nervosa represent substantial changes in diagnostic procedures based on *DSM-III-R* criteria (American Psychiatric Association, 1987). Also, there is no established interview method for diagnosing binge eating disorder, a provisional diagnostic category in *DSM-IV*. Current psychometric research on the Interview for Diagnosis of Eating Disorders–IV is designed to address these research needs.

Psychometric research for the Eating Disorder Inventory–2, the Eating Attitudes Test, and the Bulimia Test–R is quite advanced. Research on the other measures reviewed in this chapter is limited to a few research reports. We believe that there is still a need for a relatively brief self-report inventory that assesses the central features of anorexia nervosa and bulimia nervosa. On the basis of factor analytic studies of the symptoms of anorexia nervosa and bulimia nervosa (Gleaves & Eberenz, 1993; Gleaves, Williamson, & Barker, 1993; Tobin, Johnson, Steinberg, Staats, & Dennis, 1991), the central features of anorexia nervosa and bulimia nervosa are (a) negative affect, (b) dietary restraint, (c) bulimic behaviors, and (d) body image disturbance. There is also a need for psychometric research in the development of a relatively brief treatment outcome measure that assesses these same four factors. In principle, interviews such as the Interview for Diagnosis of Eating Disorders–IV or the Eating Disorder Examination 12.00 might be developed for this purpose. However, we feel that a self-report inventory with these scales might receive more widespread usage than a structured interview.

REFERENCES

Agras, W. S., Dorian, B., Kirkley, B. G., Arnow, B., & Bachman, J. (1987). Imipramine in the treatment of bulimia: A double-blind controlled study. *International Journal of Eating Disorders, 6,* 29–38.

Agras, W. S., Rossiter, E. M., Arnow, B., Schneider, J. A., Telch, C. F., Raeburn, S. D., Bruce, B., Perl, M., & Koran, L. M. (1992). Pharmacologic and cognitive–behavioral treatment for bulimia nervosa: A controlled comparison. *American Journal of Psychiatry, 149*, 82–87.

Agras, W. S., Schneider, J. A., Arnow, B., Raeburn, S. D., & Telch, C. F. (1989). Cognitive–behavioral and response–prevention treatments for bulimia nervosa. *Journal of Consulting and Clinical Psychology, 57*, 215–221.

American Psychiatric Association. (1980). *Diagnostic and statistical manual of mental disorders* (3rd ed.). Washington, DC: Author.

American Psychiatric Association. (1987). *Diagnostic and statistical manual of mental disorders* (3rd ed., rev.). Washington, DC: Author.

American Psychiatric Association. (1994). *Diagnostic and statistical manual of mental disorders* (4th ed.). Washington, DC: Author.

Beck, A. T., & Beamesderfer, A. (1974). Assessment of depression: The depression inventory. In P. Pichot (Ed.), *Psychological measurements in psychopharmacology. Modern problems in pharmacopsychiatry, Vol. 7*. Paris: Karger, Basel.

Butler, N., Newton, T., & Slade, P. D. (1988). Validation of a computerized version of the SCANS questionnaire. *International Journal of Eating Disorders, 8*, 239–241.

Carter, P. I., & Moss, R. A. (1984). Screening for anorexia and bulimia nervosa in a college population: Problems and limitations. *Addictive Behaviors, 9*, 417–419.

Cooper, Z., & Fairburn, C. G. (1987). The Eating Disorder Examination: A semistructured interview for the assessment of the specific psychopathology of eating disorders. *International Journal of Eating Disorders, 6*, 1–8.

Crocker, L., & Algina, J. (1986). *Introduction to classical and modern test theory.* New York: Holt, Rinehart and Winston.

Crowther, J. H., Lilly, R. S., Crawford, P. A., Shepherd, K. L., & Olivier, L. L. (1990, August). *The stability of the Eating Disorder Inventory.* Paper presented at the Annual Meeting of the American Psychological Association, Boston, MA.

Derogatis, L. R. (1977). *SCL-90 administration, scoring, and procedures manual-I.* Baltimore: Johns Hopkins University Press.

Eberenz, K. P., & Gleaves, D. H. (in press). An examination of the internal consistency and factor structure of the Eating Disorder Inventory-2 in a clinical sample. *International Journal of Eating Disorders.*

Fairburn, C. G., & Cooper, Z. (1993). The Eating Disorder Examination (12th ed.). In C. G. Fairburn & G. T. Wilson (Eds.), *Binge eating: Nature, assessment, and treatment* (pp. 3–14). New York: Guilford Press.

Fairburn, C. G., Jones, R., Peveler, R. C., Carr, S. J., Solomon, R. A., O'Connor, M., Burton, J., & Hope, R. A. (1991). Three psychological treatments for bulimia nervosa. *Archives of General Psychiatry, 48*, 463–469.

Fairburn, C. G., Jones, R., Peveler, R. C., Hope, R. A., & O'Connor, M. (1993). Psychotherapy and bulimia nervosa. *Archives of General Psychiatry, 50,* 419–428.

Fairburn, C. G., Kirk, J., O'Connor, M., & Cooper, P. J. (1986). A comparison of two psychological treatments for bulimia nervosa. *Behaviour Research and Therapy, 24,* 629–643.

Fairburn, C. G., Peveler, R. C., Jones, R., Hope, R. A., & Doll, H. A. (1993). Predictors of 12-month outcome in bulimia nervosa and the influence of attitudes to shape and weight. *Journal of Consulting and Clinical Psychology, 61,* 696–698.

Fichter, M. M., Elton, M., Engel, K., Meyer, A., Poutska, F., Mall, H., & von der Heydte, S. (1989). The structured interview for anorexia and bulimia nervosa (SIAB): Development and characteristics of a (semi-) standardized instrument. In M. N. Fichter (Ed.), *Bulimia nervosa: Basic research, diagnosis, and therapy* (pp. 57–70). New York: Wiley.

Freeman, C. P. L., Barry, F., Dunkeld-Turnbull, J., & Henderson, A. (1988). Controlled trial of psychotherapy for bulimia nervosa. *British Medical Journal, 296,* 521–525.

Garner, D. M. (1991). *Eating Disorder Inventory-2 manual.* Odessa, FL: Psychological Assessment Resources.

Garner, D. M., & Garfinkel, P. E. (1979). The Eating Attitudes Test: An index of the symptoms of anorexia nervosa. *Psychological Medicine, 9,* 273–279.

Garner, D. M., Olmsted, M. P., Bohr, Y., & Garfinkel, P. E. (1982). The Eating Attitudes Test: Psychometric features and clinical correlates. *Psychological Medicine, 12,* 871–878.

Garner, D. M., Olmsted, M. P., & Polivy, J. (1983). Development and validation of a multidimensional eating disorder inventory for anorexia nervosa and bulimia. *International Journal of Eating Disorders, 2,* 15–34.

Garner, D. M., Rockert, W., Davis, R., Garner, M. V., Olmsted, M. P., & Eagle, M. (1993). Comparison of cognitive–behavioral and supportive–expressive therapy for bulimia nervosa. *American Journal of Psychiatry, 150,* 37–46.

Gleaves, D. H., & Eberenz, K. (1993). The psychopathology of anorexia nervosa: A factor analytic investigation. *Journal of Psychopathology and Behavioral Assessment, 15,* 141–152.

Gleaves, D. H., Williamson, D. A., & Barker, S. E. (1993). Confirmatory factor analysis of a multidimensional model of bulimia nervosa. *Journal of Abnormal Psychology, 102,* 173–176.

Gross, J., Rosen, J. C., Leitenberg, H., & Willmuth, M. (1986). Validity of Eating Attitudes Test and the Eating Disorders Inventory in bulimia nervosa. *Journal of Consulting and Clinical Psychology, 54,* 875–876.

Hamilton, M. (1960). A rating scale for depression. *Journal of Neurology, Neurosurgery, and Psychiatry, 23,* 56–62.

Henderson, M., & Freeman, C. P. L. (1987). A self-rating scale for bulimia: The 'BITE.' *British Journal of Psychiatry, 150,* 18–24.

Horne, R. L., Ferguson, J. M., Pope, H. G., Hudson, J. I., Lineberry, C. G., Ascher, J., & Cato, A. (1988). Treatment of bulimia with bupropion: A multicenter controlled trial. *Journal of Clinical Psychiatry, 49,* 262–266.

Hughes, P. L., Wells, L. A., Cunningham, C. J., & Ilstrup, D. M. (1986). Treating bulimia with desipramine. A double-blind, placebo controlled study. *Archives of General Psychiatry, 43,* 182–186.

Kettlewell, P. W., Mizes, J. S., & Wasylyshyn, N. A. (1992). A cognitive–behavioral group treatment for bulimia. *Behavior Therapy, 23,* 657–670.

Kirkley, B. G., Schneider, J. A., Agras, W. S., & Bachman, J. A. (1985). Comparison of two group treatments for bulimia. *Journal of Consulting and Clinical Psychology, 53,* 43–48.

Lacy, H. (1983). Bulimia nervosa, binge eating, and psychogenic vomiting: A controlled treatment study and long term outcome. *British Medical Journal, 286,* 1609–1613.

Laessle, R. G., Beumont, P. J. V., Butow, P., Lennerts, W., O'Connor, M., Pirke, K. M., Touyz, S. W., & Waadt, S. (1991). A comparison of nutritional management with stress management in the treatment of bulimia nervosa. *British Journal of Psychiatry, 159,* 250–261.

Landis, J. R., & Koch, G. C. (1977). The measurement of observer agreement for categorical data. *Biometrics, 33,* 159–174.

Lee, N. F., & Rush, A. J. (1986). Cognitive–behavioral group therapy for bulimia. *International Journal of Eating Disorders, 5,* 599–615.

Leitenberg, H., Rosen, J. C., Gross, J., Nudelman, S., & Vara, L. S. (1988). Exposure plus response prevention treatment for bulimia nervosa. *Journal of Consulting and Clinical Psychology, 56,* 535–541.

Mitchell, J. E., Pyle, R. L., Eckert, E. D., Hatsukami, D., Pomeroy, C., & Zimmerman, R. (1990). A comparison study of antidepressants and structured intensive group psychotherapy in the treatment of bulimia nervosa. *Archives of General Psychiatry, 47,* 149–157.

Mizes, J. S. (1988). Personality characteristics of bulimic and non-eating disordered female controls: A cognitive behavioral perspective. *International Journal of Eating Disorders, 7,* 541–550.

Mizes, J. S. (1991). Construct validity and factor stability of the anorectic cognitions questionnaire. *Addictive Behaviors, 16,* 89–93.

Mizes, J. S., Chrisitano, B. A., Madison, J., Post, G., Seime, R., & Varnado, P. (1993, November). *Psychometric properties and factor structure of the Mizes Anorectic Cognition Questionnaire in a large sample of eating disorder patients.* Paper presented at the annual meeting of the Association for Advancement of Behavior Therapy, Atlanta, GA.

Mizes, J. S., & Klesges, R. C. (1989). Validity, reliability, and factor structure of the anorectic cognitions questionnaire. *Addictive Behaviors, 14,* 589–594.

Palmer, R., Christie, M., Cordle, C., Davies, D., & Kenrick, J. (1987). The Clinical Eating Disorder Instrument (CEDRI): A preliminary description. *International Journal of Eating Disorders, 6,* 9–16.

Pope, H. G., Hudson, J. T., Jonas, J. M., & Yurgelun-Todd, D. (1983). Bulimia treated with imipramine: A placebo-controlled, double-blind trial. *American Journal of Psychiatry, 140,* 554–558.

Pyle, R. L., Mitchell, J. E., Eckert, E. D., Hasukami, D., Pomeroy, C., & Zimmerman, R. (1990). Maintenance treatment and 6-month outcome for bulimic patients who respond to initial treatment. *American Journal of Psychiatry, 147,* 871–875.

Rosenberg, M. (1979). *Conceiving the self.* New York: Basic Books.

Schlundt, D. G. (1989). Assessment of eating behavior in bulimia nervosa: The self-monitoring analysis system. In W. Johnson (Ed.), *Advances in Eating Disorders* (Vol. 2, pp. 1–41). Greenwich, CT: JAI Press.

Schlundt, D. G., Johnson, W. G., & Jarrell, M. P. (1985). A naturalistic functional analysis of eating behavior in bulimia and obesity. *Advances in Behaviour Research and Therapy, 7,* 149–162.

Schlundt, D. G., Johnson, W. G., & Jarrell, M. P. (1986). A sequential analysis of environmental, behavioral, and affective variables predictive of vomiting in bulimia nervosa. *Behavioral Assessment, 8,* 253–269.

Schulman, R. G., Kinder, B. N., Powers, P. S., Prange, M., & Gleghorn, A. (1986). The development of a scale to measure cognitive distortions in bulimia. *Journal of Personality Assessment, 50,* 630–639.

Shrout, P. E., & Fleiss, J. L. (1979). Intraclass correlations: Uses in assessing rater reliability. *Psychological Bulletin, 86,* 420–428.

Slade, P. D. (1982). Towards a functional analysis of anorexia nervosa and bulimia nervosa. *British Journal of Clinical Psychology, 21,* 67–79.

Slade, P. D., & Dewey, M. E. (1986). Development and preliminary validation of SCANS: A screening instrument for identifying individuals at risk of developing anorexia and bulimia nervosa. *International Journal of Eating Disorders, 5,* 517–538.

Smith, M. C., & Thelen, M. H. (1984). Development and validation of a test for bulimia. *Journal of Consulting and Clinical Psychology, 52,* 863–872.

Standards for educational and psychological testing. (1985). Washington, DC: American Psychological Association.

Thackwray, D. E., Smith, M. E., Bodfish, J. W., & Meyers, A. M. (1993). A comparison of behavioral and cognitive–behavioral interventions for bulimia nervosa. *Journal of Consulting and Clinical Psychology, 61,* 639–645.

Thelen, M. H., Farmer, J., Wonderlich, S., & Smith, S. (1991). A revision of the Bulimia Test: The BULIT-R. *Psychological Assessment, 3,* 119–124.

Tobin, D. L., Johnson, C., Steinberg, S., Staats, M., & Dennis, A. B. (1991). Multifactorial assessment of bulimia nervosa. *Journal of Abnormal Psychology, 100,* 14–21.

Waller, G. (1992). Bulimic attitudes in different eating disorders: Clinical utility of the BITE. *International Journal of Eating Disorders, 11,* 73–78.

Walsh, B. T., Gladis, M., Roose, S. P., Stewart, J. W., Stetner, F., & Glassman, A. H. (1988). Phenelzine vs. placebo in 50 patients with bulimia. *Archives of General Psychiatry, 45,* 471–475.

Walsh, B. T., Stewart, J. W., Roose, S. P., Gladis, M., & Glassman, A. H. (1984). Treatment of bulimia with phenelzine. A double-blind, placebo-controlled study. *Archives of General Psychiatry, 41,* 1105–1109.

Wear, R. W., & Pratz, O. (1987). Test–retest reliability for the Eating Disorder Inventory. *International Journal of Eating Disorders, 6,* 767–769.

Welch, G. (1988). *Selected multivariate statistical techniques and eating disorders.* Unpublished doctoral dissertation, University of Otago, New Zealand.

Williamson, D. A. (1990). *Assessment of eating disorders: Obesity, anorexia, and bulimia nervosa.* New York: Pergamon Press.

Williamson, D. A., Anderson, D. A., Jackman, L. P., & Jackson, S. R. (1995). Assessment of eating disordered thoughts, feelings, and behaviors. In D. B. Allison (Ed.), *Methods for the assessment of eating behaviors and weight related problems* (pp. 347–386). Newbury Park, CA: Sage.

Williamson, D. A., Davis, C. J., Goreczny, A. J., McKenzie, S. J., & Watkins, P. C. (1989). The Eating Questionnaire-Revised: A symptom checklist for bulimia. In P. A. Keller & L. G. Ritt (Eds.), *Innovations in clinical practice: A source book* (pp. 321–326). Sarasota, FL: Professional Resource Press.

Williamson, D. A., Davis, C. J., Norris, L., & Van Buren, D. J. (1990, November). *Development of reliability and validity for a new structured interview for diagnosis of eating disorders.* Paper presented at the annual meeting of the Association for the Advancement of Behavior Therapy, San Francisco.

Williamson, D. A., Gleaves, D. H., & Lawson, O. J. (1991). Biased perception of overeating in bulimia nervosa and compulsive binge eaters. *Journal of Psychopathology and Behavioral Assessment, 13,* 257–268.

Williamson, D. A., Prather, R. C., McKenzie, S. J., & Blouin, D.C. (1990). Behavioral assessment procedures can differentiate bulimia nervosa, compulsive overeater, obese, and normal subjects. *Behavioral Assessment, 12,* 239–252.

Wilson, G. T., Eldredge, K. L., Smith, D., & Niles, B. (1991). Cognitive–behavioral treatment with and without response prevention for bulimia. *Behaviour Research and Therapy, 29,* 575–583.

Wilson, G. T., Rossiter, E., Kleifeld, E. I., & Lindholm, L. (1986). Cognitive–behavioral treatment of bulimia nervosa: A controlled evaluation. *Behaviour Research and Therapy, 24,* 277–288.

Wolchik, S. A., Weiss, L., & Katzman, M. A. (1986). An empirically validated, short-term psychoeducational group treatment for bulimia. *International Journal of Eating Disorders, 5,* 21–34.

Wolf, E. M., & Crowther, J. H. (1992). An evaluation of behavioral and cognitive–behavioral group interventions for the treatment of bulimia nervosa in women. *International Journal of Eating Disorders, 11,* 3–15.

Yates, A. J., & Sambrillo, F. (1984). Bulimia nervosa: A descriptive and therapeutic study. *Behaviour Research and Therapy, 22,* 503–517.

10

STEPPED-CARE AND DECISION-TREE MODELS FOR TREATING EATING DISORDERS

DAVID M. GARNER and LAWRENCE D. NEEDLEMAN

In a clinical setting, the process for deciding (a) which treatment should be offered to which patient and (b) under what conditions the treatment plan should be altered bears little resemblance to the typical research paradigm used to study treatment efficacy. Clinicians randomly allocate patients to two or more treatment conditions in controlled research studies. Moreover, controlled research is designed to deliver treatments in a carefully standardized manner, avoiding any alteration in the treatment protocol (usually manualized) that might accommodate the special needs of an individual patient. Clinicians avoid any unintentional blending of treatment components because it potentially renders findings meaningless, or worse, leads to possible costly false conclusions. Thus, practitioners take meticulous care to avoid altering the content, duration, and frequency of therapy sessions unless this is explicitly specified in advance in the treatment manual. Ideally, following the delivery of the standardized treatments, there is a follow-up period during which no additional treatment is provided. This allows the clinician to assess the durability of changes associated with treatment. In short, in research studies, deviations from the treatment protocol are strongly discouraged in favor of the systematic application of a standardized and time-limited treatment package.

Portions of this chapter were drawn from Garner and Needleman (in press).

Without these careful controls, the results of the treatment comparison studies are open to bias and the results are at best uninterpretable. Some admonish that conducting such methodologically flawed studies is unethical (Rosenthal, 1994).

Although the research model addresses the important question of which treatment is best for most patients, it differs markedly from the clinical approach aimed at initially offering the treatment of choice with little resistance to later modifying, adapting, or combining treatments based on clinical judgment and response to treatment. Often, factors such as the clinical training and orientation of the therapist, the nature of the facility (e.g., inpatient versus outpatient or residential), or third-party reimbursement determine the mode of treatment.

In the past decade, there have been remarkable advancements in the technology of treatment for eating disorders, allowing a clearer delineation of available treatment options. It has also led to speculations that either a stepped-care or a decision-tree approach using particular algorithms for the delivery of the various treatment options may optimize overall treatment (Agras, 1993; Fairburn, Agras, & Wilson, 1992; Fairburn & Peveler, 1990; Garner, Garfinkel, & Irvine, 1986; Tiller, Schmidt, & Treasure, 1993). The term *stepped-care* has been used in different contexts in this emergent literature. For the purpose of our review of the literature and discussion, we would like to distinguish between different multifaceted models for treatment delivery.

The *stepped-care approach* involves ordering empirically or logically derived interventions into graded levels or steps based on their intrusiveness, cost, and probability of success. Initially, a patient is provided with the lowest step intervention—one that is least intrusive, dangerous, and costly. However, the lowest step intervention may not have the highest probability of success. If the first-level intervention fails, then the second step on the treatment hierarchy is provided, either in place of or in combination with the previous intervention, and so on until the patient responds favorably.

The *decision-tree approach* provides numerous choice points that result in a number of paths for treatment to follow, depending on the clinical features of the patient and response to each treatment delivered. Several key factors may be considered at each juncture in the decision-tree approach in arriving at the final treatment of choice. For example, the first question the clinician may ask is, "Is the patient in acute medical danger?" If the answer is "yes," the patient is referred to an inpatient program. If the answer is "no," then the clinician asks, "Is the patient 18 or younger and living at home?" If the answer is "yes," the patient is referred to family therapy. If the answer is "no," the patient is referred to individual therapy, and so on. The decision-tree approach follows more closely the clinical application of treatments but has not been the subject of empirical research in the area of eating disorders.

These more complex approaches can be contrasted with the *best shot intervention approach*, which involves initially implementing the intervention that is thought to be most effective, regardless of intrusiveness or cost. At this time, proposals for integrating and sequencing different forms of treatment have been made exclusively on rational grounds; the efficacy of the stepped-care and decision-tree models have not been empirically tested in the area of eating disorders. This is a result, in part, of the formidable practical and theoretical impediments to a research protocol that would have to be developed to test the stepped-care and decision-tree models. We will discuss these impediments and possible directions for research later. Nevertheless, limited clinical resources and pressures for containing health costs are powerful incentives to develop cost-effective treatment programs in which the most expensive procedures (e.g., inpatient treatment) are reserved for the most seriously ill patients or those who fail to respond to more conservative approaches.

This chapter reviews the literature on stepped-care and decision-tree approaches applied to the treatment of eating disorders. This is followed by a flowchart illustrating the treatment decision-making process as well as a brief overview of the major treatment options for treating eating disorders.

STEPPED-CARE AND DECISION-TREE APPROACHES

As indicated earlier, delineation of which treatments should be applied initially to which subgroups of patients and which treatments should be employed if initial efforts fail has received only minimal discussion in the literature on eating disorders. In an early, uncontrolled study of cognitive–behavioral therapy for bulimia nervosa, Giles, Young, and Young (1985) found that brief cognitive–behavioral therapy was beneficial for the majority of patients but that there was a subgroup of recalcitrant patients who were exposed to a succession of procedures over a longer duration. Those patients who failed to benefit were moved to the next stage of treatment. The graded steps included (a) training a significant other to supervise in vivo exposure between sessions, (b) having an experienced therapist supervise two cafeteria meals a week, (c) introducing tricyclic antidepressants, and (d) recommending hospitalization. One of the six recalcitrant patients responded well, and three showed moderate improvement with this regimen.

Garner et al., (1986) proposed the integration and sequencing of different forms of treatment for eating disorders, which combined elements from both the stepped-care and decision-tree models. This proposal was based on the belief that there should be a progression from the least complicated and intrusive approaches to those that are more disruptive, costly, or carry greater risks. The authors recommended an educational approach as the initial intervention for the least disturbed bulimia nervosa patients and as an adjunct to treatment to other eating-disordered patients, including those with anorexia nervosa. They recommended family therapy as the primary treatment modality if the patient was 18 years old or younger and living at home. They considered pharmacotherapy as an option in bulimia nervosa (not anorexia nervosa) when patients failed to respond to psychosocial treatments. For patients with serious medical complications or for those who needed to gain substantial body weight, the authors recommended inpatient treatment as the initial intervention. Finally, they recommended day treatment as a cost-effective alternative for many patients who did not require hospitalization. Day treatment programs can provide structure around mealtimes as well as intensive therapy, without requiring the patient to become totally disengaged from the supports and the therapeutic challenges outside of the hospital. It also can facilitate the transition between inpatient and outpatient care.

The integration and sequencing model involves decision making at each step, guided by considerations such as: (a) age of the patient; (b) current living arrangements; (c) duration of the disorder; (d) current symptomatology (presence of binge eating, vomiting, or purgative abuse; stable or unstable weight; deteriorating symptom picture); (e) previous treatments; (f) premorbid functioning with particular reference to depression, problems with impulse control, and personality disorders; and (g) medical condition including, but not limited to, degree of weight loss and electrolyte disturbances. Although the model proposed by Garner et al. (1986) represents an early attempt to articulate the decision-making process in delivering different forms of treatment for anorexia nervosa and bulimia nervosa, it lacks clear criteria for determining how patients would be reliably allocated to different treatment options. Thus, it is difficult to see how it could be tested empirically.

Fairburn and Peveler (1990) briefly outlined a stepped-care approach in managing bulimia nervosa patients that consists of five levels. These are (a) self-help or written materials; (b) dietary education and advice, perhaps in a group setting; (c) antidepressant drug treatment (Desipramine or Fluoxetine) in combination with advice and support; (d) outpatient cognitive–behavioral treatment, and (e) day or inpatient care with subsequent outpatient treatment. Fairburn et al. (1992) proposed a similar model for managing bulimia nervosa that did not include antidepressant drugs "because their position in the scheme is debatable" (p. 334). The model by Fairburn and colleagues (Figure 1) is novel because it formally introduces the use of supervised self-help, which is potentially more efficient than a

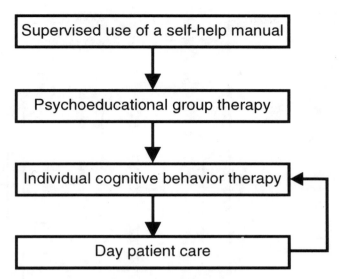

```
┌─────────────────────────────────────────┐
│  Supervised use of a self-help manual   │
└─────────────────────────────────────────┘
                    │
                    ▼
┌─────────────────────────────────────────┐
│    Psychoeducational group therapy      │
└─────────────────────────────────────────┘
                    │
                    ▼
┌─────────────────────────────────────────┐
│  Individual cognitive behavior therapy  │◄─┐
└─────────────────────────────────────────┘  │
                    │                         │
                    ▼                         │
┌─────────────────────────────────────────┐  │
│             Day patient care            │──┘
└─────────────────────────────────────────┘
```

Figure 1. A stepped-care program for managing bulimia nervosa. Antidepressant drugs have not been included in the program because their position in the scheme is debatable. They perhaps should be placed after cognitive–behavior therapy but used only with those patients with severe depressive symptoms (adapted from Fairburn, Agras, & Wilson, 1992, p. 334).

professionally delivered psychoeducational treatment. However, the reasoning behind including supervised self-help, for which there are no supportive data, and excluding drug treatments on the basis of debatable findings, is not explained.

Agras (1993) described a decision-tree model for the treatment of binge eating (Figure 2) that is more precise than earlier recommendations. However, the rationale for choice points on the decision tree may not be flexible enough to address the clinical needs of the heterogeneous patient population. According to this model, patients are assigned to psychoeducational treatment if their symptoms are mild to moderate. If their binge eating is severe, they are either assigned to cognitive–behavioral therapy or interpersonal psychotherapy depending on whether dietary or interpersonal problems predominate. The initial decision to allocate patients to psychoeducational treatment or a more intensive individual therapy is justified on the basis of one study (Olmsted et al., 1991). Although the decision to assign patients to either cognitive–behavioral therapy or interpersonal psychotherapy on the basis of principal symptoms being either interpersonal or dietary has intuitive appeal, there is no empirical evidence that these treatments are differentially effective based on these clinical features. Finally, the Agras (1993) model allocated obese patients who become *abstinent from binge eating* to *weight loss treatment,* a point that remains controversial (Garner & Wooley, 1991).

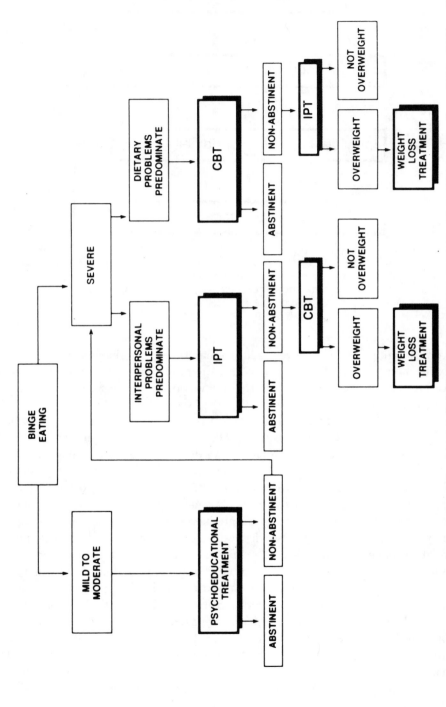

Figure 2. A flow chart illustrating a hypothetical comprehensive model of the psychological treatment of binge eating (from Agras, 1993, p. 282).

Tiller et al. (1993) outlined a stepped-care program that is similar to those presented earlier. They divided the model into five phases, adding additional treatments if patients failed to respond or if they showed only partial improvement. The first step involved minimal interventions such as psychoeducation, bibliotherapy, or referral to self-help groups. The second step involved providing the standard cognitive–behavioral therapy for bulimia nervosa. For those who fail to respond to cognitive–behavior therapy, the third step, antidepressant medication, was recommended. For those who failed to respond to the earlier treatments, cognitive–analytical therapy (Ryle, 1990) or interpersonal therapy (Klerman, Weissman, Rounsaville, & Chevron, 1984) was recommended. Finally, for those who failed to respond to earlier interventions or who presented with a medical or psychiatric crisis, inpatient or day treatment programs were recommended. Thus, the model presented by Tiller et al., (1993), actually followed earlier recommendations by combining elements of the stepped-care and the decision-tree models.

MAJOR TREATMENT OPTIONS

Although these models have clinical appeal, they are incomplete because they do not fully capture the clinical process by which different treatment options are considered. Most of the proposed stepped-care and decision-tree models for eating disorders have made provisions for bulimia nervosa but fail to include provisions for anorexia nervosa. Moreover, they do present all of the major treatment options that would be considered by most knowledgeable clinicians in the treatment decision-making process. Figure 3 is an attempt at a comprehensive decision-tree model that more clearly delineates the choice points and the options in the decision-making process in the treatment of eating disorders. It does not include all treatment options available but concentrates on those for which there is good clinical or empirical support. With this in mind, we will briefly discuss the main options and the considerations relevant to their use in a decision-tree model of treatment delivery.

Inpatient Treatment

The first major treatment consideration is whether or not the patient is in sufficient medical danger that hospitalization needs to be considered (see Figure 3). The topic of inpatient treatment for anorexia nervosa and bulimia nervosa is extraordinarily complex, beyond the scope of this overview, and has been addressed in detail elsewhere (e.g., Andersen, 1985; Garfinkel and Garner, 1982; Garner & Sackeyfio, 1993). Nevertheless, it is critical for the clinician involved in managing eating disorders to be

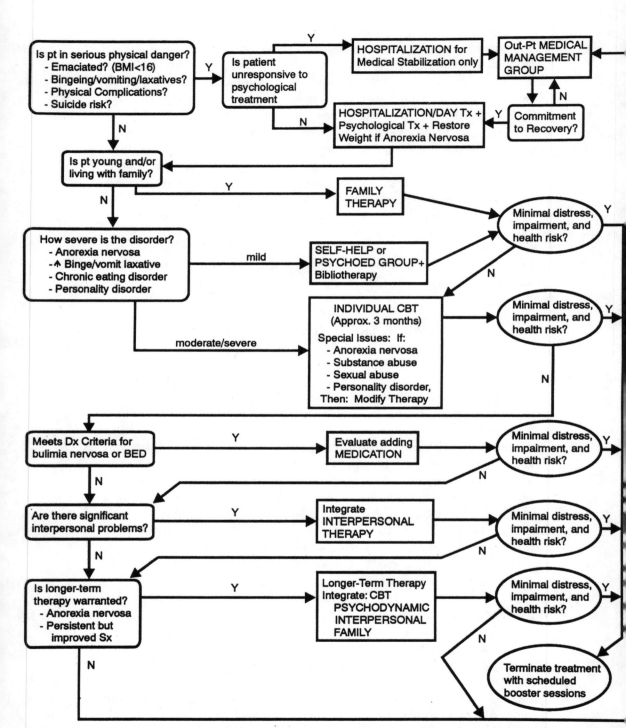

Figure 3. Decision tree illustrating the general guidelines for integration and sequencing major treatment options for eating-disordered patients (from Garner & Needleman, in press).

aware that a subgroup of patients may require or benefit from hospitalization. The primary objectives of hospitalization are (a) weight restoration or interruption of steady weight loss, (b) interruption of unremitting bingeing and vomiting, (c) treatment of medical complications, (d) management of associated conditions such as severe depression or substance abuse, and (e) at times the disengagement of patients from a social system that both contributes to the maintenance of the disorder and disrupts outpatient treatment. When the goal of hospitalization is to treat medical complications, this should be clearly distinguished from inpatient treatment aimed at recovery from the eating disorder (Figure 3). When directed strictly toward treating medical complications, it should be presented as an urgent medical priority that does not necessarily require a strong commitment by the patient to recover. If hospitalization is intended to treat the psychological as well as the physical aspects of the disorder, every effort should be made to enlist the patient's commitment to participate actively in the treatment process. Preadmission interviews should include a clear description of the program aimed at normalization of eating and weight as well as other details regarding the ward regime. Patients should be reassured that they will receive psychotherapy both during the period of hospitalization and thereafter to assist them in dealing with their concerns regarding eating and weight, as well as to address psychological issues that may be unique to them. This approach will reduce the likelihood that patients will prematurely discharge themselves from the hospital.

Hospitalization may be a prerequisite to recovery if an adequate trial of outpatient therapy fails to lead to a steady reduction in bingeing and vomiting or appropriate weight restoration. Patients may perceive the recommendation for hospitalization as a threat or as abandonment, but they should be reassured that it is a humane alternative to the tremendous emotional and financial expense of prolonged and unproductive outpatient therapy that cannot progress in the presence of the severe limits imposed by dietary chaos or starvation.

Day Treatment

Day treatment is a viable alternative to hospitalization for many patients. There are various models for day treatment programs, and they generally have many features in common with inpatient programs. The major difference is that patients receive the therapeutic services that the treatment program has to offer but do not stay overnight. This is adequate for most patients with eating disorders. However, for those who are at serious risk of self-harm, inpatient programs are still necessary to provide a protective environment. As with inpatient programs, day care programs can be structured so that they are oriented exclusively toward eating-disordered patients or so that they provide care for patients with different diagnoses.

Day treatment programs provide needed structure during meal times and evenings when many eating-disordered patients are most vulnerable to binge eating or other eating disorder symptoms. Day programs also allow the patient the flexibility to work or attend school while still receiving intensive treatment. Thus, the programs minimize the disruptive aspects of hospital confinement and allow the gradual reintroduction of normal living at a pace that meets the individual needs of patients. Day programs differ tremendously in the number of days and number of hours per day that treatment is offered, so the decision to implement day care will be greatly influenced by whether the available services can meet the needs of the particular patient. Finally, day programs have the distinct advantage of being more economical than inpatient care.

Medical Management Groups for Chronic Patients

It may be that some chronic or recalcitrant patients simply reach the point, after multiple treatment failures, that they no longer want treatment for their eating disorder or they believe that treatment has a very low probability of success. In these cases, continued treatment may be highly frustrating for both the therapist and the patient. Moreover, because the patient may not be in imminent psychological or medical danger, pressing for continued psychotherapy or inpatient care on these grounds may not be justified. Often these patients are terminated from care. Unfortunately, because these patients have failed at psychotherapy so often in the past, they are reluctant to seek further assistance if and when their medical or psychological condition deteriorates to the point that they are in grave danger. In these cases, terminating them from psychotherapy may be appropriate under the condition that they regularly attend medical management groups (Figure 3). The key for these groups is that the aim is no longer to overcome the eating disorder but rather to ensure that the patient remains medically and psychologically stable. Body weight, electrolytes, and vital signs are checked with appropriate referral to medical specialists as needed. Patients derive the added benefits of group support and friendship from similarly afflicted patients. In some cases, these groups set the stage for renewed efforts to address the symptoms of the eating disorder.

Educational Intervention

There are patients who have relatively mild symptoms and can benefit from education alone. There has been considerable variation in the content of treatments identified as educational, with some stressing dietary management techniques and others emphasizing social skills, assertiveness, and relaxation training or some combination of these approaches (Beumont, O'Connor, Touyz, & Williams, 1987; Connors, Johnson, & Stuckey, 1984;

Garner et al., 1985; Wolchik, Weiss, & Katzman, 1986). However, there are some data suggesting that minimal interventions, which provide information or education, may lead to improvement with some eating-disordered patients. Ordman and Kirshenbaum (1985) found that there was some improvement in a bulimia nervosa control group following one informational interview. Garner et al. (1985) developed a comprehensive educational treatment manual for eating disorders that emphasized the conflict between the cultural pressures on women to diet and biological compensatory mechanisms that tend to defend a set point for body weight. This educational intervention focused on challenging Western society's harsh standards for women to be thin, educating patients regarding the biology of weight regulation, structuring regular eating patterns, and implementing techniques for interrupting bingeing and purging. These were combined with self-monitoring and meal planning involving the gradual incorporation of foods that are avoided. The effectiveness of this educational approach was assessed in a study comparing individual cognitive–behavior therapy with brief psychoeducational group treatment (five 90-minute sessions during a 1-month period), delivered in a group classroom format (Olmsted et al., 1991). Results indicated for the least symptomatic 25% to 45% patients in the sample, both treatments were equally effective on several important measures of outcome.

Lassele et al. (1991) compared *nutritional management*, defined by the same methods and goals as the psychoeducational approach discussed previously, and *stress management*. They found both treatments led to significant reductions in bingeing and vomiting, as well as measures of psychopathology at the end of treatment and at a 12-month follow-up. Nutritional management produced a significantly more rapid reduction in binge eating, greater abstinence rates, and greater improvements on some measures of psychopathology.

Some bulimia nervosa patients, particularly those with less severe pathology, seem to respond favorably to information about dieting and weight regulation. Although educational treatments have varied somewhat in content and intensity, it is reassuring that a number of bulimia nervosa patients appear to benefit from a treatment that is likely to be both cost effective and to minimize psychiatric labeling.

Self-Help Manuals

The use of self-help manuals alone is not included in Figure 3 because there have been no formal studies of their effectiveness with eating disorders. Moreover, there are currently no manuals available that we would recommend as suitable. However, the enormous popularity of self-help books (Santrock, Minnett, & Campbell, 1994) would suggest that these approaches need to be exposed to empirical study. From a purely clinical point of view, we have been impressed with the improvement some patients describe after simply reading our psychoeducational manual (Garner et al., 1985). Nevertheless, these impressions do not warrant optimistic proclamations because many treatments appear effective in case reports or open trials, only to fail when put to the test in comparative trials. There is some evidence from a mail survey study that disturbed eating patterns decline over time with no intervention (Yager, Landsverk, & Edelstein, 1987). Nevertheless, controlled-outcome research on the supervised use of self-help manuals is warranted, particularly with patients who have mild to moderate symptoms of binge eating.

Individual Versus Family Therapy

The evidence on the relative effectiveness of individual and family therapy is limited; however, in anorexia nervosa there is some empirical support for family therapy as the preferred modality for younger patients (Russell, Szmukler, Dare, & Eisler, 1987). Although there is compelling clinical logic for involving the family in treating the younger eating-disordered patient, there is still little evidence for the utility of family therapy with older patients. Research is required to determine the relative efficacy of different forms of family therapy and to compare family interventions with other treatment approaches. With the decision-tree model (Figure 3), family therapy should be considered the initial treatment choice for patients who are 18 years old or younger and living at home. It also may be worthwhile to consider family therapy as an adjunct to individual therapy with older patients living outside of the home when family conflicts predominate. The decision to initiate family therapy may follow the discovery of previously undisclosed trauma, such as sexual abuse within the family, which threatens the progress of individual therapy. In these cases, the family therapy may be brief but intensive (Wooley & Lewis, 1989).

Family Therapy

Family therapy has been recommended as the preferred treatment modality in both anorexia nervosa (Minuchin, Rossman, & Baker, 1978; Selvini-Palazzoli, 1974; Vandereycken, Kog, & Vanderlinden, 1989) and bulimia nervosa (Vandereycken et al., 1989) or as an adjunct to other methods (Andersen, 1985; Crisp, 1970; Garner, Garfinkel, & Bemis, 1982; Wooley & Lewis, 1989). Family therapists have argued convincingly that the eating disorder may have a distinctive role in precipitating or maintaining certain dysfunctional roles, alliances, conflicts, or interactional patterns within the family. This can have any one of a number of manifestations. The eating disorder can deflect members of the family away from the developmental tensions that naturally emerge with the transition to puberty and the attendant preparation for emancipation. The eating disorder may serve as a maladaptive solution to the adolescent's struggle to achieve autonomy in a family in which any move toward independence is perceived as a threat to family unity. It can also provide a means by which the parents and the child avoid major sources of conflict.

For young patients, there are practical as well as theoretical reasons for recommending family therapy. From a strictly practical point of view, patients share their homes with others, and their parents or guardians are responsible for their well-being. The parents have the potential to provide environmental controls that are consistent with therapeutic goals. Regardless of theoretical orientation of the treatment setting, family members need assistance in dealing with a young eating-disordered patient. Often families have been sufficiently terrified by the weight loss that they become intimidated by the anorexic patients' demands for acquiescence to their bizarre dietary rituals. Family members may feel guilty about imposing appropriate controls because of some variant of the belief that they could not live with the anguish of their children's potential death or rejection resulting from the parental limit setting. In these cases, the individual members of the family or the entire group need to alter dysfunctional beliefs and faulty assumptions that are dominating their interactional style. In the case in which the patient is using the eating disorder symptoms to deflect away from marital problems, then the attendant problems—as well as the assumptions driving this only partially effective deflection—need to be addressed.

Cognitive–Behavioral Therapy

Cognitive–behavioral therapy has become the standard treatment for bulimia nervosa and forms the theoretical base for much of the treatment of anorexia nervosa. The earliest descriptions of cognitive–behavioral therapy for bulimia nervosa (Fairburn, 1981) and anorexia nervosa (Garner & Bemis, 1982) adapted standard cognitive–behavioral therapy methods to address the special needs of eating-disordered patients. It may be delivered in a group or individual format, and it can be integrated with family therapy.

The cognitive–behavioral therapy for bulimia nervosa has been developed further by Fairburn and colleagues (Fairburn, 1985; Fairburn, Marcus, & Wilson, 1993) and has the following major points of emphasis: (a) self-monitoring of food intake, bingeing, and purging episodes, as well as thoughts and feelings that trigger these episodes; (b) regular weighing; (c) specific recommendations such as introducing avoided foods and planning meals designed to normalize eating behavior and curb restrictive dieting; (d) cognitive restructuring directed at habitual reasoning errors and underlying assumptions that are relevant to the development and maintenance of the eating disorder; and (e) preventing relapse. Monitoring eating behavior begins in the first session with the rationale that it helps the patient and the therapist examine eating behavior and the situations in which difficulties occur and that it helps the patient alter eating behavior and associated thoughts and feelings (Fairburn, 1985; Fairburn, Marcus, & Wilson, 1993). Patients are supplied with written instructions for self-monitoring and are encouraged to record all food and liquid ingested as soon as possible after consumption. Self-monitoring sheets are reviewed in detail in the second and in all subsequent sessions.

In the case of anorexia nervosa, cognitive–behavioral therapy has been recommended largely on clinical grounds (Garner, 1986, 1988; Garner & Bemis, 1982, 1985; Garner & Rosen, 1990). There is some empirical research to provide grounds for optimism (Channon et al., 1989; Cooper & Fairburn, 1984); however, the data are insufficient to warrant any meaningful conclusions regarding effectiveness. As in bulimia nervosa, the anorexic patient's behavior is determined by the assumption that "weight, shape, or thinness can serve as the sole or predominant referent for inferring personal value or self-worth" (Garner & Bemis, 1982, p. 142). The initial emphasis of treatment is to establish a sound and collaborative therapeutic relationship. Treatment is aimed at gradually assisting the patient to normalize eating and weight through both cognitive and behavioral interventions. Cognitive interventions are aimed at beliefs that maintain extreme dieting and chronic weight suppression and also fundamental assumptions associated with feelings of worthlessness, ineffectiveness, lack of autonomy, and developmental themes that have thwarted both patient and family (Garner & Rosen, 1990). Although there is considerable overlap between the cognitive–behavioral therapy approach to bulimia nervosa and that described for anorexia nervosa, a major factor differentiating treatment for these two disorders is the need for weight gain with anorexia nervosa. This requires adaptation to the therapy, to deal with a low body weight and other symptoms that are *ego-syntonic*. In the subset of patients who do not engage in binge eating, and those who show no obvious serious physical complications, there may be extraordinary resistance to the therapeutic objectives of weight gain.

In summary, over the last decade, there has been a steady accumulation of controlled research indicating that cognitive–behavioral therapy is an effective treatment for bulimia nervosa, and this has been the subject of several reviews (Fairburn et al., 1992; Mitchell, Raymond, & Specker, 1993; Wilson & Fairburn, 1993). These reviews provide several important conclusions regarding the present state of knowledge:

1. Most bulimia nervosa patients improve following a brief course of cognitive–behavioral therapy, and a significant mi-

nority are abstinent from bingeing and vomiting at the end of treatment as well as at 1-year follow-ups.

2. Cognitive–behavioral therapy is considered the current treatment of choice for bulimia nervosa; however, not all patients benefit. Some patients do not improve, others show minimal improvement, and still others relapse following this form of treatment.

3. Cognitive–behavioral therapy has been well articulated for anorexia nervosa; however, there has been little empirical research on its effectiveness.

4) The quality of research on cognitive–behavioral therapy with bulimia nervosa has improved greatly in recent years, resulting in two major thrusts in current investigations. The first is carefully controlled treatment comparisons using treatment manuals and adequate follow-up periods. The second is dismantling trials aimed at identifying the active ingredients in treatment.

There are reports showing that cognitive–behavioral therapy is also effective in stabilizing the eating patterns of obese individuals who experience recurrent episodes of binge eating (Agras et al., 1992; Telch et al., 1990; Wilfley et al., 1993). The long-term effectiveness of cognitive–behavioral therapy in controlling binge eating for this group and the implications for body weight remain unclear.

Given the current state of knowledge, cognitive–behavioral therapy should be considered the psychological treatment of choice for eating disorders. In a *stepped-care model*, it could be argued that cognitive–behavioral therapy should be applied first since there is more evidence for its success than any other method studied to date. However, the standard 3-month cognitive–behavioral therapy protocol, delivered in an individual format (Fairburn, Jones, Peveler, Hope, & O'Connor, 1993) may be unnecessarily intense for many patients and insufficient for the needs of others. It would be logical to provide a course of cognitive–behavioral therapy for patients who fail to respond to self-help or education. In the *decision-tree model*, cognitive–behavioral therapy could be applied to patients whose age does not mandate family therapy, whose clinical picture is severe enough to expect that education alone would be insufficient, and to those patients who have failed at other psychosocial interventions.

Behavior Therapy

Behavior therapy methods are integral to the standard cognitive–behavioral therapy described in the previous section. However, there have been a number of research trials in which behavior therapy alone has been compared to cognitive–behavioral therapy for bulimia nervosa (Fairburn et al., 1991, 1993; Wolf & Crowther, 1992). Using an individual therapy format, Fairburn and colleagues found a poor outcome for behavior therapy at the end of treatment (Fairburn et al., 1991) and at 1-year follow-ups (Fairburn et al., 1993) compared to both cognitive–behavior therapy and a form of interpersonal therapy adapted to eating disorders. In a study of behavior therapy and cognitive–behavior therapy delivered in a group format, Wolf and Crowther (1992) found both treatments superior to a wait-list control group. They also found that behavior therapy was associated with greater improvements on measures of binge eating whereas cognitive–behavior therapy led to more improvement on certain attitudinal measures at follow-up. Taken together, these results suggest that there is no compelling evidence at this time for using behavior therapy in preference to cognitive–behavioral therapy in the treatment of bulimia nervosa.

With regard to anorexia nervosa, there has been little controlled research comparing behavior therapy to other methods. There have been strong proponents and critics of the operant methods to achieve weight gain and, although there is some evidence that it may lead to more rapid weight gain, there seems to be little correlation between speed of weight gain and long-term recovery (Bemis, 1987; Garner, 1985). In a study of the short-term effects of different behavioral programs, Touyz, Beumont, Glaun, Phillips, and Cowie, (1984) found that a lenient behavioral approach led to greater weight gain than a strict program during hospitalization. Again, the durability of these findings remains open to question. Bemis' incisive review of the literature concluded that operant conditioning "has established credibility as an effective, if not definitive, method of short-term intervention and appears neither as promising nor as alarming as it did to earlier commentators" (1987, p. 457). However, there has been little empirical progress since that earlier review concluded that "the research record is not particularly impressive when stretched across the 20-year span that has elapsed since the introduction of the approach . . . [and that] continued criticism must be suffered with grace until fully adequate trials have been conducted and reported" (Bemis, 1987, p. 457).

Although there has been heated discussion from advocates and opponents of behavioral intervention to promote weight gain in anorexia nervosa, the reality is that the systematic application of positive and negative reinforcement contingencies is not unique to behavioral technologists. The proper application of operant principles, within the context of a responsive psychotherapy, is less controversial than the ongoing debate implies. Nevertheless, research assessing the long-term effectiveness of an operant approach is either long overdue or the rationale for abandoning its study needs to be articulated more clearly. The use of behavior therapy alone is not included in the decision-tree approach presented in Figure 3 because evidence for applying to eating disorders outside of the cognitive–behavior therapy context is insufficient.

Interpersonal Therapy

Several studies have prompted reexamination of earlier speculations regarding the specific mechanisms of action in treating binge eating. Cognitive–behavioral therapy for eating disorders relies heavily on the premise that behavioral strategies for normalizing eating plus modification of beliefs about weight and shape that lead to restrictive dieting are fundamental to the process of recovery from binge eating. However, recent research has shown that other forms of short-term psychotherapy are effective in treating bulimia nervosa. Interpersonal psychotherapy is an approach that has received a great deal of interest in the treatment of binge eating. Interpersonal psychotherapy originally was proposed by Klerman et al., (1984) as a short-term treatment for depression. In its adaptation to bulimia nervosa, there is no direct focus on eating problems, and the interpersonal treatment process may be divided into three stages (Fairburn et al., 1991). The first involves the identification of the interpersonal problems that led to the development and maintenance of the eating problems. The second consists of a therapeutic contract for working on these interpersonal problems. The third addresses issues related to termination. Interpersonal psychotherapy does not address the eating problem directly at any stage of treatment. As mentioned earlier, Fairburn et al. (1991) found interpersonal psychotherapy somewhat less effective than cognitive–behavioral therapy at the end of treatment. However, bulimia nervosa patients who received interpersonal psychotherapy gradually improved during the follow-up period, so that after 1 year, both treatments were equally effective (Fairburn et al., 1993). In a study of non-purging bulimic patients (many of whom presented with obesity), Wilfley et al., (1993) found both cognitive–behavioral therapy and interpersonal psychotherapy equally effective in reducing binge eating assessed both at the end of treatment and at 1-year follow-ups.

Supportive–Expressive Therapy

Supportive–expressive therapy is a dynamically oriented, nondirective therapy focusing on core conflicts conceptualized in interpersonal terms (Luborsky, 1984). Garner et al. (1993) adapted supportive–expressive therapy to the treatment of bulimia nervosa, and eating symptoms were considered a reflection of underlying interpersonal problems. Results at the end of treatment indicated that supportive–expressive therapy was as effective as cognitive–behavioral therapy in reducing binge eating but was less effective on other measures of eating disturbance and psychopathology.

Unlike the 1-year interpersonal psychotherapy follow-up mentioned earlier, supportive–expressive patients did not tend to improve during the follow-up period. Many of these patients remained highly symptomatic at the end of treatment and required referral for continued care. A few who elected not to participate in treatment during the 1-year follow-up improved, but none became asymptomatic (Garner, 1989). So, although supportive–expressive therapy was less effective than cognitive–behavioral therapy in this study, there were some bulimia nervosa patients who showed improvement or discontinued their eating disorder symptoms with a treatment markedly different from cognitive–behavioral therapy in both style and content.

These findings complicate the decision-tree models. Although there is evidence that these non-cognitive–behavioral therapy treatments are effective with some patients, there is no empirical basis for suggesting that they should be applied differentially to patients on the basis of premorbid features (e.g., interpersonal conflicts). At this time, because relatively little is known about the factors predicting success with these short-term interventions, perhaps they should be used primarily for bulimia nervosa patients who fail in an initial trial of cognitive–behavioral therapy (Peveler & Fairburn, 1992).

Psychodynamic Therapy

Although there have been no controlled comparisons between long-term psychodynamic psychotherapy and other forms of treatment, it is important to mention that there have been other well articulated dynamic treatments that have been recommended on clinical grounds. These deserve mention since they may play a role in a decision-tree model based on the clinical needs of individual patients. As with the discussion of other treatment approaches presented earlier, it is impractical to provide an extensive review here; the reader is encouraged to consult original sources to obtain a full appreciation of different psychodynamic treatments for eating disorders (Johnson, 1991).

Psychodynamic treatment for eating disorders may be roughly divided into two schools of thought. The first presumes eating disorders do not require fundamental modifications to orthodox dynamic interventions because neither the symptoms nor the disorders represent a unique underlying process. The second conceptualization implies that eating disorders are distinctive in that they require major modifications to traditional dynamic therapy to meet the special psychological needs of the patient. Bruch (1973) was one of the earliest dissenters from strictly interpretive dynamic approaches, asserting that these undermine the patient's self-initiated behavior and unwittingly recapitulate earlier interactional themes that played a role in the development of the eating disorder in the first place. Bruch

(1973) emphasized a gradual fact-finding approach, allowing the patient to recognize feeling states and thoughts as self-initiated. This approach, combined with reality-oriented feedback, aimed at correcting distortions viewed as the product of deficits in self-awareness.

There has been some movement toward integrating psychodynamic therapy with active symptom management principles in treating both anorexia nervosa and bulimia nervosa (Johnson, 1991). Many psychodynamic writers advocate active management of eating disorder symptoms while using terms that are completely consistent with a dynamic theoretical orientation (Bruch, 1973; Casper, 1982; Crisp, 1980; Goodsitt, 1985; Stern, 1986; Strober & Yager, 1985). However, there are still some who espouse a traditional interpretive framework (Lerner, 1991; Sands, 1991; Sugarman, 1991). We recommend applying long-term dynamically oriented therapy as an alternative to long-term cognitive–behavioral therapy for patients who do not progress with less expensive approaches.

Feminist Therapies

Therapists who treat eating-disordered women must be sensitive to how women have been affected during the past two decades by oppressive gender roles as well as the tension inherent in rapid evolution of social roles. There has been a move beyond a general or gender-free psychology toward emphasis on qualitative gender differences and how these are especially important in understanding and treating eating disorders. A new generation of feminist therapists deviate from the traditional views by incorporating the growing literature on the psychology of women dynamics into formulations regarding the etiology and treatment of eating disorders (Fallon, Katzman, & Wooley, 1994; Wooley & Lewis, 1989). These theorists emphasize sociopolitical themes that should be considered (Perlick & Silverstein, 1994; Steiner-Adair, 1994), therapist gender and treatment (Katzman, 1994; Wooley, 1994), and the need to realign mainstream psychology to include the feminist perspectives (Striegel-Moore, 1994). They have highlighted the importance of addressing issues such as role conflicts, identity confusion, sexual abuse, and other forms of victimization in the development, maintenance, and treatment of eating disorders (Wooley, 1994). Treatments are described in interactive terms, emphasizing the importance of women's interpersonal relationships. While controlled studies are still lacking on the efficacy of feminist therapies, this is true for many other treatment approaches to eating disorders. Recent advances in articulating feminist therapeutic principles as they relate to eating disorders (Fallon et al., 1994) set the stage for evaluative studies using methods and measures that better address feminist views on treatment. At this time, the therapist's orientation, rather than the special needs of the patient, probably determine the decision to apply feminist therapy to eating disorders.

However, many of the views articulated by feminist therapists have influenced the applications of other forms of therapy. Feminist therapy offers specific treatment principles which are designed to assist patients who have a history of physical or sexual abuse (Fallon et al., 1994).

Pharmacotherapy

Discussion of pharmacotherapy for eating disorders cannot be anything but cursory here. However, there are a number of basic principles that can be derived from the literature (Mitchell et al., 1993; Raymond, Mitchell, Fallon, & Katzman, 1994). Regarding anorexia nervosa, there has been no significant pharmacological advancement to contradict earlier suggestions that pharmacotherapy has limited value with emaciated patients and should never be the sole treatment modality (Garfinkel & Garner, 1982). At times patients may benefit from medication to deal with overwhelming anxiety, severe depression, or intolerable gastric discomfort after meals, but this applies only to a small minority of patients (Andersen, 1985; Garfinkel & Garner, 1982).

The research on drug treatments for bulimia nervosa has been extensive in the past decade and leads to more complicated recommendations than with anorexia nervosa. Most of the research has been on antidepressant medications, with indications of success from some studies (e.g., Agras et al., 1992). However, for a number of reasons, we agree with the recommendation that medication should not be "the primary mode of therapy with patients with bulimia nervosa" (Raymond et al., 1994, p. 241). The reasons include (a) the effectiveness of psychological interventions, (b) the high dropout rates reported in most medication studies, (c) the risks of drug side effects, and (d) data suggesting high relapse rates with drug discontinuation. Fluoxetine hydrocholride (Prozac) is currently the first choice for treating bulimia nervosa (daily dosages of 60 mg were generally superior to 20 mg) and probably should be used at least as an adjunct to psychotherapy in cases that do not respond to a course of adequate psychological treatment (see Mitchell et al., 1993). Tricyclic antidepressants may be an alternative for some patients failing a course of fluoxetine, but side effects, high dropout rates, and greater incidence of lethality with overdose may be a source of concern when treating some patients (Leitenberg et al., 1994; Mitchell et al., 1990; Walsh, Hadigan, Devlin, Gladis, & Roose, 1991). In a similar way, Monoamine Oxidase Inhibitors may be useful in a small minority of patients who fail using fluoxitine and tricyclics. There is some evidence that patients who fail on one tricyclic may benefit from changing to an alternative medication (see Mitchell et al., 1993). However, the decision to avoid prescribing medication may be therapeutic in some cases (Raymond et al., 1994).

Psychotropic medication is generally not necessary or useful in most cases of anorexia nervosa. There is a limited role for medication with bulimia nervosa, but probably not as the initial treatment of choice (see Figure 3). The high dropout and relapse rates with studies using medication alone suggest that the best use of medication at this time is as an adjunct to one of the psychosocial treatments with proven effectiveness. Thus, in the decision-tree approach for treating bulimia nervosa, antidepressant medication should be considered as an adjunct or possibly an alternative for patients who fail to respond to psychosocial therapies or for those whose affective symptoms are impeding progress in other forms of treatment.

STEPPED-CARE AND DECISION-TREE MODELS WITH OTHER DISORDERS

It is important to point out that the concepts of stepped-care approaches and decision trees are not new and have been applied to other disorders as a conceptual framework for treatment. Brownell and Wadden (1991) have applied the stepped-care model to treating obesity. Level of obesity and response to treatment are the determinants dictating the treatment applied. A stepped-care approach has also been advocated in the pharmacological treatment of hypertension. The World Health Organization Expert Committee on Arterial Hypertension established steps for treating high blood pressure. The Hypertension Detection and Follow-Up Program Cooperative Group (1988) conducted a large study in which they randomly assigned hypertensive subjects ($N = 159,000$) to a stepped-care group or a referred-care control group. The researchers found that patients in the stepped-care group had significantly lower rates of morbidity and mortality. Currently, hypertension researchers (e.g., Kligman & Higbee, 1989; Pardell, Armario, & Hernandez, 1992) are calling for more specific treatment recommendations based on increased knowledge of the interactions between patient characteristics (e.g., race, age, other medical conditions) and medications. This new approach is more similar to a decision-tree than a stepped-care model.

PITFALLS OF THE STEPPED-CARE AND DECISION-TREE MODELS

Although stepped-care and decision-tree models for treatment delivery have received some attention in the eating disorder literature, the concept has not been well developed. The stepped-care model is predicated on the assumption that less intensive treatments should be initially applied because they are cost effective and less intrusive. Although there is some information on costs and effectiveness of several treatments, cost-effective analyses per se have not been done. Just because a treatment appears economical does not mean that it is cost-effective. Less intensive treatments actually may be more than simply ineffective because their failure might lead to the patient being more resistant to subsequent interventions. At this time, the method best studied in relation to bulimia nervosa is cognitive–behavioral therapy, and this method has been shown to benefit most patients with eating disorders. It could be argued that, with the exception of the small number of bulimia nervosa patients who require hospital or day care management, all other patients should be exposed to an initial trial of cognitive–behavioral therapy as the treatment of choice. In addition to the theoretical arguments, this has practical advantages because it is unrealistic to expect each clinical setting to have the resources to train staff competently to apply the broad range of treatments outlined earlier.

It is also important to point out that some of the more accepted treatments proposed for bulimia nervosa have gradually been integrated and consolidated. For example, the educational component of cognitive–behavioral therapy was originally quite rudimentary, but as the informational base on educational treatment has expanded, it has taken a broader place in the standard cognitive–behavioral therapy for eating disorders. In a similar way, there has been increasing agreement in the content and the format of self-monitoring in the treatment of bulimia nervosa. This may be extrapolated even further because there should be few practical problems associated with integrating some of the elements that seem to be most useful in interpersonal psychotherapy treatment into an enriched cognitive–behavioral therapy treatment model. This is not inconsistent with the cognitive–behavioral therapy model that addresses relationship problems when they are a source of emotional distress. This is a particularly important target for change in patients with personality disorders (Beck, Freeman, & Associates, 1990) .

One could start from the interpersonal psychotherapy model and incorporate elements from cognitive–behavioral therapy that seem particularly useful. The content of therapy would focus on interpersonal relationships with standard cognitive–behavioral therapy methods integrated as needed. It must be cautioned that this mix-and-match model presupposes that merging models does not have a detrimental effect. It may be that the components are really not complimentary or that integrating treatments dilutes the overall efficacy. The worst connotation of eclecticism is that it reflects a failure to understand and cogently apply any one technique. By trying to mix and match methods for bulimia nervosa patients, it may be that training therapists and implementing treatment would be weakened somehow.

One of the greatest pitfalls of the stepped-care and decision-tree models of treatment is that their complexity makes rigorous research on effectiveness exceedingly difficult. The ideal research protocol would allow testing treatment efficacy for each treatment separately and in combination. It also would allow examination of the effects of treatments presented in different sequences. Finally, complete information would be available concerning the interactions between each treatment (and treatment combination) and relevant patient characteristics. Needless to say, the resulting hypothetical matrix of treatment combinations and patient features would be enormous and completely impractical.

A more realistic approach is to conduct studies using larger sample sizes and compare different treatment sequences that are particularly relevant from a clinical point of view. It may be practical to assess the relative efficacy of the best shot treatment compared to predetermined and limited decision-tree approach. For example, it would be feasible to compare standard cognitive–behavioral therapy for bulimia nervosa with an approach that systematically adds specific components such as educational treatment, cognitive–behavioral therapy, interpersonal psychotherapy, and drug treatment.

CONCLUSION

This chapter has attempted to refine and extend the decision-tree and stepped-care models for eating disorders. Although all available treatment options have not been covered, the main treatments have been recommended based on patient–clinical features and response to treatment. We hope that this will be a useful model for making students and beginning clinicians aware of the decision-making process used in considering the major treatment options available.

REFERENCES

Agras, W. S. (1993). Short-term psychological treatments for binge eating. In C. G. Fairburn & G. T. Wilson (Eds.), *Binge eating: Nature, assessment and treatment* (pp. 50–76). New York: Guilford Press.

Agras, W. S., Rossiter, E. M., Arnow, B., Schneider, J. A., Telch, C. F., Raeburn, S. D., Bruce, B., Perl, M., & Koran, L. M. (1992). Pharmacologic and cognitive–behavioral treatment for bulimia nervosa: A controlled comparison. *American Journal of Psychiatry, 149,* 82–87.

Andersen, A. E. (1985). *Practical comprehensive treatment of anorexia nervosa and bulimia.* Baltimore: Johns Hopkins Press.

Beck, A. T., Freeman, A. & Associates. (1990). *Cognitive therapy of personality disorders*. New York: Guilford Press.

Bemis, K. M. (1987). The present status of operant conditioning for the treatment of anorexia nervosa. *Behavior Modification, 11*, 432–463.

Beumont, P. J. V., O'Connor, M., Touyz, S. W., & Williams, H. (1987). Nutritional counselling in the treatment of anorexia and bulimia nervosa. In P. J. V. Beumont, G. D. Burrows, & R. C. Casper (Eds.), *Handbook of eating disorders: Part 1: Anorexia and bulimia nervosa*. New York: Elsevier.

Brownell, K. D., & Wadden, T. A. (1991). The heterogeneity of obesity: Fitting treatment to individuals. *Behavior Therapy, 22*, 153–177.

Bruch, H. (1973). *Eating disorders: Obesity, anorexia nervosa and the person within*. New York: Basic Books.

Casper, R. C. (1982). Treatment principles in anorexia nervosa. *Adolescent Psychiatry, 10*, 86–100.

Channon, de Silva, P., Hemsley, D., & Perkins, R. (1989). A controlled trial of CB and behavioral treatment of anorexia nervosa. *Behavioral research and therapy, 27*, 529–535.

Connors, M. E., Johnson, C. L., & Stuckey, M. K. (1984). Treatment of bulimia with brief psychoeducational group therapy. *American Journal of Psychiatry, 141*, 1512–1516.

Cooper, P. J., & Fairburn, C. G. (1984) Cognitive behavioral treatment for anorexia nervosa: Some preliminary findings. *Journal of Psychosomatic Research, 28*, 493–499.

Crisp, A. H. (1970). Anorexia nervosa. 'Feeding disorder,' nervous malnutrition or weight phobia? *World Review of Nutrition, 12*, 452–504.

Crisp, A. H. (1980). *Anorexia nervosa*. New York: Grune & Stratton.

Fairburn, C. G. (1981). A cognitive–behavioral approach to the management of bulimia. *Psychological Medicine, 141*, 631–633.

Fairburn, C. G. (1985). Cognitive–behavioral treatment for bulimia. In D. M. Garner & P. E. Garfinkel (Eds.), *Handbook of psychotherapy for anorexia nervosa and bulimia* (pp. 160–192). New York: Guilford Press.

Fairburn, C. G., Agras, W. S., & Wilson, G. T. (1992). The research on the treatment of bulimia nervosa: Practical and theoretical implications. In G. H. Anderson & S. H. Kennedy (Eds.), *Biology of feast and famine*. San Diego, CA: Academic Press.

Fairburn, C. G., Jones, R., Peveler, R. C., Carr, S. J., Solomon, R. A., O'Connor, M. E., Burton, J., & Hope, R. A. (1991). Three psychological treatments for bulimia nervosa: A comparative trial. *Archives in General Psychiatry, 48*, 463–469.

Fairburn, C. G., Jones, R., Peveler, R. C., Hope, R. A., & O'Connor, M. E. (1993). Psychotherapy and bulimia nervosa: The longer-term effects of interpersonal psychotherapy, behaviour therapy and cognitive behaviour therapy. *Archives in General Psychiatry, 50*, 419–428.

Fairburn, C. G., Marcus, M. D. & Wilson, G. T. (1993). Cognitive–behavioral therapy for binge eating and bulimia nervosa. In C. G. Fairburn & G. T. Wilson (Eds.), *Binge eating: Nature, assessment, and treatment* (361–404). New York: Guilford Press.

Fairburn, C. G., & Peveler, R. C. (1990). Bulimia nervosa and a stepped care approach to management. *Gut, 31,* 1220–1222.

Fallon, P., Katzman, M. A., & Wooley, S. C. (1994). *Feminist perspectives on eating disorders.* New York: Guilford Press.

Garfinkel, P. E., & Garner, D. M. (1982). *Anorexia nervosa: A multidimensional perspective.* New York: Brunner/Mazel.

Garner, D. M. (1985). Iatrogenesis in anorexia nervosa and bulimia nervosa. *International Journal of Eating Disorders, 4,* 701–726.

Garner, D. M. (1986). Cognitive therapy for anorexia nervosa. In K. D. Brownell & J. P. Foreyt (Eds.), *Handbook of eating disorders: Physiology, psychology, and treatment of obesity, anorexia, and bulimia* (pp. 301–327). New York: Basic Books.

Garner, D. M. (1988). Anorexia nervosa. In M. Hersen & C. G. Last (Eds.), *Child behavior therapy casebook* (pp. 263–276). New York: Plenum Press.

Garner, D. M. (1989). *A comparison of cognitive–behavioral and supportive expressive therapy for bulimia nervosa at one year follow-up.* Unpublished manuscript.

Garner, D. M., & Bemis, K. M. (1982). A cognitive–behavioral approach to anorexia nervosa. *Cognitive Therapy and Research, 6,* 123–150.

Garner, D. M., & Bemis, K. M. (1985). Cognitive therapy for anorexia nervosa. In D. M. Garner & P. E. Garfinkel (Eds.), *Handbook of psychotherapy for anorexia nervosa and bulimia* (pp. 107–146). New York: Guilford Press.

Garner, D. M., Garfinkel, P. E., & Bemis, K. M. (1982). A multidimensional psychotherapy for anorexia nervosa. *International Journal of Eating Disorders, 1,* 3–46.

Garner, D. M., Garfinkel, P. E., & Irvine, M. J. (1986). Integration and sequencing of treatment approaches for eating disorders. *Psychotherapy and Psychosomatics, 46,* 67–75.

Garner, D. M., & Needleman, L. D. (in press). Integration and sequencing treatments for eating disorders. In D. M. Garner & P. E. Garfinkel (Eds.), *Handbook of treatment for eating disorders.* New York: Guilford Press.

Garner, D. M., Rockert, W., Olmsted, M. P., Johnson, C. L., & Coscina, D. V. (1985). Psychoeducational principles in the treatment of bulimia and anorexia nervosa. In D. M. Garner & P. E. Garfinkel (Eds.), *Handbook for psychotherapy for anorexia nervosa and bulimia* (pp. 513–572). New York: Guilford Press.

Garner, D. M., & Rosen, L. W. (1990). Anorexia nervosa and bulimia nervosa. In A. S. Bellack, M. Hersen, & A. E. Kazdin (Eds.), *International handbook of behavior modification and therapy* (2nd ed., pp. 805–817). New York: Plenum Press.

Garner, D. M., & Sackeyfio, A. H. (1993). Eating disorders. In A. S. Bellack & M. Hersen (Eds.), *Handbook of behavior therapy in the psychiatric setting.* (pp. 477–497). New York: Plenum Press.

Garner, D. M., & Wooley, S. C. (1991). Confronting the failure of behavioral and dietary treatments for obesity. *Clinical Psychology Review, 11,* 729–780.

Giles, T. R., Young, R. R., & Young, D. E. (1985). Case studies and clinical replication series: Behavioral treatment of severe bulimia. *Behavior Therapy, 16,* 393–405.

Goodsitt, A. (1985). Self psychology and the treatment of anorexia nervosa. In D. M. Garner & P. E. Garfinkel (Eds.), *Handbook of psychotherapy for anorexia nervosa and bulimia* (pp. 55–84). New York: Guilford Press.

Hypertension Detection and Follow-Up Program Cooperative Group (1988). *Journal of the American Medical Association, 259,* 2113–2122.

Johnson, C. (1991). *Psychodynamic treatment of anorexia nervosa and bulimia.* New York: Guilford Press.

Katzman, M. A. (1994). When reproductive and productive worlds meet: Collusion or growth? In P. Fallon, M. A. Katzman, & S. C. Wooley (Eds.), *Feminist perspectives on eating disorders* (pp. 132–151). New York: Guilford Press.

Klerman, G. L., Weissman, M. M., Rounsaville, B. J. & Chevron, E. S. (1984). *Interpersonal psychotherapy of depression.* New York: Basic Books.

Kligman, E. W., & Higbee, M. D. (1989). Drug therapy for hypertension in the elderly. *Journal of Family Practice, 28,* 81–87.

Laessle, R. G., Beumont, P. J. V., Butow, P., Lenneris, W., O'Connor, M., Pirke, K. M., Touyz, S. W., & Waadi, S. (1991). A comparison of nutritional management and stress management in the treatment of bulimia nervosa. *British Journal of Psychiatry, 159,* 250–261.

Leitenberg, H., Rosen, J. C., Wolf, J., Vara, L. S., Detzer, M. J., & Srebnik, D. (1994). Comparison of cognitive–behavor therapy and desipramine in the treatment of bulimia nervosa. *Behavior Research and Therapy, 32,* 37–45.

Lerner, H. D. (1991). Masochism in subclinical eating disorders. In C. Johnson (Ed.), *Psychodynamic treatment of anorexia nervosa and bulimia* (pp. 109–127). New York: Guilford Press.

Luborsky, L. (1984). *Principles of psychoanalytic psychotherapy. A manual for supportive–expressive treatment.* New York: Basic Books.

Minuchin, S., Rosman, B. L., & Baker, L. (1978). *Psychosomatic families: Anorexia nervosa in context.* Cambridge, MA: Harvard University Press.

Mitchell, J. E., Pyle, R. L., Eckert, E. D., Hatsukami, D., Pomeroy, C., & Zimmerman, R. (1990). A comparison study of antidepressants and structured intensive group psychotherapy in the treatment of bulimia nervosa. *Archives of General Psychiatry, 47,* 149–157.

Mitchell, J. E., Raymond, N., & Specker, S. (1993). A review of the controlled trials of pharmachotherapy and psychotherapy in the treatment of bulimia nervosa. *International Journal of Eating Disorders, 14,* 229–247.

Olmsted, M. P., Davis, R., Garner, D. M., Rockert, W., Irvine, M. J., & Eagle, M. (1991). Efficacy of a brief group psychoeducational intervention for bulimia nervosa. *Behaviour Research and Therapy, 29*, 71–83.

Ordman, A. M., & Kirschenbaum, D. S. (1985). Cognitive–behavioral therapy for bulimia: An initial outcome study. *Journal of Consulting and Clinical Psychology, 53*, 305–313.

Pardell, H., Armario, P., & Hernandez, R. (1992). Progress in the 1980s and new directions in the 1990s with hypertension management: From the stepped-care approach to the individualised programme in hypertension treatment and control. *Drugs, 43*, 1–5.

Perlick, D., & Silverstein, B. (1994). Faces of female discontent: Depression, disordered eating, and changing gender roles. In P. Fallon, M. A. Katzman, & S. C. Wooley (Eds.), *Feminist perspectives on eating disorders.* (pp. 77–93). New York: Guilford Press.

Peveler, R. C., & Fairburn, C. G. (1992). The treatment of bulimia nervosa in patients with diabetes mellitus. *International Journal of Eating Disorders, 11*, 45–53.

Raymond, N. C., Mitchell, J. E., Fallon, P., & Katzman, M. A. (1994). A collaborative approach to the use of medication. In P. Fallon, M. Katzman, & S. C. Wooley (Eds.), *Feminist perspectives on eating disorders* (pp. 231–250). New York: Guilford Press.

Rosenthal, R. (1994). Science and ethics in conducting, analyzing, and reporting psychological research. *Psychological Science, 5*, 127–134.

Russell, G. F. M., Szmukler, G. I., Dare, C., & Eisler, I. (1987). An evaluation of family therapy in anorexia nervosa and bulimia nervosa. *Archives of General Psychiatry, 44*, 1047–1056.

Ryle, A. (1990). *Cognitive analytic therapy: Active participation in change*, London: John Wiley.

Sands, S. (1991). Bulimia, dissociation, and empathy: A self-psychological view. In C. Johnson (Ed.), *Psychodynamic treatment of anorexia nervosa and bulimia* (pp. 34–50). New York: Guilford Press.

Santrock, J. W., Minnett, A. M., & Campbell, B. D. (1994). *The authoritative guide to self-help books*. New York: Guilford Press.

Selvini-Palazzoli, M. P. (1974). *Self-starvation*. London: Chaucer.

Steiner-Adair, C. (1994). The politics of prevention. In P. Fallon, M. A. Katzman, & S. C. Wooley (Eds.), *Feminist perspectives on eating disorders* (pp. 381–394). New York: Guilford Press.

Stern, S. (1986). The dynamics of clinical management in the treatment of anorexia nervosa and bulimia: An organizing theory. *International Journal of Eating Disorders, 5*, 233–254.

Striegel-Moore, R. H. (1994). A feminist agenda for psychological research on eating disorders. In P. Fallon, M. A. Katzman, & S. C. Wooley (Eds.), *Feminist perspectives on eating disorders* (pp. 438–454). New York: Guilford Press.

Strober, M., & Yager, J. (1985). A developmental perspective on the treatment of anorexia nervosa in adolescents. In D. M. Garner & P. E. Garfinkel (Eds.), *Handbook of psychotherapy for anorexia nervosa and bulimia* (pp. 363–390). New York: Guilford Press.

Sugarman, A. (1991). Bulimia: A displacement from psychological self to body self. In C. Johnson (Ed.), *Psychodynamic treatment of anorexia nervosa and bulimia* (pp. 3–33). New York: Guilford Press.

Telch, C. F., Agras, W. S., Rossiter, E. M., Wilfley, D., & Kenardy, J. (1990). Group cognitive–behavioral treatment for the nonpurging bulimic: An initial evaluation. *Journal of Consulting and Clinical Psychology, 58,* 629–635.

Tiller, J., Schmidt, U., & Treasure, J. (1993). Treatment of bulimia nervosa. *International Review of Psychiatry, 5,* 75–86.

Touyz, S. W., Beumont, P. J. V., Glaun, D., Philips, T., & Cowie, J. (1984). A comparison of lenient and strict operant conditioning programmes in refeeding patients with anorexia nervosa. *British Journal of Psychiatry, 144,* 512–520.

Vandereycken, W., Kog, E., & Vanderlinden, J. (1989). *The family approach to eating disorders.* New York: PMA.

Walsh, B. T., Hadigan, C. M., Devlin, M. J., Gladis, M., & Roose, S. P. (1991). Long-term outcome of antidepressant treatment for bulimia nervosa. *American Journal of Psychiatry, 148,* 1206–1212.

Wilfley, D. E., Agras, W. S., Telch, C. F., Rossiter, E. M., Schneider, J. A., Cole, A. G., Sifford, L., & Raeburn, S. D. (1993). Group cognitive-behavioral and group interpersonal psychotherapy for the nonpurging bulimic individual: A controlled comparison. *Journal of Consulting and Clinical Psychology, 61,* 296–305.

Wilson, G. T., & Fairburn, C. G. (1993). Cognitive treatments for eating disorders. *Journal of Consulting and Clinical Psychology, 61,* 261–269.

Wolchik, S. A., Weiss, L., & Katzman, M. A. (1986). An empirically validated, short-term psychoeducational group treatment program for bulimia. *International Journal of Eating Disorders, 5*(1), 21–34.

Wolf, E. M., & Crowther, J. H. (1992). An evaluation of behavioral and cognitive–behavioral group interventions for the treatment of bulimia nervosa in women. *International Journal of Eating Disorders, 11,* 3–15.

Wooley, S. C. (1994). Sexual abuse and eating disorders: The concealed debate. In P. Fallon, M. A. Katzman, & S. C. Wooley (Eds.), *Feminist perspectives on eating disorders* (pp. 171–211). New York: Guilford Press.

Wooley, S. C., & Lewis, K. G. (1989). The missing woman: Intensive family-oriented treatment of bulimia. *Journal of Feminist Family Therapy, 1,* 61–83.

Yager, J., Landsverk, J., & Edelstein, C. K. (1987). A 20-month follow-up study of 628 women with eating disorders. I. Course and severity of simulated diagnoses and criterion symptoms. *American Journal of Psychiatry, 144,* 1172–1177.

11

COGNITIVE–BEHAVIORAL THERAPY FOR ANOREXIA NERVOSA AND BULIMIA NERVOSA

KATHLEEN M. PIKE, KATHARINE LOEB, and KELLY VITOUSEK

In this chapter we will discuss the application of cognitive–behavioral therapy to the treatment of anorexia nervosa and bulimia nervosa. These eating disorders are multidetermined syndromes that are often severe in presentation, highly resistent to treatment, and chronic. One of the particular advantages of the cognitive–behavioral model of eating disorders is its compatibility with the conceptualization of eating disorders as multidetermined. Although acknowledging that a range of distal antecedent factors may have precipitated the psychiatric disturbance, cognitive–behavioral therapy emphasizes the proximal factors in the causation and maintenance of the disorder. Consistent with cognitive–behavioral therapy in general, the cognitive–behavioral interventions that have been developed specifically for anorexia nervosa and bulimia nervosa focus more on the current presentation of the eating disorder and the steps required for its resolution than on etiological questions.

Anorexia nervosa and bulimia nervosa have several diagnostic and associated features in common, and therefore the cognitive–behavioral treatments designed for them share many core theories and techniques. However, differences between the two treatments exist. For instance, the cognitive–behavioral therapy for bulimia nervosa that has been imple-

---

Kelly Vitousek formerly published under the name Kelly Bemis.

mented at several major clinical research centers is short term and domain specific, focusing almost exclusively on resolving the symptomatology of the eating disorder (Fairburn, Marcus, & Wilson, 1993; Wilson, 1989). However, cognitive–behavioral therapy for anorexia nervosa is typically longer in duration and includes an elaborate phase addressing a broad spectrum of developmental and interpersonal issues significant to resolving the eating disorder (Garner & Bemis, 1985; Garner, Garfinkel, & Bemis, 1982; Pike, Wilson, & Vitousek, 1995).

This chapter is divided into three major sections. The first section briefly presents the development of cognitive and behavioral theories and therapies and their applications to eating disorders. The second section reviews the extant empirical data base regarding the efficacy of cognitive–behavioral therapy in the treatment of anorexia nervosa and bulimia nervosa. The third section describes the phases of treatment and the fundamental components of cognitive–behavioral therapy for anorexia nervosa and bulimia nervosa.

COGNITIVE THERAPY

Cognitive therapy was developed by Beck to treat depression (Beck, 1967, 1976). The core principles of this treatment have been adapted for a range of psychiatric disturbances, including anxiety disorders, somatoform disorders, and eating disorders (Barlow, 1992; Hawton, Salkovskis, Kirk, & Clark, 1989).

Cognitive theory asserts that the way in which individuals conceptualize and interpret current life events is shaped by previous experiences. Early life experiences enable individuals to develop *schemas* for processing and integrating new information; these schemas are essential to learning and normal functioning. Schemas are composed of organizing principles that become automatic, operating beyond the awareness of the individual. Cognitive theory attempts to explain *how* people process information; it is not content specific and does not stipulate *what* any individual's developmental and interpersonal experiences will include.

Automatic processing is essential to normal functioning; however, problems can arise when cognitive processing is overly rigid or extreme. In such cases, the derivative thoughts can promote unrealistic expectations and result in erroneous interpretation of experiences. According to cognitive theory, these thoughts are *problematic* or *dysfunctional* and constitute core features of psychopathology. Dysfunctional thoughts alone will not result in clinical disturbance, but in combination with significant life experiences, will put an individual at risk for becoming clinically symptomatic (Fennell, 1989). Once activated, dysfunctional thoughts can lead to increased symptomatology, which can, in turn, perpetuate and increase dysfunctional thinking. The primary task of cognitive therapy in the initial phase of treatment is to identify and interrupt this self-perpetuating spiral. The long-term goal is to establish functional cognitive strategies and schemas in the context of recovery and relapse prevention.

BEHAVIORAL THERAPY

Behavioral therapy interventions are based largely on empirically tested models of normal human functioning drawing on an enormous body of research in the principles of learning. Behavioral therapy is also based on a theory of process rather than content. Behavioral theories have informed therapeutic treatments for a range of disorders, including anxiety disorders, depression, psychosexual disorders, and eating disorders (O'Leary & Wilson, 1987).

In the treatment of bulimia nervosa, behavioral treatments have been implemented alone and in conjunction with cognitive therapy techniques. The consensus in the field is that behavioral therapy interventions are more useful when applied in a fully elaborated treatment that includes cognitive therapy components. In the treatment of anorexia nervosa, behavioral therapy interventions have been implemented most extensively during the acute treatment phase requiring weight restoration. These weight gain programs, based on operant conditioning principles, are widespread and have demonstrated short-term efficacy (Agras & Kraemer, 1984; Bemis, 1987).

COGNITIVE–BEHAVIORAL MODEL OF EATING DISORDERS

Cognitive and behavioral theories have been integrated in the development of cognitive–behavioral therapy treatment programs for bulimia nervosa and anorexia nervosa. Although it is only recently that manual-based treatments have been developed for anorexia nervosa (Pike et al., 1995), the principles of cognitive–behavioral therapy for anorexia nervosa have been delineated in detail at both the theoretical and practical level of implementation for at least a decade (Garner & Bemis, 1982, 1985). Cognitive–behavioral therapy for bulimia nervosa was formulated first by Fairburn in the 1980s. With the publication of a detailed treatment manual in 1985 (Fairburn, 1985), the dissemination of cognitive–behavioral therapy for bulimia nervosa was facilitated greatly, and numerous clinical trials implementing cognitive–behavioral therapy strategies have been conducted. Although different adaptations have been developed for anorexia nervosa and bulimia nervosa, all cognitive–behavioral therapy interventions for these disorders share at least two core principles. First, all cognitive–behavioral therapy interventions hold a common view of the cognitive factors maintaining the eating disorder. Second, all cognitive–behavioral therapy treatments address both the behavioral disturbances of the eating disorders and the attitudinal disturbances regarding eating, weight, and shape.

The cognitive theory of eating disorders posits that the fundamental psychopathology of anorexia nervosa and bulimia nervosa is the attempt to compensate for deficits in self-esteem by defining and evaluating one's self excessively in terms of weight and shape (Fairburn & Garner, 1986; Garner & Bemis, 1982, 1985; Wilson & Walsh, 1991). According to this model, the pursuit of thinness becomes the central organizing principle for the individual with an eating disorder. Attitudes, beliefs, and assumptions that overvalue the meaning of appearance dominate the individual's sense of self. Such a schema serves to organize and simplify the individual's world and provides the framework for the behaviors observed in anorexia nervosa and bulimia nervosa. Cognitive–behavioral therapy is designed to help individuals with anorexia nervosa or bulimia nervosa become aware of the elaborate, rigid set of rules that govern their behaviors, challenge these rules, and adopt a more adaptive set of attitudes and behaviors (Fairburn, 1985; Fairburn, & Cooper, 1989; Fairburn, Marcus, & Wilson, 1993; Garner & Bemis, 1982, 1985).

According to the cognitive–behavioral therapy model of eating disorders, attitudes about the personal significance of weight and shape promote severe and maladaptive dietary restraint. For most individuals, this extreme dietary restraint is not sustainable, both psychologically and physically, and ultimately leads to the binge eating seen in bulimia nervosa and anorexia nervosa, binge eating and purging type. In an attempt to compensate for an episode of binge eating and resume the pursuit of an ideal body shape and weight, individuals with eating disorders employ behaviors such as vomiting, laxative abuse, or compulsive exercise. It is ironic to note that these compensatory efforts leave these individuals feeling worse about themselves—a state of affairs that they try to amend by redoubling their efforts to achieve an unrealistic weight and shape. At each point in this cycle, the individual is operating under the guiding principle of the eating disorder schema: Thinness will result in increased self-esteem.

Individuals with anorexia nervosa by definition achieve an extremely low body weight—one that individuals with bulimia nervosa have been unable to attain. It is interesting to note that if the cognitive schema that individuals with eating disorders possess indeed reflected reality, those with anorexia nervosa should manifest high levels of self-esteem by virtue of their success in accomplishing the cherished goal of thinness. However, although individuals with anorexia nervosa are often proud of their self-control around food, their overall self-esteem remains low and they lack a sense of mastery in other aspects of their lives. In fact, maintaining the eating disorder becomes their sole source of self-worth—in other words, "If I can't feel good about anything else, I might as well succeed at this."

The cognitive–behavioral therapy model for patients with anorexia nervosa, restricting type, is simplified conceptually by the absence of the binge eating and purging behaviors. In contrast to patients with bulimia nervosa and anorexia nervosa, binge eating and purging type, patients with anorexia nervosa, restricting type, report less dramatic behavioral problems with their eating because they do not experience a sense of loss of control. The absence of bulimic behaviors results in a syndrome that is more ego syntonic. Thus, despite the simplification of the model, resolving the eating disorder is a great challenge because the symptoms first must be rendered ego dystonic.

In contrast, the binge eating and purging seen in bulimia nervosa and anorexia nervosa, binge eating and purging type, are ego dystonic, and patients report high levels of motivation to eliminate these behaviors because of the associated distress. However, it is commonly the case that motivation for change is narrowly focused on eliminating the binge eating and purging without motivation for challenging the overvaluation and pursuit of thinness. If it were not for the bulimic behaviors, motivation for treatment would be compromised, as is the case for patients with anorexia nervosa, restricting type. One of the major advantages of the cognitive–behavioral therapy model of eating disorders is that it links the ego syntonic and ego dystonic beliefs and behaviors by challenging the underlying assumptions that have been central to the evolution and maintenance of the eating disorder and by showing the patient how these beliefs necessarily perpetuate the unwanted behaviors.

EMPIRICAL SUPPORT FOR COGNITIVE–BEHAVIORAL THERAPY

Bulimia nervosa has a much shorter history as a diagnosable entity than anorexia nervosa. However, in less than 15 years since bulimia nervosa was first included in the *Diagnostic and Statistical Manual of Mental Disorders* (American Psychiatric Association, 1980), it has received an enormous amount of attention from clinical researchers in the field, and viable treatments have been identified. In contrast, despite more than 50 years of scientific attention focused on anorexia nervosa, an empirical knowledge base regarding effective treatment has yet to be established. This appears to be a result of the complex nature of the disorder, the more extended course of treatment required, and the clinical pessimism regarding the possibility of achieving satisfactory results. The following section provides a brief review of the extant empirical research base for cognitive–

behavioral treatment of bulimia nervosa and reviews the rationale for applying cognitive–behavioral therapy to anorexia nervosa.

Bulimia Nervosa

In terms of treatment research for bulimia nervosa, cognitive–behavioral therapy has been the most extensively studied psychotherapeutic intervention and has become the gold standard to which other psychotherapies are compared (Craighead & Agras, 1991; Wilson, 1989). Treatment outcome studies consistently indicate that cognitive–behavioral therapy is superior to control conditions in improving binge and purge symptoms, attitudes regarding eating and shape, and general psychological functioning (Agras, Schneider, Arnow, Raeburn, & Telch, 1989; Freeman, Barry, Dunkeld-Turnbull, & Henderson, 1988; Gray & Hoage, 1990; Laessle, Zoetti, & Pirke, 1987; Ordman & Kirschenbaum, 1985; Wolf & Crowther, 1992).

Results from controlled clinical trials evaluating the efficacy of cognitive–behavioral therapy show a mean reduction in binge eating ranging from 73% to 93% and a mean reduction in purging ranging from 77% to 94%. In terms of remission rates, studies report that 51% to 71% of patients receiving cognitive–behavioral therapy are no longer binge eating at the end of the intervention and 36% to 56% are no longer purging (Agras et al., 1989; Agras et al., 1992; Fairburn et al., 1991; Mitchell et al., 1990). In addition to these measures of binge eating and purging, dietary restraint declines on average and attitudes toward weight and shape improve (Fairburn et al., 1991; Wilson, Eldredge, Smith, & Niles, 1991).

In comparison to alternative psychotherapy interventions, cognitive–behavioral therapy consistently equals or out performs other modalities in reducing the entire constellation of symptoms of bulimia nervosa, including frequency of bingeing and vomiting at the end of treatment, disturbed attitudes toward weight and shape, and dietary restraint (Fairburn, Kirk, O'Conner, & Cooper, 1986; Fairburn et al., 1991). Although cognitive–behavioral therapy is particularly effective in treating the specific features of bulimia nervosa, it does not appear to be more effective than alternative treatments in reducing associated psychopathology such as depression, social adjustment, or anxiety (Fairburn et al., 1991).

Numerous studies have been conducted to identify the active ingredients that contribute to the efficacy of cognitive–behavioral therapy. In particular, clinical researchers have tried to evaluate whether the cognitive or behavioral components of cognitive–behavioral therapy are more potent and which aspects of the cognitive and behavioral interventions are most critical. The results from these studies are equivocal. Most studies suggest that the broadest psychotherapeutic effects are achieved by integrating the major components of cognitive and behavioral interventions (Leitenberg,

Rosen, Gross, Nudelman, & Vara, 1988; Thackwray, Smith, Bodfish, & Meyers, 1993; Wilson, Rossiter, Kleifield, & Lindholm, 1986). However, some data suggest that behavioral therapy alone is sufficient to achieve psychotherapeutic benefit and that integrating cognitive and behavioral interventions does not substantially improve outcome (Cooper, Cooper, & Hill, 1989).

Findings from clinical treatment studies indicate that cognitive–behavioral group therapy is a viable and cost-effective treatment for both individuals with purging and nonpurging bulimia nervosa (Gray & Hoage, 1990; Kettlewell, Mizes, & Wasylyshyn, 1992; Kirkley, Schneider, Agras, & Bachman, 1985; Mitchell et al., 1990; Schneider & Agras, 1985; Wilfley et al., 1993; Wolf & Crowther, 1992). In addition, it appears that more general or eclectic group treatments that incorporate aspects of cognitive–behavioral therapy (such as psychoeducation regarding normalizing eating and weight, problem solving, and stimulus control procedures) can also be effective in reducing bulimic symptomotology (Fettes & Peters, 1992; Olmsted et al., 1991). Although psychoeducational group treatment for bulimia nervosa may be of benefit for a significant percentage of individuals, it appears that patients who are more disturbed either in terms of character pathology or severity of the bulimia nervosa will respond more favorably to a more intensive individual treatment (Olmsted et al., 1991). These data suggest that it may be most efficient and economical to adopt a graded-care plan for patients with bulimia nervosa, starting with psychoeducational group treatment, stepping up to individualized treatment, and finally pursuing inpatient treatment to those patients who do not respond to outpatient care.

Cognitive–behavioral therapy has been compared to and combined with psychopharmacological therapies in treating bulimia nervosa. Based on accumulating data, cognitive–behavioral therapy appears consistently more effective than medication alone in resolving bulimia nervosa (Leitenberg et al., 1993; Mitchell et al., 1990). When cognitive–behavioral therapy is combined with a psychopharmacological intervention, an incremental benefit may accrue in terms of a reduction of the specific symptoms of bulimia nervosa or associated depression and anxiety (Agras et al., 1992; Mitchell et al., 1990).

In addition to outpatient studies of the efficacy of cognitive–behavioral therapy in treating bulimia nervosa, support for its superiority over nonspecific supportive psychotherapy on an inpatient basis has been documented as well (Bossert, Schnabel, & Krieg, 1989). However, similar to the comparative outpatient psychotherapy studies, associated depression does not appear to improve significantly more when individuals receive cognitive–behavioral therapy compared to nonspecific psychotherapy.

Only limited follow-up data are available regarding the long-term efficacy of cognitive–behavioral therapy in the treatment of bulimia nervosa.

Initial studies indicate that the positive effects are mostly maintained from the end of treatment to 1 year after termination of treatment. Fairburn et al. (1993) found that 1 year after completing cognitive–behavioral therapy, patients reported a mean reduction of binge eating and purging of 90%, and 36% of patients had ceased binge eating and purging. In addition, dismantling studies indicate that cognitive–behavioral therapy is superior to behavioral therapy alone in the long term, suggesting that one or both of the features unique to cognitive–behavioral therapy (cognitive restructuring and the use of cognitive–behavioral procedures designed to decrease overconcern of shape and weight) are significant for long-term recovery (Fairburn, Jones, Peveler, Hope, & O'Connor, 1993).

Although treatment studies consistently document that cognitive–behavioral therapy is an effective psychotherapy for a majority of individuals who pursue treatment for bulimia nervosa, a significant percentage does not respond dramatically or sufficiently. Studies are just beginning to explore the individual differences among patients that may predict responsivity to cognitive–behavioral therapy. To date, it has been reported that nonresponders tend to have had a greater history of psychoactive substance abuse, low self-esteem, and borderline personality disorder (Coker, Vize, Wade, & Cooper, 1993).

Anorexia Nervosa

Cognitive–behavioral treatment for anorexia nervosa is commonly divided into two major phases: (a) acute inpatient or outpatient treatment focused on weight restoration and (b) subsequent long-term treatment focused on the broader cognitive–behavioral therapy aims of attitudinal and behavioral change related to the overvaluation of weight and shape, the normalization of eating patterns, and relapse prevention. A limited data base exists regarding the efficacy of behavioral treatments in the acute phase of weight restoration as conducted on inpatient units; there are no controlled studies of weight restoration in an outpatient setting. In regard to the second phase of treatment, only four outpatient psychotherapy trials for anorexia nervosa have been reported in the literature, and only one of these studies included an evaluation of cognitive–behavioral therapy. As we will review, methodological limitations hinder our ability to generalize from the findings.

In an outpatient study comparing cognitive–behavioral and behavioral treatment of anorexia nervosa, Channon, DeSilva, Hemsley, and Perkins (1989) failed to demonstrate significant differences between the two active treatments or superiority of either of these groups over a control treatment that was focused primarily on weight monitoring and weight restoration. Although they discussed several plausible interpretations, one simple explanation may be that their sample sizes were too small to detect group differences: There were only eight subjects in each treatment cell. Further methodological shortcomings include the fact that only one therapist provided treatment in both of the active treatment cells, and this therapist was also responsible for the assessment interviews and clinical ratings. Finally, the treatment interventions were not manual based, and although the investigators stated that the cognitive condition was patterned after the model of Garner and Bemis (1982, 1985), it is not clear how closely it *did* conform to specified procedures.

The paucity of controlled clinical trials of cognitive–behavioral therapy in the treatment of anorexia nervosa is not distinctive to cognitive–behavioral therapy. In fact, only three other outpatient trials for anorexia nervosa have been reported. Hall and Crisp (1987) conducted a study that assessed the efficacy of continuing outpatient care to prevent relapse after hospitalization by comparing 12 sessions of combined individual and family psychotherapy with 12 sessions of dietary advice. Results indicated that both groups showed significant improvement at 1-year follow-ups. The psychotherapy group showed significant improvement compared to baseline social adjustment scores, and both groups demonstrated weight gain. However the pre- to posttreatment weight gain was statistically significant for the dietary advice group only, and at follow-ups both groups remained more than 15% below the matched population mean weight. As was the case with Channon et al.'s (1989) study, the power of this study was compromised by the small sample size: 14 subjects in the psychotherapy cell and 11 in the dietary advice group. In addition, there was significant ambiguity and overlap regarding treatment conditions: (a) the psychotherapy group received some combination of individual and family treatments left to the discretion of the clinician; (b) the particular models of individual and family therapy that were employed were not clearly defined; (c) at least half of the dietary advice group received some psychotherapeutic treatment prior to the 1-year follow-ups; (d) within the psychotherapy group, eating patterns and other matters related to dieting were discussed; and (e) within the dietary advice group the dieticians discussed family and other issues.

The Eating Disorders Group at St. George's Hospital Medical School (Crisp et al., 1991; Gowers, Norton, Halek, & Crisp, 1994) reported short-term and long-term results from a controlled treatment study of 90 patients with anorexia nervosa who were assigned randomly to one of three treatment groups or to no treatment. All three treatment groups included a behavioral approach to diet and weight gain in conjunction with individual and family treatment. These conditions differed in the method of implementation. One condition was conducted on an inpatient basis initially, followed by 12 sessions of outpatient treatment. The second was an individualized 12-session outpatient treatment. The third was made up of 10 group treatment sessions delivered separately to patients and parents. At the end of 1 year, results indicated that patients in all three active treatments improved significantly in terms of weight gain, menses, and psychosocial adjustment. At 2-year follow-ups, 12 of 20 patients who had received individual outpatient treatment were still classified as significantly improved. One of the primary limitations of this study is that treatment conditions were not manual based or standardized to the extent necessary to permit replication. Also, the study reported limited assessment information, and therefore, a more comprehensive description of response to treatment is not available.

In the fourth and most carefully controlled study, Russell, Szmukler, Dare, and Eisler (1987) compared family therapy to individual supportive therapy in the treatment of 57 anorexia nervosa patients and 23 bulimia nervosa patients who had been hospitalized for their initial phase of treatment. All patients met *DSM-III* (American Psychiatric Association, 1980) criteria for their disorder. The findings from this study indicated that family treatment was more effective than individual supportive treatment for cases in which the age of onset for anorexia nervosa was 18 years or younger and the duration of illness was less than 3 years. In the bulimia nervosa group and in the anorexia nervosa groups in which the age of onset was older than 18 years or the duration of illness was 3 years or more, outcome was generally poor for both the family therapy and individual treatment groups.

Although the empirical data base supporting cognitive–behavioral therapy for anorexia is not yet established, there are several points that support the rationale for applying it to anorexia nervosa. First, as with bulimia nervosa, anorexia nervosa is characterized by high levels of dietary restraint and concern with body shape that, in the treatment of bulimia nervosa, have been shown to decline as a result of cognitive–behavioral therapy. Second, because approximately 40% to 45% of patients presenting for treatment for anorexia nervosa binge and purge (Hsu, 1988), we might expect that the components of cognitive–behavioral therapy for bulimia nervosa that address these behaviors would be applicable and effective for patients with anorexia nervosa as well. In the same way, depression and low self-esteem are common in anorexia nervosa (Hsu, Crisp, & Harding, 1979). Again extrapolating from the findings for bulimic patients, it is reasonable to hypothesize that cognitive–behavioral therapy would be an effective treatment in improving the overall emotional state of individuals with anorexia nervosa.

Data from inpatient programs designed to treat the acute phase of weight restoration and medical stabilization also offer support for cognitive–behavioral therapy for anorexia nervosa. In particular, studies suggest that behavior modification programs based on contract systems and operant conditioning procedures, in which rewards and privileges are contingent on weight gain, are effective in this phase of treatment (Agras,

Barlow, Chapin, Abel, & Leitenberg, 1974; Blinder, Freeman, & Stunkard, 1970; Halmi, 1983; Halmi, Powers, & Cunningham, 1975; Leitenberg, Agras, & Thompson, 1968). Although these behavioral techniques are not a part of conventional cognitive–behavioral therapy, we might expect that by extension similar behavioral interventions would be useful in the long-term, more broad-based treatment of anorexia nervosa.

Another source of empirical data supporting the application of cognitive–behavioral therapy to anorexia nervosa derives from basic research on thought patterns characteristic of anorexia nervosa. Cognitive distortions and idiosyncratic thinking patterns are common in anorexia nervosa (Garfinkel & Garner, 1982; Garner & Bemis, 1985; Toner, Garfinkel, & Garner, 1987). To the extent that cognitive–behavioral therapy addresses common irrational beliefs and faulty assumptions and promotes alternative, adaptive behaviors for managing the conflicts typical of these patients, it is reasonable to expect that it would be an effective treatment. For example, one of the major cognitive distortions characteristic of these patients is dichotomous thinking regarding issues of maturation, weight, body shape, and interpersonal relationships (Garfinkel, 1985). A cognitive–behavioral therapy intervention focused on helping the patient identify and challenge dysfunctional thoughts that derive from this type of thinking could facilitate adaptive behavior change and could prove to be effective in the long term.

FUNDAMENTAL FEATURES OF COGNITIVE–BEHAVIORAL THERAPY FOR ANOREXIA NERVOSA AND BULIMIA NERVOSA

The majority of patients with bulimia nervosa are treated exclusively on an outpatient basis, whereas patients with anorexia nervosa are commonly hospitalized during the course of treatment. The decision to hospitalize a patient with an eating disorder is appropriate to consider under the following circumstances: (a) when outpatient treatment fails, (b) when the frequency of purging is such that laboratory abnormalities threaten the patient's clinical safety, (c) when individuals are suicidal, (d) when weight falls below 75% of recommended weight regardless of laboratory values.

We will present the core components of cognitive–behavioral therapy, describing each phase of treatment in sequence. The intervention is designed to be more behaviorally based initially; however, even during Phase 1, the treatment relies heavily on the cognitive components of the model. Also, in the course of experimenting with behavioral change, patients have their own data and experiences that help make explicit the cognitive beliefs and attitudes that have maintained the eating disorder. In

Phase 2, as patients gain an increasing awareness of the link between the cognitive and behavioral components, and treatment gradually progresses to more cognitively based interventions focused on more inclusive maladaptive cognitive constructs and, where indicated, historical material. Phase 3 of the treatment focuses on relapse prevention. In clinical practice, treatment will need to be modified to suit particular needs of different patients. Many core features of cognitive–behavioral therapy (CBT) for bulimia nervosa described in this chapter derive from the manual-based CBT of Fairburn et al. (1993).

STRUCTURE OF THERAPY

Cognitive–behavioral therapy for bulimia nervosa is typically a time limited intervention designed to consist of approximately 20 individual sessions of 45 or 50 minutes. The treatment intervention is divided into three phases. Sessions are conducted twice per week in Phase 1 (which typically consists of 4 sessions), weekly in Phase 2, and once every two weeks in Phase 3. As noted earlier, treatment begins with a behavioral focus on normalizing eating patterns and eliminating binge eating and purging; in Phase 2, treatment is cognitively focused in terms of identifying and challenging beliefs that maintain the eating disorder. Phase 3 of treatment is focused on relapse prevention.

Cognitive–behavioral therapy for anorexia nervosa is a longer term treatment than that prescribed for bulimia nervosa. The cognitive–behavioral therapy manual for anorexia nervosa developed by Pike et al. (1995) consists of 50 sessions divided into three phases of a year-long treatment. Phase 1 of treatment specifies 10 sessions conducted twice a week for the first 5 weeks; Phase 2, 35 weekly sessions; and Phase 3, 5 sessions scheduled every two weeks. Behavioral interventions are emphasized in the early phases of treatment; however, to the extent that patients with anorexia nervosa are more overtly resistant to treatment, cognitive work tends to begin earlier with the aim of challenging the exceedingly rigid attitudes and beliefs that interfere with implementing behavioral change.

In addition to the domain-specific focus on the primary symptoms of eating, weight, and shape disturbances, cognitive–behavioral therapy for anorexia nervosa includes a broader range of intervention than is typically described for bulimia nervosa. In the latter part of Phase 2 of treatment, a schema-based cognitive therapy is applied to address the variety of developmental, interpersonal, and intrapsychic factors that may be implicated in the disorder. It is our experience that this second level of intervention is necessary given the rigid and chronic maladaptive cognitions and behaviors characteristic of most patients with anorexia nervosa.

PHASE 1

The primary components of the first phase of cognitive–behavioral therapy include (a) building a therapeutic alliance; (b) establishing the role of the patient as an active collaborator in treatment; (c) assessing the core patterns and features of the patient's particular eating disorder; (d) orienting the patient to the cognitive–behavioral therapy model of eating disorders; (e) educating patients about the importance of homework in cognitive–behavioral therapy; (f) establishing monitoring procedures for eating and weight; (g) eliminating dieting and normalizing eating throughout the day; (h) developing delay strategies and alternatives to binge eating and purging; (i) learning the skills of imagery, rehearsal, and relaxation training; (j) challenging assumptions about the overvaluation of shape and weight; and (k) providing psychoeducational information to patients.

Building a Therapeutic Alliance

Building a trusting therapeutic relationship requires continuing attention throughout the initial phase of treatment (Thompson & Williams, 1987). Patients with eating disorders frequently have significant problems in interpersonal relationships and problems with trust and intimacy will likely be evident in the process of establishing the therapeutic relationship as well.

Issues of weight can be among the greatest threats to the therapeutic relationship during the initial phase of treatment. Patients with bulimia nervosa can be extremely resistant to cognitive–behavioral interventions aimed at normalizing eating and establishing a pattern of regular meals and snacks because they continue to strive to lose weight and fear that normalizing eating will have the opposite effect. In the same way, patients with anorexia nervosa will resist behavioral normalization of their eating because they do not want to maintain a normal weight or are fearful of gaining weight. It is essential that the therapist be supportive and empathetic while maintaining a firm stance with regard to achieving the goals of the therapy intervention—in other words, normalization of eating and weight and reduction of body weight and shape concerns.

It is useful to begin to discuss explicitly the cost–benefits analysis that a patient calculates when thinking about resolving the eating disorder. Garner and Bemis (1982) have suggested that the following lines of questioning may be useful in the beginning of treatment to help patients begin to raise questions about how the eating disorder is serving them:

> What other values are important to you? How does thinness relate to achieving them? If you believe that there should be a connection be-

tween losing weight and attaining your other goals, how does it seem to be working out in practice? What role will your present concerns about weight play in your life five years from now? Ten years? Do you think that you will be able to keep up this struggle until you are forty? (p. 132)

Establishing the Role of Patient as an Active Collaborator

During the initial phase of treatment, it is important to emphasize to patients that cognitive–behavioral therapy is a treatment that requires them to be active both during and between sessions. One of the primary goals is for patients to learn the skills necessary for them to become their "own therapist." The therapist should emphasize that although treatment is time limited, it is expected that patients will continue to make progress after treatment terminates because they will have learned a wide range of skills that will allow them to carry on the work. The therapist should acknowledge that establishing personal control and normal eating can take time, and changing attitudes and beliefs may take even longer. The goal of cognitive–behavioral therapy is to make changes gradually so that they will be long lasting.

In the initial phase of treatment it is important to address any apparent problems that a patient experiences assuming an active role in the session or in completing homework tasks. Although some patients are forthcoming in their conflicts about following through with various treatment interventions, others have greater difficulty articulating the thoughts that interfere with making maximal use of treatment. To aid in clarifying the patient's motivation and resistance to change, it can be useful in the early stages of treatment to use the Decision Analysis Form (see Figure 1).

The Decision Analysis Form can help to organize thoughts around a decision point and clarify the conflicting thoughts and feelings that patients have regarding their eating disorders. In addition to identifying the positive results that patients anticipate (sources of motivation), it is useful to identify the negative consequences patients anticipate. A more complete understanding of the functions the eating disorder serves in the patient's life will help the patient and therapist work more effectively in making adaptive change. The most common problems that patients raise during the initial phase of treatment usually center around conflicts with behavioral changes in managing eating and weight. The therapist and patient can begin filling in this form in session and the patient can complete it between sessions.

Assessing the Eating Disorder

The initial session begins with evaluating the current presentation of the eating disorder. The therapist should assess the exact nature of the

	Immediate Consequences		Delayed Consequences	
	Positive	Negative	Positive	Negative
If I: (e.g., gain weight or start eating)				
If I continue to: (e.g., lose weight or refuse to eat)				

Figure 1. Decision Analysis Form

problem as reported by the patient. For patients who are binge eating or purging, the therapist needs to be sure to assess not only the binge eating and purging but also the patient's overall eating habits as well as attitudes toward weight and shape (see chapters 3 and 9, this volume). It is essential to get a history of the patient's eating disorder, focusing on how and when the eating disorder started and the course that it has taken for the duration of the illness. A medical evaluation may also be indicated (see chapter 8, this volume).

Based on the patients' descriptions of their eating disorders, it is important to acknowledge the ways in which the eating disorder has served an important function in managing developmental, familial, and interpersonal conflict. The therapist can explain that the eating disorder can be thought of as a compromise solution to difficult problems. In this context, the therapist can explain that the goal of cognitive–behavioral therapy is for the therapist and patient to work together to clarify the current problems or situations that maintain the disorder and begin to think about them in new ways so that more adaptive, less costly solutions can be tried.

Orienting the Patient to the Cognitive–Behavioral Therapy Model

During the first session, the structure and goals of cognitive–behavioral therapy are discussed. It is important to explain that the normalization and stabilization of eating patterns will be achieved by focusing on the interplay between current thoughts, feelings, and behaviors that are part of the eating disorder. The therapist should emphasize that the therapy focuses primarily on the factors that maintain the current eating disorder rather than why the eating disorder initially developed. Once the patient's current thoughts and behavior patterns relevant to the eating disorder are identified, the focus of cognitive–behavioral therapy is to help the patient challenge maladaptive attitudes and beliefs regarding the importance of weight and shape, develop alternative strategies for coping with problematic thoughts and feelings, and develop more adaptive and healthy eating patterns.

Using the cognitive–behavioral therapy model illustrated in Figure 2, the therapist presents in detail the cognitive view of the cycles that maintain the eating disorders. This is extremely useful in linking critical components of the eating disorder and providing a coherent framework that helps to account for why it has been so difficult for the patient to resolve the eating disorder. For patients with bulimia nervosa and anorexia nervosa, binge eating and purging type, the therapist should emphasize the role that dieting plays in maintaining the binge eating and purging. For all patients, it is important to link the overvaluation of weight and shape with dieting behaviors aimed at achieving an unrealistic and unhealthy weight and shape. The therapist can then explore with the patient the link between feelings of worthlessness, low self-efficacy, and low self-esteem and

Cognitive Model of Eating Disorders

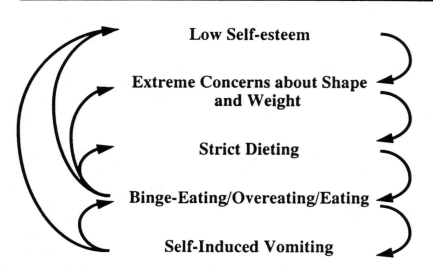

Figure 2. From Fairburn, Marcus, & Wilson (1993). Cognitive behavioral therapy for binge eating and bulimia nervosa. In C. G. Fairburn & G. T. Wilson (Eds.), *Binge eating*. New York: Guilford Press. Reprinted with permission.

the futile attempt to redress these failings by attempting to achieve a body ideal.

This model can also be used to link the ego syntonic aspects of the eating disorders with the ego dystonic aspects. The therapist can draw a dotted line between the third line of the diagram, *strict dieting*, and the fourth line, *binge eating*. The dotted line between strict dieting and binge eating is the natural dividing line between what is ego syntonic and ego dystonic about the eating disorder for most patients. Above the line, patients are invested in achieving a body shape ideal that is unrealistic and unhealthy and below the line they want to rid themselves of the binge eating and purging. By linking these components of the eating disorder, this diagram illustrates why it is that patients cannot selectively eliminate the binge eating and purging without changing other behaviors and attitudes as well.

This diagram can also be used with patients with anorexia nervosa, restricting type. The therapist can emphasize that the dotted line between strict dieting and binge eating represents the distinction between the two subtypes of anorexia nervosa. However, the therapist should inform patients that a high percentage of patients with this form of anorexia nervosa eventually start binge eating. It is useful for patients to be aware of this risk, and it can be helpful for patients who are invested in such extreme dieting to understand this behavior in the context of the whole model. Patients with anorexia nervosa, restricting type, live in perpetual fear of losing control of dieting and succumbing to binge eating. It can be explained to patients that the risk of binge eating or purging is perpetuated and intensified as a function of their extreme dieting and that their realistic fears of losing control can only subside to the extent that eating becomes less restrictive.

Educating Patients About the Importance of Homework

Homework is an essential part of cognitive–behavioral therapy interventions for both anorexia nervosa and bulimia nervosa and its importance is stressed to the patient from the start. Homework tasks are designed for the patient and therapist to identify particular patterns that are problematic and to experiment with changes in behavior in the context of a supportive therapeutic intervention. The therapist should review carefully the patient's experience with each homework assignment and build on it for subsequent assignments. The amount of effort that a patient expends on homework will be influenced by the importance and attention it receives from the therapist; therefore, it is crucial that the therapist integrate the homework assignment into each session. If a patient is resistant to complying with homework assignments, the therapist must examine the resistance, reiterate the rationale for homework, and have the patient join the therapist in designing the assignment to emphasize the collaborative nature of the task and increase compliance.

Establishing Self-Monitoring Procedures

In the first session, the therapist and patient should review the patient's current eating habits, and the therapist should introduce the concept and procedures for self-monitoring of food intake. Patients are instructed to record their food intake and associated thoughts and feelings as soon as possible after eating to maximize accuracy. The therapist should explain to patients that the self-monitoring sheets are essential because they help focus the patient and provide the patient and therapist with important information in terms of proximal antecedents that trigger or perpetuate the entire range of problematic eating behaviors. Figure 3 is an example of a self-monitoring form that organizes the most important information for the purposes of cognitive–behavioral therapy. In the first column, the individual records the time of the eating episode. In the second column, the patient records all foods and liquids. Individuals record where they were during eating episodes, whether the eating was part of a binge, and whether they engaged in any vomiting or laxative abuse to compensate for the eating. The sixth column is for recording thoughts and feelings elicited around the eating episodes.

Using the self-monitoring sheets, the therapist can help patients record during the session what they consumed over the day or two prior to the initiation of treatment. For patients who have completed an inpatient hospitalization recently, it is useful to assess the patients' eating patterns near the end of hospitalization and the changes in eating that have occurred since discharge. For homework, patients are asked to complete the self-monitoring sheets, recording exactly what they eat as well as any prominent thoughts and feelings at meal times.

The therapist should spend a significant part of the sessions in Phase 1 reviewing the self-monitoring sheets, focusing on three major points. First, the patient's own experiences can be used to exemplify the cognitive–behavioral therapy model presented in the first session. It is important to continue to refer to this model throughout treatment so that patients gain a thorough and integrated understanding of the way in which the seemingly discrete components of the eating disorder are actually interdependent. Of critical importance is that patients begin to understand from their own experience the link between extreme dieting and binge eating. For patients with anorexia nervosa who are not binge eating or vomiting, the self-monitoring sheets provide essential information about the specific rigid and avoidant eating patterns characteristically practiced by restricting anorexic

Name:		Day:				Date:
Time	Food and Liquid Consumed[a]	Place	Binge	Vomiting/Laxatives		Context

Figure 3. Self-monitoring form.

[a]Meals should be circled or bracketed.

patients. This information will provide the basis for both the behavioral tasks designed to change these eating habits and the cognitive restructuring related to the thoughts maintaining these eating habits.

Second, during the initial phase of treatment, reviewing the self-monitoring sheets with patients helps them begin to construct a hierarchy of eating situations that range from extremely difficult to comfortably manageable. In this way, therapists and patients can discuss the variables that differentiate these situations and increase the patients' awareness of the range of thoughts, feelings, and behaviors they have when eating. The purpose of this is to begin to point out the limitation and inaccuracy of labeling one's self solely *anorexic* or *bulimic*. In this way, the therapist can begin pointing out cognitive distortions such as *labeling* and *all-or-nothing thinking* to lay the foundation for subsequent sessions focused on cognitive restructuring.

Third, the self-monitoring sheets offer the opportunity to review the various forms of extreme dieting characteristic of patients with eating disorders. It is helpful to clarify with patients that extreme dieting comes in multiple forms, often including (a) setting strict limits on how much food is allowed; (b) forbidding certain types of foods; and (c) establishing strict rules about where, when, and how food can be consumed. It is important that homework tasks between sessions target the reduction of excessive restraint in all its variant forms. For example, the patient who initially was skipping dinner totally may now be eating yogurt and fruit every night. The behavioral component of subsequent assignments would entail increasing the variety and quantity of food consumed. As long as patients are progressing (and maintaining or gaining weight appropriately), the therapist should allow them to direct the behavioral change. However, if patients are losing weight or falling behind target weight-gain curves or if patients propose only minimal changes (such as increasing their intake with a glass of juice), the therapist must encourage patients to increase their efforts and explore the distortions that interfere with greater behavioral change.

One of the hallmark features common to anorexia nervosa and bulimia nervosa is excessive preoccupation with weight and shape. Cognitive–behavioral therapy addresses such overconcern with weight and shape in several ways, including monitoring weight carefully throughout treatment. In the first session for patients with anorexia and within the first few sessions for patients with bulimia, the therapist can describe in detail the weight monitoring procedures in cognitive–behavioral therapy. The logistical details for monitoring weight differ depending on diagnosis and phase of treatment; however, in all cases, the rationale is provided for patients in terms of why it is important to know one's weight, how to think about weight ranges and weight change, and why it is critical to deflate the overvaluation of weight in determining one's self-worth.

Patients should be weighed every week. The therapist can explain the rationale for weekly weighing and the purpose of refraining from weighing oneself at other times by clarifying that a total avoidance of the scale is simply the flip side of weighing oneself several times per day. In either case, weight is being imbued with excessive importance. It should be explained to patients that weight is affected by numerous factors and that it is natural for body weight to fluctuate by several pounds throughout the week. Frequent weight assessments may result in undue concern about inconsequential weight changes that nonetheless deleteriously affect one's mood and subsequent eating. Real weight change is defined as recorded shifts in the same direction for 4 consecutive weeks.

One of the primary goals of weight monitoring is to provide patients with accurate data regarding weight as they attempt to make behavioral changes in their eating. Patients with eating disorders state that they engage in their eating patterns because of tremendous fears about gaining weight. Motivating normal weight patients with bulimia nervosa to experiment with normalizing their eating can be facilitated by reviewing the clinical data indicating that, on average, recovering from bulimia nervosa is not associated with significant weight gain. By making weight monitoring an integral component of treatment, the patient's own data make it possible to identify and challenge problematic thoughts concerning weight and shape that have previously interfered with resolving the eating disorder.

Weight monitoring for patients with bulimia nervosa is usually accomplished by having patients weigh themselves on their own on a regular weekly schedule. Patients record their weekly weights on their self-monitoring sheets for discussion in the therapy session. Patients are encouraged to select the same time and scale for their weekly weighing to reduce measurement error and to reduce the likelihood that they will avoid the scale if they are feeling fat. It is usually best for patients to weigh themselves on a weekday morning. If it is too difficult for patients to commit to weighing themselves on a regular weekly schedule either because of extreme avoidance or because they are weighing themselves much more frequently, it is appropriate to try to work with the patients to shape their behavior with the aim of achieving a weekly weighing schedule. If patients still refuse to assume responsibility for weekly weighing, it may be necessary to weigh patients at the beginning of the therapy session. Patients are encouraged to write down thoughts and feelings before and after weighing themselves. This information is extremely useful in identifying the problematic thoughts and beliefs about weight and shape that are central to the eating disorder.

The treatment plan for weight monitoring needs to be discussed explicitly and thoroughly with patients with anorexia nervosa in the first session. In the treatment plan outlined by Pike et al. (1995), patients are weighed weekly by the therapist at the beginning of sessions during Phase 1 of treatment. To the extent that patients are able to maintain their weight, they gradually assume responsibility for weekly monitoring in Phase 2.

Using Crisp's (1980) weight graph (Figure 4), it can be useful to review the course of weight change and its effect on the menstrual cycle. The purpose of this intervention is to: (a) assess the extent to which developmental or maturational fears serve to maintain the disorder, (b) locate where the patient is with regard to her weight history, and (c) target the points of weight gain and return of menses (in women) as particular high-risk periods that will warrant careful attention in treatment.

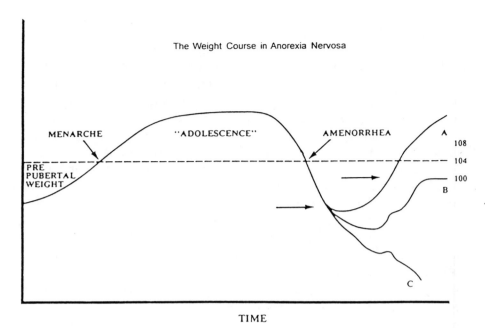

Figure 4. The Weight Course in Anorexia Nervosa

The dotted line represents the *menstrual weight threshold*, which is approximately 47 kg (104 lb) for a woman 163 cm (5 ft 4 in.) tall. Line *A* represents the weight that must be achieved for recovery; Line *B* indicates the suboptimal weight that many patients prefer, which is lower than recovery weight; and Line *C* represents the chronic course that eventually could lead to death. The two horizontal arrows represent the times when patients with anorexia nervosa express most anxiety—at the initiation of weight gain and when they approach the "menstrual threshold." (Reprinted with permission from A. H. Crisp, 1980 *Anorexia Nervosa: Let me be.* London: Academic Press.)

It is essential that the therapist offer positive reinforcement for any efforts patients with anorexia nervosa make to keep their weight stable. Even if the patient has lost weight, the therapist needs to offer positive reinforcement and encouragement for any effort aimed at recovery. It is useful for the therapist to remind patients that weight loss frequently happens immediately after discharge from an inpatient program and that it will take some fine-tuning for patients to figure out the appropriate intake to maintain their weight.

It is essential that the therapist set an explicit lower weight limit above which a patient's weight must stay in order to remain in outpatient therapy. In clinical practice this lower limit is often set at a body mass index of approximately 16.5 (body mass index equals weight [kg] divided by height squared [m^2]; Statistical Bulletin, 1984). This equates to approximately 75% of recommended weight (Metropolitan Life Insurance Company, 1959). The therapist should review with the patient the consequences that weight loss will have on the focus and structure of treatment.

If patients lose more than 5 pounds between sessions or if their weight falls below 85% of ideal, a medical evaluation, including lab work should be conducted based on the judgment of the physician who is providing medical coverage (see chapter 8, this volume). Throughout the course of treatment, when patients are having difficulty maintaining their weight, therapists and patients need to establish a weight gain protocol that returns patients to a minimally acceptable weight. It is often extremely difficult for patients to gain any more weight than the target weight established on the inpatient unit, so we recommend that the inpatient goal weight be set at a minimum of 90% of ideal weight. If patients are unable to comply with the established contract for weight restoration to the extent that their weight falls below 75% of ideal for more than 10 days, we recommend that they be evaluated for readmission to inpatient treatment. Under no circumstances is a weight of less than 75% an acceptable weight for an extended period of outpatient treatment.

Prescribing Normalized Eating

From the onset of treatment, the goal of cognitive–behavioral therapy is to help patients establish a healthy pattern of eating three meals and three snacks each day. Referring to the model of eating disorders, the therapist reiterates that normalizing one's eating—in other words, giving up extreme dieting and eccentric or narrow food choices—is essential to eliminating binge eating and purging, maintaining normal weight, and developing other positive aspects of one's life.

For patients with anorexia nervosa who are discharged from the hospital with calorie supplement drinks such as Ensure or Sustacal, the therapist and patient need to discuss a program for eliminating the high calorie drink. These changes should be incorporated into the behavioral eating tasks that the therapist and patient construct for homework. If patients are unable to comply with compensatory increases in their other eating, continuing to increase overall intake with liquid supplements may be necessary in the short term. At certain points in treatment the most important consideration is that patients keep their weight up, regardless of whether this depends on high calorie supplements. However, such supplementation is highly undesirable on a long-term basis and runs counter to other efforts aimed at normalizing eating.

Developing Delay Strategies and Alternatives to Binge Eating and Purging

An important component of treating bulimia nervosa involves helping patients generate alternative behaviors that can delay or replace destructive binge and purge episodes. For delay efforts to be successful, patients need to identify alternatives that are sufficiently active and engaging so that they may be implemented realistically and be effective. By developing a wide range of alternatives, patients will have appropriate and feasible behaviors available to substitute for binge eating or purging as needed. Although it is appropriate for the therapist to help patients generate a list of alternatives, it is also critical that the therapist encourage experimentation with the range of options that patients generate; both successful and failed efforts to avert the binge eating and purging offer important data. One of the refinements of generating alternatives includes helping patients identify more clearly the function served by the binge eating and purging and developing alternatives that can fulfill the same role more adaptively. Several common clinical problems include

1. *Alternatives that are not sufficiently engaging.* For example, a patient may suggest "sitting and relaxing" or "listening to music." It is helpful for the therapist to explore with the patient whether these alternatives will be sufficiently engaging to counteract the urgency associated with binge eating or vomiting.
2. *Alternatives that are not diverting or pleasurable.* For example, a patient may suggest "cleaning her room" or "paying bills." Although these activities may be engaging, they are not commonly pleasant or diverting, reducing the probability that a patient will be inclined to follow through with these alternatives. The therapist could help the patient choose some other alternatives such as taking a bath or writing in a journal that are similar in intensity but more positive and pleasurable.
3. *Alternatives that are not realistic.* For example, a patient may suggest "calling her best friend" or "going for a walk." However, on inquiry, the therapist discovers that the best friend lives overseas and would be sleeping during the time periods when the patient is most likely to make use of an alternative strategy. Going for a walk may be unrealistic if the patient's most difficult times occur late at night and she lives alone in a large city. The therapist can help the patient develop alternatives that can be carried out at home. For example, the therapist and patient may be able to identify some other person to call or establish some other engaging activity such as working on a crafts project.

Consistent with reports by others (e.g., Garner, 1993), it is our experience that the binge eating of patients with anorexia nervosa differs in some important ways from the binge eating described by patients with bulimia nervosa or binge eating disorder. Most important, it is our clinical impression that individuals with anorexia nervosa who do binge often consume much less food than normal-weight bulimic individuals on average during the binge episodes. In fact, it seems that many of the eating experiences described as binges by patients with anorexia nervosa would not meet the objective criteria for a binge defined by the *DSM-IV* (American Psychiatric Association, 1994). However, these eating episodes are experienced as shameful lapses for individuals with anorexia nervosa. For such patients who describe binge eating, it is our experience that they almost always vomit or engage in some other compensatory behavior to counteract the overeating. Patients with anorexia nervosa also will describe vomiting after very limited eating episodes and normal meals. For these individuals, it is never okay to eat because food interferes with their overriding desire to achieve and maintain a state of starvation.

If the subjective reports do not meet criteria for an objective binge, the goal will *not* be to alter the specific eating behavior that the patient describes as a bingeing but rather to identify and challenge the distortions that make average snacks and meals *binges* for the individual. As with normal weight patients with bulimia, for those anorexic patients whose binges are clinically large, behavioral interventions will emphasize increasing food intake throughout the day based on the rationale that if sufficient quantities of food are consumed over the course of the day the risk of binge eating will be reduced. Also, cognitive interventions can identify and challenge the distortions associated with situations that trigger binge eating.

To address compensatory purging behaviors, both cognitive and behavioral therapy interventions are useful. It is our belief that vomiting and any other compensatory behaviors, such as laxative or diuretic abuse, are driven by the same core dysfunctional thoughts as the excessive restraint characteristic of all patients with anorexia nervosa and bulimia nervosa. All of these behaviors are pursued to achieve the central aim of thinness; individuals with eating disorders believe that such efforts will provide a sense of control, mastery, and self-worth. Throughout treatment, the *cognitive* interventions directed at the vomiting and excessive restriction are analogous—in other words, they challenge the cognitive set that reveres the pursuit of thinness. The *behavioral* interventions that address vomiting versus excessive restriction differ. In the case of vomiting, the behavioral interventions—such as the use of delay strategies and alternatives—are designed to inhibit the behavior. In contrast, disinhibition is the goal of therapy efforts aimed at loosening up excessive dietary restriction and getting patients to increase flexibility in their eating behaviors.

Learning the Skills of Imagery, Rehearsal, and Relaxation

For patients who do not binge eat or purge but who engage in excessive restraint, it is appropriate to aim therapy efforts at decreasing inhibition rather than increasing control over impulsive behavior. In addition to cognitive interventions focused on identifying and challenging distortions, behavioral interventions can include the use of imagery, rehearsals, and relaxation training.

When patients describe feeling so anxious prior to eating that they are unable to follow through with their planned meals, the therapist can make use of imagery techniques and rehearsal of adaptive functioning in stressful situations. Many patients continue to report excessive anxiety prior to eating, in which case the therapist could instruct patients in progressive relaxation training (Bernstein & Borkovec, 1973).

The therapist can explain the rationale for relaxation training, and drawing on the patient's self-report, can emphasize that anxiety is interfering with the patient's ability to make maximal use of treatment interventions. It can be helpful to explain to the patient that the anxiety operates at three levels: (a) physiologically—the patient may experience increased heart rate, muscle tension, and sweating; (b) behaviorally—the anxiety is promoting avoidance that perpetuates the eating disorder; and (c) cognitively—such experiences are typically fraught with cognitive distortions that are self-deprecating and self-defeating ("I'll never be normal," "I am such an idiot"). To the extent that patients find these interventions helpful, they should integrate them in their daily routines.

Challenging Assumptions About Weight and Shape

In the first phase of treatment, cognitive–behavioral therapy aims to make explicit the attitudes and behaviors that are at the root of the body image dissatisfaction characteristic of anorexia nervosa and bulimia nervosa. Although many patients readily acknowledge their weight and shape concerns, others deny any excessive weight or shape preoccupation. One of the primary goals of therapy in the initial phase of treatment is to make explicit the model for eating disorders that posits that specific assumptions about weight and shape underlie and perpetuate the self-destructive behavioral components of the eating disorders. Using the self-monitoring sheets, completing the Decision Analysis Form, addressing weight preoccupations, and establishing a weight monitoring system are cognitive–behavioral therapy interventions that facilitate this work.

Throughout the initial phase of treatment, sessions begin with discussing the patients' thoughts and feelings about their current weights. The therapist should integrate this component of the session with reviewing the patients' food diaries. Discussions about problems in the area of eating, weight, and shape can be facilitated by the use of the Decision Analysis Form. By using the framework of this form to explore these problems, the therapist will be better able to identify the problematic assumptions and beliefs about weight and shape that underlie the behavioral component of the eating disorder.

The therapist and patient can construct collaborative behavioral tasks for homework that derive from the problems identified while reviewing the self-monitoring forms. Such tasks are designed to help the patient become more aware of the links between problematic thoughts and behaviors that make up the eating disorder. It is important that the patient feel motivated and fairly confident about accomplishing the tasks. The primary goal is for the patient to succeed. At a minimum, this means that the patient makes an effort to accomplish the goal, and ideally it means that the patient is able to complete the task.

For example, it would not be unusual for a patient to skip meals during this phase of treatment. Eating often becomes increasingly more difficult through the course of the day, with many patients either skipping dinner totally, vomiting after dinner, or not eating a sufficient meal. When this occurs, the therapist and patient need to identify and challenge the problematic assumptions that result in the perpetuation of the eating disorder. In addition, behavioral experimentation needs to be emphasized, and the patient needs to commit to making some concrete behavioral changes in eating habits. For the patient who is skipping dinner entirely, as a last resort the therapist and patient might agree on some minimal consumption such as yogurt and fruit in the interest of at least getting the patient started in establishing a more normalized eating routine. However, it must be clear to the patient that this would be unacceptable as a long-term goal and is only a first step toward eating a more complete dinner.

In the initial phase, behavioral strategies for addressing binge eating and vomiting include using delay strategies and developing alternatives to binge eating and purging. Behavioral interventions that challenge excessive restriction include systematic reintroduction of at least one additional food per insufficient meal to augment daily food intake. These behavioral interventions provide crucial information regarding how patients think about themselves, their weight, and shape. To the extent that this behavioral experimentation disrupts rigid routines, patients will have the opportunity to focus on thoughts and feelings that arise when their behavior is no longer automatic.

Providing Psychoeducation

During the initial phase of treatment, an important part of cognitive–behavioral therapy is providing the patient with accurate information regarding several important aspects of the eating disorder. Using the study conducted by Keys and colleagues at the University of Minnesota during World War II (Keys, Brozek, Henschel, Mickelsen, & Taylor, 1950), the therapist can describe to patients what is known about the physiological and psychological consequences of starvation and malnutrition, critical aspects of anorexia nervosa and bulimia nervosa.

Keys and colleagues conducted a study of malnutrition with 32 healthy male volunteers who were conscientious objectors during the war. The data from the study were to be used to inform the nutritional rehabilitation programs for individuals subjected to semistarvation during the war. The men lived on campus and participated in classes at the University of Minnesota. Initially, they were simply monitored for baseline information. During this time they consumed approximately 3500 calories per day. During the active phase of the study, caloric consumption was reduced to less than half the original calories (1570 calories per day). The effects of the undernutrition were measured by observation, personal interview, and questionnaires.

Prior to weight loss: (a) the men were interested in the educational program available; (b) they were interested in the various aspects of the study and demanded that their input be considered; and (c) social activity was high.

After the weight loss: (a) one of the first noticeable changes was that the men lost interest in social activities and became more isolated; (b) the men became reluctant to plan ahead; (c) they were less interested and less able to make decisions and participate in group activities; (d) the men became apathetic about the study and did not continue to express initiative in having a say in the rules or policies of the conduct of the study; (e) interest in sex, mental alertness, and motivation went down; (f) moodiness, irritability, and apathy increased; and especially important, (g) as interest in other aspects of living decreased, interest in food increased. The men tended to spend more time thinking, talking about, and daydreaming about food. Mealtimes became extended.

The Keys study provides an opportunity for the therapist and patient to explore the patients' experience of chronic dieting and (if they have reached anorexic weight status) their experience of having been severely malnourished. What do patients with anorexia nervosa remember from the time that they were admitted to the hospital? Do the patients notice changes in their moods, energy level, concentration, alertness, and social activity as a function of maintaining a healthy weight and normalizing their eating?

In addition to the effects of starvation, it is important to review with patients the ineffectiveness of vomiting and laxative abuse to promote weight loss. In this context, it is useful to describe the deleterious medical aspects of vomiting and laxative abuse, including the risk of dental problems, dehydration, electrolyte abnormalities, and bowel problems. Detailed information for the clinician and patient regarding the medical complications associated with eating disorders is provided in Hsu (1990) and chapter 8, this volume.

Educating patients about body image issues is also useful. For instance, it is helpful to review with patients current theories regarding the biological and genetic contributions to weight status and body shape. In this regard it is helpful to discuss with patients real limits in terms of the malleability of their bodies regardless of their eating and exercise efforts. It is also useful to review with patients the sociocultural messages conveyed in advertising and the mass media. It can be helpful to articulate the myths regarding self-improvement and the achievement of beauty promulgated by the press as well as the deception employed to create a particular image. For example, therapists can inform patients about the use of computer technology to alter models' bodies in advertising layouts so that they portray images of unnatural thinness and physical proportions. Therapists can also discuss the high levels of eating disorders among women working in modeling. This kind of information can offer a useful reference point for discussing body image concerns and can help patients begin to relinquish unrealistic and unhealthy goals regarding body image (see chapter 12, this volume).

PHASE 2

The primary components of Phase 2 of cognitive–behavioral therapy include (a) eliminating forbidden foods; (b) identifying dysfunctional thoughts; (c) cognitive restructuring; (d) problem solving; (e) continuing to challenge assumptions overvaluing weight and shape, particularly for patients with anorexia nervosa; (f) broadening the focus of treatment by identifying and challenging the eating disorder self-schema and developing alternative bases for self-evaluation.

Therapy sessions in Phase 2 are scheduled on a weekly basis. It continues to be essential that the therapist address the homework assignments between sessions and work with patients to design homework tasks that will keep the patient engaged in working on relevant challenges throughout the week. At this stage in treatment, therapy will typically become more cognitively focused.

Eliminating Forbidden Foods

Although basic discussions of eating patterns will have addressed the need to eat a range of foods, in the initial phase of treatment the primary goal is to get the patient to establish a healthy structure of eating. Once the patient is eating more normal amounts of food at more regular intervals, the therapist can confront more forcefully the problem of avoided and forbidden foods.

The therapist should discuss with the patient the concept of forbidden foods and ascertain the patient's idiosyncratic beliefs about particular types of food. Does the patient avoid meat because it is fatty? Are dairy products off-limits? Is chocolate allowed or is it a *binge food*? The first task in this discussion is simply to generate a list of forbidden or binge foods and organize the list in terms of degree. The therapist should explain why it is important not to label foods as binge or forbidden foods. It is important to identify the cognitive distortions intrinsic to concepts of binge and forbidden foods and describe how such thinking contributes to maintaining the problems of excessive restraint as well as binge eating.

It is important to review the list of forbidden foods and work aggressively on designing behavioral interventions with the patient aimed at incorporating these foods into normal, healthy eating patterns. The behavioral interventions need to be graded so that the patient begins by trying a food that is at the bottom of the list of forbidden foods. For example, this intervention should not begin with the chocolate fudge sundae but rather might begin with eating a slice of bread with butter at dinner. The primary goal of this intervention is maximizing the likelihood that the patient will attempt the task and achieve some success while minimizing the risk for experiencing feelings of failure.

Sessions during this phase of treatment should continue the graded behavioral intervention of eliminating the concept of forbidden foods and reincorporating the avoided foods into the diet. Each successive session can focus on trying another food to the extent that the patient achieved success with the previous food. If a patient did not try a given food or found it difficult to accomplish the task in its entirety, the therapist and patient need to determine what interfered with achieving greater success and modify the task for subsequent homework assignments until the patient is steadily confronting the challenge of expanding the variety of foods consumed daily.

Identifying Dysfunctional Thoughts

Problematic or dysfunctional thoughts are introduced in the context of a more general discussion of automatic thoughts. For patients who were unable to make use of more behavioral interventions early in treatment because their cognitive sets rendered them exceedingly treatment resistant, introducing the concept of dysfunctional thoughts will have been incorporated into earlier sessions. Regardless of the stage of treatment, the same principles and procedures apply. The therapist explains to the patient that automatic thoughts are necessary and useful in processing the infinite amount of information that we confront every day. Based on experience, we think about the world in particular ways that become automatic. This is an essential part of learning. These principles apply whether we are dialing a telephone or riding a bicycle or when we are engaged in more abstract cognitive processes such as anticipating a certain reaction from someone in a particular interpersonal situation. These automatic thoughts are derivatives of an overarching cognitive set or schema that governs an individual's experience and behavior. Often these schemas and the related automatic thoughts operate without the individual's consciousness or attention.

It is important to explain to the patient that automatic thoughts are fast, habitual, essential, and useful in our daily functioning. The problems arise when the individual has automatic thoughts that are not valid or adaptive. On exploration, we may be able to uncover the origins of how a particular thought became fixed in one's mind, but the major focus of cognitive–behavioral therapy is to address how it is that certain thoughts are not valid or functional in the current reality of the patient's world.

At this point it is useful for the therapist to identify one of the more straightforward cognitive distortions that the patient has identified. It may be useful to speculate briefly about how patients came to think in such a way for the purpose of reassuring patients that they are not crazy and that there are reasons why they think the way they do. Such an intervention facilitates challenging the dysfunctional way of thinking and engaging the patient in the gradual process of unlearning one cognitive set for a more adaptive set. Thus, the process of identifying, challenging, and changing distortions can be understood as a normal process based on learning principles that the patient can readily understand.

Common patterns of dysfunctional thoughts have been described by Beck, Rush, Shaw, and Emery (1979) and further articulated for patients with eating disorders by Garner (1986). Some of the most common faulty thinking patterns that occur among patients with eating disorders include all-or-nothing thinking, personalization, superstitious or magical thinking, magnification, selective abstraction, and overgeneralization. Using the list provided in Exhibit 1, the therapist can work with the patient to identify the patient's specific problematic thoughts and assumptions that reflect these faulty reasoning patterns. It is most useful to draw on homework assignments and material already offered at some point during treatment. For homework, patients should try to identify examples of cognitive distortions from their daily experiences. The primary goal at this phase is to focus on identifying the distortion—challenges and alternatives will follow shortly. The therapist should emphasize to the patient that the goal is to become aware of the dysfunctional thoughts that heretofore have been automatic. The therapist should encourage patients to examine what their underlying thoughts and assumptions are about the range of activities they engage in on a daily basis.

Cognitive Restructuring

Cognitive restructuring is a procedure whereby the patient learns to question and challenge problematic thoughts. There are four basic steps in the process of cognitive restructuring. First, the problematic thought should

EXHIBIT 1

All-or-nothing thinking: This is also referred to as "dichotomous" or "black-and-white" thinking. Rigid rules are part of all-or-nothing thinking, and no allowance is made for a middle ground. Perfectionism is a prime example of this type of reasoning. Either a job has to be done perfectly or the individual feels like a failure.

Personalization: This involves assuming excessive responsibility for events or outcomes that cannot possibly be under one's control. For example, blaming one's self for a misunderstanding with a friend that was not in one's control. Personalization involves being overfocused on one's self to the point of expecting others to notice minimal changes. For example, believing that others will notice a 2 lb weight gain.

Superstitious thinking: This is also called magical thinking. This occurs when individuals act as if there is a cause-and-effect relationship between two events or outcomes that really are not at all linked. For example, believing that eating a brownie will result in gaining 5 lb.

Magnification: This involves exaggerating the importance or significance of something negative or some undesirable event. This is a common problem around eating routines. For example, magnfication occurs when an individual who eats one cookie more than allotted decides that she has ruined her entire day, and therefore abandons all efforts to control her eating and binges.

Catastrophizing: This is related to magnification in the tendency to exaggerate the probability that something terrible will happen. This occurs when someone magnifies the importance of something and then predicts the worst. For example, if an individual decides not to go to the beach because he is afraid that he would look like a whale and everyone would notice (magnification) and that this would result in his being dumped by a new girlfriend.

Selective abstraction: This is also called *mental filter*. This involves paying attention only to certain information while ignoring contradictory information that would challenge existing beliefs. For example, this is illustrated by the belief that thinness is the sole parameter on which to base one's self-worth. Another example would be for an individual to overfocus on one critical comment in an annual review despite an overall positive review and pay raise and deciding that one's boss is not pleased.

Overgeneralization: This involves going from a specific incident or event and extracting a rule or belief that is applied to subsequent, possibly unrelated circumstances. An example of overgeneralization would be a student who fails a test and decides that he is not smart enough to continue his education.

Labeling: This involves making fixed attributions about one's self or others that interfere with a more flexible approach to problem solving. This is an extreme form of overgeneralization. Deciding that one has an eating disorder because one is a *weak* person is an example of such a label.

Should statements: Trying to motivate one's self by should statements typically derives from trying to force one's self to do what is right regardless of other considerations. Often the result is that people do not do what they think they should do and therefore feel guilty about their decisions. When others do not do what *should* be done, the result is anger.

be articulated as clearly and simply as possible. The goal is to distill the core cognitive distortions that underlie the more conscious thoughts. Second, the patient should evaluate the supporting data for the validity of the thought. Third, the patient should develop arguments and evidence that challenge the validity of the problematic thought. Fourth, the patient should aim to reach a reasoned conclusion about this data.

It is essential that patients generate the material that supports and contradicts the problematic thoughts. Using Socratic methods, the therapist can assist by asking a range of questions at each step. In assessing the support for the assumption, the therapist can ask the patient to articulate the facts ("What are the basic facts?"), make a retrospective test ("How did I feel/think/act in the past?"), and get consensual information ("Is this true for everyone?").

In challenging the problematic thought or assumption, the therapist can ask the patient whether there are any alternative explanations. This can be accomplished by reviewing responsibility, looking for other interpretations, and decentering. It is important that the therapist engage the patient in working on generating challenges that the patient really believes. It is frequently the case that a patient will know the *right* answer but will not believe the challenge as genuine or true. As a first step, the therapist might assess whether the patient can put credence in the challenge as it applies to others (*decentering*). To the extent that the patient can recognize the challenge as true for others, the therapist can work with the patient to determine why the rules are different for the patient; how the challenge can be applied to the patient; and what the distortions are in the patient's thinking that require rules that apply only to the patient. Another common problem with challenges that patients initially generate is that they tend to be overly general; they seem perfunctory and predicated on platitudes (e.g., "All women are dissatisfied with their bodies to some extent." "Things aren't really as bad as I imagine."). Although these statements may be *true*, they are not powerful or sufficiently persuasive to have any real impact on the automatic, dysfunctional thought that is being challenged.

Establishing a reasoned conclusion can be facilitated by asking questions that will make explicit what the implications are if the belief were true. Also, the therapist can help the patient question whether it is functional to act in accordance with this belief. Together they can develop a pro and con list, predict the future, and examine conflicts between other life goals and these problematic assumptions.

Structured Problem Solving: The Dysfunctional Thought Record

General problem solving procedures can be used at this stage of therapy to help patients articulate the details of the continuing problems they are having in resolving the eating disorder and constructing more adaptive attitudes and behaviors. In addition, this section describes a more structured form of problem solving that is facilitated by using the Dysfunctional Thought Record (Figure 5).

Drawing on material from earlier sessions, the therapist can introduce the Dysfunctional Thought Record and reiterate that the goal of therapy

Situation	Emotion	Automatic Thoughts	Challenges	Outcome or Alternatives
Describe: Actual event leading to unpleasant emotion or stream of thoughts Date:	Specify sad, anxious, angry, etc.	Write automatic thoughts that preceeded emotions Identify dysfunctional thoughts	Write challenges to dysfunctional thoughts	

Figure 5. Daily Record of Dysfunctional Thoughts

is to link thoughts, emotions, and behaviors to determine how it is that a particular set of thoughts affects how an individual feels and behaves within a given situation or problem. The Dysfunctional Thought Record brings together the cognitive, emotional, and behavioral components of treatment. The Dysfunctional Thought Record requires patients to focus on specific problematic situations or experiences (column 1). Once identified, the patients articulate specific feelings (column 2) and thoughts (column 3). To the extent that there are cognitive distortions influencing one's experience, patients will need to test the validity or evidence of these particular thoughts. As in simple cognitive restructuring, patients will need to formulate functional or adaptive *challenges* or responses to the dysfunctional thoughts (column 4). Once patients have generated sufficiently focused and powerful challenges to come to a more reasoned position, the final step is to identify alternative and more adaptive behaviors or options that could be employed to manage the particular situation (column 5).

A clinical example illustrates the point: Ms. A identified a situation in which she was attracted to a man on the subway who did not notice her. She felt sad and disgusted with herself. Her primary dysfunctional thought was, "I'm disgustingly fat," and her challenge was, "I'm not that disgusting. No one's perfect." This challenge had little impact. The therapist worked with her on the need to challenge more forcefully her self-denigration ("Hurling insults at myself won't do anyone any good. I am an attractive woman. John is clearly attracted to me, and I'm certainly not fat by any reasonable standard") and to examine her tendency to jump to the conclusion that the subway rider's indifference was a result of her unattractiveness ("There are hundreds of other things he could have been doing or thinking. If I really wanted to meet him, I could have said something. If I get insulted every time someone doesn't notice me, I'm going to be feeling pretty bad"). Having established a more reasoned position regarding this situation, Ms. A felt more prepared to manage similar situations by not jumping to conclusions and recognizing the need to be more assertive if she wants to meet people.

Using the Dysfunctional Thought Record, it can be useful to monitor the extent to which patients believe the challenges by having them rate on a scale of 1 to 10 their beliefs in the challenge. In addition, patients can rate the impact that the challenges have on ratings of their feelings by using a scale of 1 to 10 to describe how much they feel each of the identified feelings both before and after completing the challenges. If the patients' ratings of feelings do not change, it is likely that the challenges did not target the real problems in the automatic thoughts. In such cases, therapists and patients need to continue to work on the challenges until they have some effect on the patients' feelings and behaviors, even if the changes are small.

Continuing to Address Body Image Disturbances and Weight Issues

At this phase in treatment it can be useful to have patients address directly aspects of body image dissatisfaction and overconcern with weight and shape that have not resolved. Empirical data suggest that these can be the most refractory aspects of the eating disorders (Garfinkel & Garner, 1982). Therefore, body image dissatisfaction frequently persists even for patients who are able to engage in more adaptive behavior around issues of eating, weight management, and shape. As described by Cash (chapter 4, this volume), there are a variety of cognitive–behavioral treatment strategies to address body image disturbances. It is appropriate to try such tasks to challenge patients to reevaluate their body images and their continuing overvaluation of weight and shape.

Using cognitive restructuring techniques and the Dysfunctional Thought Records can be especially useful in challenging body image disturbances. In most people with eating disorders, recurring cognitive distortions related to shape and weight result in chronic body image dissatisfaction. For example, it can be useful to use Dysfunctional Thought Records to address thoughts such as, "I will never look good in shorts because my thighs are fat," "I feel fat [and therefore] I am fat," and "I could lose weight if only I tried harder." An excerpt from a session with Ms. R illustrates the use of dysfunctional thought records to address body image problems. Ms. R has bulimia nervosa, and at session 14 is distressed to report that she binged for the first time in 5 weeks.

T: Let's examine the week. Your food records indicate that you've started restricting again. What happened?

Ms. R: Well, on Saturday, I was cleaning out my closet and I tried on all these old clothes that don't fit me anymore. I'm so fat and I felt so ugly. . . . I decided that I needed to lose some weight.

T: How realistic is it for you to diet like this?

Ms. R: Now that I'm more in control of my eating, I thought it was going to be okay. But I think we can both see that I just don't have the willpower. The minute I was around some cookies, I ate the whole box.

Together, the therapist and Ms. R completed the Dysfunctional Thought Record and identified the problematic thoughts regarding Ms. R's body image dissatisfaction and feelings of fatness. As they completed the record, it became apparent to Ms. R that there was substantial evidence against the assertion that Ms. R was fat and ugly. For example, the clothing that Ms. R referred to was from 6 years ago when she was in high school. In addition, her current body mass index was 21, which falls toward the low end of the normal range. Acknowledging these challenges to the automatic

    KATHLEEN M. PIKE, KATHARINE LOEB, AND KELLY VITOUSEK

thought that she was fat helped Ms. R reevaluate her self-disparaging body image. Next, the therapist and Ms. R addressed the self-statement that Ms. R is a *failed dieter* with insufficient willpower.

T: (Looking together at the food diaries.) Can you show me a day that went well in terms of dieting?

Ms. R: (Pointing.) Yes—Tuesday. I had a cup of plain pasta with steamed vegetables for lunch and a salad with fat free dressing for dinner.

T: What is your experience of eating like this for an extended period of time?

Ms. R: Well, I can't stick to a diet. . . . I'm a pig.

T: You seem to be blaming yourself for binge eating this week. It seems to me that part of the problem may be that the standards you set for yourself are not reasonable. For instance, if I made a rule that you must walk around all day balancing a dictionary on your head, and at 6 P.M. you dropped it when a noise startled you, would you call yourself a failure? Or would you say that the rule was unreasonable?

Ms.R: (Laughing.) I see what you mean.

T: Going back to our model of bulimia, we know that strict dieting leads to a state of physical and psychological deprivation, both of which leave you vulnerable to binge eat.

Ms. R: I guess I've still got to work on developing more realistic weight goals for myself.

It is important to emphasize that while a single dysfunctional thought record or session of cognitive restructuring is unlikely to revolutionize a patient's thinking, there is generally an additive effect of several such interventions. Each should aim at injecting a measure of increased flexibility in the patient's cognitive schema. In addition, having the patient continue this work between sessions is extremely useful. If patients have difficulty identifying problematic thoughts when they occur throughout the course of the day, it is useful to assign a task that will elicit these cognitions, such as having patients examine their bodies in a full-length mirror at home (Fairburn, Marcus, & Wilson, 1993).

For patients with bulimia nervosa, weight monitoring should proceed with patients continuing to self-monitor their weight on a weekly basis. For patients with anorexia nervosa, to the extent that patients' weights have remained stable during the course of the outpatient treatment, patients can begin weighing themselves at home in addition to being weighed at their treatment sessions. The rationale for this is that patients should be assuming more responsibility for tracking their eating and weight because they will need to do this when treatment is terminated. Once this routine is established and patients are managing to self-monitor their weight weekly, the frequency of weighing the patient at the office can be reduced systematically until the patient is no longer being weighed at the therapist's office at all.

Broadening the Focus of Treatment

Cognitive–behavioral therapy for bulimia nervosa is typically described as a short-term, focused treatment that does not necessarily include the broadening of focus described for anorexia nervosa. The empirical data indicate that short-term therapy is effective for the majority of patients in reducing the frequency of binge eating and purging; however, for those patients who continue to report significant symptomatology or who wish to continue in treatment to address other issues, it is reasonable to broaden the focus to try to achieve greater benefit.

In anorexia nervosa, as treatment moves into the latter part of Phase 2, considerable attention is focused on identifying the continuing problem areas for each patient. The therapist and patient review how the patient is doing in terms of weight maintenance, normalization of eating, reduction of restraint, elimination of binge eating and purging (when relevant), and attitudes toward body image, weight, and shape. In the course of Phase 1 and the initial part of Phase 2, the major interventions regarding the particular problems of the eating disorder have been introduced to the patient, and homework assignments will have provided the patient with many opportunities to experiment with behavioral and attitudinal change. In the latter part of Phase 2, the therapist and patient will need to continue to focus on the specific aspects of the eating disorder with which the patient is still struggling.

In addition to the set of problems specifically linked to anorexia nervosa, the therapist and patient can also address other areas of the patient's life that have impeded complete resolution of the eating disorder. In particular, they might focus on maturity fears, developmental tasks, family problems, and career or educational issues that may contribute to perpetuating the problems associated with the eating disorder and may be affected negatively by it as well.

The Eating Disorder Self-Schema

This section applies to patients with anorexia nervosa and informs the latter phase of cognitive–behavioral therapy for these patients. However, as noted earlier, the cognitive and behavioral interventions described can be adapted for use with patients with bulimia nervosa as well.

One of the most striking features of anorexia nervosa is the all encompassing nature of the disorder. For the patient, family, and even the professionals working in the field, anorexia nervosa dominates the characterization of the individual. It is not uncommon for individuals with the disorder to refer to themselves as "anorexic" rather than refer to themselves as someone with anorexia nervosa. In the former, the anorexia nervosa comes first and serves as the umbrella under which the individual stands; in the latter, the individual constitutes the larger whole, a person with the problem of anorexia nervosa. Although the distinction may not appear significant at first, the former characterization reflects and reinforces the centrality and all-consuming nature of this disorder.

One of the major goals of therapy is to make explicit the all-encompassing role that anorexia nervosa plays in organizing and simplifying an individual's self-concept and experience. As described by Vitousek and Hollon (1990), the cognitive schema characteristic of anorexia nervosa serves several purposes. It reduces ambiguity in the individual's life by providing a structure on which to base judgments, predictions, and rules for decisions and behavior. Self-worth and self-importance are measured by the ability to achieve and maintain the state of self-deprivation associated with anorexia nervosa. Eating and weight serve to regulate the stresses, demands, and conflicts of life.

Vitousek and Hollon (1990) argue that the cognitive schema of anorexia nervosa can contribute to an understanding of both the *choice* and maintenance of the disorder. Unlike most other psychological disorders, one of the hallmark features of anorexia nervosa is the largely ego syntonic nature of the disturbance. Patients explicitly report wanting the *symptom*— in other words, they want to be thin. Individuals with anorexia nervosa choose to maintain an excessively low body weight, at least in part, by the cognitive schema overvaluing weight and thinness. Individuals with anorexia nervosa value and rely on the symptoms for their ability to simplify, organize, and manage the stresses and conflicts of life. Once established, this cognitive schema operates automatically. The automatic nature of such cognitive processing may explain, at least in part, the maintenance or stability of the psychopathology associated with anorexia nervosa and its resistance to change.

Developing Alternative Bases for Self-Evaluation and Self-Reinforcement

At this stage in treatment, it is useful to review with the patient the broad concept of cognitive schemas. Using the analogy of the construction of a house, the therapist can illustrate the way in which schemas structure and organize an individual's world. Just as the frame of a house determines all subsequent efforts in building and decorating a house, a cognitive schema is the frame with which the individual approaches the world. The therapist should explain to the patient that schemas are extremely stable and enduring ways of thinking about one's self and the environment. Schemas are formed based on an individual's previous experiences and frequently are developed in childhood. Once established, schemas often operate outside the individual's awareness. They are resistent to change, wield significant influence, and continue to be elaborated throughout an individual's life.

This stage of treatment is designed to help patients diversify their self-schemas to include a wider range of roles and activities that meaningfully enhance their sense of self. The first step in this process is to identify with patients the function that the eating disorder has played in their lives. It is important to emphasize that the patients are not *crazy*, and that the eating disorder has played a major organizing function in their lives. Although the exact details of the eating disorder schema will vary, the core of the schema is typically of the form, "I am anorexic and must stay this way because it brings me control, mastery, and somehow makes me special."

Given the ego syntonic nature of anorexia nervosa, it can be difficult for patients to connect meaningfully to anything that contradicts the belief system of the eating disorder schema—in other words, being anorexic is the one and only way to achieve control, mastery, and a sense of uniqueness. Drawing on the patient's history and current status, patients need to identify the deleterious aspects of the means (anorexia nervosa) to the end (mastery, control, special status) that they have chosen. Also, patients need to evaluate how effective anorexia nervosa is in enabling them to achieve their goals.

Cognitive–behavioral therapy interventions, including the use of the Dysfunctional Thought Records, cognitive restructuring, and problem solving, can help patients challenge the assumptions inherent in the eating disorder schema. It is helpful for patients to separate the goals of achieving control, mastery, and importance from the eating disorder. To the extent that the patient's goals are healthy and reasonable, it is important for the therapist to support the needs and desires to have control, mastery, and self-importance. In these cases, it is important to clarify that the work of therapy is not to alter these goals but to work on how to achieve these goals more adaptively. However, for those patients whose goals reflect unrealistic standards, especially in terms of asceticism and perfectionism, it is essential that the patient be urged to reevaluate such goals given their self-destructive effect.

Using the visual aid of a pie diagram, the therapist can estimate with the patient the percentage of one's self that is encompassed by the eating disorder schema. Typically, at the beginning of treatment the majority of the pie or self will be accounted for by the eating disorder, with little else elaborated. Together, the therapist and patient need to explore other achievements, experiences, roles, and relationships that the patient values. Either in session or for homework, the patient can elaborate a list of such components prior to the onset of the eating disorder and for the current situation. Once identified, the goal of this phase of treatment is to help a patient elaborate additional aspects of self-representation with the goal of encouraging the patient to resume or initiate interests, hobbies, employment, relationships, and so forth, as appropriate. It can be useful to describe to the patient the health benefits of expanding and diversifying one's self-representation. In particular, the therapist can describe to the patient that greater diversity in one's self-definition tends to be associated with enhanced coping and management of stress (Linville, 1987).

Homework during this phase of treatment is designed collaboratively between the patient and therapist with the goal of helping the patient develop additional aspects of self-schema. For example, based on a patient's history, interests, and experiences, the patient could commit to buying art supplies to resume painting to inquiring about registering for a class, or calling a friend to schedule a time to get together to begin rebuilding relationships.

General Maladaptive Schemas and Eating Disorders

In addition to the eating disorder schema that tends to be fairly explicit and accessible to the patient's conscious awareness, additional maladaptive schemas may contribute significantly to the underlying issues related to the eating disorder and therefore may be addressed in the course of treatment. For patients with anorexia nervosa, maladaptive schemas in the interpersonal realm appear to be linked intricately to the more conscious eating disorder schema. Some examples of maladaptive interpersonal schemas include (a) feeling unable to take care of oneself and undeserving of nurturance by others; (b) believing that achieving nurturing, rewarding relationships will not be possible or predictable; (c) feeling worthless and undesirable to others in terms of appearance, social skills, inner worth, and so on; (d) believing that to have any worth one must be loved by everyone and therefore one must avoid conflict at all cost: "I dare not be rejected by others."

The primary goal of these sessions is to work with patients on their specific maladaptive schemas with the goal of gaining awareness of the role that such schemas play in the eating disorder and challenging these schemas using the range of cognitive–behavioral therapy techniques. The specific details of these sessions will need to be shaped by the particular maladaptive schemas of a given patient. The therapist and patient need to remain active, and change techniques should be implemented explicitly and systematically. The therapist and patient should work collaboratively to evaluate the current data derived from experimentation and continue to use an empirical approach to evaluate the validity and functionality of the maladaptive schemas.

To the extent that patients remain symptomatic, it is important to evaluate whether maladaptive schemas are interfering with making greater progress in treatment. The therapist and patient can identify the relevant general maladaptive schemas that may contribute to the core pathology of the eating disorder. Given the rigid nature and chronic course that is characteristic of anorexia nervosa, this level of intervention, designed to address the deeper and probably more historical dysfunctional assumptions that contribute to the eating disorder, may be necessary.

Challenging the General Maladaptive Schemas

As illustrated in the examples that follow, the therapist might attempt to trigger schemas through the use of imagery, memories, the therapeutic relationship, and homework. In the following example, the therapist uses the therapeutic relationship to explore how a patient's maladaptive schema can be triggered. The therapist explores the relationship of this maladaptive schema to other relationships and the patient's eating disorder:

> Ms. A left a message on her therapist's answering machine: "I'm really sorry to take up your time, but I wonder if you might be able to call me back. . . . I have a job interview at the time of our next session, and I feel like I should go. I'm really sorry. I was wondering if maybe we could reschedule if you have some extra time, but it's all right if you can't. If you can't call me back, it's OK."

At the next session, the therapist explored this interaction with the patient, specifically her need to apologize repeatedly. By probing the patient's thoughts for dysfunctional assumptions, the therapist helped Ms. A gain awareness of the implicit message that she is undeserving of any special consideration and her expectation that the therapist would perceive her as demanding and therefore react angrily. This in turn triggered examples of similar thoughts and feelings in other aspects of Ms. A's current life and childhood and led to a fruitful exploration of her schemas of disconnection and undesirability that result in her near inability to express her needs. The eating disorder helps Ms. A to compensate for these feelings of incompetence and undesirability. It disconnects her from interpersonal situations and, by engaging in self-starvation, she attains a sense of control and mastery in this area of her life.

Once triggered, identified, and elaborated, patients should work on identifying and confronting the ways in which they attempt to maintain maladaptive schemas. Therapists and patients can work together to change the maladaptive schemas using emotive techniques, analysis of interpersonal relationships, cognitive restructuring, and behavioral change, as illustrated in the following examples.

Emotive Therapy Techniques

Emotive techniques include using imagery, role playing, and current life experiences that promote emotional expression. For many of these patients, emotional expression has been subjugated and dissociated from experience. One of the first steps in beginning the change process is connecting the emotional expression to the relevant thoughts and experiences.

For example, Ms. D described feeling "nothing" for her father despite her behavior, which suggested that she was quite hurt and angry by the way that he had treated her after her mother died. Although she said she did not care, she talked frequently about how he always denied her feelings, how he always favored her siblings, and how she hated his new wife. When asked about the day her mother died, she said she just remembers "being in a fog." The therapist encouraged the patient to remember this day in detail and connect feeling states to the experience. The therapist then asked the patient to create an imaginary dialogue with her father, expressing exactly what she wished for from her father on that day. In a role play, the therapist encouraged Ms. D to imagine expressing her current thoughts and feelings toward her father. This exercise enabled Ms. D to express unresolved grief and reconnect thoughts and feelings in a meaningful way with regard to this relationship.

Interpersonal techniques include using the therapeutic relationship as well as current relationships to evaluate which maladaptive cognitive schemas govern one's interpersonal experiences. As described by Safran and Segal (1990), using current relationships both with the therapist and significant others, the patient is encouraged to reevaluate the validity of such schemas. Using the techniques of decentering—in other words, assuming the perspective of someone else—the patient can be encouraged to develop alternative perspectives that might aid in challenging the maladaptive schemas.

In the following example, role playing and decentering are used to further elucidate the maladaptive schemas of Ms. T: The therapist asked Ms. T to imagine an interaction with her closest friend that would stimulate the previously identified schemas. Ms. T came up with the situation of asking her friend to lend her $20 until the next week and her friend refusing. They role played this situation, first with Ms. T playing the role of the friend and responding extremely negatively (as negatively as she would fear) to the request for a loan, with the therapist modeling adaptive internal and external responses to this rejection. They then switched roles, with the therapist (playing Ms. T's friend) again turning Ms. T down but in a more realistic way, and Ms. T playing herself, identifying the dysfunctional thoughts stemming from her schemas and thinking through adaptive responses to the situation.

Cognitive and Behavioral Interventions

The primary cognitive and behavioral techniques employed at this stage of the intervention include using behavioral experiments between sessions that provide current data to assess the validity and functional utility of the eating disorder schema and the more general maladaptive schemas. Once the data are in, the therapist and patient can work on identifying the derivative dysfunctional thoughts and behaviors, focus on cognitive restructuring that contradicts the maladaptive schema, and develop gradual behavioral change that is driven by the more adaptive cognitive schema.

For example, building on the case illustration of Ms. D, once the patient had expressed her unresolved grief and reconnected thoughts and feelings, she was better able to make use of the Dysfunctional Thought Record to examine the cognitive distortions that contributed to her difficulties with her father. She discovered that she had created a monster of her father by using all-or-nothing thinking ("If my father were a good person, he would have dealt with my mother's death more effectively and wouldn't have remarried"), should statements ("My father shouldn't have remarried"), and labeling ("My father is a creep"). Ms. D was able to challenge these distortions and extrapolate from this relationship to other relationships so that she was better able to express her thoughts and feelings.

In another example, Ms. C reported a series of dysfunctional thoughts (some related to food or weight and some to other domains) that reflected the idea, "If I'm not perfect, I'm a failure." As the oldest and most responsible child in a troubled family in which her father was an alcoholic and her mother was chronically depressed, Ms. C had been under a great deal of pressure to support her mother by being the perfect child. In discussing this with her therapist, she came to realize that the perfectionistic style that may have served a useful purpose during her childhood was now working against her by undermining her sense of self-worth and pride in her accomplishments.

PHASE 3

The primary focus of Phase 3 of treatment is relapse prevention in the context of termination. This includes reviewing high-risk situations and specific strategies to prevent relapse, promoting adaptive coping skills, and facilitating recovery from slips.

Relapse prevention entails reviewing the specific cognitive–behavioral therapy tools and strategies that the patient has found most helpful. It should be emphasized to the patient that the goal of treatment is not to solve all potential problems in treatment but to learn the skills necessary to manage such problems adaptively in the future. In the case of positive outcome, we would expect patients to describe an enhanced sense of self-efficacy as a result of the gains they have made in treatment. At this point, the therapist can reiterate that as long as patients continue to employ what they have learned, they will be acting as their own therapist and decrease their risk of relapse.

In the end phase of treatment, it is helpful for patients to think ahead to potentially stressful situations and challenges. During these sessions, the therapist can help patients practice and plan for particular challenges. Anticipating and planning are key elements in preventing relapse. However, it is important to emphasize that no one stays exactly on course all of the time. As much as possible, patients need to learn to identify and monitor cues that they are off-course. The more attentive and responsive patients are to such cues, the more rapidly they can implement cognitive–behavioral therapy strategies and the less likely they are to relapse. Also, it is important to emphasize that an individual episode of bingeing and purging or a day of distorted thinking does not mean that patients are headed back to where they started, (i.e., a *slip-up* is not a *failure*).

Treatment is often time limited for a range of reasons, including circumstances of the patient, limitations of economic resources, and limitations imposed by the treatment setting. Whatever the reason, the time limitation should be acknowledged throughout the treatment and focus should be on what can be accomplished in the time allotted. Often patients maintain the fantasy that if only they had more time, all their problems would be solved. Other patients will devalue the treatment, stating that whatever the time limit, it is not long enough to address their needs. The tendency to overvalue or devalue treatment in this way needs to be addressed throughout treatment but often becomes most pronounced in the end phase. In these situations, it is critical that the therapist reiterate that the goal of treatment is not to solve all potential problems but to learn the skills necessary to manage such problems adaptively in the future. The goal of cognitive–behavioral therapy is for patients to become their own therapists as they continue on in the unfinished business of life.

CONCLUSION

The goal of this chapter was to review the empirical support for cognitive–behavioral therapy in the treatment of bulimia nervosa and anorexia nervosa and describe the core features of this therapy for the eating disorders. In terms of empirical support, a significant body of data derived from controlled treatment studies document the efficacy of cognitive–behavioral therapy for bulimia nervosa. The principles of cognitive–behavioral therapy for anorexia nervosa have been described in detail for at least a decade. However, it is more recent that this therapy has been evaluated in the context of clinical treatment studies, with preliminary data suggesting that it is effective for anorexia nervosa as well.

The core components of cognitive–behavioral therapy for eating disorders have been described in this chapter. Across the range of eating disorders, cognitive–behavioral therapy focuses on both the cognitive and behavioral factors maintaining the disturbances. Identifying and challenging dysfunctional attitudes and behaviors regarding eating, weight, and shape are core components of treatment. The manual based cognitive–behavioral therapy for bulimia nervosa tends to be of shorter term and more narrowly focused than for anorexia nervosa. Cognitive–behavioral therapy for anorexia nervosa addresses a broader spectrum of developmental and interpersonal issues significant to resolving the eating disorder.

The documented efficacy of cognitive–behavioral treatment for eating disorders supports its application as a first line intervention. Further work is necessary to evaluate how cognitive–behavioral interventions could be adapted to enhance their efficacy for those who do not respond to existing treatments. In addition, adaptations of this therapy for different stages of treatment may prove beneficial.

REFERENCES

American Psychiatric Association. (1980). *Diagnostic and statistical manual of mental disorders*, 3rd ed. Washington, DC: Author.

American Psychiatric Association. (1994). *Diagnostic and statistical manual of mental disorders*, 4th ed. Washington, DC: Author.

Agras, W. S., Barlow, D. H., Chapin, H. N., Abel, G. G., & Leitenberg, H. (1974). Behavior modification of anorexia nervosa. *Archives of General Psychiatry, 30*, 279–286.

Agras, W. S., and Kraemer, H. (1984). The treatment of anorexia nervosa: Do different treatments have different outcomes? In A. J. Stunkard & E. D. Stellar (Eds.), *Eating and its disorders*. New York: Raven Press.

Agras, W. S., Rossiter, E. M., Arnow, B., Schneider, J. A., Telch, C. F., Raeburn, S. D., Bruce, B., Perl, M., & Koran, L. M. (1992). Pharmacologic and cognitive–behavioral treatment for bulimia nervosa: A controlled comparison. *American Journal of Psychiatry, 149*, 82–87.

Agras, W. S., Schneider, J. A., Arnow, B., Raeburn, S. D., & Telch, C. F. (1989). Cognitive–behavioral and response–prevention treatments for bulimia nervosa. *Journal of Consulting Clinical Psychology, 57*, 215–221.

Barlow, D. (Ed.). (1992). *Clinical handbook of psychological disorders*, 2nd ed., New York: Guilford Press.

Beck, A. T. (1967). *Depression: Clinical, experimental and theoretical aspects.* New York: Harper & Row.

Beck, A. T. (1976). *Cognitive therapy and the emotional disorders.* New York: International Universities Press.

Beck, A. T., Rush, A. J., Shaw, B. F., & Emery, G. (1979). *Cognitive therapy of depression.* New York: Guilford Press.

Bemis, K. M. (1987). The present status of operant conditioning for the treatment of anorexia nervosa. *Behavior Modification, 11,* 432–463.

Bernstein, D. A., & Borkevec, T. D. (1973). *Progressive relaxation training: A manual for the helping professions.* Champaign, Ill.: Research Press.

Blinder, B. J., Freeman, D. M. A., & Stunkard, A. J. (1970). Behavior therapy of anorexia nervosa: Effectiveness of activity as a reinforcer of weight gain. *American Journal of Psychiatry, 126,* 1093-1098.

Bossert, S., Schnabel, E., & Krieg, J. C. (1989). Effects and limitations of cognitive–behavior therapy in bulimia patients. *Psychotherapy and Psychosomatics, 51,* 77–82.

Channon, S., DeSilva, P., Hemsley, D., & Perkins, R. (1989). A controlled trial of cognitive–behavioural and behavioural treatment of anorexia nervosa. *Behaviour Research and Therapy, 27,* 529–535.

Cooper, P. J., Cooper, Z., & Hill, C. (1989). Behavioral treatment of bulimia nervosa. *International Journal of Eating Disorders, 8,* 87–92.

Coker, S., Vize, C., Wade, T., & Cooper, P. J. (1993). Patients with bulimia nervosa who fail to engage in cognitive–behavior therapy. *International Journal of Eating Disorders, 13,* 35–40.

Craighead, L. W., & Agras, W. S. (1991). Mechanisms of action in cognitive–behavioral and pharmacological interventions for obesity and bulimia nervosa. *Journal of Consulting and Clinical Psychology, 59,* 115–125.

Crisp, A. H. (1980). *Anorexia nervosa: Let me be.* London: Academic Press.

Crisp, A. H., Norton, K., Gowers, S., Halek, C., Bowyer, C., Yeldham, D., Levett, G., & Bhat, A. (1991). A controlled study of the effect of therapies aimed at adolescent and family psychopathology in anorexia nervosa. *British Journal of Psychiatry, 159,* 325–333.

Fairburn, C. G. (1985). A cognitive–behavioral treatment of bulimia. In D. M. Garner & P. E. Garfinkel (Eds.), *Handbook of psychotherapy for anorexia nervosa and bulimia* (pp. 160–192). New York: Guilford Press.

Fairburn, C. G., & Cooper, P. J. (1989). Eating disorders. In K. Hawton, P. Salkovskis, J. Kirk, & D. M. Clark (Eds.), *Cognitive behaviour therapy for psychiatric problems: A practical guide* (pp. 267–314). Oxford University Press.

Fairburn, C. G., & Garner, D. M. (1986). The diagnosis of bulimia nervosa. *International Journal of Eating Disorders, 5,* 403–419.

Fairburn, C. G., Marcus, M., & Wilson, G. T. (1993). Cognitive–behavioral therapy for binge eating and bulimia nervosa. In C. G. Fairburn & G. T. Wilson

(Eds.), *Binge eating: Nature, assessment and treatment* (pp. 361–404). New York: Guilford Press.

Fairburn, C. G., Jones, R., Peveler, R. C., Carr, S. J., Solomon, R. A., O'Connor, M. E., Burton, J., & Hope, R. A. (1991) . Three psychological treatments for bulimia nervosa. *Archives of General Psychiatry, 48,* 163–469.

Fairburn, C. G., Jones, R., Peveler, R. C., Hope, R. A., & O'Conner, M. E. (1993). Psychotherapy and bulimia nervosa: Longer-term effects of interpersonal psychotherapy, behavior therapy, and cognitive behavior therapy. *Archives of General Psychiatry, 50,* 419–428.

Fairburn, C. G., Kirk, J., O'Connor, M., & Cooper, P. J. (1986). A comparison of two psychological treatments for bulimia nervosa. *Behaviour Research and Therapy, 24,* 629–643.

Fennell, M. (1989). Depression. In K. Hawton, P. M. Salkovskis, J. Kirk, & D. Clark (Eds.), *Cognitive behaviour therapy for psychiatric problems* (pp. 169–234). New York: Oxford Medical.

Fettes, P. A., & Peters, J. M. (1992). A meta-analysis of group treatments for bulimia nervosa. *International Journal of Eating Disorders, 11,* 97–110.

Freeman, C. P. L., Barry, F., Dunkeld-Turnball, J., & Henderson, A. (1988). Controlled trial of psychotherapy for bulimia nervosa. *British Medical Journal, 296,* 521–525.

Garfinkel, P. E. (1985). The treatment of anorexia nervosa in Toronto. *Journal of Psychiatric Research, 19,* 405–411.

Garfinkel, P. E., & Garner, D. M. (1982). *Anorexia nervosa. A multidimensional perspective,* New York: Brunner/Mazel.

Garner, D. M. (1986). Cognitive therapy for anorexia nervosa. In K. D. Brownell & J. P. Foreyt (Eds.), *Handbook of eating disorders* (pp. 301–327). New York: Basic Books.

Garner, D. M. (1993). Binge eating in anorexia nervosa. In C. G. Fairburn & G. T. Wilson (Eds.), *Binge eating: Nature, assessment, and treatment* (pp. 50–76). New York: Guilford Press.

Garner, D. M., & Bemis, K. M. (1982). A cognitive–behavioral approach to anorexia nervosa. *Cognitive Therapy and Research 6,* 123–150.

Garner, D. M., & Bemis, K. M. (1985). Cognitive therapy for anorexia nervosa. In D. M. Garner, & P. E. Garfinkel (Eds.), *Handbook of psychotherapy for anorexia nervosa and bulimia* (pp 107–146). New York: Guilford Press.

Garner, D. M., Garfinkel, P. E., & Bemis, K. M. (1982). A multidimensional psychotherapy for anorexia nervosa. *International Journal of Eating Disorders, 1,* 3–46.

Gowers, S., Norton, K., Halek, C., & Crisp, A. (1994). Outcome of outpatient psychotherapy in a random allocation treatment study of anorexia nervosa. *International Journal of Eating Disorders, 15,* 165–177.

Gray, J. J., & Hoage, C. M. (1990). Bulimia nervosa: Group behavior therapy with exposure plus response prevention. *Psychological Reports, 66,* 667–674.

Hall, A., & Crisp, A. (1987). Brief psychotherapy in the treatment of anorexia nervosa: Outcome at one year. *British Journal of Psychiatry, 151,* 185–191.

Halmi, K. A. (1983). Treatment of anorexia nervosa: A discussion. *Journal of Adolescent Health Care, 4,* 47–50.

Halmi, K. A., Powers, P., & Cunningham, S. (1975). Treatment of anorexia nervosa with behavior modification: Effectiveness of formula feeding and isolation. *Archives of General Psychiatry, 32,* 93–96.

Hawton, K., Salkovskis, P. M., Kirk, J., & Clark, D. (1989). *Cognitive behaviour therapy for psychiatric problems.* New York: Oxford Medical.

Hsu, L. K. (1988). The outcome of anorexia nervosa: A reappraisal. *Psychological Medicine, 18,* 807–812.

Hsu, L. K. (1990). *Eating disorders.* New York: Guilford Press.

Hsu, L. K., Crisp, A. H., & Harding, B. (1979, January). Outcome of anorexia nervosa. *Lancet,* 61–65.

Kettlewell, P. W., Mizes, J. S., & Wasylyshyn, N. A. (1992). A cognitive–behavioral group treatment of bulimia. *Behavior Therapy, 23,* 657–670.

Keys, A., Brozek, J., Henschel, A., Mickelsen, O., & Taylor, H. L. (1950). *The biology of human starvation.* Minneapolis, MN: University of Minnesota Press.

Kirkley, B. G., Schneider, J. A., Agras, W. S., & Bachman, J. A. (1985). Comparison of two group treatments for bulimia. *Journal of Consulting and Clinical Psychology, 53,* 43–48.

Laessle, R. G., Zoettl, C., & Pirke, K. M. (1987). Metaanalysis of treatment studies for bulimia. *International Journal of Eating Disorders, 6,* 647–653.

Leitenberg, H., Agras, W. S., & Thompson, L. E. (1968). A sequential analysis of the effect of selective positive reinforcement in modifying anorexia nervosa. *Behaviour Research and Therapy, 6,* 211–218.

Leitenberg, H., Rosen, J. C., Gross, J., Nudelman, S., & Vara, L. S. (1988). Exposure plus response prevention treatment of bulimia nervosa: A controlled evaluation. *Journal of Consulting and Clinical Psychology, 56,* 535–541.

Leitenberg, H., Rosen, J. C., Wolf, J., Vara, L. S., Detzer, M. J., & Srebnick, D. (1993). Comparison of cognitive–behavior therapy and desipramine in the treatment of bulimia nervosa. *Behavior Research Therapy, 32,* 37–45.

Linville, P. W. (1987). Self-complexity as a cognitive buffer against stress-related illness and depression. *Journal of Personality and Social Psychology, 52,* 663–676.

Metropolitan Life Insurance Company. (1959). *Statistical Bulletin of the Metropolitan Life Insurance Company, 40,* 1–17.

Mitchell, J. E., Pyle, R. L., Eckert, E. D., Hatsukami, D., Pomeroy, C., & Zimmerman, R. (1990). A comparison study of antidepressant and structured group psychotherapy in the treatment of bulimia nervosa. *Archives of General Psychiatry, 47,* 149–157.

O'Leary, K. D., & Wilson, G. T. (1987). *Behavior therapy: Application and outcome.* Englewood Cliffs, NJ: Prentice-Hall.

Olmstead, M. P., Davis, R., Rockert, W., Irvine, M. J., Eagle, M., & Garner, D. M. (1991). Efficacy of a brief group psychoeducational intervention for bulimia nervosa. *Behavior Research Therapy, 29*, 71–83.

Ordman, A. M., & Kirschenbaum, D. S. (1985). Cognitive–behavioral therapy for bulimia: An initial outcome study. *Journal of Consulting and Clinical Psychology, 53*, 305–313.

Pike, K. M., Wilson, G. T., & Vitousek, K. (1995). *Cognitive behavioral treatment for anorexia nervosa.* Unpublished manuscript.

Russell, G. F. M., Szmukler, G. I., Dare, C., & Eisler, I. (1987). An evaluation of family therapy in anorexia nervosa and bulimia nervosa. *Archives of General Psychiatry, 44*, 1047–1056.

Safran, J. D., & Segal, Z. V. (1990). *Interpersonal process in cognitive therapy.* New York: Basic Books.

Schneider, J. A., & Agras, W. S. (1985). A cognitive behavioral group treatment of bulimia. *British Journal of Psychiatry, 146*, 66–69.

Statistical Bulletin. (1984). *Measurement of Overweight, 65*, 20–23.

Thackwray, D. E., Smith, M. C., Bodfish, J. W., & Meyers, A. W. (1993). Comparison of behavioral and cognitive behavioral interventions for bulimia nervosa. *Journal of Consulting and Clinical Psychology, 61*, 639–645.

Thompson, J. K., & Williams, D. E. (1987). An interpersonally based cognitive behavioral psychotherapy. In M. Herson, R. M. Eisler, & P. M. Miller (Eds.), *Progress in behavior modification* (Vol. 21, pps. 230–258). New York: Sage.

Toner, B. B., Garfinkel, P. E., & Garner, D. M. (1987). Cognitive style of patients with bulimic and diet-restricting anorexia nervosa. *American Journal of Psychiatry, 144*, 510–512.

Vitousek, K. B., & Hollon, S. D. (1990). The investigation of schematic content and processing in eating disorders. *Cognitive Therapy and Research, 14*, 191–214.

Wilfley, D. E., Agras, W. S., Telch, C. F., Rossiter, E. M., Schneider, J. A., Cole, A. G., Sifford, L., & Raeburn, S. D. (1993). Group cognitive–behavioral therapy and group interpersonal therapy for the non-purging bulimic: A controlled comparison. *Journal of Consulting and Clinical Psychology, 61*, 296–305.

Wilson, G. T., (1989). Bulimia nervosa: Models, assessment, and treatment. *Current Opinion in Psychiatry, 2*, 790–794.

Wilson, G. T., Eldredge, K. L., Smith, D., & Niles, B. (1991). Cognitive–behavioral treatment with and without response prevention for bulimia. *Behaviour Research and Therapy, 29*, 575–583.

Wilson, G. T., Rossiter, E., Kleifield, E. I., & Lindholm, L. (1986). Cognitive–behavioral treatment of bulimia nervosa: A controlled evaluation. *Behaviour Research and Therapy, 24*, 277–288.

Wilson, G. T., & Walsh, B. T. (1991). Eating disorders in the DSM-IV. *Journal of Abnormal Psychology, 100*, 362–365.

Wolf, E. M., & Crowther, J. H. (1992). An evaluation of behavioral and cognitive–behavioral treatment of bulimia nervosa in women. *International Journal of Eating Disorders, 11*, 3–15.

12

TREATMENT OF BODY IMAGE DISTURBANCE IN EATING DISORDERS

J. KEVIN THOMPSON, LESLIE J. HEINBERG, and
ALICIA J. CLARKE

In chapter 11, Pike, Loeb, and Vitousek noted the importance of intervening in the area of body image to make the most of the cognitive–behavioral treatment of anorexia nervosa and bulimia nervosa. In this chapter, we will focus exclusively on treating appearance issues as they occur within the context of these two eating disorders. Because of the relative absence of research in this area with binge eating disorder, we will leave the bulk of this discussion to Johnson and Torgrud (chapter 13, this volume) who will offer a comprehensive overview of the description, assessment, and treatment of this newly emerging syndrome.

One of the strongest findings in the entire area of body image is the significant power of cognitive–behavioral strategies to alleviate elevated levels of appearance disparagement. In the area of obesity, as detailed by Rosen (chapter 17, this volume), the findings are clear—cognitive–behavioral approaches are extremely effective in reducing body dissatisfaction among obese individuals, even in the absence of weight loss. In addition, Cash and Rosen (chapters 4 and 7, this volume) have found cognitive–behavioral approaches to be efficient in reducing the disparagement that occurs in non-eating-disordered individuals and persons with body dysmorphic disorder.

It is possible that these techniques might also be used to modify body image disturbance as it occurs in individuals with diagnosable eating disorders. However, no clinical study has addressed body image problems in eating disorders using the kind of cognitive–behavioral interventions specified by Cash and Rosen, despite empirical support of these programs for several years (Butters & Cash, 1987; Rosen, Saltzberg, & Srebnik, 1989). What may seem counterintuitive actually makes sense on closer examination. In eating disorders, in which extreme symptoms such as starvation and purging may prove life threatening, most therapies—especially cognitive–behavioral treatments—are geared toward gaining immediate control over issues such as food avoidance, self-induced vomiting, laxative abuse, out-of-control bingeing, and so on. Therefore, treatments are designed primarily to focus on aspects of the symptomatic picture other than body image disturbance (see chapters 10 and 11, this volume).

Nonetheless, as noted throughout this book, there is a strong case for including, at some point during treatment, a focus on body image concerns in *any* intervention for anorexia nervosa and bulimia nervosa. For instance, a wealth of evidence indicates that higher levels of body image disturbance are associated with a poorer response to treatment and with a greater potential for treatment relapse (Rosen, 1990). Even individuals treated successfully for anorexia nervosa and bulimia nervosa continue to express concern regarding physical appearance (see Rosen, in press). Finally, as noted earlier, the role of body dissatisfaction in the development of eating disturbance appears to have strong empirical support (chapter 1, this volume). It seems timely to offer a review of the particular methods researchers and clinicians have used to modify body image in eating disorders.

The review of this area will consist of four parts. First, we will offer a review of treatment outcome studies, focusing on the use of techniques specifically targeting appearance concerns and the measurement of the effectiveness of these procedures in modifying body image related dependent variables. Second, many potential strategies for managing body image have not received sufficient empirical testing, yet these treatments may be evaluated in the future and are also being used in individual cases by many clinicians. Therefore, we will provide a brief overview of these methods. Third, researchers are beginning to evaluate treatments for the primary or secondary prevention of eating disorders, and many of these approaches target issues related to body image. We will offer a review of these preventive approaches, along with a discussion of other possible sources of intervention, such as parents or partners of at-risk individuals. Fourth, we will offer suggestions for implementing strategies in clinical practice.

EMPIRICAL EVALUATION OF BODY IMAGE CHANGES IN OUTCOME STUDIES WITH EATING DISORDERS

As noted previously, Bruch (1962) felt that correcting body image disturbance was necessary to effectively treat anorexia nervosa (see chapter

1). However, researchers and clinicians did not immediately build on her suggestion by targeting the body image problems of individuals with eating disorders. In 1987, Garner, Fairburn, and Davis cataloged 22 different treatment components in the 19 treatment outcome studies contained in their review. None of these intervention strategies included a focus on body image issues. In his 1990 review, Rosen found that the "overwhelming majority" (p. 205) of 75 studies either (a) did not treat or measure body image or (b) did not assess body image changes, despite targeting body image problems during treatment. None of the 20 pharmacological studies measured body image (see chapter 14, this volume, for an update on this literature). Of the 40 psychological treatment outcome studies reviewed by Rosen (1990), approximately one third involved some procedure to modify body image. Many of these trials were uncontrolled, with the exception of several studies with bulimia nervosa. Of the few controlled studies, cognitive–behavioral procedures appeared to offer the most promise for improving body image concerns. Rosen (1990) concluded that it was "ironic and alarming that there is still no definite answer to questions of treatment effectiveness for body-image disturbance" (p. 208).

Rosen (in press) recently revisited this issue. His second review of this area included studies that employed an experimental design with random assignment of subjects to treatment and, minimally, one other condition. If studies did not contain specific details delineating procedures targeting body image concerns, they were not labeled as including a body image therapeutic component. It should be noted that this review procedure may have eliminated some investigations that addressed some aspect of body image in their overall treatment program, but failed to provide a discussion of the information within the text of the article. Rosen found that 21 of the 31 studies that used a psychological intervention (usually cognitive–behavioral therapy) included a body image component. However, he also found that the intervention was typically minimalistic, usually involving some psychoeducational information relevant to the sociocultural bases of eating disorders or cognitive restructuring procedures that included some focus on thoughts or beliefs about shape and body size. *None* of the studies used the set of techniques that have been found to be effective for body image problems in non-eating-disordered females, individuals with body dysmorphia, or obesity (see chapters 4, 7, and 17, this volume). For instance, no study used exposure or response prevention procedures to deal with body image avoidance or included a self-monitoring form to document relevant thoughts regarding size, shape, and weight (outside of binge eating episodes).

Our own review of the research paralleled the findings of Rosen's review (in press), suggesting little systematic effort to target body image disturbance concurrent with a selection of dependent measures capable of documenting change in this critical aspect of eating disorders. Many of the studies neither targeted body image as a treatment component nor measured changes. Some investigations included a body image component in their treatment plan but did not assess changes in this variable, whereas several studies included an outcome measure to evaluate the effectiveness of the treatment, but the intervention did not contain techniques that specifically addressed body image problems. We will focus on a brief description of some of the recent research that included both of these components in their treatment designs. The resulting outcome for various psychotherapeutic interventions offers some initial evidence of the efficacy of cognitive–behavioral therapy over other interventions. Unless otherwise noted, all of the studies were on samples of individuals with bulimia nervosa.

Fairburn, Garner, and their colleagues have provided a systematic focus on body image and included measures specifically designed to track changes as a function of treatment. In these investigations, cognitive–behavioral therapy specifically addressed unrealistic attitudes toward shape and weight and the modification of these cognitions, whereas behavior therapy and interpersonal therapy did not address body image issues (Fairburn et al., 1991; Fairburn, Jones, Peveler, Hope, & O'Connor, 1993; Garner et al., 1993). Fairburn et al. (1991, 1993) used the Eating Disorder Examination, which is an interview procedure that includes shape and weight subscales (see Cooper & Fairburn, 1989; chapters 3 and 9, this volume). Fairburn et al. (1991) found that cognitive–behavioral therapy was better than behavior therapy and just missed statistical criteria for bettering interpersonal therapy for the shape scale. Cognitive–behavioral therapy was clearly more effective than the other two conditions for the weight scale. In their 12-month follow-up of the cognitive–behavioral therapy and interpersonal therapy conditions (because of attrition, the behavior therapy group was not included in this analysis), Fairburn et al. (1993) found that both treatments produced equal improvements on the shape and weight scales.

Garner et al. (1993) compared cognitive–behavioral therapy with supportive–expressive therapy for bulimia nervosa. They noted that they "generally followed the manual described by Fairburn" (p. 40), therefore, it is likely that they included the cognitive procedures described in Fairburn et al. (1991, 1993). Outcome measures included the body dissatisfaction subscale of the Eating Disorder Inventory (Garner, Olmstead, & Polivy, 1983; see also chapter 3, this volume) and the shape and weight subscales of the Eating Disorder Examination. Cognitive–behavioral therapy produced significantly more improvement on the shape scale and barely missed statistical significance for the weight scale. However, there was clearly no difference between the two conditions on the Eating Disorder Inventory measure of body image.

Wolf and Crowther (1992) also addressed body image issues in their cognitive–behavioral approach and compared this condition to behavior therapy and a waiting-list control group. They found that body dissatisfaction was affected more positively by both the cognitive–behavioral therapy and behavior therapy than the waiting-list control group; however, the two treatment groups did not differ. Follow-up analyses at 1 and 3 months indicated that both treatments were equivalent in producing further improvements in body satisfaction. Finally, Leitenberg et al. (1994) compared three treatments: cognitive–behavioral therapy, cognitive–behavioral therapy plus medication (desipramine), and medication only. Both of the cognitive–behavioral conditions targeted cognitive aspects of body image, however, as with previous research, behavioral treatments (exposure, response prevention) were not included. On the Body Shape Questionnaire (Cooper, Taylor, Cooper, & Fairburn, 1987; see also chapter 3, this volume), only subjects in the cognitive–behavioral conditions improved on size and weight disparagement.

As this brief review reveals, the outcome research with cognitive–behavioral therapy that includes a cognitive component that addresses attitudes to weight and shape is somewhat encouraging. A small number of investigations specifically addressed body image concerns, however, these studies used techniques consisting solely of cognitive modification procedures. None of the studies actually included exposure or response prevention techniques, although these components are crucial elements of the cognitive–behavioral programs found to be extremely effective for body dysmorphic disorder, obesity, and non-eating-disordered individuals with elevated levels of appearance disparagement (Butters & Cash, 1987; Rosen et al., 1989; chapters 4, 7, and 17, this volume). Future research that involves a more comprehensive treatment approach, along with a variety of assessment measures to document any changes in body image, is certainly indicated.

OTHER TREATMENT STRATEGIES

Several treatments have received a restricted degree of analysis, primarily in case reports or uncontrolled clinical trials. We offer a brief review of these methods because they may yet receive empirical validation and may also offer useful ajunctive interventions to cognitive–behavioral approaches.

Procedures that force patients to confront their images attempt to modify the accuracy of their perceptual size estimations or their subjective feelings regarding appearance by representing visual evidence of the patients' emaciated states. In the first such use of an image confrontation procedure, Gottheil, Backup, and Cornelison (1969) filmed a 17-year-old patient with anorexia nervosa as she responded to questions such as, "How are you feeling today" (p. 240). She was then shown a film of the interview and asked a variety of questions regarding her affective response to viewing the images. There appeared to be a positive effect of this procedure on the patient's self-image—after months of therapy, she noted that "it has helped me to see what I really looked like" (p. 244). However, in this single case report, the visual confrontation treatment was combined with psychotherapy, diet modification, and medication treatments.

Biggs, Rosen, and Summerfield (1980) had anorexic patients, control subjects, and depressed individuals view a 4-minute video of themselves. No body image measures were taken; however, self-esteem levels were found to decrease in the group with anorexia nervosa, to remain the same for depressed participants, and to increase for control subjects. Fernandez and Vandereycken (1994) also exposed anorexic patients to a video of their bodies filmed in "a dark bikini" (p. 137) and evaluated multiple measures on a semantic differential scale. Although control subjects did not receive the video exposure, they were also measured for changes on the semantic differential measure. Following the exposure, the anorexic patients experienced their bodies as thinner and more active, whereas the control subjects did not change as a function of retesting.

In an interesting variation of the video procedure, Gardner, Gallegos, Martinez, and Espinoza (1989) allowed obese and normal weight subjects to self-adjust their images to match their own conceptualization of their sizes. There were two conditions—with and without the presence of a mirror. Both obese and normal weight subjects were more accurate in the adjustment of their video-presented image with the presence of a mirror.

Positive findings also have accrued by using a mirror in the absence of a video image. Norris (1984) found that anorexic and bulimic patients improved in accuracy of size perception following a phase in which they evaluated their semi-nude bodies in a full-length mirror. In a replication of this study with non-eating-disordered college females, Goldsmith and Thompson (1989) found that subjects' accuracy could be improved if they were given a combination of mirror confrontation and feedback regarding the accuracy of their body size estimations. In the mirror confrontation component, subjects evaluated their bodies for 3 minutes in a mirror while given verbal feedback to examine various "curves and contours" (p. 440).

In the second stage of treatment, the actual widths of their cheeks, waist, hips, and thighs were drawn on a blackboard in blue chalk and their estimations of the widths of these same sites were drawn immediately below the actual widths in red chalk. They viewed these discrepancies and were then reassessed on the Adjustable Light Beam size estimation apparatus (see chapter 3, this volume, for a description of this measurement procedure). Subjects repeated the second phase of the study until their perceptual accuracy was within 10%.

These specific perceptual confrontation and evaluation procedures have not been compared to cognitive–behavioral procedures. The use of mirrors is somewhat similar to Cash's (chapter 4, this volume) mirror desensitization procedure. In the former approach, subjects are asked to correct a misperception of size, whereas Cash's procedure, as with other densitization approaches, is geared to reduce the association between certain body sites and levels of heightened anxiety.

Techniques that are more nondirective in nature have received attention in the literature also. Wooley and Kearney-Cooke (1987) treated body image problems in eating-disordered women by focusing on three interpersonal and developmental areas: puberty, early sexual experiences, and the role of the mother's body image in relation to the daughter's. Guided imagery is used to help patients reenact relevant past events that were formative in the development of body image problems. In addition, they are given instructions to engage in current behaviors that reflect their improved body image, such as an increase in social activities. The issue of shame regarding the body and appearance is also addressed in the feminist–psychodynamic treatment approach for sexual abuse in eating disorders (Kearney-Cooke & Striegel-Moore, 1994).

Hutchinson (1994) also advocated an experiential approach, believing that cognitive–behavioral methods may not "address deep resistance to change, in cases where body image is entrenched in the identity and continually reinforced by social values" (p. 157). She used guided imagery in association with journal processing, group sharing, movement, and expressive media. Guided imagery is the primary mechanism for relieving isolation, heightening awareness of body issues, exploring the roots of body issues, exploring blockages and resistance to change, and reembodiment (healing the dissociation between self and the physical body).

PREVENTION PROGRAMS

Researchers are beginning to call for interventions to prevent the onset of body image disturbance. Crisp (1988) advocated information regarding "the risk factors and natural history of eating and body weight and shape disorders" and also felt that skills could be taught by "direct behavioral methods" (p. 15). Thompson (1990) felt it important to modify the "irrational expectations" regarding appearance that are "fostered by sociocultural factors" (p. 105). Brownell and Rodin (1994) felt that education was necessary to "promote acceptance of different body shapes . . . to communicate that the body cannot be shaped and molded at will and that pursuit of an unrealistic ideal increases risk for eating disorders" (p. 787).

In recent years, several investigations have attempted to intervene with adolescents to prevent body image disturbances and eating disorders (Killen et al., 1993; Moreno & Thelen, 1993; Paxton, 1993). In general, as reviewed by Smolak and Levine (1994), these programs are successful in increasing nutrition knowledge and awareness of information about weight regulation and physical development, but they have little effect on attitudes and behaviors that reflect disordered eating or might lead to eating disturbance, such as beliefs about size and weight. Smolak and Levine (1994) suggested that one reason for these disappointing results is that prevention programs for adolescents may be starting too late to preclude the onset of symptoms that may lead to eating disorders. Reviewing data that illustrate high levels of body dissatisfaction already present in middle-school girls suggests that preventive programs onset during elementary school.

Smolak and Levine (1994) recommended six specific goals for such early prevention programs:

1. Acceptance of diverse body shapes. This requires discussion of the causes of body size and shape and of prejudice against heavy people. It should also include, especially among older elementary schoolers, information concerning pubertal changes.
2. Understanding that body shape is not infinitely mutable.
3. Understanding proper nutrition, including the importance of dietary fat and of a minimum caloric intake.
4. Discussion of the negative effects of dieting as well as the lack of long-term positive effects.
5. Consideration of the positive effects of moderate exercise and the negative effects of excessive or compensatory exercise.
6. Development of strategies to resist teasing, pressure to diet, propaganda about the importance of slenderness, etc.

Smolak & Levine, 1994, pps. 301–302

Although it is certainly advisable to intervene as soon as possible, programs targeting adult women also may be beneficial. Huon (1994) developed a group discussion program that was evaluated on females, ranging in age from 18 to 25. The discussion centered on two topics: developing a more positive body image and giving up dieting. Huon also tested the effectiveness of two different approaches: focusing on strategies to facilitate change versus addressing barriers that might impede change. For instance, using the former approach, group members working on body image might be encouraged to take up sporting activities or learn to value individuality. Group members in the latter condition might focus on the media's role in promoting unrealistic expectations of thinness or society's social attitudes about shape and weight. In general, positive affect scores about the body increased after the group discussion, but only in the strategies condition.

Feminist approaches to treating eating disorders also focus on the role of body image in prevention programs. Shisslak and Crago (1994) offered a rationale and techniques for challenging the "beauty myth" (p. 421). For instance, they suggested that any prevention program should include material on the ways that clothing and cosmetic fashions are psychologically and physically damaging. They also noted that the effect of the media's images on women's physical and mental health should be explored.

Along these lines, Stormer and Thompson (1995) designed a psychoeducational intervention that involved a specific focus on informing young women (ages 17 to 25) of the strategies used by the media for promoting unrealistic standards of attractiveness. In a single 30-minute session, subjects were given a presentation that included (a) information on how the beauty ideal has changed over time; (b) biological limitations on achieving the "ideal" weight; (c) how the media modifies images with airbrushing, computer graphics, video splicing, morphing, and so forth; (d) how social comparisons to unrealistic ideals leads to body image disparagement; and (e) how the foregoing produce unrealistic expectancies and how these thought patterns lead to body image problems. Subjects who received the psychoeducational information were compared with subjects supplied with a general health education condition that consisted of information related to nutrition, exercise, stress management, and dental hygiene. The findings indicated that only subjects in the former group experienced a decrease in anxiety about their appearance and also a decrease in a measure that indexes internalization of sociocultural values regarding attractiveness (the Sociocultural Attitudes Towards Appearance Scale; Heinberg, Thompson, & Stormer, 1995, see chapter 3, this volume).

Athletes may be a particularly problematic at-risk group for the development of eating and shape-related disorders (Pasman & Thompson, 1988; Thompson & Pasman, 1991; Thompson & Sherman, 1993a). Thompson and Sherman (1993b) reviewed a variety of possible intervention areas and strategies including educating the athlete in nutrition, body fat composition, and the effects of dieting and weight loss on performance. They also suggested that coaches receive information on eating disorders, menstrual functioning, and consciousness raising (noting a particular problem with derogation used as a motivational technique—for example, a "fat pig award" for the athlete who needs to lose the most weight). Their risk reduction strategies included deemphasizing weight, eliminating group weigh-ins, eliminating unhealthy subcultural aspects (for example, wrestlers who "proudly reported their unhealthy experiences related to weight loss" [p. 73] Thompson & Sherman, 1993b), treating each athlete individually, developing guidelines for appropriate weight loss, and controlling the contagion effect (athletes copying maladaptive weight management procedures from one another).

One of the most comprehensive approaches to preventing eating disorders involves the use of a public policy approach on a widespread level. Norway is currently in the process of implementing such a plan (Gresko & Karlsen, 1994) that includes a variety of intervention components. For instance, public health officials distributed an instruction pamphlet on eating disorders to all doctors, clinics, local health agencies, and schools. Health services in schools also received a book detailing similarities and differences between types of eating problems and treatment strategies. Two other pamphlets dealing with the specific issues confronted by athletes were sent to the Norwegian Confederation of Sports. Finally, Norway is piloting an intensive study within one county that will serve as a model for nationwide implementation. This program has four components: a coordinated referral procedure, support groups for pupils with eating disorders, an education program for school and health care personnel, and an outcome evaluation of a preventive curriculum. Data on the progress of this program should be forthcoming in the near future.

FUTURE DIRECTIONS

There are several avenues for future research relevant to early intervention and prevention programs. For example, there is evidence that it might be beneficial to evaluate the role of parents and significant others (i.e., romantic partners) in the development or maintenance of body image problems. Moreno and Thelen (1993) found differences in parents of students with bulimia nervosa or bulimic symptoms versus nonclinical controls. Mothers of the two symptomatic groups were more likely to restrict their daughters' intake, encourage dieting and exercise as weight loss strategies, and perceive their daughters as overweight. (It is interesting to note there were no differences between the fathers.) Striegel-Moore and Kearney-Cooke (1994) conducted a nationwide survey of fathers and mothers and found that their evaluations of their children's attractiveness decreased with increasing age of the child. The authors found few differences with regard to the gender of the child in this self-report study, however mothers were more involved than fathers in influencing children's appearances. Smolak and Levine (1994) reviewed other evidence supporting the position that parental involvement may be an important component of prevention programs.

Tantleff-Dunn and Thompson (in press) evaluated the role of one's partner in an individual's satisfaction with appearance. They looked at several discrepancies between self and partner ratings, including ratings of self, partner, perceived partner ideal, perceived partner rating of self, and ideal opposite sex (all couples were heterosexual). The results clearly indicated that one particular discrepancy was associated with overall body dissatisfaction and eating dysfunction, but only for females. This measure was the difference between the females' ratings of the thin sizes and their perception of their partner's ideal female size. This finding indicates that a woman's *perception* of her male partner's ideal, as opposed to his *actual* ideal female size, predicts her own body image dissatisfaction. Tantleff-Dunn and Thompson's research suggests that body image intervention programs might benefit from including issues relevant to one's perception of a romantic partner's preference for body size and appearance.

Finally, although it must be handled with care, it is important to consider the role of physical activity in preventing the onset of appearance disparagement or as an adjunct to a treatment program. As noted earlier, Smolak and Levine (1994) suggested a focus on the positive aspects of appropriate exercise, along with an exploration of the contraindications of excessive physical activity. Fisher and Thompson (1994) found that a combination of aerobic exercise and anaerobic activity (weight-lifting) was as beneficial as cognitive–behavioral strategies for college women with elevated levels of appearance concern. However, they also urged caution in the use of this method because "clients might infer that use of this procedure supports the veracity of a negative view of their appearance" (p. 183).

CONCLUSION

After reviewing the literature on treating body image in eating disorders, there is one dominant conclusion that emerges. As of 1995, we know a great deal regarding the efficacy of psychological interventions for the treatment of body image disturbance in obesity, body dysmorphic disorder, and non-eating-disordered individuals (with clinically severe levels of body image concern), yet we know little about the treatment of body image problems in anorexia nervosa and bulimia nervosa. In recent years, the situation has improved slightly (Rosen, in press), and there are positive findings of cognitive–behavioral treatments that include a component that consists of cognitive restructuring of attitudes to shape and weight. However, the large controlled outcome studies have neither included a comprehensive focus on treating body image problems nor attempted to obtain a clear indication of the power of treatment to modify levels of disturbance.

Generalizing from the outcome of research trials with one clinical entity to another is often quite risky, and it would be inadvisable to assume that the cognitive–behavioral therapy methods found to be effective for the body image problems of non-eating-disordered patients (i.e., chapters 4, 7, and 17) should also prove optimal for the particular body image concerns of individuals with anorexia nervosa and bulimia nervosa. However, there is little reason to doubt that the positive findings will generalize to eating-disordered patients. Although there are some differences in the manifestation of body image issues between the clinical phenomena, particularly with anorexia nervosa patients (for example, the extreme denial and often delusional nature of the failure to acknowledge their emaciation), many of the affective, cognitive, and behavioral symptoms are quite similar across these samples (Cash & Deagle, 1995; Thompson, 1990, 1995).

Perhaps the greatest empirical support exists for the use of cognitive restructuring to challenge specific attitudes toward shape and weight. As noted earlier in the review of outcome studies, the programs used by Fairburn et al. (1991, 1993), Garner et al. (1993), and Leitenberg et al. (1994) included this ingredient to target body image in their cognitive–behavioral therapy intervention. Cash and Rosen's programs included a similar cognitive component (see chapters 4, 7, and 17, this volume). Pike, Loeb, and Vitousek (chapter 11) provide detailed guidelines for detecting and challenging faulty thought patterns that perpetuate body image dissatisfaction. Their discussion includes the important role of self-monitoring, use of a dysfunctional thoughts record, and clinical examples of cognitive restructuring. Exhibit 1 contains some common cognitions found in patients with body image disturbance.

It may be useful, in terms of preparing the patient for body image interventions, to precede the use of cognitive procedures with an orientation to the development of body image, the sociocultural factors that contribute to body dissatisfaction, or other educational material regarding body image. The manualized programs of Cash and Rosen provide some excellent material in this regard, and Pike, Loeb, and Vitousek (chapter 11, this volume) also offer guidelines (see also Stormer & Thompson,

EXHIBIT 1
Common Irrational Beliefs Regarding Body Size, Weight, and Overall Appearance

1. My value as a person is tied directly to my weight.
2. My appearance is so bad that I cannot let anyone see me.
3. If my thighs touch when I'm standing with my feet together, that means that I'm too fat.
4. If my clothes don't fit perfectly, everyone will notice.
5. I have to weigh constantly, otherwise I'll gain weight.
6. When people stare at me, it's because I'm overweight.
7. My hair should be perfect, otherwise I'll look awful.
8. When I eat carbohydrates or fats, it shows up immediately on my thighs.
9. I'm special when I'm thin.
10. My overall fitness level is dependent on the amount of fat on my body—the lower the fat content, the healthier I am.

1995). Coupled with psychoeducational and cognitive strategies, the addition of other behavioral strategies (relaxation, mirror desensitization, exposure and response prevention strategies, etc.) seems particularly appropriate for the symptoms of appearance anxiety and body image avoidant features (i.e., social situations) that are often seen in eating-disordered patients. These exposure procedures are perhaps the most empirically supported approaches for a variety of anxiety disorders and are integral to the programs developed by Cash and Rosen (Cash, 1991, 1995; Grant & Cash, 1995; Rosen & Cash, 1995; Rosen et al., 1989).

A number of other procedures reviewed in this chapter may prove useful as ancillary strategies or, given the specific case, may play a primary role in treatment. For instance, size perception training methods may be appropriate if the individual is particularly inaccurate in estimating body size (Goldsmith & Thompson, 1989). Feminist and experiential methods may be helpful in cases in which deep-rooted shame, a history of sexual abuse, or historical issues are dominant. The patient's parents or romantic partner may be a historical or concurrent factor in body image problems, and these influences certainly should be examined. An introduction of activities designed to improve body image, including exercise, dance, or other sports should be considered and carefully monitored for efficacy (Fisher & Thompson, 1994).

In sum, this review has covered a wide assortment of issues and techniques for treating body image problems in individuals with eating disorders. What can be stated unequivocally is that a focus on body image should be considered as an integral part of any comprehensive treatment program for anorexia nervosa and bulimia nervosa. These guidelines are based on a review of diverse areas of research but must be considered preliminary given the current limitations of scientific knowledge. Clinical application of these methods should be monitored closely, including periodic assessments to determine the effectiveness of the chosen treatments. Research proceeds at a rapid pace, and the conclusions included in this chapter may require modification based on newly emerging research.

REFERENCES

Biggs, S. J., Rosen, B., & Summerfield, A. B. (1980). Video-feedback and personal attribution in anorexic, depressed, and normal viewers. *British Journal of Medical Psychology, 53,* 249–254.

Brownell, K. D., & Rodin, J. (1994). The dieting maelstrom: Is it possible and advisable to lose weight? *American Psychologist, 49,* 781–791.

Bruch, H. (1962). Perceptual and conceptual disturbances in anorexia nervosa. *Psychological Medicine, 24,* 187–194.

Butters, J. W., & Cash, T. F. (1987). Cognitive–behavioral treatment of women's body-image dissatisfaction. *Journal of Consulting and Clinical Psychology, 55,* 889–897.

Cash, T. F. (1991). *Body-image therapy: A program for self-directed change.* New York: Guilford.

Cash, T. F. (1995). *What do you see when you look in the mirror?* New York: Bantam Books.

Cash, T. F., & Deagle, E. A. (1995). *The nature and extent of body-image disturbances in anorexia nervosa and bulimia nervosa: A meta-analysis.* Manuscript submitted for publication.

Cooper, Z., & Fairburn, C. G. (1987). The Eating Disorder Examination: A semistructured interview for the assessment of the specific psychopathology of eating disorders. *International Journal of Eating Disorders, 6,* 1–8.

Cooper, P. J., Taylor, M. J., Cooper, Z., & Fairburn, C. G. (1987). The development and validation of the Body Shape Questionnaire. *International Journal of Eating Disorders, 6,* 485–494.

Crisp, A. H. (1988). Some possible approaches to prevention of eating and body weight/shape disorders, with particular reference to anorexia nervosa. *International Journal of Eating Disorders, 7,* 1–18.

Fairburn, C. G., Jones, R., Peveler, R. C., Carr, S. J., Solomon, R. A., O'Connor, M. E., Burton, J., & Hope, R. A. (1991). Three psychological treatments for bulimia nervosa: A comparative trial. *Archives of General Psychiatry, 48,* 463–469.

Fairburn, C. G., Jones, R., Peveler, R. C., Hope, R. A., & O'Connor M. (1993). Psychotherapy and bulimia nervosa: Longer-term effects of interpersonal psychotherapy, behavior therapy and cognitive–behavior therapy. *Archives of General Psychiatry, 50,* 419–428.

Fernandez, F., & Vandereycken, W. (1994). Influence of video-confrontation on the self-evaluation of anorexia nervosa patients. *Eating Disorders: The Journal of Treatment and Prevention, 2,* 135–140.

Fisher, E., & Thompson, J. K. (1994). A comparative evaluation of cognitive–behavioral therapy (CBT) versus exercise therapy (ET) for the treatment of body image disturbance: Preliminary findings. *Behavior Therapy, 18,* 171–185.

Gardner, R. M., Gallegos, V., Martinez, R., & Espinoza, T. (1989). Mirror feedback and judgments of body size. *Journal of Psychosomatic Research, 33,* 603–607.

Garner, D. M., Fairburn, C. G., & Davis, R. (1987). Cognitive–behavioral treatment of bulimia nervosa: A critical appraisal. *Behavior Modification, 11,* 398–431.

Garner, D. M., Olmsted, M. P., & Polivy, J. (1983). Development and validation of a multidimensional eating disorder inventory for anorexia nervosa and bulimia. *International Journal of Eating Disorders, 2,* 15–34.

Garner, D. M., Rockert, W., Davis, R., Garner, M. V., Olmsted, M. P., & Eagle, M. (1993). Comparison of cognitive–behavioral and supportive–expressive therapy for bulimia nervosa. *American Journal of Psychiatry, 150,* 37–46.

Goldsmith, D., & Thompson, J. K. (1989). The effect of mirror confrontation and size estimation accuracy feedback on perceptual inaccuracy in normal females who overestimate body size. *International Journal of Eating Disorders, 8,* 437–444.

Gottheil, E., Backup, C. E., & Cornelison, F. S. (1969). Denial and self-image confrontation in a case of anorexia nervosa. *Journal of Nervous and Mental Disease, 148,* 238–250.

Grant, J. R., & Cash, T. F. (1995). Cognitive–behavioral body image therapy: Comparative efficacy of group and modest-contact treatments. *Behavior Therapy, 26,* 69–84.

Gresko, R., & Karlsen, A. (1994). The Norwegian program for the primary, secondary, and tertiary prevention of eating disorders. *Eating Disorders: The Journal of Prevention and Treatment, 2,* 57–63.

Heinberg, L. J., Thompson, J. K., & Stormer, S. (1995). Development and validation of the Sociocultural Attitudes Towards Appearance Questionnaire. *International Journal of Eating Disorders, 17,* 81–89.

Huon, G. F. (1994). Towards the prevention of dieting-induced disorders: Modifying negative food- and body-related attitudes. *International Journal of Eating Disorders, 16,* 395–399.

Hutchinson, M. G. (1994). Imagining ourselves whole: A feminist approach to treating body image disorders. In P. Fallon, M. A. Katzman, & S. C. Wooley (Eds.), *Feminist perspectives on eating disorders* (pp. 152–168). New York: Guilford Press.

Kearney-Cooke, A., & Striegel-Moore, R. H. (1994). Treatment of childhood sexual abuse in anorexia nervosa and bulimia nervosa: A feminist psychodynamic approach. *International Journal of Eating Disorders, 15,* 305–319.

Killen, J. D., Taylor, C., Hammer, L., Litt, I., Wilson, D., Rich, T., Hayward, C., Simmonds, B., Kraemer, H., & Varady, A. (1993). An attempt to modify unhealthful eating attitudes and weight regulation practices of young adolescent girls. *International Journal of Eating Disorders, 13,* 369–384.

Leitenberg, H., Rosen, J. C., Wolf, J., Vara, L. S., Detzer, M. J., & Srebnik, D. (1993). Comparison of cognitive–behavior therapy and desipramine in the treatment of bulimia nervosa. *Behaviour Research and Therapy, 32,* 37–45.

Moreno, A. B., & Thelen, M. H. (1993). A preliminary prevention program for eating disorders in a junior high school population. *Journal of Youth and Adolescence, 22,* 109–124.

Norris, D. L. (1984). The effects of mirror confrontation on self-estimation of body dimensions in anorexia nervosa, bulimia, and two control groups. *Psychological Medicine, 14,* 835–842.

Pasman, L., & Thompson, J. K. (1988). Body image and eating disturbance in obligatory runners, obligatory weightlifters, and sedentary individuals. *International Journal of Eating Disorders, 7*, 759–770.

Paxton, S. J. (1993). A prevention program for disturbed eating and body dissatisfaction in adolescent girls: A 1-year follow-up. *Health Education Research: Theory & Practice, 8*, 43–51.

Rosen, J. C. (1990). Body-image disturbance in eating disorders. In T. F. Cash and T. Pruzinsky (Eds.), *Body images: Development, deviance, and change* (pp. 190–214). New York: Guilford Press.

Rosen, J. C. (in press). Cognitive behavioral body image therapy for eating disorders. In D. M. Garner & P. E. Garfinkel (Eds.), *Handbook of treatment for eating disorders*. New York: Guilford Press.

Rosen, J. C., & Cash, T. F. (1995). Learning to have a better body image. *Weight Control Digest, 5*, 412–416.

Rosen, J. C., Saltzberg, E., & Srebnik, D. (1989). Cognitive behavior therapy for negative body image. *Behavior Therapy, 20*, 393–404.

Shisslak, C., & Crago, M. (1994). Toward a new model for the prevention of eating disorders. In P. Fallon, M. Katzman, & S. Wooley (Eds.), *Feminist perspectives on eating disorders* (pp. 419–437). New York: Guilford Press.

Smolak, L., & Levine, M. P. (1994). Toward an empirical basis for primary prevention of eating problems with elementary school children. *Eating Disorders: The Journal of Prevention and Treatment, 2*, 293–307.

Stormer, S. M., & Thompson, J. K. (1995, November). *The effect of media images and sociocultural beauty ideals on college-age women: A psychoeducational program.* Paper presented at the annual meeting of the Association for Advancement of Behavior Therapy, Washington, DC.

Striegel-Moore, R. H., & Kearney-Cooke, A. (1994). Exploring parents' attitudes and behaviors about their children's physical appearance. *International Journal of Eating Disorders, 15*, 377–385.

Tantleff-Dunn, S., & Thompson, J. K. (in press). The influence of romantic partners on body image: Further evidence for the role of perceived–actual disparities. *Sex Roles.*

Thompson, J. K. (1990). *Body image disturbance: Assessment and treatment.* Elmsford Park, NY: Pergamon.

Thompson, J. K. (1995). Assessment of body image. In D. B. Allison (Ed.), *Handbook of assessment methods for eating behaviors and weight-related problems* (pp. 119–148). Thousand Oaks, CA: Sage.

Thompson, J. K., & Pasman, L. (1991). The Obligatory Exercise Questionnaire. *The Behavior Therapist, 14*, 137.

Thompson, R. A., & Sherman, R. T. (1993a). *Helping athletes with eating disorders.* Champaign, IL: Human Kinetics.

Thompson, R. A., & Sherman, R. T. (1993b). Reducing the risk of eating disorders in athletics. *Eating Disorders: The Journal of Treatment and Prevention, 1*, 65–78.

Wolf, E. M., & Crowther, J. H. (1992). An evaluation of behavioral and cognitive–behavioral group interventions for the treatment of bulimia nervosa in women. *International Journal of Eating Disorders, 11*, 3–15.

Wooley, S. C., & Kearney-Cooke, A. (1987). Intensive treatment of bulimia and body-image disturbance. In K. D. Brownell and J. P. Foreyt (Eds.), *Handbook of eating disorders: Physiology, psychology, and treatment of obesity, anorexia, and bulimia*. New York: Basic Books.

13

ASSESSMENT AND TREATMENT OF BINGE EATING DISORDER

WILLIAM G. JOHNSON and LAINE J. TORGRUD

Perhaps the most salient topic in the eating disorders literature over the past few years has been binge eating, and several factors have contributed to this burgeoning interest. First, binge eating is ubiquitous, being widely distributed in both eating-disturbed and normal populations. It has long been recognized as a serious clinical problem in obesity (Loro & Orleans, 1981; Stunkard, 1959) and anorexia nervosa (Garfinkel, Moldofsky, & Garner, 1980), and binge eating is central to the diagnosis of bulimia nervosa and the newly proposed binge eating disorder (American Psychiatric Association, 1994). Furthermore, binge eating is observed with troublesome frequency in college populations (Halmi, Falk, & Schwartz, 1981; Hawkins & Clement, 1980).

A second factor promoting interest in binge eating concerns its relationship to several important clinical features. Bingeing increases with adiposity (Telch, Agras, & Rossiter, 1988), and it is associated with psychopathology in individuals with obesity (Kolotkin, Revis, Kirkley, & Janick, 1987; Marcus et al., 1990a), anorexia nervosa (DaCosta & Halmi, 1992), and nonpurging bulimic individuals (Prather & Williamson, 1988). Binge eating is also related to poor treatment outcome for obesity (Keefe, Wyshogrod, Weinberger, & Agras, 1984; Marcus, Wing, & Hopkins, 1988).

A third factor encouraging attention to binge eating is the development of diagnostic categories in which binge eating is the most prominent characteristic. Binging was a major component of bulimia nervosa in *DSM-III* (American Psychiatric Association, 1980), yet research following the publication of *DSM-III* criteria for bulimia nervosa soon identified two groups of bulimic patients: those who purged and those who did not. In *DSM-III-R* (American Psychiatric Association, 1987), bingeing and purging became criteria for bulimia nervosa, and a diagnostic impasse emerged for obese binge eaters (e.g., Marcus et al., 1988; Marcus, Smith, Santelli, & Kaye, 1992) and nonpurging bulimic patients (e.g., McCann, Rossiter, King, & Agras, 1991). Spitzer et al. (1991) proposed that such individuals be diagnosed with binge eating disorder (BED), with binge eating as its central feature.

While some have argued that the proposed BED category is premature (Fairburn, Welch, & Hay, 1993), two multisite studies support the existence of a distinct BED syndrome, with approximately 30% of the obese population and 2% to 5% of the general population satisfying diagnostic criteria (Spitzer et al., 1992, 1993). In addition, BED has been associated with severe obesity, marked weight fluctuations, impaired social and work functioning, overconcern with body shape and weight, psychopathology, amount of adult lifetime spent on diets, and a history of treatment for emotional problems. Presently, BED has been included in the appendix of *DSM-IV* as a category warranting further study (American Psychiatric Association, 1994).

CHARACTERISTICS OF BINGE EATING DISORDER

The proposed diagnostic criteria for BED are listed in Exhibit 1. In brief, the diagnosis requires that binge episodes occur at least twice weekly for 6 months and be experienced as distressing. Also, for an eating episode to be identified as a binge, it must satisfy at least three of the five associated features in section B of Exhibit 1. Because the diagnosis of BED is a recent development, only a handful of studies have targeted subjects satisfying the formal criteria for the disorder (e.g., Fichter, Quadflieg, & Brandl, 1993; Nangle, Johnson, Carr-Nangle, & Engler, 1994; Yanovski et al., 1992). Fortunately, information prior to the development of formal BED criteria can be gleaned from the literature on obese binge eaters and nonpurging bulimic patients—many of whom would satisfy current criteria for BED (Antony, Johnson, Carr-Nangle, & Abel, 1994). Together these groups will be referred to as pre-BED subjects.

Binge Eating Behavior

Central to the diagnosis of BED is binge eating, and research has addressed its frequency, size, composition, duration, and relation to antecedents and consequences in both pre-BED and BED populations.

EXHIBIT 1
Proposed *DSM-IV* Diagnostic Criteria for Binge Eating Disorder

A. Recurrent episodes of binge eating, an episode being characterized by both of the following:
   1. Eating, in a discrete period of time (e.g., within any 2-hour period), an amount of food that is definitely larger than most people would eat during a similar period of time in similar circumstances.
   2. A sense of lack of control during the episodes, for example, a feeling that one cannot stop eating or control what or how much one is eating.
B. During some of the episodes, at least three of the following:
   1. Eating much more rapidly than usual.
   2. Eating until feeling uncomfortably full.
   3. Eating large amounts of food when not feeling physically hungry.
   4. Eating alone because of being embarrassed by how much one is eating.
   5. Feeling disgusted with oneself, depressed, or feeling very guilty after overeating.
C. Marked distress regarding binge eating.
D. The binge eating occurs, on average, at least twice a week for a 6-month period.
E. Does not occur only during the course of bulimia nervosa or anorexia nervosa.

From Spitzer et al. (1993)

Frequency

Binge frequencies in excess of those required by *DSM-IV* diagnostic criteria have been reported in studies of both pre-BED and BED individuals. For example, Marcus et al. (1992), employing a semistructured interview, obtained an average reported binge frequency of approximately 16.0 episodes in 28 days for obese binge eaters. Average frequencies over 10 weeks have been found for nonpurging bulimic subjects (Rossiter, Agras, Telch, & Bruce, 1992). In a comparison of BED, nonclinical binge eaters, and normal subjects, Johnson, Schlundt, Barclay, Carr-Nangle, and Engler (1995) found that BED subjects were more likely to identify eating episodes as binges (36.2% of episodes vs. 23.2% for nonclinical binge eaters and 12.1% for normal subjects). These data translate to a weekly binge frequency of approximately 10 for BED subjects, 7 for nonclinical binge eaters, and 3 for normal subjects. Clearly, binge eating is a frequent phenomenon in clinical populations and in many normal individuals who may not satisfy other diagnostic criteria. It has been suggested that number of binge days, as opposed to the frequency of binge episodes, may be the preferred index of binge severity in nonpurging subjects because of the difficulty of demarcating binge episodes that do not end with purging (Rossiter et al., 1992). This difficulty in specifying the termination of a binge contributes to the problem of defining binge episodes, an issue that pervades research on the various aspects of binge behavior.

Amount and Composition

Studies investigating the amount of food consumed during binge episodes reveal considerable variability. Using self-monitoring records, Rossiter et al. (1992) reported an average consumption of approximately 600 kcal (range: 25–6000) in nonpurging bulimic patients. This finding contrasts with the laboratory study of Yanovski et al. (1992) on a BED sample in which an average of nearly 3000 kcal (range: 2300–3600) was observed. This difference in self-monitored versus laboratory estimates of caloric consumption is no doubt a result of methodological variables such as demand characteristics among others and is also evident in similar studies on subjects with bulimia nervosa (e.g., Rossiter & Agras, 1990; Walsh, Kissileff, Cassidy, & Dantzic, 1989). Regardless of actual size, however, it is clear that binge episodes vary greatly among individuals with BED. Variability in the size of binges and the number that are relatively small in size has led to the recommendation that size be deemphasized as an operational criterion for *binge* (Rossiter & Agras, 1990).

Data on food composition confirms that binges typically involve high calorie, fattening foods (Loro & Orleans, 1981; Marcus et al., 1988) with the likelihood of macronutrient differences between binge and normal meals. Rossiter et al. (1992) found that the binge episodes of pre-BED subjects typically involved consumption of less protein and fiber than was consumed on nonbinge days, with a difference in fat content approaching significance. The results of laboratory studies are consistent with the self-report data in showing that obese women meeting BED criteria consumed a greater percentage of energy as fat than did non-BED obese subjects (38.9% vs. 33.5%) and a lesser percentage as protein (11.4% vs. 15.4%) when both groups were instructed to binge (Yanovski et al., 1992).

Duration

Similar to the data on amount, data on the duration of binges also displays considerable variation. To illustrate, Rossiter et al.'s (1992) nonpurging bulimic subjects reported binge lengths ranging from 1 to nearly 900 minutes (averaging around 40). Binges in the upper end of this range appear to violate the *DSM-IV* specification of occuring "in a discrete period of time" (American Psychiatric Association, 1994, p. 545). Excluding binge episodes of lengthy duration may constitute a significant problem because nearly 24% of binge episodes identified by Marcus et al.'s (1992) subjects lasted the entire day. Measuring binge days has been offered as an alternative (Rossiter et al., 1992).

Loss of Control

The variability in amount and duration of binge episodes may be accounted for by subjective variables such as loss of control. Consistent with this notion, Johnson, Carr, Zayfert, Nangle, & Antony (1993) provided both non-eating-disordered peers and dieticians with 3 weeks of self-monitoring records of BED and nonclinical bingeing subjects. There was little agreement between the judgments of the subjects themselves regarding the status of their own eating episodes (binge vs. nonbinge) and the judgments of peers and dieticians based solely on amount and duration criteria. This disagreement suggests that subjective information available only to the subjects, such as the degree of perceived control during an eating episode, may significantly influence perceptions of the nature of eating episodes. This finding also raises the possibility of defining binge episodes exclusively from the patient's perspective (Johnson et al., 1993). Although clinician–patient collaborative judgments likely will continue to be the standard (Cooper & Fairburn, 1987), the literature provides compelling support for emphasizing this subjective dimension (Beglin & Fairburn, 1992).

Antecedents and Consequences

Negative emotional states, social situations, time of day, and the type of meal have been associated with bingeing in BED. Arnow, Kenardy, and Agras (1992) interviewed pre-BED individuals about their thoughts and feelings that occurred before, during, and after a binge episode. Negative moods were common preceeding binges, with the most predominant being anger and frustration, anxiety and agitation, and sadness and depression. Emotions occurring during binge episodes were evenly split between negative and positive, and those following a binge were overwhelmingly negative, with guilt, regret, and self-directed anger evident.

Johnson et al. (1995) examined emotions and other situational variables associated with eating behavior for BED, nonclinical binge eaters, and normal subjects. BED subjects were equally likely to binge whether alone or with others and whether at home or in a restaurant. BED subjects were also unique by virtue of a strong association between bingeing and snacking, particularly after midnight. Also, in contrast to the comparison groups, the BED subjects showed no relationship between feeling very hungry and bingeing. Rather, these individuals typically felt full when they were bingeing. BED subjects reported greater overall emotional distress associated with eating and a tendency to binge in response to less negative moods than did nonclinical binge eaters and normal subjects.

The eating behavior of individuals with BED and pre-BED is characterized by frequent binge episodes during which they consume snack and dessert foods. Furthermore, binge eating in BED subjects is more likely to occur in the evening while snacking and is relatively unaffected by social variables. Negative emotional states typically precede and follow binges.

Distinctiveness From Bulimia Nervosa

In addition to the lack of compensatory behavior, the research evidence suggests that individuals with BED also differ in other clinically meaningful ways from those diagnosed with bulimia nervosa. Pre-BED subjects consume approximately half the calories of those with bulimia nervosa during binges (Rossiter et al., 1992; Rossiter & Agras, 1990; Walsh et al., 1989; Yanovski et al., 1992) and they also binge less frequently (Fairburn et al., 1991; Marcus et al., 1992; McCann et al., 1991). Since the binge episodes of bulimia nervosa are easily discriminated by purges (Rossiter et al., 1992), the differences in amount and frequency may be attenuated.

Further distinctions between BED and bulimia nervosa are evident in the multisite study in which Spitzer et al. (1993) found that BED subjects reported a history of severe obesity (defined as a body mass index of 35 or greater) and greater weight fluctuations than did bulimia nervosa subjects. Higher levels of impairment in work performance, weight and shape concerns, depression, alcohol and drug abuse, and sexual abuse, however, were endorsed more often by subjects with bulimia nervosa. Interesting gender differences emerged between BED and bulimia nervosa in that BED is slightly more common in females than males in weight-control patients and occurs equally in college and community nonpatient samples. In contrast, females make up the majority of patients with bulimia nervosa (American Psychiatric Association, 1987).

There is also evidence that individuals with BED may differ from those with bulimia nervosa in dietary restraint (Brody, Walsh, & Devlin, 1994). Marcus et al. (1992) found that bulimic patients scored significantly higher than obese binge eaters on the restraint subscale of the Eating Disorders Examination, whereas scores for the two groups were similar on the other subscales. McCann et al. (1991) obtained similar data by comparing the responses of purging and nonpurging bulimic patients. Purging bulimic individuals scored higher on the restraint measure, as well as disinhibition, relative to nonpurging subjects.

Psychopathology

The distinctiveness of the BED syndrome is also evident in comparisons of BED and pre-BED patients with bulimic, obese nonbinge eaters, and normal subjects on measures of psychopathology. Individuals satisfying various pre-BED criteria have lower levels of depression (Brody et al., 1994; Katzman & Wolchik, 1984; McCann et al., 1991; Schmidt & Telch, 1990), lower rates of panic and personality disorders (McCann et al., 1991; Schmidt & Telch, 1990), higher self-esteem (Katzman & Wolchik, 1984), and less tendency toward impulsive and self-defeating behavior (Schmidt & Telch, 1990) than those with bulimia nervosa. By contrast, pre-BED individuals score higher on many measures of psychopathology relative to obese subjects (Fitzgibbon & Kirschenbaum, 1990; Kirkley, Kolotkin, Hernandez, & Gallagher, 1992; Marcus et al., 1988, 1990a) and normal controls (Prather & Williamson, 1988; Schmidt & Telch, 1990; Williamson, Prather, McKenzie, & Blouin, 1990). To summarize, while the data are not entirely definitive (e.g., see Crowther & Chernyk, 1986; Prather & Williamson, 1988), the general finding is that bulimic patients exhibit the highest level of psychopathology, followed by pre-BED patients, obese subjects, and normal controls, in descending order.

Studies employing explicit BED diagnostic criteria confirm these group differences (e.g., Fichter et al., 1993; Telch & Agras, 1994). In a prospective study, Antony et al. (1994) used the Questionnaire of Eating and Weight Patterns (QEWP) to compare BED, nonclinical binge eaters, and normal groups. The BED group reported higher levels of psychopathology than normal subjects on measures of depression, anxiety, fatigue, and confusion. In general, conclinical binge eating subjects scored between the BED and normal groups, falling closer to the subjects without eating problems. Overall, the available evidence appears to justify the conclusion that individuals with BED and pre-BED fall somewhere between bulimic patients and normal subjects on general and specific measures of psychopathology (Antony et al., 1994; Schmidt & Telch, 1990). This distinct pattern of psychopathology lends support to the integrity of the BED diagnosis and, in addition, suggests clinical levels of psychopathology that deserve therapeutic intervention.

Body Image

Body image disturbance with both size overestimation and dissatisfaction is a significant clinical feature among individuals with anorexia nervosa and bulimia nervosa (see Part I, this volume). With BED patients, however, body size overestimation appears to be less of a clinical problem, perhaps because their conspicuous obesity precludes significant perceptual distortion. In contrast, body image dissatisfaction has been a more fruitful line of investigation with the general finding that individuals meeting BED criteria are dissatisfied with their appearance, perhaps because of their objective obesity. Using the Body Image Assessment (see chapter 3, this volume) that requires individuals to select their current and ideal body sizes from a set of nine size-graded silhouettes, Williamson, Gleaves, and Savin (1992) found a mean current body size estimate of 8.83 (9 being the largest), and a mean ideal body size preference of 5.00 for subjects with BED. The difference between current and ideal body size (3.83) is considered a measure of body size dissatisfaction, and large differences consistently have been found in studies comparing BED (Antony et al., 1994) and pre-BED populations (Williamson et al., 1990) to normal controls. Indeed, greater body size dissatisfaction among those with BED occurs even when the degree of obesity is covaried (Antony et al., 1994). These data concur with alternative measures such as the body dissatisfaction subscale of the Eating Disorder Inventory (de Zwaan et al., 1994) and the shape concern subscale of the Eating Disorders Examination (Smith, Marcus, & Kaye, 1992) in which pre-BED groups score higher than normal subjects (Cooper, Cooper, & Fairburn, 1989; Garner, Olmstead, & Polivy, 1983).

The degree of body dissatisfaction exhibited by individuals with BED versus bulimia nervosa and obese groups is less clear. For example, while several studies suggest greater dissatisfaction among pre-BED and BED samples relative to bulimia (Fichter et al., 1993; Williamson et al., 1990), others show little difference (Williamson et al., 1992). Conflicting data also emerge from the literature comparing the body dissatisfaction of BED and pre-BED subjects to obese subjects. On the one hand, research supports a positive relationship between binge severity and body dissatisfaction in obese subjects (de Zwaan, Nutzinger, & Schoenbeck, 1992; Marcus et al., 1990b; but see Lowe & Caputo, 1991) and an association between BED diagnosis and weight and shape concern (Spitzer et al., 1993). On the other hand, comparisons of pre-BED and obese subjects have found similar body size dissatisfaction (Williamson et al., 1990), and comparisons of BED and obese subjects have failed to find differences in Eating Disorder Inventory body dissatisfaction scores (de Zwaan et al., 1994; Fichter et al., 1993). At present, it seems that individuals with BED are dissatisfied with their bodies and that there is some empirical justification (e.g., de Zwaan et al., 1992; Spitzer et al., 1993) to expect this dissatisfaction to be greater than that exhibited by non-binge-eating obese persons. These data suggest that any comprehensive treatment program for BED must include techniques designed to modify self-evaluative assumptions and body disparagement, as is the case in the treatment of obesity (Garner & Wooley, 1991).

ASSESSING BINGE EATING DISORDER

Assessing BED has employed a wide range of methods including questionnaires, self-monitoring, diagnostic interviews, and laboratory observation. Because the diagnosis of BED shares with bulimia nervosa a focus on binge eating, instruments measuring eating behavior have clinical utility for assessing both disorders.

Questionnaire Measures

The Questionnaire of Eating and Weight Patterns (Spitzer et al., 1992, 1993) is the sole diagnostic procedure used exclusively for identifying BED. Thirteen items serve to classify respondents with BED, purging bulimia nervosa, or nonpurging bulimia nervosa (Spitzer et al., 1993), and psychometric data on the questionnaire are encouraging. The BED diagnosis based on the Questionnaire of Eating and Weight Patterns is moderately stable over a 3-week interval (kappa = .58; Nangle, Johnson, Carr-Nangle, & Engler, 1994), correlates well with the diagnosis based on structured interview (kappa = .57; de Zwann, et al., 1993), and differentiates high- versus low-frequency binge eaters with sufficient predictive efficiency (71% to 73%; Nangle et al., 1994).

The Binge Eating Scale is a 16-item questionnaire originally designed to describe binge behavior and associated thoughts and feelings in the obese (Gormally, Black, Daston, & Rardin, 1982). This scale addresses several diagnostic characteristics of BED, including all five aspects of Criterion B (see Exhibit 1). The Binge Eating Scale has been shown to identify individuals with no, moderate, or severe binge eating as assessed by structured interview (Gormally et al., 1982). The Binge Scale is a 9-item measure of binge severity (Hawkins & Clement, 1980). This scale provides information on several aspects of Criterion B (Exhibit 1) and, unlike the Binge Eating Scale, probes for binge frequency. The Bulimia Test is a 32-item, self-report scale originally designed to measure the symptoms of *DSM-III* bulimia and to distinguish bulimic from anorexic patients (Smith & Thelen, 1984). The test was revised to accommodate *DSM-III-R* criteria for bulimia nervosa (Thelen, Farmer, Wonderlich, & Smith, 1991). Although Bulimia Test scores can distinguish obese binge eaters from obese subjects (Prather & Williamson, 1988) and BED subjects from both subclinical binge eaters and normal subjects (Antony et al., 1994), its capacity to distinguish obese binge eaters from individuals with bulimia nervosa is questionable (Williamson et al., 1990). The Bulimia Test–Revised options for binge frequency are equal to the diagnostic demands of BED, although the 6-month history of binge eating necessary for a diagnosis of BED cannot be determined. The Eating Disorder Inventory is a 64-item scale (Garner et al., 1983), recently revised to 91-items (Garner, 1991), that measures clinical features of bulimia nervosa and anorexia nervosa (see chapter 9, this volume). The validity of this instrument for BED and related populations has yet to be established, and the few questions pertaining to bingeing are confined to the bulimia subscale. The potential utility of this instrument in the assessment of BED, however, can be adduced from its increasing use in identifying the characteristics of obese binge eaters (e.g., de Zwaan et al., 1994).

The Drive for Thinness and Ineffectiveness subscales, for example, have been shown to predict binge eating severity among the obese (Lowe & Caputo, 1991) and may discriminate subjects satisfying full BED criteria from obese binge eaters not meeting criteria (de Zwaan et al., 1994). Interoceptive awareness may also relate to binge eating status (Kuehnel & Wadden, 1994; Lowe & Caputo, 1991; Marcus et al., 1990b), as may body dissatisfaction (Marcus et al., 1990b), although the latter relationship remains equivocal (de Zwaan et al., 1994; Lowe & Caputo, 1991). Body dissatisfaction and ineffectiveness scores may differ between BED and bulimia nervosa patients (with bulimic patients scoring lower on body dissatisfaction and higher on ineffectiveness), although these relationships disappear when the body mass index is controlled (Fichter et al., 1993). Among the subscales introduced in the Eating Disorder Inventory–2, impulse regulation may be associated with BED diagnosis in the obese (Kuehnel & Wadden, 1994).

Questionnaires have been developed to assess dietary restraint, a concept that occupies a prominent position in current theoretical (Heatherton, Polivy, King, & McGree, 1988; Lowe, 1993; Ruderman, 1986) and empirical (Heatherton, Polivy, & Herman, 1989; Johnson, Corrigan, Crusco, & Schlundt, 1986; Lowe, 1992) work on eating behavior and its disorders. The initial measure of dietary restraint, the Restraint Scale (Herman & Mack, 1975), has found favor among researchers because it predicts many of the behavioral phenomena that gave impetus to the concept of restraint (see Lowe, 1993). Other recently developed measures, such as the Three-Factor Eating Questionnaire (Stunkard & Messick, 1985) and the Dutch Eating Behavior Questionnaire (Van Strien, Frijters, Bergers, & Defares, 1986) are popular among researchers because, in addition to cognitive restraint, they measure functionally related variables such as disinhibition and hunger.

Several lines of evidence suggest that dietary restraint, disinhibition, and hunger are important in assessing individuals with BED. First, individuals diagnosed with *DSM-III* bulimia nervosa have elevated restraint scale scores (Ruderman, 1985). Second, some evidence suggests a relationship between dieting and binge eating in the obese. Telch and Agras (1993), for example, showed that administration of a very low calorie diet produced a subsequent increase in binge behavior in subjects identified as nonbinging obese. Finally, a number of studies have shown a positive association between indices of restraint and measures of binge behavior or BED diagnostic status (Antony et al., 1994; Goldfein, Walsh, LaChaussee, Kissileff, & Devlin, 1993; Gormally et al., 1982).

It must be acknowledged, however, that the degree of association between restraint and binge eating in individuals with BED remains debatable (Yanovski, 1993). In contrast to Telch and Agras (1993), weight-loss dieting actually has been shown to reduce the frequency and severity of binge eating among those diagnosed with BED (Yanovski & Sebring, 1994). Furthermore, of the individuals with BED surveyed by Spitzer et al. (1993), 48.6% reported that they began binge eating *before* dieting, compared with 37.0% who reported the reverse.

The utility of measures of dietary restraint in the understanding of BED will depend ultimately on their capacity to predict clinical features of the disorder that influence therapeutic interventions. At present, the disinhibition subscale of the Three-Factor Eating Questionnaire appears to have particular relevance. It measures emotional eating (Ganley, 1988), which is consistently elevated in individuals with BED and pre-BED (Fichter et al., 1993; Goldfein et al., 1993; Marcus et al., 1988). Furthermore, scores on this subscale appear to decrease in the course of both psychotherapeutic (Wilfley et al., 1993) and pharmacological (McCann & Agras, 1990) interventions that reduce binge eating. It is interesting to note that binge reduction in the obese has also been associated with elevations on the cognitive restraint subscale that brings their total scores more closely in line with the higher scores of bulimic patients (Brody et al., 1994; McCann et al., 1991).

Each of the questionnaires listed previously has potential utililty in assessing and treating BED, but no single measure provides a picture of this disorder that is both comprehensive and detailed. The Questionnaire of Eating and Weight Patterns, for example, is preferable for diagnostic purposes because it derives directly from BED criteria. However, information on psychological correlates of the disorder must be obtained from instruments such as the Eating Disorder Inventory–2, Three-Factor Eating Questionnaire, and Restraint Scale. In a similar way, the Binge Scale and the Binge Eating Scale provide multifaceted measures of binge severity, yet lack the Questionnaire of Eating and Weight Pattern's capacity to measure binge frequency. In the interest of obtaining comprehensive information, several measures are justified, particularly given the nascent state of BED assessment.

Self-Monitoring

Self-monitoring has long been a mainstay in assessing eating behavior in obesity (Bellack, 1976) and bulimia nervosa (Schlundt, Johnson, & Jarrell, 1986). The procedure typically involves recording eating episodes and their situational contexts. A primary advantage of self-monitoring is the direct measurement of eating episodes, which theoretically reduces the potential for distortion relative to recall-based methods such as questionnaires and interviews. Self-monitoring can also elicit the comprehensive information required for abstracting functional relationships between situational events and eating behavior (Schlundt et al., 1986). Given these advantages, it is not surprising that self-monitoring has been applied to such diverse topics as treatment outcome (e.g., Agras, Schneider, Arnow, Raeburn, & Telch, 1989; Leitenberg, Rosen, Gross, Nudelman, & Vara, 1988), binge characteristics (Rossiter et al., 1992), mood correlates

(Lingswiler, Crowther, & Stephens, 1987), and energy intake (Yanovski & Sebring, 1994) in populations spanning the range of eating disorders.

Although the potential reactivity of self-monitoring procedures is recognized (e.g., Wilson, 1987), several studies comparing subjects and other observers support the validity of self-monitoring as an assessment method. Crowther, Lingswiler, and Stephens (1984), for example, found excellent agreement between subjects and their partners for both the type (86.4%) and quantity (90.3%) of food consumed during eating episodes. No differences were found between partner-present and partner-absent meals, suggesting that significant reactivity did not occur. Self-monitored binging also has been shown to vary with diagnostic classification based on the Questionnaire of Eating and Weight Patterns (Nangle et al., 1994). In this latter study, a comparison of self-monitoring over a 3-week period with the questionnaire revealed a significant relationship between diagnostic categories and the recorded frequency of binge eating.

One factor ensuring the continued use of self-monitoring in eating disorders research is its amenability to functional analysis (Johnson et al., 1995; Schlundt, 1989; Schlundt, Johnson, & Jarrell, 1985, 1986). Recent findings suggest important similarities and differences between subjects diagnosed with BED and both nonclinical binge eaters and normal controls (Johnson et al., 1995). Future research using self-monitoring may elucidate similar differences between BED and other eating-disordered populations. A second factor ensuring the continued utility of self-monitoring concerns the diagnostic criteria for BED. Unlike anorexia nervosa, in which the diagnostic criteria are largely attitudinal and nonepisodic in nature, the criteria for BED (particularly Criteria A, B, and D—see Exhibit 1) require detailed information on binge frequency, size, physical and social antecedents, and associated emotions—the very characteristics self-monitoring data are suited to illuminate.

Several caveats can be offered with respect to self-monitoring. First, in constructing self-monitoring forms, the advantages of detail must be weighed against the potential aversiveness of recording demands. Ideally, self-monitoring provides information on time, physical location, type and quantity of food or drink, social and emotional context, and perception of amount consumed for any eating or drinking episode. Excessively demanding forms may compromise the validity of self-monitoring by encouraging subjects to respond carelessly rather than accurately in an effort to complete the recording process. Second, providing subjects with explicit instructions not to alter their eating habits (e.g., Johnson et al., 1995) may reduce the potential for reactivity. Third, subjects should receive precise training in self-monitoring to ensure that subject and experimenter share an understanding of the information the self-monitoring system is designed to elicit.

Interview

Of the interview formats that address binge eating (see Wilson, 1993, p. 234), the Eating Disorder Examination (Cooper & Fairburn, 1987; see chapter 9, this volume) is used most widely. Unfortunately, while this examination has been employed extensively in the study of bulimia nervosa (e.g., Wilson, Eldredge, Smith, & Niles, 1991; Wilson & Smith, 1989), data are scarce on individuals with BED and pre-BED diagnoses. Existing data suggest differences between pre-BED and normal weight bulimic patients on the restraint subscale (Marcus et al., 1992; Wilson & Smith, 1989). In addition, Wilson, Nonas, and Rosenblum (1993) demonstrated that 16 items from a questionnaire version of the Eating Disorder Examination discriminated obese binge eaters from nonbinge eaters. The largest *t* values were for items targeting preoccupation with weight and concern about being seen eating.

An interesting aspect of the Eating Disorder Examination is its use of *DSM-IV* definitions for "large amount of food" and "loss of control" to categorize overeating episodes. As shown in Figure 1, two

Amount eaten

	"Large" (EDE definition)	Not "large", but viewed by subject as excessive
"Loss of control"	Objective bulimic episodes	Subjective bulimic episodes
No "loss of control"	Objective overeating	Subjective overeating

Figure 1. The Eating Disorder Examination scheme for classifying episodes of overeating. From Fairburn and Wilson (1993).

dimensions—namely, perceived loss of control and amount eaten—are used to define a four-fold classification of eating episodes. Unfortunately, use of the *DSM-IV* definition of binge imports into the examination conceptual scheme the problems of classification mentioned earlier: How much food is definitely larger than most people would eat in similar circumstances? A number of subjective elements pervade this supposedly objective criterion (e.g., *definitely larger, most people,* and *similar circumstances*) allowing so-called *objective bulimic episodes* and *objective overeating* to become personal judgments of the interviewer. An additional concern is raised by the variable size of eating episodes identified by subjects as binges (Rossiter & Agras, 1990; Rossiter et al., 1992) and by the poor agreement between bingers and judges about the status (i.e., binge vs. nonbinge) of the bingers' own eating episodes (Johnson et al., 1993). These data suggest that the experience of bingeing may be so tied to subjective variables such as loss of control and the violation of internal dietary standards (Schlundt & Johnson, 1990, pp. 77–91) that any *objective* definition may be of questionable utility. This having been said, the depth and breadth of information generated by the Eating Disorder Examination makes it particularly suitable for the study of BED. Detailed information will become increasingly important as new and subtle diagnostic distinctions continue to emerge.

Assessment: Summary and Recommendations

Data obtained from questionnaires, self-monitoring, and interviews all may contribute to the assessment of patients with BED. Questionnaires and interviews provide diagnostic and clinically relevant information, whereas self-monitoring measures the severity, change, and associated variables. Future research should determine which measures best reflect the core symptoms of the BED diagnosis and are sensitive to changes produced by interventions.

TREATMENT OF BINGE EATING DISORDER

The treatment of BED has focused on two separate yet complimentary objectives—namely, weight management and a reduction in binge eating. Since the majority of patients meeting BED criteria are obese, treatment efforts directed at weight control are indicated, and they typically involve comprehensive cognitive–behavioral programs that attempt to modify disordered eating behaviors, among others. Also, with the recognition of binge eating per se as a clinical problem, other treatment interventions have been directed almost exclusively toward controlling eating behavior. Although these two treatment objectives and their interventions are interrelated, for the most part, the literature has addressed them separately.

Weight Management

In contrast to early evidence (Keefe et al., 1984), more recent findings show that BED and pre-BED individuals appear to lose as much weight as nonbingers over the course of behavioral weight control programs (LaPorte, 1992; Marcus et al., 1988). In some cases, these losses are quite significant (Wadden, Foster, & Letizia, 1992). Drop-out and maintenance may be more problematic. For example, both drop-out and relapse rates are higher for obese individuals with BED than those without BED (Keefe et al., 1984; Marcus et al., 1988; Yanovski, 1993). Marcus et al. (1988) employed Binge Eating Scale scores and DSM-III criteria to divide obese subjects into binge eating and nonbinge eating groups. Subsequently, subjects participated in either a standard weight control program or one modified for binge eating. While the treatments were not differentially effective, the binge eaters were more likely to drop out of treatment and regained significantly more weight at 6-month follow-up than nonbinge eaters.

Managing Eating Behavior

Both pharmacological and psychotherapeutic interventions have been evaluated for the management of eating behavior, and the results are largely consistent with those of weight control studies in demonstrating difficulty in adherring to interventions, as well as higher drop-out and relapse rates. Pharmacological treatments have relied primarily on antidepressants, and desipramine and imipramine have been shown to reduce the frequency and the duration of binge eating, respectively, in pre-BED obese subjects. McCann and Agras (1990), for example, randomly assigned women diagnosed with DSM-III-R bulimia nervosa who did not regularly purge to either a desipramine treatment or a placebo control group. By week 12 of the trial, subjects treated with desipramine reduced their binge frequency by 63%, compared to a 16% increase for control subjects. Binge frequency approached baseline rates following medication withdrawal, suggesting that either the act of taking medication or some aspect of the drug was responsible for the reduction in binge frequency.

As with weight control, psychotherapy for the management of eating behavior involves a number of cognitive–behavior therapy interventions that are designed to establish regular eating patterns. These interventions include self-monitoring, exposure to forbidden foods, challenging dysfunctional beliefs about eating, and training in relapse prevention. The response to these interventions shows a similar pattern, with clinical improvement followed by relapse—although the extent of relapse is relatively small compared to that observed following pharmacotherapy termination (McCann & Agras, 1990). Telch, Agras, Rossiter, Wilfley, and Kenardy (1990) evaluated cognitive–behavioral therapy for binge eating and found reductions in binge frequency of 94% for nonpurging bulimics compared to 9% in a control group, with many of the treated subjects eliminating binge eating entirely. Although relapse was significant—only 46% of subjects remained binge-abstinent at 10-week follow-up—binge frequency remained significantly improved over baseline levels. Similar binge frequency changes were obtained by Wilfley et al. (1993), who found comparable treatment efficacy for cognitive–behavioral therapy and interpersonal psychotherapy.

Treatment for Binge Eating Disorder: Summary and Recommendations

In light of the existing data on the characteristics of individuals with BED, it is obvious that treatment should be directed at the disordered eating and associated psychopathology. Most prominent in this regard are binge eating and its antecedents—nutrition, body image dissatisfaction, and depression. The interrelated nature of these symptoms indicates that improvement on one target such as weight reduction may yield positive changes in another. For example, depressed mood is usually elevated with weight loss. However, in a practical, programmatic sense, the idiosyncratic nature of these relationships for specific subjects appears to require a comprehensive program, and the available literature supports these inclusive efforts.

Current cognitive–behavioral therapy programs reduce binge eating during implementation (Smith et al., 1992; Wilfley et al., 1993), however, the poor maintenance of these reductions (e.g., Telch et al., 1990) suggests that further efforts at relapse prevention are needed. A fruitful avenue for preventing relapse may be the treatment of clinical problems associated with BED, including psychopathology (Schmidt & Telch, 1990; Williamson et al., 1990) and body size dissatisfaction (de Zwaan et al., 1994). Interventions directed at the psychopathology associated with BED could reduce the influence of emotional cues on binge eating (Johnson et al., 1995), and antidepressant medications may be helpful in combination with cognitive–behavioral therapy (Alger, Schwalberg, Bigaouette, Michalek, & Howard, 1991; McCann & Agras, 1990). Treatment of body size dissatisfaction, either through modification of self-evaluative assumptions (Smith et al., 1992) or weight reduction (Wadden et al., 1992), may attenuate the tendency for individuals treated only for bingeing to engage in self-imposed dieting, a practice that could contribute to future binge eating (Telch & Agras, 1993; Telch et al., 1990). Consistent with this notion, there is evidence that weight loss may reduce binge eating severity in subjects with BED (Yanovski & Sebring, 1994). In summary, the available data strongly suggest that the effective treatment of BED requires the management of clinical features beyond those defined solely by its formal criteria.

Although comprehensive interventions may increase the efficacy of current treatments for BED, these developments in treatment should be complemented with efforts at prevention to reduce the prevalence of this disorder. In their recent multisite study, Spitzer et al. (1993) found that, among individuals enrolled in weight control programs, those diagnosed with BED reported an earlier onset of both overweight and dieting than did those without the diagnosis. These data underscore the necessity of early intervention and suggest that child and adolescent weight management programs that deemphasize dieting and weight per se, and at the same time promote nutritional, activity, and lifestyle changes, may play an important prophylactic role with respect to BED (chapter 12, this volume).

Several questions regarding future developments in BED are indicated from the foregoing review. In spite of its apparent simplicity, the nature and origin of binge eating is still fraught with more than a modicum of uncertainty. As we have discussed, the definition of a binge is ambiguous because it relies on quantity and temporal criteria that are suspect and inconsistent with empirical data. Equally important is research on the development of binge eating in children, as there is compelling evidence that BED is associated with early onset of both overweight and dieting (Brody et al., 1994; de Zwaan et al., 1992; Spitzer et al., 1993).

REFERENCES

Agras, W. S., Schneider, J. A., Arnow, B., Raeburn, S. D., & Telch, C. (1989). Cognitive–behavioral and response–prevention treatments for bulimia nervosa. *Journal of Consulting and Clinical Psychology, 57*, 215–221.

Alger, S. A., Schwalberg, M. D., Bigaouette, J. M., Michalek, A. V., & Howard, L. J. (1991). Effect of a tricyclic antidepressant and opiate antagonist on binge-eating behavior in normoweight bulimic and obese, binge-eating subjects. *American Journal of Clinical Nutrition, 53*, 865–871.

American Psychiatric Association. (1980). *Diagnostic and statistical manual of mental disorders* (3rd ed.). Washington, DC: Author.

American Psychiatric Association. (1987). *Diagnostic and statistical manual of mental disorders* (3rd ed., rev.). Washington, DC: Author.

American Psychiatric Association. (1994). *Diagnostic and statistical manual of mental disorders* (4th ed.). Washington, DC: Author.

Antony, M. M., Johnson, W. G., Carr-Nangle, R. E., & Abel, J. (1994). Psychopathology correlates of binge eating and binge eating disorder. *Comprehensive Psychiatry, 35*, 386–392.

Arnow, B., Kenardy, J., & Agras, W. S. (1992). Binge eating among the obese: A descriptive study. *Journal of Behavioral Medicine, 15*, 155–170.

Beglin, S. J., & Fairburn, C. G. (1992). What is meant by the term "binge"? *American Journal of Psychiatry, 149,* 123–124.

Bellack, A. S. (1976). A comparison of self-reinforcement and self-monitoring in a weight reduction program. *Behavior Therapy, 7,* 68–75.

Brody, M. L., Walsh, B. T., & Devlin, M. J. (1994). Binge eating disorder: Reliability and validity of a new diagnostic category. *Journal of Consulting and Clinical Psychology, 62,* 381–386.

Cooper, Z., Cooper, P. J., & Fairburn, C. G. (1989). The validity of the Eating Disorder Examination and its subscales. *British Journal of Psychiatry, 154,* 807–812.

Cooper, Z., & Fairburn, C. G. (1987). The Eating Disorder Examination: A semi-structured interview for the assessment of the specific psychopathology of eating disorders. *International Journal of Eating Disorders, 6,* 1–8.

Crowther, J. H., & Chernyk, B. (1986). Bulimia and binge eating in adolescent females: A comparison. *Addictive Behaviors, 11,* 415–424.

Crowther, J. H., Lingswiler, V. M., & Stephens, M. A. P. (1984). The topography of binge eating. *Addictive Behaviors, 9,* 299–303.

DaCosta, M., & Halmi, K. A. (1992). Classification of anorexia nervosa: Question of subtypes. *International Journal of Eating Disorders, 11,* 305–313.

de Zwaan, M., Mitchell, J. E., Seim, H. C., Specker, S. M., Pyle, R. L., Raymond, N. C., & Crosby, R. B. (1994). Eating related and general psychopathology in obese females with binge eating disorder. *International Journal of Eating Disorders, 15,* 43–52.

de Zwaan, M., Mitchell, J. E., Specker, S. M., Pyle, R. L., Mussell, M. P., & Seim, H. C. (1993). Diagnosing binge eating disorder: Level of agreement between self-report and expert rating. *International Journal of Eating Disorders, 14,* 289–295.

de Zwaan, M., Nutzinger, D. O., & Schoenbeck, G. (1992). Binge eating in overweight women. *Comprehensive Psychiatry, 33,* 256–261.

Fairburn, C. G., Jones, R., Peveler, R. C., Carr, S. J., Solomon, R. A., O'Connor, M. E., Burton, J., & Hope, R. A. (1991). Three psychological treatments for bulimia nervosa: A comparative trial. *Archives of General Psychiatry, 48,* 463–469.

Fairburn, C. G., Welch, S. L., & Hay, P. J. (1993). The classification of recurrent overeating: The "binge eating disorder" proposal. *International Journal of Eating Disorders, 13,* 155–159.

Fairburn, C. G., & Wilson, G. T. (1993). Binge eating: Definition and classification. In C. G. Fairburn & G. T. Wilson (Eds.), *Binge eating: Nature, assessment, and treatment* (pp. 3–14). New York: Guilford Press.

Fichter, M. M., Quadflieg, N., & Brandl, B. (1993). Recurrent overeating: An empirical comparison of binge eating disorder, bulimia nervosa, and obesity. *International Journal of Eating Disorders, 14,* 1–16.

Fitzgibbon, M. L., & Kirschenbaum, D. S. (1990). Heterogeneity of clinical presentation among obese individuals seeking treatment. *Addictive Behaviors, 15,* 291–295.

Ganley, R. M. (1988). Emotional eating and how it relates to dietary restraint, disinhibition, and perceived hunger. *International Journal of Eating Disorders, 7,* 635–647.

Garfinkel, P. E., Moldofsky, H., & Garner, D. M. (1980). The heterogeneity of anorexia nervosa. *Archives of General Psychiatry, 37,* 1036–1040.

Garner, D. M. (1991). *Eating Disorder Inventory–2.* Odessa, FL: Psychological Assessment Resources.

Garner, D. M., Olmsted, M. P., & Polivy, J. (1983). Development and validation of a multidimensional eating disorder inventory for anorexia nervosa and bulimia. *International Journal of Eating Disorders, 2,* 15–34.

Garner, D. M., & Wooley, S. C. (1991). Confronting the failure of behavioral and dietary treatments for obesity. *Clinical Psychology Review, 11,* 729–780.

Goldfein, J. A., Walsh, B. T., LaChaussee, J. L., Kissileff, H. R., & Devlin, M. J. (1993). Eating behavior in binge eating disorder. *International Journal of Eating Disorders, 14,* 427–431.

Gormally, J., Black, S., Daston, S., & Rardin, D. (1982). The assessment of binge eating severity among obese persons. *Addictive Behaviors, 7,* 47–55.

Halmi, K. A., Falk, J. R., & Schwartz, E. (1981). Binge-eating and vomiting: A survey of a college population. *Psychological Medicine, 11,* 697–706.

Hawkins, R. C., & Clement, P. (1980). Development and construct validation of a self-report measure of binge eating tendencies. *Addictive Behaviors, 5,* 219–226.

Heatherton, T. F., Polivy, J., King, G. A., & McGree, S. T. (1988). The (Mis)measurement of restraint: An analysis of conceptual and psychometric issues. *Journal of Abnormal Psychology, 97,* 19–28.

Heatherton, T. F., Polivy, J., & Herman, C. P. (1989). Restraint and internal responsiveness: Effects of placebo manipulations of hunger state on eating. *Journal of Abnormal Psychology, 98,* 89–92.

Herman, C. P., & Mack, D. (1975). Restrained and unrestrained eating. *Journal of Personality, 43,* 647–660.

Johnson, W. G., Carr, R. E., Zayfert, C., Nangle, D. W., & Antony, M. (1993, November). *What is binge eating? A comparison of binge eater, peer, and professional judgments.* Paper presented at the annual meeting of the Association for Advancement of Behavior Therapy Convention, Atlanta, GA.

Johnson, W. G., Corrigan, S. A., Crusco, A. H., & Schlundt, D. G. (1986). Restraint among bulimic women. *Addictive Behaviors, 11,* 351–354.

Johnson, W. G., Schlundt, D. G., Barclay, D. R., Carr-Nangle, R. E., & Engler, L. E. (1995). A naturalistic functional analysis of binge eating. *Behavior Therapy, 26,* 101–118.

Katzman, M. A., & Wolchik, S. A. (1984). Bulimia and binge eating in college women: A comparison of personality and behavioral characteristics. *Journal of Consulting and Clinical Psychology, 52*, 423–428.

Keefe, P. H., Wyshogrod, D., Weinberger, E., & Agras, W. S. (1984). Binge eating and outcome of behavioral treatment of obesity: A preliminary report. *Behaviour Research and Therapy, 22*, 319–321.

Kirkley, B. G., Kolotkin, R. L., Hernandez, J. T., & Gallagher, P. N. (1992). A comparison of binge-purgers, obese binge eaters, and obese non-binge eaters on the MMPI. *International Journal of Eating Disorders, 12*, 221–228.

Kolotkin, R. L., Revis, E. S., Kirkley, B. G., & Janick, L. (1987). Binge eating in obesity: Associated MMPI characteristics. *Journal of Consulting and Clinical Psychology, 55*, 872–876.

Kuehnel, R. H., & Wadden, T. A. (1994). Binge eating disorder, weight cycling, and psychopathology. *International Journal of Eating Disorders, 15*, 321–329.

LaPorte, D. J. (1992). Treatment response in obese binge eaters: Preliminary results using a very low calorie diet (VLCD) and behavior therapy. *Addictive Behaviors, 17*, 247–257.

Leitenberg, H., Rosen, J., Gross, J., Nudelman, S., & Vara, L. (1988). Exposure plus response–prevention treatment of bulimia nervosa. *Journal of Consulting and Clinical Psychology, 56*, 535–541.

Lingswiler, V. M., Crowther, J. H., & Stephens, M. A. P. (1987). Emotional reactivity and eating in binge eating and obesity. *Journal of Behavioral Medicine, 10*, 287–299.

Loro, A. D., & Orleans, C. S. (1981). Binge eating in obesity: Preliminary findings and guidelines for behavioral analysis and treatment. *Addictive Behaviors, 6*, 155–166.

Lowe, M. R. (1992). Staying on versus going off a diet: Effects on eating in normal weight and overweight individuals. *International Journal of Eating Disorders, 12*, 417–424.

Lowe, M. R. (1993). The effects of dieting on eating behavior: A three-factor model. *Psychological Bulletin, 114*, 100–121.

Lowe, M. R., & Caputo, G. C. (1991). Binge eating in obesity: Toward the specification of predictors. *International Journal of Eating Disorders, 10*, 49–55.

Marcus, M. D., Smith, D., Santelli, R., & Kaye, W. (1992). Characterization of eating disordered behavior in obese binge eaters. *International Journal of Eating Disorders, 12*, 249–255.

Marcus, M. D., Wing, R. R., Ewing, L., Kern, E., Gooding, W, & McDermott, M. (1990a). Psychiatric disorders among obese binge eaters. *International Journal of Eating Disorders, 9*, 69–77.

Marcus, M. D., Wing, R. R., Ewing, L., Kern, E., McDermott, M., & Gooding, W. (1990b). A double-blind, placebo-controlled trial of fluoxetine plus behavior modification in the treatment of obese binge-eaters and non-binge eaters. *American Journal of Psychiatry, 147*, 876–881.

Marcus, M. D., Wing, R. R., & Hopkins, J. (1988). Obese binge eaters: Affect, cognitions, and response to behavioral weight control. *Journal of Consulting and Clinical Psychology, 56,* 433–439.

McCann, U. D., & Agras, W. S. (1990). Successful treatment of nonpurging bulimia nervosa with desipramine: A double-blind, placebo-controlled study. *American Journal of Psychiatry, 147,* 1509–1513.

McCann, U. D., Rossiter, E. M., King, R. J., & Agras, W. S. (1991). Nonpurging bulimia: A distinct subtype of bulimia nervosa. *International Journal of Eating Disorders, 10,* 679–687.

Nangle, D. W., Johnson, W. G., Carr-Nangle, R. E., & Engler, L. E. (1994). Binge eating disorder and the proposed *DSM-IV* criteria: Psychometric analysis of the Questionnaire of Eating and Weight Patterns. *International Journal of Eating Disorders, 16,* 147–157.

Prather, R. C., & Williamson, D. A. (1988). Psychopathology associated with bulimia, binge eating, and obesity. *International Journal of Eating Disorders, 7,* 177–184.

Rossiter, E. M., & Agras, W. S. (1990). An empirical test of the *DSM-III-R* definition of binge. *International Journal of Eating Disorders, 9,* 513–518.

Rossiter, E. M., Agras, W. S., Telch, C. F., & Bruce, B. (1992). The eating patterns of nonpurging bulimic subjects. *International Journal of Eating Disorders, 11,* 111–120.

Ruderman, A. J. (1985). Restraint, obesity and bulimia. *Behaviour Research and Therapy, 23,* 151–156.

Ruderman, A. J. (1986). Dietary restraint: A theoretical and empirical review. *Psychological Bulletin, 99,* 247–262.

Schlundt, D. G. (1989). Assessment of eating behavior in bulimia nervosa: The self-monitoring analysis system. In W. G. Johnson (Ed.), *Advances in eating disorders Vol. II* (pp. 1–41). New York: JAI Press.

Schlundt, D. G., & Johnson, W. G. (1990). *Eating disorders: Assessment and treatment.* Boston: Allyn & Bacon.

Schlundt, D. G., Johnson, W. G., & Jarrell, M. P. (1985). A naturalistic functional analysis of eating behavior in bulimia and obesity. *Advances in Behavior Research and Therapy, 7,* 149–162.

Schlundt, D. G., Johnson, W. G., & Jarrell, M. P. (1986). A sequential analysis of environmental, behavioral, and affective variables predictive of vomiting in bulimia nervosa. *Behavioral Assessment, 8,* 253–269.

Schmidt, N. B., & Telch, M. J. (1990). Prevalence of personality disorders among bulimics, non-bulimic binge eaters, and normal controls. *Journal of Psychopathology and Behavioral Assessment, 12,* 169–185.

Smith, D. E., Marcus, M. D., & Kaye, W. (1992). Cognitive–behavioral treatment of obese binge eaters. *International Journal of Eating Disorders, 12,* 257–262.

Smith, M. C., & Thelen, M. H. (1984). Development and validation of a test for bulimia. *Journal of Consulting and Clinical Psychology, 52,* 863–872.

Spitzer, R. L., Devlin, M., Walsh, B. T., Hasin, D., Wing, R., Marcus, M., Stunkard, A., Wadden, T., Yanovski, S., Agras, S., Mitchell, J., & Nonas, C. (1991). Binge eating disorder: To be or not to be in *DSM-IV*. *International Journal of Eating Disorders, 10*, 627–629.

Spitzer, R. L., Devlin, M., Walsh, B. T., Hasin, D., Wing, R., Marcus, M., Stunkard, A., Wadden, T., Yanovski, S., Agras, S., Mitchell, J., & Nonas, C. (1992). Binge eating disorder: A multisite field trial of the diagnostic criteria. *International Journal of Eating Disorders, 11*, 191–203.

Spitzer, R. L., Yanovski, S., Wadden, T., Wing, R., Marcus, M., Stunkard, A., Devlin, M., Mitchell, J., Hasin, D., & Horne, R. L. (1993). Binge eating disorder: Its further validation in a multisite study. *International Journal of Eating Disorders, 13*, 137–153.

Stunkard, A. J. (1959). Eating patterns and obesity. *Psychiatry Quarterly, 33*, 284–295.

Stunkard, A. J., & Messick, S. (1985). The Three-Factor Eating Questionnaire to measure dietary restraint, disinhibition and hunger. *Journal of Psychosomatic Research, 29*, 71–83.

Telch, C. F., & Agras, W. S. (1993). The effects of a very low calorie diet on binge eating. *Behavior Therapy, 24*, 177–193.

Telch, C. F., & Agras, W. S. (1994). Obesity, binge eating, and psychopathology: Are they related? *International Journal of Eating Disorders, 15*, 53–61.

Telch, C. F., Agras, W. S., & Rossiter, E. M. (1988). Binge-eating increases with increasing adiposity. *International Journal of Eating Disorders, 7*, 115–119.

Telch, C. F., Agras, W. S., Rossiter, E. M., Wilfley, D., & Kenardy, J. (1990). Group cognitive–behavioral treatment for the nonpurging bulimic: An initial evaluation. *Journal of Consulting and Clinical Psychology, 58*, 629–635.

Thelen, M. H., Farmer, J., Wonderlich, S., & Smith, M. (1991). A revision of the Bulimia Test: The BULIT-R. *Psychological Assessment: A Journal of Consulting and Clinical Psychology, 3*, 119–124.

Van Strien, T., Frijters, J. E., Bergers, G. P. A., & Defares, P. B. (1986). Dutch Eating Behaviour Questionnaire for assessment of restrained, emotional and external eating behavior. *International Journal of Eating Disorders, 5*, 295–315.

Wadden, T. A., Foster, G. D., & Letizia, K. A. (1992). Response of obese binge eaters to treatment by behavior therapy combined with very low calorie diet. *Journal of Consulting and Clinical Psychology, 60*, 808–811.

Walsh, B. T., Kissileff, H. R., Cassidy, S. M., & Dantzic, S. (1989). Eating behavior of women with bulimia. *Archives of General Psychiatry, 46*, 54–58.

Wilfley, D. E., Agras, W. S., Telch, C. F., Rossiter, E. M., Schneider, J. A., Cole, A. B., Sifford, L., & Raeburn, S. D. (1993). Group cognitive–behavioral therapy and group interpersonal psychotherapy for the nonpurging bulimic individual: A controlled comparison. *Journal of Consulting and Clinical Psychology, 61*, 296–305.

Williamson, D. A., Gleaves, D. H., & Savin, S. S. (1992). Empirical classification of disorder not otherwise specified: Support for *DSM-IV* changes. *Journal of Psychopathology and Behavioral Assessment, 14,* 201–216.

Williamson, D. A., Prather, R. C., McKenzie, S. J., & Blouin, D. C. (1990). Behavioral assessment procedures can differentiate bulimia nervosa, compulsive overeater, obese, and normal subjects. *Behavioral Assessment, 12,* 239–252.

Wilson, G. T. (1987). Assessing treatment outcome in bulimia nervosa: A methodological note. *International Journal of Eating Disorders, 6,* 339–348.

Wilson, G. T. (1993). Assessment of binge eating. In C. G. Fairburn & G. T. Wilson (Eds.), *Binge eating: Nature, assessment, and treatment* (pp. 227–249). New York: Guilford Press.

Wilson, G. T., Eldredge, K. L., Smith, D., & Niles, B. (1991). Cognitive–behavioural treatment with and without response prevention for bulimia. *Behaviour Research and Therapy, 29,* 575–583.

Wilson, G. T., Nonas, C. A., & Rosenblum, G. D. (1993). Assessment of binge eating in obese patients. *International Journal of Eating Disorders, 13,* 25–33.

Wilson, G. T., & Smith, D. (1989). Assessment of bulimia nervosa: An evaluation of the Eating Disorder Examination. *International Journal of Eating Disorders, 8,* 173–179.

Yanovski, S. Z. (1993). Binge eating disorder: Current knowledge and future directions. *Obesity Research, 1,* 306–324.

Yanovski, S. Z., Leet, M., Yanovski, J. A., Flood, M., Gold, P. W., Kissileff, H. R., & Walsh, B. T. (1992). Food selection and intake of obese women with binge eating disorder. *American Journal of Clinical Nutrition, 56,* 975–980.

Yanovski, S. Z., & Sebring, N. G. (1994). Recorded food intake of obese women with binge eating disorder before and after weight loss. *International Journal of Eating Disorders, 15,* 135–150.

14

PHARMACOLOGIC TREATMENTS FOR EATING DISORDERS

SCOTT J. CROW and JAMES E. MITCHELL

A large and complex literature has developed concerning pharmacotherapy of eating disorders, and the literature clearly suggests that pharmacologic treatments can be effective for both anorexia nervosa and bulimia nervosa. When reviewing the existing literature, it quickly becomes apparent that the majority of research conducted so far (particularly the majority of reports finding medications efficacious) has involved the study of individuals with bulimia nervosa. However, recently anorexia nervosa has been a more active focus for psychopharmacologic treatment research.

In this chapter we will review the published studies of pharmacologic treatment for eating disorders that have included a placebo control or comparison group. Also, we will touch briefly on some of the uncontrolled trials of various agents for these disorders. Finally, we will review and discuss the existing studies from the perspective of clinical relevance and provide practical guidelines to aid the clinician in treating these individuals.

Throughout this chapter we will also focus on the efficacy of medications in treating disturbance of body image, but as the reader shall find, in spite of the general clinical perception that these medications are helpful for body image disturbance, there is limited evidence in the literature to support this conclusion.

A number of studies, stretching back several decades, have examined the use of pharmacologic agents in anorexia nervosa treatment; these are summarized in Table 1. Several studies have investigated antidepressants or antipsychotics, whereas other classes of agents have been studied less widely.

Three placebo-controlled blind studies of tricyclic antidepressants have been completed (Biederman et al., 1985; Halmi, Eckert, LaDu, & Cohen, 1986; Lacey & Crisp, 1980). Two of these three did not find active medication to be significantly more effective than placebos. Lacey and Crisp (1980) used a relatively low dose of clomipramine (50 mg per day); Biederman et al. (1985) used a substantially higher dosage (175 mg per day) of amitriptyline. A third study involving amitriptyline and employing the highest reported dosage, conducted by Halmi et al. (1986), did find a significantly faster weight gain in the amitriptyline group compared to the placebo group.

Placebo-controlled trials of fluoxetine for anorexia nervosa are in progress. These were initiated following two reports (Gwirtsman, Guze, Yager, & Gainsley, 1990; Kaye, Weltzin, Hsu, & Bulik, 1991) of open trials wherein fluoxetine appeared to be helpful. Newer agents, such as the selective serotonin reuptake inhibitors, may prove particularly advantageous with anorexic patients given their medical instability and intolerance of side effects.

Antipsychotic agents have been studied in two separate placebo-controlled studies in anorexia nervosa (Vandereycken, 1984; Vandereycken & Pierloot, 1982) following various anecdotal reports of efficacy. These agents were first employed because of the observation that some anorexic symptoms, such as body image disturbance, are of psychotic proportion or suggested impaired reality testing. These controlled studies, involving sulpiride in a maximum dose of 400 mg/day and pimozide up to 6 mg/day were both performed by Vandereycken's group. Neither agent appeared more effective than placebos.

A variety of other agents have also been studied. The most frequently studied of these has been cyproheptadine, a histamine and serotonin antagonist that was investigated after anecdotal reports of weight gain using this and similar compounds. In two of these studies, cyproheptadine did appear to provide benefit (Halmi et al., 1986; Silverstone & Schuyler, 1975), whereas in two others (Goldberg, Halmi, Eckert, Casper, & Davis, 1979; Vigersky & Loriaux, 1977) it did not. It is of note that the largest study, which employed the highest dosage, did find evidence suggesting the utility of the drug.

Clonidine, an alpha-2 adrenergic agonist, has also been investigated based on its theoretical appetite-inducing effects (Casper, Schlemmer, &

TABLE 1
Placebo-Controlled Drug Trials for Anorexia Nervosa

	Drug	Duration in weeks	N	Maximum dosage	Results	Dropout rate D	P
Lacey & Crisp (1980)	Clomipramine	variable	16	50 mg	NS	25%	12.5%
Biederman et al. (1985)	Amitriptyline	5	25	175 mg	NS	NR	NR
Halmi et al. (1986)	Amitriptyline	4	72	160 mg	AMI > plc	0	0
	Cyproheptadine	4	72	32 mg	Cyproheptadine > plc	0	0
Casper et al. (1987)	Clonidine	8	4	0.5–0.7 mg	NS	0	0
Vandereycken (1984)	Sulpiride	6	18	400 mg	NS	0	0
Vandereycken & Pierloot (1982)	Pimozide	6	18	6 mg	NS	55%	0
Gross et al. (1983)	THC	4	11	30 mg	NS	27.3%	0
Gross et al. (1981)	Lithium	4	16	c	NS[b]	0	0
Stacher et al. (1993)	Cisapide	12	12	30 mg	NS	0	0
Goldberg et al. (1979)	Cyproheptadine	NR	81	32 mg	NS	0	0
Vigersky & Loriaux (1977)	Cyproheptadine	8	24	12 mg	NS	7.7%[d]	NR

NS = not significantly different from placebo. NR = not reported. a = drug given until goal weight achieved. b = NS for weight gain; active drug did decrease gastric emptying time. c = titrated to serum level of 1.0 ± 0.1. d = 2/26 withdrew, treatment status not specified.

Javaid, 1987). However, it was not better than placebos in inducing weight gain in anorexic patients at a dosage of 0.5 to 0.7 mg/day. Cisapride has been studied in a crossover design with placebos at a dose of 10 mg three times per day (Stacher et al., 1993). In this study, cisapride did not appear helpful in inducing weight gain, although—as expected—it did accelerate gastric emptying in these subjects. One inpatient study examined the use of lithium in anorexia nervosa (Gross et al., 1981), which showed a statistically significant but probably clinically unimportant benefit for lithium-treated patients. Finally, tetrahydrocannabinol was compared with diazepam as an active control and placebo, again because of its reported appetite-inducing effects (Gross et al., 1983). This study found that in doses ranging from 7.5 to 30 mg/day, tetrahydrocannabinol did not appear more effective than placebos.

Body Image Disturbance and Anorexia Nervosa

Although body image disturbance is a prominent feature of anorexia nervosa, there is little evidence in the treatment literature thus far for the efficacy of the treatments just discussed on body image disturbance. Only one of the previously mentioned studies of pharmacologic treatment in anorexia nervosa addressed changes in body image disturbance throughout treatment. Stacher et al. (1993) found a statistically significant decrease in mean scores on the body dissatisfaction subscale of the Eating Disorder Inventory for those receiving cisapride. For all the other studies, rate of weight gain or time of achievement of goal weight have been the typical outcome variables used.

Existing Literature on Pharmacologic Treatments for Anorexia Nervosa

There are several limitations to the existing literature on the treatment of anorexia nervosa with medications. One is that mentioned previously: Outcome measures in pharmacologic research in anorexia nervosa thus far have focused primarily on easily quantifiable variables such as weight gain or time to normal body weight restoration. Although this is appropriate to the extent that low weight is present in anorexia nervosa patients and can cause medical problems and lead to hospitalization, the other psychological components of the illness may well remain after weight restoration to varying degrees and presumably may predispose the patient to relapse. Body image appears particularly resistant. If the medications are proven to have an effect on body image disturbance, fear of fat and other psychological components may have a role in anorexia nervosa treatment that extends long beyond the weight restoration phase of treatment, as has been discussed throughout this book. To the extent that this is true, a second weakness in the research becomes apparent: namely, the duration of studies completed so far. Although this is a long-term illness for the majority of patients, only one pharmacologic study has extended beyond 8 weeks. In this way, the published research is markedly different than the usual clinical scenario. This speaks to the need for maintenance studies, several of which are underway.

BULIMIA NERVOSA

There is a much larger literature exploring the use of medications in bulimia nervosa than in anorexia nervosa. Most of these studies have examined the use of antidepressants, although, as with anorexia nervosa, a variety of other types of agents have also been studied.

Tricyclic antidepressants initially were the focus of experimentation in this area, beginning with the drug imipramine (Pope, Hudson, Jonas, & Yurgelun-Todd, 1983). In that study, imipramine-treated patients had a significant decrease in binge eating episodes compared to placebo-treated patients. Since that time, at least eight more studies (Agras, Dorian, Kirkley, Arnow, & Bachman, 1987; Agras et al., 1992; Barlow, Blouin, Blouin, & Perez, 1988; Blouin et al., 1988; Hughes, Wells, Cunningham, & Ilstrup, 1986; Mitchell & Groat, 1984; Mitchell et al., 1990; Sabine, Yonace, Farrington, Barratt, & Wakeling, 1983) have used tricyclic antidepressants, including imipramine, desipramine, or amitriptyline, in bulimic patients. All but one (Mitchell & Groat, 1984) found the antidepressant to be effective in reducing the frequency of binge eating and vomiting. In general, the active drug treatment has resulted in significant decreases in rates of binge eating, ranging from 40% to 90%. However, end-of-treatment abstinence rates have varied from 4% to 20%—with one exception: a study in which 68% of patients achieved abstinence (Hughes et al., 1986). Thus, the medications have some efficacy for most patients but have been somewhat disappointing in their ability to induce a complete remission of symptoms.

Selective serotonin-reuptake inhibitors have been the focus in studies of bulimia nervosa. At least five placebo-controlled studies have employed selective serotonin-reuptake inhibitors (Fichter, 1993; Fichter et al., 1991; Fluoxetine Bulimia Nervosa Collaborative Study Group [FBNCSG], 1992; Goldstein et al., in press; Kanerva & Rissanen, 1994) and each of those studies, except for Kanerva and Rissanen, found an advantage for the selective serotonin-reuptake inhibitors versus placebos. In general, these medications have been well tolerated, with relatively low dropout rates. As Table 2 shows, the rates of decrease in binge eating have been similar to those found for tricyclic antidepressants. These regimens have varied, but in the FBNCSG (1992) study, 60 mg/day of fluoxetine was compared with 20 mg/day, and the higher dose was found more effective in decreasing

TABLE 2
Placebo-Controlled Trials of Antidepressants for Bulimia Nervosa

Study	Drug	Duration in weeks	N	Maximum dosage	% Decrease in binge eating	% Abstinent	Dropout rate (%) D	P
Pope et al. (1983)	Imipramine	8	36	200 mg	70	(35%)	18	9
Sabine et al. (1983)	Mianserin	6	19	60 mg	NS	NS	30	27
Mitchell & Groat (1984)	Amitriptyline	8	32	150 mg	NS	NS	24	6
Hughes et al. (1986)	Desipramine	6	22	200 mg	91	68	30	25
Agras et al. (1987)	Imipramine	16	22	avg = 167 mg	72	30	0	17
Walsh et al. (1988)	Phenelzine	6	50	69–90 mg	64	35	26	13
Barlow et al. (1988)	Desipramine	6	24	150 mg	47	4	49	—
Blouin et al. (1988)	Desipramine	6	10	150 mg	40	10	41	
Horne et al. (1988)	Bupropion	8	81	450 mg	67	30	33	54
Pope et al. (1989)	Trazodone	6	42	400 mg	31	10	13	4
Mitchell et al. (1990)	Imipramine	10	74	300 mg	49	16	34	15
Walsh et al. (1991)	Desipramine	6	78	300 mg	47	13	23	16
Fichter et al. (1991)	Fluoxetine	5	40	60 mg		NR	0	0
FBNCSG (1992)	Fluoxetine	8	387	60 mg	67	NR	31	39
Goldstein et al. (1994)	Fluoxetine	16	398	60 mg	50	NR	11	6
		8		20 mg	45	NR	24	—
Fichter (1993)	Fluvoxamine	15	64	300 mg	NR	NR	NR	NR
Kanerva & Rissanen (1994)	Fluoxetine	8	50	64 mg	NS	NR	NR	NR

NS = not significantly different from placebo. NR = not reported.

SCOTT J. CROW AND JAMES E. MITCHELL

binge eating (67% vs. 45%). Other studies have employed high doses of fluoxetine (60 mg) (Fichter et al., 1991; Goldstein et al., in press) or fluvoxamine (300 mg per day) (Fichter et al., 1991), leading to a general perception that higher doses are likely to be more effective in treating bulimia.

Several other antidepressants have also been found to be effective in bulimia nervosa, including trazodone (Pope, Keck, McElroy, & Hudson, 1989), bupropion (Horne et al., 1988), mianserin (Sabine et al., 1983) and phenelzine (Walsh et al., 1988). All of these have been shown to be effective in double-blind placebo-controlled trials. However, a variety of clinical concerns limits the use of all but trazodone. Bupropion, while effective, was associated with seizures in 5.7% of bulimic subjects receiving it; this rate of seizures was more than 10 times that found in non-eating-disordered depressive patients receiving the medication, leading to a recommendation that it *not* be used in eating-disordered patients. Mianserin, while effective, was taken off of the market subsequently for other reasons. Phenelzine also was effective, but is little used because of concerns that bulimic patients might be prone to other dietary indiscretions that would violate the tyramine-free diet required with this medication, which could lead to hypertensive crises.

As with anorexia nervosa, a variety of other agents in addition to antidepressants have been studied (see Table 3). Four controlled studies of opiate antagonists have been conducted (Alger, Schwalberg, Bigaouette, Michalek, & Howard, 1991; Igoin-Apfelbaum & Apfelbaum, 1987; Mitchell, Laine, Morley & Levine, 1986; Mitchell et al., 1989); these grew out of the observation that endogenous opiates appear to be involved in the regulation of eating. One short-term study of the single-dose administration of naloxone decreased the size of a single binge (Mitchell et al., 1986). However, the three other controlled studies of opiate antagonists failed to demonstrate convincingly a long-term benefit in terms of bulimic behaviors. Hsu, Clement, Santhouse, and Elim (1991) used lithium in a placebo-controlled trial that suggested it may be helpful to some patients. Subjects received up to 1200 mg/day, resulting in average serum levels of .62 mEq/L. While overall binge eating rates were not significantly different between active treatment and placebo groups, 17.6% of those receiving active treatment had at least 1 week of abstinence at the completion of treatment—a rate that is similar to that achieved with antidepressants. Phenytoin appeared to provide some benefit to bulimic patients in a double-blind placebo-controlled crossover trial (Wermuth, Davis, Hollister, & Stunkard, 1977), but an order effect confused interpretation of that study. Fenfluramine yielded mixed results in two controlled studies. One group (Blouin et al., 1988) reported a 25% rate of abstinence in 6 weeks of treatment, whereas a 12-week trial did not find the medication effective (Russell, Checkley, Feldman, & Eisler, 1988). Finally, L-tryptophan in a

TABLE 3
Placebo-Controlled Trials of Other Agents for Bulimia Nervosa

Study	Drug	Duration in weeks	N	Maximum dosage	% Decrease in binge eating	% Abstinent	Dropout rate (%) D	P
Wermuth et al. (1977)	Phenytoin	19	12	varies	8/19 with moderate or marked improvement	NR	5	—
Krahn & Mitchell (1985)	L-Tryptophan	13	6	3 gm	NS	NR	0	0
Blouin et al. (1988)	Fenfluramine	12	6	60 mg	NR	25%	37	42
Russell et al. (1988)	Fenfluramine	42	12	30 mg	NS	NR	38	32
Hsu et al. (1991)	Lithium	68	8	1200 mg	NS	18%	19	32
Mitchell et al. (1986)	Naloxone	5	—	18 mg	NS	—	—	—
	CCK			20 ng/kg	229	—		
Igoin-Apfelbaum & Apfelbaum (1987)	Naltrexone	10	8	120 mg	NSª	NR	0	80ª
Mitchell et al. (1989)	Naltrexone	3	3	50 mg	NS			
Alger et al. (1991)	Naltrexone	6	6	100–150 mg	NS			

NR = Not Reported. D = Drug. P = Placebo.
ªDouble Blind, Placebo-controlled crossover trial in which significant order effect was apparent.

dose of 3 gm/day was not more effective than placebos (Krahn & Mitchell, 1985).

Combining Pharmacotherapy and Psychotherapy

Four trials have been completed to date that examined the interaction of psychotherapy and pharmacotherapy in treating bulimia nervosa. Mitchell et al. (1990) in a four-cell design using imipramine, placebo, and group cognitive–behavioral therapy with either imipramine or placebo, found that both imipramine and group therapy were effective; when combined, however, increased efficacy was not demonstrated on eating variables.

Agras et al. (1992) compared cognitive–behavioral therapy alone, desipramine alone, and cognitive–behavioral therapy plus desipramine; treatment varied between 16 and 24 weeks. In this trial, the most effective treatment condition was cognitive–behavioral therapy plus medication for 24 weeks.

Fichter et al. (1991) treated inpatients with fluoxetine or placebos while they were receiving intensive psychotherapy concurrently. No statistically significant differences in response were seen, although both groups did improve.

Finally, Goldbloom, Olmsted, Davis, and Shaw (1994) investigated individual cognitive–behavioral therapy, fluoxetine, and combination treatment with therapy and fluoxetine. While all three subject groups demonstrated improvement, psychotherapeutic treatment appeared most effective, and combination treatment was not superior to cognitive–behavioral therapy alone.

Thus, although it appears logical that combining known effective treatments for bulimia nervosa would result in improved treatment outcome, three out of four studies to date addressing this question have failed to show this. The relationship between pharmacotherapy and psychotherapy in treating body image disturbance is largely unexplored.

Body Image Disturbance and Bulimia Nervosa

There is limited evidence in the literature for the efficacy of medications on body image disturbance in bulimia nervosa, as summarized in Table 4. All of the studies addressing the issue have used the body dissatisfaction subscale of the Eating Disorder Inventory (Garner, Olmsted, & Polivy, 1983), except for Walsh, Hadigan, Devlin, Gladis, and Roose (1991) who used the Body Shape Questionnaire (Cooper, Taylor, Cooper, & Fairburn, 1987).

Four studies have demonstrated statistically significant decreases in these measures. These have involved fluoxetine (Fichter et al., 1991; FBNCSG, 1992), lithium (Hsu et al., 1991), and desipramine (Walsh et

TABLE 4
Effects of Pharmacologic Treatment on Body Image Disturbance in Eating Disorders

	Illness	Drug	Body image measure used	Statistically significant improvement?
Barlow et al. (1988)	BN	Desipramine	EDI	No
Pope et al. (1985)	BN	Trazodone	EDI	No
Walsh et al. (1991)	BN	Desipramine	BSQ	Yes
Fichter et al. (1991)	BN	Fluoxetine	EDI	Yes
Hsu et al. (1991)	BN	Lithium	EDI	Yes
FBNCSG (1992)	BN	Fluoxetine	EDI	Yes
Stacher et al. (1993)	AN	Cisapride	EDI	Yes
Goldstein et al. (1995)	BN	Fluoxetine	EDI	No
Mitchell et al. (1990)	BN	Imipramine	EDI	Trend ($p = .08$)

Note. BN: Bulimia nervosa. AN: Anorexia nervosa. EDI: Eating Disorder Inventory—Body Dissatisfaction scale. BSQ: Body Shape Questionnaire.

al., 1991). Three others involving desipramine (Barlow et al., 1988), trazodone (Pope et al., 1989), and fluoxetine (Goldstein et al., in press) did not. One study of imipramine (Mitchell et al., 1990) showed a trend ($P = .08$) that did not reach statistical significance. Thus, results are mixed regarding the efficacy of these treatments on body image disturbance.

Existing Literature on Pharmacologic Treatments for Bulimia Nervosa

Essentially the same criticisms can be made of the bulimia nervosa literature as the anorexia nervosa literature. Pharmacologic treatment studies have focused on change in frequency of eating behaviors, but the other psychological components of the illness have received less attention. It seems logical that persisting body image disturbance would increase the risk of recurrent bulimic symptoms through recurring cycles of fasting, binge eating, and purging. Whereas this seems sensible, the influence of change in body image disturbance on long-term outcome remains untested. As mentioned, measures of acute change in body image disturbance following pharmacologic treatment are limited to Eating Disorder Inventory subscales or the Body Shape Questionnaire. It would be ideal to investigate the effects of these medications on a variety of other measures of body image disturbance.

A second weakness is that, although the clinical reality is that bulimia nervosa necessitates long-term treatment, there are few long-term studies. Those that exist suggest that long-term treatment of these patients is problematic and involves frequent medication changes. Pope, Hudson, Jonas, and Yurgelun-Todd (1985) found that although one half of their subjects were in remission at 9- to 19-month follow-ups, most were still receiving antidepressants and more then two thirds had tried more than one medication. Furthermore, many subjects had attempted to discontinue medications at some point and relapsed. Walsh et al. (1991), in a study comparing desipramine with a placebo for an initial 8 weeks followed by 16 weeks of maintenance treatment and 6-month discontinuation follow-ups, found the medication to be initially effective. However, only a limited number qualified for the 16-week maintenance phase, and of those, 29% relapsed.

PRACTICAL ISSUES

A careful medical evaluation is necessary prior to medication treatment of any patient with an eating disorder (chapter 8, this volume). This is true of any form of eating disorder treatment, but it is perhaps particularly true when using pharmacologic treatments because administering medications may cause side effects or exacerbate other medical problems such as orthostasis or cardiotoxicity. Even after initial medical stability is established, it is often necessary to monitor patients medically on a regular basis. This is especially true for bulimic patients who continue to have purging behavior or anorexic patients who remain at low weight.

Intermittent weight measurements are appropriate with anorexic patients because this provides treatment efficacy information as well as some measure of medical stability. This is helpful for many low weight bulimic patients as well. For bulimic patients, self-monitoring has been shown to be somewhat effective in its own right and should be a routine aspect of treatment, whether pharmacologic or psychotherapeutic (chapter 11, this volume). This offers patients more detailed insight into their behaviors and can be helpful even if the primary treatment is pharmacologic rather than psychotherapeutic. In addition, all eating-disordered patients receiving pharmacotherapy should also receive nutritional counseling to learn about more healthy eating patterns and meal planning.

Treatment compliance is a prominent issue in the pharmacologic management of both anorexic and bulimic patients. At varying times in treatment, both types of patients may have limited investment in treatment or feel coerced into receiving it; in these instances compliance obviously tends to be low. As with other psychiatric illnesses, ensuring good compliance is essential for effective treatment.

Many patients with anorexia nervosa or bulimia nervosa have coexisting mood, anxiety, or substance use disorders; a small number have coexistent psychotic disorders. Effective treatment of these comorbid disorders probably increases the chance of good clinical outcome. The clinician should bear in mind that markedly disordered eating patterns can induce changes in mood; in particular, dysphoria can be associated with starvation and extreme low weight and the dietary chaos seen with bulimia nervosa. For this reason, many experienced clinicians will defer administration of antidepressants until a significant degree of weight restoration has been achieved for low weight anorexic patients; if depressive symptoms persist, then antidepressants are indicated. If cyclic mood disorders, severe anxiety disorders, or psychotic disorders are present, appropriate treatment should be undertaken using a mood stabilizer, anxiolytic, or antipsychotic. These disorders appear to represent the main indications for these medications in eating-disordered patients; such medications seem to be of little benefit in treating the eating disorder symptoms.

CONCLUSION

A variety of medications have been studied for treating anorexia nervosa; most have demonstrated little effect on measures such as weight gain. Antidepressants of all types are effective in treating bulimia nervosa, although rates of abstinence at the end of treatment are still relatively low and are typically inferior to those obtained with psychotherapy. Medications other than antidepressants have also been studied in bulimia nervosa; most studies have shown them to have little effect. One obvious and clinically relevant question is whether medication treatment for bulimia nervosa combined with cognitive–behavioral therapy improves outcome. This question remains unresolved.

The effect of pharmacotherapy on body image disturbance in the disorders is uncertain at this point. Four out of eight studies examining this question in bulimia nervosa found a statistically significant improvement. The only study examining this question in anorexia nervosa also found an improvement in body image disturbance.

REFERENCES

Agras, W. S., Dorian, B., Kirkley, B. G., Arnow, B., & Bachman, J. (1987). Imipramine in the study of bulimia: A double-blind, controlled study. *International Journal of Eating Disorders, 6*, 29–38.

Agras, W. S., Rossiter, E. M., Arnow, B., Schneider, J. A., Telch, C. F., Raeburn, S. D., Bruce, B., Perl, M., & Koran, L. M. (1992). Pharmacologic and cognitive–behavioral treatment for bulimia nervosa: A controlled clinical comparison. *American Journal of Psychiatry, 149*, 82–87.

Alger, S. A., Schwalberg, M. D., Bigaouette, J. M., Michalek, A. V., & Howard, L. J. (1991). Effect of a tricyclic antidepressant and opiate antagonist on binge-eating behavior in normalweight bulimic and obese, binge-eating subjects. *American Journal of Clinical Nutrition, 53*, 865–871.

Barlow, J., Blouin, J., Blouin, A., & Perez, E. (1988). Treatment of bulimia with desipramine: A double-blind, crossover study. *Canadian Journal of Psychiatry, 33*, 129–133.

Biederman, J., Herzog, D. B., Rivinus, T. M., Harper, G. P., Ferber, R. A., Rosenbaum, J. F., Harmatz, J. S., Tondorf, R., Orsulak, P. J., & Schildkraut, J. J. (1985). Amitriptyline in the treatment of anorexia nervosa: A double-blind, placebo-controlled study. *Journal of Clinical Psychopharmacology, 5*(1), 10–16.

Blouin, A. G., Blouin, J. H., Perez, E. L., Bushnik, T., Zuro, C., & Mulder, E. (1988). Treatment of bulimia with fenfluramine and desipramine. *Journal of Clinical Psychopharmacology, 8*, 261–269.

Casper, R. C., Schlemmer, R. F., Jr., & Javaid, J. I. (1987). A placebo-controlled crossover study of oral clonidine in acute anorexia nervosa. *Psychiatry Research, 20*, 249–260.

Cooper, P. J., Taylor, M. J., Cooper, Z., & Fairburn, C. G. (1987). The development and validation of the Body Shape Questionnaire. *International Journal of Eating Disorders, 6*, 485–494.

Fichter, M. M. (1993, June). *Antidepressant therapy revisited for bulimia nervosa.* Proceedings of the 9th World Congress of Psychiatry, Rio de Janiero, Brazil.

Fichter, M. M., Leibl, K., Rief, W., Brunner, E., Schmidt-Auberger, S., & Engel, R. R. (1991). Fluoxetine versus placebo: A double blind study with bulimic inpatients undergoing intensive psychotherapy. *Pharmacopsychiatry, 24,* 1–7.

Fluoxetine Bulimia Nervosa Collaborative Study Group (FBNCSG). (1992). Fluoxetine in the treatment of bulimia nervosa. *Archives of General Psychiatry, 49,* 139–147.

Garner, D. M., Olmsted, M. P., & Polivy, J. (1983). Development and validation of a multidimensional eating disorder inventory for anorexia nervosa and bulimia. *International Journal of Eating Disorders, 2,* 15–34.

Goldberg, S. C., Halmi, K. A., Eckert, E. D., Casper, R. C., & Davis, J. M. (1979). Cyproheptadine in anorexia nervosa. *British Journal of Psychiatry, 134,* 67–70.

Goldbloom, D., Olmsted, M., Davis, R., & Shaw, B. (1994, April). *A randomized controlled trial of fluoxetine and individual cognitive–behavioral therapy for women with bulimia nervosa: Short-term outcome.* Paper presented at the Sixth International Conference on Eating Disorders, New York.

Goldstein, D. J., Wilson, M. G., Thompson, V. L., Potvin, J. H., Rampey, A. H., Jr., & The Fluoxetine Bulimia Nervosa Research Group. (1995). Long-term fluoxetine treatment of bulimia nervosa. *British Journal of Psychiatry, 166,* 660–666.

Gross, H. A., Ebert, M. H., Faden, V. B., Goldberg, S. C., Kaye, W. H., Caine, E. D., Hawks, R., & Zinberg, N. (1983). A double-blind trial of D^9-tetrahydrocannabinol in primary anorexia nervosa. *Journal of Clinical Psychopharmacology, 3*(3), 165–171.

Gross, H. A., Ebert, M. H., Faden, V. B., Goldberg, S. C., Nee, L. E., & Kaye, W. H. (1981). A double-blind controlled trial of lithium carbonate in primary anorexia nervosa. *Journal of Clinical Psychopharmacology, 1*(6), 376–381.

Gwirtsman, H. E., Guze, B. H., Yager, J., & Gainsley, B. (1990). Fluoxetine treatment of anorexia nervosa: An open clinical trial. *Journal of Clinical Psychiatry, 51,* 378–382.

Halmi, K. A., Eckert, E., LaDu, T. J., & Cohen, J. (1986). Anorexia nervosa: Responses to cyproheptadine and amitriptyline. *Archives of General Psychiatry, 43,* 177–181.

Horne, R. L., Ferguson, J. M., Pope, H. G., Hudson, J. I., Lineberry, C. G., Ascher, J., & Cato, A. (1988). Treatment of bulimia with bupropion: A multicenter, controlled trial. *Journal of Clinical Psychiatry, 42,* 262–266.

Hsu, L. K. G., Clement, L., Santhouse, R., & Elim, S. Y. J. (1991). Treatment of bulimia nervosa with lithium carbonate: A controlled study. *Journal of Nervous Mental Disorders, 179,* 351–355.

Hughes, P. L., Wells, L. A., Cunningham, C. J., & Ilstrup, D. M. (1986). Treating bulimia with desipramine. *Archives of General Psychiatry, 43,* 182–186.

Igoin-Apfelbaum, L., & Apfelbaum, M. (1987). Naltrexone and bulimic symptoms [Letter to the editor]. *Lancet, 2,* pp. 1087–1088.

Kanerva, R., & Rissanen, A. (1994, April). *Fluoxetine in the treatment of bulimia nervosa: Psychological and behavioral changes after eight weeks' treatment*. Paper presented at Sixth International Conference on Eating Disorders, New York.

Kaye, W. H., Weltzin, T. E., Hsu, L. K. G., & Bulik, C. M. (1991). An open trial of fluoxetine in patients with anorexia nervosa. *Journal of Clinical Psychiatry, 52*(11), 464–471.

Krahn, D., & Mitchell, J. E. (1985). Use of L-tryptophan in treating bulimia [Letter to the editor]. *American Journal of Psychiatry, 142*, p. 1130.

Lacey, J. H., & Crisp, A. H. (1980). Hunger, food intake and weight: The impact of clomipramine on a refeeding anorexia nervosa population. *Postgraduate Medical Journal, 56* (Suppl. 1), 79–85.

Mitchell, J. E., Christenson, G., Jennings, J., Huber, M., Thomas, B., Pomeroy, C., & Morley, J. (1989). A placebo-controlled, double-blind trial of naltrexone hydrochloride in outpatients with normal weight bulimia. *Journal of Clinical Psychopharmacology, 9*, 94–97.

Mitchell, J. E., & Groat, R. (1984). A placebo-controlled, double-blind trial of amitriptyline in bulimia. *Journal of Clinical Psychopharmacology, 4*, 186–193.

Mitchell, J. E., Laine, D. E., Morley, J. E., & Levine, A. S. (1986). Naloxone but not CCK-8 may attenuate binge-eating behavior in patients with the bulimia syndrome. *Biological Psychiatry, 21*, 1399–1406.

Mitchell, J. E., Pyle, R. L., Eckert, E. D., Hatsukami, D., Pomeroy, C., & Zimmerman, R. (1990). A comparison study of antidepressants and structured intensive group psychotherapy in the treatment of bulimia nervosa. *Archives of General Psychiatry, 47*, 149–157.

Pope, H. G., Hudson, J. I., Jonas, J. M., & Yurgelun-Todd, D. (1983). Bulimia treated with imipramine: A double-blind, placebo-controlled study. *American Journal of Psychiatry, 140*, 554–558.

Pope, H. G., Hudson, J. I., Jonas, J. M., & Yurgelun-Todd D. (1985). Antidepressant treatment of bulimia: A two-year follow up study. *Journal of Clinical Psychopharmacology, 5*, 320–714.

Pope, H. G., Keck, P. E., McElroy, S. L., & Hudson, J. I. (1989). A placebo-controlled study of trazodone in bulimia nervosa. *Journal of Clinical Psychopharmacology, 9*, 254–259.

Russell, G. F. M., Checkley, S. A., Feldman, J., & Eisler, I. (1988). A controlled trial of d-fenfluramine in bulimia nervosa. *Clinical Neuropharmacology, 11*, S146–S159.

Sabine, E. J., Yonace, A., Farrington, A. J., Barratt, K. H., & Wakeling, A. (1983). Bulimia nervosa: A placebo-controlled double-blind therapeutic trial of mianserin. *British Journal of Clinical Pharmacology, 15*, S195–S202.

Silverstone, T., & Schuyler, D. (1975). The effect of cyproheptadine on hunger, calorie intake and body weight in man. *Psychopharmacologia, 40*, 335–340.

Stacher, G., Abutzi-Wentzel, T.-A., Wiesnagrotzki, S., Bergmann, H., Schneider, C., & Gaupmann, G. (1993). Gastric emptying, body weight and symptoms in primary anorexia nervosa: Long-term effects of cisapride. *British Journal of Psychiatry, 162,* 398–402.

Vandereycken, W. (1984). Neuroleptics in the short-term treatment of anorexia nervosa: A double-blind placebo-controlled study with sulpiride. *British Journal of Psychiatry, 144,* 288–292.

Vandereycken, W., & Pierloot, R. (1982). Pimozide combined with behavior therapy in the short-term treatment of anorexia nervosa. *Acta Psychiatrica Scandinavica, 66,* 445–450.

Vigersky, R. A., & Loriaux, D. L. (1977). The effect of cyproheptadine in anorexia nervosa: A double-blind trial. In R. A. Vigersky (Ed.), *Anorexia Nervosa.* New York: Raven Press.

Walsh, B. T. (1991). Psychopharmacologic treatment of bulimia nervosa. *Journal of Clinical Psychiatry, 52* (Suppl.), 34–38.

Walsh, B. T., Gladis, M., Roose, S. P., Stewart, J. W., Stetner, F., & Glassman, A. H. (1988). Phenelzine vs placebo in 50 patients with bulimia. *Archives of General Psychiatry, 45,* 471–475.

Walsh, B. T., Hadigan, C. M., Devlin, M. J., Gladis, M., & Roose, S. P. (1991). Long-term outcome of antidepressant treatment for bulimia nervosa. *American Journal of Psychiatry, 148,* 1206–1212.

Wermuth, B. M., Davis, K. L., Hollister, L. E., & Stunkard, A. J. (1977). Phenytoin treatment of the binge eating syndrome. *American Journal of Psychiatry, 134,* 1249–1318.

III

OBESITY

INTRODUCTION

OBESITY

Clinical management of obesity is a complex and controversial area. Definitive research on associated psychopathology and treatments with long-term maintenance of weight loss have proven elusive. Individuals with excessive weight (i.e., morbid obesity) have special problems, and certain individuals are at an elevated risk status (e.g., African American women). Although the significant presence of body image problems has been known for almost 30 years (see my discussion in chapter 1), researchers have turned adequate attention to this clinical feature only recently. In this last part, we examine the foregoing issues as they relate to the clinical entity of obesity.

In chapter 15, Faith and Allison tackle the issue of emotional disturbance in obesity using a "zoom lens" approach to identify at-risk subgroups, including in their analysis clinical and community samples, individuals with accompanying binge eating patterns, and patients with body image disturbance. In the second part of the chapter, they review the psychological assessment of the obese individual, detailing methods for measuring eating patterns, body image, interpersonal functioning, and general psychological functioning. Their review clarifies the issue of the association between psychological functioning and weight, offering some reliable indicators of elevated disturbance in the overweight individual. Faith and Allison's review of measurement devices also adds to the survey and descriptions contained in Williamson, Gleaves, and Anderson (chapter 9) and Johnson and Torgrud (chapter 13).

Grilo presents an integrative model for the treatment of obesity in chapter 16. He begins with an overview of the three primary treatment approaches: behavior therapy, pharmacotherapy, and very low calorie diets. A number of issues regarding the selection of an intervention strategy, such as the presence of binge eating, follows this background material. Grilo discusses several general treatment issues and interventions, providing the bulk of his approach to handling the often intractable problem of obesity. These areas include the choice of a meal plan, daily caloric allowance, weight goal, body image issues, exercise, and relapse prevention. He closes with a call for increased research, especially in the area of enhancing long-term maintenance of weight loss.

Any strategy for treating obesity should deal with the associated body image disparagement that accompanies excessive weight. Rosen follows his chapter on body dysmorphic disorder with a discussion of his work on treating body image in obesity. In chapter 17, he again offers a clear-cut, step-by-step exploration of the cognitive–behavioral approach to managing body image problems. The components include information on the development of body image, exposure via mirror to one's body, cognitive restructuring, exposure and response prevention, coping with stereotypes and prejudice, and integrating body image treatments with weight reduction strategies.

The issues involved in modifying obesity in two special groups close out this part. Fettes and Williams broach the difficult issues associated with morbid obesity in chapter 18. They provide background material on issues such as associated morbidity and mortality, presence of psychopathology and body image disturbance, and social and occupational aspects of this condition. They note that a variety of assessment issues should be considered. For instance, the interview should focus on weight history, eating patterns, symptoms of eating disorders, physical activity, expectations regarding treatment, and psychological and social history. They also emphasize the role of psychological and behavioral assessment. They couch the various options for treatment, including behavioral therapy, very low calorie diets, and surgery in terms of a variety of selection issues.

In chapter 19, Klesges, DeBon, and Meyers focus on the particular issues involved in treating African American women, a group that has one of the highest rates of obesity in the United States. These authors attack a relatively new area of research, and this chapter has little empirical basis to offer specific guidelines for assessment and treatment. The authors focus on possible determinants of the excessive weight, the role of body image issues, and potential avenues for intervention.

15

ASSESSMENT OF PSYCHOLOGICAL STATUS AMONG OBESE PERSONS

MYLES S. FAITH and DAVID B. ALLISON

Children may overeat and be obese in order to get attention. Both children and adults often use food in an attempt to solve emotional problems. Sweets can become a way of handling anxiety, depression, loneliness or fear. (Brothers, 1993)

—Dr. Joyce Brothers

My greatest failure was in believing that the weight issue was just about weight. It's not. . . . It's about not handling stress properly. It's about sexual abuse. It's about all the things that cause other people to become alcoholics and drug addicts. (Big Pain, No Gain, 1991)

—Oprah Winfrey

What is the relationship between obesity and emotional disturbance? These two testimonials suggest a positive association. Furthermore, they imply that obesity is the result of *preexisting, unresolved* psychological problems. These views, common among professionals and lay people alike (Liese, 1986), appear to stem from psychodynamic theories of obesity or lay variants thereof. These models traditionally conceptualized the obese individual as being neurotic, typically with an oral fixation (e.g., Alexander, 1934; Bychowski, 1950). But do the data support this model? Do obese persons as a group exhibit greater psychopathology than nonobese persons? If so, what is the direction of causation? And how might clinicians best assess psychological functioning among the obese to answer these questions? This chapter addresses these questions and provides practical suggestions for a comprehensive psychological assessment.

This chapter consists of two sections. In the first section, we will present a literature review on the relationship between psychopathology and obesity. Using a "zoom lens" approach, this section gradually identifies the subgroups of obese individuals that experience greater emotional disturbance, as well as their discriminating clinical features. The section begins at the broadest and least exclusionary level by examining the association between obesity and psychopathology in community samples. It then focuses on studies using clinical samples. Finally, the section zooms in on binge eating and body image disturbance and their relevance to psychopathology. We end the section with a brief discussion on causal models of emotional disturbance in obesity.

In the second section, we make recommendations for a meaningful psychological assessment. We review clinically relevant constructs, along with some instruments for their assessment. Throughout the chapter, our focus is on adults. Discussions on similar issues among children are provided elsewhere (Epstein, Klein, & Wisniewski, 1994; Epstein, Wisniewski, & Weng, 1994; Kimm, Sweeney, Janosky, & MacMillan, 1991; Wadden, Foster, Stunkard, & Linowitz, 1989).

OBESITY AND EMOTIONAL DISTURBANCE

There have been many discussions in the literature addressing the relationship between obesity and emotional disturbance (e.g., Faith, Allison, & Geliebter, in press; Friedman & Brownell, 1995; Rodin, Schank, & Striegel-Moore, 1989; Wadden & Stunkard, 1985). Over the years, empirical articles have attempted to determine whether there is a positive association between the two and, if so, what might be the direction of causation. These studies have generally investigated either community or clinical samples, both of which are discussed in the following sections.

Community Samples

Large scale community studies have assessed the relationship between body mass index (weight in kilograms/height in meters^2) and emotional disturbance in the general population. Most reviews of this literature suggest no significant difference between obese and nonobese persons in psychological functioning (O'Neil & Jarrell, 1992; Striegel-Moore & Rodin, 1986; Wadden & Stunkard, 1985). Indeed, these data, based predominantly on standardized instruments, contradict earlier psychoanalytic accounts that typically focused on unreliable idiographic measures and clinical interpretation (Smoller, Wadden, & Stunkard, 1987).

Most studies found no difference in psychological functioning between obese and nonobese persons (e.g., Hällström & Noppa, 1981; Kittel, Rustin, Dramaix, deBacker, & Kornitzer, 1978), with some studies finding *less* anxiety and depression among obese individuals (Crisp & McGuiness,

1976; Silverstone, 1968; Stewart & Brook, 1983). However, recent reports suggest that depression and anger do correlate positively with obesity among women, although the effect size is generally small—r values range from about .06 (Istvan, Zavela, & Weidner, 1992) to about .16 (Wing, Matthews, Kuller, Meilahn, & Plantinga, 1991).

Contrary to the studies suggesting no association between body mass index and psychopathology, some recent European studies are starting to paint a different picture. As part of a large sample investigation of obese persons in Sweden, the psychological status of 1,743 obese individuals was compared with 89 nonobese control individuals (Sullivan et al., 1993). The authors reported significantly greater anxiety and depression and poorer mental well-being among obese than nonobese persons. Furthermore, severely obese individuals reported poorer mental well-being than moderately obese individuals, patients with rheumatoid arthritis, cancer survivors, individuals with spinal cord injuries, and nonobese control subjects. Also noteworthy is a 10-year longitudinal study that found that children who were neglected by their parents were 9.8 times more likely to become obese in young adulthood than those who were not parentally neglected as children (Lissau & Sørensen, 1994).

Along these lines, some researchers have proposed an association between emotional distress and abdominal body fat, in particular, rather than total body mass in general (Björntorp, 1988, 1991). Indeed, some data indicate that emotional disturbance, nightmares, and antidepressant and tranquilizer use may be associated more strongly with abdominal fat than total body mass (Lapidus, Bengtsson, Hällström, & Björntorp, 1989; Wing et al., 1991). However, few large sample studies have examined both body mass index and fat distribution (i.e., the waist-to-hip ratio) in relation to psychopathology.

Thus, the data do not suggest a compelling association between obesity and psychopathology. In contrast to a number of studies suggesting no relationship, a few recent studies do report significant associations between obesity and emotional problems and *suggest* that psychological issues might even play a causal role (Lissau & Sørensen, 1994). The jury is still out on this hypothesis. However, we submit one caveat: Few of the studies tested focused on theory-driven hypotheses. That is, they generally compared obese and nonobese persons on measures of general psychopathology rather than more precise, theoretically guided constructs (e.g., arousability to stimuli—see Rodin, Schank, & Striegel-Moore, 1989). We agree with Friedman and Brownell's (1995) argument that it seems premature to assert unequivocally that there are no unique or consistent psychological correlates of obesity. What seems to be needed are more focused hypotheses and longitudinal research designs.

Clinical Samples

Several controlled studies have found that obese individuals seeking dietary treatment report greater emotional disturbance than obese persons not seeking treatment, as well as nonobese controls. For example, obese persons seeking treatment presented more symptoms of borderline personality disorder, greater binge eating, and greater depression (Fitzgibbon, Stolley, & Kirschenbaum, 1993; Prather & Williamson, 1988). Compared with normal weight control subjects, obese persons in treatment have reported more frequent sexual abuse (Felitti, 1993), obsessive–compulsive tendencies (Hart, 1991), and depression (Prather & Williamson, 1988).

These findings raise the question of whether obese persons have more psychopathology than nonobese patients receiving treatment for other disorders. The answer appears to be no (Wadden & Stunkard, 1985). For example, the Minnesota Multiphasic Personality Inventory profiles for obese patients are comparable to those of nonobese medical and clinical samples (Crumpton, Wine, & Groot, 1966; Leon, Kolotkin, & Korgeski, 1979). Furthermore, the prevalence of affective disorders among obese patients does not differ from that found in the general population (Halmi, Long, Stunkard, & Mason, 1980). Commenting on the psychological status of severely obese persons, Stunkard and Wadden (1992) tentatively concluded that "there appears to be no evidence of an increased rate of major psychiatric disorder in these severely obese persons" (p. 525S).

On balance, obese persons in treatment have a greater *tendency* toward disturbance than those not in treatment; however, not all obese persons seeking treatment experience significant emotional disturbance (Fitzgibbon & Kirschenbaum, 1990). Therefore, to better identify those with greater pathology, some researchers have turned their attention to binge eating and negative body image characteristics.

Binge Eating Patterns

Reports of obese binge eaters originated with Stunkard's (1959) classic article and have mushroomed in recent years. Indeed, this proliferation of articles has led some researchers to propose that binge eaters make up a distinct subgroup of the obese population and to support the proposed binge eating disorder (Brody, Walsh, & Devlin, 1994; Spitzer et al., 1992; Spitzer et al., 1993; see also chapter 13, this volume) introduced in *DSM-IV* (American Psychiatric Association, 1994), although others question its validity (Fairburn, Welch, & Hay, 1993). Exhibit 1 presents the diagnostic criteria for binge eating disorder.

Binge eating correlates positively with body weight among obese persons (Telch, Agras, & Rossiter, 1988) and is common among persons enrolled in weight loss programs, with prevalence estimates ranging from 23%

EXHIBIT 1
Criteria for *DSM-IV* Binge Eating Disorder

A. Recurrent episodes of binge eating. An episode of binge eating is characterized by both of the following:

(i) eating, in a discrete period of time (e.g., within any 2-hour period), an amount of food that is definitely larger than most people would eat during a similar period of time in similar circumstances; and,

(ii) a sense of lack of control over eating during the episode (e.g., a feeling that one can't stop eating or control what or how much one is eating).

B. The binge eating episodes are associated with at least three of the following:

(1) eating much more rapidly than normal
(2) eating until feeling uncomfortably full
(3) eating large amounts of food when not feeling physically hungry
(4) eating alone because of being embarrassed by how much one is eating
(5) feeling disgusted with oneself, depressed or feeling very guilty after overeating.

C. Marked distress regarding binge eating.

D. The binge eating occurs, on average, at least two days a week for six months.

Note: The method of determining frequency differs from that used for Bulimia Nervosa; future research should address whether the preferred method of setting a frequency threshold is counting the number of days on which binges occur or counting the number of episodes of binge eating.

E. The binge eating is not associated with the regular use of inappropriate compensatory behaviors (e.g., purging, fasting, excessive exercise) and does not occur exclusively during the course of Anorexia Nervosa or Bulimia Nervosa.

Note. From American Psychiatric Press (1993). Copyright 1993 by the American Psychiatric Association. Reprinted by permission.

to 46% (deZwaan & Mitchell, 1992; Marcus, 1993). Recent studies explicitly using binge eating disorder criteria report prevalences of approximately 30% among obese persons receiving treatment (Spitzer et al., 1992; Spitzer et al., 1993).

Studies using the Minnesota Multiphasic Personality Inventory report that greater binge eating is associated with greater psychopathology, particularly depression (Kolotkin, Revis, Kirkley, & Janick, 1987; Wadden, Foster, Letizia, & Wilk, 1993). In a similar way, on the Symptom Checklist-90 (Derogatis, 1977), binge eating correlates with elevated levels of somatization, obsessive–compulsive disorder, interpersonal sensitivity, depression, anxiety, hostility, paranoid ideation, and psychoticism (Marcus, Wing, & Hopkins, 1988). Obese individuals who report more binge eating also report more symptoms of borderline personality disorder (Fitzgibbon & Kirschenbaum, 1990) and, in one study, elevated rates of personal and parental alcohol abuse (Kanter, Williams, & Cummings, 1992). Studies using structured clinical interviews also have detected greater pathology among obese binge eaters (e.g., Marcus et al., 1990; Yanovski, Nelson, Dubbert, & Spitzer, 1993).

Unfortunately, few studies have teased apart the independent effects of body weight and binge eating tendencies on psychopathology. Recent research suggests that the elevated psychopathology is associated with excessive binge eating and not excessive body weight (Telch & Agras, 1994); however, this finding awaits replication. In the meantime, these data clearly pinpoint binge eating patterns as a red flag for emotional disturbance among obese persons and highlight a key area for psychological assessment.

Body Image Disturbance

Other researchers have studied body image disturbance to better discriminate psychopathology of obese persons. These studies examine the relationship between body mass and the two domains of body image—the *perceptual* and *attitudinal* components (Thompson, Penner, & Altabe, 1990). The perceptual component refers to the accuracy with which one perceives various body parts, whereas the attitudinal component refers to thoughts, feelings, and behavioral reactions to one's own body (chapter 3, this volume).

Regarding perceptual body image, obese individuals have demonstrated the tendency to overestimate body dimensions (e.g., Garner, Garfinkel, Stancer, & Moldofsky, 1976; Glucksman & Hirsch, 1969), typically by 10% to 19% of actual body size (Collins, 1987; Collins et al., 1987; Gardner, Martinez, & Sandoval, 1987). Despite these relatively consistent findings, a few caveats emerge. First, some studies report accurate body estimates by obese subjects (Brodie & Slade, 1988). Second, some non-obese subjects have been shown to overestimate body dimensions at rates comparable to obese subjects (Gardner, Gallegos, Martinez, & Espinoza, 1989), sometimes displaying even greater distortion (Thompson, Berland, Linton, & Weinsier, 1986). Third, body size overestimation correlates neither with depression (Brodie & Slade, 1988; Pumariega et al., 1993) nor neuroticism (Garner et al., 1976) among obese samples, suggesting that it has limited clinical utility for obese persons.

Turning to attitudinal body image, there does not appear to be a simple relationship between body mass index and body dissatisfaction. Although some data support such a relationship (Brodie & Slade, 1988), some large sample research suggests an alternative interpretation. Cash and Hicks' (1990) national survey on body image attitudes demonstrated a significant relationship between *perceived* overweight—rather than *actual* overweight—and body dissatisfaction. Among normal weight respondents, perceived overweight was associated with a poorer evaluation of physical appearance, poorer attitudes toward personal health and fitness, as well as poorer psychological well-being. Furthermore, self-classified and actual overweight respondents displayed few differences in body image dissatisfaction and no differences in psychological well-being. Thus, in assessing attitudinal body image disturbance, clinicians need to discriminate "being fat versus thinking fat" (Cash & Hicks, 1990, p. 327). The belief that one is overweight or obese, rather than actual overweight or obesity, might carry a greater emotional toll and should be assessed independent of body weight.

Finally, certain subgroups of the obese population are more likely to experience attitudinal body image disturbance than others. First, people who binge eat are more likely to be disturbed about their overweight (Cash, 1991). Second, obese women generally report greater body dissatisfaction than do obese men (Cash & Hicks, 1990). Third, obese adults who had been obese adolescents tend to have greater body dissatisfaction than those who were obese as children but not as adolescents (Stunkard & Burt, 1967). Finally, Stunkard and Mendelson (1967) reported that obese persons with general emotional disturbance have greater attitudinal body image disturbance.

Causality of Emotional Disturbance

Why do some obese persons experience emotional disturbance? Psychodynamic theory conceptualizes obesity as the manifestation of an underlying psychopathology. For example, the psychosomatic hypothesis (Kaplan & Kaplan, 1957) postulates that obesity is caused by stress-induced overeating. However, data to support this model are weak (Allison & Heshka, 1993a, 1993b; Greeno & Wing, 1994).

A vast literature documents the pernicious psychosocial consequences of obesity (Yuker & Allison, 1994; Yuker, Allison, & Faith, 1995). These consequences often take strong financial tolls. For example, compared with normal weight persons, obese individuals receive lower salaries (Frieze, Olson, & Good, 1990), fewer job offers (Klesges et al., 1990), and less financial support for college from family (Crandall, 1991). Obese children are often described as *lazy*, *stupid*, *dirty*, and *immature* (Sherman, 1981). Among a sample of 47 formerly morbidly obese patients, all indicated a preference for deafness, dyslexia, diabetes, acne, or heart disease over being obese (Rand & Macgregor, 1991).

More recently, Gortmaker, Must, Perrin, Sabol, and Dietz (1993) used a 7-year prospective design to compare overweight with normal weight persons on various outcome measures. Compared with normal weight women, women who were overweight in 1981 had completed fewer years of education, were less likely to be married, had lower household incomes, and experienced greater poverty in 1988. Compared with normal weight men, overweight men had completed fewer years of education, were less likely to be married, and had lower incomes at 7 year follow-up. Furthermore, comparable differences failed to emerge when normal weight subjects were compared with individuals with other chronic illnesses (e.g., asthma, diabetes mellitus, epilepsy). Taking this vast psychosocial literature into account, any association between obesity and psychopathology may reflect an emotional reaction to one's physical condition and social treatment rather than some preexisting psychosomatic condition.

PSYCHOLOGICAL ASSESSMENT OF THE OBESE INDIVIDUAL

It is difficult to propose one standard psychological assessment battery for *all* obese persons. However, based on our clinical experience and our review of the literature, we believe that certain core constructs should be considered for any assessment. The constructs are presented in Figure 1. We emphasize that this figure is not a path model per se; rather, it is a broad pictorial heuristic to aid clinicians who work with obese clients.

When working with individual clients, this heuristic might be particularly helpful for conceptualizing a relationship between obesity and depression. For example, in a national telephone survey of 2,031 household

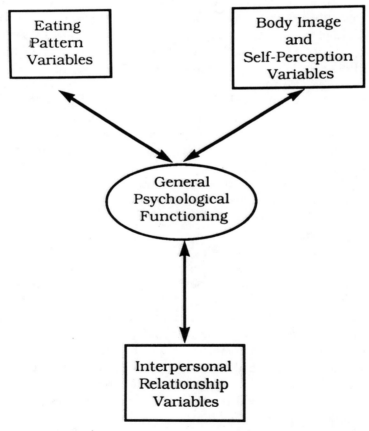

Figure 1. Pictorial heuristic to guide psychological assessment of an obese individual.

respondents, Ross (1994) found a statistically significant association between body mass index and depression. However, once dieting practices and self-perceptions of health were included in the regression equation, the association between body mass index and depression was not statistically significant.

Table 1 presents suggested instruments, as well as some psychometric properties as published in the provided sources. This is not intended to be an exhaustive list of scales but rather some of the more commonly used and psychometrically sound clinical instruments. Most of the provided references include the actual instruments. Detailed critiques of these and other assessment instruments can be found in Allison's (1995) edited volume.

Eating Pattern Variables

There are various instruments for assessing binge eating tendencies. The Binge Eating Scale (Gormally, Black, Daston, & Rardin, 1982) is a popular instrument for evaluating the cognitive, behavioral, and affective components of binge eating. Unfortunately, the scale yields only one global score, which limits its diagnostic utility (Pike, Loeb, & Walsh, 1995). The newer Questionnaire on Eating and Weight Patterns–Revised (Spitzer et al., 1993) was designed according to the criteria for binge eating disorder in the *DSM-IV* (American Psychiatric Association, 1994). Although more comprehensive than the Binge Eating Scale, there are only limited data on the questionnaire's psychometric features. Pike et al. (1995) and Wilson (1993) provide further discussions on the Binge Eating Scale, the Questionnaire on Eating and Weight Patterns–Revised, and other binge eating scales (see chapters 9 and 13, this volume).

There are surprisingly few good scales for assessing emotional eating among the obese. Van Strien, Frijters, Bergers, and Defares (1986) provided a brief, psychometrically sound emotional eating scale as part of their Dutch Eating Behavior Questionnaire. The authors provided norms for both normal weight and obese samples. However, Allison and Heshka (1993b) have questioned its discriminant validity. Glynn and Ruderman (1986) provide an alternative emotional eating scale. For further discussion on this issue, Faith, Allison, and Geliebter (in press) provide a comprehensive review of available self-report instruments for assessing emotional eating tendencies among obese persons.

Dietary restraint may be a better predictor of stress-induced eating than obesity (Greeno & Wing, 1994) and might even be a precondition for binge eating (Polivy & Herman, 1993). Herman and Polivy's (1975) Restraint Scale has been the most popular instrument to date, measuring concern for dieting and weight fluctuation. However, restraint scales by Van Strien et al. (1986) and Stunkard and Messick (1985) seem to have

TABLE 1
Sample Instruments for Inclusion in Psychological Assessment

| Instrument | Eating Pattern Variables | | Reference |
	Description	Reliability	
Binge Eating Scale	16 items tapping behavioral, cognitive, and affective components of binge eating.	α: Not available. TR: Not available.	Gormally et al. (1982)
Questionnaire on Eating and Weight Patterns–Revised	28 items tap *DSM-IV* criteria for binge eating disorder.	α: .75 and .79 in weight control and community samples. TR: Not available.	Spitzer et al. (1993) Reprinted in Pike et al. (1995)
Eating Disorders Examination (12th ed.)	Standardized interview measuring aspects of overeating and weight control. Yields four subscales: restraint, eating concern, shape concern, and weight control. Results can guide *DSM-III-R/IV* diagnoses.	α: .68–90 for subscales across various clinical samples. TR: Not available.	Fairburn & Cooper (1993)
Eating Self-Efficacy Scale: Negative Affect Subscale	13 items tap negative emotional eating.	α: .94 for undergraduate sample. TR: Not available.	Glynn & Ruderman (1986)
Dutch Eating Behavior Questionnaire (DEBQ): Emotional Eating Subscale.	15 items tap negative emotional eating.	α: .94–.95 for obese and nonobese samples. TR: Not available.	Van Strien et al. (1986)
DEBQ: Restraint Subscale	10 items tap dietary restraint.	α: .94–.95 for nonobese and obese samples. TR: Not available.	Van Strien et al. (1986)

| Restraint Scale | 11 items tap (a) diet and weight history and (b) concern with food and eatng. | α: .68, .62 for two subscales for undergraduate sample.
TR: .91 for undergraduate sample (Kickham & Gayton, 1977). | Herman & Polivy (1975) |
| Three-Factor Eating Questionnaire: Cognitive Restraint Scale (also has Disinhibition and Hunger scales). | 21 items tap dietary restraint. | α: .93 for members of a weight reduction group (*dieters*) and their referrals (*free-eaters*).
TR: .93 undergraduate sample. | Stunkard & Messick (1985) |

Body Image and Self-Perception Variables

| Multidimensional Body–Self Relations Questionnaire | 69 items tap evaluation and orientation to appearance, health and illness, and fitness. Also measures body areas satisfaction, weight attitudes, and self-classified weight status. | α: .70–.91 for adult respondents to a magazine survey (Cash, 1994)
TR: .71–.94 (1 month—Cash, 1994) | Cash (1994) |
| Body Shape Questionnaire | 34 items tap concerns about body shape, especially "feeling fat." | α: .93 for female samples.
TR: Not available. | Cooper et al. (1987) |

MYLES S. FAITH AND DAVID B. ALLISON

TABLE 1
(Continued)

Eating Pattern Variables

Instrument	Description	Reliability	Reference
Interpersonal Relationship Variables			
Social Avoidance and Distress/ Fear of Negative Evaluation Scales	28 and 30 item scales tap social anxiety.	KR-20: .94–.96. TR: .68–.94 for undergraduate samples.	Watson & Friend (1969)
Interaction and Audience Anxiousness Scales	15 and 12 item scales tap two dimensions of social anxiety.	α: .88–.91. TR: .80–.84 for undergraduate samples.	Leary (1983)
Rathus Assertiveness Scale	27 items measure assertive behavior.	SH: .77, TR: .77 for undergraduate sample.	Rathus (1973)
Inventory of Interpersonal Problems	127 items tap 6 factors: assertive, sociable, intimate, submissive, responsible, controlling.	α: .82–.94, TR: .80–.87 for clinical outpatients.	Horowitz et al. (1988)
General Psychological and Emotional Status			
Beck Depression Inventory	21 items measure depression.	α: .80–.90 for six clinical samples. TR: .48–.86 for psychiatric patients; .60–.90 for nonpsychiatric controls (Beck, Steer, & Garbin, 1988).	Beck & Steer (1994)

Measure	Description	Reliability	Reference
MMPI–II	567 items (From AX) yield 7 validity and 10 clinical scales, as well as other supplementary and content scales.	α: .33–.86 for 10 clinical scales in standardization sample. TR: .58–.92 for 10 clinical scales in standardization sample.	Butcher et al. (1989)
SCL–90	90 items tap 9 domains of psychopathology plus global severity index.	α: .77–.90 for symptomatic volunteers. TR: .78–.90 for psychiatric outpatients.	Derogatis (1977)
MCMI–II	175 items tap 22 scales corresponding to Axis I and Axis II diagnoses of *DSM-III-R*.	KR-20: .81–.95 for clinical samples. TR: .43–.85 for psychiatric inpatients and outpatients.	Millon (1987)
Extended Satisfaction With Life Scale	50 items tap satisfaction within 9 domains: general life, social life, sexual life, relationship, self, physical appearance, family life, school life, job.	α: .81–.96, TR: .74–.84 for undergraduate samples.	Alfonso & Allison (1994)

Note. For reliabilities, α = Cronbach's alpha; TR = test–retest reliability; SH = split-half reliability; KR-20 = Kuder-Richardson statistic.

better psychometric properties (Allison, Kalinsky, & Gorman, 1992). More thorough discussions on assessing dietary restraint are provided elsewhere (Allison et al., 1992; Gorman & Allison, 1995).

Body Image and Self-Perception Variables

Despite the number of body image scales available (Thompson, 1990, 1995; see also chapter 3, this volume), few were explicitly standardized on obese samples and few provide separate norms for obese persons. Still, Cash's (1994) Multidimensional Body–Self Relations Questionnaire is an excellent instrument that includes four general scales: (a) the Body–Self Relations Questionnaire, (b) the Body-Areas Satisfaction Scale, (c) the Overweight Preoccupation Scale, and (d) the Self-Classified Weight Scale. Clinicians might also consider the Body Shape Questionnaire (Cooper, Taylor, Cooper, & Fairburn, 1987), which measures concerns about body shape and the experience of "feeling fat."

A more behavioral type of assessment requires individuals to rate their discomfort level while looking in a three-way mirror (Butters & Cash, 1987). Although this procedure could be implemented easily with obese persons, limited psychometric data are available demonstrating its utility at this time.

Interpersonal Relationship Variables

A history of verbal teasing and ridicule has detrimental psychological effects for many individuals (Shapiro, Baumeister, & Kessler, 1991). Given the social stigma of obesity, this might be especially common for overweight children. Indeed, in a study of 40 overweight female adults, a significant correlation was found between being teased as a child about body weight and adulthood body image dissatisfaction (Grilo, Wilfley, Brownell, & Rodin, 1994). To understand better the psychological effect of teasing, Thompson, Fabian, Moulton, Dunn, and Altabe (1991) developed the Physical Appearance Related Teasing Scale, which measures the extent of teasing experienced about weight-related and non-weight-related features. The scale has good psychometric properties and provides clinically useful data about obese persons (see also chapters 2 and 3, this volume, for related discussions).

Social anxiety and interpersonal skills should be assessed (Miller, Rothblum, Barbour, Brand, & Felicio, 1990), particularly among obese binge eaters. There is a striking comorbidity of binge eating tendencies and *DSM-III-R* (American Psychiatric Association, 1987) anxiety disorders, especially social phobia and generalized anxiety disorder (Schwalberg, Barlow, Alger, & Howard, 1992). Along these lines, Watson and Friend (1969) and Leary (1983; Leary & Kowalski, 1993) provide brief, reliable measures of social anxiety. The Rathus Assertiveness Schedule (Rathus, 1973) can be used for assessing general assertiveness skills. Another, newer instrument has been standardized on clinical outpatients and shows sensitivity to clinical change. The Inventory of Interpersonal Problems (Horowitz, Rosenberg, Baer, Ureño, & Villaseñor, 1988) measures six domains of interpersonal distress and has good psychometric features. Of course, many other instruments are available (see Leary, 1991).

General Psychological Functioning

Although standardized instruments might lack the sensitivity to detect idiographic problems among some obese individuals (Smoller et al., 1987), they are essential for reliable and valid assessments. Along these lines, the Symptom Checklist-90 (Derogatis, 1977) is a popular instrument for assessing nine dimensions of psychological functioning. The instrument provides a global severity index of symptomatology and is useful for clinical and research purposes. Norms are provided for inpatient, outpatient, and nonclinical samples.

The Minnesota Multiphasic Personality Inventory–II (Butcher, Dahlstrom, Graham, Tellegen, & Kaemmer, 1989) was standardized on a representative sample of men and women drawn from seven states and is a useful tool for measuring psychopathology. It contains 10 clinical plus several validity scales. The instrument also offers supplementary scales, including the Anxiety and Repression scales and MacAndrew Alcoholism Scale–Revised (Graham, 1990).

The Millon Clinical Multiaxial Inventory–II (Millon, 1987) was developed specifically for use with clinical samples. It yields 13 personality and 9 clinical symptom syndrome scales that correspond, respectively, to axis II and axis I diagnoses of the *DSM-III-R* (American Psychiatric Association, 1987). The scale has been used to study psychological changes in obese persons who have undergone gastric stapling surgery (Chandarana, Holliday, Conlon, & Deslippe, 1988).

To specifically assess depression, there are several good instruments available (see Carson, 1986, for a review). The Beck Depression Inventory (Beck & Steer, 1994) is a brief self-report measure tapping the affective, cognitive, and physiological symptoms of depression. Its widespread popularity is certainly one of its strongest advantages.

Finally, psychological assessment might include a measure of happiness, or subjective well-being (see Alfonso, 1995). Alfonso and Allison's (1994) Extended Satisfaction With Life Questionnaire measures satisfaction with nine domains of life, including the physical appearance domain.

CONCLUSION

The psychological assessment of obese persons should be theory and data driven. This chapter has reviewed some reliable indicators of emotional disturbance among obese persons and has provided some suggested scales for their assessment. As we have seen, there are still unresolved questions regarding the relationship between psychological functioning and body weight. More research into the causes and correlates of obesity ultimately will yield better assessment conceptualizations and instruments to facilitate clinical work with this population.

REFERENCES

Alexander, F. (1934). The influence of psychological factors upon gastrointestinal disturbances. *Psychoanalytic Quarterly*, 3, 501.

Alfonso, V. C. (1995). Measures of quality of life, subjective well-being, and satisfaction with life. In D. B. Allison (Ed.), *Methods for the measurement of eating behaviors and weight related problems* (pp. 23–80). Newbury Park, CA: Sage.

Alfonso, V. C., & Allison, D. B. (1994). *The Extended Satisfaction With Life Questionnaire: Development and psychometric properties.* Manuscript submitted for publication.

Allison, D. B. (1995). *Methods for the measurement of eating behaviors and weight related problems.* Newbury Park, CA: Sage.

Allison, D. B., & Heshka, S. (1993a). Emotion and eating in obesity: A critical analysis. *International Journal of Eating Disorders*, 13, 289–295.

Allison, D. B., & Heshka, S. (1993b). Social desirability and response bias in self-reports of "emotional eating." *Eating Disorders: The Journal of Treatment and Prevention*, 1, 31–38.

Allison, D. B., Kalinsky, L. B., & Gorman, B. S. (1992). A comparison of the psychometric properties of three measures of dietary restraint. *Psychological Assessment*, 4, 391–398.

American Psychiatric Association. (1987). *Diagnostic and statistical manual of mental disorders* (3rd ed., rev.). Washington, DC: Author.

American Psychiatric Association. (1994). *Diagnostic and statistical manual of mental disorders* (4th ed.). Washington, DC: Author.

Beck, A. T., & Steer, R. A. (1994). *The Beck Depression Inventory Manual.* New York: Psychological Corporation.

Beck, A. T., Steer, R. A., & Garbin, M. G. (1988). Psychometric properties of the Beck Depression Inventory: Twenty-five years of evaluation. *Clinical Psychology Review*, 8, 77–100.

Big Pain, No Gain. (1991, January). *People*, p. 82.

Björntorp, P. (1988). The associations between obesity, adipose tissue distribution and disease. *Acta Medicae Scandinavica, 723,* 121–134.

Björntorp, P. (1991). Visceral fat accumulation: The missing link between psychosocial factors and cardiovascular disease. *Journal of Internal Medicine, 230,* 195–201.

Brodie, D. A., & Slade, P. D. (1988). The relationship between body-image and body-fat in adult women. *Psychological Medicine, 18,* 623–631.

Brody, M. L., Walsh, T. B., & Devlin, M. J. (1994). Binge Eating Disorder: Reliability and validity of a new diagnostic category. *Journal of Consulting and Clinical Psychology, 62,* 381–386.

Brothers, J. (1993, July 7). People's horror of others' obesity is fear they may also lose 'slip.' *Newark Star Ledger,* p. 24.

Butcher, J. N., Dahlstrom, W. G., Graham, J. R., Tellegen, A., & Kaemmer, B. (1989). *MMPI-II: Manual for administration and scoring.* Minneapolis: University of Minnesota Press.

Butters, J. W., & Cash, T. F. (1987). Cognitive–behavioral treatment of women's body-image dissatisfaction. *Journal of Consulting and Clinical Psychology, 55,* 889–897.

Bychowski, G. (1950). On neurotic obesity. *Psychoanalytic Review, 4,* 301–319.

Carson, T. P. (1986). Assessment of depression. In A. R. Ciminero, K. S. Calhoun, & H. E. Adams (Eds.), *Handbook of behavioral assessment* (2nd ed., pp. 404–445). New York: John Wiley & Sons.

Cash, T. F. (1991). Binge-eating and body images among the obese: A further evaluation. *Journal of Social Behavior and Personality, 6,* 367–376.

Cash, T. F. (1994). *Resource manual for the Multidimensional Body-Self Relations Questionnaire.* Unpublished manuscript, Old Dominion University.

Cash, T. F., & Hicks, K. L. (1990). Being fat versus thinking fat: Relationships with body image, eating behaviors, and well-being. *Cognitive Therapy and Research, 14,* 327–341.

Chandarana, P., Holliday, R., Conlon, P., & Deslippe, T. (1988). Psychosocial considerations in gastric stapling surgery. *Journal of Psychosomatic Research, 32,* 85–92.

Collins, J. K. (1987). Methodology for the objective measurement of body image. *International Journal of Eating Disorders, 6,* 393–399.

Collins, J. K., Beumont, P. J. V., Touyz, S. W., Krass, J., Thompson, P., & Philips, T. (1987). Variability in body shape perception in anorexic, bulimic, obese, and control subjects. *International Journal of Eating Disorders, 6,* 633–638.

Cooper, P. J., Taylor, M. J., Cooper, Z., & Fairburn, C. G. (1987). The development and validation of the Body Shape Questionnaire. *International Journal of Eating Disorders, 6,* 485–494.

Crandall, C. S. (1991). Do heavy-weight students have more difficulty paying for college? *Personality and Social Psychology Bulletin, 17,* 606–611.

Crisp, A. H., & McGuiness, B. (1976). Jolly fat: Relation between obesity and psychoneurosis in general population. *British Medical Journal, 1*, 7–9.

Crumpton, E., Wine, D. B., & Groot, H. (1966). MMPI profiles of obese men and six other diagnostic categories. *Psychological Reports, 19*, 1110.

Derogatis, L. R. (1977). *Derogatis Sexual Functioning Inventory.* Riderwood, MD: Clinical Psychometric Research.

deZwaan, M., & Mitchell, J. E. (1992). Binge eating in the obese. *Annals of Medicine, 24*, 303–308.

Epstein, L. H., Klein, K., & Wisniewski, L. (1994). Child and parent factors that influence psychological problems in obese children. *International Journal of Eating Disorders, 15*, 151–157.

Epstein, L. H., Wisniewski, L., & Weng, R. (1994). Child and parent psychological problems influence child weight control. *Obesity Research, 2*, 509–515.

Fairburn, C. G., & Cooper, Z. (1993). The Eating Disorder Examination (12th ed.). In C. G. Fairburn & G. T. Wilson (Eds.), *Binge eating: Nature, assessment, and treatment* (pp. 317–360). New York: Guilford Press.

Fairburn, C. G., Welch, S. L., & Hay, P. J. (1993). The classification of recurrent overeating: The "binge eating disorder" proposal. *International Journal of Eating Disorders, 13*, 155–159.

Faith, M. S., Allison, D. B., & Geliebter, A. (in press). Emotional eating and obesity: Theoretical considerations and practical recommendations. In S. Dalton (Ed.), *Obesity and weight control: The health professional's guide to understanding and treatment.* Gaithersburg, MD: Aspen Press.

Felitti, V. J. (1993). Childhood sexual abuse, depression, and family dysfunction in adult obese patients: A case control study. *Southern Medical Journal, 86*, 732–736.

Fitzgibbon, M. L., & Kirschenbaum, D. S. (1990). Heterogeneity of clinical presentation among obese individuals seeking treatment. *Addictive Behaviors, 15*, 291–295.

Fitzgibbon, M. L., Stolley, M. R., & Kirschenbaum, D. S. (1993). Obese people who seek treatment have different characteristics than those who do not seek treatment. *Health Psychology, 12*, 342–345.

Friedman, M. A., & Brownell, K. D. (1995). Psychological correlates of obesity: Moving to the next research generation. *Psychological Bulletin, 117*, 3–20.

Frieze, I. H., Olson, J. E., & Good, D. C. (1990). Perceived and actual discrimination in the salaries of male and female managers. *Journal of Applied Social Psychology, 20*, 46–67.

Gardner, R. M., Gallegos, V., Martinez, R., & Espinoza, T. (1989). Mirror feedback and judgments of body size. *Journal of Psychosomatic Research, 33*, 603–607.

Gardner, R. M., Martinez, R., & Sandoval, Y. (1987). Obesity and body image: An evaluation of sensory and non-sensory components. *Psychological Medicine, 17*, 927–932.

Garner, D. M., Garfinkel, P. E., Stancer, H. C., & Moldofsky, H. (1976). Body image disturbances in anorexia nervosa and obesity. *Psychological Medicine, 38,* 327–336.

Glucksman, M. L., & Hirsch, J. (1969). The perception of body size. *Psychosomatic Medicine, 31,* 1–7.

Glynn, S. M., & Ruderman, A. J. (1986). The development and validation of an eating self-efficacy scale. *Cognitive Therapy and Research, 10,* 403–420.

Gormally, J., Black, S., Daston, S., & Rardin, D. (1982). The assessment of binge eating severity among obese persons. *Addictive Behaviors, 7,* 47–55.

Gorman, B., & Allison, D. B. (1995). Measurement of dietary restraint. In D. B. Allison (Ed.), *Methods for the measurement of eating behaviors and weight related problems* (pp. 149–184). Newbury Park, CA: Sage.

Gortmaker, S. L., Must, A., Perrin, J. M., Sobol, A. M., & Dietz, W. H. (1993). Social and economic consequences of overweight in adolescence and young adulthood. *New England Journal of Medicine, 329,* 1008–1012.

Graham, J. R. (1990). *MMPI-II Assessing Personality and Psychopathology.* New York: Oxford University Press.

Greeno, C. G., & Wing, R. R. (1994). Stress-induced eating. *Psychological Bulletin, 115,* 444–464.

Grilo, C. M., Wilfley, D. E., Brownell, K. D., & Rodin, J. (1994). Teasing, body image, and self-esteem in a clinical sample of obese women. *Addictive Behaviors, 19,* 443–450.

Hällström, T., & Noppa, H. (1981). Obesity in women in relation to mental illness, social factors and personality traits. *Journal of Psychosomatic Research, 25,* 75–82.

Halmi, K. A., Long, M., Stunkard, A. J., & Mason, E. (1980). Psychiatric diagnosis of morbidly obese gastric bypass patients. *American Journal of Psychiatry, 137,* 470–472.

Hart, K. E. (1991). Obsessive–compulsiveness in obese weight-loss patients and normal weight adults. *Journal of Clinical Psychology, 47,* 358–360.

Herman, C. P., & Polivy, J. (1975). Anxiety, restraint, and eating behavior. *Journal of Abnormal Psychology, 84,* 666–672.

Horowitz, L. M., Rosenberg, S. E., Baer, B. A., Ureño, G., & Villaseñor, V. S. (1988). Inventory of interpersonal problems: Psychometric properties and clinical applications. *Journal of Consulting and Clinical Psychology, 56,* 885–892.

Istvan, J., Zavela, K., & Weidner, G. (1992). Body weight and psychological distress in NHANES I. *International Journal of Obesity, 16,* 999–1003.

Kanter, R. A., Williams, B. W., & Cummings, C. (1992). Personal and parental alcohol abuse, and victimization in obese binge eaters and nonbingeing obese. *Addictive Behaviors, 17,* 439–445.

Kaplan, H. I., & Kaplan, H. S. (1957). The psychosomatic concept of obesity. *Journal of Nervous and Mental Disorders, 125,* 181–201.

Kickham, K., & Gayton, W. F. (1977). Social desirability and the Restraint Scale. *Psychological Reports, 40,* 550.

Kimm, S. Y. S., Sweeney, C., Janosky, J., & MacMillan, J. P. (1991). Self-concept measures and childhood obesity: A descriptive analysis. *Developmental and Behavioral Pediatrics, 12,* 19–24.

Kittel, F., Rustin, R. M., Dramaix, M., deBacker, G., & Kornitzer, M. (1978). Psycho-socio-biological correlates of moderate overweight in an industrial population. *Journal of Psychosomatic Research, 22,* 145–158.

Klesges, R. V., Klem, M. L., Hanson, C. L., Eck, L. H., Ernst, J., O'Laughlin, D., Garrott, A., & Rife, R. (1990). The effects of applicant's health status and qualifications on simulated hiring decisions. *International Journal of Obesity, 14,* 525–535.

Kolotkin, R. L., Revis, E. S., Kirkley, B. G., & Janick, L. (1987). Binge eating in obesity: Associated MMPI characteristics. *Journal of Consulting and Clinical Psychology, 55,* 872–876.

Lapidus, L., Bengtsson, C., Hällström, T., & Björntorp, P. (1989). Obesity, adipose tissue distribution and health in women—Results from a population study in Gothenburg, Sweden. *Appetite, 12,* 25–35.

Leary, M. R. (1983). Social anxiousness: The construct and its measurement. *Journal of Personality Assessment, 47,* 66–75.

Leary, M. R. (1991). Social anxiety, shyness, and related constructs. In J. P. Robinson, P. R. Shaver, & L. S. Wrightsman (Eds.), *Measures of personality and social psychological attitudes* (pp. 161–194). New York: Academic Press.

Leary, M. R., & Kowalski, R. M. (1993). The Interaction Anxiousness Scale: Construct and criterion-related validity. *Journal of Personality Assessment, 61,* 136–146.

Leon, G. R., Kolotkin, R., & Korgeski, G. (1979). MacAndrew addiction scale and other MMPI characteristics associated with obesity, anorexia, and smoking behavior. *Addictive Behaviors, 4,* 401–407.

Liese, B. S. (1986). Physicians' perceptions of the role of psychology in medicine. *Professional Psychology: Research and Practice, 17,* 276–277.

Lissau, I., & Sørensen, T. I. A. (1994). Parental neglect during childhood and increased risk of obesity in young adulthood. *The Lancet, 343,* 324–327.

Marcus, M. D. (1993). Binge eating in obesity. In C. G. Fairburn & G. T. Wilson (Eds.), *Binge eating: Nature, assessment, and treatment* (pp. 77–96). New York: Guilford Press.

Marcus, M. D., Wing, R. R., Ewing, M. S., Dern, E., Gooding, W., & McDermott, M. (1990). Psychiatric disorders among obese binge eaters. *International Journal of Eating Disorders, 9,* 69–77.

Marcus, M. D., Wing, R. R., & Hopkins, J. (1988). Obese binge eaters: Affect, cognitions, and response to behavioral weight control. *Journal of Consulting and Clinical Psychology, 56,* 433–439.

Miller, C. T., Rothblum, E. D., Barbour, L., Brand, P. A., & Felicio, D. (1990). Social interactions of obese and nonobese women. *Journal of Personality, 58,* 365–380.

Millon, T. (1987). *Manual for the MCMI-II* (2nd ed.). Minneapolis, MN: National Computer Systems.

O'Neil, P. M., & Jarrell, M. P. (1992). Psychological aspects of obesity and very-low-calorie diets. *American Journal of Clinical Nutrition, 56,* 185S–189S.

Pike, K. M., Loeb, K., & Walsh, B. T. (1995). Binge eating and purging. In D. B. Allison (Ed.), *Methods for the assessment of eating behaviors and weight-related problems* (pp. 303–346). Newbury Park, CA: Sage.

Polivy, J., & Herman, C. P. (1993). Etiology of binge eating: Psychological mechanisms. In C. G. Fairburn & G. T. Wilson (Eds.), *Binge eating: Nature, assessment, and treatment* (pp. 173–205). New York: Guilford Press.

Prather, R. C., & Williamson, D. A. (1988). Psychopathology associated with bulimia, binge eating, and obesity. *International Journal of Eating Disorders, 7,* 177–184.

Pumariega, A. J., Black, S. A., Gustavson, C. R., Gustavson, A. R., Gustavson, J. C., Reinarz, D., Probe, L., & Pappas, T. (1993). Clinical correlates of body-size distortion. *Perceptual and Motor Skills, 76,* 1311–1319.

Rand, C. S. W., & Macgregor, A. M. C. (1991). Successful weight loss following obesity surgery and the perceived liability of morbid obesity. *International Journal of Obesity, 15,* 577–579.

Rathus, S. A. (1973). A 30-item schedule for assessing assertive behavior. *Behavior Therapy, 4,* 398–406.

Rodin, J., Schank, D., & Striegel-Moore, R. (1989). Psychological features of obesity. *Medical Clinics of North America, 73,* 47–66.

Ross (1994). Overweight and depression. *Journal of Health and Social Behavior, 35,* 63–79.

Schwalberg, M. D., Barlow, D. H., Alger, S. A., & Howard, L. J. (1992). Comparison of bulimics, obese binge eaters, social phobics, and individuals with panic disorder on comorbidity across DSM-III-R anxiety disorders. *Journal of Abnormal Psychology, 101,* 675–681.

Shapiro, J. P., Baumeister, R. F., & Kessler, J. W. (1991). A three-component model of children's teasing: Aggression, humor, and ambiguity. *Journal of Social and Clinical Psychology, 10,* 459–472.

Sherman, A. A. (1981). *Obesity and sexism: Parental child preferences and attitudes toward obesity.* Unpublished masters thesis, University of Cincinnati, OH.

Silverstone, J. T. (1968). Obesity. *Proceedings of the Royal Society of Medicine, 61,* 371–375.

Smoller, J. W., Wadden, T. A., & Stunkard, A. J. (1987). Dieting and depression: A critical review. *Journal of Psychosomatic Research, 31,* 429–440.

Spitzer, R. L., Devlin, M., Walsh, B. T., Hasin, D., Wing, R., Marcus, M. D., Stunkard, A., Wadden, T., Yanovski, S., Agras, S., Mitchell, J., & Nonas, C.

(1992). Binge eating disorder: A multisite field trial of the diagnostic criteria. *International Journal of Eating Disorders, 11,* 191–203.

Spitzer, R. L., Yanovski, S., Wadden, T., Wing, R., Marcus, M. D., Stunkard, A., Devlin, M., Mitchell, J., Hasin, D., & Horne, R. L. (1993). Binge eating disorder: Its further validation in a multisite study. *International Journal of Eating Disorders, 13,* 137–153.

Stewart, A. L., & Brook, R. H. (1983). Effects of being overweight. *American Journal of Public Health, 73,* 171–178.

Striegel-Moore, R., & Rodin, J. (1986). The influence of psychological variables in obesity. In K. D. Brownell & J. P. Foreyt (Eds.), *Handbook of eating disorders: Physiology, psychology, and treatment of obesity, anorexia, and bulimia* (pp. 99–121). New York: Basic Books.

Stunkard, A. J. (1959). Eating patterns and obesity. *Psychiatric Quarterly, 33,* 284–292.

Stunkard, A. J., & Burt, V. (1967). Obesity and body images: II. Age at onset of disturbances in the body image. *American Journal of Psychiatry, 123,* 1443–1447.

Stunkard, A., & Mendelson, M. (1967). Obesity and the body image: I. Characteristics of disturbances in the body image of some obese persons. *American Journal of Psychiatry, 123,* 1296–1300.

Stunkard, A. J., & Messick, S. (1985). The Three-Factor Eating Questionnaire to measure dietary restraint, disinhibition and hunger. *Journal of Psychosomatic Research, 29,* 71–83.

Stunkard, A. J., & Wadden, T. A. (1992). Psychological aspects of severe obesity. *American Journal of Clinical Nutrition, 55,* 524S–532S.

Sullivan, M., Karlsson, J., Sjöström, L., Backman, L., Bengtsson, C., Bouchard, C., Dahlgren, S., Jonsson, E., Larsson, B., Lindstedt, S., Näslund, I., Olbe, L., & Wedel, H. (1993). Swedish obese subjects (SOS)—An intervention study of obesity. Baseline evaluation of health and psychosocial functioning in the first 1743 subjects examined. *International Journal of Obesity, 17,* 503–512.

Telch, C. F., & Agras, W. S. (1994). Obesity, binge eating and psychopathology: Are they related? *International Journal of Eating Disorders, 15,* 53–61.

Telch, C. F., Agras, W. S., & Rossiter, E. M. (1988). Binge eating increases with increasing adiposity. *International Journal of Eating Disorders, 7,* 115–119.

Thompson, J. K. (1990). *Body image disturbance: Assessment and treatment.* New York: Pergamon Press.

Thompson, J. K. (1995). Assessment of body image. In D. B. Allison (Ed.), *Handbook of assessment methods for eating behaviors and weight related problems* (pp. 119–148). Newbury Park, CA: Sage.

Thompson, J. K., Berland, N. W., Linton, P. H., & Weinsier, R. L. (1986). Utilization of self-adjusting light beam in the objective assessment of body distortion in seven eating disorder groups. *International Journal of Eating Disorders, 5,* 113–120.

Thompson, J. K., Fabian, L. J., Moulton, D. O., Dunn, M. E., & Altabe, M. N. (1991). Development and validation of the physical appearance related teasing scale. *Journal of Personality Assessment, 56,* 513–521.

Thompson, J. K., Penner, L., & Altabe, M. (1990). Procedures, problems, and progress in the assessment of body images. In T. F. Cash & T. Pruzinsky (Eds.), *Body images: Development, deviance, and change* (pp. 21–48). New York: Guilford Press.

Van Strien, T., Frijters, J. E. R., Bergers, G. P. A., & Defares, P. B. (1986). The Dutch Eating Behavior Questionnaire (DEBQ) for assessment of restrained, emotional, and external eating behavior. *International Journal of Eating Disorders, 5,* 295–315.

Wadden, T. A., Foster, G. D., Letizia, K. A., & Wilk, J. E. (1993). Metabolic, anthropometric, and psychological characteristics of obese binge eaters. *International Journal of Eating Disorders, 14,* 17–25.

Wadden, T. A., Foster, G. D., Stunkard, A. J., & Linowitz, J. R. (1989). Dissatisfaction with weight and figure in obese girls: Discontent but not depression. *International Journal of Obesity, 13,* 89–97.

Wadden, T. A., & Stunkard, A. J. (1985). Psychopathology and obesity. *Annals of the New York Academy of Sciences, 499,* 55–65.

Watson, D., & Friend, R. (1969). Measurement of social-evaluative anxiety. *Journal of Consulting and Clinical Psychology, 33,* 448–457.

Wilson, G. T. (1993). Assessment of binge eating. In C. G. Fairburn & G. T. Wilson (Eds.), *Binge eating: Nature, assessment, and treatment* (pp. 227–249). New York: Guilford Press.

Wing, R. R., Matthews, K. A., Kuller, L. H., Meilahn, E. N., & Plantinga, P. (1991). Waist to hip ratio in middle-aged women: Associations with behavioral and psychosocial factors and with changes in cardiovascular risk factors. *Arteriosclerosis and Thrombosis, 11,* 1250–1257.

Yanovski, S. Z., Nelson, J. E., Dubbert, B. K., & Spitzer, R. L. (1993). Association of binge eating disorder and psychiatric comorbidity in obese subjects. *American Journal of Psychiatry, 150,* 1472–1479.

Yuker, H. E., & Allison, D. B. (1994). Obesity: Socio-cultural perspectives. In L. Alexander-Mott & D. B. Lumsden (Eds.), *Understanding eating disorders: Anorexia nervosa, bulimia nervosa, and obesity* (pp. 243–270). Washington, DC: Taylor & Francis.

Yuker, H. E., Allison, D. B., & Faith, M. S. (1995). Methods for measuring attitudes and beliefs about obese people. In D. B. Allison (Ed.), *Handbook of assessment methods for eating behaviors and weight-related problems* (pp. 81–118). Newbury Park, CA: Sage.

16

TREATMENT OF OBESITY: AN INTEGRATIVE MODEL

CARLOS M. GRILO

Obesity is a major public health problem. Approximately 34 million Americans are overweight (Kuczmarski, 1992) and this figure is increasing, especially in women and certain ethnic and racial groups (Flegal, Harlan, & Landis, 1988; Williamson, Kahn, Remington, & Anda, 1990) despite record levels of dieting and pervasive cultural and media pressures to be thin (Brownell, 1991a). Obesity is associated with substantial morbidity and mortality (Manson et al., 1990; Sjostrom, 1992a, 1992b), psychological and social consequences (Wadden & Stunkard, 1985), and economic costs (Colditz, 1992).

The past 30 years have witnessed the development of a variety of specific treatment programs (Wilson, 1994). Although some treatments are able to produce significant short-term weight loss, weight losses are still far from optimal and are difficult to maintain over time (Brownell & Wadden, 1992; Wadden & Bartlett, 1992; Wilson, 1994). Obesity treatment has increasingly been the target of scrutiny and criticism (Garner & Wooley, 1991). This increased scrutiny is needed and could serve to make consumers more wary and professionals more rigorous in their work. Given the magnitude of this public health problem and the reality of the need for both compassionate and improved interventions for obesity (Brownell & Wadden, 1992), this review, following Brownell and Rodin (1994), will not divert to a discussion of whether weight control is good or bad but focus instead on the issues relevant to treatment formulation and intervention with a view toward identifying specific components to increase the likelihood of success.

In this chapter I will present an overview of research findings relevant to the treatment of obesity. This review will represent the basis for the presentation of an integrative model for the treatment of obesity. I will highlight the limitations in the research literature, as well as the limitations in the current "state-of-the-art" treatment approaches. An understanding of these limitations is essential for both professional and compassionate treatment of obese persons, as well as for stimulating continued research on ways to improve the understanding of obesity in an effort to enhance treatments. This chapter will provide an exposition of interventions, based primarily on empirical research findings, targeted toward practical implementation. I will conclude the chapter with a speculation regarding the future of obesity treatment.

OVERVIEW OF TREATMENT

There exist a vast variety of treatments for obesity, including self-help programs, self-help groups (such as Overeaters Anonymous), a variety of commercial and worksite programs, dietary programs, exercise programs, behavioral treatments, drug treatments, university- and hospital-based treatments, very low calorie diet programs, residential programs, and surgery (Brownell & Wadden, 1992; Mason, 1981; Wilson, 1994). This review will focus selectively on those interventions that have received the most study, most notably dietary and exercise programs, behaviorally based programs, very low calorie programs, and drug therapies as applied primarily through university-affiliated facilities. It is possible that findings from such research may not be generalizable to the general population of slightly overweight persons who follow self-initiated programs or who attend commercial programs, although there are no data to support this caveat. If differences were to exist, it is possible that the findings from these university-based programs are more conservative than to be expected with the general population. University-affiliated programs are generally believed to treat heavier patients, many of whom have a history of failed weight control attempts. This review will not address surgery that, although data suggest is effective in many cases, is only indicated for severe obesity, representing a small percentage of obese persons (Kral, 1992; Mason et al., 1994; see also chapter 18, this volume). Even in cases of surgery, however, much of the integrative treatment I will discuss is relevant for sustaining the surgical benefits (Mason et al., 1994).

Behavioral Treatment

Behavioral treatments, dating back to the Ferster, Nurnberger, and Levitt (1962) description of the application of behavioral principles to eating behaviors and Stuart's (1967) seminal report of eight cases of successful weight loss with behavior therapy, have generally been based on the premise that learning principles can be applied to correct excessive eating that accounts for overweight (see Wilson, 1994, for a detailed history of the development of behavioral treatments for obesity). Although it is currently believed that excessive eating and insufficient exercise are but two components of a complex biopsychosocial problem with strong genetic and metabolic components (Brownell & Wadden, 1992; Grilo & Pogue-Geile, 1991), behavioral treatments continue to be used widely.

Behavior therapy is based heavily on functional analyses of behavior (Wilson, 1994), which, in the case of obesity, has generally involved examining the specifics of eating and exercise behaviors with a particular focus on identifying the antecedents and consequences of problematic behaviors. Stunkard (1992) noted that the early application of behavior therapy, which focused primarily on modifying specific eating behaviors, occurred in parallel to dietary and exercise interventions. The different approaches, however, have been integrated, and today the application of behavioral therapies generally occurs in combination with dietary and nutritional or exercise interventions (see Stunkard, 1993; Wilson, 1994). Table 1, from Stunkard and Berthold (1985), provides a summary of the various methods used in behavioral treatments.

The efficacy of behavioral therapies has been studied extensively and has been reviewed elsewhere (see Brownell & Jeffery, 1987; Brownell & Kramer, 1989; Brownell & Wadden, 1992). Table 2 summarizes a review by Wadden and Bartlett (1992; updated from Brownell and Wadden, 1986) on selected controlled studies from 1974 to 1990 of behavioral therapy and conventional moderate reducing diets. Treatments have become longer and more intensive in recent years and produce significant short-term weight losses. The increases in weight losses appear to be primarily a function of the increased length of treatment and a result of a more potent treatment (Wilson, 1994). Behavioral treatments, however, are associated with substantial weight regain posttreatment (Brownell, 1992; Wilson, 1994). Recent studies have found that patients, on average, regain one third to one half of their weight loss during the 1-year posttreatment and that most patients regain their entire weight loss by 5 years (Kramer, Jeffery, Forster, & Snell, 1989; Wadden, Sternberg, Letizia, Stunkard, & Foster, 1989).

TABLE 1

Behavioral Weight Loss Principles Described in Five Leading Treatment Manuals

Principles	Books citing	Principles	Books citing
1. STIMULUS CONTROL		3. REWARD	
A. Shopping		1. Solicit help from family and friends	5
1. Shop for food after eating	3	2. Help family and friends provide this help in the form and praise and material rewards	5
2. Shop from a list	3	3. Utilize self-monitoring records as basis for rewards	5
3. Avoid ready-to-eat foods	3	4. Plan specific rewards for specific behaviors (behavioral contracts)	3
4. Don't carry more cash than needed for shopping list	2	4. SELF-MONITORING	
B. Plans		Keep diet diary that includes:	
1. Plan to limit food intake	4	1. Time and place of eating	5
2. Substitute exercise for snacking	4	2. Type and amount of food	5
3. Eat meals and snacks at scheduled times	3	3. Who is present/How you feel	5
4. Don't accept food offered by others	2	5. NUTRITION EDUCATION	
C. Activities		1. Use diet diary to identify problem areas	5
1. Store food out of sight	5	2. Make small changes that you can continue	5
2. Eat all food in the same place	5	3. Learn nutritional values of foods	5
3. Remove food from inappropriate storage areas in the house	5	4. Decrease fat intake; increase complex carbohydrates	4
4. Keep serving dishes off the table	4	6. PHYSICAL ACTIVITY	
5. Use smaller dishes and utensils	3	A. Routine Activity	
6. Avoid being the food server	2	1. Increase routine activity	5
7. Leave the table immediately after eating	2	2. Increase use of stairs	5
8. Don't save leftovers	2	3. Keep a record of distance walked each day	2
D. Holidays and Parties		B. Exercise	
1. Drink fewer alcoholic beverages	2	1. Begin a very mild exercise program	5
2. Plan eating habits before parties	2	2. Keep a record of daily exercise	2
3. Eat a low calorie snack before parties	2	3. Increase the exercise very gradually	2
4. Practice polite ways to decline food	2		
5. Don't get discouraged by an occasional setback	2		

2. EATING BEHAVIOR
   1. Put fork down between mouthfuls   4
   2. Chew thoroughly before swallowing   4
   3. Prepare foods one portion at a time   4
   4. Leave some food on the plate   4
   5. Pause in the middle of the meal   3
   6. Do nothing else while eating (read, watch   3
      television)

7. COGNITIVE RESTRUCTURING
   1. Avoid setting unreasonable goals   4
   2. Think about progress, not shortcomings   4
   3. Avoid imperatives like "always" and "never"   4
   4. Counter negative thoughts with rational   4
      restatements
   5. Set weight goals   4

Note. From "What Is Behavior Therapy: A Very Short Description of Behavioral Weight Control" (p. 822) by A. J. Stunkard and H. C. Berthold, 1985, *American Journal of Clinical Nutrition, 41,* 821–823. Copyright 1985 by American Society for Clinical Nutrition, Inc. Reprinted by permission.

TABLE 2
Summary Analysis of Selected Studies from 1974 to 1990 Providing
Treatment by Behavior Therapy and Conventional Reducing Diet

	1974	1978	1984	1985–1987	1988–1990
Number of studies included	15	17	15	13	5
Sample size	53.1	54.0	71.3	71.6	21.2
Initial weight (kg)	73.4	87.3	88.7	87.2	91.9
Initial % overweight	49.4	48.6	48.1	56.2	59.8
Length of treatment (wk)	8.4	10.5	13.2	15.6	21.3
Weight loss (kg)	3.8	4.2	6.9	8.4	8.5
Loss per week (kg)	0.5	0.4	0.5	0.5	0.4
Attrition (%)	11.4	12.9	10.6	13.8	21.8
Length of follow-up (wk)	15.5	30.3	58.4	48.3	53.0
Loss at follow-up	4.0	4.1	4.4	5.3	5.6

Note. The data, adapted and updated, are from Brownell and Wadden (1986). Table reprinted from Wadden and Bartlett (1992) with permission.

Very Low Calorie Diets

Very low calorie diets (VLCD) represent an aggressive approach to weight loss (Wadden, Van Itallie, & Blackburn, 1990). VLCDs involve fasting supplemented with several possible methods, including powdered supplements or small amounts of lean meat or fish to provide protein. VLCDs have involved a range of calorie levels that generally fall between 400 and 800 kcal/day and generally have been used with patients 40% or more above ideal weight for their height. These programs have been found to be generally safe but should be followed under medical supervision (Wadden et al., 1990).

The efficacy of VLCDs has been studied extensively, and Table 3 summarizes a review by Wadden and Bartlett (1992) of randomized clinical trials of VLCDs that have included follow-up data. As can be seen, VLCDs tend to produce rapid and substantial weight losses in the short-term (Wadden & Stunkard, 1986), but these weight losses are poorly maintained. The combination of behavior therapy appears to decrease weight regain during the year following the VLCD, but studies with 3- to 5-year follow-up periods have found that all of the weight loss has been regained (Wadden, Stunkard, & Liebschutz, 1988; Wadden et al., 1989).

Pharmacotherapy

Pharmacotherapy has played a minor role in the treatment of overweight. Given the increased emphasis on biological aspects of weight regulation and obesity, the poor long-term success of conservative treatments and VLCDs, and an apparent paradigmatic shift toward viewing obesity as

TABLE 3
Summary Analysis of Randomized Clinical Trials of Very Low Calorie Diets That Include Follow-Up Data

Reference	Subjects	Mean pretreatment weight (kg)	Mean age (yr)	Treatment regimen	Mean treatment duration (wk)	Mean weight loss (kg)	Mean weight loss at follow-up (kg)
Miura et al. (1989)	46 F, 24 M	148% of ideal weight	35.4	VLCD for 4–8 weeks followed by conventional diet	16	8.6	1 year: 5.0 / 2 years: 4.1
				BT + conventional diet	16	4.5	1 year: 5.5 / 2 years: 5.8
				BT + VLCD for 4–8 weeks followed by conventional diet	16	10.7	1 year: 11.5 / 2 years: 12.0
Sikand et al. (1988)	30 F (21; 15)	102.7	38.8	BT + VLCD for 16 weeks	16	17.5	2 years: 0.8
				BT + exercise + VLCD for 16 weeks	16	21.8	2 years: 9.1
Wadden et al. (1989)	89 F (76; 68; 55)	106.0	42.1	PSMF for 8 weeks; 1000–1200 kcal/day for 8 weeks	16	13.1_a	1 year: 4.7_a / 5 years: +1.0
				BT + 1200 kcal/day	26	13.0_a	1 year: 6.6_{ab} / 5 years: +2.7
				BT + PMSF for 8 weeks; 1000–1200 kcal/day for 18 weeks	26	16.8_b	1 year: 10.6_b / 5 years: +2.9
Wing et al. (1991)	26 F, 10 M (33; 33)	103.8	51.0	BT + 1000–1500 kcal/day	20	10.1_a	1 year: 6.8
				BT + PSMV/VLCD for 8 weeks; 1000–1500 kcal/day for 12 weeks	20	18.6_b	1 year: 8.6

Note. Numbers in parentheses indicate the number of persons remaining at the end of treatment and at successive follow-up evaluations. VLCD = very low calorie diet; BT = behavior therapy; PSMF = protein-sparing modified fast. Dissimilar lowercase subscripts indicate statistically significant differences between conditions. Table reprinted from Wadden and Bartlett (1992) with permission.

a chronic biological disorder of energy regulation (Bray, 1992; Weintraub, 1992; Wilson, 1994), there appears to be increased interest among clinical researchers in developing safe and effective drug therapies for obesity (Atkinson, 1994). It has been argued forcefully that treatments can be improved via a more rigorous application of theory to guide research and practice (Brownell & Wadden, 1992; Wilson, 1994). Wilson notes, "Given the model of obesity as a chronic biological disorder, a more direct and potentially powerful treatment would be aimed at correcting or modifying the maladaptive biological mechanisms responsible for the cause or at least the maintenance of obesity" (1994, p. 61).

There are now 10 approved drugs for weight control in the United States (Atkinson, 1994); 9 influence the adrenergic systems and 1 (fenfluramine) influences the serotonergic system. To date, however, research on drug treatments has been limited and has focused, for the most part because of Federal Drug Administration guidelines, on short-term trials (Bray, 1992). Recent research also has begun to examine the potential usefulness of different types of serotonergic influencing agents for weight loss (Craighead & Agras, 1991).

Scoville (1975) reviewed more than 200 studies with a total of more than 10,000 patients involving clinical trials of adrenergic drugs (amphetamine-like compounds). In approximately 40% of the controlled studies, the active drug produced significantly more weight loss than placebos, which across studies averaged 0.5 lbs/week more weight loss. Other more recent reviews of these types of medications have produced similar findings (Galloway, Farquhar, & Munroe, 1984). The discontinuation of drug treatment is followed universally by weight regain (Galloway et al., 1984). There is general consensus these amphetamine-like medications are not clinically indicated because of their potential for abuse (Craighead & Agras, 1991).

Recent research has targeted a number of agents that focus on the serotonin system. One of the most promising drugs studied to date is fenfluramine (Bray, 1992; Guy-Grand et al., 1992). Fenfluramine, which partially inhibits serotonin reuptake and stimulates serotonin release, has produced impressive weight losses in several trials (Douglas et al., 1983; Guy-Grand et al., 1989). In a particularly impressive study, Weintraub and his colleagues (Weintraub, Sundaresan, Madan, et al., 1992; Weintraub, Sundaresan, Schuster, Averbach, et al., 1992; Weintraub, Sundaresan, Schuster, Ginsberg, et al., 1992) examined the effectiveness of DL-fenfluramine and phentermine (a centrally acting adrenergic drug without the addictive potential of other amphetamines) in a long-term study involving a complex design with multiple treatment components, including behavior therapy. This landmark study found that the drug treatment produced significantly greater weight loss than placebos in obese patients receiving comprehensive dietary interventions and behavior therapy. The

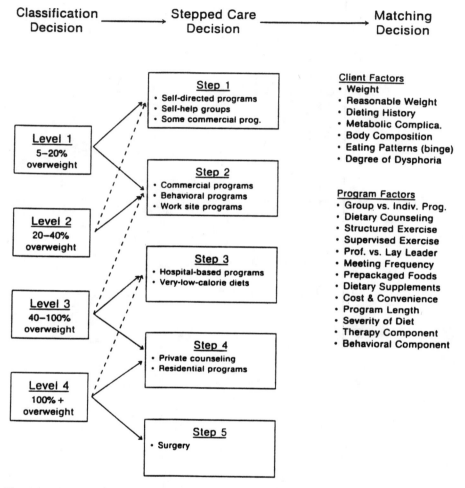

Classification Decision → **Stepped Care Decision** → **Matching Decision**

Level 1
5–20% overweight

Level 2
20–40% overweight

Level 3
40–100% overweight

Level 4
100% + overweight

Step 1
• Self-directed programs
• Self-help groups
• Some commercial prog.

Step 2
• Commercial programs
• Behavioral programs
• Work site programs

Step 3
• Hospital-based programs
• Very-low-calorie diets

Step 4
• Private counseling
• Residential programs

Step 5
• Surgery

Client Factors
• Weight
• Reasonable Weight
• Dieting History
• Metabolic Complica.
• Body Composition
• Eating Patterns (binge)
• Degree of Dysphoria

Program Factors
• Group vs. Indiv. Prog.
• Dietary Counseling
• Structured Exercise
• Supervised Exercise
• Prof. vs. Lay Leader
• Meeting Frequency
• Prepackaged Foods
• Dietary Supplements
• Cost & Convenience
• Program Length
• Severity of Diet
• Therapy Component
• Behavioral Component

Figure 1. A conceptual scheme showing the three-stage process in selecting a treatment for an individual. The first step, the Classification Decision, divides individuals according to percent overweight into four levels. This level indicates which of the five steps would be reasonable in the second stage, the Stepped Care Decision. This indicates that the least intensive, costly, and risky approach will be used from among alternative treatments. The third stage, the Matching Decision, is used to make the final selection of a program, and is based on a combination of client and program variables. The dashed lines with arrows between the Classification and Stepped Care stages show the lowest level of treatment that may be beneficial, but more intensive treatment is usually necessary for people at the specified weight level. Reprinted with permission from Brownell KD, Wadden TA: The heterogeneity of obesity: Fitting treatments to individuals. *Behavior Therapy, 22*:153, 1991.

TABLE 4
Response of Obese Binge and Non-Binge Eaters to Weight Loss Treatment

Author	Treatment, weeks (diet/program)	Type of Criteria	Pre-Rx Wt (kg) BE	NBE	Number (F/M) BE	NBE	Dropouts during program BE	NBE	Weight loss kg (% total body weight) BE	NBE	Follow-up kg regained (% of lost wt regained) BE	NBE	Number in follow-up/ number started BE	NBE
Yanovski et al., 1993 (78)	VLCD + BT 12/26	BED[a], BES[b]	114.3	104.5	21 F	17 F	2 (10%)	0 (0)	19.6 (18%)	21.3 (21%)	3 months[c] 3.7 (19%) 12 months[c] 8.5 (42%)	3 months 2.5 (13%) 12 months 10.4 (51%)	3 months 20/21; 12 months 16/21	3 months (17/17) 12 months 17/17
LaPorte, 1992 (36)	VLCD + BT 10/10	BES	108.1	109.0	19 F 6 M	15 F 9 M	5 F 3 M (32%)	1 F 3 M (17%)	18.7 (17%)	20.2 (19%)	N/A	N/A	N/A	N/A
Wadden et al. 1992 (70)	VLCD + BT 12/26	Binge eaters (BE) episodic overeaters (EO)[d]	BE: 97.8 EO: 99.0	101.6	BE: 29 F EO: 26 F	180 F	BE: 14 (47%) EO[e] 15 (58%)	68 (37%)	BE: 21.5 (22%) EO: 19.4 (20%)	21.7 (21%)	Not reported[f]	Not reported	12 months 7/29 BE 6/26 EO	12 months 73/180
deZwaan et al., 1992 (16)	CBT vs. DM ± fluvoxamine[g]	Self-report + clinical interview[h]	35.8[i] kg/m2	36.7 kg/m2	22 F	44 F	7 (32%)	9 (21%)	6.1	5.6	12 months 4.6 kg (76%)	12 months 1.6 kg (28%)	N/A	N/A
Marcus et al., 1990[j] (44)	BT ± fluoxetine 52/52	DSM-III[k]	110.1	94.8	20 F 2 M	22 F 2 M	13 (59%)	11 (48%)	Fluoxetine 3.9 (4%) Placebo + 0.25 kg (0%)	Fluoxetine: 11.5 (12%); Placebo + 0.27 (0%)	3–6 months Fluoxetine[l] +6.6 (>100%) Placebo +0.73 (>100%)	3–6 months Fluoxetine[l] +4.4 (38%) Placebo −1.4 (>100% additional loss)	3–6 months 7/22	3–6 months 8/23

| Marcus et al., 1988 (45) | BT[m] 10/10 | DSM-III | 84.2 | 81.2 | 35 F | 33 F | 9[n] (26%) | 3 (9%) | 4.7 (5%) | 5.2 (6%) | 6 months 2.8kg (60%),[o] 12 months 3 kg (65%) | 6 months 0.5kg (10%) 12 months 2.6 kg (50%) | 6 months −1.1kg (60% additional loss) | 6 month 26/35 12 months 26/35 | 6 months 30/33; 12 months 30/33 |
| Keefe et al., 1984 (34) | BT 9/9 | DSM-III | 94.4 | 86 | 23 ?M/F | 21 ?M/F | 16[p] | 1.9[q] (2%) | 4.4 (5%) | | 6 months −1.1kg (30% additional loss) | | N/A | N/A |

Note. BE = binge eater, NBE = non-binge eater, VLCD = very low calorie diet, BT = behavioral therapy, CBT = cognitive behavioral therapy, DM = dietary management. [a]BED = preliminary DSM-IV criteria for binge eating disorder as assessed by the QEWP. [b]BES = binge eating scale (26). [c]BE defined by DSM-III-R criteria for bulimia nervosa with omission of purging, episodic overeaters defined by frequent episodes of overeating without subjective loss of control. [e]EO were significantly more likely to drop out of treatment following refeeding than BE and NBE, $p < 0.003$. [f]Overall weight regain was 8.8 kg at one year; however, separate figures were not reported for BE, EO, and NBE. [g]This was a double-blind placebo controlled study evaluating effectiveness of cognitive-behavioral therapy (CBT) versus standard dietary management without behavior therapy (DM) and fluvoxamine versus placebo. No differences in weight-loss outcome measures were found as a function of treatment type. [h]Self-report of moderate to severe binge eating on questionnaire +/− criteria for bulimia nervosa without fulfilling purging or frequency criteria. [i]Weight in kg not reported. Body mass index given. [j]Some of these data are previously unpublished (M. Marcus, personal communication, December, 1992). [k]DSM-III criteria for bulimia do not require compensatory purging. [l]Refers to group which was on active drug during the study. All medications were stopped at study endpoint. [m]BT was modified or standard. No differences on outcome measure were seen as a result of treatment type (modified vs. standard therapy). [n]Binge eaters vs. non-binge eaters, $p < 0.07$. [o]Binge eaters vs non-binge eaters. $p = 0.2$. [p]Study was retrospective. Only completers interviewed, therefore dropout and follow-up rate cannot be calculated. [q]$p < 0.05$, binge eaters versus non-binge eaters.
Reprinted from Yanovski (1992) with permission.

termine the optimal combination or sequence of treatments for obese binge eaters. Nonetheless, based on available data, the presence of substantial binge eating (a psychological and behavioral problem) indicates that treatment for the binge eating should be considered rather than making weight loss the focus (Wilfley et al., in press).

GENERAL TREATMENT ISSUES AND INTERVENTIONS

A review of general treatment issues and recommended interventions, regardless of the major treatment approach or combination of approaches implemented, follows. I will discuss the following domains in turn: (a) calories and nutritional issues, (b) weight goals, (c) relapse prevention, (d) body image, and (e) exercise.

Number of Calories and Meal Plans

There exists substantial variation in how calorie levels and nutritional recommendations are made. Except for the case of VLCDs, most university-affiliated programs recommend roughly a 1200-kcal/day goal for producing weight loss. Because there are gender differences and substantial individual differences in metabolic processes and overall energy expenditure, Brownell and Grilo (1993) recommended the following approach to estimate calorie goals for a patient. Begin with a 1500-kcal/day goal for men and a 1200-kcal/day goal for women, and carefully monitor all food intake in a food diary. This information will allow for the calculation of the caloric intake necessary to accomplish weekly weight loss goals. This approach is suggested over the common recommendation to reduce daily caloric intake by 500 kcal to lose 1 pound per week. The latter type of calculation is based on average intakes and expenditures across many people and does not allow for consideration of intraperson variability over time as a result of changes in water loss, metabolic shifts, lean tissue loss, and changes in activity levels.

In addition to total caloric expenditure, any weight control program must consider balanced nutrition practices. The U.S. Department of Agriculture (1992) recently published the Food Guide Pyramid (Figure 2). This pyramid presents recommended dietary guidelines with clearly specified daily servings for five food groups.

The question of how many calories also applies to VLCD programs. One study compared the effects of three VLCDs (420-, 660-, and 800-kcal/day) in combination with behavior therapy on weight loss, body composition, and psychological functioning in 76 obese females randomly assigned to one of the three conditions (Foster et al., 1992). The three diets

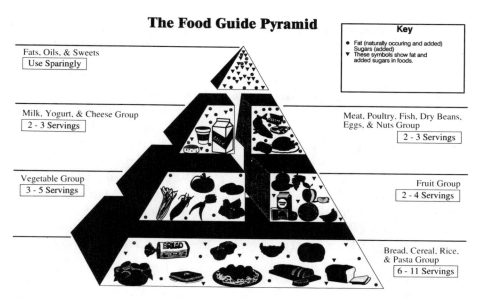

Figure 2. U.S. Department of Agriculture—Food Guide Pyramid (Reprinted with permission from *Weight Control Digest, 2,* p. 177, 1992.)

did not differ significantly in weight loss, changes in body composition, or psychological functioning. These data suggest that there do not appear to be any advantages to using VLCDs with fewer than 800 kcal/day (see Wadden & Kuehnel, 1993). A more recent study by Wadden and colleagues (1994) found that the combination of a VLCD and behavior therapy had no long-term advantage over the combination of a conventional balanced moderate deficit diet plus behavior therapy.

Wadden and colleagues (Wadden et al., 1994; Wadden & Bartlett, 1992; Wadden & Kuehnel, 1993) have speculated that the large short-term advantages of VLCDs versus conventional diets are a result, in part, of the form or structure of the VLCDs themselves. The decreased choices with the increased structure may facilitate dietary adherence (Wadden et al., 1994). A study by Wing, Shiffman, Drapkin, Grilo, and McDermott (1995) found that although patients on VLCDs and conventional diets reported lapses with equal frequency, the lapses in the VLCD patients involved fewer calories. Consistent with Wadden and colleagues' (1994) hypothesis, VLCD patients reported greater self-efficacy than patients on conventional diets about avoiding future dietary lapses and continuing to lose weight.

Convergent findings from other types of studies are consistent with the speculation that the structure of eating may be important for weight control. For instance, many persons believe that skipping meals is an efficient way to save calories to lose weight. Skipping meals, however, may lead to subsequent overeating (Schlundt, Hill, Sbrocco, Pope-Cordle, & Sharp, 1992).

Taken together, these findings suggest that structure and consistency in eating represent potentially important goals. Eating regular meals consisting of balanced nutrition, avoiding skipped meals, and planning for coping with impulsive eating (see Grilo, Brownell, & Stunkard, 1993) represent important goals for treatment. For some patients who have marked difficulty with meal planning or food choices, either a VLCD or a program involving packaged foods might be helpful (Wadden et al., 1994). This recommendation, following Wadden et al. (1994), seems viable given recent findings that these types of structured meal plans do not create binge eating problems (Telch & Agras, 1993; Wadden et al., 1994). This represents an area in which further research is needed.

Number of Calories: Revisited

Behavior therapy, which initially focused intensively on modifying eating behaviors, increasingly has become focused on a wide range of lifestyle changes relevant to weight regulation and lifestyle balance (e.g., Brownell, 1991b). The large volume of biologically oriented research from the 1980s to the present has emphasized the complex metabolic and physiologic processes that influence weight. For instance, research has found support for many metabolic processes that supported some obese persons' claims that their metabolisms were low, that their energy expenditure systems were inefficient, and that they could not lose weight on 1200 kcal/day diets (Brownell & Wadden, 1992). Recent studies, however, using complex metabolic assessment techniques such as doubly labeled water (a technique using isotopes to measure 24 hour energy expenditure in people; see Schoeller, 1988) have produced findings that seriously call into question the reliability of dietary self-report and claims that certain obese persons do not eat substantially more than lean persons. Although both lean and obese persons tend to underestimate caloric intake, the underestimation by obese persons has been found to be approximately 35%, which is substantially greater than by lean persons (Bandini, Schoeller, Cyr, & Dietz, 1990; Lichtman et al., 1992; Prentice, et al., 1986). For instance, Lichtman and colleagues (1992) found that a sample of diet-resistant obese patients underestimated the amount of food they ate during a 2-week period by 47% and overestimated their level of physical activity by 51%.

These findings suggest that the failure to lose weight could be a result in part of overeating and underactivity in addition to complex biological processes. A study by Smith and Wing (1991) found that the frequently observed pattern of less weight loss during a second trial of a VLCD versus the first trial was a result of nonadherence rather than to metabolic alterations. It is critical to stress, however, that these findings do not necessarily reflect lying per se. Rather, the important clinical implication is that professionals devote time to the detailed description of caloric values, measurement, and self-monitoring. Moreover, it may be particularly useful to have periodic reviews of caloric estimation to keep patients anchored to specific portion sizes and calorie values. My clinical impression is that although many "dieting veterans" sound sophisticated when discussing food, their estimations of serving sizes and calorie contents can be substantially incorrect.

Weight Goals

Establishing weight goals is difficult. Until recently, a common practice was to indicate to patients what their ideal weight goal was based on age, gender, and weight for height tables, such as the one published by the Metropolitan Life Insurance Company (1983). This may not be a helpful strategy, particularly for those patients who are moderately obese. Brownell and Wadden (1992) recently discussed the issue of "ideal versus healthy versus reasonable weight" (p. 509). Although research is needed to determine how best to identify *healthy* and *reasonable* weights for specific individuals, Brownell and Wadden (1992) offered a few general clinical guidelines to help patients to arrive at a reasonable weight. These guidelines take into account factors such as the degree of family obesity, the lowest weight maintained as an adult for at least 1 year, the largest size of clothes that the person would feel comfortable wearing, weights of friends or family members who look normal, and what weight could be sustained given the necessary eating and exercise changes. In addition, it might be helpful to have patients remember the lowest weights achieved during previous attempts before they achieved a plateau. In support of this departure from previous methods to establish goal weights are findings that even modest amounts of weight losses are sufficient to produce substantial health improvements (Blackburn & Kanders, 1987).

Preventing Relapse

There is consensus that long-term weight maintenance and relapse prevention represent the greatest challenges faced by patients regardless of the nature of the intervention (Brownell, 1992; Brownell & Wadden, 1992; Perri, Nezu, A. M., & Viegener, B. J., 1992; Wilson, 1994). The problem of relapse has led to the nearly universal integration of relapse prevention techniques (Marlatt & Gordon, 1985) into weight control programs (e.g., Brownell, 1991b), the development of a variety of maintenance programs (Brownell & Rodin, 1990; Perri et al., 1992), and research aimed at understanding the process of relapse (Grilo & Shiffman, 1994; Grilo, Shiffman, & Wing, 1989; Grilo, Shiffman, & Wing, 1993; Kayman, Bruvold, & Stern, 1990; Mooney, Burling, Hartman, & Brenner-Liss, 1992; Schlundt, Sbrocco, & Bell, 1989; Wadden et al., 1994; Wing et al., 1995).

Figure 3 is a simplified schematic representation (Brownell & Rodin, 1990) of the process of relapse based on the Relapse Prevention Model developed by Marlatt and Gordon (1985). This model depicts relapse as a process rather than as an outcome. In brief, patients—regardless of motivation—inevitably experience *high-risk situations*, which refer to any circumstance that threatens to divert them from their weight control program. This may involve the temptation to overeat, the decision to skip exercise, or the desire to miss a treatment session. How a person copes with the high-risk situation is the key to whether a lapse will occur and may determine whether that isolated lapse escalates into repeated lapses or relapse (Grilo et al., 1989, 1993).

Components of Marlatt and Gordon's (1985) model have received empirical support (Grilo & Shiffman, 1994; Mooney et al., 1992). Re-

The Process of Lapse and Relapse

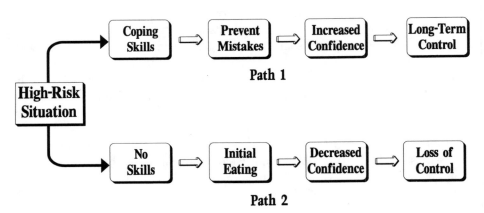

Figure 3. Schematic diagram of the process of lapse and relapse. Dieters inevitably encounter "high-risk" dieting situations in which dietary control is challenged. Two general paths are possible. The lack of coping skills or the inability to successfully apply coping during high-risk situations may result in overeating, which decreases confidence. Lack of coping skills, coupled with decreased confidence, increases the probability of continued loss of dietary control. Alternatively, the application of coping skills during a high-risk situation may help the dieter to overcome the temptation, which increases confidence. Coping skills coupled with increased confidence increase the probability of continued dietary control. Reprinted with permission from Brownell KD, Rodin J: *Weight Maintenance Survival Guide*. Dallas: American Health Publishing Co., 1990. Adapted originally from Marlatt GA, Gordon JR. (eds.), (1985). *Relapse Prevention: Maintenance Strategies in the Treatment of Addictive Behaviors*. New York: Guilford Press.

searchers have found that active coping decreases the likelihood of lapses (Grilo et al., 1989, 1993). The combination of cognitive and behavioral coping seems to be important for overcoming dietary lapses (Grilo et al., 1989). It is interesting to note that what kinds of specific cognitive or behavioral coping techniques are used seems to make little difference (Grilo et al., 1993). Grilo and colleagues (1993) speculated that instilling a readiness to cope in patients may be more useful than trying to decide what is the best coping response. Research has also found that maladaptive reactions following lapses are associated with escalations in problematic eating (Grilo & Shiffman, 1994) and weight regain (Mooney et al., 1992). In particular, patients need to be taught how to identify and to combat negative cognitive–affective reactions following lapses, referred to as the *abstinence violation effect* (Grilo & Shiffman, 1994; Marlatt & Gordon, 1985).

The addition of relapse prevention techniques to the current multi-component interventions, however, does not appear to have contributed to improved outcomes (Wilson, 1994). Although the addition of relapse prevention theory apparently has not improved the long-term efficacy of weight control programs based on weight outcome data, it is possible that the philosophy of the *process* of relapse is helpful to professionals and patients alike. As noted earlier, obesity is a complex biopsychosocial problem with powerful biological components. To view a particular time-limited intervention as the answer for lifelong weight regulation seems increasingly inappropriate (Wilson, 1994). It has been proposed by leading experts in the field that a more chronic disease continuous treatment model be considered for obesity (Weintraub, 1992; Wilson, 1994).

Body Image

Although body image concerns are likely to be present in many obese patients, this area has received surprisingly little systematic attention in weight control programs (chapters 4 and 17, this volume). In contrast to eating disorder treatment approaches (e.g., Wilfley et al., in press), body image receives little attention in assessment and treatment approaches to weight control. This is surprising given that body image concerns are common in both men and women (Cash, Winstead, & Janda, 1986; Thompson, 1990, 1992) and are cited as motivators for dieting (Cash & Hicks, 1994) and exercising (Cash, Novy, & Grant, 1994). Moreover, recent studies have found that body dissatisfaction is associated with weight regain following initial weight loss (Kayman et al., 1990; Wadden et al., 1988).

Rosen (chapter 17, this volume) provides a detailed discussion of the assessment and treatment of body image disturbance in obese patients. I will highlight only a few points in this chapter regarding this important domain relevant to the comprehensive needs of obese persons. It is my clinical impression that body image issues represent another critical client factor to be considered, along with those shown in the Brownell and Wadden (1992) treatment matching model depicted in Figure 1.

Body image concerns should be assessed during the initial evaluation, ideally by multidimensional measures that tap cognitive–affective aspects as well as behavioral aspects (e.g., Cash et al., 1986; Cooper, Taylor, Cooper, & Fairburn, 1987; see also chapter 3, this volume). If significant body image problems exist during the initial evaluation, this could signal the need for a referral for counseling in the same way that significant psychological distress or binge eating would. A self-directed cognitive–behavioral body image program could be recommended (e.g., Cash, 1991; see also chapter 4, this volume). In many cases, however, an additional body image program may not be needed, particularly if care is taken to integrate body image issues into the overall treatment. For instance, as noted above, discussion of body image concerns or embarrassment by the professional and patient will decrease the inadvertent recommendation that a particularly self-conscious patient join a crowded gym to exercise. If the feelings of embarrassment are not identified, the reasons for the apparent nonadherence will be missed and likely produce frustration in both the professional and patient. Some obese persons, especially those who were overweight as children, may have experienced teasing regarding their weight or shape, leaving them feeling embarrassed about showing their bodies or trying new physical activities (Grilo, Wilfley, Brownell, & Rodin, 1994; see also chapter 2, this volume).

Body image concerns should also be assessed, ideally through the use of consistent measures, throughout the course of treatment. In many cases, substantial body image improvement is experienced with weight loss (Cash, 1994). In such cases, the documented body image improvement could represent an additional reinforcer and motivator for the patient. In other cases, weight loss does not lead to improved body image (Stunkard & Mendelsohn, 1967). It has been suggested that obese persons who were overweight as children (Grilo et al., 1994; Grinker, Hirsch, & Levin, 1973; Stunkard & Burt, 1967) may have substantially elevated body image concerns. Cash (1994; Cash & Pruzinsky, 1990) termed this phenomenon, initially identified by Stunkard (Stunkard & Burt, 1967) as a group whose body image disparagement is refractory, as *vestigial body image*. Repeated assessments will identify those individuals who may require additional attention paid to body image concerns or who may be at risk for attrition (Cash, 1994) or relapse (Wadden et al., 1988). For instance, Cash (1994) found that certain body image variables, such as poor fitness-related attitudes and limited changes in body image early in treatment, predicted attrition from treatment independent of the amount of weight change.

Exercise

Although physical activity and weight are negatively associated, the exact nature of this relationship is uncertain (Grilo, 1994). Research, however, strongly suggests that increased physical activity is a critical component of any program for weight loss (Grilo, 1994; Grilo et al., 1993; Thompson, Jarvie, Lahey, & Cureton, 1982). Exercise alone, without dietary changes, is usually insufficient to produce significant weight loss in many obese persons. However, the combination of exercise and diet, although not consistently associated with short-term weight loss, is consistently associated with successful weight loss maintenance (Epstein, Wing, Koeske, Ossip, & Beck, 1982; Epstein, Wing, Koeske, & Valoski, 1984; Hill, Sparling, Shields, & Heller, 1987; Kayman et al., 1990; Pavlou, Krey, & Steffee, 1989). Moreover, exercise predicts weight maintenance regardless of the type of dietary program (Pavlou et al., 1989).

Grilo (Grilo, 1994; Grilo, Brownell, & Stunkard, 1993) and others (Bouchard, Despres, & Tremblay, 1993) have discussed a number of potential metabolic and psychological mechanisms linking exercise and weight control. Possible mechanisms include increased energy expenditure (Thompson & Blanton, 1987), minimization of lean body mass loss during overall weight loss, appetite suppression, increased metabolic rate, decreasing preference for dietary fat, and a number of positive psychological effects, including increased self-efficacy, decreased anxiety, and general well-being. It may be useful for professionals to provide an overview of these multiple possible effects of exercise to obese patients. Many obese patients view exercise as an additional chore, with the primary benefit being calorie expenditure. A review of the multiple benefits with patients will highlight additional outcome measures (in addition to weight) that can serve as ongoing reinforcers for the increased activity.

Exercise and Health

Health enhancement represents a major motivator and goal for persons who wish to lose weight. Recent studies have produced impressive evidence showing that exercise can reduce morbidity and mortality via a number of possible mechanisms (Blair, Goodyear, Gibbons, & Cooper, 1984; Leon, Connett, Jacobs, & Rauramaa, 1987; Paffenbarger, Hyde, Wing, & Hsieh, 1986; Powell, Caspersen, Koplan, & Ford, 1989). Moreover, the positive effects of exercise may be especially salient in overweight persons with poor health risk factor profiles, such as obese women with upper-body types of fat distribution (Kanaley, Andresen-Reid, Oenning, Kottke, & Jensen, 1993) or overweight men at risk for non-insulin-dependent diabetes mellitus (NIDDM) (Helmrich, Ragland, Leung, & Paffenbarger, 1991). Helmich and colleagues (1991) found that physical activity index (leisure time physical activity level defined as the energy used per week for walking, climbing stairs, and sports) was inversely related to the development of NIDDM in a prospective study with 5,990 men. The relationship between physical activity and NIDDM, shown in Figure 4, was strongest in those persons with a high risk profile for NIDDM (high body mass index, a history of hypertension, family history of diabetes).

Exercise may be necessary to produce the desired health outcomes of dietary interventions. Wood and colleagues (1988) found that the combination of moderate exercise and diet significantly improved lipoprotein and apolipoprotein ratios in moderately overweight sedentary persons. As shown in Figure 5, the addition of exercise to the diet appeared necessary to produce significant changes. Another important finding is that exercise can result in health improvement even with only minimal weight loss (Powell et al., 1989; Wood et al., 1988).

Exercise Intensity

Recent convergent findings from well controlled studies suggest that modest levels of physical activity may be sufficient to produce improve-

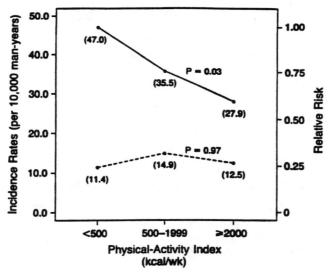

Figure 4. Age-adjusted incidence rates and relative risks of NIDDM among 5,990 men, according to high-risk (solid line) and low-risk (dashed line) subgroups and physical-activity index. The high-risk subgroup consisted of 2,634 men who had at least one of the following risk factors: a body-mass index of 25 or more, a history of hypertension, or a family history of diabetes. NIDDM developed in 135 of these men. The low-risk group included 3,356 men not in the high-risk group; NIDDM developed in 67 men in this group. (Reprinted from Helmrich, Ragland, Leung, & Paffenbarger (1991) *New England Journal of Medicine* with permission.)

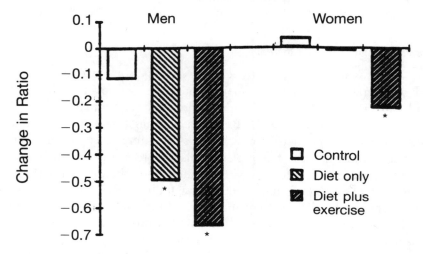

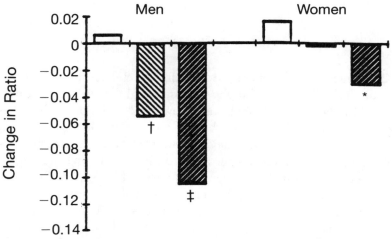

Figure 5. Changes in lipoprotein and apolipoprotein ratios in the study groups after one year. For the comparison with the control group, the asterisk denotes $p < 0.05$, and the dagger $p < 0.01$. The double dagger denotes $p < 0.001$ for the comparison with the control group and $p < 0.05$ for the comparison with the diet-only group. (Reprinted from Wood et al. (1988) *New England Journal of Medicine* with permission.)

ments in health (Blair et al., 1989; DeBusk, Stenestrand, Sheehan, & Haskell, 1990; Duncan, Gordon, & Scott, 1991; Helmrich et al., 1991; Rippe, Ward, Porcari, & Freedson, 1988). Blair and colleagues (1989) found that the greatest decrease in risk for mortality is observed between individuals who are not fit and individuals who are modestly fit with little differences occurring between modestly and highly fit individuals. In the same way, as can be seen in Figure 4, substantial decreased risk for NIDDM can be obtained via moderate activity levels (Helmrich et al., 1991).

Exercise Initiation and Adherence

Much as with the case of average weight persons, exercise initiation and adherence represent two major challenges for overweight persons (Dishman, 1991; Dubbert, 1992; Grilo, Brownell, & Stunkard, 1993; Wilfley, Grilo, & Brownell, 1994). Research findings that exercise is one of the few consistent predictors of weight loss maintenance and that exercise enhances health dictate that professionals devote significant attention to enhancing exercise adherence and maintenance in obese patients (Epstein, Wing, Thompson, & Griffin, 1980). The findings that modest levels of activity are likely to be sufficient suggest that professionals avoid traditional exercise prescription approaches that focus on intensity and duration and focus instead on modest but consistent lifestyle activity (Grilo et al., 1993). Exhibit 1, adapted from Grilo and colleagues (1993), summarizes a number of recommendations for professionals to use to increase exercise initiation and adherence.

CONCLUSION

Continued research is needed to address the issues raised by Brownell and Rodin (1995) about who should lose weight, who can lose weight, how should weight control be pursued, how much individuals should aspire to lose, and how weight can best be lost and maintained. In this chapter, I have reviewed a number of major findings relevant to treating obesity and offered practical implications. Based on current knowledge, regardless of the nature of treatment intervention (dietary, behavioral, VLCD, pharmacologic, etc.), a comprehensive program involving nutrition, exercise, body image, and behavior and lifestyle change is likely to be required continuously for maintaining successful weight loss. Greater attention to the multiple benefits (e.g., health profile, fitness, body image, psychological benefits) of such lifestyle changes, in addition to the traditional focus on weight loss, is needed to sustain the continuous effort. Research is needed to better understand the mechanisms involved in weight regulation that may lead to improved treatment. Given the complex biology of obesity, it

Strategies to Increase Exercise Initiation and Adherence in Obese Patients

A. General Strategies
1. Be sensitive to psychological barriers and body image issues (see Cash, 1994; Grilo et al., 1994; Grilo, Shiffman, & Carter-Campbell, 1994)
2. Be sensitive to physical barriers and poor conditioning
3. Be sensitive to lifespan developmental issues (see King, 1991)
4. Be sensitive to sociocultural issues (see Akan & Grilo, 1995; Kumanyika, Wilson, & Guilford-Davenport, 1992; Lasco et al., 1989)
5. Facilitate discussion of barriers and ongoing problem solving
6. Focus on initiation and consistency
7. Decrease focus on traditional exercise threshold approaches

B. Specific Interventions
1. Prescription Principles
   a. Provide clear information regarding importance of exercise and assess comprehension
   b. Focus on modest activities appropriate to physical level (see Blair, 1991)
   c. Focus on maximizing routine activities such as walking (see Rippe et al., 1988)
   d. Avoid threshold and focus on consistency
2. Behavioral Principles
   a. Introduce goal setting, self-monitoring, evaluation, and feedback and reinforcement techniques (see Dishman, 1991)
   b. Identify multiple goals (including physical changes, improved endurance, lowered heart rate, improved metabolic and biological profiles, enhanced physical and psychological well-being, improved confidence, etc.) to shift focus away from weight level as sole outcome
   c. Use physical activity to cope with temptations to overeat or to cope with stress (see Grilo et al., 1989, 1993)
   d. Introduce stimulus control techniques, such as reminders to exercise, reminders to focus on benefits of exercise, and elimination of competing cues for activities other than exercise.
   e. Introduce relapse prevention techniques, including ways to identify high-risk situations for missing exercise, ways to cope or to problem solve with these situations, and ways to prevent a lapse from escalating into relapse
   f. Schedule follow-up sessions

Adapted from Grilo, Brownell, and Stunkard (1993) with permission.

---

appears, as Wilson (1994) argued, that further enhancement of long-term outcome, as least for some patients, will need to be accomplished via the integration of pharmacological approaches into the treatment package.

REFERENCES

Agras, W. S., Telch, C. F., Arnow, B., Eldredge, K., Wilfley, D. E., Raeburn, S. D., Henderson, J., & Marnell, M. (1994). Weight loss, cognitive–behavioral, and desipramine treatments in binge eating disorder: An additive design. *Behavior Therapy, 25,* 225–238.

Akan, G. E., & Grilo, C. M. (1995). Sociocultural influences on eating attitudes and behaviors, body image, and psychological functioning: A comparison of African-American, Asian-American, and Caucasian college women. *International Journal of Eating Disorders, 18* 181–187.

American Psychiatric Association. (1994). *Diagnostic and statistical manual of mental disorders* (4th ed.). Washington, DC: Author.

Atkinson, R. L. (1989). Low and very low calorie diets. *Medical Clinics of North America, 73,* 203–216.

Atkinson, R. L. (1994). The role of drugs in weight control. *Weight Control Digest, 4,* 339–340.

Bandini, L. G., Schoeller, D., Cyr, H. N., & Dietz, W. H. (1990). Validity of reported energy intake in obese and nonobese adolescents. *American Journal of Clinical Nutrition, 52,* 421–425.

Blackburn, G. L., & Kanders, B. S. (1987). Medical evaluation and treatment of the obese patient with cardiovascular disease. *American Journal of Cardiology, 60,* 55g–58g.

Blair, S. N. (1991). *Living with exercise: Improving your health through moderate physical activity.* Dallas, TX: American Health.

Blair, S. N., Goodyear, N. N., Gibbons, L. W., & Cooper, K. H. (1984). Physical activity and incidence of hypertension in healthy normotensive men and women. *Journal of the American Medical Association, 252,* 487–490.

Blair, S. N., Kohl, H. W., Paffenberger, R. S., Clark, D. G., Cooper, K. H., & Gibbons, L. W. (1989). Physical fitness and all-cause mortality: A prospective study of healthy men and women. *Journal of the American Medical Association, 262,* 2395–2401.

Bouchard, C., Despres, J. P., & Tremblay, A. (1993). Exercise and obesity. *Obesity Research, 1,* 133–147.

Bray, G. A. (1992). Drug treatment of obesity. *American Journal of Clinical Nutrition, 55,* 538–544.

Brownell, K. D. (1991a). Dieting and the search for the perfect body: Where physiology and culture collide. *Behavior Therapy, 22,* 1–12.

Brownell, K. D. (1991b). *The LEARN Program for Weight Control.* Dallas, TX: American Health.

Brownell, K. D. (1992). Relapse and the treatment of obesity. In T. A. Wadden & T. B. Van Itallie (Eds.), *The treatment of severe obesity by diet and lifestyle modification* (pp. 437–455). New York: Guilford Press.

Brownell, K. D., & Grilo, C. M. (1993). Weight management. In American College of Sports Medicine (Eds.), *American college of sports medicine resource manual for exercise testing and prescription* (2nd ed.). Philadelphia.: Lea & Febiger.

Brownell, K. D., & Jeffery, R. W. (1987). Improving long-term weight loss: Pushing the limits of treatment. *Behavior Therapy, 18,* 353–374.

Brownell, K. D., & Kramer, F. M. (1989). Behavioral management of obesity. *Medical Clinics of North America, 73,* 185–201.

Brownell, K. D., & Rodin, J. (1991). *The weight maintenance survival guide.* Dallas, TX: American Health Publishing.

Brownell, K. D., & Rodin, J. (1994). The dieting maelstrom: Is it possible and advisable to lose weight? *American Psychologist, 49,* 781–791.

Brownell, K. D., & Rodin, R. (1994). Medical, metabolic, and psychological effects of weight cycling. *Archives of Internal Medicine, 154,* 1325–1330.

Brownell, K. D., & Wadden, T. A. (1986). Behavior theray for obesity: Modern approaches and better results. In K. D. Brownell & J. P. Foreyt (Eds.), *Handbook of eating disorders: Physiology, psychology, and treatment of obesity, anorexia, and bulimia* (pp. 180–197). New York: Basic Books.

Brownell, K. D., & Wadden, T. A. (1991). The heterogeneity of obesity: Fitting treatments to individuals. *Behavior Therapy, 22,* 153–177.

Brownell, K. D., & Wadden, T. A. (1992). Etiology and treatment of obesity: Toward understanding a serious, prevalent, and refractory disorder. *Journal of Consulting and Clinical Psychology, 60,* 505–517.

Cash, T. F. (1991). *Body-image therapy: A program for self-directed change.* New York: Guilford Press.

Cash, T. F. (1994). Body image and weight changes in a multisite comprehensive very-low-calorie diet program. *Behavior Therapy, 25,* 239–254.

Cash, T. F., & Hicks, K. L. (1994). Being fat versus thinking fat: Relationships with body image, eating behaviors, and well-being. *Cognitive Therapy and Research, 14,* 327–341.

Cash, T. F., Novy, P., & Grant, J. (1994). Why do women exercise? Factor analysis and further validation of the reasons for exercise inventory. *Perceptual and Motor Skills, 78,* 539–544.

Cash, T. F., & Pruzinsky, T. (Eds.). (1990). *Body images: Development, deviance, and change.* New York: Guilford Press.

Cash, T. F., Winstead, B. A., & Janda, L. H. (1986). The great American shape-up: Body image survey report. *Psychology Today, 20,* 30–44.

Colditz, G. A. (1992). Economic costs of severe obesity. *American Journal of Clinical Nutrition, 55*(Suppl.), 503S–507S.

Cooper, P. J., Taylor, M. J., Cooper, Z., & Fairburn, C. G. (1987). The development and validation of the Body Shape Questionnaire. *International Journal of Eating Disorders, 6,* 485–494.

Craighead, L. W., & Agras, W. S. (1991). Mechanisms of action in cognitive–behavioral and pharmacological interventions for obesity and bulimia nervosa. *Journal of Consulting and Clinical Psychology, 59,* 115–125.

DeBusk, R. F., Stenestrand, U., Sheehan, M., & Haskell, W. L. (1990). Training effects of long versus short bouts of exercise in healthy subjects. *American Journal of Cardiology, 65,* 1010–1013.

deZwann, M., Nutzinger, D. O., & Schoenbeck, G. (1992). Binge eating in overweight women. *Comparative Psychology, 33*, 256–261.

Dishman, R. K. (1991). Increasing and maintaining exercise and physical activity. *Behavior Therapy, 22*, 345–378.

Douglas, J. G., Preston, P. G., Haslett, C., Gough, J., Frasier, I., Chalmers, S. R., & Munro, J. F. (1983). Long-term efficacy of fenfluramine in treatment of obesity. *Lancet, 1*, 384–386.

Dubbert, P. M. (1992). Exercise in behavioral medicine. *Journal of Consulting and Clinical Psychology, 60*, 613–618.

Duncan, J. J., Gordon, N. F., & Scott, C. B. (1991). Women walking for health and fitness: How much is enough? *Journal of the American Medical Association, 266*, 3295–3299.

Epstein, L. H., Wing, R. R., Koeske, R., Ossip, D. J., & Beck, S. (1982). A comparison of lifestyle change and programmed aerobic exercise on weight and fitness changes in obese children. *Behavior Therapy, 13*, 651–665.

Epstein, L. H., Wing, R. R., Koeske, R., & Valoski, A. (1984). The effects of diet plus exercise on weight change in parents and children. *Journal of Consulting and Clinical Psychology, 52*, 429–437.

Epstein, L. H., Wing, R. R., Thompson, J. K., & Griffin, W. (1980). The effects of contract and lottery procedures on attendance and fitness in aerobics exercise. *Behavior Modification, 4*, 465–479.

Ferster, C. B., Nurnberger, J. I., & Levitt, E. E. (1962). The control of eating. *Journal of Mathetics, 1*, 87–109.

Flegal, K. M., Harlan, W. R., & Landis, J. R. (1988). Secular trends in body mass index and skinfold thickness with socioeconomic factors in young adult women. *American Journal of Clinical Nutrition, 48*, 535–543.

Foster, G. D., Wadden, T. A., Peterson, F. J., Letizia, K. A., Bartlett, S. J., & Conill, A. M. (1992). A controlled comparison of three very-low-calorie diets: Effects on weight, body composition, and symptoms. *American Journal of Clinical Nutrition, 55*, 811–817.

Galloway, S. M., Farquhar, D. L., & Munro, J. F. (1984). The current status of anti-obesity drugs. *Postgraduate Medical Journal, 60*, 19–26.

Garner, D. M., & Wooley, S. C. (1991). Confronting the failure of behavioral and dietary treatments for obesity. *Clinical Psychology Review, 11*, 729–780.

Grilo, C. M. (1994). Physical activity and obesity. *Biomedicine and Pharmacotherapy, 48*, 127–136.

Grilo, C. M., Brownell, K. D., & Stunkard, A. J. (1993). The metabolic and psychological importance of exercise in weight control. In A. J. Stunkard & T. A. Wadden (Eds.), *Obesity: Theory and therapy* (pp. 253–273). New York: Raven Press.

Grilo, C. M., & Pogue-Geile, M. (1991). The nature of environmental influences on obesity: A behavior–genetic analysis. *Psychological Bulletin, 110*, 520–537.

Grilo, C. M., & Shiffman, S. (1994). A longitudinal investigation of the abstinence violation effect in binge eaters. *Journal of Consulting and Clinical Psychology, 62*, 611–619.

Grilo, C. M., Shiffman, S. S., & Carter-Campbell, J. (1994). Binge eating antecedents in normal-weight non-purging females: Is there consistency? *International Journal of Eating Disorders, 16*, 239–249.

Grilo, C. M., Shiffman, S., & Wing, R. R. (1989). Relapse crises and coping among dieters. *Journal of Consulting and Clinical Psychology, 57*, 488–495.

Grilo, C. M., Shiffman, S., & Wing, R. R. (1993). Coping with dietary relapse crises and their aftermath. *Addictive Behaviors, 18*, 89–102.

Grilo, C. M., Wilfley, D. E., Brownell, K. D., & Rodin, J. (1994). Teasing, body image, and self-esteem in a clinical sample of obese females. *Addictive Behaviors, 16*, 443–450.

Grilo, C. M., Wilfley, D. E., Jones, A., Brownell, K. D., & Rodin, J. (1994). The social self, body dissatisfaction, and binge eating in obese females. *Obesity Research, 2*, 24–27.

Grinker, J., Hirsch, J., & Levin, B. (1973). The affective responses of obese patients to weight reduction: A differentiation based on age at onset of obesity. *Psychosomatic Medicine, 35*, 57–63.

Guy-Grand, B., Apfelbaum, M., Crepaldi, G., Gries, A., Lefebvre, P., & Turner, P. (1989). International trial of long-term dexfenfluramine in obesity. *Lancet, 2*, 1142–1144.

Helmrich, S. P., Ragland, D. R., Leung, R. W., & Paffenbarger, R. S. (1991). Physical activity and reduced occurrence of non-insulin-dependent diabetes mellitus. *New England Journal of Medicine, 325*, 147–152.

Hill, J. O., Sparling, P. B., Shields, T. W., Heller, P. A. (1987). Effects of exercise and food restriction on body composition and metabolic rate in obese women. *American Journal of Clinical Nutrition, 46*, 622–630.

Kanaley, J. A., Andresen-Reid, Oenning, L., Kottke, B. A., & Jensen, M. D. (1993). Differential health benefits of weight loss in upper-body and lower-body obese women. *American Journal of Clinical Nutrition, 57*, 20–26.

Kayman, S., Bruvold, W., & Stern, J. S. (1990). Maintenance and relapse after weight loss in women: Behavioral aspects. *American Journal of Clinical Nutrition, 52*, 800–807.

Keefe, P. H., Wyshogrod, D., Weinberger, E., & Agras, W. S. (1984). Binge eating and outcome of behavioral treatment of obesity: A preliminary report. *Behavioral Research and Therapy, 22*, 319–321.

King, A. (1991). Community intervention for promotion of physical activity and fitness. In K. B. Pandolf & J. O. Holloszy (Eds.), *Exercise and Sport Sciences Reviews, 19*, 211–259.

Kolotkin, R. L., Revis, E. S., Kirkley, B. G., & Janick, L. (1987). Binge eating in obesity: Associated MMPI characteristics. *Journal of Consulting and Clinical Psychology, 55*, 872–876.

Kral, J. G. (1992). Surgical treatment of obesity. In T. A. Wadden & T. B. VanItallie (Eds.), *Treatment of the seriously obese patient* (pp. 496–506). New York: Guilford Press.

Kramer, F. M., Jeffery, R. W., Forster, J. L., Snell, M. K. (1989). Long-term follow-up of behavioral treatment for obesity: Patterns of weight regain in men and women. *International Journal of Obesity, 13,* 123–136.

Kuczmarski, R. J. (1992). Prevalence of overweight and weight gain in the United States. *American Journal of Clinical Nutrition, 55,* 495S–502S.

Kumanyika, S. K., Wilson, J., & Guilford-Davenport, M. (1992). Weight-related attitudes and behaviors of black women. *Journal of the American Dietetic Association, 93,* 416–442.

LaPorte, D. J. (1992). Treatment response in obese binge eaters: Preliminary results using a very low calorie diet (VLCD) and behavior therapy. *Addictive Behavior, 17,* 247–257.

Lasco, R. A., Curry, R. H., Dickson, V. J., Powers, J., Menes, S., & Merritt, R. K. (1989). Participation rates, weight loss, and blood pressure changes among obese women in a nutrition-exercise program. *Public Health Reports, 104,* 640–646.

Leon, A. S., Connett, J., Jacobs, D. R., & Rauramaa, R. (1987). Leisure-time physical activity levels and risk of coronary heart disease and death. *Journal of the American Medical Association, 258,* 2388–2395.

Lichtman, S. W., Pisarska, K., Berman, E. R., Pestone, M., Dowling, H., Offenbacher, E., Weisel, H., Heshka, S., Matthews, D. W., & Heymsfield, S. B. (1992). Discrepancy between self-reported and actual caloric intake and exercise in obese subjects. *New England Journal of Medicine, 327,* 1893–1898.

Manson, J. E., Colditz, G. A., Stampfer, M. J., Willet, W. C., Rosner, B., Monson, R. R., Speizer, F. E., & Hennekens, C. H. (1990). A prospective study of obesity and risk of coronary heart disease in women. *New England Journal of Medicine, 322,* 882–889.

Marcus, M. D., Wing, R. R., Ewing, L., Kern, E., McDermott, M., & Gooding, W. (1990). A double-blind, placebo-controlled trial of fluoxetine plus behavior modification in the treatment of obese binge eaters. *American Journal of Psychiatry, 147,* 876–881.

Marcus, M. D., Wing, R. R., & Hopkins, J. (1988). Obese binge eaters: Affect, cognitions, and response to behavioral weight control. *Journal of Consulting and Clinical Psychology, 56,* 433–439.

Marlatt, G. A., & Gordon, J. R. (Eds.). (1985). *Relapse prevention: Maintenance strategies in the treatment of addictive behaviors.* New York: Guilford Press.

Mason, E. E. (1981). *Surgical treatment of obesity.* Philadelphia: W. B. Saunders.

Mason, E. E., Maher, J. W., Doherty, C., & Cullen, J. J. (1994). Surgical approaches to obesity: Part I. *Weight Control Digest, 4,* 371–372.

McCann, U. D., & Agras, W. S. (1990). Successful treatment of nonpurging bulimia nervosa with desipramine: A double-blind, placebo-controlled study. *American Journal of Psychiatry, 147,* 1509–1513.

Metropolitan Life Insurance Company. (1983). 1983 Metropolitan height and weight tables. *Statistical Bulletin of the Metropolitan Life Insurance Company, 64,* 2.

Miura, J., Arai, K., Tsukahara, S., Ohno, M., & Kideda, Y. (1989). The long term effectiveness of combined therapy by behavior modification and very low calorie diet: 2 year follow up. *International Journal of Obesity, 13*(Suppl. 2), 73–77.

Mooney, J. P., Burling, T. A., Hartman, W. M., & Brenner-Liss, D. (1992). The abstinence violation effect and very low calorie diet success. *Addictive Behaviors, 17,* 319–324.

Paffenbarger, R. S., Hyde, R. T., Wing, A. L., & Hsieh, C. C. (1986). Physical activity, all cause mortality, and longevity of college alumni. *New England Journal of Medicine, 314,* 605–613.

Pavlou, K. N., Krey, S., & Steffee, W. P. (1989). Exercise as an adjunct to weight loss and maintenance in moderately obese subjects. *American Journal of Clinical Nutrition, 49,* 1115–1123.

Perri, M. G., & McAllister, D. A., Gange, J. J., Jordan, R. C., McAdoo, W. G., & Nezu, A. M. (1988). Effects of four maintenance programs on the long-term management of obesity. *Journal of Consulting and Clinical Psychology, 56,* 529–534.

Perri, M. G., Nezu, A. M., & Viegener, B. J. (1992). *Improving the long-term management of obesity: Theory, research, and clinical guidelines.* New York: Wiley Press.

Powell, K. E., Caspersen, C. J., Koplan, J. P., & Ford, E. S. (1989). Physical activity and chronic disease. *American Journal of Clinical Nutrition, 49,* 999–1006.

Prentice, A. M., Black, A. E., Coward, W. A., Davies, H. L., Goldberg, G. R., Murgatroyd, P. R., Ashford, J., Sawyer, M., & Whitehead, R. G. (1986). High levels of energy expenditure in obese women. *British Medical Journal, 292,* 983–987.

Rippe, J. M., Ward, A., Porcari J. P., & Freedson, P. S. (1988). Walking for health and fitness. *Journal of the American Medical Association, 259,* 2720–2724.

Schlundt, D. G., Hill, J. O., Sbrocco, T., Pope-Cordle, J., & Sharp, T. (1992). The role of breakfast in the treatment of obesity: A randomized clinical trial. *American Journal of Clinical Nutrition, 55,* 645–651.

Schlundt, D. G., Sbrocco, T., & Bell, C. (1989). Identification of high risk situations in a behavioral weight loss program: Application of the relapse prevention model. *International Journal of Obesity, 13,* 223–234.

Schoeller, D. A. (1988). Measurement of energy expenditure in free-living humans by using doubly-labeled water. *Journal of Nutrition, 118,* 1278–1289.

Scoville, B. A. (1975). Review of amphetamine-like drugs by the Food and Drug Administration: Clinical data and value judgements. In G. A. Bray (Ed.),

Obesity in Perspective (DHEW publication NIH No. 75-708) Washington, DC: U.S. Government Printing Office.

Sikand, G., Kondo, A., Foreyt, J. P., Jones, P. H., & Gotto, A. M. (1988). Two year follow-up of patients treated with very low calorie dieting and exercise testing. *Journal of the American Dietetic Association, 88,* 487–488.

Sjostrom, L. V. (1992a). Morbidity of severely obese subjects. *American Journal of Clinical Nutrition, 55,* 508S–515S.

Sjostrom, L. V. (1992b). Mortality of severely obese subjects. *American Journal of Clinical Nutrition, 55,* 516S–523S.

Smith, D. E., & Wing, R. R. (1991). Diminished weight loss and behavioral compliance during repeated diets in obese patients with TYPE II diabetes. *Health Psychology, 10,* 378–383.

Spitzer, R. L., Devlin, M., Walsh, B. T., Hasin, D., Wing, R. R., Marcus, M. D., Stunkard, A. J., Wadden, T. A., Yanovski, S., Agras, W. S., Mitchell, J., & Nonas, C. (1992). Binge eating disorders: A multi-site field trial of the diagnostic criteria. *International Journal of Eating Disorders, 11,* 191–203.

Stuart, R. R. (1967). Behavioral control of overeating. *Behaviour Research and Therapy, 5,* 357–365.

Stunkard, A. J. (1959). Eating patterns and obesity. *Psychiatric Quarterly, 33,* 284–295.

Stunkard, A. J. (1992). An overview of current treatments for obesity. In T. A. Wadden & T. B. Van Itallie (Eds.), *Treatment of the seriously obese patient* (pp. 33–43). New York: Guilford Press.

Stunkard, A. J. (1994). Binge eating disorder and the treatment of obesity. *Obesity Research, 2,* 279–280.

Stunkard, A. J., & Berthold, H. C. (1985). What is behavior therapy: A very short description of behavioral weight control. *American Journal of Clinical Nutrition, 41,* 821–823.

Stunkard, A. J., & Burt, V. (1967). Obesity and body image: II. Age at onset of disturbances in the body image. *American Journal of Psychiatry, 123,* 1443–1447.

Stunkard, A. J., & Mendelson, M. (1967). Obesity and body image: I. Characteristics of disturbances in the body image of some obese persons. *American Journal of Psychiatry, 123,* 1296–1300.

Telch, C. F., & Agras, W. S. (1993). The effects of very low calorie diet on binge eating. *Behavior Therapy, 24,* 177–193.

Telch, C. F., & Agras, W. S. (1994). Obesity, binge eating, and psychopathology: Are they related? *International Journal of Eating Disorders, 15,* 53–61.

Telch, C. F., Agras, W. S., Rossiter, E., Wilfley, D., & Kenardy, J. (1990). Group cognitive-behavioral treatment for the non-purging bulimic: An initial evaluation. *Journal of Consulting and Clinical Psychology, 58,* 629–635.

Thompson, J. K. (1990). *Body image disturbance: Assessment and treatment.* Elmsford, NY: Pergamon Press.

Thompson, J. K. (1992). Body image: Extent of disturbance, associated features, theoretical models, assessment methodologies, intervention strategies, and a proposal for a new DSM-IV diagnostic category—Body Image Disorder. In M. Hersen, R. M. Eisler, & P. M. Miller (Eds.), *Progress in behavior modification* (pp. 3–54). Sycamore, IL: Sycamore.

Thompson, J. K., & Blanton, P. (1987). Diet, exercise, and energy conservation: A sympathetic arousal hypothesis of exercise dependence. *Medicine and Science in Sports and Exercise, 19,* 91–99.

Thompson, J. K., Jarvie, G. J., Lahey, B. B., & Cureton, K. J. (1982). Exercise and obesity: Etiology, physiology, and intervention. *Psychological Bulletin, 92,* 55–79.

U.S. Department of Agriculture. (1992). Food Guide Pyramid. In *Home and Garden Bulletin Number 252.* Washington, DC: Human Nutrition Information Service.

Wadden, T. A., Foster, G. D., & Letizia, K. A. (1992). Response of obese binge eaters to treatment by behavioral therapy combined with very low calorie diet. *Journal of Consulting and Clinical Psychology, 60,* 808–811.

Wadden, T. A., & Bartlett, S. J. (1992). Very low calorie diets: An overview and appraisal. In T. A. Wadden & T. B. Van Itallie (Eds.), *Treatment of the seriously obese patient* (pp. 44–79). New York: Guilford Press.

Wadden, T. A., Foster, G. D., & Letizia, K. A. (1994). One-year behavioral treatment of obesity: Comparison of moderate and severe caloric restriction and the effects of weight maintenance therapy. *Journal of Consulting and Clinical Psychology, 62,* 165–171.

Wadden, T. A., & Kuehnel, R. H. (1993). Very-low-calorie-diets: Reappraisal and recommendations. *Weight Control Digest, 3,* 265–270.

Wadden, T. A., & Letizia, K. A. (1992). Predictors of attrition and weight loss in patients treated by moderate and severe caloric restriction. In T. A. Wadden & T. B. Van Itallie (Eds.), *Treatment of the seriously obese patient* (pp. 383–410). New York: Guilford Press.

Wadden, T. A., Sternberg, J. A., Letizia, K. A., Stunkard, A. J., & Foster, G. D. (1989). Treatment of obesity by very low calorie diet, behavior therapy, and their combination: A five-year perspective. *International Journal of Obesity, 13,* 39–46.

Wadden, T. A., & Stunkard, A. J. (1985). Social and psychological consequences of obesity. *Annals of Internal Medicine, 103,* 1062–1067.

Wadden, T. A., & Stunkard, A. J. (1986). A controlled trial of very low calorie diet, behavior therapy, and their combination in the treatment of obesity. *Journal of Consulting and Clinical Psychology, 54,* 482–486.

Wadden, T. A., Stunkard, A. J., & Liebschutz, J. (1988). Three-year follow-up of the treatment of obesity by very low calorie diet, behavior therapy, and their combination. *Journal of Consulting and Clinical Psychology, 56,* 925–928.

Wadden, T. A., Van Itallie, T. B., & Blackburn, G. L. (1990). Responsible and irresponsible use of very-low-calorie diets in the treatment of obesity. *Journal of the American Medical Association, 263*, 83–85.

Weintraub, M. (1992). Long-term weight control: The national Heart, Lung, and Blood Institute funded multimodal intervention study. *Clinical Pharmacological Therapy, 51*, 581–646.

Weintraub, M., Sundaresan, P. R., Madan, M., Schuster, B., Balder, A., Lasagna, L., & Cox, C. (1992). Long-term weight control study I (weeks 0 to 34). *Clinical Pharmacological Therapy, 51*, 586–594.

Weintraub, M., Sundaresan, P. R., Schuster, B., Averbuch, M., Stein, E. C., & Byrne, L. (1992). Long-term weight control study V (weeks 190 to 210). *Clinical Pharmacological Therapy, 51*, 615–618.

Weintraub, M., Sundaresan, P. R., Schuster, B., Ginsberg, G., Madan, M., Balder, A., Stein, E. C., & Byrne, L. (1992). Long-term weight control study II (weeks 34 to 104). *Clinical Pharmacological Therapy, 51*, 595–601.

Wilfley, D. E., Agras, W. S., Telch, C. F., Rossiter, E. M., Schneider, J. A., Cole, A. J., Sifford, L., & Raeburn, S. D. (1993). Groupt CBT and group interpersonal psychotherapy for non-purging bulimics: A controlled comparison. *Journal of Consulting and Clinical Psychology, 61*, 296–305.

Wilfley, D., Grilo, C. M., & Brownell, K. D. (1994). Exercise and regulation of body weight. In M. Shangold (Ed.), *Women and exercise: Physiology and sports medicine* (pp. 27–59). Philadelphia, PA: F. A. Davis.

Wilfley, D. E., Grilo, C. M., & Rodin, J. (in press). Group psychotherapy for the treatment of bulimia nervosa and binge eating disorder: Research and clinical methods. In J. Spira (Ed.), *Group therapy for the medically ill.* New York: Guilford Press.

Williamson, D. F., Kahn, H. S., Remington, P. L., & Anda, R. F. (1990). The 10-year incidence of overweight and major weight gain in U.S. adults. *Archives of Internal Medicine, 150*, 665–672.

Wilson, G. T. (1994). Behavioral treatment of obesity: Thirty years and counting. *Advances in Behaviour Research and Therapy, 16*, 31–75.

Wilson, G. T., & Walsh, B. T. (1991). Eating disorders in the DSM-IV. *Journal of Abnormal Psychology, 100*, 362–365.

Wing, R. R., Marcus, M. D., Salata, R., Epstein, L. H., Miaskiewicz, S., & Blair, E. H. (1991). Effects of a very-low-calorie diet on long-term glycemic control in obese Type II diabetics. *Archives of Internal Medicine, 151*, 1334–1340.

Wing, R. R., Shiffman, S., Drapkin, R., Grilo, C., & McDermott, M. (1995). Moderate versus restrictive diets: Implications for relapse. *Behavior Therapy.*

Wood, P. D., Stefanick, M. L., Dreon, D. M., Frey-Hewitt, B., Garay, S. C., Williams, P. T., Superko, H. R., Fortmann, S. P., Albers, J. J., Vranizan, K. M., Ellsworth, N. M., Terry, R. B., & Harkell, W. L. (1988). Changes in plasma lipids and lipoproteins in overweight men during weight loss through dieting as compared with exercise. *New England Journal of Medicine, 319*, 1173–1179.

Yanovski, S. Z. (1993). Binge eating disorder: Current knowledge and future directions. *Obesity Research, 1*, 306–324.

Yanovski, S. Z., Nelson, J. E., Dubbert, B. K., & Spitzer, R. L. (1993). Association of binge eating disorder and psychiatric comorbidity in obese subjects. *American Journal of Psychiatry, 150*, 1472–1479.

17

IMPROVING BODY IMAGE IN OBESITY

JAMES C. ROSEN

ADDRESSING BODY IMAGE IN WEIGHT REDUCTION PROGRAMS

In our weight-conscious society, obesity is judged as less physically attractive and the result of personal misbehavior. Because obesity is stigmatized, it is not surprising that many overweight persons develop a negative body image. Studies of nonclinical samples show that obese persons do not differ from nonobese persons in psychological symptoms, psychopathology, and personality. The one consistent difference that does emerge in these comparisons is body image (Stunkard & Wadden, 1992). Compared with normal weight individuals, obese persons overestimate or distort their body size more, are more dissatisfied and preoccupied with their physical appearance, and avoid more social situations because of their appearance (Cash, 1990; Collins et al., 1987; Tiggemann & Rothblum, 1988). All three components of body image (Rosen, 1990)—perception; cognition and affect; and behavior—can be more troublesome for obese individuals. Body image is a concern of most overweight persons, and a desire to improve body image is often the motivation to embark on weight reduction attempts. Although body image has been neglected in traditional weight control programs, recent research on body image therapy indicates that overweight persons are capable of developing more positive attitudes about their appearance, regardless of how much they weigh or how much weight they are able to lose.

The purpose of this chapter is to review the assessment of body image in obesity. Recognizing that weight reduction is not always the complete answer to body image dissatisfaction, practical guidelines for psychological techniques, which can be used in conjunction with weight control or by themselves, will be given.

Body Image and Reasons for Seeking Weight Reduction

People generally believe that if one is overweight, the best way to improve one's body image is to lose weight. This is an outside-to-inside approach to changing body image. That is, if one can change one's outward physical appearance, one should enjoy a more positive internal self-image. Indeed, weight reduction is one of the most widely practiced body image remedies. According to a review of dieting prevalence studies, 63% of overweight women and 47% of overweight men in the United States report they are trying to lose weight (French & Jeffery, 1994). And concern about physical appearance plays an important role in these attempts (Berman, 1975; Levy & Heaton, 1993). In women, the most common reason for attempting to lose weight is the desire to improve physical appearance, especially among those who seek help in weight programs. Expectations for health benefits are more important than appearance in older and severely obese women. Nonetheless, appearance is still a reported motivation for weight loss in a large portion of even the most overweight women. The group of weight reducers least likely to be concerned about appearance is severely obese men. However, even 16% of these men stated appearance was the *most* important reason for losing weight, compared with 22% for present health and 41% for future health concerns (Levy & Heaton, 1993).

Effect of Weight Reduction on Body Image

This raises an important question of whether weight reduction is truly effective for body image change. Any answer to this must be tentative because body image has been virtually ignored in obesity treatment outcome. The most information available is on severely obese persons who have undergone gastrointestinal obesity surgery. In conjunction with their dramatic weight reduction, these subjects show greatly improved body image after surgery (Adami et al., 1994; Stunkard & Wadden, 1992). Obese subjects also showed a much improved body image when assessed immediately after they lost a large amount of weight on a liquid very low calorie diet (Cash, 1994). Beyond these studies, I was unable to find any others that reported meaningful improvements in body image with dieting or behavioral obesity treatment (that is, body image in the sense of satisfaction or social comfort with appearance). Any improvement in body image that accompanies weight reduction, unfortunately, is likely to be temporary for most overweight persons because of the high rate of weight regain. Those who do regain weight report the most negative effect is on satisfaction with appearance (Wadden, Stunkard, & Liebshutz, 1988). Therefore, based on the available data, nonsurgical weight reduction programs cannot be described as an effective treatment for negative body image in obesity.

Professionals experienced in weight reduction programs probably have heard about the experience, "I lost weight but still didn't like myself." This points out a basic fact about body image and the weight reduction enterprise. Body image is a psychological construct that refers to people's evaluations of their physical attractiveness and, although it is related to objective physical appearance, the correlation between the two is low (Feingold, 1992). It is therefore not surprising that losing weight does not guarantee a positive or normal body image. For instance, it happens that formerly overweight persons who lost their excess weight score closer to obese than nonobese subjects on measures of body image (Cash, Counts, & Huffine, 1990).

Furthermore, not all appearance concerns in overweight persons are focused on weight, which means that weight reduction is not always an appropriate remedy. Anthropometric studies indicate that frame size and hip circumference are better predictors of body dissatisfaction in women than body fat and degree of overweight (Bailey, Goldberg, Swap, Chomitz, & Houser, 1990; Davis, Durnin, Dionne, & Gurevish, 1994). In my study of body image therapy for overweight women (Rosen, Orosan, & Reiter, 1995), 35% of subjects presented non-weight-related concerns about their appearances in addition to their obesity. These included preoccupation with height, facial features, scars and other skin blemishes, and breast size and shape. In sum, dietary intervention, even when accompanied by significant weight loss, may be ineffective in reducing total body dissatisfaction, which in part is focused on shape and other appearance features rather than fatness.

Body Image Interventions in Behavioral Weight Reduction Programs

Obese persons who start weight reducing in pursuit of the ideal physique must confront and come to terms with real limits in their biological and behavioral capacities to meet their goals. Otherwise, dieting attempts will only solidify the sense of failure that accompanies obesity in the first instance. Psychosocial interventions, especially interventions to improve body image, may be helpful adjuncts for people undergoing weight loss whose concerns extend beyond strictly physical health (Brownell & Wadden, 1991). Yet obesity researchers have not incorporated these new directions into their programs. I repeated Brownell and Wadden's review

(1986) of the behavioral obesity treatment literature for 1978 and 1984, plus added a third year, 1990. No study included any psychological techniques specifically designed to modify negative body image.

One subgroup that has been targeted in recent studies of behavioral weight control is obese dieters with binge eating disorder (BED; regular binge eating without drastic compensatory weight control as in bulimia nervosa). Although the prevalence in the general population is low, persons with BED constitute a large portion of participants in weight reduction programs—about 29% (Spitzer et al., 1993)—and increase in frequency with increasing body mass index (Telch, Agras, & Rossiter, 1988). Persons with BED are a particularly difficult subgroup in weight control programs because they tend to have more severe obesity, more dieting failures, and more psychological comorbidity (Spitzer et al., 1993). Most treatment programs for BED involve cognitive behavior therapy to deal with binge eating and weight loss to deal with overweight (Agras et al., 1994).

No published studies have added body image interventions to BED treatment, although it seems especially appropriate for this subgroup of obese weight reducers. First, obese persons with BED report more body dissatisfaction and are more likely to evaluate themselves based on body weight and shape than non-BED weight reducers (Cash, 1991a; Spitzer et al., 1993). Second, although weight control and cognitive–behavioral interventions can help to reduce binge eating behavior, there is a high dropout rate in BED programs, and those who complete treatment lose little weight (Agras et al., 1994). As a result, negative body image is not likely to be remedied by weight loss. Third, the treatment theory behind cognitive–behavioral therapy for BED holds that binge eating could be reduced if episodes of excessive dietary restraint and deprivation were brought under control (Agras et al., 1994). Going further back in the chain of events, one could argue that excessive restraint could be curtailed if binge eaters were better able to manage their negative body image attitudes. Indeed, intensifying dietary restraint over time is best predicted by body dissatisfaction after controlling for psychological symptoms and body fat (Cattarin & Thompson, 1994).

Overweight persons with BED report the same type of eating and body image disorder symptoms as normal weight persons with bulimia nervosa (Marcus, Smith, Santelli, & Kaye, 1992). Therefore, they might require the same type of combined cognitive–behavioral therapy intervention for bulimia nervosa that addresses eating and body image issues. However, the cognitive–behavioral interventions currently described in the BED literature are parallel to an experimental treatment condition for bulimia nervosa that was described by Fairburn and associates (Fairburn, Jones, Peveler, Hope, & O'Connor, 1993). It focused on modifying binge eating, restraint, and vomiting, but the treatment turned out to be dramatically inferior compared with cognitive–behavioral therapy that also targeted body image attitudes.

Obese persons are not homogeneous in their motivations for weight reduction or their clinical presentation. As a result, interventions that focus strictly on changing eating, exercise, or weight will not be relevant or sufficient for everyone. Psychological intervention for negative body image seems to be a neglected, but relevant, ingredient in weight control programs.

DIAGNOSING NEGATIVE BODY IMAGE IN OBESITY

A major problem in studying body image in obese persons is the lack of a standard definition or diagnosis for a clinically significant problem. The only accepted term for body image disorder is body dysmorphic disorder (Phillips, 1991). However, body dysmorphic disorder is inappropriate for obese persons who are more than mildly overweight because the disorder refers to concern about imagined or minimal defects in physical appearance. In the *DSM* system (American Psychiatric Association, 1994), the concept of bodily preoccupation in the somatoform disorders, such as body dysmorphic disorder, assumes there is insufficient organic basis for the person's complaints of physical abnormality. There is no diagnostic category in the *DSM* that accommodates a disorder of body image in persons who possess true defects in physical appearance.

Obese persons have a real, not imagined, physical condition and are subjected to real negative social evaluation. This raises important questions about the concept of body image problems in obesity. Given the weight consciousness of Western society, are negative body image feelings in obese persons always appropriate or can they be excessive and dysfunctional? Can negative body image be overcome by obese persons without losing weight or is that a hopeless venture?

Obese persons may not imagine their obesity, as might a normal weight bulimia nervosa patient. This type of body image distortion is just one, but not a necessary component of a negative body image. The other components of negative body image refer to attitudes and behavior. Problems in these areas range on a continuum from the ubiquitous mild body dissatisfaction to a distressing preoccupation with physical appearance that impairs functioning. In a study of case histories that were identical except for body weight, psychologists rated obese patients as having more trouble with embarrassment and self-consciousness than the nonobese (Agell & Rothblum, 1991). Although there might be some reality basis to these expectations, mental health professionals must be careful to avoid trivializing body image complaints of obese patients or acting as if obese persons deserve to feel the way they do. Body image complaints can reach a dysfunctional point on that continuum where mental health intervention is warranted. To deal with the fact that some obese persons truly suffer, Thompson (1992) proposed a sensible alternative diagnosis—body image disorder—that would accommodate preoccupation with appearance in two subgroups: persons with minimal defects or body dysmorphic disorder and those with real appearance defects.

Lacking a standard term at this moment, I have been using the term *negative body image*. I am referring to a condition that is more distressing and inhibiting than ordinary body dissatisfaction. Without a set of diagnostic criteria relevant to obese persons, a negative body image could be identified objectively with cutoff scores on questionnaires. Most popular measures include norms that allow the practitioner to define negative body image statistically. However, because body image measures correlate significantly with percent overweight, cutoff scores should be based on norms for overweight persons. Unfortunately, there are no readily available obese norms for body image measures. In my research on body image therapy with obese persons, I have been using the diagnostic criteria for disorder on the Body Dysmorphic Disorder Examination (Rosen & Reiter, in press) minus the criterion that refers to normality of appearance. The features of negative body image include distressing preoccupation with appearance, self-consciousness and embarrassment in social situations, distress when appearance is noticed by other people, excessive importance given to appearance in self-evaluation, negative self-evaluation attributed to appearance, and avoidance of activities because of self-consciousness about appearance.

EFFECTIVENESS OF BODY IMAGE INTERVENTIONS FOR OBESE PERSONS

Alternatives to weight reduction to improve body image in the obese have been reported. In an uncontrolled study of their program called "Undieting," Polivy and Herman (1992) helped obese women to recognize the futility of trying to lose a large amount of weight and the negative consequences of dieting. Subjects learned to replace restrained eating behavior with natural eating. After therapy, subjects reported less restraint, binge eating, depression, and negative self-esteem; however, body satisfaction was unimproved. Ciliska (1990) randomly assigned obese women to antidieting education, antidieting education plus experiential body image exercises, and no-treatment control groups. Subjects who received either intervention decreased dieting behavior; however, they failed to show any meaningful improvement in body dissatisfaction and remained in the clinically severe range along with the no-treatment control subjects. There is an antidiet, antiweight reduction movement taking hold among psychologists who are concerned about the poor outcome in obesity treatment (Garner & Wooley, 1992; Rothblum, 1993); however, these results show that giving up dieting by itself does not lead to improved body image.

Roughan, Seddon, and Vernon-Roberts (1990) reported an uncontrolled evaluation of a program to decrease overeating and dietary restraint and to help participants accept their weight. Although body dissatisfaction was reduced, the results for obese and normal weight subjects were pooled together. Moreover, improvement could not be attributed necessarily to the body image component of therapy because the subjects also learned to change eating habits and lost weight. McCrea and Summerfield (1988) had overweight women look at video recordings of themselves and discuss their appearance while being discouraged from self-criticism. After treatment, subjects decreased size overestimation (body image distortion) more than subjects who received training in a behavioral weight loss program; however, the study was quasiexperimental. Although these two studies are somewhat encouraging, neither was methodologically adequate.

There are several controlled studies showing that cognitive–behavior therapy is an effective treatment for negative body image in normal weight college women (see chapter 4, this volume). Because these subjects complained of excessive preoccupation with weight and body shape, the same type of cognitive–behavioral body image therapy could be effective with obese subjects as well, but this remains to be tested.

My colleagues and I recently completed an evaluation of our cognitive–behavioral therapy body image program, tailored to the circumstances of overweight participants (Rosen et al., 1995). Fifty-one obese women were randomly assigned to cognitive–behavioral body image therapy or no-treatment. Patients were treated in small groups for eight 2-hour sessions. Therapy included information to challenge negative stereotypes of obesity, modification of intrusive thoughts of body dissatisfaction and overvalued beliefs about physical appearance, exposure to avoided body image situations, and elimination of body checking. No assistance was provided to change eating or exercise behavior.

At the end of therapy, 70% of the cognitive–behavioral subjects were significantly improved on body image measures—that is, their scores decreased significantly and they switched from the clinically severe range to within the normal range. Four months later, the rate of clinically significant improvement was between 68% or 78%, depending on the measure. No-treatment subjects were unimproved. Treatment benefits extended to global self-esteem and psychological symptoms.

A secondary objective of the study was to determine if body image therapy had an impact on eating habits or weight, variables that were not being targeted in treatment. It seemed possible that if subjects learned to accept their obesity, they might abandon their weight control efforts in place already and gain weight. Alternately, improved body image might facilitate weight reduction and improved eating behavior. Or body image improvement could be completely unrelated to changes in weight or eating habits. It turned out that, on average, therapy subjects' weight remained unchanged. This finding should be reassuring to obese body image therapy participants, because at the beginning most are concerned that self-acceptance will lead to even greater obesity. However, it would be inappropriate to tell them not to expect any weight change because one third of our cognitive–behavioral subjects did lose or gain at least 10 pounds. Nonetheless, weight change was not attributable to therapy (weight changes did not differ between the two experimental conditions), and weight was unrelated to the degree of body image improvement (correlations between change scores on the two variables were insignificant).

The treatment program did not address eating. Nonetheless, cognitive–behavioral therapy subjects reported more feelings of being in control of their eating, less guilt and preoccupation about eating, and less binge eating. Restraint over eating returned to baseline levels by follow-up. However, this was not accompanied by weight reduction, deterioration of body image improvement, or increased binge eating or eating guilt. This finding is noteworthy for obese persons who might seek body image therapy. The fear that they would abandon efforts to control eating was not valid.

PRACTICAL GUIDELINES FOR BODY IMAGE THERAPY WITH OBESE PERSONS

I will present a brief overview of cognitive–behavioral body image therapy and some special considerations that will help the therapist tailor intervention to overweight persons. These guidelines are based on the program for negative body image in obese women that was evaluated by Rosen et al. (1994).[1] Chapters 4 and 7 in this volume present in more detail body image therapy with normal weight college students and patients with body dysmorphic disorder.

Format of Therapy

My colleagues and I have been providing therapy mainly in small groups of 4 to 10 participants, meeting for one 2-hour session per week for 8 weeks. Although we started this practice because it allowed us to complete clinical trials more rapidly, we have discovered other advantages to

---

[1]The manual for cognitive–behavioral body image therapy and the Body Dysmorphic Disorder Examination are available by writing the author at the Department of Psychology, University of Vermont, Burlington, VT 05405. (My e-mail address is j_rosen@dewey.uvm.edu).

the group format. First, it seems to be therapeutic for participants to observe other people conquer the same type of maladaptive beliefs about appearance and self-worth that they hold themselves. Second, the group is a handy environment to provide supervised exposure to body image cues—for example, wearing a form-fitting outfit to the group session. Third, the participants invariably differ in outward appearance, which presents opportunities to examine beliefs about the relation between appearance and body image. At first, we were reluctant to combine people with different appearances—in other words, normal versus overweight persons. However, reactions to these differences can be addressed in a constructive manner. A participant might report feeling more negative about herself because other people in the group are less heavy. On the other hand, she will probably discover that less overweight participants can have exactly the same type of body image problem, even though they weigh less. The therapist can use this experience as data to counter beliefs that body image is determined by appearance and that appearance needs to be altered to develop more positive self-esteem.

Body image therapy does not need to be conducted in groups. Our experience has been positive with individual treatment, although objective data with this format have not been reported. The best way to help people make significant changes in their body image is to have them practice attitude and behavior change at home, in between sessions. To provide clients with homework, we have been using the audiotape series and workbook on self-directed body image therapy by Cash (1991b). The audiotapes repeat and solidify the self-management concepts that are presented in therapy sessions. Also, the participant is given step-by-step instructions to carry out the therapeutic exercises. This frees time in therapy sessions to explore issues in more depth and to debrief homework.

Therapy Ingredients

Information About Body Image Development

The first goal is to help participants have an overview of the concept of body image and the social and personal roots of their own body image development. Explain that overweight persons learn negative body image attitudes in part from the modeling of cultural stereotypes about obesity and that, through modeling, they learn they must lose weight to feel better about themselves. Subjects should be asked to evaluate how effective weight reducing has been in improving their body image. Using their examples, point out that changes in their physical appearance through weight reduction have not always led to improved body image; that body image is a subjective, psychological construct; that the two variables, physical appearance and body image, can be independent; and that body image can be altered without having to change physical appearance. These points will have to be reiterated throughout therapy as participants struggle with the belief that negative self-esteem is the inevitable result of obesity.

Next, participants should identify personal experiences during childhood and adolescence that preceded their negative body image—for example, being teased, criticized, or rejected for being overweight. Despite a prevailing bias against overweight, self-consciousness about appearance often does not begin until the person has been subjected individually to rejection (Cattarin & Thompson, 1994; Harris, 1982). Explain that personal experiences of humiliation condition body image distress in similar situations through generalization.

Have the participants keep a self-monitoring diary of situations in which they feel self-conscious, recording their beliefs in the situation as well as the emotional and behavioral consequences. Using the diaries, ask participants to identify current examples of negative self-statements about physical appearance or negative body talk (e.g., "My rear is disgusting"), negative implications of appearance for self-worth (e.g., "I'll never get married"), and body image avoidance and checking behavior (e.g., wearing baggy clothes and excessive weighing). Explain that these factors are responsible for maintaining their negative body image and will be the targets for the remainder of therapy. Although it might seem like blaming the victim to stress personal responsibility, it is empowering to increase the sense of control the individual has over sociocultural messages. In a study of attitudes toward counseling for weight and eating concerns, women did not necessarily prefer sociocultural interpretations. In fact, women with nontraditional gender role orientation preferred attributions to personal responsibility (Glidden & Tracey, 1989).

Exposure to the Sight of the Body

Participants should begin working through exposure of a hierarchy of body area dissatisfaction by viewing themselves, part-by-part, in front of a full-length mirror in the privacy of their own homes. The hierarchy should be completed first clothed, then unclothed, over a period of a couple of weeks. Neutral, objective self-descriptions should be generated in therapy sessions to replace unnecessarily negative body talk during these exposure assignments (e.g., "I see my round stomach" instead of "I hate that disgusting flab"). The hierarchies of many participants show them to be distressed by features other than obesity (e.g., skin blemishes). This assessment can be used therapeutically by encouraging the participant to realize the problem is a preoccupation with appearance in general, rather than simply with weight.

Cognitive Restructuring

The therapist should help the participants to identify maladaptive assumptions about their appearances and to practice cognitive restructuring. Begin with simple statements of body dissatisfaction recorded in the diary, such as "I looked really fat," and then instruct the participant to follow this thought to where it leads by asking about the implications of looking "fat" in that situation. Typically, the sequence of thinking is, "I look fat, other people notice and care about my fatness, they evaluate me negatively as a person, and consequently being fat proves something truly negative about my self and worth to other people." Some amount of body dissatisfaction is not unrealistic given their obesity. Therefore, cognitive restructuring should focus on the negative meanings attributed to physical appearance that cause them to feel ashamed or embarrassed around other people. Using standard cognitive restructuring interventions, participants can evaluate the evidence for and against their beliefs and construct alternative, disputing thoughts.

Exposure and Response Prevention

The rationale for exposure therapy is to extinguish anxiety by facing feared body image situations and to eliminate self-defeating, rigid, and inhibited physical activity, dress, and posture. Examples are wearing a form-fitting outfit instead of baggy clothes, wearing a blouse tucked-in, eating or exercising in public, and accentuating a distressing feature (e.g., wearing a colorful necklace around a fat neck). Response prevention is designed to reduce behavioral rituals, mainly checking behavior, that promote preoccupation with appearance. Examples of assignments are to decrease weighing, set a fixed time for dressing, and refrain from asking other people for reassurance and comparing oneself to other people.

Coping With Stereotypes and Prejudice

Overweight persons are confronted with situations in which people have negative expectations about them. As a result, successful cognitive restructuring of body image attitudes depends in part on bolstering efforts to cope with the stigma of obesity. Self-protective strategies used by other stigmatized subgroups are relevant to body image in obesity (Miller, Rothblum, Felicio, & Brand, 1995). First, participants can be encouraged to attribute negative reactions from others to prejudice toward the obese rather than to defects in personal traits. The real culprit is the unfair and uninformed attitude toward an entire segment of society. Obesity prejudice does not prove the existence of characterologic defects. However, because most obese persons blame themselves to excess for their overweight, it is important to provide information on the nonbehavioral, genetic, and physiological causes of obesity. Overweight individuals also might be encouraged to find examples from their own experiences to counter stereotypes—for example, the person is strong willed and self-disciplined in many other areas of life.

Second, participants will have to learn to reduce the importance of the characteristics on which they are judged—in other words, their overweight appearance. Although overweight persons are judged by peers as less attractive (Jarvie, Lahey, Graziano, & Farmer, 1983), appearance seems to be more influential in initial impressions between unacquainted persons. Peer ratings do not show obese–nonobese differences in the amount the person is liked or perceived social competence (Jarvie et al., 1983; Miller, Rothblum, Brand, & Felicio, 1995). Information such as this will help the participant to develop beliefs to dispute excessive meaning given to physical appearance.

Third, participants should be discouraged from comparing themselves only with people who are thinner. Lopsided comparisons perpetuate feelings of alienation. Instead, the participants should compare themselves with a more diverse and representative range of body types. As long as it is does not become excessive, social comparisons should be made with other overweight persons.

Fourth, persons with negative body image attribute most of their troubles to their appearance. Recovery will be facilitated if the patient can find other reasons to account for feeling uncomfortable around others (e.g., not knowing how to maintain a conversation). This discovery can help patients abandon the idea that they must look different to be happier. Although it might be distressing to admit to another dysfunction, at least it may be one that is more modifiable than physical appearance.

Integrating Body Image Therapy With Weight Reduction

Body image therapy is not an antidiet, antiweight reduction approach, even though its basic premise is that self-image can be improved without losing weight. The two goals are not incompatible and the two types of interventions can be presented simultaneously. My colleagues and I are engaged in a controlled study of weight reduction versus weight reduction plus body image therapy. So far, about one half to two thirds of participants in a short-term, community-based weight reduction program volunteer to be randomized to one of the two conditions. There seems to be a great interest in the body image component, although not all participants have a truly negative body image. In the combined intervention, the therapist needs to acknowledge that participants are experiencing more body satisfaction as they lose weight. The rationale we give for adding the body image intervention is that it will enable them to exercise their new self-image more effectively and to unlearn body image habits that do not give way to weight loss.

CONCLUSION

The most consistent psychosocial consequence of obesity is body image dissatisfaction. Not only is this a frequent motivation for weight reduction attempts, but body dissatisfaction can be a cause of significant distress and impairment. Research on the effectiveness of body image therapy indicates that it is possible to help obese persons to change their body image attitudes and behavior using a strictly psychological approach, without any intervention to change eating, exercise, or weight. Although treatment outcome is encouraging at short-term follow-up assessment, the long-term effectiveness of body image therapy in obesity is unknown. As a group, overweight men are more concerned about fitness and health benefits of weight reduction. But the difference between men and women in their desire for improvement in appearance is not dramatic. Body image is a man's issue too, but so far, all treatment outcome studies with normal and overweight subjects have been conducted on women. The benefits or disadvantages of integrating body image therapy into other obesity treatment programs is unknown. Body dissatisfaction is so common among overweight persons that some accepted definition of significant distress is needed. The prevalence of negative body image in overweight samples is unknown. Moreover, the significance of negative body image for obesity itself in terms of response to obesity treatment is unknown. Nonetheless, there is an unmet need for body image intervention. The results in our clinical trial are strong enough to warrant the use of this approach by other investigators and clinicians.

REFERENCES

Adami, G. F., Gandolfo, P., Campostano, A., Bauer, B., Cocchi, F., Scopinaro, N. (1994). Eating Disorder Inventory in the assessment of psychosocial status in the obese patients prior to and at long term following biliopancreatic diversion for obesity. *International Journal of Eating Disorders, 15,* 265–274.

Agell, G., & Rothblum, E. D. (1991). Effects of client's obesity and gender on the therapy judgments of psychologists. *Professional Psychology: Research and Practice, 22,* 223–229.

Agras, W. S., Telch, C. F., Arnow, B., Eldridge K., Wilfley, D. E., Raeburn, S. D., Henderson, J., Marnell, M. (1994). Weight loss, cognitive–behavioral, and desipramine treatments in binge eating disorder. An additive design. *Behavior Therapy, 25,* 225–238.

American Psychiatric Association. (1994). *Diagnostic and statistical manual of mental disorders* (4th ed.). Washington, DC: Author.

Bailey, S. M., Goldberg, J. P., Swap, W. C., Chomitz, V. R., & Houser, R. F. (1990). Relationships between body dissatisfaction and physical measurements. *International Journal of Eating Disorders, 9,* 457–461.

Berman, E. M. (1975). Factors influencing motivations in dieting. *Journal of Nutritional Education, 7,* 155–159.

Brownell, K. D., & Wadden, T. A. (1986). Behavior therapy for obesity: Modern approaches and better results. In K. D. Brownell & J. P Foreyt (Eds.), *Handbook of eating disorders: Physiology, psychology, and treatment of obesity, anorexia, and bulimia* (pp. 180–199). New York: Basic Books.

Brownell, K. D., & Wadden, T. A. (1991). The heterogeneity of obesity: Fitting treatments to individuals. *Behavior Therapy, 22,* 153–177.

Cash, T. F. (1990). The psychology of physical appearance: Aesthetics, attributes, and images. In T. F. Cash & T. Pruzinsky (Eds.), *Body images: Development, deviance, and change* (pp. 51–79). New York: Guilford Press.

Cash, T. F. (1991a). Binge-eating and body image among the obese: A further evaluation. *Journal of Social Behavior and Personality, 6,* 367–376.

Cash, T. F. (1991b). *Body image therapy: A program for self-directed change.* Audiocassette series including client workbook. New York: Guilford Press.

Cash, T. F. (1994). Body image and weight changes in a multisite comprehensive very-low-calorie diet program. *Behavior Therapy, 25,* 239–254.

Cash, T. F., Counts, B., & Huffine, C. E. (1990). Current and vestigial effects of overweight among women: Fear of fat, attitudinal body image, and eating behaviors. *Journal of Psychopathology and Behavioral Assessment, 12,* 157–167.

Cattarin, J. A., & Thompson, J. K. (1994). A three-year longitudinal study of body image, eating disturbance, and general psychological functioning in adolescent females. *Eating Disorders: The Journal of Treatment and Prevention, 2,* 114–125.

Ciliska, D. (1990). *Beyond dieting: Psychoeducational interventions for chronically obese women: A non-dieting approach.* New York: Brunner/Mazel.

Collins, J. K., Beumont, P. J. V., Touyz, S. W., Krass, J., Thompson, P., & Philips, T. (1987). Variability in body shape perception in anorexic, bulimic, obese, and control subjects. *International Journal of Eating Disorders, 6,* 633–638.

Davis, C., Durnin, J. V. G. A., Dionne, M., & Gurevish, M. (1994). The influence of body fat content and bone diameter measurements on body dissatisfaction in adult women. *International Journal of Eating Disorders, 15,* 257–263.

Fairburn, C. G., Jones, R., Peveler, R. C., Hope, R. A., & O'Connor, M. (1993). Psychopathology and bulimia nervosa: The longer-term effects of interpersonal psychotherapy, behaviour therapy and cognitive behaviour therapy. *Archives of General Psychiatry, 50,* 419–428.

Feingold, A. (1992). Good-looking people are not what we think. *Psychological Bulletin, 111*, 304–341.

French, S. A., & Jeffery, R. W. (1994). Consequences of dieting to lose weight: Effects on physical and mental health. *Health Psychology, 13*, 195–212.

Garner, D. M., & Wooley, S. C. (1992). Confronting the failure of behavioral and dietary treatments of obesity. *Clinical Psychology Review, 11*, 729–780.

Glidden, C. E., & Tracey, T. J. (1989). Women's perceptions of personal versus sociocultural counseling interventions. *Journal of Counseling Psychology, 36*, 54–62.

Harris, D. L. (1982). The symptomatology of abnormal appearance: An anecdotal survey. *British Journal of Plastic Surgery, 35*, 312–323.

Jarvie, G. J., Lahey, B., Graziano, W., & Farmer, E. (1983). Childhood obesity and social stigma: What we know and what we don't know. *Developmental Review, 3*, 237–273.

Levy, A. S., & Heaton, A. W. (1993, October). Weight control practices of U.S. adults trying to lose weight. *Annals of Internal Medicine, 119 (Suppl. Pt. 2)*, 661–666.

Marcus, M. D., Smith, D., Santelli, R., & Kaye, W. (1992). Characterization of eating disordered behavior in obese binge eaters. *International Journal of Eating Disorders, 12*, 249–255.

McCrea, C., & Summerfield, A. B. (1988). A pilot study of the therapeutic usefulness of videofeedback for weight loss and improvement of body image in the treatment of obesity. *Behavioural Psychotherapy, 16*, 269–284.

Miller, C. T., Rothblum, E. D., Brand, P. A., & Felicio, D. M. (1995). Do obese women have poorer social relationships than nonobese women? Reports by self, friends, and co-workers. *Journal of Personality, 63*, 65–85.

Miller, C. T., Rothblum, E. D., Felicio, D., & Brand, P. (1995). Compensating for stigma: Obese and nonobese women's reactions to being visible. *Personality and Social Psychology Bulletin, 21*, 1093–1106.

Phillips, K. A. (1991). Body dysmorphic disorders: The distress of imagined ugliness. *American Journal of Psychiatry, 148*, 1138–1149.

Polivy, J., & Herman, C. P. (1992). Undieting: A program to help people stop dieting. *International Journal of Eating Disorders, 11*, 261–268.

Rosen, J. C. (1990). Body image disturbance in eating disorders. In T. F. Cash & T. Pruzinsky (Eds.), *Body images: Development, deviance and change* (pp. 190–214). New York: Guilford Press.

Rosen, J. C., Orosan, P., & Reiter, J. (1995). Cognitive behavior therapy for negative body image in obese women. *Behavior Therapy, 26*, 25–42.

Rosen, J. C., & Reiter, J. (in press). Development of the Body Dysmorphic Disorder Examination. *Behaviour Research and Therapy*.

Rothblum, E. D. (1993). I'll die for the revolution but don't ask me to stop dieting: Feminism and the continuing stigmatization of obesity. In P. Fallon, M. A.

Katzman, & S. C. Wooley (Eds.), *Feminist perspectives on eating disorders* (pp. 53–76). New York: Guilford Press.

Roughan, P., Seddon, E., & Vernon-Roberts, J. (1990). Long-term effects of a psychologically based group programme for women preoccupied with body weight and eating behaviour. *International Journal of Obesity, 14,* 135–147.

Spitzer, R. L., Yanovski, S., Wadden, T., Wing, M. D., Stunkard, A., Devlin, M., Mitchell, J., Hasin, D., & Horne, R. L. (1993). Binge eating disorder: Its further validation in a multisite study. *International Journal of Eating Disorders, 13,* 137–153.

Stunkard, A. J., & Wadden, T. A. (1992). Psychological aspects of severe obesity. *American Journal of Clinical Nutrition, 55,* 524S–532S.

Telch, C. F., Agras, W. S., & Rossiter, E. M. (1988). Binge eating increases with increasing adiposity. *International Journal of Eating Disorders, 7,* 115–119.

Thompson, J. K. (1992). Body image: Extent of disturbance, associated features, theoretical models, assessment methodologies, intervention strategies, and a proposal for a new DSM-IV diagnostic category—Body Image Disorder. In M. Hersen, R. M. Eisler, & P. M. Miller (Eds.), *Progress in behavior modification, Vol. 28* (pp. 3–54). Sycamore, IL.: Sycamore.

Tiggemann, M., & Rothblum, E. D. (1988). Gender differences in social consequences of perceived overweight in the United States and Australia. *Sex Roles, 18,* 75–86.

Wadden, T. A., Stunkard, A. J., & Liebshutz, J. (1988). Three-year follow-up of the treatment of obesity by very low calorie diet, behavior therapy, and their combination. *Journal of Consulting and Clinical Psychology, 56,* 925–928.

18

ASSESSMENT AND TREATMENT OF MORBID OBESITY

PATRICIA FETTES and DONALD E. WILLIAMS

Morbid obesity is a serious and potentially deadly problem that until the past few decades received little attention in the scientific literature. However, there has been a dramatic increase in research on the phenomenology and treatment of severe weight disturbance recently, possibly because of the development of relatively safe and effective surgical treatments for morbid obesity. The outcome of this increased attention has been a growing awareness that morbid obesity is qualitatively different from less severe forms of obesity and requires special attention in both assessment and treatment.

The purpose of this chapter is to provide a practical outline for the assessment and treatment of morbid obesity from the perspective of the consulting mental health professional. We begin with a brief review of the literature on morbid obesity, with specific attention to morbidity and mortality, as well as psychosocial characteristics of morbidly obese patients. We will then discuss the various characteristics of the morbidly obese individual, including psychopathology, body image disturbance, and the social and occupational aspects relevant to this population. We will devote the rest of the chapter to assessment and treatment.

MORBIDITY AND MORTALITY

Morbid or *severe obesity* (these terms are used interchangeably throughout the chapter) is defined as either 100 pounds overweight or 100% above ideal weight. It has been estimated to occur in a roughly equal percentage of men and women in the general population (approximately 0.1%; Lomax, 1989), but is apparently infrequent even among the obese, accounting for approximately .5% or less of overweight persons (Stunkard, 1992).

There is little doubt that morbid obesity is associated with a number of severe health problems that place individuals in danger of disability or early death. Severely obese persons are at greatly increased risk of developing diabetes mellitus, hypertension, hyperlipidemias, coronary artery disease, and a host of other health problems such as obstructive sleep apnea, osteoarthritis, cholecystitis, and reduced fertility (Van Itallie & Lew, 1992). Morbid obesity is also associated with increased mortality from medical complications. For example, compared with the general population, the mortality rate among morbidly obese males is nearly three times higher (e.g., Lew & Garfinkel, 1979). Younger morbidly obese adults are at the greatest risk of death from obesity-related complications (e.g., Lew & Gajewski, 1990). It is clear that the significant medical risks of morbid obesity provide a striking rationale for treating this disorder.

PSYCHOSOCIAL CHARACTERISTICS OF MORBIDLY OBESE INDIVIDUALS

Psychopathology

Obesity is a complex disorder believed to be induced by any one or more of a number of biological, psychological, or social elements, including genetic makeup, metabolic factors, certain medical conditions, behavioral patterns, and psychological issues (see Brownell & Wadden, 1992, for a more complete discussion of the etiology of obesity). While genetic and other biological factors are viewed as primary contributing factors, psychological factors have long been a central component of etiological theories about obesity, dating from early psychoanalytic speculations about the oral personality. As a result, the relationship between obesity and psychopathology has been the subject of numerous investigations over the years. Despite the widespread popular belief that obesity is associated with a much greater incidence of mental health problems, several large population studies have not provided striking evidence to support this assumption (e.g., Crisp & McGuiness, 1976; Moore, Stunkard, & Srole, 1962; see also chapter 15, this volume).

However, many clinicians and researchers have questioned whether this lack of association holds for the most severely obese. Some clinicians have noted a high rate of emotional or characterological disturbance among patients presenting for treatment of morbid obesity and have speculated that such disturbance either may contribute to severe weight problems or arise as a consequence. In the past few decades a number of studies have been conducted to examine rates of psychopathology in the morbidly obese. In general, these studies have produced widely discrepant results and have been fraught with methodological difficulties such as small sample sizes, inconsistencies in methods of assessing psychopathology, and inattention to the reliability or validity of diagnoses (Black, Goldstein, & Mason, 1992; Charles, 1983). An overriding methodological concern is the fact that most research has been conducted with patients who are being evaluated for weight reduction (bariatric) surgery. In at least one study, bariatric surgery patients were found to manifest substantially more psychopathology than morbidly obese patients who did not request surgery (Rosen & Aniskiewicz, 1983), suggesting that it is inappropriate to generalize from bariatric clinic patients to the entire population of morbidly obese persons.

Nonetheless, information about the incidence of specific psychopathology among bariatric surgery patients is useful from the perspective of the consulting mental health professional who provides assessment and treatment services to morbidly obese patients. A few studies have addressed some of the methodological concerns noted previously and merit special consideration. Black et al. (1992) examined the lifetime incidence of psychiatric diagnoses among 88 bariatric clinic patients via psychometrically sound structured diagnostic interviews that conformed to the *DSM-III* classification system (American Psychiatric Association, 1987). Compared with a control group of first-degree relatives of psychiatrically normal subjects, bariatric clinic patients were more likely to have been diagnosed with major depression, agoraphobia, simple phobia, posttraumatic stress disorder, bulimia nervosa, and one or more personality disorders—particularly histrionic, borderline, avoidant, and passive aggressive personality disorders.

Further evidence of the overrepresentation of posttraumatic stress disorder among morbidly obese individuals comes from a population study conducted by Dansky, O'Neill, Brewerton, and Kilpatrick (1993). These researchers administered structured interviews to approximately 75% of a national sample of 4,009 women and found that compared with normal weight and moderately obese women, morbidly obese females evidenced a higher lifetime prevalence of posttraumatic stress disorder and history of rape or sexual assault. In a similar way, a study of medical records of adult patients of a health maintenance organization indicated that those individuals who reported a history of childhood sexual abuse on a medical questionnaire were four times more likely to be morbidly obese than a random sample of control patients (Felitti, 1991).

There is also evidence that the newly conceptualized binge eating disorder (BED) is associated with morbid obesity. BED is characterized by recurrent binge eating in the absence of purging or other behaviors used to prevent weight gain (American Psychiatric Association, 1994; see also chapter 13, this volume). Yanovski, Nelson, Dubbert, and Spitzer (1993) administered structured clinical interviews to 128 obese men and women who at the time were not in treatment. They found that severely obese individuals were more likely than those with moderate obesity to meet BED diagnostic criteria. In addition, subjects with BED had higher lifetime prevalence rates of major depression, panic disorder, bulimia nervosa, borderline personality disorder, and avoidant personality disorder, suggesting that BED may covary with other psychopathology among the obese.

Although it is tempting to speculate that certain diagnoses (e.g., depression) or experiences (e.g., sexual abuse) may play a causal role in morbid obesity by promoting excessive or binge eating (Brownell & Wadden, 1992), it must be emphasized that these studies are correlational and therefore cannot determine causality. However, regardless of whether psychopathology predated or antedated the onset of obesity, psychiatric conditions may interfere with the success of weight management interventions and may need to be resolved before obesity treatment can proceed.

Body Image Disturbance

It is the impression of many clinicians that body image disturbance is quite common among morbidly obese individuals who present for treatment. It has been only recently that standardized measures of body image (including measures of affective, cognitive, behavioral, or perceptual components) have been developed, and there has been very little research employing these assessment methods with obese individuals (Thompson, 1992; see also chapter 3, this volume).

However, the available evidence supports the popular impression noted earlier. In the seminal work by Stunkard and Mendelson (1967), negative feelings and attitudes about body and overall self were found to be present in more than 50% of a group of obese individuals, although extreme body image disparagement occurred exclusively among individuals who developed obesity during childhood or adolescence. It is surprising to note the extent of overweight did not appear to be associated with the intensity of body image disparagement. In addition, obese adults were less accurate in perceptual measures of body image in that they overestimated their body dimensions by 6% to 12%, compared to 1% to 2% for average weight individuals (O'Neil & Jarrell, 1992); this pattern of overestimation of the dimensions of body parts was found to hold true for a group of bariatric surgery patients (Leon, Eckert, Teed, & Buchwald, 1979).

Social and Occupational Aspects

Morbid obesity is associated with adverse social and occupational consequences, in large part because of the widespread prejudice against obesity in Western culture. Obese individuals are less likely to be accepted into college or to be hired for employment compared with normal weight individuals, and when employed typically earn less than equally qualified persons of average weight (Wadden & Stunkard, 1985). In some cases the physical consequences of morbid obesity prevent employment entirely, causing great financial hardship. High rates of difficulties with interpersonal relations and sexual functioning and satisfaction have also been reported among severely obese individuals (e.g., Atkinson & Ringuette, 1967). Most describe demoralizing experiences with social prejudice and intolerance, including being stared at, taunted, or criticized in public situations. As a result, social isolation is quite common.

ASSESSMENT OF MORBID OBESITY

As noted previously, morbid obesity is a multidimensional problem incorporating medical, behavioral, nutritional, psychological, and social factors. Therefore, a multidisciplinary approach to assessment and treatment is most appropriate. In the best case scenario, mental health professionals participate with physicians and dieticians in all phases of the assessment and treatment process (e.g., Thompson, 1984), along with other specialists that may be appropriate (e.g., exercise physiologists). In practice, however, the mental health professional may be called on to provide services to morbidly obese patients at any of a number of points in the evaluation and treatment process. The majority of patients are referred by physicians or dieticians, many for the specific purpose of evaluation regarding bariatric surgery or treatment by very low calorie diets. A small percentage are self-referred for weight management assistance; in these cases, the mental health professional should arrange concurrent evaluations with a physician and dietician.

The purposes of assessment are to determine the most appropriate treatment options from a psychosocial standpoint, to evaluate for the presence of psychiatric or psychological treatment contraindications, and to establish a baseline for setting treatment goals and monitoring progress. A variety of tools are available to accomplish these purposes, including clinical interviews, psychological testing, and behavioral assessment (chapter 15, this volume). We recommend the use of all three methods wherever possible because each technique can offer information potentially not available via other methods.

Clinical Interview

The clinical interview is the most important component of the mental health evaluation. During the interview, information is gathered about the weight problem, previous weight loss attempts, as well as about past and current psychosocial status and about attitudes and expectations on treatment options. A semistructured interview format is particularly well suited for collecting this information. In the paragraphs to follow, we will describe a useful framework for conducting the interview.

Introduction

We find it helpful to provide a brief explanation and description of the assessment process. We try to uncover and allay any fears that the patient may have about referral to a mental health professional. Such an introduction can help relax the patient and build rapport, ultimately improving the quality of the interview.

Weight History

A thorough weight history should be obtained by asking patients to describe weight changes over their lifetimes, beginning in childhood. Special attention should be paid to date of onset of obesity, onset events (such as life stressors, losses, etc.), highest and lowest adult weights, and current weight. Family history of obesity should also be explored. The majority of morbidly obese patients report both a family history of obesity and childhood onset of obesity (e.g., Atkinson & Ringuette, 1967), which indicate the presence of biological obstacles to weight loss and suggest the need for cautious goal setting. Onset of obesity associated with particular events such as psychological trauma may indicate the need for counseling before weight management treatment is initiated.

Weight Loss Attempts and Treatments

Specific and detailed information should be obtained about past involvement with self- or physician-prescribed diets, self-help groups (e.g., Overeaters Anonymous), commercial programs (e.g., Weight Watchers, Optifast), medications, surgery, behavior therapy, or psychotherapy. Weight loss and compliance with each method should be explored, as well as any history of diet-induced stress or psychological difficulties. This process provides invaluable information about the patient's typical attitudes about and reactions to weight management efforts and possible roadblocks to be considered in treatment planning.

Eating Patterns

Patients should be asked to describe their typical daily food consumption, including frequency and composition (type of food and amount) of meals and snacks, rate of eating, typical eating locations, and potential triggers to eating other than hunger, such as emotional distress. It is useful to have the patients list foods consumed in the previous 24 hours. This information, in conjunction with behavioral assessments, will form a baseline for purposes of treatment planning and measuring treatment outcome.

Eating Disorder Symptoms

Morbidly obese patients frequently report current or past symptoms typically associated with eating disorders, such as binge eating, self-induced vomiting, laxative abuse, diuretic abuse, or periods of fasting (see chapter 9, this volume). The presence of such symptoms, if severe or entrenched, is a contraindication to beginning weight management treatment. Psychotherapy may be an appropriate first step to help resolve these symptoms (see chapter 11, this volume).

Physical Activity

Current level of physical activity, both formal (e.g., exercise) and incidental (e.g., using stairs rather than the elevator) should be explored (see chapter 16, this volume). As with eating patterns, this information will form a baseline.

Attitudes and Expectations Regarding Treatment

An understanding of the patient's current motivations for treatment as well as expectations about the process and outcome of weight loss interventions are essential. Some patients seek weight loss assistance on the basis of inappropriate motivations, such as to save a failing marriage. Many expect to lose an unrealistic amount of weight, to experience dramatic life changes after weight loss, or to be passive treatment participants. Others have low self-efficacy, believing that they cannot lose weight no matter what they try. These attitudes and expectations need to be clarified and perhaps modified in preparation for treatment. It is essential for patients to understand the probable benefits and limits of treatment, as well as their role as active participants in any intervention before treatment begins. Individuals who continue to harbor unrealistic expectations regarding interventions or outcome may be inappropriate candidates for treatment.

Psychiatric History and Mental Status

Past and current psychiatric difficulties and treatment must be reviewed, as well as current mental status and family psychiatric history.

Certain current psychiatric problems are contraindications to treatment and should be resolved if possible before any intervention is initiated. These include psychosis, substance dependence (other than nicotine), severe depression or anxiety, severe personality disorder, or disorders involving significant cognitive dysfunction (e.g., mental retardation, dementia).

Social History

A brief social history should be obtained, with attention to marital status and satisfaction, sexual concerns, occupational functioning, educational history and learning difficulties, history of abuse (physical, sexual, emotional), current stressors, and social supports. Although problems in these areas are generally not absolute contraindications to treatment, it may be beneficial to resolve certain difficulties (e.g., marital distress) before treatment to minimize barriers to success.

Psychological Testing

Psychological testing can be a useful adjunct to the clinical interview in evaluating patients for weight management intervention. We have incorporated a number of psychometric instruments into the assessment protocol for bariatric surgery candidates as part of a clinical research project exploring psychosocial characteristics and outcomes in this population. However, in general clinical practice it is probably neither practical nor appropriate to administer a large number of psychological tests. Therefore, instruments should be selected on the basis of whether they efficiently enhance treatment decision making. Many clinicians find the Minnesota Multiphasic Personality Inventory (MMPI; Hathaway & McKinley, 1940), or MMPI–2 (Butcher, Dahlstrom, Graham, Tellegen, & Kaemmer, 1989), or the Millon Clinical Multiaxial Inventory–II (Millon, 1987) useful for eliciting critical information about general psychopathology and personality disorders, which can be further explored in the clinical interview. The Eating Disorders Inventory–2 (Garner, 1991), which assesses the presence of eating disorder symptoms, and a number of eating restraint scales (see chapter 15, this volume), are potentially useful screening instruments. Some clinicians have recommended using psychometric instruments such as the MMPI as a screening technique, with further psychosocial assessment provided only to those patients who produce abnormal results (e.g., Manolis, 1984). We would caution against this approach because tests of personality or psychopathology are not capable of gathering certain information necessary to the evaluation process, such as attitudes about treatment or experiences with previous treatments.

Behavioral Assessment

A third method of evaluating morbidly obese patients is behavioral assessment. The behaviors of interest in this context are eating and physical activity. Although direct observation of these behaviors would be desirable, indirect observation methods, such as self-monitoring, are generally more practical. Eating and exercise diaries are typical components of most weight management treatments, and we strongly recommend including them in both assessment and treatment phases (see Exhibits 1 and 2). Although patients may underreport food consumption to some extent on eating diaries, we nonetheless find this tool invaluable in identifying maladaptive eating patterns such as excessive fat or sugar consumption, binge eating, or fasting. Requiring self-monitoring during the assessment phase can also be a useful measure of compliance: Patients who fail to complete an eating diary may be expected to show poor compliance with a recommended eating or exercise regimen.

TREATMENT FOR MORBID OBESITY

A variety of obesity treatment methods have been applied to the problem of morbid obesity. The most extensively researched methods include behavioral weight management programs, very low calorie diets and a variety of bariatric surgical methods.

Behavioral Programs

Behavioral programs emphasize modifying eating and exercise patterns through the methods of behavior therapy (e.g., self-monitoring, goal setting, stimulus control) combined with nutrition education and a balanced deficit diet of 1200 ± 200 kcal/day. Typical weight loss is approximately .5 kg/week for programs of 16 to 20 weeks in duration; although 12-month follow-ups typically show moderate maintenance of weight loss on average, follow-up periods of longer durations (i.e., 3 to 5 years) often indicate a return to baseline weight levels (Brownell & Wadden, 1992; see also chapter 16, this volume). Because of the modest weight loss and high relapse rates associated with conventional behavioral programs, many morbidly obese patients fail to lose sufficient weight or maintain weight loss with this type of treatment.

Very Low Calorie Diets

Very low calorie diets (VLCDs) differ from conventional behavioral programs by restricting caloric intake to 400 to 800 kcals/day provided

EXHIBIT 1
Sample Eating Diary

Date	Time	Food and Amount	Location	With Whom	Hunger Level[a]	Speed[a]	Feelings

Note. [a]Use letters or abbreviations to indicate hunger (NH = not hungry, H = hungry, VH = very hungry) and speed (S = slow, A = average, F = fast).

EXHIBIT 2
Physical Activity Diary

Date	Time	Activity	Time Spent	Distance[a]

Note. Indicate distance for walking, bicycling, canoeing, or cross-country skiing.

either in liquid form or as prepackaged solid foods. VLCDs typically incorporate behavioral treatment methods and are provided in commercial weight loss centers or in university or hospital settings. Weight loss over the course of programs lasting 12 to 26 weeks is approximately twice that of standard behavioral programs (Wadden & Kuehnel, 1993), although many patients fail to maintain weight loss in the long term (Brownell & Wadden, 1992). However, as with behavioral programs, a small percentage of patients appear to be able to maintain weight loss over an extended period following VLCD treatment.

Surgery

Surgical treatment of morbid obesity was pioneered in the 1950s with the development of the jejuno-ileal (or small bowel) bypass, which is rarely used today because of frequent medical complications. Since that time there have been significant advances and improvements in surgical options for morbid obesity. Two different general surgical approaches are available today: (a) *gastric restriction* (e.g., vertical-banded gastroplasty; see Figure 1) involves reducing the capacity of the stomach to a small pouch by partitioning it with a surgical stapler; and (b) *gastric bypass* (see Figure 2) entails stapling the stomach across the top to create a small pouch to which a part of the small intestine is sewed. A more radical version, pancreatobiliary bypass, involves removing 75% of the stomach and bypassing 50% of the small intestine, producing weight loss through both gastric restriction and malabsorption. Two of the most recent refinements in bariatric surgical treatment are the use of laparoscopic methods and adjustable gastric bands (e.g., Belachew, Legrand, Defechereux, Burtheret, & Jacquet, 1994).

Although gastric bypass is associated with greater weight loss compared to gastroplasty, initial weight loss following all of the bariatric surgeries is typically quite impressive. Average weight loss in the 12 months following surgery is between 25% and 35% of preoperative weight, which corresponds to approximately 100 pounds and approximately 50% of excess weight (Kral, 1992). Although most patients remain at least mildly (and generally moderately) obese, the medical risks of obesity are reduced greatly. In addition, many clinicians have reported positive psychological changes following bariatric surgery, including reduced depression (Bull, Engels, Engelsman, & Bloom, 1983), improved self-image (Hafner, 1991),

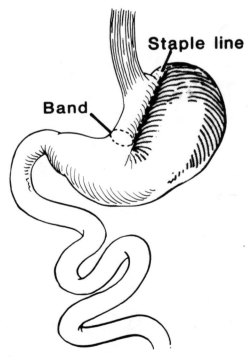

Figure 1. Diagram of surgical procedures in vertical-banded gastroplasty.

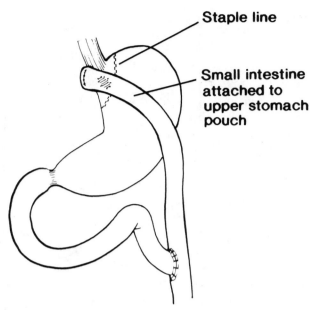

Staple line

Small intestine attached to upper stomach pouch

Figure 2. Diagram of surgical procedures in gastric bypass.

increased social activity (Hawke et al., 1990), and improved social relationships (Gentry, Halverson, & Heisler, 1984). Weight loss following bariatric surgery also appears to be associated with improved feelings and attitudes about one's body, although the perceptual overestimation of body size may remain (Leon et al., 1979).

Research suggests that maintenance of weight loss following bariatric surgery may be better than that associated with other treatments for morbid obesity. Andersen, Backer, Stokholm, and Quaade (1984) conducted a randomized treatment study of gastroplasty versus a VLCD in 60 morbidly obese patients. Although maximum weight losses did not significantly differ between the two groups, the gastroplasty group regained less weight over the course of the 2 years following treatment compared to the VLCD group. At 2-year follow-ups, 58% of available gastroplasty patients were less than 40% overweight compared with 7% of available VLCD patients.

Longer-term studies show a trend toward gradual weight gain, however. In a study of 153 gastric bypass patients, the average weight loss at 1 and 5 years were 48.5 kg and 37.0 kg (Reinhold, 1994). In a long-term study of 60 vertical-banded gastroplasty patients, 31% had returned to or were above their preoperative weight at follow-up approximately 10 years after surgery, with only 40% maintaining initial weight loss (Ramsey-Stewart, 1995). A 10-year outcome study of 119 patients showed mean weight losses of only 9 kg, 31 kg, and 25 kg, respectively, for horizontal gastroplasty, transected gastric bypass, and stapled gastric bypass procedures (Wolfel, Gunther, Rumenapf, Koerfgen, & Husemann, 1994).

Although the authors of the latter study concluded that none of the bariatric operations they studied provided adequate or prolonged control of morbid obesity, these results are more encouraging than the long-term outcome of other weight management strategies for morbid obesity. In addition, even those patients who ultimately regain weight over 10 or 15 years may nonetheless experience reduced risk of medical complications and mortality and improved quality of life for a significant period of time.

Despite the generally positive outcome of bariatric surgery, some complications have been reported. Whereas most patients regain a portion of their weight in the long term, some patients fail to lose significant weight or regain much or all of their weight relatively quickly because of continued overeating or consumption of high calorie liquid meals (Brownell & Wadden, 1991). Therefore, behavioral weight management therapy before and after surgery is appropriate to help maximize weight loss and maintenance (e.g., see Carmody & Brischetto, 1986, and Tucker, Samo, Rand, & Woodward, 1991, for discussions about combining behavior therapy with bariatric surgery treatment).

Iatrogenic vomiting and bulimia nervosa have also been reported following bariatric surgery in a number of patients (Powers & Rosemurgy, 1989; Thompson, Weinsier, & Jacobs, 1985). Other psychiatric complications (e.g., depression, anxiety) may occur in up to 15% of patients (Dubovsky & Liechty, 1985), and there is some indication that patients in previously unstable marriages may experience increased marital problems (e.g., Rand, Kuldau, & Robbins, 1982). Given the possibility of psychosocial complications, the mental health professional should work with the physician and dietician in monitoring patients during the months following bariatric surgery. Although quarterly follow-up appointments for 1 year will be sufficient for many patients, the frequency of appointments should be dictated by clinical need.

Treatment Selection

Although research suggests that bariatric surgery may be more effective on average than less intensive treatments for morbid obesity, we do not recommend that every morbidly obese patient be referred for this intervention. The choice of treatment should be made on the basis of a variety of factors, including previous treatments, medical status, psychiatric considerations, psychosocial support, eating and physical activity patterns, cost and availability of treatments, and patient preference (e.g., Brownell & Wadden, 1991). For example, a less intensive intervention such as a behavioral program certainly would be warranted for an otherwise healthy patient who has never undergone formal behavioral weight management therapy. However, a psychologically stable patient with extensive medical complications who has a long history of failures with behavioral and VLCD treatments may be a good candidate for evaluation for bariatric surgery.

Along these lines, Brownell and Wadden (1991) provide an excellent discussion of the heterogeneity of obesity and a comprehensive conceptual scheme for selecting obesity treatments for different individuals. This approach involves a series of decisions based on the extent of obesity, a stepped-care scheme (i.e., least intensive treatments are provided first), and individual characteristics of the client and available programs. Although this scheme has not been evaluated formally, it provides a useful structure for the complex process of selecting obesity treatments.

Regardless of the specific treatment selected (i.e., behavioral programs, VLCDs, or bariatric surgery), cognitive–behavioral methods are likely to be a component of the intervention. For additional information, LeBow (1989) provides a detailed, data-based, practical review of adult obesity therapy; Thompson (1990) provides guidelines for the assessment and treatment of body image disturbance in general with methods that easily could be adapted to the morbidly obese population, and Wadden and Van Itallie (1992) provide a comprehensive view on the treatment of the seriously obese patient, including pharmacological intervention.

CONCLUSION

Morbid obesity is a biopsychosocial problem that demands the attention of a variety of disciplines as a serious health concern. However, outcome data for existing weight management programs are notoriously poor. A variety of interventions have been researched, although none has provided a complete, effective, lasting treatment for morbid obesity as a health problem. Therefore, developing a multidisciplinary model that may account for the refractory nature of obesity and that may generate a sound rationale for multidisciplinary intervention is an appropriate focus for future efforts.

One promising theoretical approach is applying the notion of a *set-point* to physiological functions such as body weight (Keesey & Powley, 1986) as well as to psychological functioning (Williams & Thompson, 1993). As applied to weight regulation, the set-point theory predicts that body weight is governed at a constant level, similar to blood pressure or temperature, by a complex interaction of physiological factors. As a result, the set-point for body weight is likely to resist change; deviations from the set-point are likely to be met by regulatory, compensatory mechanisms intended to maintain that set-point.

In parallel to the set-point theory of obesity, psychological function might also be described from a homeostatic perspective, involving biological and behavioral regulatory factors. Although descriptions of the mechanisms of energy regulation from a psychological perspective are not as easily enunciated, the analogy is more clear. Human psychological resources, regardless of theoretical definition, may be subject to a variety of fluctuations. They are likely to be available and readily mobilizable, yet may be limited in nature with obligatory costs in terms of both utilization and endurance. Deviations from the psychological set-point also might be met by regulatory, compensatory mechanisms intended to maintain that set-point (Williams & Thompson, 1993). However, just as many physiologically regulated variables can be shifted (Keesey, 1986), psychological function might also be shifted by manipulating contributing variables such as environmental contingencies.

It is clear that the treatment of the morbidly obese patient must address these complex biopsychosocial issues. Lasting reductions in weight might be achieved only through alterations of both physiological and psychological set-points. This premise suggests that biological and behavioral therapies need to be integrated effectively to maximize therapeutic outcome with morbidly obese patients. Future research might be directed toward uncovering variables that contribute to both physiological and psychological set-points in obesity and toward identifying optimum combinations of biological and psychological treatment elements for altering these set-points.

REFERENCES

American Psychiatric Association. (1987). *Diagnostic and statistical manual of mental disorders* (3rd ed., rev.). Washington, DC: Author.

American Psychiatric Association (1994). *Diagnostic and statistical manual of mental disorders* (4th ed.). Washington DC: Author.

Anderson, T., Backer, O. G., Stokholm, K. H., & Quaade, F. (1984). Randomized trial of diet and gastroplasty compared with diet alone in morbid obesity. *New England Journal of Medicine, 310*, 352–356.

Atkinson, R. M., & Ringuette, E. L. (1967). A survey of biographical and psychological features in extraordinary fatness. *Psychosomatic Medicine, 29*, 121–133.

Belachew, M., Legrand, M. J., Defechereux, T. H., Burtheret, M. P., & Jacquet, N. (1994). Laparoscopic adjustable silicone gastric banding in the treatment of morbid obesity: A preliminary report. *Surgical Endoscopy, 8*, 1354–1356.

Black, D. W., Goldstein, R. B., & Mason, E. E. (1992). Prevalence of mental disorder in 88 morbidly obese bariatric clinic patients. *American Journal of Psychiatry, 149*, 227–234.

Brownell, K. D., & Wadden, T. A. (1991). The heterogeneity of obesity: Fitting treatments to individuals. *Behavior Therapy, 22*, 153–177.

Brownell, K. D., & Wadden, T. A. (1992). Etiology and treatment of obesity: Understanding a serious, prevalent, and refractory disorder. *Journal of Consulting and Clinical Psychology, 60,* 505–517.

Bull, R. H., Engels, D., Engelsman, F., & Bloom, L. (1983). Behavioural changes following gastric surgery for morbid obesity: A prospective, controlled study. *Journal of Psychosomatic Research, 27,* 457–467.

Butcher, J. N., Dahlstrom, W. G., Graham, J. R., Tellegen, A., & Kaemmer, B. (1989). *Minnesota Multiphasic Personality Inventory (MMPI–2). Manual for administration and scoring.* Minneapolis: University of Minnesota Press.

Carmody, T. P., & Brischetto, C. S. (1986). Combined behavioral and surgical treatment of morbid obesity: A case of backsliding. *The Behavior Therapist, 4,* 79–80.

Charles, S. C. (1983). The psychological status of morbidly obese patients. *Integrative Psychiatry, 1,* 122–125.

Crisp, A. H., & McGuiness, B. (1976). Jolly fat: Relation between obesity and psychoneurosis in general population. *British Medical Journal, 1,* 7–9.

Dansky, B. S., O'Neil, P. M., Brewerton, T. D., & Kilpatrick, D. G. (1993, April). *The nature of the relationship between obesity and victimization in a national sample.* Poster presented at the meeting of the Society of Behavioral Medicine, San Francisco, CA.

Dubovsky, S. L., & Liechty, S. L. (1985). Psychiatric evaluation in gastric surgery for obesity. *Psychotherapy and Psychosomatics, 44,* 144–150.

Felitti, V. J. (1991). Long-term medical consequences of incest, rape, and molestation. *Southern Medical Journal, 84,* 328–331.

Garner, D. M. (1991). *Eating Disorder Inventory–2: Professional manual.* Odessa, FL: Psychological Assessment Resources.

Gentry, K., Halverson, J. D., & Heisler, S. (1984). Psychologic assessment of morbidly obese patients undergoing gastric bypass: A comparison of preoperative and postoperative adjustment. *Surgery, 95,* 215–220.

Hafner, R. J. (1991). Morbid obesity: Effects on the marital system of weight loss after gastric restriction. *Psychotherapy and Psychosomatics, 56,* 162–166.

Hathaway, S. R., & McKinley, J. C. (1940). A multiphasic personality schedule (Minnesota). I. Construction of the schedule. *Journal of Psychology, 10,* 249–254.

Hawke, A., O'Brien, P., Watts, J. M., Hall, J., Dunstan, R. E., Walsh, A. H., Slavotinek, A. H., & Elmslie, R. G. (1990). Psychosocial and physical activity changes after gastric restrictive procedures for morbid obesity. *Australian and New Zealand Journal of Surgery, 60,* 755–758.

Keesey, R. E. (1986). A set-point theory of obesity. In K. D. Brownell & J. P. Foreyt (Eds.), *Physiology, psychology, and treatment of the eating disorders* (pp. 63–87). New York: Basic Books.

Keesey, R. E., & Powley, T. L. (1986). The regulation of body weight. *Annual Review of Psychology, 37,* 109–133.

Kral, J. G. (1992). Surgical treatment of obesity. In T. A. Wadden & T. B. Van Itallie (Eds.), *Treatment of the seriously obese patient* (pp. 496–506). New York: Guilford Press.

LeBow, M. D. (1989). *Adult obesity therapy.* Elmsford, NY: Pergamon Press.

Leon, G. R., Eckert, E. D., Teed, D., & Buchwald, H. (1979). Changes in body image and other psychological factors after intestinal bypass surgery for massive obesity. *Journal of Behavioral Medicine, 2,* 39–55.

Lew, E. A., & Gajewski, J. (Eds.). (1990). *Medical risks: Mortality trends by age and time elapsed.* New York: Praeger.

Lew, E. A., & Garfinkel, P. E. (1979). Variations in mortality by weight among 750,000 men and women. *Journal of Chronic Diseases, 32,* 563–576.

Lomax, J. W. (1989). Obesity. In H. I. Kaplan & B. J. Sadock (Eds.), *Comprehensive textbook of psychiatry, Vol. 5.* Baltimore: Williams and Wilkins.

Manolis, D. C. (1984). Psychiatric considerations. In J. H. Linner, *Surgery for morbid obesity* (pp. 17–22). New York: Springer-Verlag.

Millon, T. (1987). *Manual for the MCMI-II (second edition).* Minneapolis, MN: National Computer Systems.

Moore, M. E., Stunkard, A., & Srole, L. (1962). Obesity, social class, and mental illness. *Journal of the American Medical Association, 181,* 138–142.

O'Neil, P. M., & Jarrell, M. P. (1992). Psychological aspects of obesity and dieting. In T. A. Wadden & T. B. Van Itallie (Eds.), *Treatment of the seriously obese patient* (pp. 252–272). New York: Guilford Press.

Powers, P. S., & Rosemurgy, A. S. (1989). Psychological sequelae of surgical procedures for obesity. In M. Deitel (Ed.), *Surgery for the morbidly obese patient* (pp. 351–358). Philadelphia: Lea & Febiger.

Ramsey-Stewart, G. (1995). Vertical-banded gastroplasty for morbid obesity: Weight loss at short- and long-term follow up. *Australian & New Zealand Journal of Surgery, 65,* 4–7.

Rand, C. S. W., Kuldau, J. M., & Robbins, L. (1982). Surgery for obesity and marriage quality. *Journal of the American Medical Association, 247,* 1419–1422.

Reinhold, R. B. (1994). Late results of gastric bypass surgery for morbid obesity. *Journal of the American College of Nutrition, 13,* 326–331.

Rosen, L. W., & Aniskiewicz, A. S. (1983). Psychosocial functioning of two groups of morbidly obese patients. *International Journal of Obesity, 7,* 53–59.

Stunkard, A. J. (1992). An overview of current treatments for obesity. In T. A. Wadden & T. B. Van Itallie (Eds.), *Treatment of the seriously obese patient* (pp. 33–43). New York: Guilford Press.

Stunkard, A. J., & Mendelson, M. (1967). Obesity and the body image: I. Characteristics of disturbances in the body image of some obese persons. *American Journal of Psychiatry, 123,* 1296–1300.

Thompson, J. K. (1984). The psychologist as a member of a clinical nutrition outpatient services team. *The Journal of Practical Application in Clinical Nutrition, 4,* 20–24.

Thompson, J. K. (1990). *Body image disturbance: Assessment and treatment.* Elmsford, NY: Pergamon Press.

Thompson, J. K., Weinsier, R., & Jacobs, B. (1985). Self-induced vomiting and subclinical bulimia following gastroplasty surgery for morbid obesity: A case description report of a multi-component cognitive–behavioral treatment strategy. *International Journal of Eating Disorders, 4,* 609–615.

Tucker, J. A., Samo, J. A., Rand, C. S., & Woodward, E. R. (1991). Behavioral interventions to promote adaptive eating behavior and lifestyle changes following surgery for morbid obesity: Results of a two-year outcome evaluation. *International Journal of Eating Disorders, 10,* 689–698.

Van Itallie, T. B., & Lew, E. A. (1992). Assessment of morbidity and mortality risk in the overweight patient. In T. A. Wadden & T. B. Van Itallie (Eds.), *Treatment of the seriously obese patient* (pp. 3–32). New York: Guilford Press.

Wadden, T. A., & Kuehnel, R. H. (1993). Very low calorie diets: Reappraisal and recommendations. *The Weight Control Digest, 3,* 265–270.

Wadden, T. A., & Stunkard, A. J. (1985). Social and psychological consequences of obesity. *Annals of Internal Medicine, 103,* 1062–1067.

Wadden, T. A., & Van Itallie, T. B. (Eds.). (1992). *Treatment of the seriously obese patient.* New York: Guilford Press.

Williams, D. E., & Thompson, J. K. (1993). Biology and behavior: A set point hypothesis of psychological functioning. *Behavior Modification, 17,* 43–57.

Wolfel, R., Gunther, K., Rumenapf, G., Koerfgen, P., & Husemann, B. (1994). Weight reduction after gastric bypass and horizontal gastroplasty for morbid obesity. Results after 10 years. *European Journal of Surgery, 160,* 219–225.

Yanovski, S. Z., Nelson, J. E., Dubbert, B. K., & Spitzer, R. L. (1993, October). *Psychiatric comorbidity in obese men and women with binge eating disorder.* Paper presented at the meeting of the North American Association for the Study of Obesity, Milwaukee, WI.

19

OBESITY IN AFRICAN AMERICAN WOMEN: EPIDEMIOLOGY, DETERMINANTS, AND TREATMENT ISSUES

ROBERT C. KLESGES, MARGARET DeBON, and ANDREW MEYERS

Obesity is a significant health disorder (Bray, 1976) with an impact on a wide variety of diseases (Van Itallie, 1979). Bray (1976) indicated that obesity decreases lifespan by increasing mortality from related conditions such as hypertension, diabetes, arthritis, and increased surgical risk (Drenick, Bale, Seltzer, & Johnson, 1980). Although the specific mechanisms that link obesity and these health problems are not well known, many of these complications may be reduced by weight loss (Stunkard & Stellar, 1984; Van Itallie, 1979). Recent evidence also suggests that body fat distribution, independent of the amount of body fat, is associated with coronary heart disease and Type II diabetes. Individuals with upper-body obesity have higher blood pressure, triglycerides, fasting and stimulated glucose and insulin levels, and lower levels of HDL cholesterol than individuals with lower-body obesity.

There are many reviews available on the assessment and treatment of obesity (Brownell & Wadden, 1992; see also chapters 16 and 17, this volume). However, there is surprisingly little written on issues related to obesity in minority and low-income populations. There is a need for a

Preparation of this book chapter was supported by a Centers of Excellence grant awarded to the Department of Psychology, University of Memphis, from the State of Tennessee. Address all correspondence to: Robert C. Klesges, PhD, The Universities Prevention Center, Department of Psychology, The University of Memphis, Memphis, TN 38152.

better understanding of the causes of obesity in these populations. Intervention and prevention strategies also need to be designed, implemented, and evaluated.

We will focus on African American women[1] for three important reasons. First, a detailed discussion of the issues of prevalence, determinants, treatment, and body image in *all* ethnic and minority groups is beyond the scope of a single book chapter. Second, one of the highest incidence rates of obesity in the United States is found among African American women (Heckler, 1985; Kumanyika, 1987; National Heart, Lung, and Blood Institute, 1990; Wadden et al., 1990). Third, there appears to be a large gender difference in the prevalence rates of obesity for African American males versus females. That is, although the incidence rate of obesity in African American males is approximately that of Caucasian males (Heckler, 1985), by far the greatest racial discrepancy in obesity is between African American women and Caucasian women. Depending on the study and age range investigated, African American women, relative to comparably aged Caucasian women, are between 1.6 to 2.5 times more likely to be obese. For example, Kumanyika (1987) estimated that over a 10-year period, African American women were likely to gain anywhere from 15 percent (for older women) to 61 percent (for younger women) more weight than Caucasian women. In a recent study of 10-year incidence of obesity and weight gain in U.S. adults (n = 9,962; Williamson, Kahn, Remington, & Anda, 1990), the incidence of major weight gain was twice as high in women relative to men and was highest (men = 3.9%; women = 8.4%) in persons 25 to 34 years of age. African American women gained more weight than Caucasian women and were 40% more likely to have experienced a major weight gain (relative risk [RR] = 1.4). These differences remain *even after* statistical adjustment for socioeconomic status (Kahn & Williamson, 1991).

The purpose of this review is four fold. First, we will present an overview of the prevalence of obesity in African Americans. Given that a review of all minority groups is beyond the scope of this chapter, we will focus on one minority group—African Americans—because it appears that risk for obesity varies markedly in African Americans depending on gender. Second, we will discuss what is known, or more accurately, what is *not* known about the determinants of obesity in African Americans. Third, we will highlight and discuss the few studies that have attempted to treat

---

[1]The terms *Black* and *African American* are used throughout this review. *African American* refers to those of African, but not Caribbean, descent. *Black* is a more generic term and will include those of both African and Caribbean descent. However, studies vary markedly in their definitions, and in many studies it cannot be ascertained what precisely is meant by *Black*. For the sake of simplicity and the fact that studies differ in their definitions (or typically provide no definition), in this review, we will use these terms synonymously.

obesity in African Americans. Fourth, we will discuss what is known about body image and its relationship to obesity in African Americans.

PREVALENCE OF OBESITY IN MINORITY POPULATIONS

Prior to a discussion of ethnic differences in any health-related disorder, it is important to make an important caveat. There is an increasing awareness of the part cultural diversity plays in people's behaviors, especially as they affect morbidity and mortality. As pointed out by Melnyk and Weinstein (1994), the United States was once considered a *melting pot* in which ethnic groups would be assimilated slowly into the mainstream culture. However, the nation currently may be viewed best as a *tossed salad* in which individual and cultural differences are recognized and preserved. When one discusses an ethnic group such as African Americans, it is important to note that one is still discussing a diverse group of ethnicities and cultures. For example, the term *Black American* includes not only those with ancestral roots from multiple African regions but immigrants from Caribbean countries. Even among African Americans, each subculture has its own unique characteristics (Melnyk & Weinstein, 1994). The same cultural diversity is found in Hispanic Americans, Asian or Pacific Islander Americans, Native Americans, and Alaskan Indians (Kumanyika, 1994).

It is also important to point out that minority group classifications are not specific for any systematic group of the genetic, or for that matter, environmental variables that might be implied by the terms *race* or *ethnicity* (Kumanyika, 1994); minority classifications do not follow conventional definitions of race (biological) and ethnicity (sociobehavioral). Many times race and ethnicity are treated as mutually exclusive, and they are not. When discussing obesity in minority populations, it is important to keep in mind the enormous complexities that produce these differences.

With this introduction, large amounts of epidemiologic data suggest that on average minorities in general and African Americans in particular have higher (and in some cases, much higher) incidence rates of obesity than non-Hispanic Whites (Kumanyika, 1993). Depending on the survey and minority group, rates of obesity range from about 10% to 300% higher in minorities than non-Hispanic Whites (Kumanyika, 1993). The highest rates of obesity are observed among Somoans, Native Hawaiians, and Pima Indians, in which the majority of the adult population is overweight or obese (Knowler et al., 1991; Kumanyika, 1993).

Associated with these high rates of obesity are increases in cardiovascular disease and a variety of obesity-related disorders such as hypertension and Type II diabetes (Kumanyika, 1994). However, the severity of the health risk varies markedly by minority group. For example, the Pima Indians have high rates of obesity and at least one third suffer from non-insulin-dependent diabetes (Knowler et al., 1991). However, among Black women, three large-scale studies are consistent in reporting *no* association between relative levels of obesity and either total or cardiovascular mortality (Johnson, Heineman, Heiss, Hames, & Tyroler, 1986; Stevens et al., 1992; Weinpahl, Ragland, & Sidney, 1990). In these surveys, Black women all had higher rates of mortality. They also had higher rates of obesity and obesity-related conditions such as diabetes and hypertension but lower cholesterol levels. After adjusting for other factors associated with mortality, no relationship between obesity and mortality was observed in Black women. In addition, in one study (Stevens et al., 1992), fat patterning (waist-to-hip ratio) predicted mortality in White women but not Black women. However, such factors as hypertension and diabetes did predict mortality, so obesity is likely an indirect risk factor for mortality in Black women. Nonetheless, although it appears that obesity is a risk for disease in Black women, its relationship to disease appears weaker than in other ethnic groups (Kumanyika, 1994). Because African Americans have higher bone densities and muscle mass than other ethnic groups (Ortiz et al., 1992), the weaker relationship could be attributed to an overestimation of the prevalence of obesity in this group. As discussed in the following sections, whereas the overall relationship between obesity and mortality is not clear, obesity in African American women is associated with a host of cardiovascular and other risk factors.

To examine further the relationship between gender and obesity in Black individuals, we analyzed the incidence rates of obesity in Blacks versus Whites from the National Health and Nutrition Examination Survey (NHANES II; National Center for Health Statistics, 1981). NHANES II was a study of approximately 24,000 subjects and was conducted by the National Center for Health Statistics from 1976 to 1980. Survey participants, aged 6 months to 74 years, were sampled to represent noninstitutionalized U.S. citizens. Clinical, anthropometric, and biochemical measures were obtained, and a personal interview, including dietary intake, was conducted for each subject. We then calculated the prevalence rates of obesity (defined as a body mass index of 30 or greater) separately by race and gender, adjusted for energy intake and activity.

As can be seen in Figure 1, rates of obesity in Black men are just slightly higher than Caucasian men. In marked contrast, the rate of obesity in Black women is more than double that of any other group.

Because smoking has a major effect on body weight (Klesges, Meyers, Klesges, & LaVasque, 1989), we also assessed body mass index in nonsmokers versus heavy smokers.

As is shown in Figure 2, among nonsmokers, Black women had the highest average body mass index. Consistent with the extant literature, in heavy smokers body mass index decreased among Black men, White men,

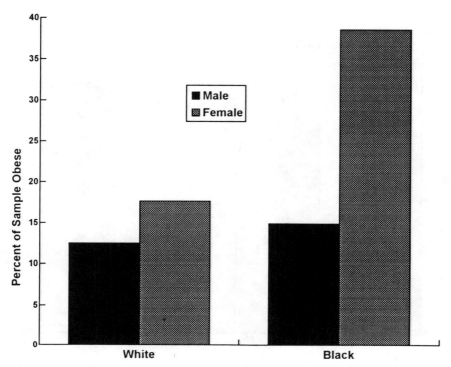

Figure 1. Prevalence rates (%) of obesity in NHANES II by race and gender.

and White women. However, heavy smoking among Black women was associated with an increased body mass index, relative to nonsmoking Black women.

Thus, the data analyzed from NHANES II confirms other reports that suggest that obesity is much more prevalent among Black women than Black men. Moreover, Black women who smoke heavily have a higher body mass index than nonsmoking Black women. This increased incidence of obesity in African American females is likely to contribute to a number of health-related problems that have a higher incidence in the African American population.

As mentioned previously, whereas the direct relationship between obesity and mortality has not been well established (Stevens et al., 1992), obesity has been related to a number of known risk factors that, in turn, predict mortality and morbidity. For example, African Americans have a greater risk of hypercholesterolemia (Heckler, 1985; Morrison et al., 1979), are less cardiovascularly fit (Farrell, Kohl, & Rogers, 1987), are more likely to be hypertensive (Cornoni-Huntley, LaCroix, & Havlik, 1989; Heckler, 1985), are more likely to exhibit the suspected risk factor of heightened cardiovascular reactivity (Arensman, Treiber, Gurber, & Strong, 1989), and are much more likely to suffer from Type II diabetes (Pi-Sunyer, 1990). As

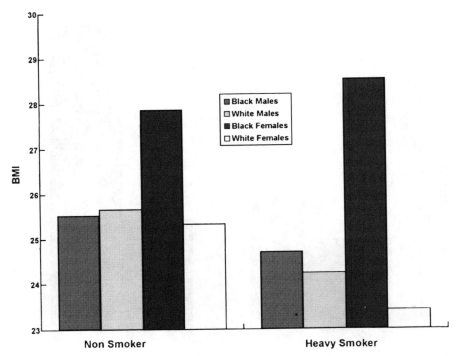

Figure 2. Body Mass Index (BMI) as a function of gender, race, and smoking status in NHANES II.

a group (both obese and nonobese) African American women are at higher risk for cardiovascular disease mortality than Caucasian women. African American women, for example, are more likely to suffer from heart disease deaths (RR = 1.5), cerebrovascular disease deaths (RR = 1.8), and death from diabetes mellitus (RR = 2.5; Kumanyika, 1987) than Caucasian women.

Given the consistent pattern of increased obesity in African American versus Caucasian women and the observation that African Americans are more likely to suffer from obesity-related disease, there is a tremendous need to understand more fully the obesity process in African American women.

DETERMINANTS OF OBESITY IN AFRICAN AMERICAN WOMEN

Prior to discussing any issues regarding the determinants of weight gain, it is important to distinguish between *direct* versus *indirect* mechanisms of weight gain. *Direct mechanisms* are variables of the energy balance equation: either energy intake (or components, such as fat intake) or energy expenditure (physical activity or metabolic rate). Direct mechanisms studies, although extremely important, are difficult (and expensive) to conduct and, as a result, are rare relative to studies assessing indirect mechanisms. *Indirect mechanisms* are those that correlate to body weight but do not cause weight gain directly. Examples of indirect mechanisms include such factors as age, educational level, and socioeconomic status. Age, education, and socioeconomic status may affect components of the energy balance equation, which, in turn, affect weight gain. Given the relative ease with which indirect mechanisms can be assessed, there are relatively more studies in the literature on these factors.

The paucity of research on the mechanisms of obesity in African American women is unfortunate. There is not a single prospective study on the direct determinants of weight gain in African American women, and we are aware of only two prospective studies of indirect mechanisms of weight gain in African American women (Kahn & Williamson, 1991; Kahn, Williamson, & Stevens, 1991). No study has assessed prospectively both direct and indirect mechanisms of weight gain. We must rely on the few cross-sectional investigations of direct and indirect mechanisms of weight change in this minority population. Cross-sectional studies, while useful, tell us nothing about the dynamic nature of weight gain, may relate more to the consequences rather than the causes of obesity (e.g., lowered physical activity levels in the obese as cause or result of obesity), and often present confusing, confounded results. For example, a common finding in cross-sectional research is that the obese eat less than the nonobese (Shah & Jeffery, 1991). This counterintuitive finding could relate to deception on the part of the obese in their reporting, an inability among the obese to report food intake accurately, or to the fact that a large percentage of the obese are dieting at any given point in time (Klesges, Mizes, & Klesges, 1987).

Even more serious, to our knowledge there is not one study comparing the components of energy expenditure across race: namely, resting metabolic rate, the thermic effect of food, and the thermic effect of exercise. The lack of comparative data on resting metabolic rate, which accounts for the majority of kilocalories burned in a day, is particularly disturbing. We are aware of one study that assessed metabolic rates in African American girls, but this study compared obese with nonobese girls and did not make an ethnic comparison (Manos et al., 1992). We were unable to find any studies comparing African American women with other ethnic groups on the thermic effect of food or the metabolic effects of exercise. Note that levels of physical activity and the kilocalories burned in exercise are not the same. Two people can be engaged in identical amounts of exercise yet produce markedly different levels of energy expenditure (Thompson, Jarvie, Lahey, & Cureton, 1982). Assessing the mechanisms of obesity in African American women should be a high priority for future research.

Direct Mechanisms

There are no prospective studies on direct mechanisms of weight gain in women, so all data presented are cross-sectional surveys. In the area of energy intake, the data are inconclusive. We are aware of four studies in the literature, all of which reported African American women weighing more than Caucasian women. However, the similarities among these studies end there. Two studies have found that African American women report less total intake and lower intake from fat than Caucasians (Block, Rosenberger, & Patterson, 1988; Gartside, Khoury, & Glueck, 1989). Another recent study reported that dietary intake among African American women was higher than that of Caucasian women in general. However, obesity levels were negatively associated with dietary intake in African American women (i.e., as dietary intake goes up, body mass goes down; Burke et al., 1992).

Extant studies also fail to show agreement on racial differences in the area of physical activity. Two studies have reported that African Americans in general report lower levels of physical activity than Caucasians (Folsom et al., 1991; Washburn, Kline, Lackland, & Wheeler, 1992). However, these studies were not interested in obesity per se and did not report relationships between physical activity and obesity. Three studies assessed the relationship between obesity and activity in African American women (Burke et al., 1992; Croft et al., 1992) and girls (Wolf et al., 1993). Two of these studies reported lower levels of activity in African American females in general (Burke et al., 1992; Wolf et al., 1993). However, levels of physical activity were not related to levels of obesity in any of the three studies.

We could find no studies of energy expenditure in African American women, so the relationship between this important variable and obesity in this population could not be evaluated. This again highlights the necessity for investigation in this area.

Indirect Mechanisms

There are two prospective studies looking at indirect mechanisms of weight gain for African American women. It is interesting to note that both surveys report that African American women—after adjustment for income, education, and marital factors—are not at risk for major weight gain but are significantly less likely to experience a significant weight loss (Kahn & Williamson, 1991; Kahn et al., 1991). Major weight gain was associated with low income, low education, and marital changes, but race did not predict weight gain in these adjusted models (Kahn & Williamson, 1991; Kahn et al., 1991). However, African Americans were less likely to experience a weight loss. Thus, factors routinely given as explanations for the discrepancy between African American and Caucasian obesity rates explain the weight gain, but not the lack of weight loss.

Cross-sectional studies in this area vary in what they find. In one study, socioeconomic status was inversely correlated with obesity in African American women but not in men (Croft et al., 1992). In a large study (Burke et al., 1992), an earlier age of menarche, more children, and an earlier age of first childbirth were all related to increased obesity among African American women. There is some evidence that the media is specifically targeting African Americans, encouraging them to increase alcohol intake and foods with high fat contents (Williams, Achterberg, & Sylvester, 1992). Whether or not this relates to actual changes in intake and subsequent increases in adiposity is unknown. Finally, one *could* conceptualize body image as an indirect mechanism of obesity, and there is some emerging research on body image differences among Black versus White women. These issues are discussed at the end of the chapter.

Thus, the literature to date give little cogent evidence as to the mechanisms of weight gain among African American women. Prospective studies, using both direct and indirect mechanisms, are needed to answer this important question.

BODY IMAGE ISSUES

One common reason cited for the large difference in the incidence of obesity among African American women compared with Caucasian women relates to body image. That is, there is a common belief that obesity in African American women receives a high level of cultural acceptance and is, perhaps, encouraged (Heckler, 1985). However, there is little empirical evidence to support this assumption.

Several recent studies have suggested that African American and Caucasian women view their body weights differently. For example, among adolescents who were overweight, 100% of the Caucasian young women accurately viewed themselves as overweight. In contrast, only 40% of the African American young women perceived themselves to be overweight (Desmond, Price, Hallinan, & Smith, 1989). It should be stressed that the evaluation of surveys such as these must be considered within the cultural context of the African American community. When related to weight issues, much depends on the reference group used. If African American women are comparing themselves with women in general (or Caucasian women), a high rate of obesity may be reported. However, if African American women use other African American women as their reference group, a low rate of obesity may be accurately reported, given the high rate of obesity among their peers. Thus, assessing body image is extremely complex, particularly when assessing body image issues cross-culturally (see chapter 6, this volume).

There is evidence to suggest that cultural references, and thus the wording of assessment questions, are extremely important. In a carefully collected study in adolescents (a time when body image is particularly important for girls), an interesting pattern emerges. For example, the female body size considered ideal by African American adolescent girls was significantly larger than the size selected as ideal by white females (Kemper, Sargent, Drane, Valois, & Hussey, 1994). It is important to note that on a task in which subjects were asked to rate nine female body drawings, the means between the African American and Caucasian samples were similar. However, in this same study, Black adolescent females were more likely to perceive that friends and family viewed them as thin, were more likely to perceive that friends and family wanted them to be larger, and were more likely to perceive that friends and family wanted them to gain weight compared with Caucasian adolescent girls (Kemper et al., 1994). Given these perceived pressures, perhaps it is not surprising that African American girls rate the ideal body type slightly higher than Caucasian girls.

A similar pattern emerges on studies conducted on adults. For example, a recent study reported that although African American women are weight conscious, at the same time they report an absence of negative social pressure to become thin and report a relatively positive body image (Kumanyika, Wilson, & Guilford-Davenport, 1993). In a study of 6,758 men and 14,915 women who reported trying to lose weight (Williamson, Serdula, Anda, Levy, & Byers, 1992), active attempts to lose weight were common among all ethnic groups. In women, actively trying to lose weight was unrelated to ethnicity. However, consistent with the research on intervention efforts (Kumanyika, Obarzanek, Stevens, Hebert, & Whelton, 1991), African American women reported being less successful in their actual weight loss attempts (Williamson et al., 1992). Finally, in a study of 2,801 African American and Caucasian women (Burke et al., 1992), both African American and Caucasian women were likely to report the health effects of obesity as "very harmful" (45.1% for African American women, 46.7% for Caucasian women). When asked about self-perceived fatness, African American women were almost three times more likely to report themselves to be "much too fat" (31.4% vs. 10.7%, respectively).

In summary, although much research still needs to be conducted, it appears that concern about body weight, perceptions of degree of obesity, and weight loss attempts are fairly prevalent among African American women. However, body satisfaction is relatively higher and the perceived pressure to lose weight is lower than for Caucasians. It should be noted

munity center) are increasing in popularity because they are familiar sites for participants and can provide a safe place for conducting exercise. Other recent recommendations include changes at the policy level (Jeffery, 1991). For example, it has been recommended that policies should be implemented that mandate health education curricula in all public schools, ensure universal access to treatment, and enhance minority access to healthful foods and recreational opportunities (Jeffery, 1991). Regulation of food advertising and taxing high fat or calorically dense foods have also been suggested (Jeffrey, 1991). However, it is clear that if we are to reduce the incidence of obesity in African American women, we need to implement interventions and prevention programs at the individual, family, and community levels.

CONCLUSION

The incidence of obesity among minorities is typically much higher than the incidence among Caucasians, with African American women having extremely high rates of obesity. Little is known regarding the mechanisms of action and virtually nothing is known regarding effective intervention strategies. Research is needed to begin to fill the large gaps in this literature.

REFERENCES

Arensman, F. W., Treiber, F. A., Gurber, M. P., & Strong, W. B. (1989). Exercise-induced differences in cardiac output, blood pressure, and systemic vascular resistance in a healthy biracial population of 10-year-old boys. *American Journal of Diseases in Children, 143,* 212–216.

Block, G., Rosenberger, W. F., & Patterson, B. H. (1988). Calories, fat, and cholesterol: Intake patterns in the US population by race, sex, and age. *American Journal of Public Health, 78,* 1150–1155.

Bray, G. (1976). *The obese patient.* Philadelphia: W. B. Saunders.

Brownell, K. D., & Wadden, T. A. (1986). Behavior therapy for obesity: Modern approaches and better results. In K. D. Brownell & J. Foreyt (Eds.), *Handbook of eating disorders* (pp. 180–197). New York: Basic Books.

Brownell, K. D., & Wadden, T. A. (1992). Etiology and treatment of obesity: Understanding a serious, prevalent, and refractory disorder. *Journal of Consulting and Clinical Psychology, 60,* 505–517.

Burke, G. L., Savage, P. J., Manolio, T. A., Sprafka, J. M., Wagenknecht, L. E., Sidney, S., Perkins, L. L., Liu, K., & Jacobs, D. R. (1992). Correlates of obesity in young Black and White women: The CARDIA study. *American Journal of Public Health, 82,* 1621–1625.

Cornoni-Huntley, J., LaCroix, A. Z., & Havlik, R. J. (1989). Race and sex differentials in the impact of hypertension in the United States. *Archives of Internal Medicine, 149,* 780–788.

Croft, J. B., Strogatz, D. S., James, S. A., Keenan, N. L., Ammerman, A. S., Malarcher, A. M., & Haines, P. S. (1992). Socioeconomic and behavioral correlates of body mass index in Black adults: The Pitt County Study. *American Journal of Public Health, 82,* 821–826.

Desmond, S. M., Price, J. H., Hallinan, C., & Smith, D. (1989). Black and White adolescents' perceptions of their weight. *Journal of School Health, 59,* 353–358.

Domel, S. B., Alford, B. B., Cattlett, H. N., & Gench, B. E. (1992). Weight control for Black women. *Journal of The American Dietetics Association, 92,* 346–350.

Drenick, E. J., Bale, G. S., Seltzer, F., & Johnson, D. G. (1980). Excessive mortality and causes of death in morbidly obese men. *Journal of the American Medical Association, 243,* 443–445.

Fardan, L., & Tyson, Y. (1985). Drew program for obesity treatment. *Journal of The National Medical Association, 77,* 737–741.

Farrell, S. W., Kohl, H. W., & Rogers, T. (1987). The independent effect of ethnicity on cardiovascular fitness. *Human Biology, 59,* 657–666.

Folsom, A. R., Cook, T. C., Sprafka, J. M., Burke, G. L., Norsted, S. W., & Jacobs, D. R. (1991). Differences in leisure-time physical activity levels between Blacks and Whites in population-based samples: The Minnesota Heart Survey. *Journal of Behavioral Medicine, 14,* 1–9.

Garner, D. M., & Wooley, S. C. (1991). Confronting the failure of behavioral and dietary treatments for obesity. *Clinical Psychology Review, 11,* 729–780.

Gartside, P. S., Khoury, P., & Glueck, C. J. (1989). Determinants of high-density lipoprotein cholesterol in Blacks and Whites: The Second National Health & Nutrition survey. *American Heart Journal, 108,* 641–653.

Heckler, M. M. (1985). *Report of the secretary's task force on Black and minority health.* Bethesda, MD: U.S. Department of Health and Human Services.

Holm, R. P., Taussig, M. T., & Carlton, E. (1983). Behavioral modification in a weight-reduction program. *Journal of The American Dietetics Association, 83,* 170–174.

Jeffery, R. W. (1991). Population perspectives on the prevention and treatment of obesity in minority populations. *American Journal of Clinical Nutrition, 53,* 1621S–1624S.

Johnson, J. L., Heineman, E. F., Heiss, G., Hames, C. G., & Tyroler, H. A. (1986). Cardiovascular disease risk factors and mortality among Black women and White women aged 40–64 years in Evans County, Georgia. *American Journal of Epidemiology, 123,* 209–220.

Kahn, H. S., & Williamson, D. F. (1991). Is race associated with weight change in US adults after adjustment for income, education, and marital factors? *American Journal of Clinical Nutrition, 53,* 1566S–1570S.

Kahn, H. S., Williamson, D. F., & Stevens, J. A. (1991). Race and weight changes in US women: The roles of socioeconomic status. *American Journal of Public Health, 81,* 319–323.

Kemper, K. A., Sargent, R. G., Drane, J. W., Valois, R. F., & Hussey, J. R. (1994). Black and White females' perceptions of ideal body size and social norms. *Obesity Research, 2,* 117–126.

Klesges, R. C., & DeBon, M. (1994). *How women can finally stop smoking.* Alameda, CA: Hunter House.

Klesges, R. C., Meyers, A. W., Klesges, L. M., & LaVasque, M. (1989). Smoking, body weight, and their effects on smoking behavior: A comprehensive review of the literature. *Psychological Bulletin, 106,* 204–230.

Klesges, R. C., Mizes, J. S., & Klesges, L. M. (1987). Self-help dieting strategies in college males and females. *International Journal of Eating Disorders, 6,* 71–79.

Knowler, W. C., Pettitt, D. J., Saad, M. F., Charles, M. A., Nelson, R. G., Howard, B. V., Bogardus, C., & Bennett, P. H. (1991). Obesity in the Pima Indians: Its magnitude and relationship with diabetes. *American Journal of Clinical Nutrition, 53,* 1543S–1551S.

Kumanyika, S. (1987). Obesity in Black women. *Epidemiologic Reviews, 9,* 31–50.

Kumanyika, S. K. (1993). Special issues regarding obesity in minority populations. *Annals of Internal Medicine, 119,* 650–654.

Kumanyika, S. K. (1994). Obesity in minority populations: An epidemiologic assessment. *Obesity Research, 2,* 166–182.

Kumanyika, S. K., & Charleston, J. B. (1992). Lose weight and win: A church-based weight loss program for blood pressure among black women. *Patient Education Counseling, 19,* 19–32.

Kumanyika, S. K., Obarzanek, E., Stevens, V. J., Hebert, P. R., & Whelton, P. K. (1991). Weight-loss experience of Black and White participants in NHLBI-sponsored clinical trials. *American Journal of Clinical Nutrition, 53,* 1631S–1638S.

Kumanyika, S., Wilson, J. F., & Guilford-Davenport, M. (1993). Weight-related attitudes and behaviors of Black women. *Journal of the American Dietetics Association, 93,* 416–422.

Lasco, R. A., Curry, R. H., Dickson, V. J., Powers, J., Menes, S., & Merritt, R. K. (1989). Participation rates, weight loss, and blood pressure changes among obese women in a nutrition-exercise program. *Public Health Reports, 104,* 640–646.

Manos, T. M., Gutin, B., Rhodes, T., Spandorfer, P. R., Jackson, L. W., & Litaker, M. S. (1992). Energy expenditure and intake in obese and nonobese African American girls. In C. L. Williams & S. Y. S. Kimm (Eds.), *Prevention and Treatment of Childhood Obesity: Annals of the New York Academy of Science, Vol. 699* (pp. 275–277). New York: New York Academy of Sciences.

Melnyk, M. G., & Weinstein, E. (1994). Preventing obesity in Black women by targeting adolescents: A literature review. *Journal of the American Dietetics Association, 94,* 536–540.

Morrison, J. A., deGroot, I., Kelly, K. A., Mellies, M .J., et al. (1979). Black–White differences in plasma lipoproteins in Cincinnati schoolchildren (one-to-one pair matched by plasma cholesterol, sex, and age). *Metabolism, 28*, 241–245.

National Center for Health Statistics. (1981). *Plan and operation of the Second National Health and Nutrition Examination Survey (NHANES II), 1976–1980* (Vital and Health Statistics, Series 1, No. 15; DHHS Publication No. PHS 81-13-17). Washington, DC: U.S. Government Printing Office.

National Heart, Lung, & Blood Institute (1990, August). *Obesity and CV disease in minority populations.* NHLBI Consensus workshop, Bethesda, MD.

Ortiz, O., Russell, M., Daley, T. L., Baumgartner, R. N., Waki, M., Lichtman, S., Wang, J., Pierson, R. N., & Heymsfield, S. B. (1992). Differences in skeletal muscle and bone mineral mass between Black and White females and their relevance to estimates of body composition. *American Journal of Clinical Nutrition, 55*, 8–13.

Pleas, J. (1988). Long-term effects of a lifestyle-change obesity treatment program with minorities. *Journal of the National Medical Association, 80*, 747–752.

Pi-Sunyer, F. X. (1990). Obesity and diabetes in Blacks. *Diabetes Care, 13*, 1144–1149.

Shah, M., & Jeffery, R. W. (1991). Is obesity due to overeating, inactivity, or to a defective metabolic rate? A review. *Annals of Behavioral Medicine, 13*, 73–81.

Stevens, J., Keil, J. E., Rust, P. F., Tyroler, H. A., Davis, C. E., & Gazes, P. C. (1992). Body mass index and body girths as predictors of mortality in Black and White women. *Archives of Internal Medicine, 152*, 1257–1262.

Stunkard, A. J., & Stellar, E. (Eds.). (1984). *Eating and its disorders.* New York: Raven Press.

Sullivan, J., & Carter, J. P. (1985). A nutrition-physical fitness intervention program for low-income Black parents. *Journal of the National Medical Association, 77*, 39–43.

Thompson, J. K., Jarvie, G. J., Lahey, B. B., Cureton, K. J. (1982). Exercise and obesity: Etiology, physiology, and intervention. *Psychological Bulletin, 92*, 55–79.

Van Itallie, T. B. (1979). Obesity: Adverse effects on health and longevity. *American Journal of Clinical Nutrition, 32*, 2723–2733.

Wadden, T. A., Stunkard, A. J., Rich, L., Rubin, C. J., Sweidel, G., & McKinney, S. (1990). Obesity in Black adolescent girls: A controlled clinical trial of treatment by diet, behavior modification, and parental support. *Pediatrics, 85*, 345–352.

Washburn, R. A., Kline, G., Lackland, D. T., & Wheeler, F. C. (1992). Leisure time physical activity: Are there Black/White differences? *Preventive Medicine, 21*, 127–135.

Weinpahl, J., Ragland, D. R., & Sidney, S. (1990). Body mass index and 15-year mortality in a cohort of Black men and women. *Journal of Clinical Epidemiology, 43*, 949–960.

Williams, J. D., Achterberg, C., & Sylvester, G. P. (1992). Target marketing of food products to ethnic minority youth. In C. L. Williams & S. Y. S. Kimm (Eds.), *Prevention and Treatment of Childhood Obesity: Annals of the New York Academy of Science, Vol., 699* (pp.107–115). New York: New York Academy of Sciences.

Williamson, D. R., Kahn, H. S., Remington, P. L., & Anda, R. F. (1990). The 10-year incidence of overweight and major weight gain in U.S. adults. *Archives of Internal Medicine, 150,* 665–672.

Williamson, D. R., Serdula, M. K., Anda, R. F., Levy, A., & Byers, T. (1992). Weight loss attempts in adults: Goals, duration, and rate of weight loss. *American Journal of Public Health, 82,* 1251–1257.

Wolf, A. M., Gortmaker, S. L., Cheung, L., Gray, H. M., Herzog, D. B., & Colditz, G. A. (1993). Activity, inactivity, and obesity: Racial, ethnic, and age differences among schoolgirls. *American Journal of Public Health, 83,* 1625–1627.

AUTHOR INDEX

Numbers in italics refer to listings in reference sections.

Irvine, M. J., 226, 249, *251, 302*
Irving, L. M., 38, *43*
Istvan, J., 367, 383

Jack, A. B., 109, *126*
Jackman, L. P., 20, 214, *223*
Jackson, L. A., 36, *44*
Jackson, L. W., *475*
Jackson, S. R., 214, *223*
Jacobs, B., 454, *459*
Jacobs, D. R., 409, *418, 473, 474*
Jacquet, N., 452, *456*
James, S. A., *474*
Janda, L. H., 5, *16*, 31, *42*, 84, *103*, 150, *167*, 407, *415*
Janet, P., 149, *168*
Janick, L., 321, *340*, 369, *384*, 398, *418*
Janosky, J., 366, *384*
Jarcho, H. D., *75*
Jarrell, M. P., 209, *222*, 331, 332, *341*, 366, *385*, 444, *458*
Jarvie, G. J., 409, *421*, 436, 439, 468, *476*
Jasper, K., 36, 37, *44*
Javaid, J. I., 348, *357*
Javanovic, J., 85, *154*
Jeffery, R., *418*
Jeffery, R. W., 391, *415*, 426, 439, 456, 467, 473, *474, 476*
Jennings, J., *359*
Jensen, J. A., 120, *124*
Jensen, M. D., 409, *417*
Jerome, L., 156, *168*
Jimerson, D., *200*
Jimerson, D. C., *200*
Johnson, C., 218, *222*, 242, 243, *250*
Johnson, C. L., 234, *248, 249*
Johnson, D. G., 461, *474*
Johnson, E. E., 180, *200*
Johnson, J. L., 454, *474*
Johnson, S., 5, *19*, 31, 46, *77*
Johnson, W. G., 71, *72*, 209, *222*, 322, 323, 325, 330, 331, 332, 334, 336, *337, 339, 341*
Joiner, T. E., 62, *75*
Jonas, J. M., *200, 221*, 349, 355, *359*
Jones, A., 6, 8, *16*, 398, *417*
Jones, K. H., 35, *44*, 133, *146*
Jones, P. H., *420*
Jones, R., *219, 220*, 239, *248*, 260, *300*, 306, *316, 338*, 428, *438*
Jonsson, E., *386*

Jordan, R. C., *419*
Josimann, J. E., 34
Jourard, S. M., 161, *169*
Jovanovic, J., 86, *105, 168*

Kaemmer, B., 379, *381*, 448, *457*
Kaeser, A. C., 109, *126*
Kahn, A. S., 11, *18*
Kahn, H. S., 389, *422*, 462, 467, 468, 469, *474, 475, 477*
Kalick, S. M., *125*
Kalinsky, L. B., 378, *380*
Kalucy, R. S., 29, *42*
Kamal, N., 187, *200*
Kanaley, J. A., 409, *417*
Kanders, B. S., 405, *414*
Kanerva, R., 349, *359*
Kanter, R. A., 369, *383*
Kaplan, H. I., 371, *384*
Kaplan, H. S., 371, *384*
Kaplowitz, C., 85, *106*
Karlsen, A., 312, *317*
Karlsson, J., *386*
Karp, L., 191, *198*
Kaslow, F., *125*
Katz, J., *199*
Katz, J. L., *199*
Katzman, M. A., 10, 12, *16*, 223, 235, 243, 244, 249, 250, 251, 252, 326, 340
Kaye, W., *200*, 322, 328, *340*, 428, *439*
Kaye, W. H., 187, *199, 200*, 346, *358, 359*
Kayman, S., 406, 407, *417*
Kaynar, A., 187, *201*
Kearney-Cooke, A., 10, 12, *17*, 309, 312, *317, 318, 319*
Keck, P. E., 150, *169*, 351, *359*
Keefe, P. H., 321, 335, *340*, 401, *417*
Keenan N. L., *474*
Keesey, R. E., 455, 456, *457*
Keeton, P., 93, *103*
Keeton, W. P., 50, 70, *72, 75*, 93, *105*
Keil, J. E., *476*
Kelly, E., 33, 36, *45*
Kelly, K. A., *476*
Kemper, K. A., 470, *475*
Kenardy, J., *252*, 325, 336, *337, 342*, 398, *420*
Kenrick, J., 207, *221*
Kern, E., *340, 418*
Kern, J. M., 32, *43*

Nasser, M., 135, *146*
National Academy of Sciences, National Research Council, *17*
National Center for Health Statistics, 464, 476
National Heart, Lung, & Blood Institute, 462, 476
Nee, L. E., *358*
Needleman, L. D., *249*
Neer, R. M., 189, *202*
Nelson, J. E., 11, *20*, 369, 387, 398, *423, 444, 459*
Nelson, R. A., 189, *199*
Nelson, R. G., *475*
Nemeroff, C. J., 10, *17*
Netemeyer, R. G., *20*
Nevo, S., 131, *146*
Newton, T., 76, 214, *219*
Neziroglu, F. A., 88, *105, 153, 156, 157, 158, 161, 163, 164, 165, 168*
Nezu, A. M., 405, *419*
Nickl, N. J., 187, *201*
Nieman, L. K., *200*
Niles, B., *223, 258, 302, 333, 343*
Nolen-Hoeksema, S., 5, 10, *17*
Nonas, C. A., 333, *342, 343*, 385, *420*
Noppa, H., 366, *383*
Norris, D. L., 308, *317*
Norris, L., 209, *223*
Norsted, S. W., *474*
Norton, K., 261, 299, *300*
Notti, L., 191, *198*
Novy, P., 407, *415*
Nozoe, S., 191, *202*
Nudelman, S., *221, 259, 301, 331, 340*
Nunnally, J., 69, *75*
Nurnberger, J. I., 391, *416*
Nussbaum, S. R., 189, *202*
Nutzinger, D. O., 328, *338, 416*

Obarzanek, E., 470, *475*
O'Brien, P., *457*
O'Connor, J., *199*
O'Connor, M., *219, 220, 221, 234, 248, 250, 258, 306, 428, 438*
O'Connor, M. E., 239, *248, 260, 300, 316, 338*
Oenning, L., 409, *417*
Offenbacher, E., *418*
Offer, D., *75*
Ohno, M., *419*

O'Laughlin, D., *384*
Olbe, L., *386*
O'Leary, K. D., 255, *301*
Olivier, L. L., 210, *219*
Olmsted, M. P., 7, *16, 74*, 131, *146*, 213, *220*, 229, 235, 249, *251*, 259, *302*, 306, *316, 317, 328, 339, 353, 358*
Olson, J. E., 371, *382*
O'Neil, P. M., 366, *385*, 443, 444, *457, 458*
Orbach, S., 35, *44*
Ordman, A. M., 235, *251, 258, 302*
Orleans, C. S., 321, 324, *340*
Orosan, P., 6, 8, *18, 88, 106, 151, 169, 427, 439*
Orsulak, P. J., *357*
Ortiz, O., 454, *476*
Ossip, D. J., 409, *416*
Overman, S. J., 133, *146*

Paffenbarger, R. S., 409, 410, *414, 417, 419*
Pahl, J., *201*
Pahl, J. J., *200*
Palese, V. J., *199*
Palmer, E. P., 193, *202*
Palmer, P. A., *186*
Palmer, R., 207, *221*
Pamuk, E. R., *18*
Pantano, M., 150, *168*
Pappas, T., *385*
Pardell, H., 245, *251*
Pasman, L., 11, *17*, 66, 67, *77*, 311, *318*
Pate, J., *146*
Patterson, B. H., 468, *473*
Pavlou, K. N., 409, *419*
Pawlik, G., *200*
Paxton, J. C., *310*
Paxton, S. J., *20, 318*
Pearson, P. H., 186, *201*
Penner, L., 5, *17*, 49, *77*, 370, *387*
Penner, L. A., 29, *44*, 67, 68, *74, 75*, 92, *106*
Perdue, L., 33, 36, *45*
Perez, E. L., 349, *357*
Perkins, L. L., *473*
Perkins, R., 248, 260, *299*
Perl, M., 218, 247, 298, *357*
Perlick, D., 243, *251*
Perri, M. G., 405, *419*

Sidney, S., 454, *473, 476*
Siever, M. D., 36, *45*
Sifford, L., *20, 252, 302, 342, 422*
Sikand, G., 395, *420*
Silber, T. J., *147*
Silberg, N. T., 90, *106*
Silberstein, L. R., 5, 7, *18, 19, 33, 35, 38, 44, 45, 46*
Silverstein, B., 36, 37, *45,* 243, *251*
Silverstein, G., 36
Silverstein, M. J., 120, *124*
Silverstone, J. T., 367, *385*
Silverstone, T., 346, *359*
Simmonds, B., *317*
Simmons, M. S., 203
Simpson, G. M., 152, *168*
Singh, D., 62, *75*
Sjostrom, J. E., 389
Sjöström, L., 386
Sjostrom, L. V., *420*
Slade, P. D., 3, 4, *18,* 29, *45,* 49, 50, 64, 67, *72, 76,* 150, *169,* 214, *219, 222,* 370, *381*
Slator, R., 109, 111, *126*
Slatzberg, E., 89
Slavotinek, A. H., *457*
Smilack, K. M., 10, *17*
Smith, D., 87, *107,* 223, 258, *302,* 322, 333, *340, 343,* 428, *439, 469, 474*
Smith, D. E., 6, 12, *18,* 328, 329, 336, *341,* 404, *420*
Smith, M. C., *222,* 259, *302,* 329, *341, 342*
Smith, S., 213, *222*
Smolak, L., 31, *44, 45,* 310, 312, 313, *318*
Smoller, J. W., 366, 379, *385*
Snell, M. K., 391, *418*
Sobkiewicz, T. A., 87, *104*
Sobol, A. M., *383*
Soejima, Y., *202*
Solomon, L. J., 11, *15*
Solomon, R. A., *219, 248, 300, 316, 338*
Solyom, L., *73*
Sørensen, T. I. A., 367, *384*
Sorenson, T., 62, *76*
Spalter, A. R., 189, *203*
Spana, R. E., 28, *42, 46,* 64, 67, *77,* 132, *145*
Spandorfer, P. R., *475*
Sparling, P. B., 409, *417*
Specker, S. M., 238, *250, 338*
Speizer, F. E., *418*

Spence, J. T., *45*
Spence, R. J., 35, 41, *42*
Spitzer, R. L., 11, *18, 20,* 322, 326, 328, 329, 330, 337, *342,* 368, 369, 373, *385, 386, 387,* 398, *420, 423,* 428, *440, 444, 459*
Sprafka, J. M., *473, 474*
Spratt, E. G., *18*
Srebnik, D., 50, *75,* 89, 90, 93, *106,* 250, 301, 304, *317, 318*
Srole, L., 442, *458*
Staats, M., 218, *222*
Stacher, G., 348, *359*
Stampfer, M. J., *418*
Stancer, H. C., *74,* 370, *383*
Stancin, T., 86, *105*
Starke, H., 186, *201*
Statistical Bulletin, *302*
Steer, R. A., 379, *380*
Stefanick, M. L., *422*
Steffee, W. P., 409, *419*
Stein, E. C., *422*
Stein, R. I., 10, *17*
Steinberg, S., 218, *222*
Steiner-Adair, C., 243, *251*
Steketee, G., 99, *106*
Stellar, E., 461, *476*
Stenestrand, U., 412, *416*
Stephens, G., 90, *106*
Stephens, M. A. P., 332, *338, 340*
Stern, J. S., 406, *417*
Stern, S., 243, *251*
Sternberg, J. A., 391, *421*
Stetner, F., *222, 360*
Stevens, J., 454, 465, *476*
Stevens, J. A., 467, *475*
Stevens, V. J., 470, *475*
Stewart, A. L., 367, *386*
Stewart, D. E., 197, *203*
Stewart, J. W., *222, 223, 360*
Stewart, M., 154, *168*
Stokholm, K. H., 453, *456*
Stolley, M. R., 368, *382*
Stormer, J. M., 311
Stormer, L. J. S., 32
Stormer, S., 39, 40, *44, 45,* 66, *74, 77,* 311, *317*
Stormer, S. M., 314, *318*
Strauman, T. J., 140, *147*
Striegel-Moore, R., 33, 35, 36, 38, *45,* 366, 367, *385, 386*

SUBJECT INDEX

Appearance preoccupation (*continued*)
    rituals in, 98
Appearance Schemas Inventory, 59, 64, 96
Assessment
    behavioral, 63
    in cognitive–behavioral therapy, 92–93, 266–267
    innovations in, 64–67
    methodological issues in, 67–69
        instructional protocol, 67
        reliability and validity, 68–69
        subject's actual size, 67–68
    of obese individual
        body image and self-perception variables in, 378
        eating pattern variables in, 373, 378
        heuristic guide to, 372–373
        instruments for, 374–377
        interpersonal relations variables, 378–379
        psychological functioning, 379
    size perception measurement in, 63–64
    subjective and attitudinal measures in, 49–63
        proportional, 62
        site-specific, 62
Assumptions
    about weight and shape, 278–279
    cognitive–behavioral therapy and, 278–279
    identification and challenge of, 95–96
Athletes
    body image disturbance in, 10–11
        prevention programs for, 311–312
    eating disorders in, 10–11
        prevention of, 311–312
        risk for, 311
Attitudes
    Eating Attitudes Test and, 216, 217
    negative body image and, 85, 86
    in obesity, 370–371
    sociocultural, 60, 66
Average-weight body-dissatisfied women, outcome studies of, 89–92
Avoidance behavior
    assessment of, 162
    in body dysmorphic disorder, 153, 162–163
    case example of social, 2

exposure for, 162–163
Fear of Negative Evaluation Scale, 376
Physical Appearance Behavioral Avoidance Test and, 59
self-defeating aspect of, 163
Social Avoidance and Distress Scale, 376

Bariatric surgery
    complications of, 454
    efficacy of, 454
    evaluation for, 443
    gastric bypass, 452–453
    gastroplasty, 452, 453, 454
    psychopathology and, 443
    weight loss maintenance following, 453–454
BDD. *See* Body Dysmorphic Disorder (BDD)
Beck Depression Inventory, 216, 217, 376, 379
BED. *See* Binge eating disorder (BED)
Behavioral therapy
    for anorexia nervosa, 240
    and bariatric surgery, 454
    for body dysmorphic disorder, 161–163
    for bulimia nervosa
        comparison with cognitive–behavioral therapy, 239–240
    for obesity, 391–394, 427–429
        bases of, 391
        efficacy of, 391
        principles of, 392–393
        studies of, 394
Beliefs
    in body dysmorphic disorder, 160, 161
    in body image education, 94
Best shot intervention approach, description of, 227
Binge eating
    in anorexia nervosa, 276–277
    cognitive–behavioral therapy in, 239
    criteria for, 5–6
    DSM-IV criteria for, 369
    Eating Attitudes Test for, 216, 217
    Eating Disorder Examination in, 216, 217

Eating Disorder Inventory-2 for, 216, 217
interpersonal therapy for, 241
patterns of, 368–370
physical signs and symptoms of, 178, 179, 180
differential diagnosis of, 183–184
subjective versus objective measure of, 216
supportive–expressive approach in, 241
Binge eating and purging
alternatives to, 275–277
clinical problems with, 276
generation of, 275–276
Binge eating disorder (BED)
assessment of, 328–224
questionnaires in, 328–332, 333–334
self-monitoring in, 331–332, 334
associated concerns and, 322
behavioral characteristics in
amount and composition, 324, 333, 334
antecedents and consequences, 325
duration, 324
frequency of, 323
loss of control, 324–325, 333, 334
body image concerns in, 12
body image disturbance in, 327–328
versus bulimia nervosa, 326–327
characteristics of, 322–328
cognitive–behavioral therapy for
body image intervention in, 428–429
dietary restraint in, 330–331
DSM-IV proposed criteria for, 323
gender and ethnicity in, 11
interest in, 321–322
morbid obesity and, 443
psychopathology in, 326–328
questionnaires in, 328–331, 333–334
treatment of
eating behavior management in, 335–336
recommendations for, 336–337
weight management in, 335
weight loss treatment of
in obese versus overweight patients, 398, 400–402
Binge Eating Scale, 329, 373, 374

in binge eating disorder, 331
Binge Scale, in binge eating disorder, 331
BN. See Bulimia nervosa (BN)
Body Cathexis Scale, 161
Body dissatisfaction
in average-weight women
cognitive–behavioral therapy for, 89–92
group versus self-directed therapy for, 90–91
Eating Disorders Inventory-Body Dissatisfaction Scale and, 55
in obesity, 3
risk for, 8–9
teasing and, 7–8
in women
non-weight-related concerns in, 427
predictors of, 427
Body dysmorphic disorder (BDD)
assessment of, 155–157
versus body dissatisfaction, 160
clinical features of, 150–153
behavioral, 153
cognitive and affective, 152–153
development of, 154–155
diagnostic classification of, 153–154
historical overview of, 149–150
outcome studies of, 88
pharmacotherapy for, 157–158
psychotherapy for, 158
outcome studies of, 88
response prevention in, 163–166
screening for plastic surgery and, 117
treatment of
behavioral procedures in, 161–163
cognitive restructuring in, 159–161
guidelines for, 158–166
initial phase, 159
outcomes research in, 157–158
Body Dysmorphic Disorder Examination, 156–157, 158, 162
¬negative body image and, 430
Body Esteem Scale, 56
Body Exposure in Sexual Activities Questionnaire, 61
Body image. See also Negative body image
assessment of
in binge eating, 327-328
in obese patients, 408
components of

Body image (*continued*)
  in obesity, 425
  in overweight persons, 425–426
  in eating disorders and obesity
    historical perspective on, 3–6
    integration of, 6–9
  gender and ethnicity role in, 9–12
    issues in eating disorders and obesity, 2
  obesity and, 7–8, 425
  overweight and, 425-426
  vestigial after weight loss, 8, 408
  weight reduction and, 426–427
  in weight reduction programs, 425–429
Body Image Assessment, 54
  in binge eating disorder, 327–328
Body Image Automatic Thoughts Questionnaire, 57
  in body dysmorphic disorder, 159
Body Image Avoidance Questionnaire, 59
Body Image Detection Device, 51, 64
Body image disorder, versus body dysmorphic disorder, 430
Body image disturbance
  in average-weight body-dissatisfied women, 89–92
  in binge eating disorder, 327–328
  in bulimia nervosa
    pharmacotherapy and, 353–355
  clinical implications of, 84
  cognitive–behavioral theory in, 92–101
  determinants of
    historical, 84–86
    proximal, 85, 86–87
  future of, 312–313
  negative body image development and, 84–87
  in obesity, 370–371
    attitudinal component, 370–371
    perceptual component, 371
  obesity therapy and, 88–89
  outcomes studies of, 87–92
  parents and significant others in, 312–313
  physical activity and, 313
  prevalence of, 84
  prevention of
    parents and significant others in, 312–313
    physical activity in, 313

  prevention programs and, 309–312
    for adolescents, 310
    for adult women, 310–311
    for athletes, 311–312
    educational, 309–310
    feminist approaches in, 311
    goals for, 310
    physical activity and, 313
    psychosocial, 311
    public policy and, 312
  treatment of, 83–101, 303–315
    guided imagery in, 309
    mirror technique in, 308–309
    nondirective techniques in, 309
    outcome studies of, 304–307
    video image confrontation in, 308
    video mirror combined in, 308
Body image disturbance theories. *See also* Perceptual theories; Sociocultural theories; Subjective theories
  perceptual, 28–29
  subjective, 29–39
    developmental, 29–32
    sociocultural, 32–39
Body Image Ideals Questionnaire, 58
Body Mapping Questionnaire and Colour-the-Body Test, 55
Body mass index, in nonsmokers versus heavy smokers, 464–465
Body Satisfaction Scale, 56
Body Shape Questionnaire, 56, 375
Body-Image Ideals Questionnaire, 64
Bowel dysfunction, in eating disorders, 186–187
Breast/Chest Rating Scale, 54
Bulimia Cognitive Distortions Scale, 213, 214
  Physical Appearance Subscale of, 57
Bulimia nervosa (BN)
  binge eating disorder versus, 326–327
  case example of, 1
  cognitive–behavioral therapy for, 237-238, 256–257
    versus alternative treatments, 258
    empirical support for, 258–260
    long-term results of, 259–260
    versus medication alone, 259
    versus psychoeducation and group therapy, 259
    versus psychopharmacologic therapy, 259
  diagnostic criteria for, 4

differential diagnosis of, 183–184
educational intervention in, 235
family therapy in, 235–236
hospitalization in, 195
interpersonal therapy for, 241
nutritional counseling in, 194
pharmacotherapy for, 244, 349–355
pharmacotherapy in
  body image disturbance and, 353–355
  literature on, 355
  psychotherapy and, 353
physical signs and symptoms of, 178–179
post bariatric surgery, 454
prevalence and incidence of, 9
stepped-care in, 228–229, 231
supportive–expressive approach in, 242
treatment outcomes studies of, 216–218
weight monitoring in, 273
Bulimia Test, 329
Bulimia Test-Revised, 212, 213–214, 329
Bulimic Investigatory Test, Edinburgh, 213, 215
Bupiron, for bulimia nervosa, 351

Calories
  estimation of goal, 402
  underestimation of intake of, 404–405
  in very low calorie diets, 402–403
Cardiovascular complications, of eating disorders, 185-186, 193
Cardiovascular disease, obesity and, 463, 464, 465, 466
Catastrophizing, 283
Checking behavior
  in body dysmorphic disorder, 152
  prevention of, 163, 164, 165–166
Cisapride, for anorexia nervosa, 348
Clonidine, for anorexia nervosa, 346, 348
Cognitive distortions
  in anorexia nervosa
    cognitive–behavioral therapy for, 263
Cognitive restructuring
  as behavioral weight loss method, 393
  for body dysmorphic disorder, 159–161

in body image therapy
  for obesity, 435
steps in, 283–285
Cognitive–behavioral therapy, 253–297
  for anorexia nervosa, 238, 256–257
    versus bulimia, 253–254
  behavioral therapy and, 255
  for binge eating disorder, 428
    with body image intervention, 428–429
  for body dysmorphic disorder, 158
  body image enhancement activities in, 99–100
  for bulimia nervosa, 237–238, 256–257
    as treatment of choice, 246
  cognitive therapy and, 254–255
  comprehensive assessment in, 92–93
  core principles of, 255–256
  education and self-discoveries in, 93–94
  empirical support for, 257–258
    in anorexia nervosa, 260–263
    in bulimia nervosa, 258–260
  exposure and desensitization in, 94–95
  features of, 263–254, 265–297
  identification and challenge of appearance assumptions, 95–96
  identification and correction of cognitive errors, 96–97
  for modification of self-defeating behaviors, 97–99
  for morbid obesity, 455
  for negative body image, 431–342
  phase 1 in, 265-281
    assessment of core patterns and features in, 266–267
    collaboration in, 266, 267
    delay strategies and alternatives development in, 275–277
    homework in, 269–270
    imagery, rehearsal, relaxation skills in, 277–278
    prescription of normalized eating in, 265, 275
    psychoeducation in, 279–281
    self-monitoring procedures in, 270–275
    shape and weight assumptions in, 278–279
    therapeutic alliance in, 265–266

for body dysmorphic disorder, 158
imaginal, 95
mirror, 95
Desipramine, for bulimia nervosa, 349,
350, 354, 355
Developmental theory(ies)
negative verbal commentary, 31–32
puberty and maturation timing,
30–31
sexual abuse, 32
teasing and, 32
Diabetes. *See also* Non-insulin-dependent
diabetes mellitus (NIDDM)
eating disorders and, 197
non-insulin-dependent diabetes mellitus, 409–410, 412, 464
Diabetes insipidus, in anorexia nervosa,
189
Diet
exercise and, 409
Food Guide Pyramid and, 402, 403
Diet pill abuse, complications of, 185, 193
Dietary guidelines, 402, 403
Dietary lapses, abstinence violation effect
following, 407
Dietary restraint
in binge eating disorder, 330–331
versus bulimia nervosa, 326
in bulimia nervosa, 330
questionnaire assessment of, 330
Dieting
strict
cognitive–behavioral model and,
268–269
success of
in African American women ver-
sus Caucasian women, 470, 471
Discounting, in body dysmorphic disorder,
165
Distorting Mirror, 53
Distorting Photography Technique, 53
Distorting Video Technique, 53
Distorting Videocamera, 52
Diuretic abuse
in bulimia nervosa, 180
complications of, 185, 192–193
Drive for Thinness and Ineffectiveness
Scales, The, 329–330
Dutch Eating Behavior Questionnaire
(DEBQ), 330

Emotional Eating Subscale, 373, 374
Restraint Subscale, 374
Dysfunctional thought
identification of, 282–283, 284
record of and problem solving,
285–287
restructuring of, 283–285, 288, 289
Dysfunctional Thought Record, in
cognitive–behavioral therapy,
285–287, 288–289
Dysmorphophobia, 149–150. *See also* Body
dysmorphic disorder (BDD)

Eating Attitudes Test, 212, 213
in binge eating, 216, 217
Eating diary, in behavioral assessment,
449, 450
Eating Disorder Examination, 63, 207,
208, 209
in binge eating, 216, 217
description of, 207, 208, 209
DSM-IV definitions in, 333, 334
Eating Disorder Inventory-2, 210, 212, 213
in binge eating, 216, 217, 331
Eating Disorder Inventory, body dissatisfaction subscale of, 328
Eating disorders. *See also* Anorexia nervosa
(AN); Binge eating disorder
(BED); Bulimia nervosa (BN)
assessment of
initial physical, 181–182
cognitive–behavioral model of,
255–257
complications of
cardiovascular, 185–186, 193
dental, 196–197
dermatologic, 190
gastrointestinal, 186–187, 193
hematology and immunology, 191
neurologic, 191–192
pulmonary, 190
renal, fluid, electrolyte, 187–188,
193
diabetes in, 197
differential diagnosis of, 183–184
feminist explanation of, 10
hospitalization in, 195
laboratory examination in, 183, 193
medical management of, 193–198

body image and, 34-36
eating disorders and, 9–10, 11
obesity and, 462, 463, 464, 465, 469
consequences of, 371
Goldfarb Fear of Fat Scale, 57
Grooming behavior, prevention of, 163–164
Group therapy
for bulimia nervosa, 259
versus self-directed therapy, 90–91
Guided imagery, in body image disturbance, 309

Hamilton Rating Scale-Depression, 216, 217
Hand Appearance Comparison Scale, 60
Homework
in body image therapy, 433
in cognitive–behavioral therapy, 269–270
Hospitalization, in eating disorders, 195

Image Marketing Procedure, 52
Information processing
in behavioral therapy, 255
in cognitive therapy, 254
Informed consent, for cosmetic plastic surgery, 119
Inpatient treatment, 231, 233
Insatiable patient, cosmetic plastic surgery, 122
Interaction and Audience Anxiousness Scales, 379
Inventory of Interpersonal Problems, 376, 379
Interpersonal relations
Inventory of Interpersonal Problems, 379
variables in
in obesity assessment, 378–379
Interpersonal therapy, 241
Interview. See Structured interview(s)
Interview for Diagnosis of Eating Disorder, 207, 208, 209
Ipecac abuse
in bulimia nervosa, 180, 185
complications of, 185, 193

Labeling, 283
Laxative abuse

in bulimia nervosa, 180
complications of, 185, 192–193
Lithium
for anorexia nervosa, 346, 348
for bulimia nervosa, 351, 353
Loss of control, in binge eating, 324–324, 333, 334
Loss of identity, after cosmetic plastic surgery, 122–123
L-tryptophan, for bulimia nervosa, 351, 352, 353

Magnification, 283
Maladaptation. See Self-schema, maladaptive interpersonal
MAOIs. See Monoamine oxidase inhibitors (MAOIs)
Maturation timing, development of disturbance and, 30–31
Meal plans, calories and, 402–404
Million Clinical Multirotational Inventory, 377, 379
Minnesota Multiphasic Inventory-2, 369, 377, 379
Minority populations, obesity in, 463–466
Mirror Distress Rating, 66
Mirror Focus Procedure, 57
Mirror technique, in body image disturbance, 308
Mitral valve prolapse, in anorexia nervosa, 186
Mizes Anorectic Cognitions Questionnaire, 213, 215
Monoamine oxidase inhibitors (MAOIs), for bulimia nervosa, 244
Morbid obesity, 441–456
assessment of, 445–449
behavioral, 449, 450, 451
behavioral programs for, 449
binge eating disorder and, 444
body image disturbance in, 444
clinical interview in, 446–449
morbidity and mortality in, 442
occupational aspects of, 445
posttraumatic stress disorder and, 443
psychological characteristics of, 442–445
psychological testing in, 448
psychopathology in, 442–444
social aspects of, 445
surgery for, 451–454

Morbid obesity (*continued*)
   treatment of, 449, 451–454
      selection of, 454–455
   very low-calorie diets for, 449, 451
Mortality, obesity-associated, predictors of, 464–465
Movable Caliper Technique: Visual Size Estimation, 51–52
Multidimensional Body–Self Relations Questionnaire, 375, 378
   Appearance Orientation in, 62–63
   Body Areas Satisfaction Scale in, 161

Naloxone, for bulimia nervosa, 351, 352
Negative body image
   cognitive–behavioral therapy for, 431–432
   in obesity
      versus body dissatisfaction, 430
      diagnosis of, 439–430
      features of, 430
   overweight and, 86
Negative verbal commentary, in development of disturbance, 32–32
Neurology, in anorexia nervosa, 191–192
Non-Caucasians in Caucasian countries
   body image studies of, 130–133
   physical appearance discrepancy, 144
Non-insulin-dependent diabetes mellitus (NIDDM)
   obesity and
      in Pima Indians, 463–464
   risk for
      in overweight men, 409–410
      physical activity ami, 409–410, 412
Nutritional counseling
   in anorexia nervosa, 194–195
   as behavioral weight loss method, 392
   in bulimia nervosa, 194
   in eating disorders, 194–195
   pharmacotherapy and, 356

Obesity. *See also* Morbid obesity
   in African American women, 461–472
      versus African American males, 462
      body image issues in, 469–471
      versus Caucasian women, 462

determinants of, 46–469
direct mechanisms in, 466–467, 468
energy expenditure and, 467–468
indirect mechanisms in, 467, 468
physical activities and, 468
socioeconomic status and, 469
treatment issues in, 471–474
assessment of psychological status in, 365–380
binge eating and, 398, 400–402
binge eating disorder in, 428
body dissatisfaction and, 3
body image and, 7–8
   assessment of, 408
body image therapy for, 88–89
   effectiveness of, 430–432
   format of, 432–433
   homework in, 433
   ingredients of, 433–436
   studies of, 430–432
   weight reduction integration with, 436–437
cardiovascular disease and, 463, 464, 465, 466
case example of, 2–3
consequences of
   emotional, 371
dexamethasone suppression results in, 188–189
emotional status in, 365–370
   binge eating patterns in, 368–370
   body image disturbance in, 370–371
   causality in, 371–372
   clinical samples of, 368
   community samples of, 366–367
   psychopathology of, 369–370
incidence and prevalence of
   in Black women versus Black men, 464–465
   race and gender in, 462, 463, 464, 465, 469
in minority populations
   prevalence of, 463–466
   rates of, 463
negative body image in, 429–430
pharmacotherapy for, 394, 396–397
   ideal drug in, 397
prejudice and, 435–436
prevalence of, 11, 389
psychological assessment of, 372–379

Physical Appearance Discrepancy Questionnaire, 143

Physical Appearance Related Teasing Scale, 59, 378

Physical Appearance State and Trait Anxiety Scale, 58, 66

Physical Appearance Subscale, of Bulimia Cognitive Distortions Scale, 57

Pima Indians, obesity in, 463–464

Posttraumatic stress disorder, morbid obesity in, 443

Pregnancy, eating disorders and, 197–198

Prejudice
obesity and, 445
coping strategies for, 435–436

Psychodynamic therapy
integration with active symptom management, 243
schools of thought in, 242

Psychoeducation
body image and, 93–94
issues in, 280–281
in cognitive–behavioral therapy, 279–281
in effects of malnutrition and starvation, 280

Psychometric development process, 206–207

Psychometric research
issues in, 205–207
psychological tests in, 210–215
self-monitoring procedures in, 209–210, 211
structured interviews in, 207–209
treatment outcome measures in, 216–218

Psychopathology
in binge eating disorder, 326–328
in morbid obesity, 442–444
in obesity, 369–370

Psychopharmacologic therapy, in bulimia nervosa, 259

Psychotherapy, for body dysmorphic disorder, 158

Psychotic decompensation, after cosmetic plastic surgery, 123

Puberty, development of disturbance and, 30–31

Public policy, body image disturbance and,

prevention programs and, 312

Purging, alternatives to, 277

QEWP. *See* Questionnaire of Eating and Weight Patterns (QEWP)

Questionnaire of Eating and Weight Patterns (QEWP)
in binge eating disorder, 327
in binge eating disorder assessment, 328–329, 331, 332

Questionnaire of Eating and Weight Patterns–Revised, 373, 374

Race
African American versus Caucasian women, 469–472
obesity and, 462, 463, 464, 465, 469

Rathus Assertiveness Scale, 376, 379

Reassurance seeking, in body dysmorphic disorder, 165

Refeeding cardiomyopathy with heart failure, in anorexia nervosa, 186

Relapse
in behavioral programs, 449
prevention of
in cognitive–behavioral therapy, 296–297
in weight control programs, 405–406
process of, 406

Relapse Prevention Model
empirical support of, 406–407
in long-term weight maintenance, 406

Relaxation training, 278

Reliability
interrater in structured interview, 206
intraclass correlation in, 206
relation to validity, 206
of test instrument, 205–206, 207

Reproductive function, eating disorders and, 197

Research. *See* Psychometric research

Resistance to change, therapeutic alliance and, 265

Restraint Scale, 330, 375

Reward, as behavioral weight loss method, 392

Role play, for maladaptive schemas, 295
Rosenberg Self-Esteem Scale, 216, 217

Schemas. *See also* Self-schema
    Appearance Schemas Inventory and, 64
    in cognitive therapy, 254
SCL-90. *See* Symptom Checklist-90 (SCL-90)
Selective serotonin reuptake inhibitors (SSRIs), for bulimia nervosa, 349–350
Self-defeating behaviors, modification of, 97–99
Self-discrepancy theory, 139–140
Self-esteem, Rosenberg Self-Esteem Scale and, 216, 217
Self-evaluation
    alternative bases for, 291–293
    negative body image and, 96
Self-help manuals, 235–236
Self-ideal, disturbance and, 38–39
Self-Image Questionnaire for Young Adolescents Body Image Subscale, 56
Self-monitoring
    as behavioral weight loss method, 392
    in binge eating
        advantages of, 331
        applications of, 331–332
        caveats in, 332
        utility of, 332
    in cognitive–behavioral therapy, 246, 270–275
        experiences in, 270–271
        hierarchy of eating situations in, 271
        review of extreme dieting in, 272
    comparison with Questionnaire of Eating and Weight Patterns, 332
    in psychiatric studies of eating disorders, 209–210, 211
    of weight
        in cognitive–behavioral therapy, 272–275
Self-monitoring diary
    in body image therapy
        for obesity, 434
    checking behavior and, 164
    in cognitive restructuring, 159

Self-perception
    in obesity
        Multidimensional Body-Self Relations Questionnaire, 375, 378
    variables in
        in obesity, 378
Self-reinforcement, alternative bases for, 291–293
Self-schema. *See also* Schemas
    diversification of, 292–293
    in eating disorders, 290–291
    maladaptive interpersonal, 293–295
        challenging, 294
        cognitive–behavioral interventions for, 296
        emotive therapy techniques for, 295
Setting Conditions for Anorexia Nervosa Scale, 213, 214
Sexual abuse
    development of disturbance and, 32
    morbid obesity and, 443
Sexual orientation, body image dissatisfaction and, 36
Shape
    assumptions about, 278–279
        and cognitive–behavioral therapy, 278–279
    Body Shape Questionnaire and, 56, 375
    Eating Disorders Examination subscale and, 328
Should statements, 283
Situational Inventory of Body Image Disturbance, 66
Situational Inventory of Body Image Dysphoria, 58, 64
    in body dysmorphic disorder, 159–160
Size
    measurement of, 63–64
    Movable Caliper Technique: Visual Size Estimation and, 51–52
    overestimation of
        in morbid obesity, 444
    perception of, 3–5, 63–64
Smoking, effect on body weight, 464
Social anxiety, in obesity assessment, 378–379
Social Avoidance and Distress/Fear of Negative Evaluation Scales, 376

ABOUT THE EDITOR

J. Kevin Thompson, PhD, is a professor in the Department of Psychology at the University of South Florida in Tampa, Florida. He received his PhD in clinical psychology from the University of Georgia in 1982 and has been at the University of South Florida since 1985. His research interests include eating disorders, body image, and psychotherapy integration. His current research involves a variety of topics in the area of body image, including, etiological factors (especially in the areas of social–developmental and sociocultural pressures), assessment issues, and cognitive processing models of body image disturbance.

Thompson has written over 60 articles in the areas of body image, eating disorders, and obesity. He has been on the editorial board of the *International Journal of Eating Disorders* since 1990. He has previously published six chapters in the area of body image and is the author of *Body image disturbance: Assessment and treatment* (Pergamon, 1990).